The Practical Handbook of Library Architecture

ALA Editions purchases fund advocacy, awareness, and accreditation programs for library professionals worldwide.

The Practical Handbook of Library Architecture

CREATING **BUILDING SPACES** THAT WORK | SECOND EDITION

ALA Editions
CHICAGO 2024

FRED SCHLIPF
JOE HUBERTY
JOHN A. MOORMAN

© 2024 by Fred Schlipf, Joe Huberty, and John A. Moorman

Extensive effort has gone into ensuring the reliability of the information in this book; however, the publisher makes no warranty, express or implied, with respect to the material contained herein.

ISBN: 978-0-8389-3966-6 (paper)

Library of Congress Cataloging-in-Publication Data

Names: Schlipf, Frederick A., author. | Huberty, Joseph, author. | Moorman, John A., author.
Title: The practical handbook of library architecture : creating building spaces that work / Fred Schlipf, Joseph Huberty, and John A. Moorman.
Description: 2nd edition. | Chicago : ALA Editions, 2024. | Includes bibliographical references and index. | Summary: "This definitive resource on library architecture provides extensive how-to guides for library building design, construction, remodeling, and more"—Provided by publisher.
Identifiers: LCCN 2023029937 | ISBN 9780838939666 (paperback)
Subjects: LCSH: Library architecture—Handbooks, manuals, etc. | Library buildings—Design and construction—Handbooks, manuals, etc. | Library fittings and supplies—Handbooks, manuals, etc. | Library architecture—United States—Handbooks, manuals, etc. | Library buildings—United States—Handbooks, manuals, etc.
Classification: LCC Z679 .S33 2024 | DDC 727/.8—dc23/eng/20230714
LC record available at https://lccn.loc.gov/2023029937

Book design by Kim Hudgins in the Oswald, Freight Sans Pro, and Freight Text Pro typefaces.

♾ This paper meets the requirements of ANSI/NISO Z39.48-1992 (Permanence of Paper).

Printed in the United States of America

28 27 26 25 24   5 4 3 2 1

Contents

Acknowledgments / xi
Introduction / xiii

PART I — Nearly Endless Observations on Good Library Design

Ch. 1 More than 250 Snappy Rules for Good and Evil in Library Architecture — 3

Ch. 2 Essentials of Good Library Design — 17
Introduction | Flexibility | Expandability | Accessibility | Effective Lighting | Good Acoustics | Staircases That Are Pleasant to Climb | Functional Room Shapes | Simple Connecting Hallways | Safe Environments | Low-Maintenance Designs | Avoiding Popular Designs That Cause Problems | Snappy Rules on Essentials of Good Library Design

Ch. 3 The Basic Configuration of Successful Library Spaces — 25
Introduction | External Configuration | Internal Layout and Room Shapes | Features That Require Extreme Care in Order to Be Functional | Traffic Flows | Artistic Ceiling Shapes | Snappy Rules on the Basic Configuration of Successful Library Spaces

Ch. 4 Evaluating Library Buildings by Walking Around — 45
Introduction | Reasons for Evaluating Buildings on Your Own | The Problems with Asking the Staff | Evaluation Criteria | Snappy Rule on Evaluating Library Buildings by Walking Around

Ch. 5 Dysfunctional Designs — 59
Bad Lighting | Bad Acoustics | Bad Ventilation | Inflexibility | Unexpandability | Soffits of All Kinds | Bad Staircases and Handrails | Cheap Substitutes for Real Elevators | Bad Shelving | Bad Balconies and Walkways | Nasty Ramps |

Bad Sight Lines | Bad Security | Bad Wiring | Insufficient Storage Space | Indoor Water Features | Funny-Shaped Interior Spaces | And Many More | And a Few Designs That Can Be Made to Work but Require Serious Preliminary Exploration by Architects, Engineers, Owners, Librarians, and Building Consultants

---

PART II From Overcrowding to Ribbon Cutting

Ch. 6 Essential Teamwork — 67
Introduction | How Do Libraries Avoid Serious Problems? | What Can You Do to Prevent Serious Problems Due to Bad Communication or to Elimination of Essential Players from Crucial Decision-Making?

Ch. 7 Building Programs — 71
About Building Programs | Purposes of Programs | Input on Programs | Typical Contents of Programs | Methods of Space Estimating | Who Should Write Your Building Program | How to Hire Library Building Consultants | Programming Methods | Two-Phase Building Programs | What to Do When Owners and Architects Ignore Your Building Program | Quick Space Estimates Using Formulas | Conclusions | Snappy Rules on Building Programs

Ch. 8 Hiring an Architect — 97
Introduction | Locating Architectural Firms | Investigating the Prior Work of Architectural Firms | Proposals from Architectural Firms | Special Problems with Teams | Evaluating Proposals | Interviews | Final Selection | Contracting with Architects | Design Competitions | Snappy Rules on Hiring an Architect

Ch. 9 Site Selection — 125
Introduction | Evaluating Potential Sites | Special Site Needs of Various Types of Libraries | Summary | Snappy Rules on Site Selection

Ch. 10 Design — 161
Introduction | Basic Steps in the Design Process | Schematic Design | Design Development | Contract Documents | Snappy Rules on Design

Ch. 11 Accessibility — 189
Introduction | The Americans with Disabilities Act | Access for People with Limited Mobility | Access for People with Limited Eyesight | Access for People with Limited Hearing | Access for People with Acrophobia | Access for People with Vertigo |

Access for People with Claustrophobia / Access for People with Limited Senses of Direction / What You Can Do to Protect Your Library's Accessibility / The Central Point of All This / Snappy Rules on Accessibility

Ch. 12	**Surfaces and Materials**	209

Introduction / Health Problems / Exterior Walls / Roof Coverings / Interior Walls / Floors / Ceilings / Snappy Rules on Surfaces and Materials

Ch. 13	**Building Codes**	237

Introduction / Building Codes / Additional Codes / Snappy Rules on Building Codes

Ch. 14	**Bidding**	243

Introduction / Delivery Methods / Getting Ready to Bid / The Bidding Process / Bid Openings / Bid Evaluation / Alternatives to Bidding / Awarding Contracts / Snappy Rules on Bidding

Ch. 15	**Construction**	261

Introduction / The Contractor's Role in Construction / The Architect's Role in Construction / The Librarian's Role in Construction / Coordination and Quality Control / Money / Recurring Tasks / Construction Close-out / Post-occupancy Inspection / Public Events during and after Construction / Snappy Rules on Construction

Ch. 16	**Remodeling and Expanding Library Buildings**	289

Introduction / Comparative Costs / Problems with the Reuse and Expansion of Existing Library Buildings / Phasing Expansion Projects / Snappy Rules on Remodeling and Expanding Library Buildings

Ch. 17	**Converting Non-library Buildings to Public Libraries**	307

Introduction / Rationales for Conversions / Common Problems in Conversions / Types of Buildings Often Suggested for Conversion to Libraries / Summary / Snappy Rules on Converting Non-library Buildings to Public Libraries

Ch. 18	**Shared Buildings**	327

Introduction / Types of Shared Facilities / Things You Can Do / Snappy Rules on Shared Buildings

Ch. 19	**Building Costs**	343

Introduction / Capital Costs / Anticipating Operating Costs / Anticipating Capital Renewal and Replacement Costs / Snappy Rules on Building Costs

| Ch. 20 | **Funding** | 355 |

Introduction / Sources of Money / Snappy Rules on Funding

| PART III | **Essential Spaces All Libraries Need** |

| Ch. 21 | **User Seating** | 371 |

Introduction / How Much User Seating? / How Library Furniture Is Ordered / Tables / Chairs / Placement of User Seating in Library Buildings / Snappy Rules on User Seating

| Ch. 22 | **Collection Storage and Display** | 393 |

Introduction / Steel Cantilever Shelving / Alternatives to Steel Cantilever Shelving / Shelving Placement / Other Types of Storage / Super High-Density Storage / Estimating Required Space for Collection Storage / Snappy Rules on Collection Storage and Display

| Ch. 23 | **Public Service Desks** | 417 |

About Public Service Desks / Typical Functions of Public Service Desks / Placement of Public Service Desks / Evaluating Proposed Public Service Desks / Types of Public Service Desks / Public Service Desks and Security for Staff / Common Problems in the Design of Public Service Desks / Library Supply Company Service Desks / Snappy Rules on Public Service Desks

| Ch. 24 | **Program, Activity, and Study Rooms** | 443 |

Introduction / General Features of Typical Rooms / Types of Program, Activity, and Study Rooms / Private Use of Program, Activity, and Study Rooms / Snappy Rules on Program, Activity, and Study Rooms

| Ch. 25 | **Display and Exhibit Areas** | 483 |

Introduction / Open Exhibit Areas / Display Cases / Wall Spaces for Hanging Artworks / Pinnable Surfaces / Security Issues / Permanent Works of Art / Exterior Displays / Combined Libraries and Museums / Policies on Displays and Exhibits / Snappy Rules on Display and Exhibit Areas

| Ch. 26 | **Restrooms** | 491 |

Introduction / Building Codes / Fixtures and Equipment / Accommodations for Children and Infants / Family Restrooms / Size and Locations of Restrooms / Security / Lighting / Planning for Maintenance / Snappy Rules on Restrooms

CONTENTS | ix

Ch. 27 **Staff Workrooms** 511
Introduction | General Considerations for Staff Workrooms | Individual Workrooms | Workroom Furnishings | Staff Conference Rooms | Specialized Workrooms | Workspaces in Otherwise Public Areas | Required Workroom Sizes | Snappy Rules on Staff Workrooms

Ch. 28 **Staff Facilities** 533
Introduction | Staff Lunchrooms | Staff Restrooms | Staff Coat and Purse Storage | Staff Mailboxes | Staff Bike Storage and Showers | Snappy Rules on Staff Facilities

Ch. 29 **Storerooms** 545
Introduction | Locations of Storage Spaces | Assigned Storage Spaces | Meeting and Program Room Storage Spaces | Mechanical Equipment Storage Spaces | Describing Storage Spaces in Building Programs | Protecting Storage Spaces from Looters Who Covet Your Space | Snappy Rules on Storerooms

PART IV Technical Issues

Ch. 30 **Elevators, Staircases, Railings, and Ramps** 561
Introduction | Elevators | Staircases | Railings | Ramps | Snappy Rules on Elevators, Staircases, Railings, and Ramps

Ch. 31 **Lighting** 583
Introduction | An Impressively Short History of Library Lighting in the Last Century | A Quick Formula for Good Library Lighting | General Lighting Concepts | Types of Light Sources | Lighting Strategies | Energy-Saving Ideas | Common Lighting Problems and How to Avoid Them | Working with Natural Light | A Final Word on Lighting | Snappy Rules on Lighting

Ch. 32 **Electrical Systems** 627
Introduction | Electrical Circuits | Snappy Rules on Electrical Systems

Ch. 33 **HVAC** 637
Introduction | Basic HVAC Vocabulary | HVAC Basics | Energy Conservation | Considerations of Function | Common HVAC Systems | Old Libraries | Operations and Maintenance | Snappy Rules on HVAC Systems

Ch. 34	**Plumbing Systems**	655

Introduction | Water Supplies | Wastewater | Stormwater | Special Room Considerations | Water "Features" | Snappy Rules on Plumbing Systems

Ch. 35	**Security**	667

Introduction | Security through Building Design | Theft-Control Systems | Theft of Personal Possessions | Entrance and Exit Control Equipment | Intrusion Alarms | Fire-Protection Systems | Humidity Control | Video Surveillance Systems | Miscellaneous Issues in Patron and Staff Security | Public Relations Implications | Staff Training on Security | Snappy Rules on Security

Ch. 36	**Insurance**	705

Introduction | Types of Insurance Coverage | Possible Property Coverages | Non-property Insurance | Action in Case of Loss | Snappy Rules on Insurance

About the Authors / 717
Index / 719

Acknowledgments

A LARGE NUMBER of people have helped us with this book.

Many librarians gave us advice over the years, taking time to show us through their libraries, pointing out both the wonderful and the not-so-wonderful features.

Many others took time to read portions of the book and tell us where we were either dead wrong or omitting vital facts or difficult to understand. Without their help, we could never have finished the book, and we would be terrified that we got things seriously wrong.

Here, in alphabetical order, are some of the people who helped us by reading chapters in one or both editions of the book.

- *Clayton Copeland*, faculty at the School of Library and Information Sciences at the University of South Carolina, Columbia, who brought her experience teaching courses on accessibility and on library buildings to commenting on chapters of the book.
- *Jim Derden* of State Farm of Bloomington, Illinois, and a retired contractor, who read and commented on the chapters on design, construction, security, and insurance.
- *Julie Derden*, retired librarian at Illinois State University at Normal, and professional editor, who read and commented on a number of chapters in the book.
- *Diane Hillard*, a biologist and Fred's wife, who read chapters of the book and told us (in the very friendliest sort of way possible) where we were clear as mud.
- *John Howard*, director, Mahomet Public Library, Illinois, and professional fundraiser, who expanded and improved the chapter on money.
- *Ben Huberty*, a mechanical engineer and Joe's son, who helped review multiple versions of the HVAC chapter and convinced Fred and Joe to keep it simple.
- *Amanda McGrory*, a winner of international wheelchair marathons and a master's graduate of the iSchool of the University of Illinois, who read and commented on the chapter on accessibility.
- *Mark Misselhorn*, retired from Apace Design, Peoria, Illinois, and architect on many library construction projects, who provided a set of sample floor plans.
- *Bev Obert*, retired director of an Illinois multi-type library system and of Illinois public libraries, who read and commented on almost all of the chapters in the book.

- *Karl Schlipf*, a computer expert for the University of Illinois and Fred's son, who rescued Fred on a number of (often very late-night) occasions when Fred embroiled himself and his computer in electronic messes, some merely stupid but several others genuinely serious and manuscript threatening.
- And many of the architects and designers at Engberg Anderson who helped review, fact-check, and keep Joe on the straight and narrow. Special thanks to *Isela Catania, Bridget Greuel, Shaun Kelly, Sarah Ponto, Alex Ramsey, Kristin Richardson,* and *Bill Robison.*

We also want to thank our editor at ALA Editions, *Jamie Santoro*, who provided support and help and exhibited extraordinary patience as we struggled to finish writing, and thanks to *David Aretha* for his thoughtful copyedits. Thanks to everyone on the ALA Editions team who helped in the production and marketing of this work. Special thanks to *Rob Christopher, Kim Hudgins, Samantha Kundert,* and *Ramon Robinson.*

Since we occasionally ignored really good advice from people who read sections of the book, it's important to point out that any errors are due exclusively to our stubborn attitudes and behavior.

Introduction

THIS IS A how-to-do-it book on library buildings. It's intended primarily for use by professional librarians. Our goal is to help our readers work effectively with the wide range of people engaged in balancing the technical, aesthetic, and functional aspects of any building project. As such, it emphasizes the pragmatic aspects of the decisions that go into defining the effectiveness, longevity, and affordability of a building project. We obviously hope that library owners, managing boards, and architects will read it as well as librarians, but we are particularly interested in working with librarians, who we feel are too often nearly ignored when it comes to planning the spaces they know best and work in constantly.

The first edition of this book was written by Fred Schlipf and John Moorman. Both were public library directors and library building consultants, and Fred taught courses on library buildings as a faculty member at the University of Illinois. Starting in 1998, Fred and John gave a number of illustrated programs at Public Library Association conferences on good and bad ideas in library architecture, including "The Seven Deadly Sins of Library Architecture" (1998), "(Un)desiderata: 27 Snappy Rules for Good and Evil in Library Architecture" (2000), "Let There Be at Least Half-Way Decent Light: How Library Illumination Systems Work—And Don't Work" (2002), and "The Curse of Carnegie: Can Modern Public Libraries Find True Happiness in Historic Buildings: 21 Useful Aphorisms" (2006).

They had so much fun writing "snappy rules" that they included a couple of dozen at the end of nearly all the chapters in this book.

The second edition of this book is written by Fred Schlipf and Joe Huberty. Joe and Fred first worked together on a suburban Chicago library and found they agreed endlessly on the functional essentials of library design. As an architect, Joe has worked on over 200 library buildings looking to provide both the pragmatic and the inspirational within a project budget. To be effective, library building should embody the traditions of learning and the aspirations of individuals and communities served. Library architecture should not be a choice between practical and inspirational.

One question we always ask ourselves is how so many dysfunctional ideas have managed to permeate library buildings. We're convinced that part of the problem is the nature of librarians. By and large, librarians are friendly and helpful people, not given to complaining. When we ask directors of new buildings about dysfunctional features, what we hear is almost never a rueful

"Yes, we know," but rather an appreciative "But it's so much better than our old building." Unfortunately, "better than our old building" doesn't always make it good enough.

In writing this book we've assumed that very few people will read the entire thing straight through. As a result, some chapters repeat important points that appear in other chapters. However, we've tried to remove excessive repetition from individual chapters (not always succeeding), and we've tried to tell favorite war stories only once.

The first edition of this book was far longer than originally expected, and the second edition is longer than we had planned. Much of the problem appears to be due to the fact that there are very few sweeping rules of functional library design, but rather a nearly endless number of useful details. The sweeping rules are repeated endlessly in the book, but just in case people feel that there should be rules in the introduction, here are some of the basics:

- *Keep space flexible.* Use all-purpose, low-glare lighting. Ensure ceilings are a minimum of 10 feet high. Make all floors strong enough for books. Don't build stuff in when movable furniture works just as well. Avoid monumental service desks. Never use soffits (lowered sections of ceilings). Have electrical outlets everywhere. Tell your architects that libraries move stuff around all the time, and they'll have to plan for that. Have enough storerooms.

- *Design for security.* One public entrance is almost always enough. (If you have two, provide security and staffing for both.) Pay attention to sight lines. Provide glass walls for study rooms. Avoid places where users or staff can be cornered. Control humidity at all times. Don't build "reading terraces" that are accessible through secure areas of buildings. Don't force people to grope their way into dark rooms to activate automatic lights. Have exterior book return slots lead to fireproof receiving areas. Keep floors wide and open. Avoid basements. Provide storm shelters. Be wary of shared buildings; never have shared elevators. And never have railings you can climb like ladders.

- *Provide bright but low-glare lighting.* All exterior pieces of glass that face any direction except straight north require movable blinds or roller shades. Tinted film is not a substitute. Cute little windows need cute little blinds. Avoid harsh, direct lights, such as recessed downlights. Bounce almost all light off ceilings. Saving energy by making lights too dim involves missing the entire point of libraries: inviting community spaces that require lots of light to help highlight their resources and services. By all means, provide daylight and views of the outside world, but always have ways to block direct sunlight. Beware of skylights and high windows.

- *Make library users comfortable.* Provide pleasant places to sit. Don't frighten people who have acrophobia. Don't create places where people can be cornered. At all costs, avoid atria and floating staircases; they increase noise problems and can lead to injuries. Keep indoor air fresh and comfortable. Always try chairs out before buying them. Use round tables only for coffee. Provide elbow room.

- *Keep libraries accessible.* Remember that accessible features benefit all users. Avoid ramps in general and outdoor ramps in particular. Never try to combine staircases with seating or with book shelving. Never use gratings for floors. Make all restrooms accessible.

- *Keep things simple.* The sequence of call numbers in shelving needs to be easy to figure out. Service desks need to be easy to find. Build no more partitions than necessary. Don't create labyrinths unless you have Minotaurs. Provide clear directional signs in modest numbers. Beware of courtyards, which tend to lead to beads-on-a-string room arrangements.

- *Plan for growth.* Despite digital enthusiasms, book collections continue to grow and libraries continue to run out of space for books. Sooner or later, all libraries need extra workspaces for extra staff. And they need new spaces for users. Don't let political pressures lead you to construct a building that is full the day it opens. (We were tempted to say "fiscal or political pressures," but most fiscal pressures are actually political pressures.) Construct the building so that it can meet building codes even if expanded.

- *Never lose control.* Do preemptive building programming. Make sure that someone who knows a lot about how libraries occupy space plays a central role in your library's planning team. Beware of exciting new design concepts that you can't view in action in existing buildings. Never give your designers any rights to your building after the ribbon is cut. Avoid design competitions and other building beauty contests. And never let aesthetics trump function.

Most of the book is based on the authors' personal experiences during lifetimes of working in library buildings, consulting on library building design, designing library buildings, and teaching how-to-do courses on library buildings, rather than on the published library literature.

The problem with library buildings is that bad decisions can last a century. Poorly selected books can be dumped into the next book sale, uncomfortable furniture wears out or can be transferred to the library staff lunchroom, but buildings last for generations. If we get only one chance to do it right, we need to make sure that we really do get it right the very first time we do it.

But sometimes we get it wrong. As a library director said, "Once a week we tell ourselves how great it is to work in a library designed by a world-famous architect. The rest of the time we hate the place."

We hope that this book reduces your chances of hating the place.

We've tried hard to make this book helpful and friendly and usable. Remember that each library building and site is different. The opinions and advice offered here must be reviewed in the context of your project's parameters and with professionals focused on those specific circumstances. Our goal with this book is to make those discussions more effective. And since we tend to have strong opinions, here is a friendly disclaimer written by a reasonably friendly lawyer:

> The information contained in this book is for general informational purposes only. No reader should act or rely upon the information in this book for their own particular situation. All liability in connection with a reader's actions taken or reliance upon the information in this book is hereby expressly disclaimed. Additionally, the authors disclaim liability for any errors or omissions in the content of this book. The information contained in this book is provided on an "as-is" basis with no guarantees of completeness or accuracy. There are multiple authors of the book, and the views expressed by each of them are their own.

So there.

Keep in touch. Please call or email us if you have questions. Tell us what we've left out. Tell us (particularly if you are a practicing librarian) what you think we got wrong and should change. If we live long enough to write a third edition of the book, we'll try to incorporate all sorts of ideas that people send us. Although we're connected to social media, we almost never look at it, so the way to get in touch with us is by telephone, US mail, and email.

Fred Schlipf
PO Box 816
Urbana, IL 61803-0816
217-898-1393 | fschlipf@illinois.edu

Joe Huberty
Engberg Anderson Architects
8618 West Catalpa Ave, Suite 1116
Chicago, IL 60656
847-704-1300 | joeh@engberganderson.com

PART I

Nearly Endless Observations on Good Library Design

PART I
Nearly Endless Observations on Good Library Design

CHAPTER 1

More than 250 Snappy Rules for Good and Evil in Library Architecture

SINCE WRITING SNAPPY RULES is always fun, here are over 250 of them. Most of them can be found in the various chapters of the book, but others are here alone.

1. Don't be led astray by winsome but dysfunctional designs. As P. J. O'Rourke said, "It's always tempting to impute unlikely virtues to the cute."

2. A badly designed and constructed building is a pain forever. Or until it falls down, whichever comes first. Never cut planning time short.

3. Select your architect with care. There are some amazingly competent designers around.

4. Having the same firm write your building program and design your library is always a seriously bad idea.

5. You will have a far better balanced project if your consultant is a librarian with a knowledge of buildings rather than an architect with a knowledge of libraries.

6. Never have an architect write your building program. With a tiny number of exceptions, architects don't know enough about libraries, even if they've designed a few. And few architects can divorce themselves from design issues that should come later.

7. If you hire a world-famous architect, you'll probably get a lot less library than you pay for and have a lot higher operating costs than you hope for.

8. The single most important construction material is money.

9. In addition to being functional disasters, atria with dramatic staircases are one of the most overworked clichés in unoriginal library architecture. If one is inflicted on your library, you'll be gaining five minutes of "wow" and suffering endless decades of problems.

10. When you are planning a building, always think in terms of project cost and never in terms of construction cost. And make sure all your hired help (building consultants,

architects, and construction managers) do the same.

11. You have only one chance with naming opportunities. Plan first and negotiate second. All too often, libraries initially give things away too cheaply and find themselves short of money but fresh out of places to name.

12. Donors would rather pay for a new college library (think shining city on the hill) than for a new dormitory (think restrooms on Friday night). This is probably why dormitories are often named after early college presidents.

13. Never begin with a project cost and design a building that fits. Start with needs, estimate costs, and ask whether you can afford them, and *only if and only when you decide it's too expensive*, compromise on needs.

14. Skylights are too bright by day, too dark by night, and noisy, but they make up for all that by leaking.

15. Unless you have a particularly nasty turn of mind, there's no real need to terrify all your users who have a fear of heights.

16. Reading terraces accessible from inside libraries are golden doors to the theft of library materials. "Secure reading terrace" is a total oxymoron.

17. Saying that a new library "meets all applicable codes" is a little like saying that it's right on the edge of being illegal.

18. Even if it's stupid, as long as it's legal you can have anything you want.

19. Creating excitement with light in a library is like creating excitement with steps in a nursing home.

20. Unless your library is so far south that you worry about Burmese pythons lurking in the parking lot, you need an entrance that faces south. Under duress, settle for east.

21. Regardless of initial intent, *all library floors need to be strong enough to bear the weight of books.* Flimsy floors are never a good investment.

22. When the time comes to replace sections of your carpet, it will no longer be in production. That's why people invented attic stock.

23. There's no such thing as too many electrical outlets in a library. Or too many electrical circuits in a library kitchenette.

24. When your architects ask you where you want to put computers, the correct answer always is, "Anywhere we want."

25. Preparing building programs and selecting architects can take a surprising amount of time and cost surprisingly little. It's a lot easier to have a program completed and an architect waiting in the wings than to suddenly have to rush madly about.

26. *NEVER build a library on land to which you do not hold a completely clear title.*

27. For financing public library buildings, know the spirit of your community. Some angrily anti-tax people can be amazingly generous when asked for voluntary donations.

28. Any project larger than a woodshed will be called a Taj Mahal and a monument to the inflated egos of managing boards. It's good to have people handy (usually consultants and architects) who can point out the actual modesty of your plans.

29. Unless your name is "Library of Congress" or "British Museum," you don't need a round reading room or a dome.

30. *All* windows that don't face directly north need blinds, including especially little tiny windows high up that look innocent on the plans. "Modern glass" is not a substitute. (You can often expect a fight from your architects on the unshaded windows issue. They will be wrong, but they will be impressively determined.)

31. Most departmental libraries benefit from a "T"-shaped interior furniture layout. Enter from the center of the broad side of the department, facing the service desk. Walk to the desk and then turn left or right for the rest of the department.

32. A "monitor" is a structure that rises above the roof and has glass on one or more sides. Any glass that does not face straight north needs an adjustable blind. Unfortunately, many monitors shine uncontrolled sunlight directly into the eyes of the people below.

33. A schematic design without furniture placement is *totally useless*. Reject it.

34. Beware of designing buildings that are just small enough to slither under code requirements. Sooner or later, you'll need to expand, and the cost of upgrading the existing building can be painfully high.

35. Trying to weasel out of building codes is not a good idea, as the choice of verb suggests.

36. In addition to potentially spreading Legionnaires' disease, indoor "water features" have many other nasty aspects. For example, mayors tend to fall into them.

37. Anyone who has dealt with children in a library knows that "infectious" does not apply just to lilting laughter. All staff workrooms need sinks.

38. If you have an open exterior staircase leading down to a basement door, sooner or later the drain at the bottom of the steps will plug up and rainwater will flow into your basement.

39. The most important place for childproof (tamper-resistant) electrical outlets is in public library adult departments because that's where parents hand their keys to their children to play with while the parents are otherwise occupied.

40. There's no such thing as too many electrical circuits in kitchenettes.

41. If your library has balconies a dozen stories above the main level, you will terrify your users with acrophobia, and sooner or later someone will jump off.

42. Study rooms and staff rooms need individual thermostats. If two rooms share one thermostat, the people in the room without the thermostat are likely to be seriously unhappy.

43. High-quality cantilever steel shelving can last a century, but it's extremely difficult to repaint. This tells us why bright orange and vivid magenta are seriously bad color choices.

44. Don't ever buy cheap or flimsy shelving. If it isn't steel cantilever shelving, the right price to pay is free.

45. If you arrange shelving around the walls of a room, know how you will prevent people sitting at tables from blocking access to the shelves.

46. It's hard to shelve books on spinners because there are so many small pockets. Spinners also tend to tip over in the presence of enthusiastic teenagers.

47. When as a library user you're trotting along a range of shelves and they end at 327.8, it should be extremely clear where to find 327.9.

48. Libraries are inherently flat rather than vertical. A 12-story library on a small piece of land is Not a Good Thing.

49. If anyone who does not work for a library is authorized to have a key to the building, there will be trouble.

50. Dead-end aisles in shelving areas are a particularly nasty threat to the personal safety of both library users and staff. And they're seriously rude to people in wheelchairs.

51. If you've never worked in a library, you have no right to object to plans to include a staff restroom.

52. Outside of study rooms, program rooms, and restrooms, libraries don't benefit from small spaces for public use. Wide, flat, and open makes a happy library.

53. Study tables are rectangular with chairs on two sides only. Round tables are for conversation only. Pleasant libraries may need a few round tables, but only a few.

54. If your windows are custom-made on a different continent, you'll have an interesting time after the Big Hailstorm.

55. A reading table without electrical outlets on top is just about as modern as a reading room with kerosene lighting.

56. A building project can absorb the full attention of a library administrator for years. Don't expect staff to add it to their regular duties.

57. One of the truly fine places for a special library (such as a law or medical library) is next door to the cafeteria.

58. Understanding your space needs is inexpensive, and proactive programming is invaluable.

59. Thank all of your donors. For some donors, $100 was a greater stretch than $100,000 for other donors.

60. The planning process begins with enumerating needs. Then estimate costs, ask whether you can afford them, and, finally, *if and only if it's too expensive*, compromise on needs.

61. Protect your expansion space with the fierceness of a mother grizzly bear with cubs. You'll need the fierceness, for many people cast covetous eyes on open spaces.

62. Starting your project by asking how much money you have to spend is often totally backward planning.

63. If you know you'll be expanding your library, have your library building consultant write a two-phase building program and have your architects prepare schematic designs for both phases. If you don't do this, you may find that you've painted yourself into a corner, and that your Phase I design makes it impossible to construct Phase II.

64. Restrooms with tornado-resistant construction are a good way of protecting users and staff in small buildings. And unlike other kinds of rooms, when people rush in they won't find the space full of puppet stages and boxed books.

CHAPTER 1: MORE THAN 250 SNAPPY RULES FOR GOOD AND EVIL IN LIBRARY ARCHITECTURE

65. Outside of counters with sinks, none of the furniture in library workrooms should be built in.

66. A toilet stall without two sturdy hooks for coats, purses, book bags, jackets, coats, etc., is an abomination.

67. "Design first, program second" is an easy recipe for a seriously bad building.

68. If your owners or architects announce that there's no time for your consulting librarian to review the latest set of plans, explain to your owners or architects that they are wrong.

69. Forcing a contractor to honor a mistakenly low bid may lead to nothing but trouble.

70. If your contractor messes up, be extraordinarily careful about accepting cash in lieu of corrected work. You have a right to a building that works the way it is supposed to, and it's easy to bargain away proper performance for far too little money.

71. When it comes to ground breaking and ribbon cutting, short public ceremonies followed by extensive eating and drinking make everyone happy.

72. Most soffits are a seriously bad idea, including in particular all perimeter soffits and all soffits over service desks. Recessed downlights in soffits just make things a lot worse.

73. Buy strong furniture. There is no theoretical upper limit to the number of teenagers that can occupy a single armchair.

74. All library glass surfaces that do not face straight north need blinds or similar methods of eliminating glare. Some owners and architects may argue with you on this point, but they will be amazingly (not to mention spectacularly and extraordinarily) wrong.

75. Sofas in libraries have two uses—sleeping and necking. Unless you are eager to create opportunities for sleeping and necking, never buy sofas.

76. The number of architects who understand libraries is exceeded by several thousand percent by the number of architects who don't understand libraries but are confident that they do.

77. The least expensive source of good library security is good sight lines.

78. The right number of entrances into a library is anything up to one.

79. Staircases with open risers are a tribute to everyone who loves to terrify people who suffer from fear of heights. Very few people like looking down to the floor below between their feet. Don't go there.

80. If you don't want to climb the stairs, the elevator should be immediately next door. (Sometimes designers hide the elevator down the hall and around the corner, apparently hoping to encourage people to climb the cute stairs.)

81. If you put your reading room light switches where kids can play with them, kids will turn off your reading room lights.

82. Light switches that require user training are a bad idea in meeting rooms shared with the general public.

83. If the lights in a room are controlled by sensors, they should turn on *before* people enter the room, rather than forcing them to grope their way into a dark space.

84. The fact that some people occasionally walk to the public library on perfectly

lovely spring days does not mean you don't need a parking lot.

85. Angry historical preservationists should come accompanied by checkbooks.

86. The rights of people with disabilities overrule the rights of designers to be cute.

87. Before you start remodeling, always ask your architects what it would cost to simply start over. Sometimes starting over is cheaper, and with lower long-term operating costs to boot.

88. Legitimate fundraising consultants always work for agreed fees or hourly salaries and never (as in NEVER) for a percentage of fees raised.

89. Curved and diagonal exterior walls lead to all sorts of problems with shelving placement, light fixture location, workroom shapes, acoustics, and other good things. On the other hand, they cost a lot more than straight walls.

90. Clarify contractually that your architects have no rights to your building once it's completed. This is a building, not fine art. You must have the right to alter anything you want at any time you want, whether your architects like it or not.

91. If your restroom washbasins aren't strong enough to bear the weight of adults, sooner or later someone will break one off the wall.

92. Owners who can't unload vacant buildings often have special epiphanies about what wonderful libraries they'll make.

93. Unfortunately, there's often no such thing as a "free" building, and lots of "free" buildings can end up costing more than starting over from scratch.

94. When a building is standing vacant, there is likely to be a very good reason. Or many very good reasons.

95. Converting a building that has no expansion space and no off-street parking space into a library involves making two impressively major errors at the same time.

96. Punch listing tries the previously warm social relationships between owners and contractors.

97. Until polyurethane foam is banned, be wary of extensively padded furniture.

98. At ground breaking and ribbon cutting events, what people want to hear is probably more important than what you want to tell them.

99. One of the first and most vital decisions in library planning is stack aisle width, because it determines structural column spacing.

100. No matter how short your library is of space, never have book aisles with dead ends.

101. To the intense chagrin of some designers, end panel indicators you can actually read are far more important than indicators that provide aesthetic gratification.

102. Shelving does best in long, continuous ranges. Dividing it up into lots of separate chunks in lots of separate spaces is A Very Seriously Bad Thing.

103. Shelving needs to be in parallel rows. Always. Libraries have already experimented with radiating shelving aisles, and we should have learned our lesson.

104. When your owners or architects suggest that librarians won't need to be present at

a forthcoming meeting, be sure they actually are there.

105. Shelves supported by pegs or clips on the end panels, or slipped into slots in the end panels, have a tendency to fall, dumping books on the place (or persons) beneath.

106. Triangular and round interior spaces cost a lot more to construct, but they compensate for it by not holding much.

107. You need a good excuse for internal partitions. "Functional necessity" is often a good excuse. "Architectural concept" is almost never a good excuse.

108. Funny-shaped buildings may be architecturally interesting, but they're usually expensive and dysfunctional. Curved and diagonal walls are funny shaped.

109. Basements in new libraries cost about the same amount as extra floors, but they have many fewer advantages, *as in no advantages whatsoever*. A happy library is a basement-less library.

110. A public library had a young adult study room with one tiny window. The library staff called it "the sex room."

111. If you have to install dark gray film on a window to block the glare, you should be asking yourself why you allowed someone to install the window in the first place.

112. Libraries always need more storage space than their boards of trustees, university administrations, school principals, or hospital administrators think they need.

113. If you have study rooms that can't be supervised by your staff from service desks, they'll spend a lot of time running back and forth, peeking into study room windows.

114. High-density storage connected to your library is infinitely better than high-density storage two counties off.

115. Always have your consulting librarian check your schematic design for functionality.

116. For any library construction project larger than a bicycle shed, you need an architect.

117. If your architects have little or no library experience, decide how you will fill the gap.

118. Of all architectural words of tongue or pen, "We will reinvent the library" are among the most terrifying.

119. Good librarians can be seriously annoying to architects who start off with little intention of listening to them.

120. Be particularly wary and aggressive when your library is a small element in a large building. Do proactive programming. Insist on being heard.

121. Sometimes the word *concept* should bring terror to your heart.

122. Clarify contractually what will happen if your lowest bid is significantly higher than your architects' estimate.

123. Complete honesty in architectural renderings is of mixed value. Sometimes it's better to leave off the HVAC penthouse.

124. One way to design a library building is to lay out all the needed spaces and then wrap an attractive exterior around them. Another way is to design an attractive exterior and then cram all the library spaces into it. The latter approach was invented by Procrustes, and you will not enjoy the results.

125. Soaring spaces with monumental staircases provide a few moments of "wow," followed by endless years of problems with heating, lighting, maintenance, acoustics, getting from point A to point B, unusable but expensive space, and (for many users) a paralyzing fear of heights. Say "no" early and often.

126. Make sure that your library staff have enough time to work on your building project.

127. Don't pressure architects to do something illegal.

128. If your architects have to labor mightily to talk you into their design concept, it may be because it's a crummy concept.

129. Design competitions for less than truly major libraries may simply drive off good architects. (They may also be a sign of excess owner pomposity.)

130. Working with your architects to list words that will define your project is fun, but don't engrave them on the front of your building.

131. If users have to shield their eyes from the glare anywhere in your library, something is wrong.

132. If you stand at the top of a staircase, looking down, and start fantasizing about tumbling down head over teakettle, this is Not a Good Thing.

133. Water features may be exciting and desirable, but only in someone else's library. If you're stuck with one, convert it to a planter.

134. If a railing can be climbed like a ladder, someone will. And fall off.

135. Never allow anyone to put perimeter soffits in your library.

136. Your architects and engineers are your experts on codes of all sorts.

137. Screened porches sound romantic, but they're not. They ceased to be useful with the invention of library air conditioning. Always say "No."

138. Book stacks don't fit into non-rectangular spaces.

139. Sight lines are vital, whether they're cute or not.

140. *Ars longa, technologia brevis est.* (Fake Latin for technology is fleeting but art—as in architecture, for example—endures.)

141. Rooms with dark ceilings are hard to light. Historic dark ceilings probably need to be preserved, but we don't need to create any new ones.

142. There are no desirable, cheap substitutes for elevators. If you don't want to spend the money on a genuine elevator, you need a one-story library.

143. As with other building codes, the requirements of the Americans with Disabilities Act are legal minimums, not ideals. Don't feel seriously smug about things if your building just squeaks through.

144. The undersides of floating staircases are wonderful places to bump one's head.

145. Steps that serve no necessary purpose whatsoever serve no purpose whatsoever.

146. Staircases should not terrify library users, who are nice people and deserve better treatment.

147. A member of a governing board envisions a balcony overlooking a library atrium as

an inspirational vantage point. A library manager wonders how long it will be before someone falls off.

148. There's no excuse for staircases with funny-shaped treads.

149. For people with a serious fear of heights, a glass-walled elevator is not a kindly alternative to a vertiginous staircase.

150. Beware of providing eternal exhibit space for things you don't own.

151. Never compromise with color rendering index (CRI). There's no need to accept anything less than 85.

152. And never compromise with color temperature in lighting. Anything higher than 3500K is too cold.

153. Be sure your lighting is bright enough. Anything less than 50 footcandles of soft, even light is unacceptable, and 60 footcandles is a lot better.

154. Know how you will change your lamps. If your designer says, "Use a lift," that is about as helpful as being told to "Use a screwdriver" when you ask how to rebuild the carburetor on your XKE.

155. Entryways need to be brightly lit and welcoming, even though all most people do is just move on through.

156. Avoid tricksy switching of lights in meeting rooms that will be used by people who have not received special training. Most intelligent and well-educated people have not received special training.

157. With the exception of study rooms and program rooms, put light switches where library users can't play around with them.

158. When it comes to a bond referendum, making sure your friends all vote works a lot better than trying to convert your enemies.

159. Remodeling is almost always more expensive than either your critics or supporters expect.

160. Some people suggest you begin with your project cost and design a building that can be built for that cost. This is almost always backward thinking. Begin by listing needs and then estimate costs. Compromise on needs only when you have no other choice.

161. Construction costs tend to increase faster than the value of money in the bank.

162. Some donors come equipped not only with money (good) but also with weird structural ideas they want to inflict on you (bad). Some want to pay only part of the cost of the building but still get to inflict their unfortunate ideas on you. It hurts to say "no" to money, but sometimes that's the only sane option.

163. Bake sales and book sales are fun and make everyone feel involved and appreciated, but they don't bring in much money. Construction projects rely on seriously big bucks from a more limited range of sources.

164. You can't get through any funding for a new library without hearing "The book is dead." Be prepared to point out how packed your library is, but don't expect to convert everyone.

165. Know what you'll do if you end up with the larger library of tomorrow but yesterday's operating budget.

166. Local non-experts are frequently eager to estimate construction costs on your behalf. Run away quickly.

167. Some sinks may require garbage disposals, particularly in staff lunchrooms.

168. If you construct an open terrace next to your library, below grade level, you will regret it deeply. Sooner or later the storm drains will fail, and water will fill your library.

169. Install enough electrical outlets. Fire marshals will not appreciate your extension cords.

170. Wall-mounted computer counters with outlets at the back force users to sit with their backs to the room. Lots of users don't like this much.

171. Heating with propane is a lot more expensive than heating with natural gas. If you have a choice of sites, pick one with access to natural gas.

172. Never buy a site or a building without input from an architect (and a consulting librarian, if possible).

173. When possible, use the term "workroom" rather than "office." It's a lot more accurate and creates far fewer emotions on the part of observers.

174. Floor-mounted toilets are cheaper than wall-mounted toilets, but only if you don't count the cost of maintenance.

175. Always use flush-valve toilets unless your community suffers from low water pressure.

176. Unless your building successfully bans infants, your restrooms will need changing tables. And receptacles for dirty diapers.

177. Even in tiny libraries, staff do not want to share restrooms with library users. Unless you've spent your life working in libraries, you have no right to regard this as an unreasonable attitude.

178. Restrooms must never open directly into reading rooms, program rooms, or staff lunchrooms.

179. The only acceptable restroom floor covering is anti-slip ceramic tile with very dark grout.

180. Be sure all of your toilet stalls are large enough for actual human beings.

181. Written building programs for expanding existing buildings should always be written without regard to those structures. *It's always a matter of what you need, not what you have.*

182. Remodeling and expanding a historic library is difficult. Trying to merge it with a second historic building is seriously scary, but the concept has an evil appeal to the inexperienced.

183. Once they've been expanded, historic buildings frequently have too many floors and too many rooms, with resulting expensive implications for access, supervision, and excessive elevators and staircases.

184. The walls of most historic libraries are uninsulated, and you probably won't be able to do anything about it.

185. The great temptation in dealing with historic buildings is to construct what you can have rather than what you need. Starting with a written building program is particularly vital.

186. A bargain building in a bad location is a bad building. A beautiful building in a bad location is also a bad building.

187. A contemporary addition to a historic building will frequently—with the passage

of time—become a painfully dated addition to a historic building, the architectural equivalent of avocado shag carpet.

188. A service desk is a service desk, not a monument.

189. Most service desks need occasional rearrangement, relocation, readjustment, and repurposing. Inflexibility of construction is not a virtue.

190. A matching soffit with recessed downlights over a service desk ensures a strong and happy combination of inflexibility and glare.

191. Atria are rotten places for service desks.

192. All program rooms need adequate storage closets for all furniture and program supplies.

193. Movable room dividers in program rooms are expensive and hard to maneuver, do a bad job of acoustical separation, change the shapes of rooms in weird ways, and are hard to repair. But outside of that they sound like a pretty good idea.

194. Funny-shaped meeting rooms are less amusing than one might hope. Nature loves rectangles.

195. Very few libraries complain that their meeting rooms are too large.

196. Unless you have a large and pompous library, conference rooms with large and pompous conference tables and with large and pompous chairs tend to look extremely silly.

197. Few public libraries complain that they have too many study rooms, but most of them complain that they have too few.

198. Be careful that parent agencies like universities or city governments don't take over control of your program rooms. But set things up so there won't be any serious security problems when they overrule you and take over anyway.

199. Study rooms need to be terrariums—glass boxes that can be supervised from every possible angle.

200. Workable staircases need to be exclusively staircases, not combined with reading rooms or shelving areas. Never confuse the functions, or let other people confuse them for you.

201. Good architects can envision solutions to design problems in ways that would never occur to the rest of us. Make your needs very clear and then see what happens.

202. When you are planning a library, always ask what additional building codes will come into play when you expand it.

203. All entrances need to be staffed, whether or not they have security gates.

204. Never let your library be a passageway to someone else's turf.

205. The lowest cost theft prevention system is keeping something that's theft-worthy in an area limited to staff.

206. Avoid places where staff and users can be trapped.

207. Workrooms need internal windows with Venetian blinds to adjoining areas.

208. If you plan your new building for 30 years of collection growth but no staff growth, the fact that workers eventually end up on each other's laps shouldn't come as much of a surprise.

209. When people are waiting to see the library director, where will they sit?

210. Access lanes to drive-up book returns and book pickups need to have curves wide enough for real vehicles to handle.

211. Good shapes for all library rooms are simple rectangles.

212. A staff lunchroom without a powerful exhaust fan is not as gross as a staff restroom without an exhaust fan, but the general principal is the same.

213. Staff toilets located directly next to staff lunch areas are depressingly prevalent and one of the most easily avoided library design idiocies.

214. Staff mailboxes need to be large enough for 8½-by-14-inch documents. Pigeonholes don't work.

215. A bad site for a nice store is a bad site for a nice public library.

216. Whether you have a campus library, a school library, a business library, or a public library, if you have a great site, everyone always wants to steal it.

217. Never let anyone else relieve you of your vacant land, and never let nearby land slip through your fingers.

218. High-quality movable room dividers can do a good job of separating large meeting rooms into smaller rooms. Unfortunately, high-quality dividers are amazingly scarce.

219. Exterior entry ramps on library buildings should have been banned in 1990. The fact that they're still being constructed speaks ill of everyone involved.

220. When you are planning a service desk, know what your staff will do between customers.

221. If you plan outdoor program spaces, know how you will deal with excess heat and cold, excess wind, excess precipitation, excess insects, and excess sounds of passing traffic drowning out presentations. Hot, wet, buggy, and noisy is not romantic.

222. Light fixtures hidden in ceilings look great, but they work terrible.

223. It's hard to find an excuse for the lack of a lactation room in a large library. A chair tucked behind the furnace is not an acceptable substitute.

224. Some libraries have tried to save money by sharing elevators with adjacent non-library buildings. Unless your library consists exclusively of lockable rooms on every floor, this is an insane idea.

225. Having a multi-floor open area in your library is a bad idea. Putting a scary public bridge across it is amazingly unfriendly. Providing glass walls on the sides of the bridge and requiring users to cross it compounds the felony.

226. If you decide to equip your public library with a coffee shop, know what you'll do with the space when the shop fails.

227. When evaluating proposed multiuser restroom plans for your library, always ask what simply removing the entry door would do.

228. The combination of a monumental library atrium and a monumental library staircase helps to demonstrate that two wrongs don't make a right.

229. Books and floods are not good friends. Be extremely wary of all proposed sites.

230. Cute buildings are fun, but function comes first. A good architect can give you both.

231. One of the great things about following disability requirements is that all users and staff benefit.

CHAPTER 1: MORE THAN 250 SNAPPY RULES FOR GOOD AND EVIL IN LIBRARY ARCHITECTURE | 15

232. When the author of the "Battle Hymn of the Republic" spoke of "dim and flaring lamps," she could well have been describing the recessed downlights in some libraries.

233. Building programs tend to be long because there's a lot to cover. Tiny programs are for library buildings tinier than yours.

234. If you decide to have a cash bar at public events, you'll need dram shop insurance, which the press may find fun to report.

235. Never seek architectural solutions to furniture problems.

236. Beware of "surveys" in library studies. Many appear to be irresponsible nonsense. A good quick indicator of total garbage is any percentages reported after the decimal point. If anyone gives you public library "survey" results that include numbers after the decimal point, throw them away.

237. Even in a properly constructed survey with a good sample size, 45 percent and 51 percent are usually the same number.

238. Any library building planning meeting that excludes librarians is a sign of impressively serious problems.

239. Stop bad design ideas the second they are proposed. The longer they hang around, the more people will start to accept them.

240. Library buildings need to be shaped by librarians. If your staff does not include a librarian who can shape your library, hire a librarian who specializes in library buildings.

241. Some amazingly innovative and unusual ideas for building designs are innovative and unusual because they should never have been proposed in the first place.

242. A comfortable height for a reading table is 29 inches. Leg clearance that meets ADA requirements is 27 inches. This is one reason to find a new home for lots of old library tables with thick tops.

243. Getting needs into print helps people to see where they disagree. As Francis Bacon said, "Truth emerges more readily from error than from confusion."

244. Recessed downlights (can lights) lead to elegant, unobstructed ceilings. But they also lead to impressively crappy lighting, a triumph of glamor over function, of glare and shadows over visibility. Ban them from day one (but expect to hear them suggested anyway).

245. Once people try to talk you into what you think is a bad design idea, start by visiting a library that has one. If no library has one, consider not letting your library be the innocent victim of ill-considered experimentation.

246. If your library has an unenclosed ramp or staircase leading down to a basement entrance, sooner or later you'll have a flooded basement. And most libraries don't have flood insurance.

247. Never store book sale books in your library's attic without first consulting your engineers or architects on whether your attic will handle the weight. Finding out experimentally that it doesn't work is not much fun.

248. If you decide to build a wood-framed library without a tornado shelter, have your rationale ready for your press interview the day after the tornado.

249. Historic restoration enthusiasts often have major plans for other people's money.

250. With the exception of branch libraries, most libraries need expansion sooner or later, despite what mayors or provosts assuredly contend to the contrary.

251. If your owners or architects tell you that you won't need your library building consultant at the next meeting, always be sure that your library building consultant is present at the next meeting.

252. If you have to choose, storerooms are more useful than water features, and innocent, unsuspecting people almost never fall into storerooms.

253. No matter what you plan to put on your library's floors on opening day, all floors need to be strong enough for books everywhere. Double check with your engineers.

254. Converting a non-library building to a library can be impressively more expensive than most people anticipate. And involve far more functional compromises than most people expect.

255. Having to carefully explain to users where your library's one and only accessible table is located won't impress a lot of people.

256. Some library floor plans feature furniture in places where it won't fit. Pay special attention to the space that will be occupied by chairs when they're pulled out for access. And the challenges of circumnavigating occupied chairs.

257. If your town has riverside sites and bluff top sites, remember that library books always prefer the view from bluff tops.

PART I
Nearly Endless Observations on Good Library Design

CHAPTER 2

Essentials of Good Library Design

I. Introduction

The history of library buildings is full of architectural ideas that are really essential and work extremely well, architectural ideas that work well if they're done right, and architectural ideas that should immediately be shown the door (if you can even find it).

This chapter is a quick summary.

In virtually all cases, the ideas dealt with here are dealt with somewhere else in the book, but finding all of them mentioned in one fairly condensed chapter may be useful for readers who don't want to spend days beating through the entire 800-page book, even though most of the ideas in this chapter are mentioned somewhere in the 800 pages.

A central point of this chapter is that making your building compatible with essential needs is not a burden. And most design concepts that deal successfully with the needs here improve other aspects of the library at the same time. Making libraries flexible cuts the long-term costs of remodeling and usually cuts the cost of staff oversight. Making libraries more easily accessible to users with disabilities benefits all users.

One of the best ways to construct libraries that are functionally well designed is to involve all the major parties in all major decisions. The major parties include more groups than one might first think, including:

- ***Owners,*** including universities, cities, schools, and corporations.

- ***Users,*** including people who borrow materials, work or study in libraries, depend on libraries for assistance, spend time in libraries, attend events in libraries, and have coffee in libraries while watching the world go by. And people who don't use libraries, sometimes for very relevant reasons.

- ***Librarians,*** including local library managers, library staff, and hired experts on library building functionality. If none of the library staff have experience with library building planning, a librarian with a background with library building planning needs to be hired and participate in the process.

- **Architects** and all the specialists who work with them, including engineers, interior planners, and landscapers. While architects with no experience with libraries can design very workable buildings, the chances of success are vastly greater if the architects have prior and successful experience constructing library buildings that owners and librarians can visit before selecting architects.

- **Administrators,** including university boards of trustees, university administrations, faculty library committees, city councils, mayors, public library boards, school boards, and school administrators.

- **Technical experts,** including campus architects, university and city planning staff, city technical staff, and code enforcement specialists, all of whom play a crucial role in defining what types of buildings can be built where and how.

Although not typically included in the routine decision-making process, there are two groups that are essential to the viability of many projects—fundraising experts and donors. Keep these groups in the loop and be aware of their needs.

- **Fundraising experts,** including university and city fundraising offices and library foundations.

- **Donors,** including library foundations, library friends groups, and individual donors, may accompany their gifts with strong opinions. On occasion, donor opinions are totally unworkable, pointing to the wisdom of designing first and finding a donor second.

Unfortunately, dysfunctional designs are sometimes pushed with extraordinary vigor, and it's the duty of everyone involved to stop them as quickly as possible. Far too many people with axes to grind push for sites subject to flooding, sites that are too small, flimsy construction decisions, designs that make maintenance of collection security nearly impossible, bizarre staircases, and many other problems.

In this chapter, we'll focus on the features of good design.

II. Flexibility

The most effective libraries are flexible. While a good building may last a century, libraries seem to change every decade. The way to make things work is to make it easy for library buildings to adapt to change. Among other things, this means:

- Build libraries that are wide, flat, and open.

- Create partitions only when they are functionally necessary.

Although it is warm and welcoming, this children's department can be completely rearranged in minutes.

SOURCE: ENGBERG ANDERSON

- Avoid architectural solutions to furniture problems. Built-in service desks are an example of things that cause problems.

- Make all floor areas strong enough to support book shelving, whether or not they will have shelving there on opening day.

- Avoid underfloor air ducts because the grills can limit furniture relocation.

- When possible, have wider column spacing, although the cost of really widely spaced columns can be a problem in multistory buildings when you need floors strong enough to support books.

- Avoid lighting designed to light specific items of furniture unless it is built into the furniture.

III. Expandability

Almost all libraries run out of space sooner or later. If it isn't extra space for collections, it's extra space for readers, space for meeting rooms, space for storage, space for staff, and other predictable or unexpected needs.

If you have expansion space, no rules say when and how you can use it. But if you have no expansion space, because you couldn't purchase or protect the land, or if your building can't be expanded because it wasn't designed for expansion—you're out of luck.

Expandability is especially essential to central academic and public libraries. By contrast, academic departmental libraries and public library branches can meet local needs and transfer all of their less-used materials to central libraries. School libraries are often pretty well off if they start off big enough (although many are too small from the beginning), and special libraries tend to be more movable.

IV. Accessibility

Making new libraries accessible is a straightforward design decision.

Making older and inaccessible libraries accessible can be more difficult, but that doesn't mean libraries can evade the situation.

Equally important are all of the library features that technically meet accessibility requirements but still fail users with disabilities in significant ways. Users in libraries that comply with the Americans with Disabilities Act may still be forced to struggle up narrow, icy ramps, walk beside terrifying drop-offs, or hunt for hidden elevators.

Accessibility means real elevators, not toy substitutes. Elevators should open into main library areas, not into strange back corners or directly out of doors.

V. Effective Lighting

All libraries need bright, low-glare lighting that works nearly interchangeably with reader seating, book shelving, computers, staff workspaces, special events, and other uses.

V-A. ARTIFICIAL LIGHTING

Modern lighting systems usually use LED illumination, which is unusually efficient. Although cheap LEDs can put out nasty light, the best are excellent.

A variety of ways exist to save energy by turning off LEDs when they are not needed. There are two basic points: First, LEDs are energy efficient. And second, lots of systems that are designed to turn off lights when they are not needed tend instead to turn off lights when they are actually needed, or fail to turn on lights when they are needed. And third, good lighting control systems are possible, so don't let the ghastly screw-ups of the past completely defeat you.

The main approach to artificial lighting in libraries is to bounce the light off the ceiling. If your ceiling heights don't allow this, you'll need carefully selected and arranged fixtures that light individual shelving units and individual tabletops.

V-B. NATURAL LIGHTING

Almost everyone likes natural light. They like the fact that colors are more realistic under daylight. And they like looking out windows at the real world outside.

Over the years, libraries have had a lot of problems with uncontrolled natural light. In particular, any window that can admit direct sunlight requires some sort of movable shade that can block any direct sunlight that creeps through.

Problems caused by natural light are especially apparent with designs like monitor windows and clearstory windows that face any direction except straight north. And with skylights. Unfortunately, a lot of libraries have one or more of these features, and users and staff learn to hate them.

If a skylight is important to your library, electrically lighted "artificial skylights" are widely used and can avoid the nasty glare and erratic illumination associated with real skylights. If you want a real skylight, the issues can be extremely complex. Coordinated work by your architects, engineers, librarians, and library consultants is important.

VI. Good Acoustics

Libraries need to have pleasant acoustics. Many do.

Many libraries rely on a combination of carpeted floors and acoustic ceilings to do the job. When you can't have both, include an acoustic consulting engineer in the design of your building.

Round rooms and oddly proportioned rooms can have nasty acoustics. So can atria and large openings around staircases. Always involve an acoustic consulting engineer.

VII. Staircases That Are Pleasant to Climb

Staircases are essential in all libraries on more than one level, and if they are well designed they are pleasant to climb. Staircases help users understand how libraries are laid out internally.

Unfortunately, there are a lot of seriously bad library staircases out there, enough to fill many pages of this book. Among the many problems are:

- Staircases that are designed to be impressive to view but ignore user comfort in the process.

- Staircases that are merged with irrelevant functions. No staircase should ever be combined with library shelving or user seating or any other non-staircase function, although a number of impressively ill-advised staircases have been.
- Staircases that float in midair and have places underneath where users can bump their heads.
- Staircases with funny-shaped treads that lend themselves to people tripping. Or worrying about tripping. These can include all treads that are not simple rectangles, treads that end short of side walls, treads with ends that curve up into sidewalls, and so on.
- Staircases with railings that can be climbed like ladders.
- Staircases with open or transparent risers.
- Staircases with handrails that cannot be grabbed easily.
- Elevators that are too far or hidden from staircases that people really don't want to climb.
- Staircases that cause acoustic problems, with noise migrating between floors on the openings around staircases.
- Staircases that are too long for comfort. A staircase that makes a turn halfway up is usually far more comfortable than one that leaves people staring down what looks like an endless flight of steps.

Some staircase problems are due to staircases constructed before current building codes, while other staircases are technically legal but still bad ideas.

VIII. Functional Room Shapes

With very few exceptions, libraries always do best with rectangular rooms. Rectangular rooms make the most efficient use of space, and most library contents fit best into rectangular spaces.

A room always works best when users enter close to the center of the longer side, walk up to the service desk in the center of the room, facing the entrance, and then turn left or right as needed.

Round reading rooms can be impressive and fun, but the architect needs to have built them for other libraries before doing yours. Typically, round rooms are for user seating rather than for book shelving, which fits badly in round spaces.

Some round rooms have shelving arranged like the spokes of a wheel. It is always a mistake.

Nothing fits well into triangular rooms.

IX. Simple Connecting Hallways

Connecting hallways need to be straight, simple, and driven by functional need rather than building design decisions.

Rooms should never be arranged as beads on a chain. One of the main places this happens is when libraries have courtyards. There may not be enough space for both rooms and the corridors that serve them, and the result can be walking through one room to reach another. Or the owners may want rooms that have views of both the courtyard and the outside world.

X. Safe Environments

There are a huge number of ways to make libraries safe for their users and staff. A lot of them involve maintaining wide-open spaces that can be easily supervised and where people cannot be trapped.

Study rooms, for example, need glass walls rather than occasional windows.

Shelving aisles and service desks must always have two ways out.

Staff workstations must provide staff with the best possible sight lines.

Indoor water features and outdoor fountains need to have ways to keep people from falling in. (A lot of librarians feel that by far the best way to keep people from falling into water features is to avoid having water features entirely.)

There are important ways to protect libraries from fire. Meet all building codes for a building larger than your initial project. Build with fire-resistant materials. And have a sprinkler system.

Protect your library from groundwater. Never build on anything even remotely resembling a floodplain. Avoid basements; they're just as expensive as upper stories, and upper stories have daylight and don't flood.

XI. Low-Maintenance Designs

A good library is one that makes the custodial forces happy, and that saves money. Some things that help include:

- Door handles and handrails made of brushed stainless steel. Nothing else works for long. Painted handles and handrails always look shabby. Brass is extremely high maintenance.
- Flush-valve toilets rather than flush tank toilets.
- Easily replaceable soap dispensers.
- Light fixtures that are easy to reach.
- Dark grout in ceramic floor tile.
- Devices to protect plaster walls, including chair rails, baseboards, and corner protectors.

XII. Avoiding Popular Designs That Cause Problems

A number of these are discussed extensively in the text. Among them are:

- Atria, which are multi-floor openings, often with dramatic staircases in the middle. Atria in libraries have led to expensive HVAC problems, acoustic problems, lighting problems, users and staff having to detour around open areas, safety problems, waste of expensive space, terrified people who fear heights, and suicides.
- Showoff staircases, which can lead to an impressive variety of problems.
- Courtyards, which get in the way of internal circulation and are often extremely difficult to supervise.
- Balconies. People fear falling off balconies. Unless the room faced by the balcony is well over 20 feet high, the ceiling of the balcony and the space beneath it will be too low for library purposes.

- Screened porches. Some libraries love them. Others hate them because they can lead to HVAC and supervision problems. They were a lot more appealing before the advent of air conditioning.

- Reading terraces. These are frequently proposed, but they work only if the terraces are entered from an area outside the library's security gates. Otherwise, users can carry books to the terraces, pitch them over the edges into the bushes below, and then retrieve them later from out of doors.

- Soffits are lowered ceiling sections, often with recessed downlights. They lead to inflexibility and to bad lighting.

XIII. Snappy Rules on Essentials of Good Library Design

1. This is a lot of material crammed into a few pages. Luckily, the rest of the book awaits, with far more detail. Perhaps even more than you really want.

2. If users or staff have to shield their eyes from glare anywhere in a library, something is wrong.

3. Prevent your staircases from becoming major design elements.

4. If you stand at the top of a staircase, looking down, and start fantasizing about tumbling down head over teakettle, this is Not a Good Thing.

5. You can always convert water features into planters.

6. "How will we change the lightbulbs?" is a legitimate question. "Use a lift" is not a sufficient answer.

7. If a railing can be climbed like a ladder, someone will climb it.

8. Good libraries shouldn't terrify people with a mild fear of heights.

9. No matter what people say about electronic books, libraries always run out of space sooner or later. Before you construct a new building, know how it will be expanded.

10. If you need perimeter ornamentation on a room, crown moldings are vastly better than soffits.

11. Perforated vinyl white roller blinds are an amazing cure for blinding sunlight. And you can still see images of the outside world.

12. Skylights are too bright by day and too dark by night, and they are noisy when it rains. But they make up for all that by leaking.

13. Multiple entrances into a library will make users happy, but they're expensive to supervise.

14. No matter what some people insist, almost all libraries sooner or later run out of space.

15. Glass surfaces are a lot noisier than drywall surfaces, and you can't add sound-absorbing panels.

16. Rooms with dark ceilings require expert lighting.

PART I
Nearly Endless Observations
on Good Library Design

CHAPTER 3

The Basic Configuration of Successful Library Spaces

I. Introduction

This chapter provides a quick overview of some general options for the physical layout of library buildings.

Many of the issues discussed here are easy to review when you are going over early versions of schematic designs. If you think your staff, owners, or architects are proposing room shapes and arrangements that may cause functional problems, the time to deal with this is as early as possible in the design process.

Essential drawings from your architects include:

- *Schematic design* indicating furniture placement. Without furniture placement, library spaces are often nothing more than large open spaces, and it's impossible to judge their effectiveness.

- *Elevations*, showing what the outside of the library looks like from all four sides.

- *Cross sections.* For all but extremely simple buildings with fairly flat roofs show the vertical relationships between floors, ceilings, and roofs. Trying to work without cross sections is impossible when rooms do not have flat ceilings or buildings are more than one story tall.

- *Site plans*, showing how the building fits onto the land the library owns. Among other things, site plans tell a lot about essential space for long-term expansion.

Occasionally architects will argue that schematic designs should not include furniture placement, which should come later in the process. But they are wrong. Be sure that your contracts with your architects make clear that furniture placement is part of schematic design work.

It's unfair to everyone to keep your mouth shut and let an unfortunate early concept develop and take shape, only to be abandoned when your staff or owners or architects have devoted a lot of time to it.

A basic rule of good design is to keep things simple. Have a good reason for every shape. Not all rectangles are the same (proportions matter). And always pay attention to the third dimension.

II. External Configuration

II-A. BUILDING SHAPES

Rectangular structures are less expensive to construct than more complex structures, and they're a lot easier to arrange internally.

Constructing buildings with curved walls can be expensive, and sometimes very expensive, especially when curves are so sharp windows can't be made of sections of flat glass.

But it's not just curves that cost money. Many attractive details, such as windows, dormers, and all sorts of revived historic features, can also cost money to construct and maintain.

As chapter 22 on collection storage indicates, trying to fit shelving into curved spaces is a miserable experience. Concave curved walls also tend to lead to weird acoustics.

Curved walls in reading areas can be welcoming and functional, although with small buildings spaces can serve both as reading areas and collection areas, leading to problems with curved walls in general.

Similarly, rooms with diagonal walls are hard to use. Libraries with a lot of triangular or trapezoidal spaces have problems with furniture placement, staff workrooms, and placement of hallways.

The other side of the issue is that rectangular buildings can also be more boring to look at, particularly if your designer is in love with buildings with no surface ornamentation.

The main thing is to be aware of your choices. Be sure that your architect reviews your options and relative costs, and be sure that all schematic designs show how your necessary furnishings will fit in. And then make an informed decision.

II-B. COMPASS ORIENTATION OF ENTRANCES

Except in areas where winter never comes, south entrances always work best.

South entrances help protect your users and staff from wintry blasts when doors are held open.

South entrances also discourage ice buildup right outside the doors because the south sun shines directly on the pavement all winter.

If you can't have a south entrance, strive for east or southeast, and do your best to avoid north and west entrances.

> This really matters. Fred worked with one library with a long (and fairly modern) flight of exterior steps facing northwest. The steps are coated with ice all winter (because the sun doesn't fall all that much on staircases facing northwest). As a result, the steps are roped off about three months a year, and users must enter through a basement door. When the architect was asked why he designed a huge exterior flight of steps facing northwest, he responded, "Don't they look great!"

If you are forced to have a north or west entrance, investigate ice-melting systems with fluid in heated pipes buried below the pavement outside the door. Or do as many libraries with west or north entrances do and budget for substantial amounts of ice-melting chemicals. And have a closet for ice-melting chemicals right by your main entrance.

If south doors include a lot of glass, the glare from the low southern sun in the winter can be fierce. One approach is to make the entry vestibule a zigzag, which helps prevent direct glare from blinding people inside the library. Because the doors are further apart, the possibility of having both open at the same time is also reduced, saving drafts and energy. The greater the number of people entering the building here, the deeper the vestibule or offset needs to be, in order to prevent both doors from being open at the same time and sending winter winds howling around users and staff.

II-C. WHERE TO PUT ENTRANCES

It's always better to enter a rectangular building or room on the long side. This allows service desks to face entrances and allows users to divide into separate groups the moment they enter the space. For example, in a small public library, children can immediately turn one way and adults the other, without having to traipse through each other's spaces.

If users have to enter the narrow end of a space, it's much harder for library staff to supervise the space, and users have to walk through more irrelevant spaces to reach the spaces they want. Entering the narrow side of a library building is a little like entering the airplane through a door right by the cockpit and having to thread your way past endless rows of seats.

II-D. THE NUMBER OF ENTRANCES

"The right number of entrances to a library is anything up to one" is one of the most central tenants of library design, along with "no skylights" and "don't smirk while you terrify people with acrophobia."

A few exceptions to the single-entrance rule exist. Huge buildings that consist of hallways leading to lockable departments sometimes need more than one way in. Libraries with historic entrances accompanied by flights of stairs need second entrances that are accessible to users with disabilities. Library buildings that have streets on one side and parking lots on the opposite side are more popular with two entrances.

The primary reason for the single-entrance rule is money. All public entrances need to be staffed at all times by people who are within a few feet of the entrance. Even if extra entrances work out when the library opens, the fiscal burden of staffing two entrances may wear thin over the years.

All security gates at entrances need to be staffed, so adding gates to an entrance doesn't eliminate the need for staffing. (Some architects, city planners, and campus planners don't realize this fact, which means that librarians and building consultants have to keep an eye on schematic designs.)

If you need two entrances, some sites will support a building with two outside entrances leading to a single vestibule, with the vestibule in turn having a single entrance to the actual library. This makes one security point possible and avoids the cost of staffing two entrances.

III. Internal Layout and Room Shapes

III-A. AVOID STRANGELY SHAPED SPACES

Designers are frequently tempted to create interesting interior spaces by avoiding simple rectangles. Sometimes these work well, but often they don't.

L-shaped rooms are often a bad idea. Some libraries have tried L-shaped meeting rooms, with program locations at the juncture of the two sides of the L. Inevitably, all the members of the audience see the speaker at a 45-degree angle, and no one can see the projection screen well. The audience in one arm of the L cannot see the audience in the other arm. L-shaped rooms will typically hold fewer pieces of furniture than rectangular rooms with the same square footage. Be prepared to say "No." Loudly.

Triangular rooms also make extremely bad use of available square footage. Shelving and study tables are all rectangular. And nothing fits into sharp interior corners.

In addition to L-shaped rooms and triangular rooms, we've also seen libraries with banana-shaped rooms, oval rooms, pie-shaped rooms, trapezoidal rooms, and other non-rectangular geometric shapes. In all cases, the rooms worked poorly. In many cases, the owners spoke unkindly of the rooms, despite their strong motivation to speak well of their buildings.

Some libraries have very successful spaces with curved walls, but they take extremely careful planning. Curved walls are incompatible with shelving, it's usually impossible to add on a space with a curved wall, rooms with curved walls can have horrible acoustics, and nearly all windows will require blinds. On the other hand, round reading rooms can be extremely attractive.

So be extremely careful. Unfortunately, curved walls are the bane of some libraries, and once constructed they won't go away.

Curved walls are expensive to build, and library contents don't fit well into curved spaces. With curved spaces it's hard to install lighting, almost impossible to position stacks, hard to position furniture, and frequently hard to keep an eye on things because non-rectangular shelving spaces lead to bad sight lines. Curved walls can also lead to sounds carrying in undesirable ways.

If your library is constructed with curved walls, they'll be around for the lifespan of the building, making life miserable for users and staff and maintenance budgets in decades to come. Or you'll spend a lot of money getting rid of them or building a totally new library. Cuteness is not a sufficient excuse for curved walls.

Summing up, funny-shaped rooms cost more to build per square foot. They are hard to light, since rows of light fixtures don't fit well into oddly shaped spaces. Funny-shaped rooms often have strange acoustics. Library furnishings are almost all rectangular, and fitting them into non-rectangular spaces is difficult. A funny-shaped room with 3,000 square feet of floor space will hold less furniture than a rectangular room with 3,000 square feet of floor space.

Reconfiguring space is a lot harder with funny-shaped rooms, so think carefully about them.

III-B. AVOID LABYRINTHS (AND THE RESULTING CONFUSION)

How rooms are grouped together is as important as the geometry of individual rooms. Clusters of related spaces (administration, study rooms, multipurpose rooms, etc.) need simple organization. Twisting corridors make access confusing, expansion difficult, and eventual reconfiguration more challenging.

Avoid bearing walls as much as possible. Bearing walls have the structural function of holding up buildings, but they interrupt sight lines and limit flexibility. And in the long term, they are almost inevitably in the wrong places, leading to endless questions in the form of, "This is a neat room, but what can we possibly fit into it?"

Library buildings that have bearing walls and have been repeatedly expanded sometimes end up as labyrinths, but there's no excuse for a labyrinth in a new building. In an existing building with bearing walls, it may be worthwhile replacing the internal bearing walls with columns and beams, often called a "structural frame," to provide long-term usability.

> One interesting version of the labyrinth is provided by a Midwestern academic library. The library has two identical two-story spaces, each consisting of a main floor and a central balcony. The trouble is that the two spaces are identical in appearance, and neither one is at the building's entry level. Both are arrived at by elevator or totally enclosed staircases, and users arriving in one of the two spaces may take a considerable amount of time to puzzle out that they are actually in the wrong space. Fred spent several hours in the building and became lost on a number of occasions. He likes to blame his problems on the building.

> The San Francisco Public Library has two entrances, one from Market Street and a second from the city hall plaza one flight up. People entering from the plaza walk to the great atrium at the center of the building. Across the way is the children's department. But you can't get there, because there's no way around the atrium. To reach the children's department, users retrace their steps to the plaza entrance, go down one floor, walk the length of the building, pass through security, and then go back up by a different elevator. Fred spent 15 minutes figuring things out and then spent half an hour watching other visitors struggle with the same confusing layout.

Staff supervision requires excellent sight lines, and that means the absence of unnecessary walls. Patron orientation requires excellent sight lines, and that means the absence of unnecessary walls. User and staff security require excellent sight lines, and those also require the absence of unnecessary walls.

We've met owners, consultants, and architects who are mad wall builders. "Beware! Beware!" as Mr. Coleridge might say, were he with us today.

III-C. MAINTAIN SIGHT LINES

In many library situations we need to maintain sight lines, often while simultaneously blocking noise.

Study rooms require acoustic separation but no visual privacy. The solution is glass walls on all sides, acoustically insulated walls above the ceiling, and appropriate sealants and doors.

Walls separating staff areas and public areas can have windows to allow staff supervision of adjacent public areas, while the walls themselves can be acoustically insulated. Staff windows can be equipped with Venetian blinds. Staff can always close blinds when privacy is essential, but they usually can't create new windows when better sight lines are necessary.

At the same time, windows into staff rooms provide security for occupants and protection for people visiting occupants.

Good sight lines are also essential for security. Libraries do not benefit from lurking places. Far too many libraries require that librarians take frequent tours around the place, just to be sure that everything is safe. We've had librarians tell us, "We have to be careful who uses that study room" because there's no glass wall facing the reference desk.

The time to start evaluating sight lines is during the schematic design phase. Sometimes you need to be really aggressive. Most design these days is done with three-dimensional modeling that will provide drawings showing what sight lines will be like from various points of view.

III-D. ASSIST WAYFINDING

Good sight lines are essential for wayfinding. Wayfinding is knowing where you are in a building, knowing where your desired destination is, and knowing how to get there from your present location. This should be as intuitive as possible if you want an inviting, effective building.

It's no fun to have to give users complex instructions when they ask how to find things. It's a lot easier to answer the favorite reference question of all time ("Where's the restroom?") when you can point to a distant sign and have the user say happily, "Oh yes, I see the sign!"

There are a couple of time-tested organizing strategies that people instinctively recognize when they come into a building:

- **The Main Street.** One convenient way to lay out the interior of a library space is to arrange various elements along a wide central aisle through the space, with individual elements butting up against the aisle. Some architects have referred to this approach to building layout as "Main Streets," and it seems to work very well.

- **The Wonderful, T-Shaped Aisle Pattern.** One of the best ways to lay out the interior of a small library building or a department in a large library is to lay it out in a T shape. The entrance to the room or library is in the center of the wide side of the room. Facing the entrance, about halfway from the entrance to the back wall, is a service desk. Reaching to the right and left of the desk, aisles provide user access to the various areas of the department or library.

Spaces arranged in this fashion maximize interaction between users and staff. Users see the service desk straight ahead when they enter the space, and staff at the desk see arriving users. Staff at the desk can also look down the left- and right-hand aisles to see what's going on. And various areas of the library or department can abut the aisles.

And there are organizing patterns to avoid:

- **"Beads-on-a-string."** Far too many libraries have floor plans that force users to wander through irrelevant spaces.

Homemade signs are awkward and often unnecessarily ugly. (But at least these are legible.)

Always be sure that extra signs to match those in your new library are available at a reasonable cost. Many libraries are driven to improvisation when it turns out that a group of signs was affordable but a single extra sign would be impossibly expensive.

This odd choice of a temporary tripod with a temporary sign pointing the way to the permanent location of the restrooms suggests that this library may have agreed to let the architects dictate all built-in signage forever. (The moral is to never give your architects any rights to your building once the ribbon is cut. If you want to paint it pink, you should never need to ask your architects' permission before picking out the special shade of cerise you want.)

Sometimes this results from having to enter the narrow end of a building. Instead of entering and being offered options to turn left, turn right, or go straight ahead, users have to enter the spaces one after another.

Sometimes this kind of unfortunate beads-on-a-string room arrangement is the result of putting obstacles such as courtyards or atria in the way, forcing users and staff to circumnavigate the spaces. Despite their occasional beauty, courtyards and atria can be impressively dysfunctional pains in the neck.

In any case, the result is not only awkwardness but also problems with wayfinding, acoustics, flexibility, and security. As an example, if the adult and children's departments in a public library have to be entered sequentially, either children run noisily through the adult department to reach their department (bothering readers) or adults walk through the children's department to reach the adult department, raising fears of the security of children.

See also section IV-A, "Courtyards."

III-E. ALWAYS AVOID BASEMENTS

One of the seriously bad ideas in library architecture is basements. Putting things as simply as possible, you don't want a basement in your library for any purpose whatsoever.

The rule is to never build a new library with a basement, never convert a building with a basement to a library, and never build a basement in the new wing of your library.

Most libraries with basements regret the situation. Basements have humidity problems. Basements leak. Basements flood, and floods suddenly occur in areas that have never before been flooded. Basements are dark. Staff members who are relegated to basement workspaces are either unhappy staff members or uncomfortable and angry and deeply resentful staff members. Sloped exterior ramps and open exterior staircases leading to basements always lead to water intrusion, even when there's no flood going on. Books and documents that are stored in basements can have short lifespans. And older basements frequently have unpleasant (and dysfunctional) low ceilings.

In Carnegie-era libraries, the half-basements were often gloomy. Unfortunately, the first response to overcrowding often led to moving the children's department into the basement meeting room, both eliminating program spaces and giving children a worm's eye view of libraries.

Departments that are moved to basements because that's the only remaining space can always ask, "Since expansion space could have been provided on an upper floor for the same cost as this dismal, sunless, dank, and flood-prone hole, what's your excuse?" And the people who picked the basement instead of an upper floor should be expected to answer.

As a friend of Fred's who is retired from a large insurance company says, "Basements are places you put things you really don't want."

In Carnegie-era libraries, first floors were several feet above grade level and basements only a few feet below ground. But in modern libraries with grade-level entries, basement floors may be anything from 14 to 15 or more feet below grade. By comparison with Carnegie-era basements, modern basements have no natural light (except for the occasional perimeter light well or skylight) and suffer from far greater hydrostatic pressures.

Some libraries build basements because they aren't allowed to add extra floors. If you have a limited site and a zoning restriction on building height, you may feel forced to have a basement. But it's far better to look for a new site.

Basements require elevators in order to meet accessibility codes. If you have a one-story library, having to add an elevator to provide access to your new basement may cost as much as adding an additional 500 to 1,000 square feet to your main floor. And your new elevator will require annual expenditures for both inspections and periodic maintenance, neither of which will be required if you have a one-story library.

Unlike home construction, basements in libraries are nearly as expensive as upper floors. With basements in houses, the crawlspace is just made larger. The foundation walls are simply extended a few feet downward, and a concrete floor is poured. (It also requires footing drains, underfloor drains, a sump, and a sump pump, but they're not a huge deal.)

By contrast, *modern* libraries use slab-on-grade construction. Pouring concrete on compacted fill means that the immense weight of books is born by the soil rather than by a strong floor. But if you add a basement, the slab-on-grade floor must be replaced by a floor strong enough to hold 150 pounds per square foot—a floor just as strong as a second-story floor. The only real difference in cost between a basement and an extra story in a library is the cost of the windows and more attractive sheathing, and from that we deduct the extra cost of sealing the basement walls. The upshot is that by building a basement instead of an extra floor you save probably less than 10 percent in construction cost for the space involved. If you have a high water table, you don't even save the 10 percent. And you get a dark and potentially dank space, missing the advantages of natural light and dry spaces.

A common response to dark basements is windows with light wells—openings in the ground leading down to basement windows. Unfortunately, the views through windows into light wells are dismal. Even with gratings at ground level to keep trash out of light wells, it still blows in, and light wells require a lot of cleaning. And they can leak during heavy rains.

Because basements are dark, some library buildings have basement-level outdoor spaces or terraces attached, something like very large light wells. These bring in light, but they're typically not pleasant spaces. And they may need sump pumps designed to handle large amounts of water.

Storm drains don't work on terraces at basement level because water from higher drains in nearby streets and less ambitious light wells backs up into your basement-level terrace. Backflow valves, designed to prevent the storm drains from operating in reverse, can be blocked by twigs. And when the valves work correctly, the pressures in the system can literally blow the valve units out of the ground. And then water fills the library. (The exploding valve and subsequent flood happened to a library that Fred inherited, so don't think we're just assuming the worst.)

Sooner or later, most basements get wet. Wet books don't smell as bad as wet dogs, but they're still no fun. Wet dogs can be dried off, while wet books (unless they have seriously major value) go into the dumpster. When the river is over its banks, it's comforting to know that your library has no basement.

Another advantage of upper floors over basements concerns flood insurance, which is not offered by commercial insurance companies. For political reasons, the federal flood insurance program is operated at a major loss, but if reasonable premiums are ever charged, you may find it hard to afford them.

Floods are not a trivial matter. People who used to talk about "hundred-year floods" are now talking about "thousand-year floods."

> There's a lot of talk about freeze-drying books as a way of rescuing wet books. For school and public libraries in particular, this appears to be a dubious idea. Freeze-drying is expensive. Books with coated paper can't be rescued. And rescued books never look the same. When you are making plans for disasters, know what the real costs and benefits of rescue are. And wish all of your books were stored above grade. There are a variety of devices to limit dangers due to floors below grade, but you can avoid all of them—and their occasional unreliability—by simply building above ground.

Workable responses when basements are suggested include:

- When your site's height restrictions force you to construct a library with a basement, find a larger site or seek political relief from height restrictions.

- When you have a historic library with a half basement, and you can't just walk away, build an addition at ground level and provide an elevator where the original building and new addition meet.

- Never buy an existing building with a basement.

III-F. LET FUNCTIONAL NEEDS DRIVE STRUCTURAL SPACES

Ideally, the exterior shape of the library will be driven by the spaces that have to fit within.

An architect friend of ours said it's a matter of laying out all the spaces you need and then wrapping an attractive exterior around them, rather than creating an attractive exterior and then cramming everything inside any old way.

In reality, of course, it's a bit of back and forth. If you want a simple rectangular building, you do need to keep that in mind as you lay out interior spaces. The point is that there is no exterior aesthetic that should overwhelm a functional plan. There is no reason you can't have both function and beauty. Settling for one or the other is a disservice to all involved for generations to come.

III-G. DON'T LET INHERITED WALLS FILL YOUR BUILDING WITH TINY SPACES

One of the problems with expanding library buildings is that the original rooms end up too small to meet any of the library's current needs.

One easy thing to do is to remove unnecessary walls. With modern buildings with post and beam construction and with simple interiors, this can be easy, but with older buildings with bearing walls—interior walls that hold up the building—this can be difficult. As a result, many historic libraries that have been expanded consist of elegant front reading rooms with the original library entrances closed off, followed by rabbit warrens of small spaces that can't be altered because of bearing walls, followed at last by wide-open modern spaces. In essence, the building consists of three parts: the modern entrance and library rooms, a wasp waist with tiny rooms on both sides, and then the original reading rooms.

Libraries can have trouble figuring out what to do with the original reading rooms, and sometimes users entering through new wings don't even realize that the historic rooms are there.

The problem is that the entire structure of the original buildings is extremely difficult to alter because the walls between the rooms are holding up the buildings.

The workable options appear to be:

- Abandon the original building, creating a new library with post and beam construction on a new site.

- Expand the original building by building a major new grade-level addition with a new main entrance to the rear, converting the original building to reading rooms or departments small enough to fit the existing space.

- Keeping the original entrance as the main entrance to the expanded building is usually a seriously bad idea. Among other things, the entrance may be unpleasantly inaccessible, and many users may end up funneled into the back of the building through what looks like a basement door. (See chapter 11, "Accessibility.")

- And buildings with widely separated historic and modern sections can be expensive to staff.

- Restructure the original building, replacing the interior (including all the interior bearing walls) with modern post and beam architecture. This retains historic exteriors but allows functional, modern interiors.

Of the three options, the first is easiest and least expensive, the second more expensive but resulting in awkward buildings, and the third the most expensive but preserving the building without creating a variety of unusable spaces.

III-H. NEVER CONSTRUCT A LIBRARY THAT CAN'T BE EXPANDED

Judging whether expansion space exists requires a site map as part of support documents.

If your proposed building has no indication of site boundaries, immediately ask owners and designers where additions will be added to the building.

Owners and designers with bad proposals will often claim that the building in question will never need to be expanded. (It's okay to imply they're lying through their teeth, but be subtle about it.)

A possible exception to the absolute need for expansion space is branches of public and academic libraries, where older materials can be sent to the main library stacks.

Some libraries have problems due to the lack of adjacent expansion land, or land that requires permission of the donor of initial land. Both situations need to be avoided from the outset. Libraries without clear title to their buildings (and essential expansion space) are not happy libraries.

IV. Features That Require Extreme Care in Order to Be Functional

Any proposed plans involving features like the ones listed below must always be accompanied by cross sections. If you don't get them, tell your designers you'll need to see them. And then discuss with your designers how the potential problems listed below will be avoided.

IV-A. COURTYARDS

Courtyards are spaces open to the air in the middle of buildings. Before the coming of modern lighting systems, courtyards played an essential role as sources of reading light.

Modern lighting systems provide far more consistent and workable light than courtyards ever did, but some people like courtyards for the open air (and plantings) they can provide.

When a courtyard provides an essential connection between two areas of a building, it can be unpleasant to use much of the year. Sometimes it's 75 and sunny, but too much of the year it's unpleasantly hot, cold, dark, or wet.

And when it's dark, who knows who's lurking behind the ornamental plantings? Many library courtyards are kept locked, suggesting that they are security issues.

Some courtyards are essentially deep and small. They are often difficult to light, and it can be hard to find plants that flourish in the frequently shadowed spaces. And the courtyards may strike many people as spooky rather than attractive.

When modern additions are attached to historic libraries, the connection between them may be filled by a courtyard, either open to the air or glassed over. Constructions bridging spaces between historic buildings and new additions can therefore result in empty rooms with glass ceilings. The question that always arises is whether the courtyard was intended primarily to avoid having to make the original and new architecture compatible. And to whom was this important?

The large openings between the original and new sections of buildings sometimes give the impression that no one has figured out what to do with them. Some are simply empty, glassed-over, vacant spaces en route from one section to another.

Courtyards can often become spaces that are simply in the way and require users and staff to detour while passing through the library—the usual beads-on-a-string pattern of badly configured spaces. At their worst, courtyards can force rooms that should be the ends of the line to become passageways. Fred worked with one library where the courtyard required access to the library's conference room to be through the library's main meeting room. People were forced to interrupt large meetings in the main meeting room while they were on the way to smaller meetings in the conference room.

What you can ask your designers to do:

- Carefully evaluate proposed courtyards for oversight problems, problems interfering with internal traffic in buildings, and likely appearance.
- If courtyards serve as connections between new and old wings, evaluate whether the courtyards will serve an important function or whether they will be empty spaces serving only as corridors.

Courtyards can be beautiful, but they can lead to long, narrow interior spaces that are hard to use and frequently complicate access to other parts of the building. The result is rooms laid out like beads on a chain.

IV-B. CURVED WALLS AND ROUND ROOMS

Curved rooms can be extremely attractive, but they can cause design challenges. Among other things:

- Curved walls can lead to unpleasant acoustics. Remember the "whispering gallery" at St. Paul's Cathedral, where a whisper spoken on one side of the room can be heard clearly on the far side, and ask if that would improve your library. An Illinois public library had a children's program room shaped more or less like a silo, and it was a miserable place for programs.

- Rooms with curved walls are completely incompatible with book shelving. We can't afford to create non-rectangular spaces that might eventually be used for shelving.

- Rooms with curved walls can be hard to light. Simple rows of uplight fixtures are not compatible with round spaces.

- Curved walls are more expensive to construct than flat walls.

- Practical curved walls need to have curves gentle enough to have windows with flat sheets of glass. The extremely high cost of curved glass has led to the construction of buildings with curved single-pane windows, resulting in impressive temperature control problems.

The basic point is that round rooms can be great, but they require unusually competent design work.

What you can ask your designers to do:

- Use round spaces as dramatic spaces for reading and socializing, but never for everyday library purposes like book shelving or staff workrooms.

- Make sure that there are ways to expand libraries without ruining the round spaces.

IV-C. ORNAMENTAL BUT OFTEN DYSFUNCTIONAL OPENINGS BETWEEN FLOORS

With any proposed design, always check cross-section drawings for large openings between floors. These are frequently proposed by architects, often appeal to owners, and reliably fail to appeal to the people who should matter most: library users and staff.

Multi-floor openings come in a variety of versions. Many are photogenic, but many also cause problems. Among the most common design concepts featuring multi-floor openings are:

- Atria
- Dramatic staircases (which frequently accompany atria)
- Balconies
- Overhead bridge walkways

Among other common problems, openings between floors lead to:

- Unwanted noise transmission. Unless the space between an upper-story open area and the rest of the upper story has a glass wall, noise can be a major problem. When in doubt, show the concept drawing to an acoustical consulting engineer.

- Difficulty in lighting. Elaborate chandeliers in areas like atria are expensive to construct and hard to service. Some are on lifts so they can be dropped to the floor for relamping, but many are not. Some simply hang there as artifacts of bygone enthusiasms, eternally switched off.

- Floor spaces that are difficult to use because they are all basically donut shaped. Fitting furniture and shelving into a torus is a lot more challenging than fitting everything into a single, large floor.

- Terrifying users and staff who have acrophobia. This can be alleviated by having wide walking spaces around atria and opaque railings up to chest height. But you may have to fight for both. And people can still climb over and jump.

- Providing sites for suicides. Atria and other openings between floors are frequent sites for suicides, including in libraries. One infamous example is the New York University's Bobst Library, by world-famous architect Philip Johnson. After three user suicides, the library had to install an extraordinarily expensive screen to keep more people from jumping.

- Floor openings may be difficult to circumvent. If getting from one area of the library to another constantly involves walking around an atrium or a major opening for a staircase, library users and staff are far more likely to be annoyed at the extra walking than be artistically engaged by the opening.

- Some large spaces have balconies all around, leading to tunnel-like upper-story spaces. While the most practical library spaces result from entering the broad sides of rectangular areas, it's hard to imagine anything that technically qualifies as a single room but is harder to deal with than a long, narrow, winding space. But they exist.

- In the case of balconies, inadequate ceiling heights on balconies or the spaces below them. For flexibility and good lighting, all library floors need ceilings an absolute minimum of 10 feet high, including both balconies and the spaces beneath balconies. If a library room has a balcony, it will probably need to be a minimum of 24 feet high.

- Sometimes complicated accessibility. Large openings between floors can lead to problems for users with disabilities. Elevators can be nearly hidden by grandiose staircases. The long and snaky configuration of elaborate balconies can be miserable for users in wheelchairs.

- Along with atria go monumental staircases. When you are evaluating options, ask your library users and library staff rather than your owners, your designers, or your visiting sightseers.

Opinions on dramatic openings between floors differ.

- Basically, if you can't explain the underlying reason for the size and height of the opening, you don't need it.

- If you can't explain what alternatives to a dramatic opening were considered as part of the design effort, you need your design team to go through the alternatives and explain why they don't meet your needs.

- If you picked the dramatic opening without involvement of library users or librarians because you knew they might object, shame on you.

What you can ask your designers to do:

- Always have acoustical engineers evaluate the impact of large open spaces between floors.

- Unless there will be obvious and extremely accessible alternative routes, always say "no" to walking bridges over architectural chasms. Or just say "no" up front, since amazingly few library users and staff find bridges appealing.

- Beware of public balconies. They tend to combine lack of easy accessibility, narrow spaces, fear of falling, unworkably low ceilings, and difficult supervision. If they're deep enough for occupancy, use them for staff workspaces.

- In some libraries that are part of larger buildings, access to library balconies is from other parts of the building. Unless the balconies have monitored access doors, the library loses all security.

- If you absolutely must have atria and monumental staircases, place them on one side of a building rather than have them serve as the focus of the building. Glass them in on upper levels. Beware of dramatic light fixtures. Always have well-marked elevators right next door to exciting staircases. And see chapter 11, "Accessibility."

- To prevent noise transmission problems, you may need to glass in upper floors on atria and dramatic staircases.

- Never create situations that will frighten people with acrophobia.

- Never create a design that facilitates suicides. Any drop-offs should be short enough that people jumping off the edges would expect (at worst) broken ankles.

- And never, ever, create potentially dangerous situations that construction without ornamental openings between floors could avoid.

- In Fred's always outspoken opinion, one of the worst popular designs in modern libraries is atria. Tell your designers from the beginning that you don't want any. Ever.

IV-D. HUGE READING ROOMS

Huge reading rooms with high ceilings have been a standard feature of large library buildings for many years. They are impressive. They lend themselves to attractive windows high on the walls. And they provide rooms where the relationship between size and height is comfortable, avoiding rooms that feel like bomb shelters.

Many reading rooms are on top floors, in order to avoid having to fill them with architectural columns supporting the rooms above. This can lead to reading rooms that are off the beaten path, but it can in turn lead to reading rooms that are the amazingly satisfactory ends of long approaches.

Other reading rooms are on ground floors and take advantage of long-span structural systems that free the floors of columns. This approach places reading rooms in more accessible locations without including the interruptions of columns.

While huge reading rooms are great when seen from floor level, not everyone agrees on the fun of viewing them from above. But there is no real need to force people to view them from above.

Great reading rooms can have lighting systems that are difficult to service. With the long lives of LED lighting systems, lamp maintenance can be minimal, but dusting may be more fun.

What you can ask your designers to do:

- Avoid situations where people have unsought access to overlooks in reading rooms.

IV-E. LARGE ENTRY ROOMS WITH RADIATING WINGS

Some historic public libraries have been constructed with great central entry halls and with radiating wings, sometimes attached to all three of the non-entry sides of the central halls. Many of these libraries are historic and handsome, such as many "revival" style buildings.

Unfortunately, with a building design of this type, it may be impossible to expand the building without removing one of the historic wings or having a building with a major addition at the end of a long, narrow wing.

If the main exterior entrance to the central hall is inaccessible, creating an accessible entrance without an offensive exterior ramp is important, and the two entrances are likely to be widely separated. See chapter 11, "Accessibility."

If the library follows the lead of many Carnegie-era libraries and closes the historic front entrance, it's left with a historic building with architecture that cries out, "This way in," but there is no in.

If the library removes a wing in order to construct an addition, the usual problems that accompany the expansion of historic buildings occur. The library becomes an increasingly complex structure, with many spaces to supervise and to find uses for. After-hours access to meeting rooms will almost certainly require locking the historic entrance at closing time, unless the historic wings are converted to meeting rooms.

What you can ask your designers to do:

- If you can't figure out how to do it well, don't ruin historic libraries by trying to expand them. Preserve them as historic library branches and construct functional main buildings somewhere else.

IV-F. WINDOWS SET INTO CEILINGS

When you examine cross sections of libraries, watch in particular for glass incorporated in ceilings. Vertical glass facing north (but not in other directions) can work extremely well. All other glass needs a way to block all direct sunlight.

Skylights require a great deal of light control, with a very high percentage of total light blocked. They also require substitutes for daylight under skylights at night, on cloudy days, or in the middle of the winter. Lots of skylights have awkward lighting at times when daylight is dim. But it's balanced by bad lighting at times when daylight is bright.

Asking questions of your owners and designers on day one is essential, and being told not to worry is unacceptable. Photometric studies are mandatory.

See chapter 31, "Lighting."

IV-G. ROOMS WITH DIAGONAL WALLS

Always say "No." And mean it.

V. Traffic Flows

When you are evaluating proposed floor plans for libraries, it helps to consider the flow of users and staff and books through the building.

Users need simple, efficient routes that don't force them to detour through unwanted spaces in order to reach their destinations. They need simple rather than complex routes, so that way-finding is as easy as possible.

While staff routes are often shared with users, all but the smallest libraries have additional routes that are closed to users. Much of this is for security. Libraries don't need users wandering through the service corridors that provide access to staff workrooms, staff lunchrooms, staff restrooms, panel rooms, HVAC spaces, water rooms, custodial workrooms, and so on. Usually these end up being somewhat more complex routes than are routes for users, but it helps to evaluate schematic designs by imagining how staff members will get around and whether the spaces that various subgroups of staff use are conveniently close.

Occasionally, staff areas double as fire escape routes. In this case, doors providing emergency access to staff areas need to be equipped with alarms.

The final major traffic flow in a library building is books. Technical services departments are ideally near loading docks, although elevators can keep libraries from tying up valuable main floor space with tech services workrooms. The general flow of processed materials from technical services to public shelves is far less massive than lending, and the paths may be longer because of that.

Lending operations must deal with major flows of incoming and outgoing interlibrary loans, carts full of returned materials brought from book returns to lending departments, and carts used to return materials to shelves. To be convenient for users, lending desks need to be close to main entrances, but what happens to returned books afterward can vary a lot. Having to trundle quantities of materials by awkward pathways may be an avoidable problem.

VI. Artistic Ceiling Shapes

Although this chapter has focused on floor plans, the third dimension of buildings always matters. When you are reviewing floor plans, be sure to check the elevation and section drawings.

Creative roof and ceiling shapes can lead to odd valleys in roofs that may tend to leak, but a more immediate problem is weird indoor acoustics.

A few libraries have had rooms with barrel vault ceilings. A barrel vault is a curved ceiling that runs the length of a room, much like the top of an old railroad tunnel. Barrel vaults can transmit sounds in amazing ways.

Domes also have weird acoustics, transmitting sounds up and down and around.

Many libraries with cathedral ceilings have serious problems. A "cathedral ceiling" is a ceiling with a center ridge pole and two sloped roof sections, similar to a house with a simple pitched roof. Cathedral ceilings are attractive and homelike, but they tend to have nasty acoustics. Sounds rise, are reflected by one side of the ceiling, are reflected again by the second side, and descend upon innocents below. In buildings with complex patterns of cathedral

> Fred worked with a library that had a reference desk at one end of a plaster-surfaced barrel vault and (about 50 to 75 feet away) a group of armchairs at the other end of the vault. Every word spoken by people sitting in the armchairs could be heard with amazing clarity at the reference desk, and all reference questions could be heard by users sitting in the armchairs.

ceilings, sounds can bounce around in strange ways and carry for surprising distances. Conversations in one part of a library can be heard unexpectedly in areas far away.

All of these problems can be cured (or at least minimized) by using sound-absorbing ceiling materials, but your designers may resist sound-absorbing surfaces because they won't provide the look they want.

> This can come to a real showdown. In desperation, one client of Fred's hired her own acoustical consulting engineers who reported that without acoustic surfaces, the proposed cathedral ceiling in her library would be an acoustic nightmare. In the process she forced the architect to grudgingly agree to acoustic surfaces.

The difficulty and extra costs of artistic ceilings vary. Construction costs may include extra structural steel, attractive cladding for the roof, and managing water at ridges, valleys, and eaves.

VII. Snappy Rules on the Basic Configuration of Successful Library Spaces

1. Funny-shaped buildings may be architecturally interesting, but they're usually expensive and often dysfunctional.

2. All good library rooms that house any books are rectangles.

3. Extra entrances are often popular with users, but because all public entrances require extra staffing, extra entrances are more expensive than many people realize. The costs continue forever, and some libraries are forced to eventually close entrances as a result.

4. Most departmental libraries benefit from a T-shaped interior aisle layout. Enter from the center of the broad side of the department, facing the service desk. Walk to the desk and turn left or right for the rest of the department.

5. The same thing works for entire buildings. Enter a library building from about the center of one of its long walls.

6. Everyone knows that cathedral ceilings are noisy, but libraries with horrible acoustics sometimes blithely deny that they have a problem.

7. Triangular interior spaces cost a lot more to construct, but they compensate for it by not holding much. The best interior spaces for libraries are simple rectangles.

8. Unless your library is so far south that you worry about Burmese pythons lurking in the parking lot, you need an entrance that faces south. Under terrible duress, settle for southeast or east.

9. Curved exterior walls lead to all sorts of problems with shelving placement, light fixture location, workroom shapes, weird acoustics, and other good things. On the other hand, they cost a lot more than straight walls.

10. Round reading rooms and domes can have predictably strange acoustics. If your name is not "Library of Congress" or "British Museum," be careful when you want a round reading room with a dome.

11. The reason for reading rooms on top floors is to avoid forests of support columns

filling the rooms. Otherwise, main floor reading rooms seem friendlier.

12. Dysfunctional configurations may be chosen by governing bodies without input from librarians. Figuring out how to prevent this can be challenging, but it's very much worth it, since this is how some seriously awful ideas are established.

13. You need a good excuse for interior partitions. "Functional necessity" is a good excuse. "Architectural concept" is not a good excuse.

14. Outside of study rooms, program rooms, faculty studies, and restrooms, libraries don't benefit from small interior spaces for public use.

15. Wide, flat, and open makes a happy library.

16. Good sight lines in public areas are essential. Study rooms need glass walls—not windows here and there but glass walls on three sides. Hidden spaces available to library users have an impressive potential for assault (really bad), fooling around (probably fun, but nonetheless not a good idea), and long-term inflexibility.

17. Basements in new libraries cost about the same amount as extra floors, but they have many fewer advantages. As in no advantages whatsoever. One of the most important snappy rules in this book is "Never build a basement, and never buy an existing building with a basement."

18. If your library has a basement, sooner or later someone will store books there. And sooner or later, you'll have a lot of soggy books.

19. An Illinois public library had a YA study room with one tiny window. The library staff called it the "sex room" and eventually converted it to a storeroom.

20. Try to cluster staff workspaces next to relevant public spaces.

21. Main floors are prime commercial space. Don't use them for tech services.

22. If you have impressively identical public rooms in locations where you can't see both rooms at the same time, your users are likely to become totally confused. This is not A Good Thing. If you consider different paint colors for the two spaces, how will people with visual handicaps cope? It takes differences in physical designs to help users keep oriented.

23. You always need a lot more storage space than your board of trustees, university administration, school principal, hospital administrator, mayor, or architect think you need.

24. A schematic design without furniture placement is worthless.

25. If you arrange things right, the staff at the service desk in a small public library also can see many of the reading tables, can see through the glass walls of the entry foyer (where they can see who's entering the building, who's entering the restrooms, and who's entering the meeting room), can see the screens of the public computers, can see (through a conveniently placed glass wall or group of windows) into the meeting room itself, and can see into study rooms with glass walls. And with a little walking back and forth, they can see down all the book aisles.

26. If you have study rooms that don't have glass walls and can't be supervised by your staff from their service desks, they'll spend a lot of time running back and forth, peeking into study room windows. This annoys both library users (who by and large don't

enjoy being peeked at) and librarians (who by and large don't enjoy peeking).

27. It's a good thing to position shelving so staff members seated at service desks can see down as many aisles as possible. But NEVER use radiating aisles.

28. Never arrange rooms like beads on a chain. (One of the reasons to be extremely wary of courtyards and atria is that they can lead to this arrangement.)

29. There are libraries where it's quicker and easier to go from one room to another by walking outside the building than through the building. This is Not a Good Thing.

30. It's better to lay out all the spaces you need and wrap an attractive exterior around them than to create an attractive exterior and then cram everything you need inside, whether it fits or not.

31. Beware of ornamental columns. They get in the way and block sight lines. Purely functional columns are bad enough, and you don't want any extras.

32. When in doubt, hire an acoustical engineer to review your drawings.

33. Always have your consulting librarian check your schematic design for functionality.

34. Owners and designers frequently assume that they have just invented the concept of reading terraces. Unfortunately, reading terraces have been around for a long time, and they're all unfortunate, unless the approaches to reading terraces are from points outside the library's security gates. (Defending their concepts, some designers use the phrase "secure reading terrace," but it's an oxymoron.)

35. Screened porches in libraries are a romantic idea but also a miserable idea. The need for screened porches ended with the advent of air conditioning.

36. Don't put large staff workrooms on the entry floor of the library. Can you imagine a department store doing this? (It sounds remarkably silly, but libraries have done it.)

37. You'll never be able to look down every aisle or over the top of every range from a chair at any service desk. Plan on getting up and even moving around a bit.

38. When someone says of a proposed design, "Walking through this library will be like floating through a cloud," tear up the design. And consider exhibiting extremely visible annoyance.

39. Know when you're breaking rules. If you can't explain why and can't explain how you will avoid the resulting problems, don't do it.

40. Bad ideas can come from anyone at any time. Never let your guard down.

41. Bad ideas can come from anyone, including you. Self-awareness is a skill we all need.

42. And because it's worth repeating endlessly, ALWAYS AVOID BASEMENTS.

PART I
Nearly Endless Observations on Good Library Design

CHAPTER 4

Evaluating Library Buildings by Walking Around

I. Introduction

One good way to evaluate existing library buildings is to simply wander around and make your own judgments. Although you can miss a great deal by being limited to public areas, you have the advantage of people not trying to sway your opinions before you have formed them or distracting you by pointing out things that don't matter to you.

The ideas in this chapter are all repeated somewhere or other in the book, but it would take a few days to find them.

In older buildings, some of the problems noted in this chapter can be the result of inherited features rather than bad planning decisions.

II. Reasons for Evaluating Buildings on Your Own

- Librarians, library users, library board members, city officials, university administrators, and others sometimes need to evaluate library buildings.

- In addition to evaluating their own buildings or spaces within buildings, people frequently evaluate other libraries when they are considering hiring architects and want to get some idea of the kind of work they can expect from specific firms. Or they evaluate buildings to see what ideas they want to adopt or avoid.

- Most librarians and library governors who set out to evaluate library buildings do so for practical reasons. They need to determine whether the buildings are successful as functioning libraries.

- It's possible to tell a great deal about a library building by just looking at it, and you can find out a great deal without asking staff members, board members, or other officials. Many staff members—including directors and governors—are very hesitant to discuss problems. And sometimes they are blinded by the elegance of new buildings. It's useful, therefore, to be able to draw your own conclusions just by walking through library buildings.

- The items listed below are some that you can evaluate without consultation with library management or staff. Obviously, there are a great many things you can't evaluate—such as staff workspaces or storage spaces—without making special arrangements to go behind the scenes. And problems like structural strength, recalcitrant HVAC systems, and so on are not usually susceptible to informal evaluation.

III. The Problems with Asking the Staff

- Library staff members sometimes have a very hard time coming to grips with the fact that their buildings have problems. Librarians who participated in the design and construction of buildings are sometimes extremely attached to them, despite dysfunctional problems that are immediately obvious to most other librarians.

- Library staff members may fail to recognize that functional problems are the direct result of architectural errors.

- Library staff members may be hesitant to point out design problems. They may be driven by loyalty to their institutions or by administrative instructions to not complain.

- Library staff members are often brilliant at developing workarounds. The building may have major problems, but staff members have figured out how to make things work pretty well in spite of all that.

- Librarians who specialize in providing outstanding public service may tend not to grumble about things.

IV. Evaluation Criteria

IV-A. APPEARANCE

- Do you find the building attractive? Many people want library buildings that look warm and welcoming. If a building strikes you as ungainly or cold or awkward, this makes a difference.

- Does the building look nice primarily just because everything is new? It may help you if you try to envision how the library will look when it's somewhat worn.

- If the building is brand new, does it look nice because it exhibits the most recent styles? Or does it give the impression that its looks will outlast its newness?

- Does the building seem suited to its environment, or does it seem discordant? No matter how much aluminum and glass are in fashion, the effect may be out of place on a Georgian campus. Just as a new Georgian library may look out of place in a severely Bauhaus campus.

- Do the interior and exterior work well together? Is there a sense of comprehensive design?

- Are decorative elements pasted on, or do they follow naturally from the design of the building? Does it appear that the architect and the interior designer were a team, or that the building was first constructed and then interior elements were pasted on like the crepe paper décor at a sock hop in the high school gym?

- Do the interior spaces strike you as either too open (like a barn) or too close (like a tunnel)?

- Do you see signs of water intrusion? Look for stained ceiling tiles, plaster damage around windows, water-damaged drywall, and so on.

- If there are signs of wear and tear, do they appear to be due to inadequate maintenance or to flimsy materials?

- Whether you personally like the looks of a building is just as important as the opinions of professional critics.

- If the building won a design award, that doesn't necessarily make it a good library. Most design awards are simply architectural glamour contests and can be heavily influenced by passing design vogues. Award committees may have little or no interest in issues of practical library function.

- Do the prominent design features fit with library functions, or do they appear irrelevant?

IV-B. SENSE OF WELCOME

- Does the building look attractive as you approach it?

- Is the entryway warmly lit? If you arrive after dark, does the entryway glow invitingly?

- Can you see staff members when you enter the library, or are they hidden away?

- When you enter the library, do you immediately feel good about it? Is it pleasant and welcoming?

- Is there an obvious place to get help from a real person?

- Are there enough signs to guide you through the building, but not so many that it reminds you of wading through all the options on telephone answering equipment? If the signs look homemade, it may be because the architects talked their clients into agreeing that all signs will be designed by the architect, and the result is temporary, homemade signs stuck up in desperation. Or it may be because the original signs were so expensive that the library could not afford to purchase additional ones of the same type. (And of course, some libraries may just not get around to it.)

- Do you see a lot of places where you would like to sit and read or study? Many readers like armchairs or tables beside windows, but the main thing is whether the library has a place where *you* would personally like to be.

- Do the places you want to sit have power for your laptop?

- Can you get a good WiFi connection everywhere you go?

- Is the layout of the library relatively easy to figure out, or are you still puzzled after hanging around for a couple of hours? Is it easy to find the area of the collection you want? When you get to 317.8 at the end of a range of shelves, is it obvious where to find 317.9? If the building is complex, are clear maps posted? Are the maps oriented to match the building?

IV-C. STAFF SERVICE POINTS

- Can you find library staff when you need help?

- Are service points located with careful consideration to staff supervision of spaces? Do staff members have good sight lines? Is a staff service point located close to every alarmed exit?

- Although good sight lines are extremely important, they can be overdone. For example, stacks that radiate like the spokes of a wheel around service points are a seriously bad idea.

- Can service points be relocated, or are they monumental constructions? Look for signs of modular desk construction.

- Matching soffits above service desks are very popular with designers, but they make it extremely expensive to reconfigure or relocate desks, and they often lead to harsh downlights over desks.

- Does the library have more than one entrance in use? Unless one entrance is an inaccessible historic entrance, this may be a design problem.

- In most situations, every entrance has to be staffed, and this can be a very expensive proposition. Some libraries have simply had to lock entrances. Security gates are not a workable substitute for staffed entrances. However, if two entrances lead to a common foyer, which in turn has only one entrance to the library, that is effectively one entrance.

IV-D. NATURAL LIGHT

- Can you see the outside world? One of the many reasons not to put libraries in basements is everyone—patron and staff alike—wants natural light. (There are a lot of other important reasons to avoid basements, including avoiding flooding, dealing with access issues if there's no elevator, and recognizing that basements are nearly as expensive to construct as floors above ground.)

- Are there places where the natural light is unpleasant? All glass surfaces that do not face north need some kind of movable shielding, such as blinds. It's often impossible to install adjustable blinds in high windows, and such windows frequently cause major problems if they don't face north. Sometimes the only solution is to apply extremely dark film to the glass, which doesn't work as well as people hope and still makes one wonder why a window was installed in the first place. If direct sunlight hits lending desk staff in the face at any time of day, there are real problems.

- Particular problems arise with skylights. Skylights are beloved by many owners and architects, but they always cause serious problems because (among other things) they are too bright by day and too dark by night. If skylights are located over book stacks, people may be blinded by the light and unable to read spine labels. If a skylight is located over a service desk, staff can't move to a different place to avoid the blinding glare. Skylights also cause echoes, and they often leak.

- So-called "fritted" glass is very popular now. The general effect is areas of frosted glass or glass with a pattern of black dots, as used on the upper and lower edges of some automobile windshields.

- Allover black or white dots can be effective, but patterns of frosted glass cause serious problems with glare. If the library has glass with this type of fritting, try to find a window facing direct sunlight to see how things work.

- If you are blinded by direct daylight anywhere in the library, it's a sign of bad design.

- Glass with ornamental fritted patterns may also prove to be amazingly expensive to replace if one or more panes are broken. To us, fritted glass is an indication of badly designed windows.

- Do the long sides of the building face north and south? At middling latitudes in the northern hemisphere, north light is the best reading light and west light is the worst. Buildings therefore work best if the long direction is east-west and the short direction north-south, with north windows for reading and with sheltered south entrances.

- Entrances that face north or northwest in climates that have snow may also suffer from ice.

- Are there any signs that the library has had to take extraordinary steps to block light through ill-conceived windows?

IV-E. ARTIFICIAL LIGHT

- Can you see to read everywhere?

- Is the light soft, bright, and even? Libraries need pleasant light everywhere. The best library lighting at the time this book was written was achieved by bouncing LED lighting off white ceilings at least 10 feet high. It's important that you can look straight at all lighting fixtures without being blinded.

- Is light in the stacks bright enough to allow you to read the spines on all of the books—even the bottom rows?

- Are there any places where highly concentrated lights shine directly in your eyes, including when you look straight upward? This is called "direct glare," and there's no excuse for it in any library.

- Is stack lighting functional? Because book shelving is often high, using a library often means looking at books over your head. If in the process, you have to stare into a bright light fixture or a skylight overhead, you can be so blinded by the light that you can't read the book spines.

- Does the lighting allow furnishings to be relocated without altering the lighting?

- Are there a great many different types of light fixtures? In some libraries, one gets the impression that people went through light fixture catalogs to see how many different fixtures they could use. The result can be far too many different types of components for the library to stock.

- Are any of the lights funny colors? This is easiest to spot where light hits walls or is reflected off ceilings. A variety of now-obsolete lighting technologies led to weird-colored lighting, but some cheap LEDs can do so as well.

- Are there any light fixtures that appear to be hard to reach? Look for high fixtures that are burned out. Ask yourself how you would get at fixtures that are over staircases or in multistory atria. If fixtures are above book stacks, remember that the lifts that are frequently used to service high light fixtures may have outrigger legs that make them too wide to use in stack aisles.

- Many buildings have light fixtures that are nearly impossible to service once the construction scaffolding is removed. This is one of the most common and most frustrating design errors in library architecture. (Look for fixtures with a lot of burnt-out lightbulbs, assuming it's not just a sign of bad maintenance.)

- Are there shiny surfaces that reflect unpleasant images of light fixtures? (If the building has totally indirect lighting, the problem is the surfaces, not the lighting.)

- If the restrooms have motion sensor lights, do the lights go on BEFORE you enter the restroom and never go off while you are in there? Having to grope your way into or out of dark restrooms is a sign of sloppy engineering.

- Are any of the light fixtures full of dead bugs? Some light fixtures display every dead bug with cheerful clarity, and no maintenance staff can keep ahead of the problem. Watch particularly for chandeliers with completely translucent bowls, for there's no need for them.

- It's easiest to evaluate artificial lighting if you visit a library after dark.

IV-F. ACOUSTICS

- Do any areas of the library echo? Listen for reverberation. When you enter a room, can you hear the openness? (Clapping your hands helps reveal echoes, but you may not be welcome when you do it.)

- Can you overhear distant conversations? Some design features that cause serious problems are hard-surfaced ceilings (particularly sloped ceilings, barrel vaults, and cathedral ceilings), skylights, domes, rooms with curved walls, and hard-surfaced floors. Atria (open areas connecting floors) often carry unwanted sound in unpleasant ways (in addition to having lights that are hard to change and terrifying people who suffer from acrophobia).

- Do noises from children's areas bother people in adult areas?

- Are there quiet reading rooms or study rooms for people who want to hold small meetings or get away from the constant noises of telephones, computers, users talking with each other, and conversations at service desks? Do the reading and study rooms have glass interior walls (not little windows but completely glass walls) to provide security for users and to allow staff supervision? Are the rooms stuffy?

- Do walls block noises? For example, see if you can hear conversations from adjacent rooms when you're standing in a restroom or sitting in a study room.

- Do staircases transmit sound in unwelcome ways?

IV-G. ELECTRICAL WIRING

- Does the library have enough electrical outlets and data ports? In the era of the laptop, almost every reading table needs places to plug in computers. Are extension cords strung about the place for laptop use or other purposes? Are laptop cords stretched across walkways? (Remember that fire marshals regard extension cords as serious evils.)

- Are light switches located where users can mess around with them? Typical good locations for light switches are behind service desks or in staff workrooms.

- Are there outlet boxes in floors in addition to those around the walls and on the support columns? Is the grid of floor boxes no larger than 10′ by 10′ or 12′ by 12′?

- Are floor outlet boxes totally flush with the floor, so furniture can be placed over the outlets until they're needed, and so no one can trip over them?

- Are there outlets in reserve, in areas that are now used for shelving but may have computers or other equipment in the future?

- Is there exposed wire mold in public areas?

- Are electrical outlets childproof ("tamper resistant")? This is particularly important in public library adult departments, since it's there that preoccupied parents hand their toddlers their car keys to play with. Look for a blue dot on the receptacle.

- Does the library have good WiFi service throughout all public service areas? Your laptop or phone will tell you. It's also interesting to watch for people parked outside the building to take advantage of the library's WiFi.

IV-H. HVAC (HEATING, VENTILATING, AND AIR CONDITIONING)

- Are places in the library unpleasantly drafty? Do you find yourself changing seats because of drafts? Pay most attention to areas around windows.

- Are areas of the library too hot or too cold?

- Does the library seem stuffy?

- Does overly positive or negative air pressure cause outside doors to stand ajar or be difficult to open? Do you hear whistling air when you start to open a door?

- Do study rooms and similar spaces have individual thermostats? One thermostat for two rooms is at least one thermostat too few.

- Are space heaters scattered about? Common places are service desks, where space heaters may be tucked beneath to keep the legs of staff members warm.

- If the entire building is too cold in the winter or too hot in the summer, this may represent a management decision to save energy rather than represent bad design.

- HVAC systems in new libraries represent about 25 percent of the entire construction cost of the building, and it's a shame when a system performs in unsatisfactory ways.

IV-I. FURNISHINGS

- Are the chairs at tables comfortable? Do they slide easily? Many users prefer padded seats and backs.

- Are tables a comfortable height? Many people prefer about 29 inches.

- Do the tables have aprons? Accessibility codes require a minimum of 27 inches of leg clearance, and there's no excuse for providing less, especially because most people prefer it. Meeting accessibility codes is impossible with old tables with aprons. Ancient library tables may look impressive, but because they usually have aprons they often have either no legroom or uncomfortably high tops.

- Are armchairs the right size for human beings? If you sit in a large armchair, is it so deep that your legs stick straight out in front of you like a three-year-old's? Is it so close to the floor that you are forced to roll out of it to stand up? Can older users get out of armchairs only with agony?

- Does upholstery appear to be fragile? Is it stained or worn? Does it give the impression of being hard to clean? (Remember that the age of the building makes a major difference here.)

- Most armchairs in libraries have wooden arms to avoid rapid wear of the upholstery, so rating armchairs down due to wooden arms is not realistic.

- Are the surfaces on service counters wearing out? Ordinary high-pressure laminates are too fragile for lending countertops. Unfortunately, that's what you often get when you order from a library supply company catalog.

- Are there furnishings that lend themselves to misuse? A common example is the use of sofas in public library adult departments. Strangers won't share sofas, but sofas offer a great place to neck or to sleep.

- Are the shelving aisles comfortably wide? Aisles as narrow as 36 inches may be legal, but 42 inches or more works better. If a library plans to have 36-inch aisles, inevitably some will be a little over 36 while others are somewhat under 36 (and consequently illegal).

- Are shelves sufficiently deep? Outside of shelving for pocket-sized paperbacks, most shelving should be at least nine inches ("nominal 10 inches") deep. Many libraries with seven-inch-deep shelving have books that stick out over the edges of the shelves all over the place, effectively narrowing aisles. The ends of double-faced shelving units should be at least two feet wide.

- Are individual shelves sufficiently far apart? Nonfiction books tend to be taller than fiction books. If books are being shelved on their fore edges, the shelves are too close together. Sometimes this overcrowding represents failure to allow enough floor space for shelving.

- Were shelving colors selected for functionality rather than to make decorator statements? Were they chosen to stand the test of time? Are they so dark that they show dust and absorb light? Are they white and hard to keep clean? (Neutral pale gray or cream are ideal colors for steel shelving. They don't show dust or dirt, don't soak up light, and don't interfere with future redecorating.) Steel shelving is coated with powder paint and is very difficult to repaint, so most libraries get just one chance to pick a color.

- Are there any tables placed so that users can back up their chairs and block access to shelving?

- Are there any building support columns in the middle of shelving aisles? This is a sign of bad architectural planning (unless, of course, the library has altered aisle width after moving in).

- Do the tilting shelves for magazines lock up and open, or do you have to attempt to hold the shelf up with one elbow while looking through older issues?

- Does the library have standard steel cantilever-style shelving? Cantilever shelving has sturdy central posts. Individual shelves hook onto the posts.

- One of the tremendous advantages of cantilever shelving is that it can be picked up and relocated fully loaded by using hydraulic stack moving equipment. Many other types of shelving have to be unloaded and disassembled, the books and shelving components relocated individually, and then everything reassembled on the new location. It's an amazingly miserable undertaking.

- Is there a lot of overstuffed furniture? The problem with modern upholstered furniture is that it is usually made with polyurethane foam, which is extraordinarily flammable and releases toxic gases when it burns. (Chemicals added to make it less flammable are also toxic, and some are now banned.) Overstuffed furniture also provides good lurking crevices for creatures like bedbugs. The central question is how we can provide attractive and comfortable furniture with a minimum of padding.

IV-J. STORAGE

- Are items that should be stored out of sight piled around the edges of rooms? One of the most common places to see this problem is in meeting rooms, which may have furniture and equipment piled around the edges because there aren't adequate furniture and equipment storage closets. The addition of maker space equipment to meeting rooms has made inadequate storage even worse.

- Are boxes or other shipping containers piled in public areas of the library?

- In public libraries, do children's services areas appear to be short of storage space? (This is actually a two-edged sword, since some children's librarians are notoriously unable to toss anything out.)

IV-K. FRAGILE CONSTRUCTION MATERIALS

- Are there any signs of fragile materials that are showing premature signs of wear?

- Do you see things that appear to be worn or battered because they are hard to repair?

- Since modern drywall with latex paint is extremely fragile, do walls in public areas have chair rails?

- Is any natural wood trim, such as baseboards, worn and battered?

- Is the building covered with EIFS? (External Insulation Finishing Systems consist of a coat of stucco over plastic foam. EIFS frequently has trouble with water intrusion and damage from mild bumping. Look for unsightly dents and peeling surfaces. If the wall looks like stucco, rap on it with your knuckles to see if it sounds lightweight or hollow.)

- Are door handles, railings, and newel posts finished in colors that are coming off? Tubular metal handles, railings, and newel posts need to be brushed stainless steel.

IV-L. FLEXIBILITY

- One of the characteristics of libraries is their tendency to move things around as functional needs change. Some buildings enable this, while others make it nearly impossible to adapt to change.

- Can desks be moved easily? One thing that makes this nearly impossible is soffits that match the shape of the desk below. And some desks are too monumental to move.

- Do carpet patterns tell you where things must be located?

- Can you see signs of obsolete and inflexible storage places for things the library no longer owns? For example, do lending desks have cutouts in their tops for the card tubs that were used in lending systems a generation ago? Are there special provisions for long-gone card catalogs?

- Are there outdated decorative elements? The trendier the design, the easier it has to be to change. (Teenagers have the attention span of gnats, and spaces for them need to recognize this fact.)

- Are spare electrical outlets located everywhere? Many owners and designers balk at providing sufficient numbers of electrical outlets upfront, even though it's vastly more expensive (and sometimes impossible) to add more later.

IV-M. FUNCTIONAL ARRANGEMENT OF ROOMS

- Can you use the library meeting rooms when the rest of the library is closed? This requires access to both the meeting rooms and the public restrooms from the main entry foyer.

- Do you have to walk through the children's department to get to the adult department, or vice versa? Or are there other awkward beads-on-a-chain room arrangements?

- Adults in children's departments can lead to security problems, and children in adult departments can lead to distracting noise.

- Are departments divided for no good reason? (This is a better question to ask in entirely new buildings. Expansion of existing buildings can force designers into an awkward arrangement of spaces.)

- Is the flow of materials clear from shelving unit to shelving unit? If a shelving unit ends at 327.1, is the location of 327.2 obvious? (If the Dewey or LC range is broken in illogical ways, people may have a hard time finding books.)

- Do you enter rooms through the long sides, facing a service desk, then turn left for one group of services and right for another?

- Are all rooms rectangular? Fitting shelving and furniture into oddly shaped rooms is extremely difficult. Oddly shaped rooms are expensive to construct and make less efficient use of space. Watch for such bad choices as triangular rooms, circular rooms, L-shaped rooms, or banana-shaped rooms.

- Are there perimeter soffits with inset downlights? These are a popular but seriously undesirable design feature, leading to dark room perimeters and spotty illumination. To ornament the junction between walls and ceilings, crown moldings work vastly better.

IV-N. CEILINGS

- Are all ceilings at least 10 feet high? Lower ceilings lack necessary clearance for shelving, lighting, and fire control.

- Are all ceilings white, to enable reflected uplighting? (Some historic libraries have dark ceilings, but there's little excuse for any of that in new buildings.)

- Are all ceilings acoustic? This is particularly important when ceilings are sloped or curved.

- Are most ceilings made of acoustic tile? In addition to muffling sound, acoustic tile provides access to the vast quantities of mechanical, electrical, and plumbing equipment located above ceilings. Historic ceilings may be ruined if acoustic tile is added, but in most situations, acoustic tile is fine.

IV-O. ACROPHOBIA

- Is the library considerate of the vast numbers of people who have at least a mild fear of heights? If you are fearless around heights, try to bring someone with you who is not.

- Are railings by drop-offs made of glass?

- Can you see downward through staircases as you are walking upward? The vogue for transparent risers has been around for decades and seems to be one of the most permanently silly features in library design.

- Has the library had to install kiddy gates at the heads of staircases?

- Do you have to skirt the edges of atria on narrow walkways?
- Do staircases consist of vertiginously long runs of steps, or do they double back, reducing images in the minds of those who fear heights of tumbling downstairs headfirst forever?
- Are elevators glass boxes or do they provide a sense of protection?
- If staircases are frightening, are elevators nearby, or are they hidden away?
- Do the floors bounce underfoot?

IV-P. FLOOR COVERINGS

- Are the floors comfortable underfoot, or do you soon find yourself looking for a place to sit and rest your feet?
- Is carpeting of solid colors that show every speck of dust? Most libraries do better with patterned carpeting.
- Do carpets in areas in front of copy machines or service desks show signs of heavy wear? If so, does that appear to be due to the use of broadloom carpet rather than carpet squares?
- Are carpet patterns so bold that they are unpleasantly distracting?
- It's hard to evaluate carpet at a glance because so much depends on maintenance and on frequency of replacement.

IV-Q. ORNAMENTAL SPACES

- Are there any dramatic or decorative areas that are either heavily used or appear to be little occupied? What seems to cause the difference?
- If the library has a fireplace, is it in a suitable place? Are the controls for staff use only? Does it have a protective glass front?

IV-R. PROTECTION FROM THE ELEMENTS

- In the winter, do blasts of cold air through the front door freeze users and staff? If the library has power assist doors, are both of two successive doors frequently open at the same time?
- The best entrances face south or southeast. The worst face north or northwest.
- Does the library have trouble with ice forming on shaded sidewalks or (even worse) steps? South entrances prevent many evils.
- Does the building have cold drafts? One sign of good architecture is attention to sealants.

IV-S. SECURITY

- Does the building appear to be easy for staff to supervise? Are there hidden corners? Do study rooms have opaque (bad) or transparent (good) walls? Can you keep an eye on users of the study rooms while you're seated at a service desk?
- Some libraries have tried to assist supervision by arranging stack aisles like the spokes of a wheel. It turned out to be a singularly bad idea.
- Do any of the stack aisles have dead ends? Libraries cannot afford situations where a user or staff member could be trapped in an aisle. Dead-end stack aisles are always a viciously nasty idea.
- Can users open the windows? A standard way thieves bypass security gates is by

dropping books out of windows and picking them up later.

- If the library is over 12,000 square feet, does it have a sprinkler system? The ideal sprinkler system for a library is a pre-action system, but you can't tell by looking at the sprinkler heads. (This may not be much help, because it can be hard to guess library sizes.)

- Are sprinkler heads concealed or are they exposed? Concealed heads are less prone to vandalism. And they're cuter. Look for three-inch white metal discs mounted flush on the ceilings.

- Is there only one public entrance? Multiple entrances are the bane of libraries because every one of them must be staffed at all times a building is open. Unstaffed security gates don't work, although designers sometimes don't believe it.

- Can people obtain 100 percent privacy by locking themselves into single-user restrooms? Even single-user restrooms can have stalls and provide for better staff oversight. Many libraries now prefer airport-style restrooms, with zigzag entries rather than doors.

- Do restrooms have unfortunate sight lines? Watch out both for direct views of fixtures and stalls and for indirect views by way of mirrors.

- If the restrooms have doors, do you have to grab dirty handles when you leave the restrooms after you have finished washing your hands? A restroom door should swing outward, or there should be a wastebasket by the door where users can drop paper towels after using them to open the door.

- Are there railings by drop-offs that can be climbed like ladders? Children have fallen while climbing handrails. All balusters should be vertical.

- Are there places where users can bump their heads, such as the undersides of staircases?

- Are there any reading terraces accessible from inside the building? If users can carry books out onto terraces, they can always toss them over the edge and retrieve them later from outside. (No matter what planners contend, there is no such thing as a "secure" reading terrace.)

- Can library users easily wander into what should be secure staff areas? Lending work areas and technical services areas are particularly vulnerable. (Of course, if you test this by trying doors marked "staff" during your tour, you may call attention to yourself.)

- Do all exit doors have illuminated "Exit" signs?

- Is there a fire extinguisher located near each exit door?

- Do any exit doors swing inward? (By law, all exit doors must swing outward.)

- If the library has revolving doors, are they designed so the panels will swing open to create passageways that allow people to exit the building quickly?

- Do any of the exit doors have double-cylinder locks? (Double-cylinder locks have keyholes on both sides. If an exit door has a keyhole facing inward, this is a serious life-safety problem.)

IV-T. EXPANDABILITY

- Is there space around the library for later expansion?

- Will expanding the library in the obvious direction involve the removal of many small rooms (expensive) or the opening up of large reading rooms (much less expensive)?

IV-U. WATER FEATURES

- Some designers enjoy installing water features both inside and outside library buildings. A "water feature" is any design element that includes water.

- If a water feature is inside a building, is it turned off and empty? Some libraries turn off water features almost immediately after construction is completed.

- Among other things, library users fall into water features. Visitors can plug up water features with coins or debris. Water features can harbor various pathogens. Water features can leak. And the sound of running water can send staff members rushing repeatedly to the restroom.

IV-V. ACCESSIBILITY

- If you are in a wheelchair, can you get into all areas of the library, including the book stacks and restrooms?

- To get into the library, can you simply enter, or do you have to use some kind of unpleasant ramp?

V. Snappy Rule on Evaluating Library Buildings by Walking Around

1. This whole chapter strikes us as one extended set of snappy rules.

PART I
Nearly Endless Observations on Good Library Design

CHAPTER 5

Dysfunctional Designs

THIS CHAPTER IS an extremely brief list of design concepts that have led to problems in libraries. Our intent is to simply list concepts here, without long explanations of why they are bad ideas. For more information, check the index or the cited chapters.

Some dysfunctional designs are traditional, but others are new and exciting. At any rate, here they are. None listed here are essential to good library design, but people can be angrily strong partisans of bad concepts. As Mr. Yeats might observe, were he with us today, "The best lack all conviction, while the worst are full of passionate intensity."

And as Seattle architectural critic Lawrence Cheek ended his 2007 review of the central library of the Seattle Public Library, "A mistake has been made."

Here are things you don't ever want, regardless of what your provosts, mayors, board members, school superintendents, tourists, donors, local news, librarians, architects, and building consultants happen to like. When in doubt, mark this list "Never under any circumstances whatsoever" and attach it to your building program. (And watch out for people blithely ignoring the list anyway.)

I. Bad Lighting
(See chapter 31, "Lighting")

- Any windows that admit uncontrollable direct sunlight. Windows without blinds must all face straight north. (Tinting these windows doesn't help, because direct sunlight can overcome tinting, and when the sunlight is from other directions, tinting removes any reason for windows.)

- Skylights, which cause endless problems with glare by day and gloom by night. (If they're inescapable, roof them over and light them electrically from behind.)

- Downlights. Lights shining straight down blind people looking up at book shelving, and they often lead to seriously irregular lighting all over the place. Always bounce all of the light off white ceilings. Watch out in particular for recessed downlights—round holes in the ceiling with brilliant lights inside. (If you have an existing building with ceilings too low for reflected uplighting, see chapter 31, "Lighting.")

- Monitor windows. Raised sections of roof that have glass on some or all sides can lead to blinding glare. (Make sure no monitor will admit direct sunlight at any time of day or year.)

- Clearstory windows that face any direction except straight north.

- Funny-shaped windows that blinds won't fit.

- Dark ceilings that prevent the best way of lighting libraries, which involves pointing 100 percent of the light upward and bouncing it off ceilings.

- Task lighting that is architecturally mounted rather than fastened to furniture. Libraries are always moving things around, and special lighting has to automatically move with them. (Remember that photos of people reading happily in direct sunlight in new buildings are all staged fakes. As are photos of library users in wheelchairs joyously using ramps. Or photos of library users happily using staircases that combine steps with seating or with book shelving.)

II. Bad Acoustics

- Atria are high-ceilinged spaces connecting two or more floors. Sometimes they have extravagant staircases. Usually they transmit noises in unpleasant ways. (They also waste energy and are hard to maintain. And they frighten people with fear of heights. Some people have committed suicide in library atria.)

- Rooms without acoustic ceilings. Most libraries use acoustic tile, which also gives easy access to all the stuff above the ceilings. (Watch out for curved ceilings, which may not have acoustic surfaces.)

- Huge openings around staircases.

- Some projects that badly need acoustical engineers don't have them. Such as round rooms.

III. Bad Ventilation
(See chapter 33, "HVAC")

- Too many library spaces have to be aired out after people leave. Or have HVAC systems that respond too slowly to sudden crowds.

- Not enough thermostats. (Many library spaces that need two have only one.)

IV. Inflexibility

- Libraries that can't change over the years. Service desks or counters or seating or shelving that can't be relocated sooner or later cause problems.

- Libraries that don't have enough electrical outlets or electrical circuits. Barely enough outlets to meet opening day needs is not enough. Libraries should never need extension cords.

- Libraries where only some floors are strong enough to support the weight of books. Sooner or later, libraries may want to put books there.

- Libraries with underfloor air ducts that limit where furnishings can go.

- Curved or diagonal walls are inflexible because all sorts of furniture doesn't fit.

[*Above*] In the alley behind this library, users first encounter a parked bookmobile. Hidden behind the bookmobile is a trash container and then (finally) a book return. For some reason, this struck some citizens as a dysfunctional arrangement.

[*Left*] Inflexibility appeals much more to designers than to librarians. Some designers want to build for the ages, while most libraries move things around every few years. For years, this obsolete card catalog blocked an important path between a lending desk and a reference desk because it was perched on a concrete plinth that was too difficult to remove. (The same library had a small display case—which should have been a simple piece of furniture—mounted on I-beams sticking out of a wall. Moving it required a cutting torch, and the cut-off I-beams still stuck out of the wall afterward.)

V. Unexpandablity

- Sooner or later, almost all libraries run out of space. Finding out that your library has painted itself into a corner and can't expand is not a good feeling.

VI. Soffits of All Kinds

- Soffits around the edges of rooms lead to bad lighting.
- Soffits over service desks lead to bad lighting. And terrible inflexibility.

VII. Bad Staircases and Handrails
(See chapter 30, "Elevators, Staircases, Railings, and Ramps")

- Dramatic staircases, whether or not they're paired with atria, can be very expensive. They cause problems for people who fear heights. Some have open risers, which appear to please none of the actual users. Some have funny-shaped treads, which serve no purpose and encourage falling. Many design concepts now banned by safety codes were introduced by designer staircases.
- Staircases combined with shelving or seating are trendy but an awful idea. Among many other failings, they don't meet accessibility codes. If your designers suggest one, this is a good time to hire new designers.
- Staircase railings (or balcony railings) that can be climbed like ladders have no advantages over railings with vertical posts. Children can climb up and fall off (and they have). Railings like this should have been banned by building codes long ago, but they're still being built.
- Staircase railings that are not perpendicular to the stairs. Some extreme examples encourage users to cross their legs while climbing up and down.
- Floating staircases where people can bump their heads underneath. They no longer meet building codes, but there are a lot left hanging around.
- Balconies and staircases with balusters so widely spaced people can fall through. These are also banned by codes, but they're still around.
- Funny-shaped staircase treads that end before the wall, or curve upward at their ends, or are not rectangular are disconcerting and pointless.
- Staircases with transparent sides or with open risers, both of which frighten people with fear of heights. (Open risers provide no interesting views, making their persistent appeal to designers puzzling.)
- Handrails that are too large to grab. New ones are no longer allowed by codes, but many older examples remain to frustrate or frighten users.
- Handrails at uncomfortable heights. Modern codes are specific about heights, but lots of horrible old handrails are still in use. (For many libraries, having an extra rail at child height helps a lot.)
- Painted handrails (and hand grabs, for that matter). Regardless of the owners' color preferences, the only thing that works is brushed stainless steel.
- Generous staircase openings that transmit all sorts of noises between floors.

- Staircases with light fixtures that can't be reached for servicing.
- Staircases with essential nearby elevators hidden to discourage their use.

VIII. Cheap Substitutes for Real Elevators
(see chapter 30, "Elevators, Staircases, Railings, and Ramps")

- Unfortunately, there are lots of these, including elevators without automatic doors, elevators that open directly into the out of doors, elevators that don't meet accessibility requirements, and elevators that are too small for people in wheelchairs and those who accompany them, or for parents with strollers and baby carriages.
- Proper elevators are expensive, but the only alternative is starting over with a new one-story building.

IX. Bad Shelving
(see chapter 22, "Collection Storage and Display")

- Shelving aisles with dead ends are a safety threat and usually illegal.
- Shelving systems with shelves supported by pegs protruding from end panels. Shelves can fall dramatically when the panels flex.
- Shelving with unadjustable shelves.
- Shelving aisles that are not parallel. Radial aisles cause an impressive variety of problems.
- Shelving not specifically engineered for library use.

X. Bad Balconies and Walkways

- Balconies with low ceilings. Squeezing in a balcony between two floors often results in substandard ceiling heights.
- Walkways with steel gratings for floors. Users may complain about someone trying to look upward through the floors to peep under their dresses or skirts, or users may complain about shoes with narrow heels getting caught in gratings.
- Walkways with glass sides over open spaces. (Walkways over open spaces shouldn't exist at all.)

XI. Nasty Ramps
(see chapter 11, "Accessibility")

- Exterior ramps may meet accessibility codes. But they shouldn't.
- Interior ramps are almost all pains as well.
- Ramps (or stairs, for that matter) that lead downhill to lower-level entrances usually cause floods. And make users feel like they've been sent around to the back door.
- Sloped spaces that combine ramps with shelving or seating are an amazingly foolish concept. (Just like staircases combined with shelving or seating.)

XII. Bad Sight Lines
(see chapter 35, "Security")

- Excess partitions.
- Study rooms that are not glass boxes.
- Unwelcome views into restrooms.

XIII. Bad Security
(once again, see chapter 35, "Security")

- Shared buildings. In particular, elevators shared by a library and any other agency.
- Basements, which are dark and dank, tend to flood, and cost just about as much as extra floors.
- Rooms under terraces, because terraces inevitably leak.

XIV. Bad Wiring
(see chapter 32, "Electrical Systems")

- Too many libraries have too few electrical outlets in too few locations, and often not enough available amperage.

XV. Insufficient Storage Space
(see chapter 29, "Storerooms")

- Libraries need all sorts of storage rooms and storage closets, but many don't have them. Meeting rooms alone need separate locking closets for furniture, program equipment, and electronic equipment.

XVI. Indoor Water Features

- People toss things in, or they fall in themselves. The sound of running water sends people rushing for the restrooms. And some water features are accused of harboring Legionnaires' disease.

XVII. Funny-Shaped Interior Spaces

- No library contents are designed to fit into triangular or round rooms. Some carefully designed rooms with curved walls make great reading rooms, but no library space ever benefits from diagonal walls.

XVIII. And Many More

- Architectural solutions to furniture problems.
- Screened porches.
- Monumental service desks.
- Designs that lead to maintenance problems, including lighting you can't reach, under-slab air ducts that fill with water, and mechanical things hidden above plaster ceilings.
- Reading terraces that allow users to carry books outdoors without checking them out.

XIX. And a Few Designs That Can Be Made to Work but Require Serious Preliminary Exploration by Architects, Engineers, Owners, Librarians, and Building Consultants

- Courtyards, which often just get in the way of movement through buildings. Some courtyards lead to beads-on-a-chain room arrangements. Many courtyards cause problems and are simply left dark and locked. Or are left as unoccupied passageways.
- Multiple public entrances may be very welcome, but they all need to be staffed. So there are cost tradeoffs involved. Some libraries end up just locking them.

PART II

From Overcrowding to Ribbon Cutting

PART II
From Overcrowding
to Ribbon Cutting

CHAPTER 6

Essential Teamwork

I. Introduction

Designing and constructing a library is a lot like making a big-budget motion picture. It's not the work of a single individual of startling genius. It's the work of a large number of competent people working together to coordinate their knowledge and priorities. Among others, there are boards of trustees, university administrators, mayors, library users, librarians, architects, engineers, code enforcement specialists, fundraisers, donors, landscapers, library building consultants, faculty library committees, library foundations, and many more.

The central ones are owners, librarians, architects, and library building consultants, none of whom can be omitted from any decisions.

One of the things that can go most seriously wrong is when some people try to keep other people out of the decision-making process. Whenever someone says, "We won't need XXX at the next meeting," the planning group should consider whether the presence of that person or group may actually be absolutely essential, more so than they had initially realized.

Major decisions should never be made by a small subset of the planning groups. If the board of trustees of the university and the architects get together to make decisions that will have a major impact on how the new library will function, the absence of librarians should make everyone cringe.

II. How Do Libraries Avoid Serious Problems?

- ***Never have planning meetings that make major decisions while omitting major players in the project.*** In particular, if the librarians, owners, and architects are not present, the meeting should be informational only. Or not held at all.

- ***Never allow any group or individual to present a major recommendation for the first time at a meeting.*** It's essential that a building program or a new floor plan be

67

distributed before the meeting, so that the people present are not blindsided by unexpected ideas. This is obvious in the case of documents like building programs, but it's equally essential in the case of single sheets like architectural floor plans. All of these things take time to examine and digest, and none of them should ever be sprung on people.

- **When specialists, such as engineers, say, "It has to be this way," always question them.** Sometimes "this way" is simply easier or cheaper or more common rather than required. And the needs of libraries may be totally different from the needs of those agencies that the experts have worked with before. Laws are laws, but they often have options.

- **Never allow donors to get together privately with owners to make major functional decisions about libraries.** All decisions require the input of the relevant major parties. And some potential donors want to inflict such seriously awful ideas on libraries that the libraries have to turn down major gifts.

- **Keep meetings controlled.** Opening up major planning meetings to the outside world may lead to something resembling chaos. Someone has to risk annoying the outside world by saying that a would-be contributor is off the subject of today's meeting.

- **Beware of situations where team members can be intimidated.** This happens in particular to librarians, who can be threatened with dismissal by mayors or provosts. The answer is to always have a library building consultant on the planning team.

- **Be aware of owners' motivations, which may have more to do with saving money or improving a bad area of town or campus than providing library service.** Some concepts appear to be driven only by visions of bargains rather than by visions of fine libraries.

- **Beware of proposed designs that excite the designers but nobody else.**

- **Never let an architect initially propose a single idea.** Ideas need to emerge through discussion, not be revealed in a sudden blaze of glory.

- **Beware of librarians who demand everything every staff member requests, regardless of cost.**

- **Site selection is always a group process.** Never let a non-library agency dictate your site without discussion of functional needs by librarians, library users, and architects.

- **The unworkability of ideas can be made clear by simple architectural sketches and accompanying cost estimates.** If you don't test ideas this way, some people will never abandon them.

Here are a few (true) examples of how the absence of team players can lead things astray.

- The university board of trustees selects an architect for the new campus library without including librarians in the decision. When architects being considered for the job see how the decision will be made, they logically speak only to the interests of trustees.

- The architect prepares a single proposed floor plan for initial distribution at a board meeting, limiting discussion to minor variations rather than testing the effectiveness of the underlying concept by comparison with true alternative approaches.

- A building consultant sends out copies of an 80-page building program three days before the next meeting of the owners and librarians, giving no one enough time to review the document or to challenge any of what may turn out to be the consultant's pet ideas.

- The mayor or library board announces the cost of the new project without any input from the architects or construction management firm, the only two agencies with any rational knowledge of what things tend to cost.

- The architect informs the owners that the absent donor specifically wants a feature that the owners dislike. After the building is constructed, including the feature, the donor asks the owners why the strange feature was included.

III. What Can You Do to Prevent Serious Problems Due to Bad Communication or to Elimination of Essential Players from Crucial Decision-Making?

- Never make essential decisions without the presence and input of all player groups, especially owners, librarians, and architects.

- Always be extremely alert to the serious danger of one of the participants trying to twist the project in a direction that other players don't agree with.

- Be prepared to tell specific members of the group at a meeting that they are out of order when they insist on raising irrelevant issues.

At one of Fred's projects, meetings were open to the public because the entire public library board was present. One member of the public wanted to have the board discuss abortion at every meeting, even though the topic was totally irrelevant to the planning of a library building. It took the board a long time to face up to the fact that it had simply to declare some speakers out of order.

- Never allow anyone to spring major decisions unexpectedly on people at meetings.

Inform all groups in advance that major documents must be distributed a week or more before meetings, and that anything with complex implications that is distributed at a meeting will be referred to everyone for study and evaluation at the next meeting.

At one of Fred's projects, the architects would arrive at planning meetings with floor plans that the board had never seen before and that they had had no time to evaluate. Often there would be two plans representing very minor variations on the same concept, perhaps with different window designs. Fred was convinced that the architects' intent was to stifle discussion by implying that a single plan out of a huge number of possibilities was the only way to do things.

- Always require engineers and architects and building consultants to be prepared to discuss other options if requested.

Members of various planning groups frequently contend that there are fewer options than there really are.

When new ideas are presented at a meeting, always allow time for all of them to be questioned or challenged.

- Save incredible amounts of time by always including all essential people at every meeting where decisions are made, including library owners, library managers, librarians, architects, and library building consultants.

- Unless your librarian is completely immune to threats (and some threats can be impressively nasty), always have your library building consultant on the planning team.

All of the examples of how bad teamwork hurts library projects are based on real life. So beware.

PART II
From Overcrowding to Ribbon Cutting

CHAPTER 7

Building Programs

I. About Building Programs

A "building program" is a written description of the spaces required in a new or expanded building. For each space, the program provides information on the functions of the space, a list of the required contents of the space, the estimated square footages required for each space, the physical nature of each space, and the location of each space in relation to the locations of other spaces in the proposed building.

A program can also provide extensive information on the basics of functional library design.

Programs are one of the ways in which libraries can work to make sure that library buildings respond to user and staff needs.

While some libraries have professional staff members who have the background to write building programs, many hire professional library building consultants who are professional librarians with extensive personal experience in how libraries occupy physical spaces.

In addition to preparing building programs, consulting librarians frequently walk library boards through the design and construction process, including serving on building committees that evaluate construction options.

Programming achieves a number of important things:

- Libraries are complex buildings, and without a carefully drawn up list of necessary functions, some important features are easy to leave out.

- The act of getting all the details into print helps make sure that all participants agree on what the library needs. Sometimes they don't even know they disagree until the library's needs are spelled out clearly.

- Building programs provide a way of establishing a library's needs before another agency decides to take unilateral action and dictate to the library.

- A building program on file in college or school or hospital or city administrative offices can also remind everyone that the library has space needs and that it has done its homework.

- Building programs can help with selecting architects. If you interview architects who (a) have never read the program or (b) clearly disagree with it, this is useful information.
- Building programs provide yardsticks for evaluating whether current library buildings can be realistically remodeled and expanded, whether existing non-library buildings can be converted to libraries, and whether proposed architectural designs correspond with the library's needs.
- Programs serve important functions during architectural design work. Without a program, the decisions about how a library building will function may be driven by what looks good rather than by functional needs.
- Having your library building consultant who wrote the program present at meetings as part of the planning team provides an essential evaluation of the design from the point of view of a librarian with personal knowledge of how libraries function in space.
- Written building programs provide strong support for grant applications and may be required by the agencies giving the grants.
- Written building programs help prevent dysfunctional designs from going unrecognized until a building is actually constructed—and it's too late to fix problems.
- For effective planning, a library should arrange for the production of a building program before selecting an architect, or at least before holding planning meetings with its architect.
- The best building planning teams consist of the owners (such as public library board members or university provosts), library staff, architects, engineers, and consultants. Working without any one of these can lead to problems.

It's unfortunately easy to come up with real-life examples of what can go wrong when experienced librarians are not involved in projects.

- Essential but unexciting features like storage spaces or exhaust fans can be omitted because they were not listed anywhere in print. (The number of small libraries that have been forced to install prefab garden sheds behind their buildings is impressive.)
- Excitingly innovative features can turn out to have unexpected functional problems.
- Functions can be divided unwisely. For example, the architect for one academic library Fred knows thought it would be a really neat idea to divide the collection among many dozens of small rooms, each with a table in the middle. He was furiously angry when his idea was rejected by all the librarians.
- Solving some problems can create others.

The basic points are:

- One of the main benefits of programming is actually getting things into print in detail. When printed words replace conversation, differences in opinion stand out. As Francis Bacon observed, "Truth emerges more readily from error than from confusion."
- Always have a librarian with a lot of experience with buildings act as your library building consultant and write your building program. This can be a staff member of your library or a hired consultant.
- The disadvantage of hiring your own staff members as consultants is that they may

not have the nerve to look library boards or provosts in the eye and criticize their pet ideas. Or tell library boards they have to provide elevators whether or not they want to spend the money.

- Get to know programmers before you hire them, in case they completely differ with your concept of library functions.
- Beware of cookie-cutter programs. You want programmers who take time to understand your own library's problems and needs, not programmers who haul out concept #3.
- Start with a clear understanding of what your library does for its users.
- Never start a building project by drawing pictures.
- Be sure that your program lists what you DON'T want, in addition to what you do want.
- Form a design team consisting of your library staff, architects, owners (public library board members, university staff, school administrators, and so on), and consultants. Never allow anyone to insist that any of the four should not attend meetings. Involving everyone in meetings may cost a little more, but the cost of meetings is miniscule compared with the cost of construction. If meetings prevent even very minor errors, the savings are immense. (Some provosts or library board presidents want to meet privately with architects. This provides a slippery path to disaster.)
- Beware of architects who want to "reinvent libraries," ignoring the needs of the library staff and users expressed in their written building programs.
- In particular, beware of owners who want to get together privately with architects,

ignoring both their own library staff and their own users. This has happened over the years, and the results have been some spectacularly unworkable library buildings.

II. Purposes of Building Programs

II-A. FRAMEWORKS FOR LIBRARY DESIGN

The primary purpose of a building program is to convert the service needs of the library to a detailed and thorough list of architectural spaces, including their sizes, physical characteristics, adjacencies to other spaces, and contents.

The written program provides the owners with a chance to see whether everyone agrees on what is wanted. Without the formality of a written program, the various parties involved can never be sure that they are all talking about the same thing. Once things appear in written form, unrealized differences in understandings become more obvious.

Using the program, the owners, architect, and library staff can test whether all of the spaces required are included in the proposed design.

When libraries are limited by existing structures, programs are particularly important, helping prevent existing features from dictating future library functions. Planning always needs to ask, "What does our library need?" rather than "What can we do with this space?"

The failure to foresee possibilities can occur particularly if library staff members have spent years coping with an inadequate building and thinking about how it might be tweaked to make it function more effectively. The kinds of changes that emerge from this approach are often too narrowly focused and miss out on the opportunities for major reassignment of spaces that starting with a written building program makes possible.

Due to the presence of existing buildings, successful programs must be carefully written to specify needed spaces rather than to make plans and suggestions for the use of existing spaces.

It's essential to avoid confusing the concepts of building "programs" and building "plans." The purpose of a program is to define the problem, not to develop a solution to the problem. A program is a written document, not a drawing. A "plan" in turn is a drawing illustrating architectural spaces. These are common definitions used in the architectural community. If you keep referring to your building program as a "plan," sooner or later one of the experts you hire will get confused about what you're talking about.

In architectural terminology, programs *define the problem* and building designs *solve the problem.*

Once you have a written program, you should expect your architects to design spaces that respond to the program. If they disagree with the program, it is their professional responsibility to tell you so before design work begins.

Occasionally architects present designs that clearly fail to meet programmatic needs but do not point this out to owners. This is one of the reasons why it's important to have your consultant present at planning meetings.

Programs also help owners separate functional architectural design from razzle-dazzle. It's easy for owners to be enchanted by a dramatic staircase or a swoopingly curved wall when a quick check of a written program might remind them that those features have nothing to do with library needs.

The great challenge of library architecture is to design a building that is artistically appropriate while still meeting all of the library's needs.

II-B. PRESENTATIONS TO YOUR COMMUNITY

A building program provides an early way to show members of your community what you have in mind.

Unfortunately, comprehensive programs can be pretty dry reading. To combat this, programs should always include executive summaries. Because summaries are really for library users and for administrators of larger service units, they can stress those details that will be of particular interest to library users and to academic or city planners.

Even if many readers will not read past the executive summary, distributing the entire program is important because it provides evidence of the careful and comprehensive planning that supports the summary. Readers who want more detail about an area in the executive summary can page to the full explanation in the main body of the document.

II-C. PROACTIVE STATEMENTS OF NEEDS

Programs often benefit from being created proactively, particularly for libraries that are part of larger organizations, such as school libraries, special libraries, academic departmental libraries, and so on.

Decisions to alter or relocate libraries that are small elements located in large buildings can come with virtually no warning, and librarians need to be prepared. By the time the head of a library learns that change is planned, there may already be an architect drawing plans. In situations like this, having a building program on file long in advance may help.

The situation is made worse by space poaching. In large buildings with small libraries, someone always needs space and is casting covetous eyes on desirable locations. In buildings located on sites with essential expansion space, some other agency may be planning to take over the vacant land.

To deal with situations like these, it's useful to have building programs on file with administrative offices, or to be able to whip one up at a moment's notice when possible changes are announced.

> As an example, a medical library with which Fred worked found out on a Friday morning that a meeting had been scheduled for the following Monday afternoon to review relocating a number of hospital units, including the library. The director of the library and Fred spent the weekend on the project, and by Monday morning they had a written program in the hands of the hospital administration. While the other departments turned up only to complain and to demand more space, the librarian was able to smile and say, "Here's what we need."

In order to be proactive, programs have to confront central issues and changing service patterns. Programs need to include how libraries are changing over time in the way they deal with changing collection sizes, changing patterns of usage, changing spaces needed for various user groups, changing collection arrangements, and many other changes—both spaces that can be cut and new spaces that are badly needed. Outside groups that are interested only in cuts and not in additions are a danger to libraries.

II-D. REQUIRED DOCUMENTATION FOR GRANT APPLICATIONS

Depending on circumstances, written building programs may be required as part of construction grant applications or for other purposes.

For this reason, a program may contain information not strictly needed by the architect, such as brief descriptions of the business, university, or community to be served; executive summaries to enable quick reviews; or comments on how the program matches requirements of external agencies. A program for an academic or special library may need to demonstrate that it meets the requirements of an accrediting agency or of a professional group from which the school or organization is seeking accreditation. A program for a public library may need to demonstrate that the library meets state standards for public libraries.

II-E. MEANS OF SORTING OUT DIFFERENCES OF OPINION

It's highly unlikely that all the players in a library project will agree. Frequently, extensive discussion among all of the planners can help sort things out. On occasion, it reminds us of discussions with citizens who want books removed from libraries—sometimes being listened to carefully disarms tense situations.

II-F. OPPORTUNITIES FOR USER INPUT BEFORE DESIGN

Programming is a good time for user input because it separates discussion of the library's service and space needs from possible arguments over locations and sites and building appearance.

In some cases, members of owners' boards, governing boards, and communities have strong and widely divergent views about where libraries should be built and what buildings should look like, or whether old buildings should be expanded or replaced. Starting with a program focuses attention on functional needs rather than artistic decisions.

Getting people involved in planning when the discussion concerns how the library will work and what kind of space is needed can help the same people realize later that certain options they originally liked are simply not workable.

III. Input on Programs

There all many sources of information for library programs. The primary source for all programs is information from library staff and management, plus knowledge of library spaces, trends in the field, and successes and failures in library design. Other possible sources include focus groups, surveys, strategic plans, and available non-library data.

III-A. OBSERVATIONS BY CONSULTANTS

Many consultants will want to begin by simply exploring existing library buildings, either alone or in the company of library administrators and staff. Programs should describe existing buildings, whether the libraries expect to remodel and expand them or start over. A lot of this description can be prepared by consultants without major input from library staff.

In these situations the consultants' knowledge of library buildings is particularly vital. A consult who has firsthand knowledge of hundreds of library buildings is in a vastly better position to assist a library.

See chapter 4, "Evaluating Library Buildings by Walking Around."

III-B. INTERVIEWS WITH STAFF AND MANAGEMENT

The most direct way to figure out what spaces are needed in a new or expanded library is to simply ask the staff and administration.

It's the responsibility of the consultant in this situation to know enough about libraries to be able to ask endless "do you want this" or "do you really need this" sorts of questions. And consultants need to be aware of continuing changes in the field. What are the implications of changes in technology? What is the impact of remote storage on study and research? How are library services for children changing? Will the library want to save money and space by farming out technical services or will it want to have bestsellers available for borrowing by street date rather than many weeks later?

The number of questions can be immense. As an example, Fred's lists of questions for a public library children's department staff and users can run to about 200 questions.

Sometimes, library staff members have trouble divorcing themselves from the existing library building. After many years of asking themselves, "How can we tweak this building to make it more functional?" they may have problems thinking of new buildings in the abstract. One approach Fred has used is the "tornado" approach. He asks library staff to imagine that a tornado has demolished the library and to tell him what kinds of spaces they need in a new building.

Another problem with discussions of needed spaces occurs when library staff who have developed ingenious workarounds for badly designed buildings want to repeat those workarounds in new buildings.

> In one library with which Fred worked, the space for cataloging was completely insecure, and the cataloger kept a cart of uncataloged DVDs locked in the computer server room near her cataloging workstation. This was an ingenious solution, and she insisted that the server room in the new library be located next to technical services so she could continue storing DVDs there. When Fred suggested a locking storage cabinet or closet could be provided in the technical services room, the staff member instead insisted on using a server room.

Some library staff have a tendency to omit from the program statement things they already have. When consultants ask, for example, "Does your department need a storage closet?" staff members may respond, "We already have one." This puts a lot of pressure on the consultant to make absolutely certain that staff members are not omitting things they need, since anything not listed in the program won't be included in the design for a new building. Once again, the "tornado" approach may help.

One problem with evaluating options occurs when the library's staff and governors and users disagree on what the library needs. To take a public library example, storing children's picture books in flip bins with the front covers of the books exposed requires more space and leads to vastly higher use, but library staff may dislike the idea because this browsing-friendly arrangement can make it harder for staff to keep books in order or locate individual items.

Avoiding assigning specific uses to specific spaces in existing libraries is important because an ingenious architect may end up reassigning all of the existing spaces.

One pitfall with distributing lists of possible features in advance of programming sessions is the desire of owners and staff to meet proactively without the consultant present and decide on answers for all of the questions. The problem with this approach is that the questions cannot ever explain all of the implications of decisions. If board members of a public library, for example, get together to decide all by themselves, they may select features without realizing how things might work. And once they've decided, they may balk at changing.

A solution to this problem is to not give people time to meet in advance of discussions of library needs. Fred often sends libraries the lists of options only a few days in advance, specifically asking library directors to distribute the questions to board and staff members just long enough in advance for the board and staff to quickly skim the lists before they meet with Fred.

Lists of options can come from many sources. Fred usually develops them himself, but a good source is the most recent edition of William Sannwald's *Checklist of Library Building Design Considerations*.

III-C. FOCUS GROUPS

A focus group consists of five or 10 people with a similar interest, such as parents of preschool children for a public library, nursing training staff for a hospital library, or student study groups for a college library.

With a group of people with similar interests, the people leading the focus group can get them to discuss the various ways they prefer to see services offered.

In addition to reviewing library services, focus groups can also help develop community support. People who have participated in focus groups will have a vastly greater knowledge of the library's needs and plans, and their response is likely to be positive.

Focus groups usually take place by public announcement, but invitations are also essential. Without inviting participants and confirming attendance, libraries sometimes find that almost no one turns up. While having too many people attend a focus group session can make things somewhat unwieldy, even worse is having almost no one turn up.

It's sometimes difficult to make sure that focus groups include a real cross section of the service community. Once Fred was asked to lead a focus group of junior high and senior high students for a new public library, only to find that the library had invited only honor students, all of whom saw the library exclusively as a place to study alone rather than a place to also hang out with friends, read manga, or play video games.

It's also a good thing to be sure that friends and supporters of the library are present in focus groups. If all the people who attend a focus group session are anti-construction, it won't be a productive meeting.

Focus groups need to be driven by questions to which the library needs answers. Sometimes the group can be given a list, or the library may simply prefer to have a list of questions on hand.

One of the advantages of focus groups is that the person leading the group can take time to explain concepts. For example, one of the most popular innovations in library design in recent decades is study rooms, but they may require some explanation before all of the people in the focus group can be asked whether they might use them.

Focus groups are intended to gather input, not to make decisions. This is usually understood, but occasionally a participant will say something to the effect of, "Well, what are you going to do about this?" Or, "Well, are you going to have a coffee shop or not?"

Occasionally, one or two aggressive people attempt to take over a focus group, making one point repeatedly and arguing that everyone else is wrong or that the library is clearly up to something. At times like this, the group leader needs to find a way to say something equivalent to "You've made your point, and we need to hear from other people."

It's sometimes hard for leaders of focus groups to avoid arguing with seriously bad suggestions from the group. Even if as librarians we know that a specific idea has been a disaster in other libraries, the purpose of focus groups is to find out what people think. If someone in a focus group is enthusiastic about an unusually bad idea, we can smile, write it down, say thank you, and then not act on it.

It can be distressing for libraries when new ideas that particularly excite librarians and owners fall like lead balloons in focus groups.

> As an example, when Fred led a focus group for a public library, one of the people present talked about the importance of a coffee bar as a major financial support of the library in lieu of taxes, but also talked about the importance of keeping prices lower than in commercial coffee shops. Fred was tempted to point out that, even when charging full prices, coffee bars in public libraries almost always lose money, but he managed to force himself to keep his mouth shut and say, "Thank you."

Sometimes the participants in the groups just don't get it or happen to be the wrong group of people. But it's also possible that the new ideas really don't appeal much to the community, and that the library has learned something useful.

Some libraries have summarized focus group input and posted it on their websites, along with thanks to all the people who participated.

If focus groups work well, they may lead to changes in building programs, but even if that doesn't happen, people always like being asked, and in that way focus groups can help bring goodwill to the library and remind community members of the necessity of the proposed project. It also gives libraries the opportunity to point out that members of the public were indeed involved in the project.

III-D. SURVEYS

This book strongly discourages most surveys. If you're planning to avoid surveys, skip the rest of this section, but if you're considering surveys, read it.

Unfortunately, a great many surveys in the library world appear to be totally worthless.

Here are some basics of surveys.

- Designing reliable questions for use on surveys is difficult, for it takes work to be sure that questions are clear and unbiased. Many questions are not. (This work is called "pretesting.")
- People responding to a survey should have no idea that you're hoping for a specific answer. If they know what you want to hear, or if you activate their emotional buttons before asking questions, there's danger of a so-called "push survey."

> The world of politics is awash in push surveys. The main thing to do is to not let people know what answers you want. We've seen surveys like, "Help our library qualify for a grant by telling us how you like our service," and no one running a survey should get by with asking something like that.

- Many "surveys" that arrive in the mail ask a few provocative questions and then ask for money. The only good thing about them is that the people running them probably deposit the checks and totally ignore the "survey" results.
- Every question that offers a choice of answers has to include the answer "none of the above." If this is not the case, you may be forcing people to pick from among answers, with all of which they may disagree.
- The group of people whose opinions you want make up the "universe," and the people in the universe that you select to speak with are the "sample." Each person in the

universe needs to have an equal chance of becoming part of the sample. For public library surveys, this can be extraordinarily difficult, and one suspects that vast numbers of library surveys are invalid for this reason alone.

- If a lot of people in your sample don't respond to your survey, you have to ask whether there's any reason they could be different from those who do respond. If there is, you may have to throw out your survey.

- The accuracy of survey responses is typically subject to "confidence intervals" of 95 percent. National opinion surveys typically survey about 1,200 people and have confidence intervals of about plus or minus 3 percent, meaning that if you asked everyone in the universe, in 95 percent of the cases the percentage of all the people in the universe would be within plus or minus 3 percent of the survey result.

- Because of this, any survey that reports any findings past the decimal point is garbage.

Many surveys in library publications—including strategic plans—feature horrible mis-uses of data by people who are not professional survey designers and statisticians.

If your library wants statistically valid surveys of the entire community—particularly a community of people served by a public library—it needs to hire a professional survey firm like NORC with a national reputation for unbiased findings.

III-E. STRATEGIC PLANS

Strategic plans are compact statements of library goals, objectives, and long-range plans. They are a source of inspiration. They are usually brief and to the point.

However, strategic plans are not a substitute for building programs. They are far too short. They do not identify needed spaces. And many strategic plans in the library world rely on survey data that is extremely suspect.

Strategic plans are a source of ideas for building programs, but they have far too little information to be helpful.

III-F. DATA FROM NON-LIBRARY SOURCES

All programs need to include basic information on the community served, particularly those aspects of the community that can affect library use.

For example, a public library may serve a town where almost all parents work, and where children come to the library after school to work until their parents finish work, and a new library may therefore need larger children's and teen reading areas. People often combine public library and shopping trips, and a town's plans for new shopping centers can have an impact on library use.

A university library's reading room needs will be strongly affected by the nature of campus housing. Comfortable, quiet dormitories mean less demand for library study space than do crowded, noisy dormitories. A community college with commuter students may find that students study in the library between classes because they have no dorm rooms. Students may seek out library spaces when they are particularly serious about their efforts.

IV. Typical Contents of Programs

This chapter uses the children's department of an imaginary library to demonstrate how information can be clearly presented and what you need from your consultant.

IV-A. DESCRIPTION OF THE AGENCY THE LIBRARY WILL SERVE

A brief description of the existing library is usually a good thing. It helps architects looking for commissions understand something about the university or city or another agency planning a new library building. And it helps grant committees gain a quick understanding of the nature of the project.

Usually a description of the agency to be served will include basic numbers:

- The number of students or researchers or citizens or employees.

- The number of users of specific age or occupational groups.

- The size of the collection to be housed. Or the sizes of the collections to be housed, if different materials require separate housing.

- Current use levels in numerical terms.

- For campuses, whether most of the students study in the library or in their dorm rooms, and how many are likely to crowd into the library during exam weeks.

- Expected future changes. Anticipated changes in student body size, public library service populations, the boundaries of service districts, and many other areas can help clarify the long-term needs of libraries. One of the major challenges in programming is determining what's likely to happen next.

This is also a good place to include some very basic information on the library's existing building.

IV-B. LONG-RANGE PLANS AS THEY RELATE TO SPACE NEEDS

A few elements in long-range plans apply directly to space needs, and these plans always need to be taken into account during programming. One of the responsibilities of the building consultant is to sort out those elements that need to be reflected in space projections.

For example, if a long-range plan calls for more public computer workstations, extra space needs to be provided. But if the long-range plan calls for access to an increased number of databases, this has little or no space implication, unless it will lead to a reduction in the sizes of reference collections or to a greater number of computer workstations.

Although they are important to planning, existing long-range plans or strategic plans are extremely insufficient to serve as programs because they do not examine every aspect of library operations and do not convert plans to space needs. Long-range plans and strategic plans are an important input to programming work but provide far too little information.

IV-C. REVIEW OF APPLICABLE SERVICE STANDARDS AND RESTRICTIONS

Depending on circumstances, there may be applicable standards that will affect the library. Some states may specify minimum user seating and minimum collection sizes for public libraries.

Accreditation standards may apply to academic libraries. Some professional associations may specify book collection sizes for academic programs seeking accreditation.

This is a useful place for the program to list the library's actual planning numbers, clarifying many of the numbers in the program.

IV-D. FUNCTIONAL EVALUATIONS OF CURRENT FACILITIES

Whether the program calls for the reworking of an existing library or the construction of a new library, a functional evaluation of the existing library is always a useful feature of a written building program.

When architects set out to remodel and expand an existing library, detailed information on the functional failings of the current library will help them design a structure that improves on the current building. Although architects usually do a good job noting problems with existing structures, they are not librarians, and they may overlook serious functional problems that can be identified by a consulting librarian working with the staff and owners.

If the library plans to abandon its current building, a written evaluation of the functional problems with the current space helps the owners explain to the community why abandoning the existing library is a necessary decision. Sometimes the number of functional problems posed by a building can be overwhelming when everyone involved takes time to enumerate them.

A written evaluation of an existing building can also help owners and architects decide whether expansion is even feasible at all.

IV-E. STRUCTURAL EVALUATIONS OF CURRENT FACILITIES

In addition to a functional analysis, the owners may also want a structural analysis of an existing building. In general, this calls for a very different set of skills and a different report. Determinations of such things as structural soundness, condition of heating and ventilating systems, conditions of roofs, presence of asbestos and lead paint, adequacy and condition of power supplies, problems with water infiltration, etc., go far beyond the scope of building programming and call for hiring separate technical experts in these various fields.

Before a final decision can be made regarding the remodeling and expansion of an existing library, or the conversion of a non-library building to a library, owners will need to know all of this information.

However, we believe that engineering studies should be part of the design process, not the programming process. The purpose of the program is to provide a careful description of all the functional spaces necessary to meet the library's long-range needs. Deciding whether to abandon an existing building or remodel and expand it is a job for the entire planning team—owners, staff, architects, engineers, and building consultants.

When the program is complete, it can be used as a yardstick to evaluate the suitability of a proposed site or building. But architects and engineers will need to review each specific site or building to be sure that it also meets the library's structural needs.

IV-F. ENUMERATION OF REQUIRED SPACES AND CONTENTS

For each space in the library, the program should provide a written description, including the purpose of the space, the activities that take place in the space, the contents of the space, and notes on adjacencies—the location of the space with regards to other spaces in the library.

Programs should provide for each space in the library a table listing the elements in that area that lead to the recommended size of the space.

If programs don't do this, people can say, "Let's cut it by 10 percent," without having any idea of what that will actually mean. If the program has a list of features for each area, libraries can verify that everything they have requested is present, and they can use the list as a shopping list if they have to reduce the size of the program.

Space calculations for a space in the library might look something like table 7.1. Once again, the example is for a children's department in a small public library. The list of spaces for the entire building could look like table 7.2.

TABLE 7.1
Services for older children

Functions	1. Seating for older children 2. Seating for parents, caregivers, and teachers 3. Collections for older children
Location	1. On the opposite side of the departmental service desk from services to younger children.
Features and Equipment	1. Two adult-sized reading tables, each with four side chairs. Tables will be three by five feet, with two chairs on each long side. Tables will not have aprons. Table legs will be attached with metal-to-metal fasteners. Tables will have high-pressure laminate tops and bottoms, with solid lumber core construction. 2. Two armchairs 3. Game tables with two side chairs. 4. Two computers on individual tables. Computer screens will be oriented to face library staff at the departmental service desk. 5. Storage for 3,000 j fiction books on the equivalent of eight double-faced 60-inch shelving units (assuming 40 books per shelf and five shelves vertically) 6. Storage for 2,000 j nonfiction books on the equivalent of five double-faced shelving units (assuming 50 books per shelf and four shelves vertically)
Estimated Space Required	1. 2 reading tables at 100 sf each = 200 sf 2. 2 armchairs at 40 sf each = 80 sf 3. Game table at 60 sf = 60 sf 4. 2 computers at 30 sf each = 60 sf 5. 13 shelving units at 23.5 sf each = 306 sf **Subtotal** = 706 sf Circulation space = 69 sf **Total: 775 square feet**

TABLE 7.2
Total square footage of library spaces

Foyer	unassignable space
Lending	875
Adult department	5,900
Young Adult department	600
Children's department	3,150
Program room	950
Public restrooms	unassignable space
Director's workroom	150
Staff workroom	725
Staff lunchroom	300
Server closet	100
Storage	900
Custodial space	unassignable space
Total assignable space*	**13,650**
Unassignable space* (25% additional)	3,450
Total gross space	**17,100**

*See section V for definitions of "assignable" and "unassignable" space.

IV-G. THINGS THAT DON'T BELONG IN PROGRAMS

The danger in writing programs is that authors may become bored with describing what's needed and start designing the building.

The purpose of the program is to define needs in extremely thorough detail but not to start drawing pictures. This occasionally happens when architects try to write building programs, because they tend to think in terms of design rather than just function. Building programs benefit from functional diagrams showing the relationships between spaces, but they should never have floor plans.

As an example of things that don't belong in programs, we've seen programs that provide a lot of information about landscaping decisions that are really a matter of architectural design rather than functional space needs.

One exception to this general rule of separating functions and aesthetics is the owner's desire to have the library fit in with existing architecture of a campus or civic center or historic neighborhood. In this case, the program might say (for example) that "the new library will match the Georgian revival architecture of the rest of the campus." Among other things, this statement may warn off architects who would rather die than match campus Georgian architecture. (Or, more likely, they will take the job and then strive in every possible way to ditch the requirement. See chapter 8, "Hiring an Architect.")

Of course, a campus may be seeking desperately to break away from its bleak physical character.

> If the new library doesn't match the rest of the campus, it may look great when it's new and trendy, but 30 years later it may stand out like white brick with turquoise doors, avocado shag carpet, and bright orange shelving.

V. Methods of Space Estimating

An essential component of all building programs is an estimate of the space required for each section of the library.

Although space estimation is sometimes viewed as the great challenge of programming, it can be a fairly mechanical undertaking. The real challenge is determining what features and items are needed in the library to meet the library's long-range plans and needs, and the final estimate of the space all of these features and items will take requires far less thought.

Most programs list specific spaces for library components like collections, furniture, service desks, meeting rooms, staff workrooms, and storage spaces. The library literature provides information on spaces required for a wide variety of library needs, but occasionally people preparing programs need to measure actual items, adding necessary space for people using the items and for other people to pass by.

By getting required spaces for library elements in print in substantial detail, libraries can help prevent situations where spaces are stolen for non-library purposes. For example, a monumental staircase may require far more space than the program estimates. If user seating or collection storage is shortchanged to enable the staircase, this needs to be immediately apparent to everyone concerned.

In calculating total space, three elements are particularly important:

- "Assignable space" is total space required for all of the library functions, including reader seating, collection storage, service desks, staff workspaces, storage, and so on.

- "Circulation space." Most standard figures for estimating the space required for furnishings don't provide the extra space needed to allow people to move comfortably between the furnishings. Depending on the feeling the owners want, the extra space may range from an extra 10 percent for a comfortable feeling to even 20 or 30 percent for a sense of real spaciousness.

- "Unassignable space." In addition to these library functions, however, there are many other things that require space, including hallways, staircases, restrooms, elevators, mechanical spaces, custodial spaces, the thickness of walls, etc. After adding up all the assignable space, consultants need to add a factor for unassignable space, typically somewhere in the range of 25 percent of unassignable space for one-story buildings and 30 to 35 percent for multistory buildings. But unassignable space can be much larger if your library wants a lot of ceremonial open space. For example, if your library wants an atrium with a monumental staircase, you will need a substantially larger building.

If the issue of open space is not settled, or if the building has a lot of historic spaces that are hard to use, your written program may want to stress the fact that unassignable space is a very rough estimate.

It's important that your program not merge circulation space and unassignable space into a single planning number, since your architects may end up repurposing essential circulation space to expand dramatic open spaces.

Space estimates must be based on an enumeration of contents. If estimates are merely offhand guesses, there is no reason to believe that the space listed for each section of the library is sufficiently accurate for the architect to follow.

Due to COVID, libraries may want to provide extra space so that users and staff can be slightly farther apart. For example, a library may want to increase spaces between reading tables by one or two feet.

V-A. PLANNING SPACE FOR COLLECTIONS

This is an example of how estimating space needs can progress. In a complete program, square footages need to be calculated for a wide variety of spaces.

Calculations for collection space involve converting from long-term collection numbers to display and storage needs.

- Libraries need to decide how many books they want to store on a shelf. Planning on less than six inches open at the end of a shelf is dangerous, for it leads to problems reshelving books. Libraries also need to decide how they will plan for collection growth and whether they want space for cover-out displays of books at the ends of shelves.

- The library staff or consultant needs to determine the number of books of each type that will fit in 24 or 30 inches. The results can sometimes be surprising. For example, collections in research libraries often contain thinner books than those in public libraries. The important thing to remember is that the average number of books per shelf varies from library to library and from collection to collection.

> We read about one research library that got itself into planning troubles by basing all calculations on the works of a famous local author, not considering whether those books were typical in size for the collection as a whole.

- Work with the consultant to determine the number of shelves vertically each type of material requires. This depends on library philosophy and shelving choices. For example, shelving height for adults can vary from 60 inches to 90 inches. Nonfiction shelves can be placed further apart to avoid separate shelving for "oversized" books.

- Some libraries have based shelf-need projections not on collection sizes but rather on how many books are actually in the library at a given time. The problem with this approach is that to avoid serious trouble one has to base calculations on times when the maximum number of books are on the shelves. (August and December for public libraries, and summertime for academic libraries.) In addition, different areas of the collection are out at different times. The number of items out also depends on how the collection is displayed: materials on face-out displays are lent much more frequently than those packed into spine-out arrangements. Don't count on high lending rates to reduce your space needs for collections if you are not going to implement a retail-based approach to display. Finally, use patterns can change both seasonally and over the longer term. All of this means the staff of a library that bases its shelving on books actually in the library at one time may have to do a lot of back-spacing at certain times to make things fit. If you take this approach, be a bit conservative and leave yourself some room on each shelf to make that back-spacing less frequent and easier. The big message here is that programming, space planning, and operational planning need to be in alignment.

- Review how the library wants to indicate shelving contents. The typical method is framed cards at the end of each aisle indicating the range of books in that aisle. Since the contents of individual aisles vary over time, it's important that the indicators are easy to adjust. Make sure that the program indicates this. (Some libraries have designer shelf labels that can't be altered, and this is an amazing mistake.)

- Programs need to specify aisle width in stacks and the frequency of cross aisles. Aisle width is particularly important to determine early, since it can determine support column spacing. Collections with extremely low use per title can have less frequent use of cross aisles in the stacks. For busy shelving areas, about one cross aisle for every seven units may be about right.

- Make sure your program has unambiguous terminology for shelving units. In particular, always specify whether shelving units are single faced or double faced. After a bad experience with an architect who converted the specified number of double-faced shelving units to the same number of single-faced shelving units, Fred began using phrases like "double-faced 84″ shelving units" every time he mentioned shelving.

Programs also need to calculate space for collections that will not be stored on standard book shelving. Map cases, flip bins for children's picture books, archival document boxes, bound newspapers, atlases, and other materials have special storage needs.

V-B. PUTTING NUMBERS TOGETHER

Programs should make clear exactly how total spaces were arrived at. For example, the programmed space estimate for a small adult reading room in a public library might look something like Table 7.3.

Some program writers specify overly precise sizes. For example, a reading area may be listed as 427.75 square feet. Although this may be the exact outcome of using available estimating

TABLE 7.3

Total square footage for a small adult reading room

8 armchairs at 40 sf each	320
2 reading tables at 100 sf each	200
Fireplace	50
Small counter for coffee service	25
Subtotal	**595**
Circulation space (about 10% extra)	55
Total	**650**

information, it is a figure with some seriously insignificant digits. Space estimates with numbers this specific are a bit of a fraud, because none of the planning numbers are that accurate to begin with. Fred's programs round off every area to a multiple of 25 square feet.

> Commercial businesses have used the overly specific number technique for years in sending bills. Even though $30,000.00 is sufficiently accurate, the company knows that a bill for $29,987.58 is (a) more attractive because it's just under $30,000.00, making it seem like more of a bargain, and (b) more credible because the unusual number implies extraordinarily careful calculation. Some people feel that this is particularly evident in their telephone, hospital, and funeral home bills.

No matter what source of square footage is used, consultants always run into situations where no data is available and they have to make estimates. The main thing to remember is that most of the space required by a piece of furniture is due not to the furniture itself but the space around it, both for people to sit or stand while using it and for people to circumnavigate the piece of furniture and the people sitting or standing there. In the case of items that are associated with crowds—such as new book racks or video selection areas—this extra space can be considerable.

Space projections in programs can be reasonably accurate, but the final test is always the design of your building. Sometimes problems are due to inaccurate programming, but they can also be due to adventurous designs that make it difficult to arrange furniture without wasting space. For example, an office that is not a simple rectangle will probably include square footage that cannot be used effectively, and the room will need to be larger as a result. Almost any space with curved or diagonal walls will be less efficient, in addition to displaying other major problems.

VI. Who Should Write Your Building Program

VI-A. PROGRAMS BY LIBRARY BUILDING CONSULTANTS

Programming is a common service provided by independent library building consultants. Usually these are professional librarians with a great deal of experience in working with library buildings.

Having a librarian rather than your architects prepare your building program has some very significant advantages:

- A librarian will have a different perception of space needs than your architect or sponsoring agency. No matter how excellent these people are, they may tend to see buildings in terms of public images or architectural spaces rather than of library services.

- If you hire a consultant who does not work for your architect, you have a much better chance of hearing an essential second opinion on a problematic design concept. (And if things get dull, you can encourage your architects and consultants to argue with each other.)

- Although architects can create exciting and interesting library spaces, they sometimes fail to understand how libraries occupy spaces on a daily basis.

- Working with a consultant will give you someone to critique proposed floor plans and building designs. This is a critical function of consultants, because very few practicing librarians or governing bodies have extensive experience with library designs.

- Be alert to architects who try to prevent your consultant from attending planning meetings or critiquing drawings. If your architects balk or always say, "There's no time," be prepared to inform them otherwise.

Hiring an independent library building consultant may also protect staff librarians who have good reasons not to speak up and disagree with mayors or provosts.

VI-B. PROGRAMS BY ARCHITECTS

There are at least two problems associated with having your architect prepare your building program.

The first is that by having your project architect program your building, you lose the vital second opinion that comes from separate people doing the programming and design.

The second is that architects and librarians see library buildings in different ways. Apart from any unproductive contentions about who is right and who is wrong, having two different perspectives on your building is almost certainly a better idea than having only one. Unless your architects . . .

- have master's degrees in librarianship accredited by the American Library Association, and

- have worked for many years as librarians, and

- have programmed a number of successful library buildings

. . . you may find that their knowledge of libraries and how library contents occupy space and (in particular) what goes on every day in libraries may be extremely inadequate.

We feel strongly that most architects are not qualified to write building programs. If your program is written by an architect rather than by a librarian, your program and your design may share similar misapprehensions about how libraries work.

VI-C. PROGRAMS BY OWNERS

If you are experienced in program writing, you may want to prepare your own building program, but it's a bad idea not to have a consultant check your work.

For example, when Fred wrote a building program for his own library, he had written about 50 earlier programs for other libraries. Nonetheless, Fred insisted that his library hire a second consultant to review Fred's own work. In the process, the second consultant discovered a couple of places where Fred had been myopic—or just not thinking clearly. So it was a good investment.

If you don't have experience writing several building programs for other libraries, it's almost certainly a serious mistake writing a program for your own library unassisted.

And it may be hard for an employee to point out to the university or city that the library needs a half-million-dollar elevator.

Because programming is the first step in library design and construction, taking the time to do it right is very important. Errors and omissions are amazingly cheap to correct during the program stage but increasingly expensive and difficult to correct as architectural design work progresses. By the time the building is built, it's basically too late.

VII. How to Hire Library Building Consultants

One of the best ways to find out about consultants is through professional word of mouth. Talk with directors and governing board members of other libraries.

State library agencies may have lists of people who have served as consultants on library design projects, but they are unlikely to provide any evaluations of the quality of consultants.

Library building consultants need appropriate backgrounds:

- Master's degrees in librarianship from programs accredited by the American Library Association.

- Extensive personal experience with how libraries function in buildings. Most consultants have been library administrators.

- Time to carefully investigate specific libraries and talk extensively with owners, staff, and users about the long-term functional plans and corresponding space needs of libraries.
- Demonstrated ability to put these plans and space needs into print.
- Unlike architects, library building consultants have no professional accreditation, and libraries need to pay close attention to the credentials of the people they consider hiring.

In addition to the obvious questions about qualifications, there are a number of other questions you can ask about their experiences with consultants.

- Did you enjoy working with the consultant?
- Did your consultant listen to you?
- Did the consultant respond to your needs rather than thrusting personal enthusiasms upon you?
- Was your consultant adept at sorting out differences of opinions among library staff and between library staff and governing bodies? (Sometimes this is nearly impossible when members of governing bodies are strongly against spending any money whatsoever and have no real interest in library services, but in most cases it goes surprisingly well.)
- Did your consultant suggest all kinds of possibilities? (We think that one of the jobs of a consultant is to give libraries a chance to consider a wide variety of options. If you reject many of them, at least you won't find yourself asking later why you'd never considered them.)
- Did you and your consultant have similar philosophies of library service? If you had philosophic differences of opinion with your consultant, what was the result?
- If a staff member insisted on an ill-considered idea, was your consultant able to deal effectively without making the person angry and at the same time not simply giving up and putting the idea in the program?
- If some members of the community were vehement in pushing a bad concept, could the consultant represent you effectively?
- Was the building program complete, clear, well organized, and literate?
- Did your consultant write generic programs that could be resold repeatedly?

> A town Fred worked with hired a consulting firm that specialized in methods of reviving small towns. The town received a standard report recommending that it become a tourist mecca with cute shops. The first draft of the report even betrayed its creators' recycling when it included the name of a different town. The first local reaction was, "Can every small town in the state become a tourist mecca with cute shops?"

- Was your consultant prepared to attend most (if not all) planning meetings with your staff and architects?
- Was your consultant familiar with architectural drawings? Was your consultant able to review drawings and make suggestions for functional improvements?
- Did your consultant have an extensive knowledge of what kinds of architectural features are successful in libraries and what kinds tend to cause trouble?

- Could your consultant help you present your project to your community? (Remember that it's the job of your consultant and architects to take the blame when people are angry, leaving the library staff and local government to take credit when things go well.)
- Was your consultant regarded positively by the grant-giving authorities?
- Did your consultant provide thoughtful analysis of your ideas or just scribble down anything you mention and move right along?

Your state may have legal requirements that limit the ways in which consultants can be hired by public agencies. Check with your state library or university administration or an experienced library attorney.

VIII. Programming Methods

VIII-A. SUCCESSIVE PROGRAM DRAFTS

No program is complete and correct the first time it is written. It's hard to be complete in initial conversations. And participants sometimes don't realize they disagree when they're talking in groups.

Getting drafts into print is therefore essential. When programs are in print, missing elements are far more likely to stand out, and the people providing input are much more likely to realize that they disagree.

For this reason, good programs cannot be completed in a single, intensive working session. For a small library with a limited budget, having a consultant who is close enough to make three or four visits is very much to its advantage.

Because programs may go through many drafts, it's vital that you can identify specific drafts. For that reason, all program drafts must have page numbers and running heads that include the date of the draft.

VIII-B. CUTTING BUILDING PROGRAMS

The majority of the first drafts of building programs need to be cut in size.

Although the contents may be appropriate and logical, by the time libraries have listed everything they need and want, the proposed building is almost always larger than people can afford.

The right way to cut a program is in a meeting with the owners, staff, and consultant present. If the program is well constructed, every section shows how estimated space requirements were developed, and it's possible to work through the program, crossing things off as you go.

Some things can be cut almost by rote, with space for collections, user seating, and other parts of the building cut by fixed percentages.

A few things, however, can't be cut by simple formulas. Workrooms for individual staff members, for example, will usually need to be cut in number rather than reduced in size.

A dangerous tendency is for people to say, for example, "I think this room should be cut to 800 square feet." The response has to be, "What listed items do you want to eliminate?"

Our experience has been that unless people fight to retain certain major features undiminished in size, even large programs can be cut in a few hours. Usually the owners and staff and consultant decide what needs to be cut, and then the consultant revises the written program accordingly.

One thing that makes the space-cutting process less painful is the percentage add-ons. If each area of the library is increased by 10 percent to provide circulation space, and then the entire program is increased by 25 percent to allow for unassignable space, cutting 100 square feet of space from user seating may result in cutting about 138 square feet from the total program.

VIII-C. FINAL REVIEW WITH LIBRARIANS, OWNERS, ARCHITECTS, AND CONSULTANTS

One of the first working meetings with your consultant and architects should include a review of the program. A program review provides your architects with an opportunity to raise questions about your building program. Your architects may find some aspects of the program unclear, and they may have alternate suggestions.

This meeting is an important step. Your consultant may have made errors, and your architect may have interesting alternatives to suggest.

The most vital aspect of this meeting is that your consultant be present to respond to suggestions or questions from your owners, staff, and architects, and to question them in turn.

It's also a good thing to make clear to your architects from the beginning that you expect proposed changes in the program to be discussed directly in this meeting. Very occasionally, architects will employ a form of passive resistance, ostensibly accepting the written program but then presenting drawings that ignore or violate sections of the program. Fred has had a couple of experiences where public library boards were nearly driven to distraction by long series of proposed architectural designs that ignored the boards' programmed spaces.

Occasionally, architects will balk publicly at written programs, contending that the consultant is "designing the building." This can be a genuine problem, but in our opinion it is completely reasonable for a program to include a list of design features that have failed widely in other libraries. A program that specifies a "two-story prairie school revival building" may be intruding in design, but one that says "no recessed downlights, no atria, and no indoor water features" is dealing with function, not aesthetics.

IX. Two-Phase Building Programs

Frequently, libraries cut the sizes of their building programs not because the programs include unneeded features but because the results will simply be too expensive to construct at one time.

Rather than simply cut a building program in situations like this, ask your consultant to prepare a two-phase program, listing first all the spaces for the Phase I version of the building and then all the spaces in the Phase II version.

A good two-phase program will include:

- Notes throughout the Phase I version on what changes will be made for Phase II.

- Recognition that many smaller spaces cannot be stretched between Phase I and II. While large reading rooms are easy to expand, small meeting rooms, public restrooms, staff workrooms, and similar areas are hard to expand.

Some solutions to the inability to stretch small spaces in second phases include:

- If you have two meeting rooms, omit one from Phase I.

- If you have only a single meeting room, you'll almost certainly need to construct it full size in Phase I or put up with the smaller size in Phase II.

- If your state plumbing code dictates the number of toilets in your restrooms, have your architect calculate how many will be necessary in Phase II. To avoid having extra toilets placed in unfortunate locations in Phase II, build your Phase I restrooms large enough to handle Phase II needs.

- General storage spaces can easily be added to piecemeal, with additional storerooms constructed in Phase II rather than expanding existing Phase I storerooms.

- For staff workrooms for groups of staff, it may be possible to build a single workroom in Phase I, shared by staff from two areas of the library, and then construct a second workroom in Phase II, allowing separate spaces for the staff of each area.

Fred has written a number of two-phase programs. He finds them complicated to write (with tricky calculations of spaces) but very useful for libraries. Library needs must outweigh consultant comfort.

If you have a two-phase program, you will want your Phase I construction drawings to be accompanied by a Phase II floor plan, so you can check for conflicting designs. Over the years, Fred has found problems with sloppy two-phase architectural planning.

X. What to Do When Owners and Architects Ignore Your Building Program

Most librarians and consultants have had experiences with owners or architects who simply ignore the aspects of programs they don't like.

When owners or architects disagree with programs, the proper thing to do is sit down in a room with the owners, library staff, architects, and consultant and review differences of opinion.

Some common methods for preventing owners and designers from ignoring programs include:

- Hold a formal program review during the first meeting with your architects, with your consultant present. If it becomes apparent at the meeting that the architects have not read your program with care, this is the best time for a serious discussion of what you expect from your architects.

- If your architects want to alter program details, explain that this will be a group undertaking.

- Require that every schematic design be accompanied by a table comparing the designed square footage in each area of the building floor plan with the square footage in the building program. This is extraordinarily easy for an architect to do, and resistance or outright refusal can easily be an indicator of serious trouble.

> In one of Fred's projects, the architects flat-out refused to provide such a table. They were later replaced on the job for being unwilling to do what the owners wanted in a number of other areas as well.

- Include your building consultant in *all* architectural planning meetings. It's amazing how much faster planning progresses when owners, library staff, architects, and library building consultants sit around the same table. Among other things, having your consultant present can stop ill-considered design ideas before they become so established that it's difficult or impossible to change them.

- Insist that your architects provide enough time for your consultant to review construction drawings.

- Ask your designers to provide initial floor plans that show which items won't fit by leaving icons for the items around the edges of the plan.

XI. Quick Space Estimates Using Formulas

Some formulas exist that use a few data elements to estimate total space needs for libraries. A formula like this can give you an order of magnitude estimate of how much space your building may occupy, particularly if it is a small, single-story building.

However, formulas may be based on standard plans that don't reflect your community's or library's needs, or its attitude toward public buildings.

A serious problem with using formulas to estimate space needs is that owners may be tempted to skip full programming and go directly to an architect with their quick space estimate. This is an extremely serious error.

One of the main purposes of quick estimates based on formulas appears to be to get the consultant's foot in the door, not to do any serious space planning.

XII. Conclusions

Programming is a vital step in the design and construction of library buildings. Never be tempted to save a few dollars and a few weeks of time by launching directly into architectural design. Careful planning takes time and money.

Well-built library buildings are characterized by permanence, and many serve for over a century. Ill-considered books or software can be discarded and uncomfortable chairs can be put in the staff lunchroom, but an ill-considered building can live to torment multiple generations of library users and staff yet unborn.

It's essential that the planning team include people who are trained librarians (a) with a strong knowledge of the functional aspects of library buildings and (b) who do not report to your architects. In addition to programming, one of the major functions of library consultants is to provide comments on the functionality of proposed designs.

A building can be both functional and inspiring if all the planners—owners, librarians, architects, and space consultants—can work together.

XIII. Snappy Rules on Building Programs

1. Among other things, a program provides a second opinion. Having the same firm write your program and design your library is always a seriously bad idea.

2. Some consultants make their money by selling the same reports over and over. When you read sample programs and studies and preliminary space estimates, look for reports that could apply to almost any library, or for reports that tell all about the consultant's methods and almost nothing about the specific library in question.

3. When you are hiring a consultant, always ask for a sample building program.

4. If your consultant gets on your nerves, you will not enjoy programming.

5. Some consultants have one solution to all problems. When you talk with previous clients, ask if consultants refused to listen to their special interests and needs.

6. Avoid quickie space estimates based on formulas or templates.

7. You will have a much better balanced project if your consultant is a librarian with a knowledge of buildings rather than an architect with a knowledge of libraries.

8. Never have an architect write your program. With a tiny number of wonderful exceptions, architects don't know enough about libraries, even if they've designed a few. And few architects can totally divorce themselves from design issues.

9. If your architect and consultant are the same person, you lose the tremendous advantage (and occasional entertainment) of having them argue with each other.

10. Even though the word *survey* sounds scientific, the vast majority of surveys in the library world appear to be anything but, and many appear to be total nonsense. Never use surveys to plan public libraries, and be very wary of them when it comes to other types of libraries.

11. If your consultant is a librarian with a deep knowledge of library buildings, always use that person to provide ongoing functional reviews of your developing building plans.

12. Focus groups are a good way to talk with library users, but you can't just count on people just turning up. Make sure they attend, and make sure that a few of them are real friends of the library.

13. The best sources of programming ideas are usually staff and administration, rather than users. But even if you don't learn much from user input, it's still important.

14. The two least expensive elements in building a new library are programming and selecting an architect, but both take time. If you're not sure when you'll have to hit the ground running, prepare a building program, go through the legal steps in selecting an architect, and then wait to see what happens next.

15. Programs with big blocks of text are miserable to read. Programs structured like outlines work best and are easiest to follow. You don't want important points buried in the middle of long paragraphs.

16. Because programs are frequently revised, every version should use running heads that include the date of the version of the program and the page numbers. There's

nothing less fun than finding out that different people are using different versions of the same program.

17. In addition to writing your building program, a good consultant can help you hire your architect, take part in architectural planning meetings, provide the perspective of a professional librarian when reviewing proposed architectural designs, and help with grant applications.

18. If a program needs to be cut in size, the right group consists of the owners, staff, and consultant. Leaving any one of the three out can lead to serious problems.

19. If you know you'll be expanding your new library, write a two-phase building program and have your architects prepare schematic designs for both phases. If you don't do this, you may find that you've painted yourself into a corner, and that your Phase I design makes it impossible to construct Phase II.

20. If people above you in the hierarchy insist that each section of your written building program be limited to a specific length, ignore them. It's a seriously bad idea.

21. Writing and revising building programs can take a lot of paper, since everyone needs to get a copy of each version in type large enough to read. This is a bad time to save a tree. (Try telling yourself it's an evil tree.)

22. Getting things into print helps clarify situations where people don't agree—or don't even know that they disagree. Francis Bacon said the best thing about library building programs: "Truth emerges more readily from error than from confusion."

23. There's a current vogue for "strategic plans," but they are not an acceptable substitute for building programs. They make things look easy because they're shallow.

24. Constructing a library is more like a movie (with a collaborating crowd of professionals) than like a poem (with one author). The public at large is a lot more in love with movies than with poems.

25. Having a library building consultant on your planning team can be very helpful in situations where mayors or provosts are bullies and threaten library directors with dismissal if they speak up. Consultants speak with more weight and can afford to be fired.

26. If anyone gives you public library "survey" results that include numbers after the decimal point, throw them away.

27. With the exception of branch libraries, most libraries need expansion sooner or later, despite what mayors or provosts assuredly contend to the contrary.

28. Building programs tend to be long because there's a lot to cover. Tiny programs are for library buildings tinier than yours.

PART II
**From Overcrowding
to Ribbon Cutting**

CHAPTER 8

Hiring an Architect

I. Introduction

Finding and hiring the best architects for your project is one of the most critical tasks facing library owners. If you hire the right architects, the whole process can be relatively straightforward and extremely rewarding. By the end of many projects, librarians are convinced that their architects can walk on water (or at least barely get their ankles wet).

But with the wrong architects—firms that know little about libraries (and don't admit it), ignore your requirements, fight you at every turn, or let cute design enthusiasms overcome functionality—the experience can be miserable.

A substantial number of architects specialize in library buildings, and this can be very much to your advantage. Although architects who know little or nothing about libraries can design functional libraries, they have a great deal to learn on the job, and you may wish they hadn't done so at your expense on your project.

If your architects don't bring significant knowledge of libraries to the job, you will need other people who have this knowledge. The most common people are your library building consultants, who you will probably need to attend many design meetings. Some libraries also hire "owner's representatives" with extensive experience in library design to provide this double-checking.

One major problem is that some architects are unwilling to admit that any special knowledge is required to design a library. This is why it's so extremely important to do extensive research on the prior work of firms before selecting one.

> The approach of some architects to library design reminds us of someone's comments on women's shoes in Britain: "They look like they were designed by someone who had often heard women's shoes described but had never actually seen one."

One of the main reasons to hire architects with little or no library experience is because you want to hire local architects. In situations like this, local architects without library experience frequently form "teams" with out-of-town architects who are library specialists. The local architects serve as local point of contact and are always nearby during construction when things go wrong, but the out-of-town library architects are present during the design process to be sure that good library practices are followed. However, working with teams is not always a great experience; see section V, "Special Problems with Teams."

Special and school libraries, of course, frequently have to deal with architects who have no particular knowledge of libraries, because the library is just one small element of a much larger project. In this case, having a very detailed building program ready before design work begins is particularly vital—as is finding a way to make sure that the architects pay attention to your program. Having your consultant around may also help, particularly if you have your consultant play the "bad librarian" role and fight the architects and administrators when dysfunctional library design ideas are proposed.

Some states have very specific laws concerning how public bodies hire architects. Your state library may have this information, or if you have in-state consultants, those people may know. When in doubt, you need to check with your attorney.

> Good librarians can be annoying to those architects who start off with little intention of listening to them. One architect who specializes in schools told Fred that school librarians were the hardest crowd to deal with during school design. Fred cheered, but to himself, in a polite sort of way.

Architects are only one of the groups important to library construction projects. For information on hiring a library building consultant, see chapter 7, "Building Programs," and for information on hiring a construction management firm, see chapter 14, "Bidding."

II. Locating Architectural Firms

Typically, architectural firms keep a constant ear to the ground. If you are considering a new or expanded library building, many firms will find out about it through the grapevine. But this is like waiting for emergency services to wander by after your accident, and it's better to be proactive.

Many librarians rely on word of mouth from other libraries. A morning on the telephone, calling libraries that have recently completed buildings, may give you a quick idea of who the major players are, including which architects librarians tend to like and which ones honk them off. Be careful at this point, however, since many librarians are in love with their new buildings—even buildings that are surprisingly badly designed—while other librarians can be crabby about reasonably workable projects.

Independent library building consultants are also good sources of information, since they spend much of their time with library buildings and keep up with library architects.

One of the potential dangers for library building consultants is developing overly close ties with architects, since they may see them on many successive jobs. Consultants work for owners and should always take the owners' sides and be deeply committed to the owners' needs, even when the architects involved are old friends.

It's good to ask other libraries about this when you're hiring a consultant.

Many architects have booths in the exhibit halls at state library conferences, and you can make contact with excellent firms this way. Since architects usually practice regionally, you are more likely to encounter them at state than at national conferences, unless this year's national conference happens to be in your part of the country.

Unlike, for example, some insurance or copy machine sellers, architects are generally too civilized to seize you by the arm and draw you into the dark recesses of their exhibit hall booths at library conferences. But they will be interested, friendly, receptive, and given to keeping in touch extensively after they meet you.

Libraries can publish advertisements indicating their interest in hiring architects. Depending on laws in your state, government-owned libraries may be required to do so.

Many state library agencies keep lists of library architects, and these can be a useful starting point. Such lists, however, often contain all firms known to have designed libraries in the state. Because the lists are not evaluative, they may not be of much help until you get to know the individual libraries personally.

For all architects, one of the biggest challenges in the profession is actually getting the job—beating out other firms for commissions. Once hired, relatively few are fired, even on those occasions when they thoroughly deserve it. Because of the critical importance of getting commissions in the first place, some architects spend a lot of money on marketing.

III. Investigating the Prior Work of Architectural Firms

Before you send out requests for proposals to architectural firms, or after you've received proposals from firms you don't know, you want to conduct personal research on the work of the architects you are considering.

III-A. REFERENCES

Librarians have a tremendous advantage here because they tend to have long-term, friendly social contacts in the profession. If you are evaluating an architectural firm that specializes in libraries, there's a good chance that someone you've known for years has worked with the firm.

This is why it's important to have the right people call references. Library directors speaking with library directors are more likely to get a straight response, because none of us likes lying to friends and colleagues.

For a different and useful view of libraries, it can be a very good idea to have your maintenance staff call the maintenance people at libraries designed by architects you are considering hiring. Your maintenance people are the ones likely to hear about lightbulbs that can't be changed, floor coverings that are impossible to clean, and other expensive structural or maintenance miseries.

Your consultant may also help you evaluate firms, but consultants have to work with architects, and you should expect quiet private comments rather than loud public comments.

> Consultants are nervous about this sort of thing. Once Fred worked for a library board that pressured him for comments on a specific architectural firm. After they promised him they would never tell anyone what he said, he said some bluntly negative things, and the board didn't interview the firm. When the head of the architectural firm asked why the firm wasn't being interviewed, the board said, "Fred told us not to."

III-B. TOURS

It's sometimes very hard for directors who had libraries built under their aegis to admit that things went badly. In this case, a tour with informal conversations with rank-and-file staff may lead you to hear about features everyone hates. We've both had experiences touring new libraries where the directors were busy telling us how well everything worked while staff members were muttering about major dysfunctions. (At one major library conference, staff members giving tours of a new library building had to admit to using flashlights to read call numbers in the stacks.)

Your library building consultants can organize tours of appropriate library buildings.

You can learn a lot about architects by visiting their libraries, and that's an important part of fact finding. A good firm, however, can deliver a variety of building styles, so it's dangerous to base your entire opinion of a firm on one building you think looks a little weird. If you don't like the aesthetics of a building, consider that the architects may have done their best to give the clients what they wanted.

While you're visiting a library, ask staff members about how the project went. Did the architects listen to them when they made suggestions? Did the architects have pet ideas and refuse to abandon them? Did the architects know anything about libraries, and, if not, were they aware of the fact?

It always helps to look for some of the architectural features that make good libraries:

- Good sight lines for library staff, including lots of interior glass partitions
- Long-term flexibility of use
- Single public entrances
- Accessibility
- Easy navigation
- Impressive numbers of electrical outlets, including in the tops of all reading tables and in the middle of open floors
- Soft, bright, extremely low-glare lighting
- Pleasant places to sit
- Comfortable acoustics
- North light
- Blinds on all exterior glass that faces any direction except north (including tiny blinds on tiny areas of glass)
- Light fixtures that are easy to reach
- Adequate staff workspaces
- Adequate storage space
- Flexibility
- Expandability

You can also carry a checklist of architectural ideas that almost always cause problems in libraries. It's probably safe to assume that when you find these in a library, most of them were suggested by architects rather than librarians. Common errors in library architecture are mentioned throughout this book, but here for quick reference are a few of the worst (and—unfortunately—most beloved by some designers):

- Atria
- Skylights
- Balconies
- Courtyards
- Reading terraces accessible from inside the building
- Indoor water features
- Non-rectangular rooms
- Monumental staircases
- Features that terrify people with acrophobia
- Railings that can be climbed like ladders
- Architecturally mounted task lighting
- Intense downlights, including recessed downlights of all sorts
- Soffits that determine the location of service desks
- Perimeter soffits
- Curved or diagonal walls
- Dark ceilings (except for historic ceilings)
- Non-acoustic ceilings (except, again, for historic ceilings)
- Windows of any size or shape or height that can admit direct sunlight but don't have blinds

Many of these are summarized in chapter 4, "Evaluating Library Buildings by Walking Around," and chapter 5, "Dysfunctional Designs."

III-C. REQUESTS FOR QUALIFICATIONS

When you are considering hiring an architect, a standard way to gather information is to formally request information from architectural firms. Most libraries will send out something variously identified as an RFP (request for proposals), RFI (request for information), or RFQ (request for qualifications).

When you send out an RFQ you embark on what sometimes approaches a game. You are trying to find out a number of things, while architects will try to convince you that whatever they have done in the past is exactly what you want. (Some people say that the architects are "being responsive," while others are more cynical.)

Here's what you ideally want to know about each firm:

- How much actual library work the firm has done. Finding this out can be surprisingly difficult, because firms tend to list every library they've ever touched, ranging from major new buildings designed and completed to preliminary studies for remodeling men's restrooms, when nothing was ever done.

  One way you can deal with this is to ask the firm to list only new library construction jobs or major library remodeling and expansion jobs. If you ask that all the projects be already completed, you will avoid a great many preliminary studies. But firms with little experience may dodge this question. Some firms will want to talk about buildings currently being designed or under construction. These may be interesting, but you can't drive over and take a look at them. And some turn out to be a lot less fantastic when completed than when described.

We suggest that when you schedule interviews, you ask to hear about finished projects only and avoid hearing about projects that are just in the planning stages.

When two firms merge, even if their offices remain scattered across the nation, they often combine their lists of previous projects. For any firm with more than one office or with a recent merger, your job becomes one of finding out which people in the firm built its library reputation and whether those specific people will handle your project—or are even still with the firm.

Some firms will include in their responses to your RFQ libraries that were worked on by the engineering firms they propose to work with. This information can be somewhat useful, but it can also be regarded as serious resume padding.

- What people the firm is proposing to do your work. In your RFQ, you want to request specific biographical information on the people who will lead your project. In particular, you want to know about the project architect and partner in charge. Who will be responsible for the actual work? Who will be present at all planning meetings?

If the firm has an overworked star library designer, you sometimes need to watch out for "bait and switch" situations. The star attends the initial interview with the owners, but the rest of the crowd does the actual work. Often these stars have tremendous personal charisma, and you need to be wary of situations where you won't see much of them once the contracts with your architects are signed.

You also want a list of the architects' sub-contractors or sub-consultants. Common ones include engineers and estimators. Geotechnical engineers are frequently hired locally, because they know local soil conditions and have necessary equipment, but in many cases other engineers will be from out of town.

Increasingly, architects hire independent cost estimators, since the volatility of the construction business makes it hard to project costs accurately, and since owners seldom forget the experience of receiving a low bid three times larger than the estimate.

- Whether the firm's clients are satisfied. Some architects will send photocopies of letters from clients. However, clients who like their architects socially can be "satisfied" with dysfunctional buildings, so you need to tread carefully. Call references, and also call people who are not listed as references.

- How much work of this type the firm has done. As noted above, some firms list projects that no one currently associated with the firm ever worked on. When you have doubts, ask which member of the current staff was the project architect or partner in charge.

- Whether the buildings the firm designs actually work. Instead of asking previous clients, "How do you like your architects?" ask, "How do you like your building?"

It also helps to ask specific questions. Do your staff members like their workspaces? Do users find the building confusing? Is it hard keeping an eye on things? Are there maintenance problems (such as difficulties maintaining light fixtures)? Is the building inflexible? Does it have problems with acoustics and with overly direct sunlight? Are people with acrophobia uncomfortable when using the building? Is energy usage exceptionally high? What was the most frustrating thing about your experience constructing this building?

Because owners are typically in love with their new buildings, it helps to visit and judge for yourself. If the building is brand new, try to see past the gleam of fresh carpet and clean paint and look for places where trouble can occur. Directors of new libraries can actually be extraordinarily defensive. On several occasions, we've asked whether a specific feature causes trouble, and the director's response has been a completely irrelevant "You should have seen our old building!" or "But it's so much better than what we had before!" Don't buy into this kind of talk. Successful building design is not a relative thing. A bad design is not better because your building used to be a lot worse.

One thing that complicates this is that while some seriously bad ideas are due to architects, many are also due to clients that insist on impressively dysfunctional designs and essentially force their architects to go along.

- Whether previous clients found the architects in the firm responsive to client requests. This is an extremely important point but sometimes a surprisingly difficult one to get at. As a profession, architects have developed a reputation for being poor listeners. It's impressive how many times owners get into a situation where their architect appears with a design idea, the owners say "no," the architect returns with new drawings featuring the same idea, the owners say "no" again, and the architect ignores them and brings back the same idea a third time.

- The moral is, when architects simply ignore clients rather than reviewing issues with them, it's time to talk with the firm bluntly about (a) whether the architect will follow the client's wishes, (b) whether the firm will assign a new architect, after that person meets with the client, or (c) whether the client will hire a new firm.

> The architect for one library Fred worked with was in love with atria. The first suggested design had an atrium. The board of trustees responded, "No atrium, please." The second design still had an atrium, but in a different location. Only mildly testy at this time, the board repeated, "No atrium." The cycle continued through eight successive designs with eight different atria, until the board president, a woman given to modest speech, pounded her fist on the table in fury and shouted, "NO DAMN ATRIUM!" The architect's feelings were hurt. The ninth design had no atrium, but one could clearly see where an atrium could be inserted when the members of the board changed their minds. The board eventually found a different designer.

- Whether the members of the firm are good listeners. When you are interviewing firms, most will tell you what good listeners they are. Many may be. A few may not be. And some stress "good listening" because, as a group, architects can be notoriously bad listeners. Ask the references you call.

- Whether artistic design tends to trump function. Everyone wants library buildings that are great looking, but libraries have to function as well. To us, the real challenge of library design is having libraries that look great but also work well. A knock-your-socks-off library that doesn't do its job is a failure rather than a success. Library design awards are given for appearance rather than function, and this is a good reason to pay limited attention to them. It's also a good reason to ignore publications that consist just of pretty pictures of new library buildings.

- Whether the firms tend to have an excessive number of change orders due to sloppy preparation of construction drawings. Change orders are due to many things, and a great many of them are no fault of the architect. Innocent change orders are particularly prevalent in remodeling, where unexpected problems are frequently found when walls are opened. Other innocent change orders are frequently due to clients changing their minds. Sometimes this happens only after a feature is constructed and the owners shout, "What is this? We hate it." (One could also argue, of course, that if owners are that surprised, their architects failed in their communication roles.) Other change orders result from extra money. If bids come in unusually low, a library may decide to add extra features, and these may appear as change orders.

Given the amazing number of details in a set of drawings, a few errors are bound to creep in, and we have to deal with them. Technically, it's the fault of the people who prepared the drawings, but ensuring perfect drawings would be far more expensive than dealing with a few minor mistakes.

However, omissions that can be rectified later by simply adding things rather than also ripping things out are sometimes called *betterments*. The general idea is that under betterment situations owners are not paying for things twice. They just didn't get them the first time around. The implication is that owners should have to pay for things that were never in the original construction contracts. The problem occurs when adding things retrospectively costs a lot more than if they had been included up front in the original contract. At what point should architects be held responsible for the extra cost of what amounts to a change order rather than part of a competitive low bid? This is where the the legal principal of Standard of Care comes into play. Perfection is in excess of the performance requirement established by most standard contracts and an allowance is made for some level of error within construction documents.

At any rate, what you want to find out is: If your architects get you into alteration trouble because of careless work, will the firm take fiscal responsibility for the extra costs that exceed the Standard of Care? Unfortunately, very few do.

In interviews with prospective firms, try a question on the order of, "If you specify the wrong size of window, and it doesn't fit the space where it goes, will your firm be responsible for the cost?"

> In one project John Moorman was involved with, the architects forgot to provide ventilation in a restroom. The result was grim. The architectural firm contended it was not at fault, but after strong words of the what-in-the-Sam-Hill-were-you-doing-designing-a-restroom-without-ventilation variety, they paid for retrofitting the proper ventilation.

Local contractors know which architectural firms tend to make a lot of errors in their drawings, and they may bid extra low to get a job, knowing that they're sure to make a good profit on change orders. If you have a connection among local contractors, you can ask them about the reputations of various architectural firms for accurate drawings.

- Who the firm is proposing as the team to do your work. All but the tiniest of firms have several architects. If the firm's reputation for library design is based on the work of one or two architects, you may want to be sure that those particular people are on your job.

- Who will do construction oversight? In some firms, the partner in charge or project architect also takes the responsibility for assuring that the building is being constructed in accordance with the drawings, but other firms have employees who provide this service. We think having the actual designers keep an eye on things works better because they know the actual design far better and they're more personally involved in the success of the project.

To get at this information, what can you ask for in your RFQ?

- A list of completed projects, particularly libraries

    This can be hard to get at, since project lists from architectural firms tend to be full of projects that involved remodeling a restroom, doing a preliminary study for construction that never took place, and so on.

    One way to nail things down is to ask for (a) a list of library construction projects that are completed or under construction, (b) the scope of each project, (c) whether any other architectural firms were involved in each project, and (d) if other firms were involved, which firm was the lead architect.

    Some firms submit impressively long project lists but have relatively few completed buildings. There's nothing necessarily wrong with this, but you want to know specifically about completed buildings.

- Accreditation

    If your state requires registration with a state agency in order to apply for state work, you can ask firms for copies of their registration certificates. Unfortunately, many state certificates represent a vast amount of work by architectural firms rather than any measure of quality. We suggest you skip them, in part because many firms have decided not to bother.

    Architects who are members of the American Institute of Architects will consistently place "AIA" after their names. Remember that AIA indicates membership in a professional organization and not licensure in your jurisdiction. Individuals identified as "Architect" or "RA" (an abbreviation for Registered Architect) are true indicators of legal standing and capability.

    You will occasionally see "FAIA" after the name of an architect. This stands for "Fellow of the American Institute of Architects." It's a major honor for architects to be named fellows, but it reflects more service to the profession and the AIA as an organization rather than owner-centric achievement, and you may wish not to be swayed by it.

    Architects are licensed to practice in specific states. If the proposed project architect or partner in charge is not licensed to practice in your state, you will want to know what's going on. Someone in the firm must be in responsible charge of your project, and that person must to licensed to practice in the state where the project is constructed. You want to know this person and see the name on your project.

If you plan to construct a LEED-certified building, you can specify LEED-accredited architects. Most architects with LEED accreditation put the initials "LEED" and some reference to the level of accreditation achieved after their names.

- A list of the people who will make up the team proposed for your project

For all members of the team, you want to know their credentials, training, and personal experience.

You can also ask for a list of projects this specific team has completed. Known compatibility is important. (Fred has attended architect interviews with teams who scarcely had been introduced to each other before the interview.)

You should expect the relevant credentials for each individual team member.

- As part of this list, specific information on who will be in charge

Watch out when responses to this question get vague, or firms say something like "In our firm, everyone works on everything." Someone has to take the lead, and if this is the first time for that person, you want to know it.

- List of outside consulting professionals in the team

Few architectural firms have a wide range of engineering skills within the firm, and this is not a reason to discount the capabilities of the firm.

Among the firms you may find mentioned are structural engineers, mechanical engineers, geotechnical engineers, electrical engineers, lighting consultants, construction cost estimators, and so on. It's common that geotechnical engineers will be from your immediate area, because knowledge of soil and drainage and local construction conditions is very much a local specialty, but the other firms will probably be from the architects' area and work with the architects on a regular basis.

Some architectural firms with little or no library experience will list the library experience of their engineering firms. This is relevant, but not very relevant, and you want to watch out for it.

Watch out in particular if an architectural firm lists your library building consultant as reporting to the firm. If this is how they're thinking, the result can be serious trouble, since they may hope to squelch people who disagree with them.

- Directions on where to send copies of proposals

If your library building consultant will be participating in architect interviews—which is always a good idea—you will want to ask firms to send copies of their proposals to your consultant so that you don't have to repackage them and ship them yourself.

Also include the following specific information in your RFQ:

- The specific day and time that proposals are due

Always make this time a time when your library will be open and staff members present to note when proposals turned up. "Midnight" is never a satisfactory time because you have no one present to receive and time stamp submissions. (This may seem a petty requirement, but in case of controversy, it's important to know who was on time and who was not. When it comes to formal bids of any kind, this information can have major importance.)

- The number of firms you plan to interview

The right number of interviews is three or four. In extreme circumstances (such as irresistible political pressure to interview a firm you wouldn't hire on a dare) you might have another interview, but we don't recommend it.

If you plan to interview a large number of firms, it will make your job far less attractive to architects. When firms feel that there is little chance of being hired, they will be less likely to spend the money to submit credentials and attend your interviews.

If you try to interview too many firms you will not give each firm enough time to make a good presentation. You may forget who said what. And you may be tempted to interview them over a period of days or weeks—always a bad approach, because the people doing the interviewing will not always be the same group, and the people doing the interviewing may forget their impressions of some firms.

- The day on which interviews will take place

The time to tell firms about interview schedules is far in advance, so that they can pencil the interviews into their calendars, and so the interview team will also commit to those times.

If you tell them at the last minute, you'll have a far poorer chance of interviewing every firm on the same day.

Don't schedule interviews for days when travel conditions are likely to be poor. Keep away from winter months if your part of the country has snow and ice in the winter.

By announcing interview times far in advance, you also prevent attempts by a handful of firms to angle to be the last firm interviewed. (Some firms feel that the last firm interviewed is the one most likely to be selected.)

We think it's also a good idea to let architects know that you are planning serious interviews, not 20-minute wonders. If you say in your RFQ, for example, that 90-minute interviews will be conducted at 9:00 a.m., 11:00 a.m., 1:30 p.m., and 3:30 p.m., architects will know they have a reasonable amount of time to describe themselves and their services, and that the half-hour break between interviews means they won't be treading on the heels of other firms.

Since the arrival of COVID, more clients may be interviewing architects by Zoom. Large state agencies may save significant travel time in this manner. It saves time for architects too, but you may miss something that provides insight into how a relationship may play out. We are fans of in-person interviews whenever possible.

- Sources of additional information

Architects need to know where to go for additional information not included in your RFQ. Usually this is a hired professional—library director, university architect, or similar. You want this to be a single person for consistency of responses. (You also want to warn your staff to refer all architect questions to this single person. Staff members making offhand and partially informed comments to architects who "stop by" can lead to problems.) So provide the mailing address, phone number, email address, and so on, of the person who will be available to answer questions.

All responses to questions should be in writing. Post them on the library's website, right where the RFQ is posted.

Expect that architects who are seriously interested in your project will want to visit your library for a tour and conversation. This is a very reasonable request, and you should make time available.

You should also offer to provide interested architects with copies of your building program, including contact information for your building consultant. (Since architects routinely contact consultants, you will want to let your consultant know if you would prefer to handle all contacts with architects personally. Most consultants will be happy to simply tell architects that questions are being handled by the library, but you have to warn your consultant in advance.)

Many firms will provide an organizational chart of the planning team. This will help clarify the relationships. It can also warn you of potential problems if people you regard as reporting to you directly (such as your building consultant) appear in the chart as reporting to the architects. Or aren't there at all.

Fred is old-fashioned and likes physical copies of proposals rather than electronic copies. If you want hard copies, include in your requirements that each firm send hard copies of its proposal to the library and a separate copy directly to your consultant.

However, many libraries now use digital distribution because of its speed, ease, and lower environmental impact. Some libraries and agencies issue tablets to their board members to facilitate their deliberations. Libraries may now request electronic copies of proposals, with perhaps hard copies only for the library files and for anyone on the selection committee who does not have access to a computer.

IV. Proposals from Architectural Firms

Most architectural firms will send you elaborate pamphlets in response to your requests for proposals.

Proposals will include photos and resumes of key staff members, with specifics about their professional experience. Proposals will also include pictures and floor plans of completed projects, information on the firms' track records in the areas of accurate estimating and change orders, statements of design philosophies (which are pretty much slogan writing), and other materials.

V. Special Problems with Teams

Some architects submit proposals involving multi-firm teams. "Teaming" is standard jargon in the field, although not necessarily grammatically elegant.

A common multi-firm team arrangement involves local architects with little library experience and an out-of-town firm with more experience.

Multi-firm teams can be great, especially if the out-of-town firm is experienced and plays a major role in the work.

However, we often suspect that the team is formed for reasons of competition with other firms, not because the local architects have any doubts about their ability to design a library all by themselves. The local firm needs the out-of-town's credentials to get the job, but it may plan to use the out-of-town firm as little as possible thereafter.

What can you ask when presented with a team proposal?

- Have the two firms ever worked together before? If this is a first time, it may be a marriage of cynical convenience in order to line up a job in a competitive environment rather than a healthy working relationship.
- If the two firms have not worked together, describe similar teaming experiences for each of the firms.
- Which specific people are the members of the team?
- How much will you see the out-of-town firm during the project? We've seen situations where the out-of-town firm attended a single meeting and never turned up again. You should expect the out-of-town firm to be present throughout the project, with heavy involvement in the design phases, in particular for all schematic design meetings.
- What is the implication of the team for your costs? This evaluation should emphasize qualifications. If the best opportunity for a successful project is a team, then expenses are a minor cost. Most teams know they need to come in at a comparable fee and will work to limit the financial impact of the team approach. If there is a local team that is truly qualified (expert library design and knowledge of the local construction industry), then go with that firm. If not, pay a little extra and get the benefits of both. This is a long-term investment and requires a full range of expertise. Focus more on whether this is just a sales pitch or a real collaboration to address your needs. Can they can function as a real team?

Sometimes mild confusion occurs because the word "team" is used in slightly different ways by architects. Some architectural firms will refer to the group that will be assigned to your project as a "team," while other firms talk about working with a second firm as "teaming."

VI. Evaluating Proposals

Once the proposals have been received, typically representatives of the owner will evaluate them in order to select firms to be interviewed. Among the things you can look for are:

- Does the firm have a company style, or does it do a variety of different designs? There's absolutely nothing wrong with a company style if you like it, but if, for example, you think serpentine glass walls are too expensive (and they *are* expensive), you will in all likelihood be unhappy with a firm whose previous buildings all have serpentine glass walls.
- What kind of library experience does the firm have? Remember that you want to find out what library projects have been completed, or are at least under construction. And you want to know about new buildings or major expansion jobs, not minor remodeling. If your RFP is worded correctly, the proposal should contain this data.
- What library experience do the people in the team proposed for your project have? You particularly want to know about the partner in charge or project architect, the person

> Unfortunately, in some cases the out-of-town expert is mostly window dressing. The one time that Fred teamed with an architect, it turned out that the architect needed Fred's credentials to get the job, but thereafter he expected Fred to shut up while the architect informed the client about all things library. When Fred sent a report to the architect, the architect simply deep-sixed it and told the client the opposite. In desperation, Fred sent the same report directly to the library. The architect then screamed (literally) at Fred over the phone, claiming that Fred had no right to speak with the client. And the team ended.

who will be in charge of design on a daily basis. Sometimes it's hard to tell this from proposals, and that's a good time to ask the firm for written clarification. (It's perfectly fine to respond to architects' submissions with specific questions, particularly in areas such as prior experience with libraries, where firms can be amazingly evasive.)

Sorting out experience is much harder with very large firms, which may have library experience scattered among many offices and many architects. What you want to know is what your office and your architects have done.

This is also a time to start sorting out the working architects from the sales architects.

- Is the group proposing to replace your library building consultant with one of their own? This is a bad sign.
- Much of evaluation consists of contacting people listed under previous projects to see whether they are happy with the experience. Because librarians are basically sweet people, it's sometimes hard to get unvarnished opinions. They may also be unwilling to say anything negative about their new library buildings.

A firm may feature two or three libraries, providing names and phone numbers of directors. Call them, but also call libraries that are not featured, because they may be less successful projects.

Remember that more librarians like their architects than like their buildings. So it's always a good idea to ask about the building itself.

- Your gut reaction matters. If you find staff members of an architectural firm to be dishonest, bullying, evasive, or poisonously full of themselves, don't bother with an interview, because you would never want to work with them.
- If you haven't done so already, try to visit buildings designed by the firm in order to judge for yourself. This is especially important because many owners and directors may fail to level with you.

Take a copy of chapter 4, "Evaluating Library Buildings by Walking Around," with you.

- Architectural firms with no library experience will sometimes argue that their lack of experience is a Good Thing. They may be right, but we don't think so.
- Ignore AIA awards and most other design awards. Although recognition from the American Institute of Architects and other groups is always impressive, these awards may not be for things you find important. If you want a library that is cozy, pleasant, functional, easy to maintain, architecturally in keeping with your community, and popular with your users, you will probably find that awards are not given for any of these attributes.

VII. Interviews

The first and most important rule for interviewing architects is to strictly limit the number of interviews and provide enough time for each firm to make a reasonable presentation.

We recommend holding a maximum of four interviews. By the time you interview a firm, you should feel that the firm is a strong potential candidate. This is why it's essential to do your homework before scheduling interviews and select only firms you suspect would do good work for your library and be a good fit.

One of the worst ways to interview architects is to run a large group of firms through at high speed, meeting a new firm every few minutes. This wastes the firms' time and money, and it gives you no time to evaluate them.

It costs architectural firms a substantial amount of money to attend interviews. The best firms are therefore much more likely to be interested in your project if they learn you plan to interview only three or four firms. This greatly increases their chance of being selected and makes the investment in the interview less of an expensive long shot.

Although you may assume that the large number of interviews is just the architects' problem, it can hurt you as well, because some of the best firms may simply lose interest if they learn that you plan to interview more than four or five.

For this reason, we think it's important to tell firms in your RFQ both when you plan to conduct interviews and how many firms you plan to meet.

Remember also that (as with marriages) there will be more than one firm out there with whom you could probably cohabit happily. By the time you interview, you should be feeling around for the best fit, not wasting everyone's time talking to firms you know you would never hire.

Any interview less than 90 minutes long is unfair to everyone concerned.

We recommend that you:

- Strictly limit the number of firms interviewed to three or four. However, one thing that can occasionally lead to additional interviews is the presence of local firms that politics say must be interviewed but that the owners of the library don't want to hire. It may be better to interview an extra firm than to antagonize the local community.

- If a firm drops out at the last minute, invite another firm. You want to interview an absolute minimum of three firms.

- Interview all of your architectural firms in a single day. Among other things, this ensures that all members of the interview group will meet all of the architects. It also helps keep all the firms fresh in everyone's mind.

- Be sure that the same group of evaluators is present for all interviews. People who miss some of the interviews are of no help when the time comes to select a firm. This is one of the reasons to interview all firms on the same day.

- Schedule interviews at two-hour intervals. Two hours leaves time for a 45-minute presentation by the firm, 45 minutes for questions and answers, and 30 minutes for the first firm to pack up and depart, the next one to set up, and the interviewers to refill their coffee cups and/or rush to the restroom. (Under duress, one hour and 45 minutes also works, but you may feel rushed.)

- Be prepared for high-tech presentations. Virtually all firms of any size will have PowerPoint presentations. They may bring projection screens with them, but many expect you to have one. You will also need proper electrical supplies and a way to partially darken a room. (Libraries that have meeting rooms with two light levels—blazingly bright and medieval dark—will have trouble meeting with architects who want to simultaneously show pictures and converse with you.)

- Some architects take all their own photographs, while others hire professional photographers to focus on one or two areas of the building that were designed to be particularly photogenic. It helps to know what's going on, especially because professional architectural photographers tend to bring in portable lights that completely change the look of the spaces photographed. You can always ask at interviews whether the pictures were taken with available light or whether the photographers brought in their own lighting equipment.

- Many architects will also bring boards with mounted photos, samples of carpet and tile, and so on, all of which have to be set up on portable easels. (You should not be asked to provide easels, but you'll need to provide adequate floor space.)

- Prepare sets of questions in advance. To be sure you cover the same material with each firm, prepare advance questions. (Many of these will usually be answered by the architects in their presentation, so you will need to pick and choose when the time comes for Q&A.) A list of possible interview questions appears below.

- Select the order of interviews yourself. Some architectural firms are convinced that the last firm interviewed is the most likely to be hired. Most firms that ask for later interviews have valid reasons for doing so, but occasionally a firm will angle to be last for a perceived advantage. (It's always considerate not to schedule the farthest-away firm for the first interview of the day.)

- Always have your library building consultant present at the interviews. Consultants can bat cleanup, asking questions that have been omitted in the conversation. They're also good at asking questions no one wants to ask, such as "Is your firm currently subject to any litigation?" or "What went so terribly wrong in the job at Port Amazing?"

- Be sure that the people asking questions know how libraries work. The great danger in having architects selected by (for example) university boards of trustees is that boards of trustees usually know absolutely nothing about libraries. The result may be the employment of an architect primarily on the basis of glamor.

What are you trying to find out at interviews?

- The interview gives you a chance to meet the members of the architectural firm. Everything else being equal, it's always better to work with people you like. If you can detect signs of serious egomania, that's useful information.

- The interview is designed to show you what the team can do for you by what it has done for other libraries in the past. It can also show that the team understands the special challenges facing your library. It may even bring along a couple of idea sketches to show that it's been thinking about you.

- Pay more attention to the firm's recently completed work than to descriptions of work in progress. We've listened to hundreds of architect interviews, and it's interesting to see how some excited descriptions of great works in the planning stages vanish from presentations once the buildings have been completed and things didn't work out quite as well as the designers had hoped.

- The interview is not a time for the architect's team to present a design for your library. The presentation should stress their past successes with other difficult situations, not possible solutions to your library's problems. Stress on your library's specific needs may also indicate a lack of previous experience.

- Any architectural team that arrives at an interview with an elaborately finished rendering of "your library" is either trotting out a cynical sales pitch or is the kind of team that leaps to conclusions. There's no way most firms can learn enough about your library before the interview to allow them to come up with a serious conclusion about designs. You are interviewing for demonstrated aptitude in past efforts, and the work to design your library is still to come.

- The interview is also not a time for the architects to learn more about your library and its needs. It's always fun and good for the ego to talk about your library, but the purpose of the interview is for you to learn about the architects. Having architects learning about your needs comes during previous visits to your library and in meetings after you've selected a firm.

- By watching the interactions within the architect's team, you can often learn how they work together—and sometimes that they've never worked together before. (A good question to ask during the interview is the prior experience of the proposed team as a working group.)

- Watch for demonstrated flexibility. You want a firm that can design the kind of building you want, not one standard structure.

- Watch for indications that the firm may fight your aesthetic ideas. If you want a prairie-style building or a Georgian revival building, you want to find out whether the firm will fight you.

- Watch for signs that the members of the firm listen to you. You can find out some of this during the Q&A period. Try to base your opinions on how they respond to the questions rather than exclusively what they say.

- Watch for signs that the members of the firm have reviewed your building program, and be very concerned if they have not. It doesn't hurt to ask the team specific questions about the program. (If your program has some controversial features, it's interesting to see how the team deals with them.)

- Watch for signs that the members of the firm dislike working with experts on library design. For example, if they clearly bridle at the consulting librarians who wrote your building program, that can be a bad sign. And it's a *very bad* sign if they want to bring in their own consulting librarian to replace yours. (If you have your special needs in print, you don't want an architectural firm that has no interest in responding to them.)

- Discount standard architectural talk. The world is full of architects who have a "passion" for libraries. In addition, many firms will stress in their presentations what good listeners they are. This is nice to hear, but we think firms say it because too many architects have well-earned reputations for not listening to their clients.

- You may not want to ask the following important question because it seems impolite. But ask anyway. Or stick your consultant with it. "Are you currently subject to any lawsuits or litigation? And if so, why?" You want to know whether a firm is being sued, and whether it's for a good reason. If the last library the firm built has filed suit because the building has a wet basement, leaky roof, malfunctioning detention pond, terrible acoustics, bad lighting, and expansion space that's unusable (this describes a library Fred knows that sued its architects), you want to know about it. In actuality, however, most firms are probably sued because workers are hurt on the job and the workers' lawyers sue everyone involved in the project. Once things get sorted out, the suit against the architect is usually withdrawn. So always follow through on this question and find out the nature of the legal problem.

VII-A. POSSIBLE QUESTIONS FOR ARCHITECT INTERVIEWS

Here are some questions you can use when interviewing architects. Many are intended to help you pin things down if you feel that people are avoiding responding to questions.

If you divided your architect interviews into formal presentations and then Q&A, many of these questions will probably be answered during the interviews. But you want to ask questions that are not covered during presentations.

A couple of libraries have interviewed architects simply by asking questions, with no opportunities for the architects to make preliminary presentations. Architects have told us they found this a very unsettling and somewhat random experience. We suspect it's not a good idea.

The italic-faced items are the actual questions, and the rest are just comments.

- *Who will be your project architect and partner in charge? How long has this person been with the firm? For what other projects has this person been partner in charge? Who will be present on a regular basis at all planning meetings? Are there any occasions when the partner in charge will not be present?*

If the partner in charge is not present at the interview, or plays no real role in the interview, find out why. If you prefer that another member of the firm than the one proposed as partner in charge serve in that capacity, you can make that a condition of employment. If someone on the team suggests there will be no partner in charge—saying something like "we all work on projects together"—that's just being evasive.

In your contract with the firm, you will want to specify that the partner in charge lead all of the planning meetings.

- *What will your firm do if this person cannot continue as partner in charge throughout the project?*

Architects leave firms for many reasons. If you are selecting the firm because of a specific person, you want to have contingency plans. You want assurance that you will get to meet and "interview" replacements and assess their ability to pick up the project and continue without having to start over.

- *Who will your consulting engineers and other specialists be? If these are not employees of your firm, what prior experience have you had with these firms?*

Commonly, firms hire their geotechnical engineers—whom they sometimes identify as "civil engineers"—locally, so they may not have worked with them before.

- *Who will be your interior designer? Is that person present at the interview today? What experience has this person had with library design?*

Interior designers are far more than interior decorators. For instance, they may be responsible for all of the furniture layouts in your library, for specifying furnishings, and so on. Meeting the designers is important.

- *Do you do your estimating in house, or do you hire the work done? How accurate have your estimates at the end of the schematic design process been in recent projects? How about your estimates at the end of the construction document phase?*

Estimating is vital. Many architects rely on specialized firms to do the work, but architects with geographically concentrated practices—particularly in areas of similar small towns—often can do a good job estimating.

Architects should be prepared to provide examples of projects including initial estimate, final estimate, and actual cost.

- *What are you prepared to do for us if the low bid for our project is higher than your estimate? Will we be billed for the extra redesign costs?*

- *Are you prepared to design a building that makes an architectural statement in accordance with our preferences? In keeping with the character of our campus or town?*

You can always try out some kind of design you suspect they will not like, just to see how they react. If they say, "It's a terribly passé design, but we can do it if you want," that's a good sign. (White brick with bright turquoise doors is a 1950s enthusiasm that should make good architects wince.)

If you say, "We want an addition that matches our existing building," and they say, "We'll design the kind of addition your original architect would design if he were working today," this is a seriously weaselish response and not a good sign, because it places no limits whatsoever on the architects.

- *Are you comfortable with designing a building that does not feel contemporary? That appears strongly influenced by earlier designers?*

Some architects are extremely uncomfortable with the appearance of lack of originality. This is a good time to watch their reactions.

- *We will continue to use our building consultant as a member of our planning team throughout the design process. We intend to have him or her present at most if not all planning meetings. Will you accept this working relationship?*

Watch out for firms that hope the consultant will butt out during the design process, although they are unlikely to ever say so outright, particularly during an interview with the consultant sitting right there.

- *Do you have any questions or problems with the written building program?*

Try to figure out whether the firm has actually read the program. For instance, you can ask what they think of a proposed feature without describing it. You can also ask your consultants to raise questions about elements they think the architects may not like, in order to see how they respond.

- *What experience has your firm had designing libraries? Libraries of our specific type? How many have been completed? Were any of these projects carried out by a different office of your firm? Were any done by a firm you acquired after the projects were designed and built?*

Firms with little experience can be straightforward or evasive. Personally, we're very fond of straightforward. Although a track record of good library buildings is always the best thing, firms with little experience can do a great job if they know their limits and your consultants are actively involved during the project.

- *How much experience have your proposed partner in charge and project architect had with library design projects? For which of those projects were they the partner in charge or project architect?*

- *Of your library building projects, how many have been completed? Of these, how many in the last 10 years?*

- *What libraries have you completed in about our size range?*

A good way to describe size is in gross square feet.

- *What design errors have you seen in recent library construction projects? What design mistakes do you foresee tempting us in this project?*

This is a somewhat mean question, because you are asking the firm to criticize current designs. Architects hoping to be hired will be very wary of stepping on the toes of those people conducting the interview. You should expect the response not to simply repeat problems with your structure that are listed in your building program.

- *Can you help us with presenting our design to the community? What experience have you had in this area?*

- *What is the capacity of your firm? What other projects are currently underway? How major a role will our project play? What other projects will your proposed partner in charge be working at the same time?*

Architects can end up either hunting for extra work or being overextended.

A standard response can be "Our services are in high demand, but we can fit you in." But it's still a good question to ask.

- *Of your last five completed library projects, how many came in on time and under budget? If they were not on time or under budget, what happened?*

If the firm has fewer than five library projects, broaden the question to a larger category, such as campus buildings, city government buildings, and so on.

"On time and under budget" is a magic phrase in building construction. In the case of library construction, over budget leads to particular problems. (Our impression is that some of the poorest records in this area are held by the firms with the largest international reputations, but we could be wrong.)

- *Is your firm currently party to any lawsuits or litigation? Please explain.*

No one likes asking this, but it's a good question. If you don't want to ask it, get your consultants to do it.

- *Are you prepared to make frequent trips here if this proves essential for design work or for construction administration? If something goes really wrong on the job, how fast can you be here?*

- *What experience have you had with construction grants?*

- *The library will reserve the right to alter the building in any way it sees fit after construction is over. Can you live with this?*

Some architectural firms have managed to get libraries to agree that all changes of any kind—even colors on workroom walls or signs saying "restroom"—will be controlled indefinitely by the firms. This is a seriously crummy situation.

- *If you are proposing a team project with another architectural firm, have your firms ever worked together in the past? If so, what buildings have you completed? How often will we see the second firm? Will there be extra charges for that firm's attendance at meetings?*

- *Are the architects on your team all licensed to practice architecture in our state?*

    This should be clear from credentials, but if the credentials are vague, you need to know.

- *What's currently happening in the construction industry that may impact this project?*

    All kinds of things affect construction costs and schedules, ranging from changes in the labor market to shortages of materials like drywall. This should be an easy question for busy architects.

- *Why are you the best firm for the job?*

Ask your consultants or attorneys or state library whether there are any questions that are illegal. In Illinois, for example, you cannot ask firms what they will charge for the work until after you have rank ordered the applicants and are ready to enter negotiations with the top-ranked firm.

VIII. Final Selection

The final selection is completely in the hands of the governing body.

- Frequently, you will have a pretty good idea of who you like best by the time the interviews are over. If you did your homework before scheduling interviews, and all the firms have good reputations, you still will be strongly influenced by the proposed partner in charge and design team, by the degree to which responses are straightforward rather than evasive, and by your perceptions of where overweening egos may make it difficult for you to work smoothly with a particular firm.

- Some owners find themselves ready to make a decision as soon as the interviews are over, while others find that they have additional questions they want to ask previous clients.

- Either way, it's a good idea to make a decision reasonably soon, while memories of the interviews are still strong. And within a few days of the interviews, the firms you met will start to call to see if you've made a decision. Making a reasonably speedy decision should not lead to timetable problems because the fact that you've designated a preferred firm does not obligate you to start work at any particular time.

- In fact, if laws in your state make hiring architects a slow process, it makes very good sense to hire them early, so that you can start design on almost a moment's notice, or carry out a quick study of some kind.

- Despite occasional hints from architectural firms that they have a special political relationship that should be recognized, you are limited only by existing laws and regulations and contracts. (Our reaction to claims of political connections is to take deep offense, but every situation is different.)

- It's useful to have first and second choice firms, in case something happens that makes it impossible to hire your number one firm. If, for example, the partner in charge or project architect you want is no longer available at your preferred firm, or if you cannot arrive at a satisfactory contractual agreement with the firm, it's better to have a second firm in mind than to start over. Some states have QBS (qualifications based selection) laws that require public agencies interviewing architects to rank order the firms they meet.

- There is no legal obligation to hire anyone at all. If you are unhappy with all of the firms you interview, you have the right to start the entire process over. (However, if you have brought in what appear to be the best firms, you may not be any happier with a new group. And because it costs firms a great deal of money to attend interviews, libraries that get a reputation for jerking firms around may find a significant loss of interest among good firms the second time around.)

- Once you have made a decision, let everyone know which firm was your first choice. For architects, the major hurdle is being hired in the first place, and all of the firms you interviewed will be eager to know your choices.

- Architectural firms that are not hired will frequently ask you why. They will ask, for example, how they might improve their presentations or proposals. Fred recommends very strongly that you do not ever get involved in discussions of this type. Hiring an architectural firm is like hiring a library employee, and the correct response to "Why wasn't I hired?" is always a friendly but noncommittal "Because we felt that the firm we hired was the one that best met our needs for this project."

Even if you were singularly unimpressed with a firm, it's a good idea to be friendly and non-judgmental, since you never know when you'll need help with something else. You can always tell firms that you appreciate their taking time to attend the interviews and that you enjoyed meeting the team, but getting involved in the specifics of evaluation is a major mistake.

IX. Contracting with Architects

Although in some states it may be legal to select architects by low bid, this always strikes us as an extraordinarily bad idea for several reasons:

- The scope of the architectural process is elastic. If your architects want to renegotiate their contract every time you request a small additional study, this may be counterproductive.

- Architectural services are far less specific than construction. When you are constructing a library building, your architects will spend months preparing detailed bid documents, leaving as little as possible open to interpretation. By contrast, your contract with your architect will of necessity involve some generalities.

- The personalities of your architects and their approach to design are important because you are exploring ideas together. By contrast, contractors execute projects already described in detail. If you hire your architects by low bid, you may have to take whatever annoying person they send you.

In the United States, most contractual relationships with architects are by means of standard contract forms prepared by the American Institute of Architects (AIA). These standard forms are part of a family of agreements that will cover the future steps in the project, such as the owner's agreement with the contractor or construction manager, and with other entities such as furniture vendors.

The family of documents also includes the "general conditions" that apply to all parties to all the agreements. This is a set of basic definitions and responsibilities. Unfortunately, it is often overlooked in the contract review.

The problem, of course, is that everyone assumes AIA forms are written against them. They are in fact the product of a documents committee that includes 25 to 30 members representing insurers, legal experts, academics, state facilities construction commissions, building code consultants, and developers. In the end, this represents a balanced effort to arrive at something workable for most parties. There is the added benefit of "downstream agreements" that coordinate with construction agreements and forms.

Whatever the source of the forms, you will need the assistance of an attorney who has a thorough knowledge of those forms.

The AIA forms divide the process into the five steps mentioned elsewhere in this book. The contract should specify the percentage of the contract amount attributable to each step. See table 8.1 for an example.

We have run into several situations where architects insisted that schematic design did not include placement of all furnishings. For libraries in particular, schematic designs without furniture placement are worthless, and you will need to make extremely clear in your contract with your architects that your definition of schematic design includes furnishings. (Some architects may feel this calls for a higher percentage of total fees.)

In addition to these costs, your architects can reasonably expect to have a separate contract for feasibility studies if a number of alternate

TABLE 8.1

Example of percentage of contract amount attributable to each step

Schematic design 15%
Design development . . . . 10 to 20%
Construction documents . . . . 35 to 40%
Bidding 5%
Construction administration . . . . . . 25 to 30%

sites need to be formally evaluated and tested for their ability to hold the sort of library you want.

Here are some things you want to be sure are covered in your contract with your architects:

- Your intent to stop work after the completion of the schematic design and not continue until construction funds have been raised. Schematic designs are all you need to raise money, and if you fail to raise the money you need, you don't want to pay for unneeded design work.

- The schematic design will include scale drawings of the floor plan, elevations, and perhaps cross sections, plus a preliminary cost estimate and outline specifications.

- The floor plan of the schematic design will include furniture placement.

- What happens if the architect makes an error that will cost you money? This means a mistake that has to be rectified by tearing something out and replacing it. Simple omissions are not mistakes of this type, because you can still add the item to the project. But if the construction drawings put the footings in the wrong place, and they have to be ripped out and poured again, will the architect take responsibility?

- Who will be the partner in charge? Because many architectural firms have charismatic sales architects and more humdrum working architects, you want to make this very clear. (This doesn't mean that the humdrum architects will be disappointing, but you want to be sure about the firm's commitments. Bait and switch is a very serious possibility, particularly with very large firms.)

- If you select a firm because you like the proposed partner in charge, what happens if that architect leaves the firm and goes to a different firm? Among other things, you may want to have the right to transfer the project to the partner in charge's new firm.

- How will fees be determined? Discussions should start with "scope," a fancy term for what you need to have done. You don't want to pay for services you do not need. You don't want to find out that the low initial fee did not include a realistic set of required services. And you don't want a never-ending stream of additional fee requests. Avoiding these issues involves consideration of a number of components:

    » What level of detail do you need?

    » How many entities are involved in ownership, public participation, review, and approvals?

    » How many phases of construction will there be?

    » Is this a new building or a renovation?

    » And many more...

    Many contracts with architects start with an understanding of general fee levels based on a percentage of construction cost. Typically, small remodeling jobs have the highest percentage fees and large jobs with repetitious elements (such as residence halls) can have substantially lower fees.

    One common method is to agree on a time-and-materials-not-to-exceed (NTE) charge, where you and the architects agree on a maximum cost and a schedule of fees for individuals of the firm. The firm then bills you for its time and costs, up to the not to exceed the agreed fee. Joe thinks this is a bit misleading: It always takes more time than the not-to-exceed framework suggests, and you will pay the maximum cost in almost every instance. You should also be careful to understand if, at the point when the NTE limit is reached, whether the scope must be completed at that point or if you are simply notified that an additional amount will be required to complete all the tasks. Also, any new project requirement or change in direction can be the basis for a change in fee.

    Another method is a flat fee method. This is particularly common for preliminary studies (such as feasibility studies), for schematic designs, and for entire projects. This is a better way to keep the architects from drawing fantasy projects on your time. There is incentive for the architect to focus on the library's needs and get into real options for addressing those needs.

    We have outlined an extensive, intensive process in this book for design and construction phase services. We also recognize that everyone likes a bargain. You can see where this is going. Some snappy rules have been known for ages: "You get what you pay for."

- What expenses are reimbursable? These are amounts that will be billed in addition to those covered in the basic percentage or dollar contract. Typically, renderings and models and printed sets of bid documents are billed separately to the owner, but find out if you will be billed for mileage, lodging, meals, and so on. Travel and lodging costs

- can be a major item if the architects have a long way to travel. (If you select a team that includes both a local firm and an out-of-town firm, you may be asked to pick up a lot of extra airfare and lodging costs for the second member of the team.)

- What activities will involve extra fees, and how will these be determined? This is a tricky area. Will your architect charge you extra for evaluating alternate sites, helping with referendums, attending public hearings, preparing master plans for long-term expansion, and other essential services that are not exactly part of designing and constructing the building?

- What will you do if the architect does not deliver everything promised? This can happen when firms never get around to providing record drawings ("as-built" drawings). As with contractors, you may want to hold back a percentage of fees until all the work for which you've contracted is delivered. Record drawings are a particular problem because when the work is over, exciting new projects are beckoning your architects, and this kind of tidying up is a bore.

- A problem can also occur when architects feel that schematic design work is getting nowhere and (despite the lack of progress) they feel they've done all the work their fees justify.

> Fred knows one firm that handed the library a collection of rough sketches and contended that this constituted a "schematic design." The library then hired a new architect. But in the original architect's defense, the board had dithered endlessly, with no decisions emerging from meetings.

- How will the contract be dissolved? As with your library building consultants, you want to be able to pay your bills for work to date and walk away if you become dissatisfied.

- What is the schedule of payments? As with contractors, you want to be sure that the bills are not running ahead of work. For example, if your contract says that schematic design will be 15 percent of architectural fees, you want to be sure that at the end of the schematic design process you will have not paid more than 15 percent of total fees.

- Who owns the plans, and what does "ownership" mean? Can the architect use the plans to build an identical building for another library? Can your library sell the plans to another library?

- What happens if the library decides to paint the building pink three months after it's finished? Some contracts give architects residual rights to buildings, and this is a disastrous idea. It's your university or town or high school and your library and your money, and the architects work for you. If they don't like your new signage or color scheme or whatever, they've got to be just out of luck.

To repeat: developing a contract with architects is not an amateur undertaking. You will need an attorney who is familiar with construction contracts. This may be a university attorney or city attorney, but it may also be an independent attorney with significant experience in the area. Ideally it's not an attorney out to reinvent the wheel.

IX-A. UNDERSTANDING ARCHITECTS

There's no way to walk on thinner ice than to conduct amateur psychoanalysis of a profession, but here goes.

When library construction projects are complete, librarians are sometimes unhappy with the experience and the results.

They complain about many of the things mentioned throughout this book: architects who won't listen, buildings that are nightmares to maintain, buildings that terrify users with acrophobia, buildings that are hard to supervise, buildings that end up on the covers of architecture magazines but fail as libraries, buildings with gimmicky details that get in the way of performance, buildings with oddly shaped rooms or confusing floor plans, complex buildings that require too many staff members to supervise, and so on.

Vast numbers of architects perform brilliantly in finding ways to design the buildings that libraries would design for themselves if only they knew how. But other architects are more focused on their own goals than on yours.

Some architects are attracted to novel solutions to library problems, even if the solutions turn out not to be solutions.

A very few architects want to create Great Art, and they regard the functional needs of their clients as nuisances to be ignored when Art is underway. This attitude appears to be far more characteristic of "signature architects" or "starchitects" than of the great mass of the profession, but it can also be found almost anywhere, particularly among young architects short on practical experience and long on exciting visions of design.

Some architects are also deeply offended by the idea of imitating the work of previous architects. The arguments architects raise against matching existing architecture are legion. Some of these are perfectly reasonable—clients may not be able to afford the styles of 1910—but Fred suspects that underlying this argument is the powerful desire not to be seen imitating the styles of other times. As a result, for example, some university campuses that maintained a fairly uniform Collegiate Georgian or Tudor Revival look through the Second World War now feature odd conglomerations of buildings representing a variety of fleeting post–World War II design enthusiasms. If you want one of the "enthusiasms" that is fine, but don't let it be imposed upon you by the architect. Make these decisions in the broader context of what the appearance of the building says about its role in the community or campus.

An architect with a vision or "concept" you dislike can be hard to derail. It helps to say "no" the first time you see something you dislike, but you may have the feeling that you are reacting too negatively too soon, failing to grasp the innovative brilliance of the idea. By the time you are convinced that you are right and that the concept is a disaster, things have moved on and it is hard to recover.

Remember that you are doing no one a favor by letting unwanted design concepts continue. Your architects will end up wasting their time pursuing a concept you have no intention of using, and you will waste expensive meeting time and perhaps delay your project.

As Fred picturesquely suggests, some architects are modern Svengalis, entrancing owners—particularly public library and university boards of trustees—with exciting architectural details that will lead to serious functional problems or terrible cost overruns.

Other architects strive to speak only with people who don't understand libraries. They bypass librarians, public library boards, campus architects, faculty library committees, library building consultants, and similar people to speak directly with city fathers and with university boards of trustees and with school boards.

These are major reasons why libraries can benefit from having relationships with people who know construction and/or library building needs extremely well but do not work for architects. These people may include independent building consultants, construction management firms, and similar specialists. Be warned though, each of these participants are just as subject to myopia and self-interest. Consider your team carefully and look for their willingness to contribute their knowledge in service of your goals. Finally, don't overlook the importance of introspection. Just as an architect is not a librarian, a librarian is not an architect. Collaborate, don't isolate, and trust but verify are practical guides to frame your approach.

X. Design Competitions

For major projects, owners may occasionally hold design competitions.

The greatest problem with design competitions is that they lead to choice of design on the basis of external appearance rather than function. They are pretty much glamor competitions and nothing more.

Design competitions can be exciting, but they can lead to problems if aesthetically popular submissions are also clearly dysfunctional.

If your circumstances call for a design competition, one thing you can do is provide a very detailed building program and require that proposed designs meet the program. It will help if your program specifically bans some of the features that are popular with designers but cause real problems in libraries, such as skylights, atria, direct lighting, overdone staircases, and so on.

A major problem with design competitions is that they may not bring out the best firms, who may be too busy with work to take time out for what looks like something little better than a lottery. It's a shame when entrants in the competition are all folks with time on their hands.

Moreover, the world may regard design competitions for less than highly prestigious jobs as simply examples of the owners' overwhelming hubris.

Our strong recommendation is that when the phrase "design competition" occurs, everyone involved in the project shouts "No!" in unison.

XI. Snappy Rules on Hiring an Architect

1. For any library construction project larger than a bicycle shed, you need an architect.

2. You get what you pay for.

3. Failing to plan is planning to fail. Invest appropriately.

4. Treat your architects fairly. Don't expect them to take on major unexpected tasks for no additional money.

5. Some architects have a brilliant ability to envision complex structures in three dimensions. Watching them work is fun.

6. You can have a comfortable and functional library. You can have a library designed by a world-famous architect. But you can't have both.

7. If you hire a team consisting of two architectural firms, be very sure you know who will actually be doing what and when—and what the extra costs will be.

8. If your architects have little or no library experience, decide how you will fill the gap. The consulting librarian who prepared your building program is the most likely person.

9. Of all architectural words of tongue or pen, "We will reinvent the library" are among the most terrifying.

10. Be particularly wary and aggressive when your library is a small element in a large building.

11. You will often see architectural awards hanging in the offices of architects. None of the awards were given for outstandingly functional buildings.

12. When interviewing architects, always be alert to bait and switch. Insist that the proposed "project architect" or "partner in charge" be the main presenter at the interview.

13. Clarify contractually what will happen if your partner in charge or project architect leaves the firm.

14. Clarify contractually what will happen if your lowest bid is significantly higher than your architects' estimate.

15. Clarify contractually that *your architects have no rights to the building once it's completed*. This is a building, not fine art. You must have the right to alter anything you want at any time you want, whether your architects like it or not.

16. While your architects should not have the right to stop you from altering your building once it's completed, you don't have the right to sell their plans to another library.

17. Clarify contractually that all color schemes, signage choices, and similar aesthetic decisions are your library's business. Your designers provide suggestions, not orders.

18. If architects bring a picture of "your new building" to an initial employment interview, ignore it. Or ask why they brought it when you had asked them not to.

19. Many states have specific laws concerning how government agencies employ architects. Check with your lawyer or consulting librarian.

20. Always hire consulting librarians and architects separately rather than as part of a single team, where you will not have the benefit of independent opinions.

21. When interviewing architects, find out where your project fits into their work. If you are their only project, things are not well with the firm. But if they have too many projects, yours may receive short shrift.

22. Design competitions for less than truly major libraries may drive off good architects. (For smaller libraries, design competitions come across as manifestations of excessive owner pomposity and ego.)

23. When architects are hired, all members of the selection committee must be present for all interviews in their entirety or not participate in the selection process. This is another reason it's important to establish interview schedules far in advance.

PART II
From Overcrowding
to Ribbon Cutting

CHAPTER 9

Site Selection

I. Introduction

Probably the two largest challenges that face most library construction projects are site and money.

Library sites can be hard to find because libraries occupy large quantities of space in crowded towns or schools or campuses or businesses, because they draw a lot of people, and because to be at their most successful, libraries should be convenient to as many potential users as possible. This puts them in competition with other land uses for desirable locations.

Generally speaking, all libraries need sites that are central, easily reached, safe, convenient to similar services, sufficiently large, relatively quiet, provided with adequate parking (if relevant), and not adjacent to problem areas.

Because other agencies are in competition with libraries for good sites, people with other plans for the most desirable sites will argue that libraries (a) have plenty of space already or (b) don't really need attractive sites. Unless libraries and librarians are able to hold their ground in the face of political and social pressure, libraries often end up in poor locations.

Examples of problematic sites are found everywhere. The most serious concern is sites that may limit user access. Libraries should never be located where the number of visitors, the frequency of visits, or the length of visits is reduced by the location or character of the site.

- Public libraries are sometimes built on sites that have no room for expansion—let alone parking. They may be built in locations far from other heavily visited buildings. They may be built on soil unsuited for structures, particularly massive structures like libraries. They may have neighbors that lead to endless troubles. They may be in locations that users are afraid to visit after dark.

- School libraries sometimes have common walls with gymnasiums or band practice rooms. They may be located in places buried deep within buildings, guaranteeing that they can never be open when the rest of the school is closed. Or they may be designed to serve as passageways to other areas of the school, completely ignoring the necessity of security for collections and equipment. And at least a certain amount of quiet.

- College and university libraries are sometimes built far from the center of campus or in locations with no room for expansion. They may be divided into scattered elements, not because service plans call for libraries on separate subject areas but because there's not enough space for a single central library.

- High-density storage units are too often located at considerable distances rather than nearby, resulting in substantial delays in the delivery of requested items, impacting the use of the collection and the effectiveness of researchers. Good sites are close by, but the best sites are actually attached to main buildings, where users can find them just down the hall.

- Special libraries are sometimes built so far from the center of user activity that nobody finds them. Because they are often located in buildings not engineered to hold the weight of books, special libraries can be buried in odd corners of basements or find themselves severely limited as to where shelving can be installed.

Unfortunately, most library locations involve compromises. The important thing is being aware of what compromises are involved and when it is essential that you stand your ground.

One good way to protect your library from inappropriate sites is to have your needs in print and on file before site issues arise. If necessary, a carefully prepared building program, one that identifies critical site characteristics, with a site evaluation process ready and circulated (or better yet, accepted before site issues arise), can solve problems by forestalling unworkable ideas.

II. Evaluating Potential Sites

This section is concerned primarily with selecting physical sites for the construction of buildings. It therefore applies primarily to public and academic libraries.

Careful evaluation of site is vital because construction decisions can last for a century. Or several centuries.

Unfortunately, while you are investigating sites, people will be pushing you to approve sites that may represent extremely poor choices. This is particularly true for public libraries, where political pressures to purchase sites that are too small, in inappropriate locations, or involve the remodeling of unsuitable existing buildings can be immense.

II-A. ALWAYS EMPLOY PROFESSIONALS

Although it's tempting to simply pick a site, there are so many technical considerations involved that libraries *always* need professional assistance. Among other things, your architects, engineers, and building consultant (all three, not just one or two) will help you determine:

- How much space you actually need (consultants and architects).

    Remember that if you cannot afford to build enough space now, you need to set aside for future growth both the extra space you need to build a sufficiently large building today plus the additional space you need for long-term expansion, including not only structure, but also parking, setbacks, landscaping, water runoff control, and so on. A carefully prepared building program will help you defend your space needs. One of the reasons for programming early is to be prepared when people abruptly start talking about sites. If you can spell out and defend your space needs when the topic first comes up, you can prevent other people from simply taking over your planning for you. Nevertheless, some people will blithely assume that all of your planning work is of no merit, even though they (a) have done no actual space planning themselves and (b) know little or nothing about libraries. In our experience, the political pressures to occupy undersized sites or derelict buildings can be immense.

Building programs rarely list all of the various non-building spaces required on a site. Determining initial and future areas required for parking, stormwater, open space, setbacks, and the like is a complex process that requires a coordinated review of zoning, planning, and environmental ordinances. These need to be discussed with and acceptable to a variety of jurisdictions that have authority over the project. You don't have a viable site until the various jurisdictions agree, in writing. Anything less is an educated presumption and comes with some risk. Do not be taken in by the "We're the library. They'll approve what we want" arguments from trustees, council members, or people trying to sell you sites.

Most municipal authorities will be up front about their processes. Early reviews often qualify for a conditional approval, subject to final design calculations and details needed for a final, binding approval. This is reasonable. You get some assurances without having to invest in expensive engineering on a site that you may not be able to acquire.

> A two-phase building program is an important tool to make sure you have enough space not only for construction but also for long-term expansion. See chapter 7, "Building Programs."

- Whether you can physically construct a building on the proposed site (engineers and architects).

The world abounds in sites that are unsuited for massive structures. The most convenient location in town is not a good choice if the library slowly sinks into the ground. (In actuality, relatively few libraries sink, but the extra cost of building on bad soil can be immense.) The input of local civil engineers (specifically geotechnical engineers) is particularly essential here because they know the idiosyncrasies of local sites.

> One of the popular rumors in the wide world of urban legends concerns hundreds of different libraries where the architects and engineers supposedly forgot to calculate the weight of the books when the buildings were designed, and that the libraries are now sinking into the ground. Almost all of these stories appear to be total hogwash, but it's fun to say, "And now as our library sinks slowly into the turf, we say goodbye to plans for long-term service."

- Whether the site comes with a building already on it and whether that building is suitable for use as a library (architects, engineers, and consultant).

Unfortunately, there are true stories of libraries assuming that buildings like former car dealerships can support the weight of books because cars are so heavy. Fred has heard the same claims made aggressively about old churches, "because pews are so heavy." But cars and pews aren't all that heavy. Only a few other types of buildings like warehouses and factories are engineered to be strong enough to serve as libraries. And even then, you want an engineer to check. (What sometimes gets people on other projects off the hook is the fact that lots of concrete floor slabs in old one-story buildings are stronger than they needed to be for their original uses.)

See also chapter 16, "Remodeling and Expanding Library Buildings," and chapter 17, "Converting Non-Library Buildings to Public Libraries."

- Whether the shape of the site lends itself to the construction of a library (architects and consultant).

Long, narrow sites, for example, may technically have sufficient square footage but not lend themselves to the construction of functional libraries with easy access from parking lots. If local zoning requires setbacks, long and narrow sites may have little land on which buildings can actually be constructed. (Oddly shaped sites have led some designers to have fun with correspondingly oddly shaped buildings, and these appear to be mostly mistakes.)

Oddly shaped sites are often thought of to be usable because "we can put parking over there," when in fact the realities of vehicle movement and the regulations governing parking lot layout are so rigid that this is the least forgiving aspect of site use.

- Whether portions of the site are unbuildable (architects, engineers, and consultants).

A surprising number of sites include space that is sloped or swampy or bordering on a crick or otherwise unusable for building purposes. When owners or agents quote site sizes, be sure to find out how much of the site is actually usable, including far above any imaginable floods. When you are getting serious, rather than trusting people hoping to sell to you, bring in an engineer to verify the actual workable size of the site. (Actually, given the long-term danger of flooding, any site that has any areas that are swampy or near a crick should be nowhere near your library site.) Interestingly, some sites by lakes with visible drainage are extremely stable, and Joe has worked on libraries in many locations like this.

- Whether zoning and code regulations and other laws will allow you to build there (architects).

Zoning and building codes will specify setbacks, total square footage (frequently as a percentage of site size), maximum building height, minimum off-street parking, water detention, construction types, and many other aspects of your library building. Often libraries are able to obtain necessary rezoning, particularly because they are not regarded as detrimental to neighbors, but you will be in bad shape if you purchase land on the assumption that you can have it rezoned, only to find that other interests stand in your way. Sometimes those interests are well funded and special, but usually it is more a matter of municipalities being wary of enforcing regulations on anyone if it will not hold itself to the same requirements. Joe has found very few jurisdictions willing to offer special consideration to libraries.

- Whether existing buildings you plan to remove or alter are protected by federal, state, or local historical preservation regulations (architects).

  Constructing a library in a historic district almost always adds to the challenge. You may find, for example, that groups insist that a specific structure on your site remain there forever, even if the new library will have to coil in a serpentine fashion around it. And some local, state, or national requirements can turn out to be incompatible with your plans for the site. Find out the situation and your appeal options before making commitments.

- Whether your location in a historic district will permit you to construct the library you need (architects).

  The limitations imposed by historic districts can be significant. Typically, you will need to deal with local agencies that have significant authority to allow or deny a wide variety of aesthetic and land occupancy considerations.

- Whether there are any concealed historic remains on the site that can prevent its development (architects, archaeologists, and local or campus historians).

  Previous burials or other hidden archaeological remains may limit or prevent use of the site for construction of a library. For example, if your site has Native American graves or a paupers' cemetery, you are highly unlikely to be able to use it.

- Whether you can afford the extra technical costs of building on the proposed site (architects and engineers).

  Coping with difficult soil situations or distant utility connections, for example, can have a major effect on construction costs. And so can having to relocate existing utilities within your site.

- Whether adjacent land uses will operate to the detriment of the library (consultants and architects).

- What the likely cost of removing any existing buildings is likely to be (architects and engineers).

  Removing buildings can be far more expensive than many people expect.

- What is the likely cost of removing the buried remnants of previous buildings that are now buried politely out of sight but will need to be removed before anything new is constructed?

The following sections of this chapter examine the practical implications of a number of these issues.

> Always consider using your hired professionals to deliver the bad news about proposed sites. They can make everyone mad and then leave town.

II-B. SOIL CONDITIONS

When you are considering a site for your library, you will need to know whether the soil is suitable for construction. Some sites that initially appear lovely are vacant because they are unbuildable.

If you manage a public library, always begin by checking with your city engineering staff. Because they are involved with issuing building permits, they often know where problem soil conditions exist. For academic libraries, check with your campus planning or facilities department.

Before you purchase property for your library, you will want your architects and engineers to test the ability of the soil to bear loads. This is done by boring holes in a number of locations around the site, removing core samples, and having them checked in a laboratory.

Soil conditions will also affect your ability to use geothermal heating systems. If you are considering a geothermal heating and cooling system, it's extremely important that you have an engineering firm evaluate your site for that purpose before you purchase it. Your architect can arrange this.

II-C. UTILITIES

One of the major costs of constructing a building is bringing utilities to the site.

Libraries commonly need access to water for domestic use and fire suppression systems, gas, electricity, storm sewers, sanitary sewers, telephone lines, and data.

If a site is half a mile from all of these utilities, the cost of connecting them to the library may be very high.

While bringing distant utilities to a site can be expensive, so is relocating utilities to make way for a new structure.

- Relocating utilities is often necessary when libraries are expanded or are constructed on brownfield sites. As with bringing utilities to a new site, the cost of relocating utilities can be extraordinary.
- Utilities are typically located under streets or alleys. If your library plans to expand across a street or alley, your architects and engineers will determine which utilities must be relocated and how much this is likely to cost. The locations of modern utilities can often be located electronically, but some older stuff is seriously hidden.
- Relocating existing sewers can be so expensive that it actually affects building locations.

> Some cities have only limited knowledge of what's underground. In the past, they prided themselves on not wasting money maintaining maps of underground utilities. Even if determining the location of utilities after the fact costs 10 times as much as making maps in the first place, one still had the advantage long ago of bragging about not wasting taxpayers' money.

Occasionally, libraries are constructed or expanded without relocating utilities that cross the building footprints. For example, sewer lines or even small brooks are sometimes located beneath floor slabs.

The cost of locating and relocating utilities is a particular problem because many people who give you forceful good advice on your project may have no idea how much money is involved in utility connections—or even that utilities exist. This is why you need opinions from your architects and engineers and city or campus engineering staff as soon as any site is seriously considered.

Even your planners may fail to mention the cost of connecting utilities while they are involved in the early phases of design, because utility connections are considered part of project costs but not construction costs. This is another reason why it's so important to be sure your architects are quoting you full project costs rather than just construction costs from the very first.

> Fred worked with one library that had previously constructed two basements divided by an underground stream running through a large pipe. Ironically, it was the newer basement that had flooded. Unfortunately, the library could have built a new third floor with natural light and views for about the same price and with the same staffing costs as the basement. Because of the massive pipe, there could be no direct connection between the two basements anyway, so traveling from the old basement to the new third floor by elevator would have been no time waster.

Occasionally, architects will indicate future expansion areas on site plans, then proceed to locate utilities directly under these areas. Always compare your architects' dotted line "master plan" future expansion locations with your engineers' utilities plans.

> Errors in this area can be amazing. For example, in one library Fred worked on, the designers planned to locate all of the utilities and the AC compressors on (and under) an area that their other drawings designated for future building expansion. From this experience, Fred concluded that the architects' indication of a building expansion area was a matter of lip service rather than genuine interest.

II-D. SURFACE WATER RUNOFF DETENTION AND RETENTION

Local regulations may require that your site include an area where rainwater can accumulate temporarily until it can drain away. If you need to provide a detention or retention basin, this can add substantially to the size of the site necessary to construct your library.

- Detention basins: Detention basins are low areas designed to control the accelerated water runoff that occurs when a permeable surface is replaced by impermeable buildings and pavement. The basin fills with water during rainstorms, and the water slowly drains away, percolates into the ground, or evaporates.

- Retention basins are like detention basins, except the water stays there all the time. Be prepared for the inevitable side products of goose occupation.

- There are alternatives to basins. Depending on local ordinances, you may be able to avoid providing a detention or retention basin if you are building on a site with previous construction or on a brownfield site. For sites with existing impervious surfaces, if you will not increase the total space occupied by impervious buildings and paving, you may not need to provide stormwater management. In essence, the non-absorbent percentage of the site is grandfathered in.

- For brownfield sites, the real concern is keeping stormwater out of the ground, where it can leach contaminants from the site and carry them into watercourses, water tables, adjacent properties, and the like. More often than not, new construction is expected to cap the hazard and prevent water from percolating into the contaminated ground—often with a new stormwater management system above the cap, and occasionally by diverting stormwater into existing municipal infrastructure.

There are also engineering alternatives to detention basins. For example, some parking lots have permeable paving that slows water runoff by letting the water directly into porous soils below the pavement or into a reservoir constructed below the pavement. The porous soil or reservoir performs the same function as detention basins.

Green roofs may also meet local requirements for controlling runoff. The nature of the plantings and the capacity of the system to absorb water determine what contribution this could make to the overall stormwater management plan for your site. The roof structure will need to be designed to carry the weight of the fully saturated roof system, you will want a root barrier to keep the plants from working their way into the actual weather barrier, and you will need some sort of watering regimen to keep your plants from dying before they are established. Your local building authorities will have the final say as to whether they will accept this type of roof as part of your stormwater management plan.

> Retention basins in subdivisions have led to a major ecological shift in the United States. Faced with the attractive new habitat offered by thousands of new basins, many Canada geese have become year-round residents rather than migratory waterfowl, perhaps becoming a subspecies in the process. People who once rushed from their houses to marvel at V formations of geese passing overhead now rush from their houses to curse geese passing in their yards.

Calculating the area required for surface water detention requires the assistance of architects and engineers because the size of the basin required depends so heavily on the size and the construction of structures and paving.

II-E. SUBSURFACE WATER

Subsurface moisture conditions are also important, even if you don't plan to create any basement space. Moisture can affect footings and floor slabs, and it can lead to water infiltration. Concrete slabs generally need a layer of porous crushed stone and a vapor barrier underneath them to keep water and water vapor from migrating into the slab.

> Fred worked with one Carnegie library that had been constructed next door to a concealed underground stream. Seventy years after the library was built, groundwater had undermined the building's footings. The result was stairstep cracks in the brick walls, massively cracked and heaving terrazzo floors (the library covered the worst cracks with heavy rubber mats), and roof beams that were pulling apart. When dropped on the floor, round pencils inevitably rolled off into dark corners. Given the condition of the library and site, the only option was a new building on a new site.

Water infiltration in basement walls can lead to hidden mold formation, particularly if the inner face of the basement wall is covered over with studs and drywall and a vapor barrier.

We argue strongly against basement space elsewhere in this book. If you have an old library, you may be stuck with a basement, but there's a very great deal to be said for not doing any more of that sort of thing, particularly because adding an extra floor costs very little more than adding a basement.

> You can laugh at subsurface seepage a great deal more easily if your library does not have a subsurface.

II-F. FLOODPLAINS

Although it's possible to build on floodplains with the right sort of design, you don't want to do it. Ever. Or, more specifically, EVER.

Given world climate changes, it seems possible that floodplains will expand in the future, and even building *close* to a floodplain may be a dangerous idea.

Insurance maps showing the locations of floodplains are available for communities throughout the US. You may even find state regulations that forbid library construction on floodplains.

Even when avoiding floodplains, however, many libraries end up wet when flooding spreads beyond the limits of official floodplains. In recent years, the phrase "100-year flood" has become almost a joke, with 100-year floods seeming to occur in some communities every decade. And now people are speaking of "1,000-year floods."

Many riverside towns have dike systems to protect low-lying areas, but (as demonstrated by the Mississippi River in Louisiana in 2007 and the Cedar River in Iowa in 2008) dikes fail. We think that blissfully counting on the eternal efficiency of dikes to protect library collections is on par with believing everything one reads on the internet.

Resist political pressure to build libraries in historic areas that can flood. If your town has a historic riverside section and a modern blufftop section, you may find yourself under tremendous pressure from local historical organizations to locate your library where floods will sooner or later find it, rather than to locate it safely on high ground. Stand your (dry) ground.

II-G. SITE CONFIGURATION

Most libraries fit best on fairly square sites. Mere acreage is not enough. The longer and thinner the site, the less chance there is of fitting a successful library onto it.

Non-rectangular sites are also difficult places to locate libraries. Some people have thought it was fun to have buildings with curved or diagonal walls to echo sites with curves or diagonals, and the result is almost inevitably either a Bad Idea or a VERY Bad Idea.

When a site is proposed for your library, one of your architects' first responsibilities is checking to see whether it's possible to actually fit the building you need on the site. This is another very important reason to hire your architect before you make a final site selection.

On the other hand, you may need your consultant to fend off your owners' or architects' enthusiasm for non-rectangular buildings.

II-H. SITE TOPOGRAPHY

Although the world frequently looks like a fairly flat place, it seldom is. Even a city block that looks almost totally flat may slope a dozen or more feet from one side to the other. As a result, libraries must be fitted to the contours of sites, and many plans are developed in response to existing conditions.

Sloped sites offer both problems and opportunities. For example:

- Will the site lead to a multilevel building when your programmatic needs called for a single-level building? Multilevel buildings need elevators, staircases, and second stories that are strong enough to bear the weight of books. And all are very expensive.

While flat sites are always easiest to work with, very successful libraries can sometimes be built on irregular sites. The site for this branch library in Evansville, Indiana, was on two widely separated levels, neither of which was large enough for both the library and the parking lot.

Putting the library on one elevation and the parking lot on the other would have led to amazing accessibility problems, with a staircase either leading from a lower-level parking lot up to a bluff-top library or a staircase leading from the bluff-top parking lot down to a library far below.

CHAPTER 9: SITE SELECTION | **135**

The solution was to bury the library in the bluff-top. People park on the lower level and simply walk into the library. From the street, all that's visible of the library is the roof over the center of the building. Not only does the whole arrangement work extremely well, with pleasant lighting, but the fact that much of the library is buried in the dirt leads to low HVAC costs.

SOURCE: ENGBERG ANDERSON IN ASSOCIATION WITH VPS ARCHITECTURE

In addition, overseeing a multilevel library building may require extra staff and therefore raise occupancy costs forever.

- What are the implications for accessibility for users with disabilities or with children in strollers? A long uphill ramp from the parking lot or the street to the library entrance may be technically legal, but it will also be extraordinarily uncivilized.

- If the site slopes down away from the street front, will it lend itself to a construction of a parking area under the building? On a site like this, the parking area beneath the building may be open to daylight on one side and therefore less spooky to library users.

- Are there opportunities for green construction using bermed walls, green roofs at grade level, and so on?

- A number of libraries have been built on slopes with the entrances and reading rooms on the top floor and book stacks beneath. This permits the high ceilings and open structures that make reading rooms attractive. (By contrast, many great research libraries constructed on flat ground have reading rooms far above entry level, to eliminate the problem of supporting heavy floors above the reading rooms.)

Again, before you commit to a site, you will need (a) a building program to define the necessary functional spaces and (b) preliminary studies by your architects and engineers to test how the library you need might be fitted to the site. Once your architects have completed their studies, you can ask your consultant to double-check the functionality of the possible structures that can be fitted to the site.

II-I. BROWNFIELD SITES

A site that has existing buildings (or has been occupied by previous buildings) and may be complicated by the presence or potential presence of a hazardous substance, pollutant, or contaminant is often referred to as a "brownfield" site. By contrast, sites that have been used only for agriculture or wild vegetation are called "greenfield" sites.

There are several major dangers in dealing with brownfield sites.

- ***Existing structures.*** The first problem with brownfield sites is existing structures. Even if the structures have no historic merit, they may be very expensive to remove, particularly if they have asbestos or lead paint. Taking down a medium-sized old school building, for example, can easily cost half a million dollars, all of which must be deducted from the value of the empty site when purchase price is considered. Remember that any building constructed before the late 1970s may have asbestos or lead paint. That's why old school buildings often stand empty for years. The cost of taking them down can be greater than the value of the resulting empty site.

- ***Buried remains of previous buildings.*** Brownfield sites that appear innocuous are sometimes full of hidden remains of previous structures. In the past, buildings may have been knocked down, the resulting rubble pushed into basements, and everything covered neatly by a clean layer of dirt. Unfortunately, all of this will have to be dug out and removed and replaced with compacted fill before you can construct a building there.

One constant fear when excavations for new buildings begin is that workers will discover buried fuel tanks, forgotten until work begins. Removing fuel tanks is not very expensive if they're empty, but if they have ancient fuel in them, the whole issue falls under the jurisdiction of the EPA—the US Environmental Protection Agency.

Soil borings can easily miss buried chunks of old buildings. Most borings are made where the corners of the new building will go, and perhaps the location of the elevator, but not much more. If you know the locations of pervious buildings on the site, borings in the centers are worthwhile, particularly if the buildings had basements. It often turns out that the basement slab of the old building is still there, trapping water and full of broken pieces of the building. If you are unsure about previous buildings, check for aerial photos on file with local governments, old Sanborn atlases, and any other records. And ask the library's local history department.

- **Serious pollution.** Many brownfield sites are badly polluted. Although it's perfectly possible to construct a library on what was once an EPA Superfund site, the cost of cleanup can be spectacular. And, as with the demolition of asbestos-laden buildings, the costs of cleaning up a polluted site can be vastly more than the value of the resulting empty land.

> Never make assumptions on the costs of site cleanup, and always get prices in writing. Unfortunately, it's hard to know what's under there until you actually dig there. Have contingency funds available.

Polluted sites are jobs for serious experts. Never commit in any way to a polluted site until you know what the problems are and who will be cleaning things up *before* you own the site. Hire experts and rely on them.

The main thing is to be sure your site is genuinely clean before you acquire it, and that you don't get stuck with any of the cleanup costs.

- **Who's responsible?** As part of the evaluation of your proposed site, your architects or engineers should do a historical check to evaluate the likelihood of underground problems. Libraries are well set up to participate in such studies if they have long runs of old city directories, old telephone books, old Sanborn atlases and similar fire-insurance publications, or other historic materials. For example, if a review of old city directories indicates that there was once a gas station or a manufacturing plant on your proposed site, the chance of a forgotten underground storage tank or of general site pollution increases immensely. Fire insurance atlases give diagrams of buildings' footprints and provide information on type of construction, helping you know where to explore for problems. If a large building once stood on the site, you need soil borings to check that it was totally removed rather than simply pushed down into the basement and covered with earth.

- **REALLY bad ideas.** When faced with polluted buildings or sites, a few owners are tempted to conduct midnight removals. "The old high school is full of lead and asbestos," someone argues, "so we'll bring in a backhoe on Saturday night, knock the structure down, load it into trucks, and dump it in the crick." (In other words, an unauthorized landfill.) This kind of activity will almost certainly lead to an intimate acquaintance with the EPA. You will not enjoy an intimate acquaintance with the EPA. (As usual in this book, this story is a true one.)

II-J. ADJACENT USES

Just as homeowners worry about inappropriate neighbors, libraries have to ask whether adjacent property uses are likely to cause service problems.

Some adjacent users that affect all kinds of libraries include:

- Noisy neighbors. Although libraries are not as quiet today as they were in years back, people still need to find quiet corners and study rooms.
- Neighboring sites that may drive away library users, such as parks that are extremely dark at night.
- High crime areas
- Polluting neighbors. Pollutants can range from dangerous chemicals (for example, benzene) to bad smells (such as pig farms). Unfortunately, pollution can spread widely, and moving the library may not help a great deal.
- And many others. See section III-A on public libraries.

> Fred worked with a school library where every iteration of the architect's drawings included a new (but always extremely noisy) neighbor next door to the library, with the two spaces sharing a common wall. First it was the band practice room (remember that the sound of people learning the saxophone sounds a lot like seriously unhappy cats) and then it was the gymnasium. In desperation, the library finally arranged to have the wall between the library and the gym consist of a row of athletic department offices and library storerooms.

> Another school library Fred worked with occupied part of a large room that had originally been a garage. To keep the cost of HVAC modifications down, the school had built a partial partition between the library and the rest of the garage. Because the partition ended about six feet below the ceiling, all sounds were shared. Many neighbors would have been good neighbors. Office personnel would have been fine. So would sewing classes, or plane geometry, or studio art. Unfortunately, the school used the space for the weight training room for high school athletes. As a result, users of the library were treated to the constant grunting of students attempting to hoist heavy weights, punctuated occasionally by the ringing crashes of barbells being dropped by young athletes who had bitten off more than they could hoist. Each time a barbell dropped, all the occupants of the library leapt as if electrocuted.

> Fred worked with another library next to a busy railroad track with about three unit coal trains passing every hour—each one a string of honking diesels followed by about 125 heavy cars. In addition to the constant noise, the vibrations from passing trains led objects to fall off shelves, and sections of the building eventually started pulling apart.

II-K. SIZE

When the time comes to build your academic or public library, many people will have difficultly believing how much acreage many libraries need. Rural and suburban libraries tend to have more spread-out buildings and need more space for parking and stormwater management. Urban libraries may have multiple floors and parking that is shared with other agencies or located in parking structures.

The important point is that the library building itself often occupies a relatively small portion of the site.

Here are some of the factors that contribute to necessary site size.

II-K-1. Building Footprint

The "footprint" of a building is the physical space it occupies.

Your building program will give you a rough idea of the likely footprint of your library. Because many libraries are inherently flat structures, for anything up to about 30,000 to 50,000 square feet in rural or suburban communities, begin by assuming that the building will be all on one floor, and that the footprint will therefore be as large as your programmed building size.

When they get a great deal larger than 50,000 square feet, one-story libraries start resembling big box retail stores. Horizontal distances become too great, and libraries start expanding upward.

Public libraries need to limit the total number of public floors in order to limit the cost of staff oversight. For a medium-sized public library, two floors is ideally enough for public areas, although offices, workrooms, storage, HVAC, and other functions can be on a third floor.

For a public library of anything from 40,000 to 80,000 or even 100,000 square feet, you might start by guessing a 40,000-square-foot footprint. For an academic library, more vertical stacking may be feasible, since supervision is a less significant issue.

Estimating footprint size is complicated by the fact that certain areas of a building—typically public library meeting rooms—may need to be in single-story sections of the building. Meeting rooms need to be at grade level to allow after-hours access and easy emergency exits. Placing other functions above meeting rooms is difficult or impossible because making the upper floors strong enough will probably lead to unwanted columns in the meeting rooms, and meeting room ceilings often need to be higher than other ceilings in the building.

The real test of required footprint, of course, is the actual building design.

II-K-2. Parking and Driveways

Virtually all academic and public library buildings require some space for parking, deliveries, and driveways.

- On-site parking. The amount of parking required for academic libraries will depend on campus planning. Many academic libraries use shared parking rather than library parking. Public library parking is strongly affected by local zoning requirements. If your public library is in an area that requires off-street parking, you may have to provide two to four parking spaces for every 1,000 square feet of library space. (Even if you are in a central business district location where zoning does not require off-street parking, you still need to know where your users will park.) Assuming that each parking space requires 300 square feet, a library in a town that requires four spaces per 1,000 square feet will have a parking lot larger than the library. If you are planning for expansion, don't forget that if you expand your library building by 75 percent, you will probably also need space to expand your parking area by 75 percent. Under conditions of extreme crowding, some libraries save space by providing parking beneath their structures. Be sure to review all of the implications with your architect, consultant, and local planning officials before assuming that you can save space this way. Know the extra cost. And keep in mind that underground parking floods a lot more easily than surface parking, and that the idea of parking underground spooks many users because they are concerned about who may be lurking in the dim recesses of the garage.

- Drive-through services. Drive-through book returns and similar services require far more turning space than is often provided, and the world is full of libraries with drive-up services that simply don't work. Unfortunately, designers often underestimate required turning radiuses for cars that need to pull up closely to book returns. (If you stand and watch people using drive-through returns, it's impressive to see how many have to get out of their cars because they can't get close enough to the returns to reach the chutes through open car windows.)

> Fred dealt with one library where the twisted drive-through lanes required contortions that no driver could manage. When he complained to the people who designed the drive-through, they said that the lanes were fine but that the drivers were all "timid."

- All libraries need additional driveway space for deliveries, staff arrivals, dumpsters, and so on.

II-K-3. Setbacks

Except for central business districts, most zoning codes require that buildings be set back from the street to provide open space and a uniform line of facades along streets. This applies primarily to public libraries.

If zoning in your area requires that your library be set back 20 feet from the sidewalk, you will require a substantial amount of extra land.

Checking to be sure that your site can contain the library you need while maintaining legal setbacks is a job for your architects. Don't guess without them.

II-K-4. Plantings and Landscaping

Public and academic libraries need to set aside space for grass, trees, flowerbeds, foundation plantings, terraces, fountains, statuary, and other civilized details. These also require space.

Depending on zoning codes, you may be required to include plantings around your public library building.

Some public library branches in cities are installed in storefronts that are located directly on sidewalks, but many of these are rented spaces rather than custom-built libraries.

II-K-5. Expansion Space

As we mention frequently, one of the major mistakes libraries make is assuming that they will never need to expand.

Spending a vast amount of money on a new library with no possibility for future expansion is a great demonstration of the remarkable power of short-term thinking.

It's hard to know how much space to allocate for long-term expansion, but with a brand new building, in a community likely to see increases in population, planning for a 100 percent increase in size is not unreasonable.

When you are planning a new library, well-meaning (and frequently very aggressive) people will insist that your library's next construction job will be its last. These people are inevitably wrong, but they are hard to deal with. Many of them deeply believe that they are right, and this gives them righteous conviction. (Others, of course, have axes to grind.)

There are a number of solid reasons why you should always plan space for outward rather than upward expansion.

II-K-5-a. *Expanding Outward*

Remember that when it comes to expanding library buildings, outward expansion is almost inevitably less expensive than upward expansion. People who argue that if you run out of space you can easily expand upward better know that capacity was built in for such a purpose. More often than not they know pretty much nothing about library buildings. Floors, columns, and footings all need to be capable of supporting another level of use in order for this to be a viable strategy.

The approaches for most libraries are obvious:

- *Never* build a library with an architectural design that prevents outward expansion. Of all errors that prevent expansion, this is by far the most easily avoided, for it simply involves holding owners and designers to the requirement that buildings be designed for expansion.

- *Always* obtain and protect sites large enough to accommodate outward expansion, make clear from the beginning that the empty site is reserved for expansion, and fight any group that proposes alternative uses for the space. This can be a special problem on crowded campuses, where academic units are always casting greedy eyes on open spaces.

- However, sometimes when the otherwise perfect site is located in a congested area, and outward expansion may be impossible, providing for later vertical expansion may be the only possible option. See the following section, "Considerations with Expanding Upward."

- Be extremely wary of expansion underground. As in never do it.

- If you can see that your library will need to be expanded in the foreseeable future, a two-phase building program will help you make sure that expansion will be as easy as possible. See chapter 7, "Building Programs."

Expanding a two-story public library outward can work particularly well if (a) the adult and children's departments are on separate floors and (b) offices and other small rooms do not abut the wall to be removed. (All of this, of course, requires proper planning of the original building.)

II-K-5-b. *Considerations with Expanding Upward*

If your existing building design and construction did not anticipate vertical expansion, you will encounter many problems if you try to expand upward. If you are starting new on a constrained site, build as much of the needed structural infrastructure as you can afford. This can make many of the challenges listed below significantly less expensive and disruptive.

- Upward expansion requires massive surgery. Roofs have to be removed and replaced with floors that can hold the weight of books. One-story libraries will require the addition of elevators and staircases in proper locations. To protect existing libraries, new roofs have to be installed before existing roofs are removed. Because steel beams are often involved, the spaces below the new beams need to be closed to the staff and public while the work is going on.

  It helps a great deal if the locations of all the necessary elevator equipment were determined during Phase I, since the equipment can otherwise be difficult to retrofit.

- Existing footings and columns are almost never strong enough to support additional levels, despite beliefs to the contrary. When people tell you, "Our building was engineered to carry an additional floor," *never* believe them. Among the reasons for disbelief are:

  » When the building was initially planned, the owners may have discussed providing footings and columns capable of holding additional levels. These were deleted to save construction costs, but the memory of the change is overwhelmed by the memory of the original concept.

  » If the building was initially planned for anything other than library functions, the footings may still not be strong enough. Footings strong enough for a two-story office structure are usually too weak to support a two-story library.

  » Columns in buildings are usually the structural components with the most excess capacity, but even so, they may not be strong enough to support an additional floor. This is particularly true with one-story buildings, where the existing columns have to support only a roof. Increasing the capacity of columns is generally easier than strengthening roofs, floors, or footings, but it is still neither simple nor inexpensive.

  » In a one-story library, supporting the weight of books on a concrete slab on grade is easy. When we have to build upward, it's suddenly a different structural world because we have to support the weight of books in midair.

  » In some libraries, sections of the floor that were not initially intended to hold book stacks are too flimsy to do so. This violates one of the most basic principles of library design, but it happens all the time and can have a major impact on the ability to rearrange functions.

  » When additional stories are mentioned, always have a structural engineer verify that this can be done. Never believe anyone else.

- For public libraries, upward expansion may increase the number of floors to be supervised. Operating a public library with an unsupervised floor is a recipe for major problems. To make extra public floors work, you need a service desk on each floor. Unless these are desks that currently exist and are staffed whenever the library is open, you will have to hire additional staff members just to watch the new floor.

- If you need to expand upward, it may be much cheaper to demolish all or part of the building and build a new two-story or three-story section from scratch.

II-K-5-c. *Few Critics Are Disinterested*

Much of the talk against the need for expansion space comes from people with axes to grind.

Public libraries can be victimized by people who have white elephant buildings to unload. If the proposed building and site are too small, the owners will argue that expansion will never be needed, or that the spaces listed in the written program are unnecessary. Often the owners will pitch their arguments directly to local governments or to chambers of commerce, contending that the only reason the library doesn't want the owner's building is the desire of the board of trustees to build an expensive monument to its own ego.

For example, Fred worked with a public library in a town that had an abandoned church that would have made an incredibly poor library. Not only was the church building unworkable, but the site was too small, even if the building were demolished. In addition, many of the ceilings were too low, the building would have required a very expensive elevator, and the complexity of the structure would have meant hiring extra staff to supervise. The congregation, hoping to unload their former church at a high price, formed an unholy alliance with a local real estate firm, which started a whispering campaign against the library board. Fred ended up having to document all of the reasons why both the building and the site were unworkable and why the cost would be greater than starting over with an empty site, and then holding public meetings to explain everything. (After the public meetings, the only holdouts were the real estate agents, who saw some really major sales commissions going down the tubes. When the building was eventually sold to another congregation, it brought only a small fraction of the price the real estate firm hoped to extract from the library.)

In general, when public libraries are seeking new sites, boards of trustees need to be prepared in advance with responses to the "Why haven't you considered X building or X site?" sort of questions. Armed with a written building program and a list of likely suggestions, architects can help boards by preparing a priori lists of the "yes, we considered X, and here's why it won't work" variety.

Always be prepared to tell everyone in advance the absolute and non-negotiable basics of functional library design:

- Floors that can uniformly hold 150 pounds per square foot (and much more for compact shelving).
- Wide open floors for easy supervision and stack placement.
- Rectangular spaces.
- Ceilings at least 10 feet high (higher for meeting rooms), plus available vertical space for air ducts or plenums.

> One classic example of turf problems occurred at the University of Illinois in Urbana. In the 1960s, the university wanted to construct an undergraduate library adjacent to the main graduate library. Unfortunately, the only available site was located between the graduate library and a historic agricultural experiment plot. The agriculture department had enough political clout to force the library to be built physically underground, where it would not cast a new afternoon shadow on the corn.

- Vast numbers of electrical outlets.
- Single entrances.

II-K-5-d. *Necessity of Strong Floors*

Expanding school and special libraries requires access to adjacent space strong enough to carry appropriate loads.

While academic and public libraries need open land reserved for expansion, small libraries that consist of rooms in large buildings need to expand horizontally into adjacent areas.

For many special libraries, however, relocating the library to a larger space may be simpler and cheaper than trying to expand an existing library. As usual, the major problems may lie in:

- Finding space strong enough to support the weight of books.
- Finding a space that facilitates use of the library by members of the organization.

School libraries can sometimes be expanded by absorbing adjacent classrooms. Here the problem may be as much one of completely opening walls as of the ability of floors to carry loads. Given limited staffing and the variegated social enthusiasms of students, school libraries cannot afford to be complex places with areas that are difficult to supervise. Basically, a good school library space is mostly one big room.

II-K-6. Rules of Thumb for Estimating Site Acreage

People will frequently push you to specify a site size before you know anything about the nature of available sites or about your library design. The only good way to come up with an opinion on site size is to involve your architects, engineers, and consultants. If you're under severe pressure to respond prematurely, here are a few suggestions:

- Tell people that you cannot make a commitment or even a comment without professional input. If you have a written building program and an architectural site study, you will be far more able to tell whether a site is large enough to actually work.

- As with all situations when you deal with the news media and politicians, never make any offhand comments, and never agree with other people's proposals until you have solid information. Never respond "Yes" to any "Would you say X?" question. And there's no shame in repeating, "We won't know until our architects and consultants have studied the situation."

- Guess big to start. It's a lot easier to eventually agree you can get by with less space than to have to say, "Oops. We *meant* to say that the space you suggested actually isn't big enough."

- But if you guess too big, that can lead to bad publicity as well.

- Rules of thumb can be dangerous. If people push you as to whether you can fit the library on less space, tell them you'll have to work with your architects to determine how many stories, size of setbacks, amount of landscaping, amount of on-site parking, stormwater management plans, future expansion space, and other details before you can provide an estimate. (Many libraries work well on less space, but you can't just whip off an estimate.)

II-L. HISTORIC BUILDINGS AND NEIGHBORHOODS

Any site with existing buildings needs to be investigated for possible historic protection. Although it's perfectly possible to demolish structures regarded as historic, trying to do so can sometimes lead to bad feelings and/or legal entanglements.

The most difficult problems occur when existing libraries need to expand onto adjacent property with historic structures, because the library may feel that it cannot simply elect to build elsewhere. For a more extensive discussion of expanding historic libraries, see chapter 16, "Remodeling and Expanding Library Buildings."

If there's a historic building next to your library, many people will contend that you can solve all of your space problems by linking the two, both saving money and protecting a community treasure.

As a basic rule, remember that (no matter what local enthusiasts claim) it can be extremely difficult and expensive to join a library to a historic building—especially one that was never designed to be a library—and that the resulting structure is far more likely to be very seriously dysfunctional. You will almost certainly have major problems with different floor levels, overly divided interior spaces, and difficult oversight.

Nothing here is meant to suggest that a handsome historic structure cannot be converted to a handsome and functional library building, but it will almost certainly be a complex and expensive job. Once again, it helps to have a building program in print and approved and ready to be used as a yardstick for evaluating options *before* discussions of possible conversions begin.

II-L-1. Jurisdictional Authorities and Self-Appointed Groups

One thing that complicates dealing with historic structures is the number of different groups that can be involved.

- Depending on circumstances, existing buildings can be protected by federal, state, or local laws.
- Many states have historical preservation agencies and many municipalities have preservation ordinances.
- Buildings and neighborhoods may be listed on the National Register of Historic Places.
- Whether or not they are on the National Register, historic neighborhoods can have extremely specific legal limits on construction and remodeling.
- Even in the absence of legal limits and controls, ad hoc local preservation groups with absolutely no legal standing can still be avidly involved.

While federal and state rules and regulations are usually straightforward, local preservation ordinances can be unpredictable. Sometimes local preservation groups can be far more emotional and difficult to deal with than state or federal agencies because they are less process bound and see themselves as protecting their local communities.

If your library is considering a new site with surviving structures, it will be wise to check with local and state preservation groups to see whether you are likely to encounter adverse reactions. Until you have completed a building program and at least architectural feasibility studies, NEVER let yourself be cornered into agreeing to retain existing non-library structures as part of a new or expanded library.

Connecting two existing buildings can be extremely difficult and likely to lead to complex structures that are on too many levels and have too many irrelevant and disconnected spaces. It may also involve difficult problems with codes, because construction types in existing buildings may not meet code requirements for larger buildings—or may not even meet requirements at all. The gross square footage of an expanded or combined building will probably be much larger than the gross square footage of a comparable new building that meets the same program needs.

Existing laws may allow the adverse (against the wishes of the owners) addition of old structures to registers of historic buildings, particularly if the structures are publicly owned. This means that a public body can purchase a privately owned structure not listed as historic, only to find it suddenly added to the National Register of Historic Places.

II-L-2. Sources of Assistance

When your proposed site has historic buildings, a number of people and agencies can help.

- State historic preservation agencies. Well-developed state historic preservation agencies can be of great assistance. They are prepared to balance competing interests, they have a broad perspective that comes from dealing with large numbers of historic structures, and they may have experts on library design who understand how libraries occupy spaces. If you have a historic library building, get to know the library expert in your state preservation agency.

- Local planning agencies. Local government agencies are good sources of information on actual local codes and local preservation ordinances.

- Experts on historic architecture. If you need a strong person in your corner, or just an impartial observer, one place you can turn is architects with expertise in this field. If you see problems with historic structures arising in your project, you can limit your search for architects to firms that have resident experts.

- Local activist groups. In our experience, if older buildings need to be demolished, the greatest difficulties can be found in dealing with local activist groups. They are more likely to be passionate and unreasoning and to lack the balance that comes from the wider experience and professional training of state agency staffs.

> On the other hand, if you are seeking to expand your historic library and are convinced you can do it with proper support, local preservation groups can be powerful friends. But there's always the danger of loose cannon behavior.

- Issues of standing. Not all agencies and groups have legal standing. Even if a building is listed on the National Register of Historic Places, it's possible that no state or federal agency will have standing if you will not be using state or federal money on your project. Many local activist groups have no standing at all.

- Politicians. Every once in a while, a library finds itself in a situation where it becomes the prisoner of a decaying or ancient-but-unworthy structure on an essential site. In situations like this, sometimes the only feasible course of action is to bypass the preservation process and seek political relief. John has done this in the past.

II-M. ARCHAEOLOGY

In addition to visible structures, ostensibly empty sites may have buried remains that limit or eliminate their use as library sites.

II-M-1. General Archaeological Issues

If your site has any historical significance, you can rest assured that you will need an archaeological study.

Depending on circumstances, you may be required to have an archaeological compliance survey conducted of your property. The field of cultural resources archaeology has expanded rapidly in the last 40 years, with contract archaeologists conducting, for example, rapid surveys of proposed highway rights of way for evidence of possible archaeological significance.

One of the major careers available to professionally trained archaeologists is checking sites.

Your architect can assist you in finding necessary experts and complying with relevant laws. More and more sites are being protected. Check with your state preservation office to see if your site is listed.

II-M-2. NAGPRA

The discovery of Native American graves on your building site will probably end any possibility of constructing a library on the site.

The Native American Graves Preservation and Repatriation Act (NAGPRA) of 1990 was designed to eliminate the practice of treating Native American burials as little more than engaging sites for archaeological investigations.

Reactions to NAGPRA have varied widely. Some people regard the act as a tremendous handicap to the study of American history, while others see it as a long overdue way to keep people from simply poking around in ancestral graves, much as more recent inhabitants would resent the scientific excavation of their church cemeteries.

From the library construction point of view, it's best to assume that if there are Native American burials on your property, you won't be able to build there.

For this reason, it's important to:

- Do some preliminary historical checking. Ask local government officials, local civil engineers, and local historical societies about stories of local Native American burials. Stories may be little more than unfounded rumors, but they may give you impetus to do further checking.
- Your state may have a registry of Native American graves.
- You can include a statement in your bill of sale that the site is warranted not to include Native American graves, but trusting the seller can be a serious mistake. Be sure that the people providing the authority know what they're doing.

II-N. ORIENTATION TO THE COMPASS

Frequently, sites dictate how library buildings can be oriented. The comments here apply to temperate areas of the northern hemisphere, such as the contiguous 48 US states.

Generally speaking, the best sites permit:

- Library buildings with south or southeast entrances. In many parts of the United States, prevailing winter winds from the north and northwest make sheltered entrances on the south or southeast sides of buildings far more practical and comfortable. If the wind howls into your library every time the door is opened, even a foyer or vestibule may not be enough to prevent bitter blasts from hitting the staff facing the entrance. And if the sun doesn't hit your entrance in the winter, you may end up fighting The Ice That Never Melts. Icy steps and ramps are particularly vicious.

- Library buildings with north light for reading. In the northern hemisphere, the only natural light that is dependably pleasant for reading is north light. If the back side of your library faces north, this provides an opportunity for rows of windows and bright but low-glare light.

- Depending on latitude, even north windows may be a source of direct sunlight, particularly around the summer solstice. As part of preliminary design sketches, your architects should indicate when north sunlight might be a problem.

- Library buildings with the least possible west light. In most of the US, western sunlight is nasty for much of the year, particularly the summer. Most libraries are closed for business until long after summer sunrises, limiting the problems of eastern light, but they are open when the sun sets, and the brutal light blasting in from the west is enough to sear retinas. If you have western windows in your library, they will all need effective shades, including in particular cute windows set far above the floor. This is frequently forgotten by architects, who blissfully install small clearstories in sloped ceilings, ornamental curved windows above rectangular windows, and monitor windows facing in all directions. The fewer western windows you have, the easier it is to avoid the very worst that natural daylight has to offer.

- Library buildings with their long axes running from east to west. In order to maximize northern and southern exposure, and to minimize western exposure, most libraries do best if the longer dimension of the building runs east-west rather than north-south. (However, most small library buildings are somewhat square.)

- General problems with excess glass. If you are worried about excess glass in your building, beware of the assertion that "with modern glass" glare is no longer a problem. We've heard this for decades, but when the buildings are complete, unshielded glass hit by direct sunlight is *always* a problem, regardless of how modern it is. When your architects tout "modern glass," always insist on seeing an existing installation using the same glass.

Get your needs for lack of direct glare in print and point them out to everyone firmly, for large numbers of libraries suffer from the glare of uncontrolled direct sunlight.

II-O. EASEMENTS

Easements are legal rights to use someone else's property. Typical uses might include driving through the property to access another piece of property, running a sewer through the property, or running power lines over the property.

Other easements limit the ability of a property owner to affect neighboring property, such as agreements not to block the view.

Libraries need to be aware of any easements on their proposed sites, and information on easements should be required in all surveys.

II-P. LAND OWNERSHIP

Public libraries do not always own the land they occupy. Sometimes, as in the case of rented buildings used for library branches, this can work very well. On other occasions, when libraries construct their own buildings on land to which they do not have clear title, the result can be a mess.

II-P-1. Rented Buildings

Many public library branches are housed in rented buildings. Typically these are retail spaces, either storefronts or shops in strip malls.

One of the advantages of rented spaces is that they give libraries a chance to try out locations. If the branch would do a lot better six blocks north, the branch can pick up and move when its lease expires.

To keep the library's investment in the site to a minimum, virtually everything can be movable, including not only all of the furnishings but also even the lighting system. If the library moves, it can literally strip the entire space down to the bare walls.

Joe has worked on a number of spaces like this, and they have worked well for their institutions. Because the library's investment is small, its risk is also small.

Most libraries in leased situations are probably city branch libraries.

II-P-2. Library Buildings Constructed on Land to Which Their Libraries Do Not Have Title

Things can go much more poorly when a library constructs its own building on land it doesn't own.

One common pattern is that an organization or family gives the library land for a building, but only as long as it serves as a library. If the library moves, the land reverts to the original donor. The donors may also make other restrictions that limit the effectiveness of the library building.

At the time the libraries are built, a free site can look great. And sometimes the donors may even help with construction cost or donate a house or other building as a nucleus for the library.

However, accepting an offer like this is always a difficult decision. If libraries do not own their sites, any significant amount of money they spend on their buildings is essentially thrown away, for the libraries cannot sell their buildings if it becomes essential to move.

Fred has worked with a couple of small public libraries caught in this situation. Any investment they make in their buildings will be lost if they leave their buildings. This is very much like the dilemma of farmhouses for tenant farmers: the tenants don't want to spend money on buildings they don't own, and the owners don't want to spend unnecessary money fixing up tenant farmhouses.

The rule is a simple one: If you build a library on a site to which you do not have full and clear title, know what your rights will be if you decide you need to move. If the owners of the property place unacceptable limits on the operations of the library, or if the location becomes unworkable for functional reasons, know what you can do.

Over the years, libraries on land to which they do not have clear title can expand and improve their buildings, but each time they do so they end up with more assets they can't take with

> If a library has no immediate need of an adjacent structure it owns, it can always lease it temporarily, but there's a lot more to be said for quick demolition and conversion to parking while the demolishing is good.

them, and the pressure to stay put may be substantial.

Among other things, before you enter into any arrangement of this kind, hire a very good lawyer.

> Land ownership can lead to difficult situations. For example, a city planned to demolish its public library and sell the site to a developer. The developer would build a new multistory building with the library on the ground floor. The developer would not charge the library rent for the first few years, but the city announced that when the developer began to charge rent, the library would have to do its own annual fundraising, since the city couldn't afford the rent out of its own budget. Essentially, the city would sell the building, keep the proceeds, and let the library try to cope.

II-Q. ACQUISITION OF EXPANSION LAND

One of the most common mistakes public library boards of trustees make is to not acquire adjacent land when it comes on the market. Many boards have turned down the opportunity to buy land next door to the library for a song, only to find that when they desperately needed it 10 years later it was not available at any price—or at least not at a rational price.

Buying land when the owner wants to sell also keeps libraries away from the ugly face of eminent domain. Although a public body can often take needed land against the will of the owner, the resulting bad feelings and bad publicity can linger for years.

If you have land for future expansion set aside next to your library, be careful that it isn't converted to a temporary asset that becomes a permanent asset. For example, if a local garden group constructs a mini-park on the site, the area may take on a life of its own and be harder to convert to library building functions when the time comes.

Existing buildings can be used temporarily for storage or leased out until the time comes to demolish them, but there are always pitfalls. Although a building was purchased for expansion, it may come to be regarded as an asset of value. And leasing out space turns the library into a landlord—a function some libraries enjoy more than others.

With the passage of years, existing buildings of no distinction scheduled for eventual demolition may also slowly gain status as "historic" structures.

Leasing space to a local business can lead to problems if the local business becomes popular with the community and local citizens want the business to stay where it is forever.

II-R. COVENANTS

The majority of new neighborhoods of single-family homes or condominiums have covenants that apply to all of the properties in the neighborhoods. Covenants are rules that are said to "ride with the deeds."

Covenants are agreements among landowners concerning construction and activities in the neighborhood. They may cover the number of vehicles the owner of a particular piece of property can maintain in the neighborhood, whether vehicles must be stored in garages, the number of pets per household, minimum home size, required setbacks, limits on outbuildings, mechanical equipment such as satellite dishes, exterior color choices, and so on.

Covenants can add restrictions on land use not required by the local municipality, but they cannot relax municipal restrictions.

Under the terms of neighborhood agreements, most covenants are enforced by neighborhood associations.

Some older neighborhoods have embarrassing covenants, such as racial requirements, that are quietly ignored because changing covenants can take a great deal of effort.

III. Special Site Needs of Various Types of Libraries

In addition to the issues listed in section II, a number of site selection concerns apply specifically to certain kinds of libraries.

Most of the issues listed here apply primarily to public libraries, since these are the primary libraries to have completely independent sites. The locations of academic libraries, school libraries, and special libraries are limited by the institutions they serve, which both define a limited range of sites and protect libraries as part of larger buildings or campuses.

III-A. PUBLIC LIBRARIES

Public libraries in particular need to consider security issues when selecting sites, but all libraries can be affected by the problems that result from insecure locations.

Public libraries are particularly vulnerable to neighborhood problems because they are open to anyone who wants to enter the library. By contrast, academic institutions, schools, and the proprietors of special libraries can usually turn away people who are not authorized to enter their buildings.

The problem with many of the issues raised in this section is that they sound illiberal. But they all are based on extremely widespread problems.

Here are a handful of site situations that affect primarily public libraries.

III-A-1. Retail Sites

About 75 years ago, Joseph Wheeler argued that the best place for a public library was a good place for a dime store. His basic point was that libraries benefit from being located where people go shopping. While a school may benefit from a slightly out-of-the-way location, public libraries benefit from being highly visible and accessible.

In turn, commercial sites benefit from nearby libraries. For example:

- Fred and Joe worked with a library that moved into a couple of empty stores in a nearby strip mall during construction. When the library moved in, merchants in the strip mall varied from indifferent to concerned about competition for parking. But when the library moved out a year later, the local merchants were dismayed to see

- it leave. Sales had boomed while the library was there.

- Naestved, Denmark, has a public library that shares a large, two-story building with a supermarket. The first floor is retail and the second the library. Both are entered through the same door, with library users taking the stairs or elevator to the upper level. Both the store and the library are packed with users. The Council Tree Library in Fort Collins, Colorado, has a similar arrangement.

- The sad thing about all of this is that too few people recognize this extremely useful juxtaposition.

- Merchants are frequently surprised to find that business increases when libraries move in nearby.

- Mayors and city planners want to save good retail sites for the exclusive use of businesses, not realizing that public libraries boost business and would improve the mix of land uses. In a world of fewer anchor retailers, the library should be even more prized as a part of a retail neighborhood.

- Governing bodies may also want to reserve the best sites for property-tax-paying entities. Unlike libraries, retail stores pay both sales and property taxes, but the existence of a library can make a lot of adjacent retail stores a lot more successful.

III-A-2. Government Sites

Frequently, developers of new sites for local government suggest including libraries. Often the plan is to provide a "campus" arrangement for the city hall, police department, fire department, and public library.

Libraries can benefit from being adjacent to other governmental buildings.

- Public libraries may find it easier to find large new sites in a government campus. With luck, the site will be free to the library.

- A group of new government buildings will be attractive, reducing the risk that the library may end up with run-down neighbors.

- Of all the buildings in a government campus, the public library may be the most popular with local taxpayers. This may provide local government with a greater incentive to fund the new library building as part of the project.

- Because a number of governmental buildings are located together, the cost of the library's access to utilities may be paid by the municipality, or at least shared.

- A location next to the police department may increase users' and librarians' sense of security.

- When libraries are adjacent to local government buildings, opportunities for shared meeting spaces are possible. For example, a city government and public library may share a large meeting room.

There are also a few potential problems.

- Shared governmental sites offer few opportunities for citizens to make multiple-visit trips that include the library. Stopping by the hardware store, the cleaners, and the library on a single trip makes sense, but there are few shared visits to libraries and other local government buildings.

> It's hard to imagine people saying, "Since we're stopping by to see Uncle Bert at the jail, let's get some books from the library. It's right next door."

- Because total space may be limited, developers of shared government sites may announce that the library's required space is unreasonably large, or that no expansion space can be provided. Libraries need to have carefully developed two-phase building programs in order to be prepared to defend their space needs, and they need to stand their ground.
- To obtain a uniform appearance among buildings, local governments may insist that their architect serve as the library architect, regardless of prior experience. In such situations, public libraries can agree to provide designs that are compatible with the general exterior appearance of the other government buildings on the site, but compatibility is vastly better than uniformity. If your library is frequently confused with the police station, this is Not a Good Thing. Among other things, it's absolutely essential that libraries have their own architects and their own consultants.
- A shared meeting room can be a major problem if an agency other than the library takes over the management of the room.
- Shared parking can be a problem at times of heavy use of adjacent government buildings.
- While the logic of grouping municipal government buildings is attractive, the logic breaks down because there are always a few types of buildings that are excluded, such as those dealing with utilities or sewage.

On balance, local government sites can be very successful locations for public libraries. The important factors are visibility, access, independence of architectural design, adequate acreage for expansion, and independence of meeting room management.

III-A-3. "River City" Sites

Some people have idyllic images of sort of Norman Rockwell libraries, not unlike the River City public library in *The Music Man*.

When public libraries are seeking sites, or considering abandoning undersized sites, someone will inevitably attack all change, painting a rosy picture of a sort of Never-Never-Land Public Library—a classic building with pediment and columns, facing the courthouse, close enough to homes so all children in town can walk to the library and obtain improving books.

Some sites of this type are still around and work. Historic libraries can feel wonderful.

However, most such surviving libraries appear to stand on sites that are far too small and offer far too little parking. And a lot are more or less inaccessible.

If you sense that the "beloved traditional tiny library" argument will arise, you can be prepared in at least two ways:

- Have data prepared on how many people actually walk to the library. One way to develop data is to conduct a parking survey, asking (in the course of the survey) whether users walked or drove to the library the day of the survey. If you know that only a small percentage of your users walk, even given the library's perfect traditional location, you will be in a much better position to argue. Doing the survey twice, once in summer and once in winter, may provide persuasive data if people never walk except in nice weather.
- Have a building program prepared to defend your space needs and describe your building's current shortcomings. One problem with all library locations is that someone

always lives nearby and doesn't want the library to move. If that person speaks passionately enough in a public hearing, however, other people in the room will realize that they don't live close to the library, and that may help take care of things.

III-A-4. Sites near Shelters

In recent decades, America has frequently done extraordinarily badly by "mainstreaming" people who were institutionalized for mental illnesses or substance abuse problems.

The result has been institutions stepping in to help, many of which maintain shelters.

Unfortunately, many shelters are closed during the day, and the residents have no place to go. Many of them end up at local public libraries, which often struggle to provide necessary help, but often lack the specialized staff training, specialized spaces, and funding necessary to take care of people. Building planning, operational planning, staff training, and funding all go hand in hand.

While some people with problems end up in libraries although they have no interest in library services, it's important that anyone who wants to use library collections or computers can do so.

There are limits to what library staff are trained to provide. In some communities, libraries have banded together with other community and social agencies to provide daytime shelters. John Moorman, coauthor of the first edition of this book, was director of an Illinois public library that worked with other local agencies to make this possible. It was a success.

Another step libraries can take is insisting that their community governments refuse to license shelters that are not open to their residents 24 hours a day.

Some libraries have replaced some of their upholstered furniture with molded plastic furniture, the best of which can be extremely comfortable for almost everyone. And be vastly easier to sanitize. See chapter 21, "User Seating."

III-A-5. Secure Locations

Never build on sites that people are afraid to visit. No matter how attractive your new building, people won't go there if they regard its location as unsafe. Some security issues can be addressed successfully through planning and funding. Others may not. Be realistic.

- A library in a park, for example, may seem charming by daylight, but few people want to enter parks after dark. This means that any library in a park must be located on a sidewalk at the edge of the park with the entrance on the sidewalk. And the exterior of the library must be well lit.

- Depending on the neighborhood, if the library is surrounded by bushes or trees, users may worry that people are lurking in the underbrush, waiting to leap upon passers-by.

- Underground parking spooks many users, and similar rules apply. Provide lots of easy ways out, lots of light, lots of exposure to passers-by to provide passive surveillance, and additional measures such as camera systems and emergency call stations.

- Some planners envision libraries as pawns in the redevelopment or improvement of unpleasant neighborhoods. Although the presence of the library in a rough or unsafe neighborhood can contribute to bringing desirable functions to the community, it should be one part of a broad and multifaceted approach to local issues and not a standalone effort. In the short term, some people may not want to visit the library (or let their children walk there unescorted). Acknowledge this concern.

- If you are planning a library building in an area that people find insecure, be sure to factor in the added long-term operational cost of extra security measures and get a commitment from local government to foot the extra cost on a permanent basis.

III-A-6. Locations near Schools

Public libraries and schools should be good neighbors. Service to students is a central focus of public libraries.

Some public libraries serve as places for students to gather between the times schools let out and working parents can pick up their children. Libraries can offer after-school programming and study spaces.

However, libraries for students above grade school may need to be far enough from school buildings to give kids a chance to expend pent-up energy or unwind and calm down before they reach the library. If a school and a library are two or three blocks apart, students can easily walk to the library, but it's not the first thing they encounter when they leave school.

Junior high schools may make the most difficult neighbors in situations where students are waiting to be picked up. High school students can often travel on their own, and grade school students are easier to entertain, but junior high students can feel stuck. Libraries need to allocate enough space so that the tech-heads, readers, group studiers, social butterflies, and gamers can all find something of interest. Or not build directly next door to junior highs.

III-A-7. Adjacent Transportation

Always consider the implications of adjacent transportation.

Both highways and railroads offer problems (and occasional benefits) for public libraries.

- General implications. A busy highway near a library can bring visibility and (depending on signaling) easy access, but it can also bring noise and concerns about safety. If a toddler wanders out of a library, a nearby highway can pose a real threat. Railroads provide noise, and those without grade separation lead to blocked crossings. Towns located on suburban railroad lines complain endlessly about the noise of locomotive horns, even though they are usually essential from a life-safety viewpoint. Towns on freight lines complain about the rumble and noise of passing trains and about long interruptions of automobile traffic as freight trains pass slowly through town. The transport of massive amounts of crude oil by train means that derailments can be major disasters.

> The distant whistles of passing trains are a lot more romantic if they're genuinely distant.

- Changes in traffic patterns. Railroad traffic patterns change. The fact that a railroad line is lightly used today does not prevent it from becoming a major thoroughfare tomorrow. Road traffic patterns can also change abruptly, particularly if highways are relocated or streets widened.

For example, one library with which Fred worked purchased a much larger site than it actually needed. The board of trustees envisioned selling part of the site for housing, but within a few months the state department of transportation announced that it was taking about a third of the site for road realignment, leaving the library with just the right amount of total space.

Although most transportation routes are well established, it's impossible to predict all changes, and compensations for heavier traffic or widened rights of way may be inadequate. For example, if a highway project takes most of a library's parking lot, the library may be compensated only for the value of the lot. If the library cannot acquire compensating space at a similar price, it may find that it owns a building that is almost unusable.

- Anticipating changes. The best way we know to predict what will happen next is to keep as many communications lines open as possible. Make sure that everyone knows how your library is vulnerable. Talk with local, county, and state traffic planners. Have friends in engineering firms. And talk with local railfans, who often have a pretty good idea of what railroads are likely to do (and who aren't subject to corporate confidentiality requirements).

III-B. ACADEMIC LIBRARIES

Because campuses are controlled environments, academic libraries may face fewer special location issues. However, central locations are important. They should have easy connections to residential and instructional areas of campuses and be the anchors for academic cores of campuses.

However, because academic libraries require a lot of turf, finding an adequate space can be difficult, and this may push the library to an undesirable part of campus. Libraries need to be central, not off in a far corner behind the stadium.

Academic libraries may have particular problems protecting their long-term expansion space. With empty space by the library on a crowded campus, other departments may constantly try to take it over.

Once in a while, an academic library lucks into a central space. In 1970, for example, the University of Chicago opened its new library on the site of Stagg Field, the university's one-time athletic field. All of this was helped, of course, by the university's earlier decision to get out of interschool athletics.

Fred, who got his PhD at the University of Chicago, thinks the sign of a great university is bulldozing the stadium to build a library. And not building a new stadium.

In recent years, many academic libraries have constructed high-density storage units. Some of these are located on inexpensive land, far from their main campus libraries, introducing delays on the order of 24 or more hours for retrieving materials. Others, however, have been constructed directly next to their main libraries, sometimes allowing retrieval even more rapid than from the main stacks.

Most universities have space planning offices that will play a major role in library location decisions.

III-C. SCHOOL LIBRARIES

In addition to the problem of nailing down sufficient space, school libraries are constantly threatened with being located next to truly undesirable functions.

One problem school librarians encounter is that their libraries are just one element in a complex mix of school functions. In many cases, spaces for many different functions are planned simultaneously. School librarians angling for good sites are up against science, athletics, music, drama, computer instruction, and lunch, in addition to all the departments that just need better classrooms. In this kind of space-needs-free-for-all, getting the attention of the superintendent of schools can be a struggle.

In addition, while academic and public libraries are usually designed by architects with special experience in library design, the architects designing school libraries are selected for their general knowledge of school design challenges and regulations. Compared to the difficultly of laying out gymnasiums and band rooms and wet labs, libraries may appear to deserve just a quick glance.

One common problem is planners' visions of shared spaces. For example, they may decide that the library can be part of an all-hours learning commons, a cafeteria, or a social center, with all the potential security issues. (To be fair to designers, some school libraries have been intended all along to be part of larger centers.)

Or the library may be viewed as the center of the school, with doors entering the library from multiple directions. This violates the basic principle of library design that libraries need single entrances, but the planners may simply try to overrule the librarians.

> Avoiding multiple entrances seems logical, but architects have ignored this basic security need over and over again.

Another common location problem school libraries face is noisy neighbors. If walls aren't designed to block sounds, a beginning saxophone class next door can contribute to the general library atmosphere in unsavory ways. The worst neighbors tend to be:

- Music rooms. A common wall with a music room can lead to perpetual unwelcome noise in the library.

- Athletic spaces. The noisiest spaces in schools are probably gymnasiums, but other athletic spaces can cause similar problems.

- Cafeterias.

If you are stuck with noisy adjacencies in a proposed new building, here are some things you might try to add to reduce possible problems:

- Convince the planners to bring in an acoustic consulting engineer.

- Introduce an intermediate row of storerooms between the athletic or music or cafeteria space and the library. You might also suggest athletic or music department offices or cafeteria storerooms.

- Make sure that the entrance to the noisy neighbor space is not immediately adjacent to the entrance to the library.

- Be sure that the dividing wall is designed to diminish sound transmission. As noted elsewhere in this book, some common methods include staggered stud walls, double walls, and making sure that the wall between the library and the noisy facility continues past the ceiling to the bottom of the roof above.

III-D. SPECIAL LIBRARIES

Because most special libraries occupy relatively small spaces, finding a site is often a matter of finding a space that is large enough and that can bear the weight of the collection.

Many special libraries are located in basements, where the weight of the books doesn't threaten the poured concrete slab-on-grade floor.

As with public libraries, a good special library location is often a busy location that staff members of the organization frequently pass. A hospital library, for example, may be far more successful just down the hall from the cafeteria than in a somewhat larger space in an outbuilding.

Because professional organizations are frequently pressed for office space, special libraries are occasionally asked to fit into smaller spaces. The success of this change typically depends on whether the library can give up hard copy of long runs of such materials as medical journals or court reporter series without diminishing service to its clientele.

Both to protect turf and to be prepared for sudden developments, special libraries may want to have at least partially completed building programs ready for rapid deployment at all times. Unlike school libraries, public libraries, and academic libraries, where the mills of governmental gods grind slowly, special libraries may find themselves in situations where response to proposed change must come virtually overnight.

Once the director of a hospital library and Fred put together a quick building program over a single weekend when the hospital announced a plan to relocate several departments, including the library. Although the hospital abandoned its plans to relocate the library, the fact that the library appeared with a written study while the other departments appeared only with angry arguments left the library looking particularly good to the administration.

IV. Summary

When the time comes to select a site for your library, it's important to include your architect, engineers, and consultant in addition to your librarians, your governing board and local campus, school, or municipal officials. Each party sees things somewhat differently. Even if you choose to ignore the advice of one or more people you hire, it's always worthwhile getting their input and having specific information on why they like a proposed site—or object to it.

It's extremely important to have a building program ready before you begin site discussions. You and your architects will need to know in specific detail what kind of space your library needs. Without a program, you will have a hard time convincing the rest of the world that you really need that much space.

It's also vital to have architects. You may be sorely tempted to agree to a site without the help of architects (and the engineers they retain), but you are likely to make serious errors. For example, architects can create quick sketches to test how your library might fit on proposed sites, and engineers can check whether the site can support a library.

As we've said endless times, when local people argue with you, always use your hired professionals to deliver the bad news. And always deliver your own good news.

When deciding between a number of possible sites becomes difficult, your architectural firm may have a scoring system for giving points to various aspects of each site.

It is essential to understand that site evaluation criteria can vary greatly based on your mission, your community, and the environments within which the library will sit. Few project follow all of these "rules" and most break more than one. However, there are certain aspects of sites that are essentially non-negotiable. Regardless of other considerations, your site has to be large enough for long-term expansion, above all possible floods, capable of supporting the weight of books, convenient to users, and safe.

V. Snappy Rules on Site Selection

1. Preemptive programming is almost always essential. When people start talking seriously about specific sites, you will need a building program to explain your space needs, but it may be too late to start writing one. Hiring a consultant to write a program, or writing your own program, is cheap, and delaying can lead to troubles.

2. A bad site for a nice store is a bad site for a nice public library.

3. Most empty buildings suggested for conversion to libraries are empty for very good reasons.

4. Whether you have a campus library, a school library, a special library, or a public library, everyone always wants to steal your site. Be wary and unforgiving of interlopers. One advantage you may have is psychological surprise, since many people don't expect to encounter librarians who go for the jugular.

5. Most sites suggested for libraries are too small. But the people who suggest them will refuse to believe you. Have a building program handy to show them why they're wrong, and an architect to explain how much acreage it will take to house the library described in the program.

6. The electronic revolution does NOT mean that your library will never run out of space.

7. Keep comfortably away from riverbanks, seacoasts, and floodplains. "100-year floods" have seemed to come along about once every two or three years. And now we're having "1,000-year floods." (Luckily, many lakeside locations are stable.)

8. Even if it's more conveniently located, you will regret building on a low area of your site. You will not enjoy the scenic effect of seeing water run downhill straight into your library.

9. If your site is so limited that your library will need to plunge underground, you will have windowless and wet basement spaces that staff and books and users will all hate. (Remember that basements in libraries cost nearly as much as extra floors above ground.) Robert Frost, were he with us today, would no doubt remark that something there is that does not love a basement.

10. Wet books are even less fun than wet dogs.

11. High-density storage next to your library is infinitely better than high-density storage two counties off.

12. Charming, historic sites for public libraries are no good unless their charming, historic parking lots are large enough to hold everyone who wants to use the libraries.

13. Converting an existing non-library structure to an academic or public library often costs just about as much as starting over. If the result is a cumbersome or awkward library, no one wins except the person who sold you the structure. Among possible choices for conversion, empty big box stores are probably best.

14. Sites required for new academic and public libraries can be very large and will frequently involve the demolition of other buildings. Expect squabbles.

15. Neighbors matter.

16. One of the truly fine places for a special library is next door to the cafeteria.

17. Never let anyone else relieve you of your vacant land, and never let nearby land slip through your fingers. Never sell off part of your land to help fund construction; in the long run, the money is trivial and the space is irreplaceable.

18. People with axes to grind will challenge your program. The credentials of your programmer may therefore be politically important.

19. Many proposed sites look sweetly benign but are truly evil below the surface.

20. Never build a library on land you don't own. Land that reverts to someone if the library leaves is just as bad. Never get involved with either situation.

21. State law may make hiring an architect for public work a slow process. You can run through the selection process at almost no cost, then lie in wait to pounce when people pressure you for quick designs.

22. Whenever architects quote building costs, always make sure you know whether they're talking about construction costs or project costs, and always insist on project costs.

23. Never agree to a site for a public or academic library without the advice of your consultants and architects.

24. If a library has no immediate need of an adjacent structure, it can always lease it temporarily, but there's a lot more to be said for quick demolition and conversion to parking while the demolishing is good.

25. If your library is close to a homeless shelter that is closed during the day, it will become a homeless shelter.

26. The right price to pay for a building to convert to a library is often free, and sometimes that's far too much.

27. If you are going to wait for a perfect site, pack a lunch. It's going to be a while.

PART II
From Overcrowding
to Ribbon Cutting

CHAPTER 10

Design

I. Introduction

I-A. DEFINITION OF "DESIGN"

"Design" is used in many ways over the course of a project.

In a broad sense of the process, it means everything between the end of programming and site selection to the start of bidding.

At points in the project, it refers most directly to the development, comparison, and refinement of options that will become a set of drawings and specifications.

The end product is a set of instructions to bidders and contractors on how to price and determine how to construct rooms, buildings, and sites.

It is both synthetic and analytical, rational and creative, collaborative and yet channeled through a small group of key people, one of them the architect.

The architect not only produces much of the product of this process but is responsible for planning and managing the activities of other participants in the process, ensuring their meaningful participation in a series of incremental steps that leads from the approved program statement into what are known as bidding and construction documents.

In addition to providing the good advice and experience needed to accomplish all of this, state and provincial law almost always requires that bid and construction documents for a government construction building for public use be prepared by a licensed architect or engineer. In most parts of North America, any new construction or alterations of existing buildings need to be designed by an architect registered in the state or province where the project will be constructed. Some very small projects, some repairs or replacements, and updates to many finishes do not need the services of an architect. Some states allow some of this work (finish replacement) to be designed and supervised by an interior designer. A smaller group of jurisdictions certify interior designers based on experience and successful completion on an examination to provide renovation design services. Be sure to understand the requirements in your area.

State law may also specify how public bodies may hire architects. Your state library may have information on the subject, as will the Board of Architects for your state or your building consultant.

Always avoid the dangerous temptation to go straight to a contractor for any library construction project, whether it's a new building or just a couple of windows. Design is almost always far more complex than it appears. If a building is larger than a specified minimum size, or if the project consists of more than cosmetic improvements, laws and regulations will require that construction documents be prepared professionally. Preparing bid documents even for something as straightforward as a storage closet is a complex undertaking.

Good architects are always a good investment. For any project bigger than a woodshed, good architects are an absolutely essential investment.

I-B. WORKING WITH ARCHITECTS

There are other good reasons for an architect leading the design effort on a project. Architects have a broad training in the pragmatic and artistic aspects of the built environment with an emphasis on buildings. Buildings are in themselves only a small part of the spectrum of spatial design disciplines, but it is the one at which urban plan, landscape design, and interior design intersect. Architects tend to be generalists with an awareness and appreciation of the specialty expertise of other participants and training at how to integrate that knowledge into a cohesive, intentional environment.

This cannot be underestimated. Design and construction is rarely (and in the case of a library, we think we can say never) the result of one person's work. This is a team effort. Keeping the members of a team focused on accepted goals is critical throughout and essential during the design phase. If the result of the design effort is confused, how is anyone expected to construct something that is not confused?

Architecture is always about people. Whether it is the owners, occupants, buildings, funders, passers-by, or a member of society at large, the process, decisions, and results of the person-to-person interactions of design are felt well beyond the design or construction timeframe. This demands skills that include communication (listening, discussion, presenting), visioning (anticipating the form, function, and behavioral impact of spaces that are not yet built), and management (of people, time, money, issues).

Clearly, things will go much better with the right architect. Selecting the architect that is right for you is a topic unto itself, and we address it in chapter 6, "Essential Teamwork." Here we want to focus on how to effectively work with our selected firm.

Although architects are absolutely essential to any library design and construction job, things don't always go well between librarians, owners, and architects. Any of the groups can be at fault. Strengths are usually related to weaknesses, and while some of this will be a matter of perspective (if you are with me, I think you are determined, and if you are against me, I think you are stubborn), more often than not it is someone on the team going a bit too far and forgetting the balance needed to achieve project goals rather than individual goals. Because the architect plays such an essential and central role in the process, often called upon to keep the team focused on the project goals, it is imperative that the architects know how to keep themselves in tune with those same goals. Knowing what you can expect from the architect and knowing how you are expected to interact with the architect can be a great boon. Knowing the common pitfalls is even better. A few warning signs recur throughout this chapter and in the book as a whole.

- Listening is important in design. Enough so that seeing drawings before you've had conversations where you are the primary speaker should be a big warning.

- Drawings are not precious in the process. They are tools. Anyone (architect, client, donor, consulting librarian—it doesn't matter) who falls in love with a drawing (plan, site plan, elevation, perspective—it doesn't matter) at any point in the project (interview, schematic design, contract documents—it doesn't matter) is not helping the process, the product, or the project. Drawings are two-dimensional tools to investigate and communicate the arrangement of three-dimensional spaces. While some are beautiful, they are meant to be critiqued and set aside in favor of a more refined iteration of the design. Nothing springs full formed from someone's forehead. You should expect to see, mark up, and toss away a lot of drawings over the course of design.

- Design has multigenerational impacts on people, society, and the environment. You, your architect, and your consulting librarian are expected to think in those time scales and acknowledge the complexities inherent in building anything, much less an important civic building and vital resource for the most heavily used essential service on campus or in the community. Acknowledge

the expertise of the architects with high expectations, active participation, and respect for their extensive training and experience.

I-C. DESIGN IS A TEAM SPORT

Design is a complex undertaking because it involves the interaction of a wide range of people and agencies. For example, a project may easily involve most (or even all) of the following:

- Governing bodies, ranging from university boards of trustees to faculty library committees, school boards, public library boards, city councils, and so on.

- Administrators such as mayors, provosts, school superintendents, school principals, and corporate officers responsible for structures.

- Library users

- Librarians

- National, state, and local codes and their enforcement agencies

- Other regulatory agencies

- Programmers (library building consultants)

- Architects

- Construction management firms

- Contractors

- Engineers (structural, civil, mechanical, electrical, etc.)

- Campus architects, city engineering firms, and other local experts

- Self-appointed community pressure groups

- Library foundations

- Donors

- LEED and other freelance programs

- State agencies, such as historical preservation agencies and state libraries
- Friends of the library groups

But you can't give all of these folks a direct role in your project. The absolutely vital groups are librarians, architects, and owners. Any design process that intentionally excludes any of these three groups is a potential disaster.

Most building planning takes place in a series of meetings between architects, owners, and librarians.

The library needs to be represented by:

- Representatives of owners, including public library boards, school administrators or school boards, campus architects, and campus administrators. Usually this amounts to one or two people—not enough people from any one board to make the planning meetings subject to your state's open meetings act.
- Library staff. In order to have essential continuity, you need two administrators, so you can count on at least one being present at every meeting.
- Hired experts on the functional design of library buildings. Someone in the library's group needs to be an expert on how library buildings occupy spaces. This can be your library's staff, building consultant, construction management firm, or owner's representative. The main thing is that someone in the room in addition to the architects needs to have serious expertise. No planning meeting should take place without librarians present. If an owner tends to be a bully, the hired library building consultant needs to be present.

The main problem is that a wide variety of groups have an interest in the design of your new library. Most of these will have no representation on the planning group, but they may expect to be informed on progress and decisions. Sorting all of this out can be interesting.

Planning groups can easily become too large. For everyday meetings, probably a maximum of six to eight people in addition to architects is recommended, with occasional meetings to report to all the major players.

Architects will take minutes of each meeting and circulate copies for everyone to sign.

Libraries should do the same. Take your own minutes of the meeting and have everyone present—including your architects—sign copies. If something goes wrong, having the library's own records helps.

Although architects are absolutely essential to any library design and construction job, things don't always go well between librarians, owners, and architects. All the groups can be at fault.

I-C-1. Architects Behaving Badly

Architects who refuse to listen to owners and librarians are not unusual. One of the reasons why so many architects stress what good listeners they are is that a few architects have well-earned reputations for ignoring their clients. If you feel that your architects are refusing to listen, here are some things you can do:

- Always have librarians present at all building planning meetings. If your provost wants to hold meetings privately with your architect, it may be a sign of serious trouble.
- Keep your own minutes of design meetings and have all the parties sign testifying accuracy. Architects do this all the time, but you

should do it too in order to be sure that your wishes are clear in the minutes. Even if you don't have bad feelings about how things are going, bring someone to meetings to take notes on your behalf.

- Stop end runs. Sometimes architects try to bypass librarians and city or university engineers and deal with people as remote from the project as possible. Make clear from the beginning to whom the architects report, and stop any attempt to go around you.

- Don't put up with situations where you turn down a design concept but the architect ignores you. If a concept that you totally rejected comes back again, it's time to sit down immediately with your architects and discuss the nature of your future relationship.

- If your architect keeps coming up with ideas you don't like, keep asking why things have to be this way.

- Stop concepts you don't like instantly.

- Ask point blank why the concept you suggested is not the one the architects are presenting. Occasionally, a library's architects will dislike the entire concept that the library has in mind, but instead of being upfront will share one alternative concept design after another, hoping that one will appeal to the owners and make it unnecessary for the architects to openly reject the owners' ideas. This happened to one library board Fred worked with, and the delays and frustrations wasted a year while the architects passively resisted the library board, coming up with one unwanted alternative concept after another.

- Find a new architectural firm. This is the most extreme response, but occasionally it's the best one.

> Some architects brush off what librarians want by saying, "You just don't understand architecture." Your response is to force them to explain why their ideas are essential, ideally with your library building consultant present.

- Architects who ignore building programs are a problem. After spending months discussing every aspect of your library's planned services and having this converted to an extremely detailed document, you have every right to expect your architects to read and follow your written building program.

If your architects disagree with the program, you should expect them to do so in a meeting with you and your library building consultant, so that the architect and consultant both get to explain the reasoning for their different views.

Frequently, a program review is included in the first meeting with architects. Some architects take this very seriously, but others totally blow it off. Be sure to ask your architects formally if there is anything in the program with which they disagree, and get their response into your meeting minutes. If you have a good program, it will include a list of those design features librarians hate but some architects love, and you don't want a firm that says, "Sure, we agree," and then proceeds to include some of the features you specifically don't want.

Some architects may work hard to keep consultants away from planning meetings.

In all of this it's important to remember that the best projects are collaborative. If the owners, library staff, architect, and building consultant are all present at planning meetings, the chances of having everything go right are greatly improved.

- Some architects are bullies and raging egomaniacs. While most architects are great, it's also a field that attracts more than its share of egomaniacs, people who are spectacularly full of themselves, often with no justification and frequently with little or no knowledge of libraries and how they work.

Over the years we've met architects who feel that they are slumming by dealing with librarians. Architects who feel justified in ignoring everything librarians say. Architects who come up with impressively dysfunctional designs and then angrily refuse to budge. Architects who want to deal only with people who know nothing about library buildings, bypassing librarians in the process. Architects who insist that their contracts allow them to ignore librarians and do whatever they darn well please. Architects who truly feel "Function be damned."

Some architects can be amazingly arrogant when dealing with librarians, who they clearly regard as their serious intellectual inferiors. One architect we know (not even hired yet) called the director of a library "little missy" and threatened her with dismissal if she didn't shut up and do as he said. (The fact that she was well educated and had extensive experience in both business and library management didn't slow him down.)

Some architects announce that they are a part of the community power structure, and that nothing will get done if they don't personally approve.

Some architects feel that they are slumming by doing anything less than the Library of Congress, and that the least that the local folks can do is shut up While The Great Men Are at Work.

It may sound like we're exaggerating, but problems with rampant and unjustified egos abound in the profession.

One useful function of library building consultants with strong credentials is to have them attend all or many of your planning meetings with your architects. Egomaniac architects will probably want to tromp all over your consultants as well, but it's easier for consultants with a hundred library projects under their belts to look architects in the eye and say "Hogwash!" And if everything blows up, it's a lot better for librarians if their consultants get fired than if the librarians get fired. If necessary, sacrifice the outsiders.

- Some architects do sloppy work. Many architects do painfully accurate work, creating construction documents that represent carefully accurate engineering and impressive consistency in detail and that leads to projects with a minimum of change orders.

But occasionally, things that you want may be missing, sections of the drawings may be out of agreement with each other, or measurements may be off.

- Some architects cut corners to increase profits. To be fair, architecture is a business. Expenses need to be covered and a reasonable profit should be expected, but occasionally we encounter architects who see ways to make extra money on fixed-price projects by simply skipping essential steps or by moving ahead when owners aren't ready.

Initially, all projects involve a lot of noodling around, trying out sketches of various possible designs and reviewing functions and likely costs. If your architects start with a completed schematic floor plan, they are cutting off valuable (and time-consuming) discussion. Instead of asking whether the entire concept needs rethinking, owners can end up debating the shape of a window.

- Some architects try to keep library building consultants from attending planning meetings or commenting on designs. This may streamline the process, but it eliminates one of the owners' major sources of professional opinions on how libraries occupy spaces, and on what kinds of features work and don't work.

- Some architects find projects more time-consuming than they want and try to get owners to accept bundles of loose sketches as "schematic designs."

- Some architects don't want to stop with schematic designs but get on with design development or construction documents before schematic designs are final. Remember that a schematic design (including the cost estimate that accompanies it) is all you need to raise funds for your project. If you are unable to find the money, any money you spent on design development or construction documents is wasted.

- Some architects move directly from schematic design to construction documents, skipping the vital area of design development. At best, this is sloppy. At worst, there are all sorts of important decisions that are never discussed.

- Some architects blow off punch listing, turning in a page or two of uselessly vague remarks like "Repair damage to wall finishes" when every specific dent needs to be mentioned (and ideally photographed), so that contractors can't claim at a later time that all the dents are the fault of the owners.

I-C-2. Owners Behaving Badly

Owners need to be conscientious participants in the design process. There are a number of potential pitfalls.

- Some owners refuse to pay attention to the process. For instance, we've had a number of experiences with librarians who let the short-term pressures of daily life dominate their lives during building planning. Faced with decisions that may affect the library and its work for 50 or 100 years, librarians announce that they have no time to review plans because they're "busy with summer reading."

For good planning to take place, libraries need to enable their administrative staffs to devote nearly full time to architectural projects, and librarians in turn cannot hide behind familiar activities. This means that the governing boards of libraries must make specific plans for the extra expenditures that will result from tying up their most expensive employees.

Having library building consultants or owners' representatives fill in for administrators helps, but the focus of an administrator has to be the new building.

One useful thing some administrators do is to maintain a diary of the entire process, both design and construction, listing major events and dates. If disagreements later arise, it helps to know what happened and when it happened.

- There are owners who think they know it all (but don't). We'd like to think that all librarians and library governors are modest and well-informed, but the field has a few amazingly unjustified egos.

We've seen it primarily in public library boards, but individual board members can be amazingly insistent on dysfunctional ideas.

Sometimes it's logical. For example, basements in library buildings are a really bad idea, but they make good practical sense in private homes constructed in areas with low water tables. Board members who have a good understanding of the construction of houses can insist on similar concepts in libraries. And it can be hard to dissuade them. Even though they're wrong.

- There are owners who refuse to be realistic about costs. Architects tell us about problems with owners whose desires are larger than their finances and balk whenever architects start providing cost estimates.

Libraries are inherently more expensive than many other types of buildings. They need high-quality air handling systems, lots of light fixtures, a huge number of electrical outlets, unusually solid floors, ceilings a minimum of 10 feet high, and many other features that set them apart from inexpensive structures like many retail stores. Library owners need to come to grips with this.

- Owners with no practical experience with buildings (but who deny it to themselves) can frustrate the process. Most day-to-day library building planning includes frequent meetings between architects, owners, and librarians. For practicality, the owner's group has to be of reasonable size, anything from half a dozen to a maximum of perhaps eight people.

Among those representing the owners at these meetings has to be someone who knows about the practical side of buildings, particularly library buildings, someone who can understand proposed designs and who can point out potential problems.

Some libraries have a professional staff member with wide experience in the functional design of library buildings.

- Public libraries can sometimes find building committee members who are retired contractors or school superintendents, or they can arrange to have their building consultants or construction managers or owners' representatives attend all meetings.

- Universities can rely on campus architects or construction management firms or building consultants.

- Other libraries rely on their library building consultants.

The reason these people are important is that planning committees must include members who understand everything architects say. And occasionally to point out the problems with suggested ideas.

One great way to keep library owners from being Led Down the Garden Path is for them to have their own experts on hand.

- Owners who are painfully indecisive put the process at risk. Occasionally, owners are nearly unable to make up their minds or keep changing their minds, and the architectural design process slows to a halt.

To be fair to your architects, be available for meetings at reasonable times and make sure that all decision makers turn up. If you don't like a proposed idea, say so immediately, before your architects have spent many hours pursuing a concept that is doomed from the start. If a new member of the planning group wants to throw everything out and start over, you may have to tell that person that *it's too late.*

> At one public library Fred worked on, the owners' members of the committee included a former contractor who was a member of the board of trustees, a library director who was forceful and knowledgeable, and Fred. At least once or twice in every meeting, the three said "No!" in unison to proposed ideas. The good thing is that they were always right. The building was successful, but the architects skipped the ribbon cutting.

If your architects are working for a fixed fee, creating endless delays by being unable to attend planning meetings or make up your mind is seriously unfair.

- There are owners who want to do illegal things. Good architects have an intensive mastery of the vast array of legal standards that surround buildings and construction. Building codes, prevailing wage laws, accessibility codes, zoning regulations, and other regulations place severe limits on the freedom of action of library owners.

Occasionally, owners push pet ideas that are strictly illegal, placing their architects in awkward situations. For example, Fred has encountered library boards that want to evade prevailing wage acts, ignore or argue about building codes, not install required sprinkler systems, or cut corners on accessibility.

Occasionally, owners and directors want to steer work to family and friends. We've seen it happen particularly with interior work and furnishings, but there are probably all sorts of other bad examples out there.

If you and your architects are facing off, good sources of insight may be your construction management firm and your attorneys.

- Some owners want to deal privately with architects (cutting their librarians and other library experts out of the process). One sign of serious problems to come is owners who meet with architects privately.

- Some owners practice passive resistance. Say what you mean, say it out loud, say it face to face, and mean what you say.

II. Basic Steps in the Design Process

Although this chapter covers design work, architects also provide many vital functions during the construction process and during occupancy. For the role of architects in programming, construction, and occupancy, see the appropriate chapters.

Among other services, your architects can:

- Help you evaluate your options.

- Help you determine whether your site is suitable for the building you have in mind. This is a surprisingly complex undertaking, as the chapter on site selection indicates.

- Evaluate your existing structure, if you are considering expansion rather than starting over. (Your programmer should have already done this from a library function point of view, but your architect will bring additional viewpoints, particularly the technical feasibility of expanding your building and bringing it up to current codes.)

- Develop a design for your building. This includes arranging and coordinating the work of a variety of engineers.

- Help with presenting your design to voters, the local press, and so on.

- Convert the design to construction documents—drawings and written specifications that will assure that bids from different contractors are for exactly the same structure.

During construction your architect will usually do the following, as described in chapter 15, "Construction." (If you hire a construction management firm, however, much of this work may be done by a construction manager.)

- Assist in soliciting, receiving, and evaluating bids. Bidding for public construction usually is subject to laws providing for competitive bidding. Private construction does not require this, but competitive bidding will almost certainly bring private owners a lower price and prevent situations where the brother-in-law of the college president is allowed to install woefully substandard carpeting.

- Provide construction administration. In particular, this involves making sure that the building described in the construction documents is the building you get. (Note that "construction administration" is not "construction supervision," which is the job of the general contractor or construction manager.)

- Sort out problems during construction. If the owners and contractors disagree, the architects are the people who need to explore the situations and propose solutions.

- Deal with change orders. Sooner or later in every project, the contractor is asked to build something that was not in the original specifications. Your architect will write the change order and help you negotiate a price with your contractor.

- Approve "draws" from your contractors. Before bills are paid, your architect will verify that the work was actually done.

- Carry out punch listing and other project closeout tasks at the end of the project.

II-A. ENGINEERING SERVICES

Architectural fees usually include engineering services. Be very careful that your agreement with your architects includes necessary engineering work.

Some architectural firms have a variety of engineers on their staffs, while others subcontract almost all of these services. Firms with many engineers claim that this improves their services, but firms with no engineers on their staffs do very good work as well. Our personal feeling is that both ways work.

Most engineering specialties required for building construction fall into the general area of "civil engineering." The name is an ancient one and comes from the distinction between military and civil engineering. In the modern design and construction industry, however, "civil engineering" most commonly refers to site design and engineering, including such areas as site utilities, earthwork, paving, stormwater drainage, and so on.

Among the sub-areas of building engineering are:

- Geotechnical engineering, concerned with soils, drainage, and foundations. (Frequently identified as "civil engineering" in architectural documents.)

- Structural engineering.

- Engineering of MEP systems. These include mechanical engineering (HVAC—heating, ventilating, and air conditioning), electrical, and plumbing.

- Acoustical engineering, which is almost always underutilized in library design projects. (Acoustical engineering is a specialized area of expertise. Except for auditoriums, acoustical engineers are often not involved in library projects, although they may be needed in situations with sloped ceilings that don't absorb sound.)

II-B. PROGRAM REVIEW OR VERIFICATION

A written building program is a detailed description of all the spaces in your proposed library, including their functions, sizes, furnishings, and adjacencies. Before architects start design work, it's essential that everyone involved in your library project—governing boards and library administrative staff—understand the program and agree on its contents.

The creation of written building programs is covered in detail in chapter 7, "Building Programs."

Usually the first meetings with your newly hired architects will involve review of your building program. This is a critical meeting, because your program defines in serious detail what you want in your new library building.

In many cases, architects do not agree with everything in building programs, and this first meeting is the proper time to sort this out. You need to let your architects know that you expect them to either speak up at this time or follow your program as it is written. More about this later.

To make this meeting work, it is essential that your consultants (or whoever wrote your building program) be present to explain the reasons for the information in the program. And to sometimes stand their ground.

Spending time with your architects and your programmer to go through the nuances of the program and answer questions is an essential step.

One thing that can go seriously awry in architecture is if the architects disagree with the program but prefer to quietly ignore the program rather than face issues directly. Fred has worked with libraries that had to fire architects who persistently ignored programs without admitting they were doing so.

A few architects clearly resent building programs. Frequently these architects are people who want not only to design a library but also to determine what it will do. Unless your architects have an impressive track record building highly functional libraries, their desire to redefine your library's purpose and intent should be a chilling experience—a dangerous sign of hubris that needs to be stopped before things get seriously out of hand.

Program verification occurs through the design process. One way to work with your architects in making sure that the proposed building is compatible with your building program is to ask you architects to indicate on their drawings, or in tabular form, which items in the program have been added, deleted, or relocated. In some drawings, you'll notice icons for items of furnishings floating in midair around the edges of the drawings, outside the enclosed floor area of the building, indicating that the items are in the program but don't fit into the drawings.

Keeping your library building consultants around during the design process is an extremely good idea, because they may be the only people who have the knowledge and experience to question your architects' concepts.

> Little white lies may make the world go more smoothly in many areas of life, but the only way architecture succeeds is if all issues are faced directly as soon as they emerge.

Occasionally, a firm of architects will provide both programming and design. *We think this is an extremely bad idea.* If your programmer is a librarian with wide experience with library architecture rather than an architect, the program is more likely to be driven by functional needs. In addition, if your programmer and architects work independently rather than as members of the same firm, you will have a valuable second opinion on design concepts.

Having said all this, good architectural firms tend to welcome well-thought-out building programs because programs help them understand clients (and sometimes save them a lot of work).

II-C. BASIC SERVICES PHASES

The standard AIA (American Institute of Architects) contracts divide standard architectural services for building projects into "Basic Services" and "Additional Services." Basic services are the typical steps common to most projects. They usually include five phases.

- Schematic design
- Design development
- Construction documents
- Bidding
- Construction administration

We are dealing with the first three in this chapter. These are the three phases most frequently included in the colloquial "design" phases you will hear referenced. Bidding is the means by which the project is procured. Construction administration is a set of administrative and quality control tasks that runs parallel to the construction of the project. Bidding and construction administration are covered in chapter 14, "Bidding," and chapter 15, "Construction."

II-D. PRELIMINARY SERVICES

Preliminary services are some of the possible additional services. Before you get into basic service, you may need a number of investigations before design can start. These preliminary services are in addition to basic building design and should not be overlooked. The temptation to "roll them in" to the basic building design does not do justice to the complexity of any of the tasks. Plan time and budget professional fees to cover these efforts.

II-D-1. Evaluation of Existing Structures

If you are considering remodeling and expanding your current library building, or converting a non-library structure to a library, one of the first and most important functions of your architect is evaluating your structure. Your programmers may have included evaluations in their reports, but these are likely to be from the point of view of effective library service. Your architects will add to this an evaluation of the library as a physical structure, including the opinions of professional engineers as needed.

If your architects disagree with the evaluations provided by your programmers, you need to sort this out with both parties as quickly as possible.

Among the many questions that need to be answered before buildings can be considered for expansion are:

- The physical stability of the structure. Architects will evaluate the condition of footings, walls, windows, roof, and so on. For example, if brick walls need to be completely reworked, the cost of moving into an existing building can be greatly increased.

- Floor strength. Library buildings require greater floor loading strength than almost any other type of structure. In particular, if a non-library building is being considered for conversion to a library, an evaluation of floor strength is vital. Outside of slab-on-grade structures, few non-library buildings are strong enough. In addition, some libraries have floors that are strong enough to hold books in some places but not strong enough in others, and you need to find this out immediately.

- Problems with water infiltration. One of the most serious problems with buildings is water. Your architects will inspect your roof, walls, windows, and foundations. They will check the condition of flashings, caulking, mortar, and other elements that resist water problems. If you have maintained your building properly, you will be aware of many of these, but lots of library buildings have structural problems that have been politely ignored. It's important that you tell your architects about any problems your library has had with water infiltration and what was done about them.

- Environmental contamination problems that will require remediation, such as asbestos, mold, mercury, and lead paint. Many of these materials can be present in large quantities and lead to significant expense. EPA regulations will apply not only to existing structures but also to undeveloped sites, particularly sites that have been contaminated by previous users. Problems with buried fuel tanks are unfortunately common. (Typically, your architects will arrange for inspections for asbestos and lead paint by licensed third-party firms.)

- The condition of MEP systems. Remember that the cost of mechanical, electrical, and plumbing systems can be about 40 percent of the cost of building a library, and HVAC alone about 25 percent. In many older buildings, all MEP systems are obsolete and will need to be replaced.

- Conformance with local zoning. Zoning can be a major problem for libraries, even though they are government owned. Many municipalities will hold any public entity to the highest standard so as to avoid favoritism or setting a precedent of exempting any user from their ordinances. Even with a sense that the library will be exempt from many requirements, you still need to face problems before you begin spending serious money. For example, if you intend to open a small coffee shop in your new library, zoning may have to be altered to make this retail function legal. If your building is in a residential neighborhood, height and setback regulations may apply. In many cases, zoning may require off-street parking. And so on.

- Conformance with current building codes. Because codes are numerous, overlapping, and frequently updated, your building may no longer be entirely legal. This is the time to find this out and to look at the legal implications of expansion. Older buildings are sometimes rated differently if they are historic structures, but even then there are thresholds that will require major renovations to come into compliance with key aspects of the current code. Just because you've been allowed to operate with antiquated egress, inadequate emergency exits, minimal restrooms count, and limited accessibility does not mean your next project will not trigger the need to be compliant.

- Whether your building currently meets codes but will not do so if it is expanded. For example, if expansion will increase your building from 10,000 to 15,000 square feet, you will probably need to retrofit a sprinkler system to the entire building.
- Although zoning can sometimes be negotiated, most governments will be unyielding when it comes to code compliance for a public building as heavily used as a library.

Your architects' findings at this stage of your project can have a major impact on your planning. If, for example, you will be required to bring your building up to code requirements when you expand it, it may prove to be massively expensive to do so. Or bringing the building up to code may compromise the design features that made people want to expand the building rather than just start over.

See chapter 16, "Remodeling and Expanding Library Buildings."

II-D-2. Feasibility Studies

Owners sometimes ask architects to conduct separate studies evaluating whether specific buildings can be converted or specific sites utilized.

Even if certain ideas are obviously preposterous, you may still need to check them out in order to convince your community that you have checked all possible options. People often turn up and accuse libraries of not considering specific options, and it helps a great deal to be able to say, "Our architects checked this possibility, and we had to reject it for the following reasons."

Feasibility studies are a valuable architectural service. If you need much more than a series of quick trial sketches, you should expect to pay extra, particularly if there have to be a large number of studies or if they have to be very detailed.

Feasibility studies cannot be undertaken before programs are prepared. The whole point of a study is to explore whether a specific building or site can be used for your library, and this cannot be done until your architects have detailed information on what kind of library you need.

See chapter 17, "Converting Non-library Buildings to Public Libraries."

III. Schematic Design

Schematic design involves the basic decisions about how the building will solve the problems described in detail in the building program. Since there are many ways to arrange things, and few if any are without some compromise, this phase is about exploring and comparing options in sufficient detail that the overall functionality, adaptability, image, and cost are defined with some measure of precision and confidence.

Although schematic design is supposedly only about 15 percent of total architectural services, it involves many of the most important decisions in the project, and it can often cost more, particularly because schematic designs for libraries must include furniture layouts. Projects involving complex remodeling of existing structures can also cost more. Because of both of these factors, it can be reasonable for schematic design charges to be about 20 percent.

In preparing schematic designs, architects should meet extensively with owners, staff, and building consultants as a group to study ways in which the functional requirements in the building program can be converted into actual designs. Even for a very small library, this can involve several long meetings.

Having your building consultant (programmer) attend design meetings will do a great deal to speed the process, avoiding wasted meetings where the architect brings designs to a library to a library board, the board approves one, the programmer later points out functional problems, the architect then redraws the design, and on and on. Some of the most successful design meetings we have seen involve four critical groups—owners, library staff, architects, and building consultant—sitting around the same table at the same time.

III-A. PROCESS

One popular method of developing design ideas is a process called a "charrette." In a charrette, architects will lead group discussions, posting all sorts of ideas in the form of quick sketches all over the walls of a room.

Another method used by some architects is to create a series of simple rectangles representing the size of an element described in the building program.

Some architects lead off the design process by asking owners to list words that describe the library the owners want. The result may be a dozen or two words, ranging (as possible examples) from "traditional" to "friendly" to "important" to "spacious" to "inspiring" to "permanent" to

> *Charrette* is a French word for "cart." Its current application to architecture comes from the concept of tossing all sorts of ideas into a cart. It derives from the days of the Ecole des Beaux Arts. In their final days of cranking out drawings before the design jury was convened, students placed their drawings on a cart and continued to work on their drawings while they were wheeled into the presentation.

"educational." And so on. We've seen this done frequently. It may help designers get a feel for what you want, but it may also be just a way to get conversation started. (Some owners enjoy this process so much that they display the words on the walls of the library. This may or may not be a smart idea.) However they start, the important thing is you don't want to show up with a finished drawing at the first meeting!

All schematic designs should always progress through a series of steps, from simple layout concepts to more carefully developed floor plans. Architects should begin with a large number of rough concept sketches, showing how various approaches might work. Many ideas can be discarded at this point, but you'll want to keep all of the sketches so you have a response to people who propose design ideas that you've rejected for good reason.

Beware, beware of architects who want to present finished floor plans as the first drawings you see. Starting with finished drawings tends to stifle discussion and move things along too quickly. If architects are working on a flat fee basis, starting out with a finished drawing may save the architects' time and improve their income per hour, but it's a major disservice to the client. When the first thing a client sees is a finished drawing, the tendency is to get hung up on discussions of small details rather than of basic conceptual issues.

Architects who skip preliminary sketches and begin with semi-finished drawings are not earning their money and are stifling proper consideration of options. It's intimidating to find yourself looking at a finished drawing and realize that you need to reject the entire thing. The mere fact that the drawing is elegant is no reason to accept it. If you feel it doesn't meet your needs, you need to say so immediately, even if it means tossing out a finished-looking piece of work. (All of this assumes, of course, that you are paying a fair fee for architectural services. If you selected your architect based on who had the lowest fee, you already decided what effort your project is worth, and the process will reflect your priorities.)

In all dealings with architects, it's vital to stop ideas you dislike as soon as possible. The longer your architects work with an idea, the more time and imagination and money they will have invested in the concept, and the harder it will be for them to abandon it. If things you don't like go on too long, the architects' time has been wasted, and that's not fair to them.

Occasionally, you may deal with architects who essentially refuse to abandon design concepts you dislike. You need to put a stop to this quickly and firmly. We've seen stubbornness over design ideas lead to the dismissal of architects, and you should be prepared to do so if your architects consistently ignore your instructions. Luckily, things very seldom get to this point.

You have a right to expect technical explanations from your architects. If you ask for a specific feature and your designers say you can't have it, or if your designers propose something you don't like, it's completely reasonable to expect a full explanation.

> One librarian Fred knew had a great way with designers. Although she understood a great deal about construction, when she saw concepts with which she disagreed, she'd say something like, "I'm sorry, but I'm new at all this, and I really don't understand why it has to be this way. You'll have to take time to explain to me why we can't do things another way."

One thing that helps a great deal during the schematic design process is to ask your architects to provide a small chart comparing the space required for each major area of the library in the building program with the space provided in the design. Fred once worked with an architect who categorically refused to provide this information. The library board eventually severed the relationship.

At all meetings with your architects, someone must prepare minutes of the meeting. Typically, architects will prepare minutes and circulate them for signatures by the owners or other parties involved. We think it's a good practice for owners to do the same thing, making sure that things important to them are not omitted from the minutes, and also collecting signatures.

Almost all construction drawings are prepared using digital software. CADD systems (computer-aided drawing and design) have been around since the 1970s, and these have frequently been updated to BIM systems (building information management). BIM systems have the added advantage of portraying the three-dimensional nature of all building objects and keeping better track of competing locations for ductwork, wiring, and plumbing. They also make it easy to generate lists of materials in buildings, which in turn help with accurate cost estimating.

"Outline specifications" are summaries of the types of construction materials or products proposed and their quality. Not all bricks are equal so it is important to tell the estimators and contractors which ones you want. This happens in the specifications. They may be as short as two or three pages for a relatively small project. They are important because the cost of buildings depends heavily on materials. If you've been thinking of a limestone exterior and the architect is thinking of precast concrete (concrete imitations of stone) or even EIFS (external insulation finishing systems—basically a skim coat of mortar over Styrofoam), you need to know this right away.

Cost estimating is vital at every stage of a design project and should become more accurate at the end of each stage—schematic design, design development, and construction documents. When you are researching possible architectural firms to hire, their track records in cost estimating are of serious importance.

Some designers will attempt to present schematic designs without furniture placement. Because libraries consist of a lot of big, open spaces with furniture, schematic designs without furnishing are worthless.

In the trade, schematic design is often referred to as "SD," as in "We're in SD right now."

Some architects contend that furniture layouts are part of design development rather than schematic design, and your agreement with your architects must make clear that furniture layout is part of schematic design. Without furniture layouts, a schematic design for the public areas of a library can be basically a big, empty rectangle. You will have no idea of how book stacks and seating and workstations and service desks fit into the space, or even *if* they fit into the space.

Some architects propose oddly shaped spaces that actually have the right square footage but won't hold the furnishings listed in your program. By insisting that the schematic design include all furnishings, you will protect yourself from embarrassing news later.

The understanding that furniture layout is included in schematic design should be made clear in your written contract.

When you are dealing with architects, watch carefully that required furnishings are not altered in the schematic design. Rectangular tables must not be converted to square or (even worse) round tables. Tables with chairs on two sides must not be converted to tables of the same size with chairs on four sides. Double-faced shelving units must not be converted to single-faced units. Square footages must not be altered without discussion involving owners, architects, and consultants.

> Fred has experienced all of these problems repeatedly during the schematic design phases of various building projects.

Architects will want to know at the schematic design stage whether you plan to seek a LEED rating for your library, since that has implications for building design and costs. (LEED stands for Leadership in Energy and Environmental Design.)

178 | PART II: FROM OVERCROWDING TO RIBBON CUTTING

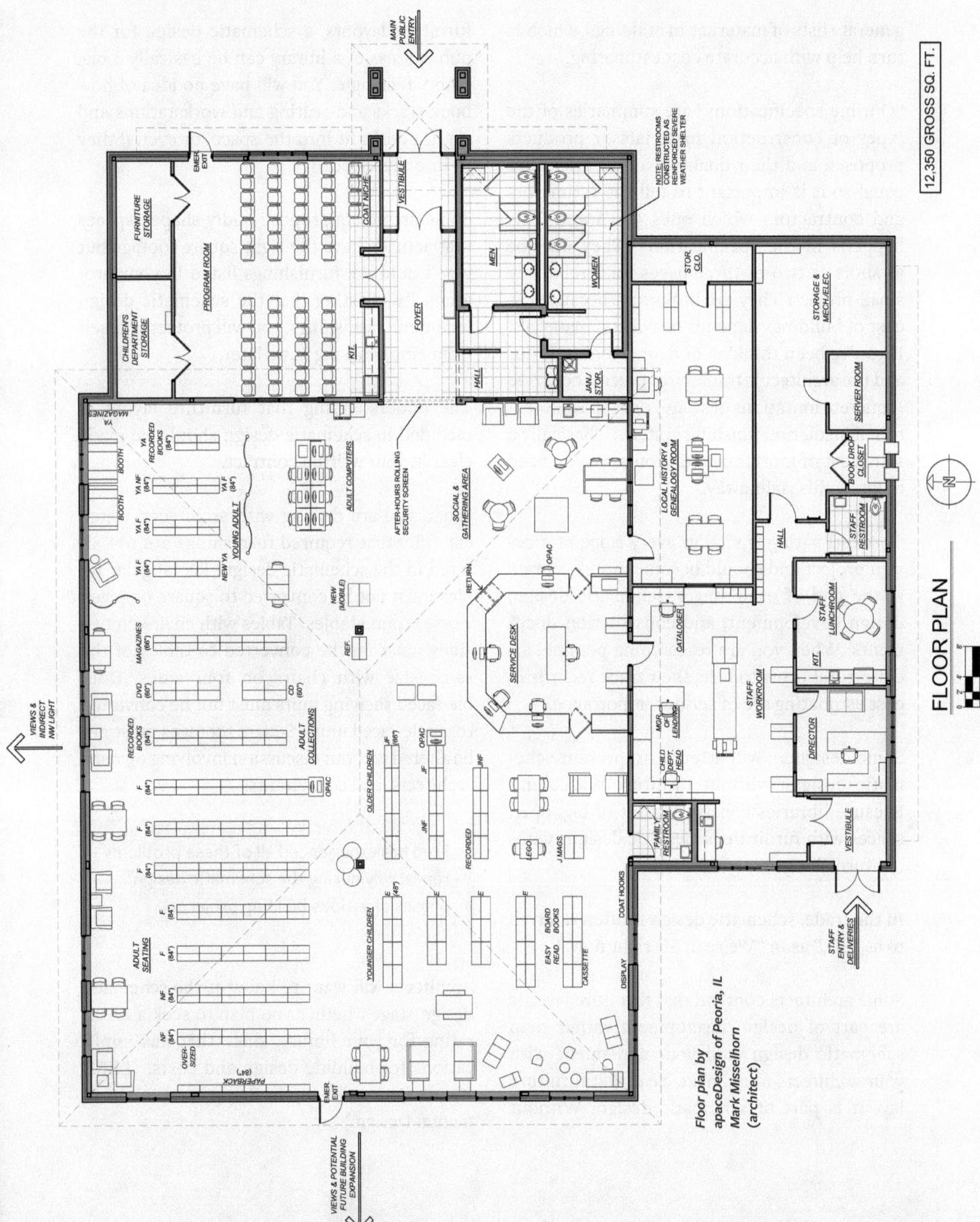

Floor plan by apaceDesign of Peoria, IL
Mark Misselhorn (architect)

This floor plan for the Allerton District Library (Monticello, Illinois) illustrates many basic principles of functional library design. The 12,350-square-foot building was designed by Mark Misselhorn (architect) and Julie Coogan (interior designer) of apaceDesign in Peoria, Illinois, and completed in 2016. Fred wrote the building program. The design principles illustrated here apply to libraries in a wide range of sizes.

General Features
- The building consists entirely of rectangular spaces. Triangular and curved spaces are much more expensive to construct and much harder to use effectively.
- The building faces east, sheltering library users and staff from the prevailing winter winds in the Midwest, which come from the north and west.
- The library building is designed for easy expansion to the west by knocking out a single wall.
- The opening between the foyer and the main library room can be closed by a security screen, allowing the program room and restrooms to be used when the rest of the building is closed.
- Because the site is sufficiently large, the building could be constructed on a single level, significantly reducing long-term staffing costs (which are about two-thirds the cost of library operations) and eliminating the very substantial construction cost of staircases, an elevator, and an upper floor strong enough to bear the weight of books.
- The building has no basement, eliminating the high cost of constructing a main floor with a basement below it, eliminating the cost of construction of staircases (and perhaps an elevator), and eliminating the problem of flooded basements.
- The drive-up book drops lead into a room designed to contain fires. (Incendiaries in book returns have caused fires in libraries.)
- The library has a large number of wall and floor outlets (which don't show on the plan, but are vital) and security gates are roughed in for possible later installation.

Program Room
- The program room includes storerooms for furniture and for program supplies. (The functionality of program rooms in many libraries is reduced by the inability to store furniture and program equipment out of the way when it is not in use. Program rooms without adequate storage closets end up with stacks of unused furniture and equipment piled around the edges.)

Main Library Room
- The main library room is a simple rectangle, maximizing flexibility of use.
- The north wall of the library has a large number of windows that provide low-glare north light for reading. The furniture arrangement places readers (who like light) close to windows and books (which don't like light) away from windows.
- The main library room is extremely flexible in design. All of the shelving and seating and computers can be relocated. This is particularly easy because there are only two support columns to get in the way. (It doesn't show in the drawing, but the room also has large numbers of electrical outlets, which are essential for flexibility in modern libraries.)
- The single service desk is immediately visible to users entering the main library room. In turn, library staff at the desk have direct oversight of the main library room, the entry foyer, the local history room, and the entrances to the restrooms and meeting room.
- The connection between the main library room and staff work areas is at the back of the service desk, discouraging library users from wandering in.
- The service desk has two access points, making it difficult for staff members to be cornered behind the desk.
- A public photocopier is located at the entrance to the main library room, making it unnecessary for people who stop by the library just to make photocopies to walk through the rest of the library.
- Public computers are close to the service desk for ease of staff supervision and assistance.
- In accordance with good seating practices, round tables are provided only for socializing, while chairs at rectangular tables are on two sides of the tables only.
- Soft seating includes easy chairs for adults and a mixture of easy chairs and loveseats for children and their parents or caregivers. (Parents and children like reading together on loveseats. Adult readers on the other hand don't like sharing soft seating, and sofas therefore tend to be used either

by single readers or used for sleeping and necking.)

- Shelving aisles are a maximum of 21 feet long, making it easy for a user to approach an aisle from the opposite end when another user is blocking the aisle.
- The open design of the room leaves no place where users can be cornered. None of the shelving aisles have dead ends.
- The young adult area is as far as possible from the children's area, a feature young adults strongly prefer. It is also easy for adults to use the YA area, since many adults make heavy use of YA materials.
- The social area is between the service desk and the entrance to the main library room, keeping social conversations away from reading areas.

Restrooms
- The two restrooms are designed to serve as storm shelters, which is particularly important in one-story buildings without sturdy second floors that protect people on first floors below. (The unusual thickness of the restroom walls indicates concrete construction. The ceilings of the restrooms are concrete slabs.) The only rooms that provide good storm shelters are restrooms because they are never used as storerooms. And they can be built without windows, avoiding flying glass shards when storms hit.
- The open space in the wall between the restrooms provides space for brackets supporting wall-mounted toilets. Wall-mounted toilets make restroom cleaning easier because they eliminate the unsanitary joints between toilets and floors.
- The restrooms are laid out so that there are no unwanted sight lines between the access hall and the interiors of the two restrooms.
- Restroom doors swing outward, eliminating the problem users face when trying to open doors as they leave restrooms with freshly-washed hands.
- The mop basin (required by building codes) is located as close as possible to the restrooms.
- The library has a staff restroom. No matter what outsiders think, all but the tiniest libraries need staff restrooms. (Ask any experienced librarian.)
- A "family rest room" is located by the children's area. Restrooms of this type are useful for situations where a person of one gender is assisting a person of a different gender, including parents with children and elderly couples.
- The library's eight sinks are concentrated in a relatively compact area of the building, which simplifies plumbing.

By the end of the schematic design phase, the owner should have received the following "deliverables":

- Site plans.
- Floor plans (with furniture layouts, which are absolutely essential).
- Elevations (drawings of the building's exterior seen squarely from each side).
- Cross sections if needed to clarify the proposed structure of the building.
- Outline specifications. (This means a description of the major systems materials and quality standards anticipated for the project. Systems include such items as structure type, MEP, and enclosure—walls, windows, roofs, and so on.)
- A preliminary cost estimate. It's important that costs be project costs, not just the much lower construction costs. Project costs will include such items as furnishings, site work, fees, contingencies, and escalation (estimated inflation in costs by the time the project is bid).

With all this in hand, owners have enough information to raise money. They can show donors or voters what the building will look like and be able to tell them what it is likely to cost.

At this point, many owners temporarily stop architectural service until fundraising is complete.

III-B. ESTIMATING

Accurate cost estimating can make the difference between joyous and miserable construction.

By the time bidding takes place, you will have found your site, presented your plans to your public, lined up your funding, completed your construction documents, and be ready to go. If your low bid is triple your estimate, there is no way that omitting some add alternates will fix things. You will then be faced with returning to your funding source, completely redesigning your library, or some other desperate measure. If donors find out that their gifts will purchase only a third of what they were promised, they may decide to skip the whole thing. If you have government grants, you may find yourself trapped in situations where you are required to start construction by a specific date or lose the grants.

Total screw-ups in estimating don't often happen, but even minor screw-ups can lead to major problems. (Buildings that cost three times the estimated amount sound impossible, but it happened to a library Fred knows.)

Because of the critical importance of estimating, many architects use separate estimating firms or rely on construction management firms for help. Estimating firms have a reputation for being hard-nosed rather than optimistically hopeful that things won't be too expensive, and that's a good reason to use them.

As we've mentioned in other places in this book, it's vital that everyone agrees on what "budget" means. Actual construction is only one part of the cost of building a new library. *Be sure everyone agrees that all budget numbers discussed will be for a "project budget" or "comprehensive budget," including not only construction but all the other inevitable costs, including site work, permits, furnishings, professional fees, contingencies, utility connections, moving, and so on.* If the project won't start in the near future, budgets need to provide for escalation—expected inflation in costs. Construction costs alone may be interesting to know in an abstract sort of way, but they aren't helpful in planning.

As an unusually competent architect friend of Fred's says, "Estimate early and estimate often."

III-C. ASSISTANCE WITH FUNDRAISING

Many architects are skilled in helping clients make presentations to donors or to voters.

Architects are very aware that buildings can't be constructed without funds, and that their incomes and reputations depend on the completion of projects. Having a resume consisting only of schematic designs for structures that were never built does not indicate a successful architectural firm.

- Renderings. Many architects will prepare renderings, which are pretty pictures of completed buildings. These are vital for elections and donors because relatively few people can look at architectural drawings and visualize the resulting structure. Even owners who work extensively with architects may be surprised by the way things actually look.

  Preparing renderings used to be a job for highly skilled artists who could see in their minds' eyes how completed buildings would look, but the coming of computer-aided drawing and design changed all of that, and modern design systems can easily show you how buildings will look from a wide variety of angles of view and perspectives.

  One of the downsides of computer-generated renderings is that they can look very mechanical and even stilted. But they have the advantage of costing relatively little extra. Computerized drawing programs can even provide people, automobiles, landscaping, flagpoles, blue skies with white clouds, and other persuasive details.

Many architectural firms will use computers to generate drawings with the proper perspective and then redo them in a more artistic medium, occasionally with hand-drawn lines and soft watercolors rather than hard computer colors and increasingly using software programs designed for illustration rather than construction. This used to be expensive, but it is increasingly affordable, and the artistic images can provide a better understanding of what the completed project will look like. And they can exert a powerful appeal that old-school computer-generated images cannot.

One of the major criticisms of renderings is their tendency to lie attractively. The used car lot next to the library site is magically transformed to virgin woodland. The ungainly HVAC penthouse on the roof of the library conveniently vanishes. If the front of the library will actually be butted against the curb, the rendering may include an elegant but imaginary expanse of green lawn between the library and the street.

> These are common misrepresentations in renderings, all drawn from Fred's consulting experience. In the case of the green lawn, the architect angrily insisted it would be there when the building was finished. But it wasn't.

The problem with misrepresentation in renderings is that people may call you on them. You hope this happens only after the building is completed, but it's embarrassing to be caught lying when a tax referendum is just around the corner.

A similar problem occurs because most completed library buildings do not match the renderings exactly. Since renderings will usually be prepared at the end of the schematic design phase, the actual buildings are likely to be somewhat different. However, this seems to be a much less severe problem than deliberate misrepresentation. The most common reason for mismatched renderings and buildings is probably lack of time invested in schematic design.

Because renderings are never exactly like the finished buildings, some people argue they should be vague. But users need to see what they'll get.

- The power of renderings is impressive. People who look at floor plans and elevation drawings may say, "Very nice," in a controlled sort of way. But when shown the same thing in perspective as a rendering, they cry, "That's what we want!"

- Models. Many library construction projects, particularly those that require fundraising or referendums or competitions, also include physical models.

Architectural models can be lovely objects and persuasive when it comes to convincing people that their money will be well spent on the new library. Some models even have lift-off roofs to allow people to see the interiors of buildings.

In design competitions, models are of critical importance, and they may be required as elements of submissions.

Models are sometimes displayed in libraries at times leading up to referendums. Others migrate about like garden gnomes, sitting in windows of local businesses, attending PTA meetings, and so on.

Architectural models are impressively expensive. A simple model of a small library may cost as little as $5,000, but a large model of a major structure may cost $50,000 or more. Many models are displayed in custom-made enclosures of heavy transparent plastic.

Simple models can be built in architectural offices, but large models are often built by firms that specialize in architectural models.

Even transporting large architectural models is difficult. We hear of them being transported in vans or occupying a couple of first-class seats in airplanes.

Once the building is constructed, the owners have to decide what to do with the models. Many of them kick around library administrative workrooms, protected by their original transparent plastic boxes. Others—particularly those from design competitions—end up on permanent display. Because models are extremely expensive, no one wants to chuck them out. (And most are too stylized to serve as scenery on model railroad layouts.)

Make sure your contracts with your architects specify who owns the models when the project is completed.

- Participation in public meetings. Architects are often gifted at making public presentations. This is particularly true of those architects who specialize in representing architectural firms at job interviews. Having your architect attend public meetings can add a strong dimension to your presentation, as can having your consultant present. In fact, having your consultant first describe your needs at a meeting, and then having your architects show the proposed building and explain how it will enable the library to meet its needs, can make an effective presentation.

Always find out in advance what your architects and consultants will charge you for attending meetings of this type.

- Responding to questions from the media. Dealing with the media requires spokespeople who are knowledgeable and not given to off-the-cuff responses. Your library will want to designate a small number of people who respond to media questions and tell other participants that all questions will be handled by this group.

Architects often deal effectively with reporters because the information they have does not have to be filtered through the owners of the building. Some sort of established media plan should be in place before your architect goes rogue in front of a camera or microphone.

And, as mentioned repeatedly in this book, architects can explain why beloved ideas of some local people won't work, secure in the knowledge that the architects do not live in town and won't have to confront angry faces at the next Rotary meeting.

IV. Design Development

The second phase of architectural work as specified in AIA contract documents is design development.

From the point of view of the community, this is a far less exciting time than schematic design, because most decisions about room arrangement and exterior appearance have already been made.

In design development, a wide range of technical refinements are made. What kind of physical structure will the library have? How will the HVAC system work? How will the building be lighted? What provisions will be made for electrical power? How will foundation problems be dealt with? And on and on.

If schematic design is typically only about 15 percent of total architectural services, design development is 20 percent. Some architectural firms will sometimes skip design development and move from schematic design straight to construction drawings. Don't put up with this, and don't put up with a firm that wants to do it. (If they're doing it because you're paying them badly, shame on you and the firm.)

Even if the questions raised for design development may not excite the outside world, from the owners' point of view they are of major importance, and you should expect to be deeply involved in the planning that moves your project through design development. It is here that functional or dysfunctional lighting can be selected. Electrical outlets can be plentiful, or they can be so few that users will be tripping over laptop cords everywhere. The floors can be solid, or they can bounce underfoot because of HVAC plenums beneath. West-facing windows may have perforated vinyl blinds, or they may have partial fritting (patterns of printed dots) that results in spotty but blinding glare.

If your building program is a complete one, it should have some information on what technical solutions are of particular importance to libraries, but vast areas of decision-making will be left to the architects and their engineers to develop and make recommendations.

Librarians should approve design development documents, just as they approve schematic designs. You can also involve your programmers.

Just as schematic design is often referred to as "SD," design development is called "DD."

V. Contract Documents

Construction documents are used by contractors both for preparing bids for constructing your building and for actually constructing the building. The documents typically include both a set of drawings and a book of specifications.

Construction drawings are grouped by the area of construction they represent. Some groups of sheets may be prepared by engineers or other specialists, rather than by your architects. Individual drawings are often identified first by the series (such as A for architectural, M for mechanical, and so on) and second by the number in the series.

Typically, a set of drawings might include:

- ***A cover sheet***, identifying the library and listing all the drawings that comprise the complete set.

- ***Site plans***, showing how the library building will occupy its site; how the site drains; how utility connections are made; where paving, landscaping, and site signage are placed; and how the design conforms with zoning ordinances. There should also be a clear indication of expansion plans, indicating areas reserved for intended growth of the building, parking, and other site features.

- ***Demolition plans***.

- ***Structural drawings***, including foundation plans, floor framing plans, reinforcing schedules, and details.

- ***Architectural drawings***, including code compliance plans, floor plans, reflected ceiling plans, roof plans, exterior elevations, building sections, interior elevations, enlarged floor plans and sections at stairs and elevators, floor finish plans, equipment plans, door and hardware schedules, construction details, and so on.

- *Plumbing drawings*, showing the details of installation of supply, waste, and venting piping (for each floor and under the floor of the lowest level) fixtures, diagrams of piping, and so on.
- *Sprinkler system drawings*. (Fire suppression sprinkler systems are typically specified separately and installed by specialist contractors.)
- *HVAC drawings*, showing the location and sizes of HVAC ductwork, heating and cooling equipment, sensors, and so on.
- *Electrical drawings*, including lighting, switching, power distribution, communications, fire alarms, and so on.
- *Furniture layouts* should be included for informative purposes to remind everyone where things will go, even though furnishings will be bid separately. (These are left out of some sets of construction drawings, making the drawings far harder to interpret.)

For remodeling work, there will also be:

- *Drawings of the existing building.* This is an area where rushed work by architects can lead to problems if they use surviving original plans that may not represent what was actually built or what has been changed since the building was new. If you do not have current drawings of actual conditions, it is well worth the money to have the building surveyed and drawn. This is typically not part of the basic services fee.
- *Demolition drawings*, showing which existing parts of the building need to be removed during the construction process.

Remodeling is amazingly complex, and it's reasonable for your architects to charge a higher percentage of construction costs for remodeling than for new construction.

Although construction drawings do not typically include furniture placement drawings, it's a very good thing to specify that a sheet showing furniture placement be part of the construction drawing set. Because libraries frequently consist of large open spaces, knowing how the furniture will fit is vital. (Such drawings will be marked as for information only, since your construction firm will generally not supply your furniture.)

Preparation of construction documents is an immense job because nothing can be left vague or uncertain. If your library is requesting competitive bids, each prospective bidder must sift through the drawings and specifications, asking how the building can be built for the least possible cost while still meeting specifications. If there is a nice feature you want, but it's not in the drawings or specifications, you won't get it.

Because of the amount of labor involved, construction drawings are assumed to be 35 to 40 percent of the entire cost of architectural services.

Much of a bid set or construction set is not drawings. Specifications, contained in a "project manual," are verbal instruction on material selection, installation processes, and quality assurance standards. Assembling the specifications should involve as much participation by the library as the construction drawings.

All planned items of manufactured equipment, such as light fixtures, plumbing fixtures, and so on, will be illustrated with catalog pages called "cut sheets." Insist on seeing all of these before the products are included in your bid documents.

Often the specifications will include two or three acceptable brand names and model numbers for each item required. This promotes competition, which helps to control prices. The acceptable models, however, should not lead to sacrifice of performance or durability. If different items are proposed, be sure you receive and approve cut sheets.

State or local laws may require that the owners accept alternative equivalent products in addition to those specified. Be sure to require that any substitution of equipment proposed by the bidder or contractor include provision of new cut sheets for your approval. The burden of proof in establishing equivalence is on the contractor.

The bid documents will include a section on "substitutions" that lists the evaluation criteria that contractors must address when requesting approval an alternate product. Criteria can include size, shape, power requirements, output, control, fit with other products and systems, compliance with codes, national standards, minimum performance criteria established by the drawings and specifications, access, ease of maintenance, availability of qualified repair services, aesthetics (available standard colors being the most common), durability, and cost.

In the case of furnishings, there are additional performance criteria such as comfort, ergonomics, and adjustability.

Including a list of evaluation criteria helps the contractor prepare the request, the architect review the request, and the owner consider the architect's recommendation. You can see a lot of factors are considered in selecting the acceptable products, and any request to substitute something else needs to be taken seriously by all parties.

Serious problems can result when a contractor talks the owners or architects into using an inferior product, claiming it is an "equivalent." Most often the primary motivations for a substitution request are availability and cost. Occasionally the supply chain does break down, and none of the acceptable products listed in the specification will be available in time to keep construction moving. Sometimes this is due to poor scheduling by the contractor, but at other times it is more of a manufacturing issue. Each reason is considered differently when evaluated by the design team.

Many times a substitution request is based on the cost of a product, with the contractor hoping to increase the profit margin on the project. If there is a cost saving to be had, and the product is truly equivalent, by all means take the alternative but insist that the savings be passed along to the owner.

Be sure that your library building consultants (programmers) see all the construction documents and let you know if they see any potential problems. Let your architects know that you want your consultants to see the drawings, and insist that your architects leave enough time for this to take place. Occasionally, your architects may contend that there is "no time" for your consultants to review drawings, and you will need to refer your architects to your prior agreements.

The next steps in your project and your use of the building for decades to come depends on the quality of your construction documents. Thorough review is essential.

VI. Snappy Rules on Design

1. Some architects have a brilliant ability to mentally envision complex structures in three dimensions. Watching them work is fun.

2. You can have a comfortable and functional library. You can have a library designed by a world-famous architect. But you can't have both.

3. Communication is the soul of architectural planning. Always speak up.

4. Of all architectural words of tongue or pen, "We will reinvent the library" are among the most terrifying.

5. Good librarians can be seriously annoying to architects who start off with little intention of listening to them.

6. You have a right to understand what's going on. Although mansplaining is passé, even a remark like "Don't worry your little head about it" is totally unacceptable.

7. Saying "I'm sorry I don't understand these things, so you'll have to explain to me why we need to have this in words I understand" is a great technique.

8. Always beware if the first drawing you see is a completed drawing rather than a few conceptual sketches. Rushing things this way may save your architect time, but it does you no favors.

9. If your architects refuse to answer your questions about their designs, you have a serious problem.

10. Be careful when your library is a small element in a large building. Be particularly careful and wary and aggressive when your owners and architects meet to discuss the library without the librarians present.

11. Be sure that decisions made in meetings are reflected in plans. Take your own minutes in meetings and have everyone sign off on them.

12. If you see a building that has some seriously awful concepts, the fault may lie entirely with the client rather than with the architects. Find out before you jump to conclusions.

13. You will often see architectural awards hanging in the offices of architects. None of the awards were given for outstandingly functional buildings.

14. Charettes are fun, but they can lead to serious rushing to judgment.

15. Sometimes the word "concept" should bring terror to your heart.

16. Clarify contractually what will happen if your lowest bid is significantly higher than your architects' estimate.

17. Clarify contractually that all color schemes, signage choices, and similar aesthetic decisions are your library's business. Your designers provide suggestions, not orders.

18. Complete honesty in renderings is of mixed value. Sometimes it's better to leave off the HVAC penthouse.

19. One way to design a library building is to lay out all the needed spaces and then

wrap an attractive exterior around them. Another way is to design an attractive exterior and cram all the spaces into it. The latter approach was invented by Procrustes, and you will not enjoy the results.

20. When your designers talk about "modern glass," ask to see an existing installation. Too many new libraries have had to replace their windows or cover them with dark gray film.

21. Soaring spaces with monumental staircases provide a few moments of "wow," followed by endless years of problems with heating, lighting, maintenance, acoustics, getting from point A to point B, and unusable but expensive space. Say "no" early and often.

22. Make sure that your library staff have enough free time to work on the project. Even if your director's responsibilities can be handed off to other staff members, those staff members may need to pass things off in turn. At the end of the handing-off chain you'll need more staff hours somewhere.

23. Don't pressure your architects to do something illegal. (Unfortunately, it happens.)

24. Schematic designs without furniture placement are worthless, particularly in libraries, which are basically large open spaces. Make sure that your contract with your architects specifies that your schematic design will include furnishings.

25. If your program calls for rectangular four-person tables but your architects' schematic design converts them to round four-person tables or square four-person tables, you have a very serious problem, probably involving trying to cram too much furniture into too little space. Shout "Stop that!" immediately.

26. If your architects have to labor mightily to talk you into their design concept, it may be because it's a crummy concept. Ask people who have worked in library buildings, such as the library building consultant who wrote your building program.

27. If your architects infuriate you on a regular basis, tell your colleagues. That's one of the great strengths of the social networks of professional librarians.

28. When you have planning meetings with your architects, always have your own expert on library buildings in the room.

29. Working with your architects to list words that will define your project is fun, but don't engrave them on your building.

30. Beware of designers who spend all of their time on the exterior of your library and just dump the contents in at random.

31. Just because you can manage to build some kind of library with your limited funds doesn't mean it's a good idea.

32. Once people try to talk you into what you think is a bad design idea, start by visiting a library that has one. If no library has one, consider not letting your library be the innocent victim of ill-considered experimentation.

PART II
From Overcrowding to Ribbon Cutting

CHAPTER 11

Accessibility

I. Introduction

Far too many library buildings pose unnecessary difficulties for their users and staff.

Some of these are the result of people coping with traditional disability issues, but many issues that affect many people are simply ignored or swept aside in the interest of artistic design or minor cost savings.

The most significant approaches to coping with disabilities have been through building codes. For example, the Americans with Disabilities Act (ADA) of 1990 provides a wide range of requirements for the access and safety of people using buildings, and these have resulted in significant improvements in building design. And building codes in general provide many requirements for building safety.

But there are a wide range of other design issues that are still not covered by codes and make it difficult for many library users and staff members to spend time in library buildings.

One of the problems with codes is that many are not retroactive. In many cases, as long as alterations to a building are below a certain minimum, buildings do not need to be brought up to current codes.

In general, too many library buildings:

- Are too old and too small and lack modern equipment. Hundred-year-old library buildings are likely to be inaccessible simply because they are technically out of date. The only people at fault are those who have failed to spend any money during the past century. (Before committing to spending any money today, see chapter 17, "Converting Non-library Buildings to Public Libraries." And always bring in an architect, an engineer, and a building consultant.)

- Never change to meet accessibility requirements because they are exempted pending major reconstruction. (But a few buildings constructed long after the passage of the ADA have even blithely ignored requirements.)

189

- Are difficult for use by people with wheelchairs, walkers, canes, baby carriages, strollers, book trucks, or any other equipment designed for use on flat surfaces, in addition to people simply with bad senses of balance or muscular problems climbing.
- Include totally unnecessary barriers to movement through buildings, such as reading or shelving areas constructed on slopes.
- Are inaccessible because they are overcrowded. If there is not enough space to even maintain the minimal legal 32-inch spaces between furnishings, a library is too small.
- Have inaccessible furniture. For example, tables with deep aprons may be historic, but if a user in a wheelchair cannot pull up to a table, the library needs a different table.
- Include surfaces that can lead to falls and injuries, such as floors that are unusually slippery or have irregularities that lead to tripping.
- Have unnecessarily upsetting carpet patterns. Some carpets and carpet squares have such extreme patterns that many users are bothered by them.
- Use cheap and inadequate substitutes for real elevators.
- Terrify users with acrophobia, who find some library buildings almost impossible to use. (At least one American library with a monumental atrium has even successfully enabled—if not actually encouraged—several suicides.)
- Disorient people with vertigo.
- Have lighting that is either too dim or too harsh for comfortable use by people with even mildly limited vision. Bright, low-glare lighting is easy to install, but some people fight it. Or simply ignore the problem.
- Have light fixtures selected on the basis of how they look rather than how they work.
- Make it unnecessarily difficult for people with limited vision to climb stairs—or even to walk safely.
- Have unpleasant acoustics that make it difficult for library users who are bothered by noises to spend time in buildings.
- Fail to provide the physically cozy and friendly environments that library users and staff members need.

This chapter discusses the nature of frequently encountered accessibility problems and what libraries can do to prevent them. Unfortunately, once users are driven away by inaccessible library buildings, libraries may have to make unusual efforts to let them know that things have changed.

Correcting problems after the fact is sometimes possible, but by far the best and most cost-effective way to make buildings accessible is to head bad ideas off at the pass. For this reason, suggestions by owners and designers that "We can deal with that later" are usually completely wrong.

Much of the protection of library users and staff with disabilities falls on librarians, who may be the only people who work with disabled users on a regular basis. Because many disabilities not covered by the ADA (and other building codes) are occasionally ignored by owners and designers, the input of librarians is vital. Sometimes, the only way to construct a workable library is to have the staff make enemies of the owners and designers.

Other chapters with material relevant to disabilities in libraries include chapter 13, "Building Codes"; chapter 16, "Remodeling and Expanding Library Buildings"; chapter 17, "Converting Non-Library Buildings to Public Libraries"; chapter 21, "User Seating"; chapter 26, "Restrooms"; chapter 30, "Elevators, Staircases, Railings, and Ramps"; chapter 31, "Lighting"; chapter 33, "HVAC"; and chapter 35, "Security."

II. The Americans with Disabilities Act

When the ADA was passed in 1990, many libraries panicked, concerned that they could never afford to provide the specified features. As buildings are constructed or remodeled, they are usually brought up to codes, but many libraries still remain unchanged and inaccessible.

One of the great advantages of features required by the ADA and state accessibility codes is that they tend to benefit all library users and staff. For example:

- The wider stack aisles needed for wheelchair access also provide better space to read book labels, especially on bottom shelves, and for people with stiff joints to stoop down.
- Minimum clearances of 32 inches are helpful to all library users.
- Railings of the right diameter to be gripped tightly are great for all users, even those without diminished senses of balance or weak knees. (Many pre-ADA library buildings have strangely massive handrails that are nearly impossible to grab.)
- Protective railings under floating staircases protect not only people with limited eyesight but pretty much all those who wander under staircases, only to find their heads creased. (Some floating staircases in libraries have even had sharp-edged balusters that hung down below their lower edges like icicles, occasionally tearing open the scalps of passers-under.)
- Bat handles on washbasins, which enable users to shut off faucets with their closed fists, also make it unnecessary for users to place their freshly washed fingertips on dirty handles.
- The use of levers rather knobs for door handles also makes it possible for all users to avoid grasping dirty knobs with their fingertips. People who have just washed their hands in the restroom don't want to be forced to grab door handles used all day long by people who never wash their hands.
- Some stall doors in otherwise accessible restrooms have tiny latches that are hard for some users to handle.
- Old, inaccessible tables are unpleasant for all users, not just for people in wheelchairs.
- A great many users who may not be technically disabled still benefit greatly from elevators. (Ramps are better than nothing, although often only slightly better.) While a relatively small proportion of library users and staff members may use wheelchairs, large numbers use walkers, canes, strollers, baby carriages, and book carts. And even more are just unsteady on their feet or find climbing stairs hard work.
- Requirements that limit the degree to which objects can protrude from walls protect not only vision-impaired people but also many sighted people and running children.
- Doors that open at the push of a button help many people who are struggling with

armloads of books, or who simply have trouble with massive doors.

Even while following the ADA, however, some buildings are only marginally accessible.

- Buildings sometimes have ramps where elevators are really needed, particularly for access to historic buildings where no floors are at grade level. Unfortunately, ramps can be a real pain. With a maximum slope of 1:12, a ramp that deals with more than a foot or so of rise or fall can present a real challenge to some library users. Exterior ramps in the winter can be almost totally unusable, and they can be miserable to use during rain.

  Far too many library buildings have nasty exterior ramps, perhaps because locating the ramps indoors will cost far more money (although still less than an elevator). To be decent to library users and staff, an entrance ramp needs to be indoors and a minimum of seven feet wide to enable people to pass in opposite directions.

  Historic buildings that are worth preserving require the expense of elevators. Often this means two elevators—one to lift people from street level to the main floor of the library and security gates, and the second to move people between floors after they have passed through security.

- Sometimes elevators are hidden away. Occasionally this appears to be due to the desires of owners or designers to have everyone climb dramatic but terrifying staircases.

- Some staircases represent amazing tripping hazards. (The ADA provides some standards for staircases, but many building codes include detailed requirements as well. It's a complicated issue.)

- Shelving heights specified in accessibility codes are a compromise. Some specify accessible heights only for reference books and current magazines. Making all shelves wheelchair accessible would benefit most users but would probably come close to doubling the square footage of library stacks.

- Some users who have both manual and motorized wheelchairs find that distances to the stacks are too great for manual chairs, but that motorized chairs are too big to fit into the stacks once they finally get there.

- Stack aisles with widths that barely meet minimum codes don't work. They're hard to bring off successfully, since a library aiming for aisles of a minimum required 36-inch width will end up with some stack aisles that are 36½ inches wide and others that are 35½ inches wide—and technically illegal.

  Even with totally legal spacing, minimum width stack aisles can sometimes be made illegal by books that stick out slightly into aisles. This can be a particular problem in libraries with very shallow shelves. (Any shelving unit with shelves shallower than 10 over 12 inches is probably a serious mistake. See chapter 22, "Collection Storage and Display.")

  The minimum workable aisle width when codes say 36 inches is probably something like 38 inches. But 42 or 48 inches is a lot better.

  Providing aisles where people headed in opposite directions can pass each other comfortably takes substantially more width. The best solution is probably to be sure you have frequent cross aisles.

- Because accessible stalls in restrooms are large, some libraries save space by making all the other stalls uncomfortably small. Some library owners worry about the large amount of space restrooms can take up, but that's just the price of accessibility. (Similarly, buildings are notorious for saving space by not providing a sufficient number of stalls in women's restrooms, particularly adjacent to concert halls, sports arenas, and meeting rooms, where women are sometimes forced to stand in long lines during intermissions.)

Any stall where the door nearly scrapes the front edge of the toilet is a disaster.

- Locating baby changing tables in accessible restroom stalls leads to problems. Since most restrooms have only one accessible stall, someone taking a long time to change a baby can cause serious problems for disabled users kept waiting. And sometimes the changing tables even make access to the stalls difficult.

Only a couple of ADA requirements can be difficult for people not in wheelchairs:

- "Truncated domes" are raised bumps about an inch in diameter, installed at the edges of streets to warn blind people they are about to step out into traffic. Some people contend that these bumps are dangerous and may lead to tripping and to difficulties with moving wheelchairs and other wheeled equipment.
- Icy curb cuts. People on foot prefer to step down from sidewalks to streets rather than trying to keep their balance on icy slopes. Occasionally some libraries turn entire curbs into curb cuts, but most offer a choice.

There appear to be very few examples of new library buildings where the ADA is simply ignored. One in the news in recent years is the Hunters Point branch of the Queens Borough (New York) Public Library, which was completed in 2019 at a cost of more than $40 million and led to a great deal of uproar. Despite the importance of access and the long tradition of the ADA, the branch was designed with areas of public shelving accessible only by staircases, purely for reasons of cuteness. After the uproar, a spokesperson for the architects who designed the building said that the library would be "a new standard for libraries," and that the lack of accessibility was "an evolution" (*New York Times*, November 5, 2019, page A21).

Luckily, stories like this are very rare, but one wonders how architects and owners and librarians and engineers and building consultants and local code enforcement officials in Queens managed to ignore the issue when the library was being designed and construction permits issued.

III. Access for People with Limited Mobility

Despite their compliance with the ADA, some libraries are extremely difficult for people who use wheelchairs, walkers, and similar equipment. The most common problems appear to involve cheap substitutes for elevators.

The ADA permits ramps that meet designated standards, but many ramps are extraordinarily difficult for many users to use. Many of the worst offenders are exterior ramps leading to building entrances. While relatively few people may need to use a 12-foot ramp leading to a speaker's platform in a meeting room, everyone needs to get in and out of the building itself.

Many historic library buildings do not have grade-level entrances. The proper way to cope with this in a small building is to have an accessible entrance with an elevator that can lift users to the main floor of the library or lower people to the basement. Elevators of this type have doors on two sides, one that opens at grade level and the other that opens on the two or more inside floors.

All but small libraries not located at ground level require two elevators, one to carry people from the ground level to the main floor, and a second elevator to carry people between floors after they have passed through security.

Stories of amazingly unpleasant ramps and cheap elevator substitutes are everywhere. Good specifications in your written program or specifications might be:

- All entry ramps will be indoors and wide enough for users to pass each other in opposite directions.
- All elevators will be fully automatic rather than enclosed lifts.
- Stack end labels will tilt downward slightly so that users in wheelchairs aren't troubled by reflections.

By the time a library decides to construct the space large enough to install a seven-foot-wide indoor ramp, it may decide that an elevator is not as expensive as it feared.

One unfortunate result of the ADA was libraries adding poor-quality substitutes for actual elevators. Unfortunately, standard elevators are expensive due to the cost of the equipment, the difficulty of incorporating them into existing buildings, and the required maintenance and inspections. As a result, some libraries end up purchasing cheap (but seriously unpleasant) equipment.

Enclosed lifts of one sort or another and other elevator substitutes bring many problems.

For example, staff and users in libraries with various sorts of lifts complain about difficulties introduced by lifts accessed directly from outside of buildings rather than from lobbies or vestibules. If lifts are accessed directly from out of doors, the entry areas may be dangerously icy, and library staff lose much of their visual control over the building because they can't see people entering the lifts.

Many lifts have manual doors that are hard to operate, particularly by people who have disabilities.

Some librarians in buildings with cheap lifts report having to rush up and down stairs to assist users in and out of the lifts. If the only access to the grade-level entrance to the lift is out of doors, staff may end up dashing in and out of the building to help people. They may have to install doorbells so that people who cannot operate the lifts by themselves can call for assistance, and there are always circumstances where staff are away from the desk helping other patrons and don't hear the doorbells.

Some inexpensive lifts are barely large enough to hold single wheelchairs. If someone is accompanying a person in a wheelchair, the attendant may be forced to dash up and down stairs to be available for assistance when the lift arrives at another level of the library building.

If the lifts are not close to staircases, things can be even more difficult for people providing assistance. We've seen retrofitted lifts that were far from staircases, as awkward a situation as locating an elevator far from a grandiose central staircase.

A few libraries have installed the sort of chair lifts one might find riding on a rail along the staircase in a private home. With this kind of equipment, an assistant needs to help the wheelchair user into the lift, haul the wheelchair upstairs by hand, and then be waiting at the top when the user arrives at the top of the stairs. With heavy or motorized chairs, this may be completely impossible. For all of these reasons, chair lifts appear to be particularly ill-considered choices.

For many older libraries, the cost of transporting people between floors is clearly one of the major issues resulting from the ADA. The solution is to either add a genuine elevator or start over with a one-story building, not to introduce some sort of unpleasant makeshift device.

IV. Access for People with Limited Eyesight

Although the ADA makes some strong provisions for people who are blind, perhaps the major problem in providing accessible library service is the vast number of people who just have limited eyesight.

Taking care of people with weak or aging eyes is pretty straightforward, but many libraries seem to fight it all the way.

When we ask library users and staff what they need, they tell us they want bright, low-glare, reliable lighting. They want to be able to see in all areas of the library without having to hunt around for locations with adequate illumination, and they don't want to be blinded by direct sunlight. They don't want to look up only to be blinded by harsh, artificial lighting or skylights. They don't enjoy having lights suddenly go out while they are trying to read or use restrooms. They don't want to be forced to grope their way into dark rooms in order to turn on the lights. And they don't want to trip over things.

So some good basic rules are:

- Libraries need to have enough light to read by. Everywhere.

- Library users want light that enables them to read books held vertically as well as horizontally. Light that blasts straight down from above fails to do this, but it may make it easier for designers and engineers to achieve specified brightness levels.

- Libraries need even lighting from the top to the bottom shelf with no variation in light on the spines of books.

- Libraries need to avoid glare. Library users should never be blinded by ill-considered light. This includes both unwanted direct sunlight and harsh spotlights, such as so-called "recessed downlights." And some light fixtures give users unpleasant direct views of concentrated light sources, such as unshielded LEDs. Any area of a library where staff and users cannot look straight up or in any other direction without being blinded is a badly lighted area.

- Libraries need to avoid tripping hazards. It's amazing how many staircases seem particularly designed to make life unnecessarily difficult for people with limited eyesight or mobility.

Despite what some standards say, adequate light seems to call for about 60 foot-candles of even, low-glare, non-directional lighting on tabletops and on books held somewhat vertically. Stack lighting needs to provide about 20 foot-candles on book spines and 60 foot-candles for books held open horizontally.

Some people have argued that children's areas need less bright light because children have good eyesight, but this seems to ignore children with limited eyesight, as well as all the adults—parents, grandparents, library staff, and teachers—who work with children and tend to spend time in public library children's departments or in school libraries.

All artificial lighting needs to be uniform and low glare, but getting this in your library may involve battles with your owners and designers, who frequently want the excitement of dramatic (and correspondingly evil) lighting. An easy way to achieve low-glare lighting is to bounce most (or ideally all) of the light off the ceilings. In your written building program, ban such unpleasant devices as recessed downlights (can lights) and troffers (fixtures inset in the ceiling grid, leading to wide areas of dark ceilings interrupted by occasional bright rectangles of light). You can also ban fixtures with parabolic lenses, although the ill-considered vogue for them came and went a number of years ago.

Any user should be able to look straight upward anywhere in the library without being blinded by artificial light.

Daylight is wonderful in libraries, but designers have an unfortunate tendency to allow direct daylight to blind users, not to mention fade books. Direct glare is miserable in libraries, and unfortunately it exists in many buildings. It's easy to specify your needs:

- Absolutely no windows of any kind that face east, south, or west that do not have adjustable blinds. Windows like this are frequently cute, and you may have to battle to prevent them. But far too many libraries have had to retrofit dark film to windows like this at great expense, making one wonder why the designers provided the windows in the first place. And even when the windows have dark film, direct sunlight can still be too bright.

- Absolutely no monitors. (A monitor is a section of roof that is raised to allow glass on all four sides. Inevitably, direct sunlight streams through the east, west, and south sides of monitors and blinds the people below.)

- Absolutely no clearstory windows that do not face straight north. (A clearstory window is a window set vertically in a roof to bring skylight to the middle of a floor. Clearstories are great if they don't admit direct sunlight. And horrible if they do.)

- Absolutely no windows with etched areas designed to created interesting patterns on the floor when the windows are hit by direct sunlight. Although the patterns can indeed be created, being in a room when the patterns are created this way is a lot like looking directly into the beam of a high-wattage projector.

- Absolutely no skylights. Except artificial skylights. (Skylights can work well if they are roofed over and lighted artificially. Architects have also designed lower-glare skylights by using translucent materials and blocking a high percentage of the light.)

- Ceilings an absolute minimum of 10 feet high, providing enough vertical clearance to bounce light off the ceilings. Eleven or 12 feet works better. (You'll probably also need ten-foot or higher ceilings for proper clearance between shelving and fire sprinklers.)

- Absolutely no recessed downlights. Some people call them can lights. Looking up at a ceiling with recessed downlights is a little like staring at oncoming cars when the drivers forget to dim their headlights. When recessed downlights are combined with soffits, the result can be seriously evil.

- Absolutely no troffers in reading areas. "Troffers" are rectangular light fixtures in acoustic ceilings. A room lighted by troffers has a dark ceiling with occasional rectangles of light when it really needs an evenly lighted ceiling. But troffers are everywhere.

- No small-cell parabolic fixtures. Large-cell parabolic fixtures are better, but they're still far inferior to light bounced off ceilings. Luckily, small-cell parabolic lenses are out of fashion. For good reason.

- Light that is everywhere bright enough for people with somewhat compromised vision to read by, including books held nearly vertically.

- Lights with a color temperature of around 3000K to 3500K. (Higher numbers are not better. Lots of cheap fluorescents and LEDs have overly high color temperatures.)

- Lights with a CRI (color rendering index) of no less than 85. (Both fluorescent and LED lights can meet this requirement. If the packaging doesn't mention CRI, the manufacturers' websites should. Take a look at the wavelength distribution diagram for the light source you are considering, and if lots of wavelengths of visible light are simply missing, look for a better source.)

- Lighting fads. It's hard to write this section because every few years another lighting gimmick turns up. Most of them don't work well, but they leave a trail of dysfunctional gadgetry behind them.

Unfortunately, no matter how loudly you mention the need to avoid blinding light, your owners and architects may simply ignore you, assuming that you won't notice unwanted windows in the plans, or informing you that they have hired a lighting design firm that clearly knows more than a mere librarian (Fred has heard that on a number of occasions) or assuming they can override you by speaking directly to people who will not actually use the library.

Fred attended the grand opening of a public library where users were seated in a large reading room to listen to speakers. Many of the users had to hold their programs in front of their faces to shield themselves from blinding sunlight through high windows without blinds.

People who want to save energy often end up making buildings too dim. However, LED lighting is so efficient that this is not as great a problem as it was a few years ago.

Users and staff with limited eyesight can be spared problems in many ways in addition to providing sufficiently bright light:

- Make the lead edges of steps a different color, so that people with limited eyesight can see them. This is especially important for people headed downstairs, where the dangers resulting from tripping can be especially great. (This is more complex than just having risers and treads of different colors, since the different colored risers can't be seen by people walking downstairs.)

- Never have funny-shaped steps. Carnegie-era libraries were notorious for basement stairs with pie-shaped steps. Other libraries had curved staircases with impossibly tiny treads on the insides of the curves and uncomfortably deep treads on the outsides. Even today, a century or more later, people are tempted to make stairs that are more fun to look at than to use.

- Never have unexpected steps. Because of the ADA, these don't happen as often as they used to, but libraries in years gone by sometimes had silly things like steps in the middle of reading rooms, just to create visual interest, or unexpected steps a few feet past the ends of ramps.

- Never have unexpected holes in the floor, such as "reading pits." Ask the librarian who has fallen into one. Luckily, existing pits can be filled in.

- Never have glass partitions without decals at eye level for users of a variety of heights, to make sure that everyone sees the partition.

- Never allow the use of ramps merely to create architectural interest. Just because Frank Lloyd Wright used ramps in similar situations, this doesn't mean that they are A Good Thing.

- If you want book stack lighting to turn off automatically when users are not present, use pressure switches rather than motion sensors. Or failing that, use dual function sensors for two levels of lighting. The incredible annoyances people suffer due to motion sensors or timers for lighting are a standing joke, and libraries don't need to participate. Plunging people into unexpected darkness or forcing them to grope their way into dark rooms in order to turn on the lights are both nasty and dangerous designs, even if some code writers thought they were great energy-saving ideas.

- Use extra-legible lettering on directional signs and on stack end labels. Low-contrast lettering is not very legible, nor is lettering in artistic fonts, such as cursive. Patterned backgrounds on signs are a bad idea.

Remember also that shelf contents vary over the years, and permanent stack end labels become outmoded. (Never sign an agreement with your architects that allows them to dictate signage once the building has been completed.)

V. Access for People with Limited Hearing

Accessibility codes include important provisions for users who are deaf, including fire alarm units that include flashing lights and the provision of loop antennas for listening.

When we talk to library users and staff who are not deaf, the main complaints we hear about sound concern unwanted noise transmission. People complain about:

- Large openings between floors, including atria and grandiose staircases, both of which do an amazing job of funneling unwanted noise up and down.

- Cheap movable partitions, such as most meeting room dividers, which typically do a very bad job of blocking sound.

- Poorly designed study rooms, which frequently do a bad job of blocking sound transmission while simultaneously providing too much visual privacy, failing to meet both essential basic needs of study rooms at the same time. (Many study rooms also provide bad ventilation, sometimes to the point of having to be aired out between users, but this is not a hearing issue.)

- Ceilings without acoustic surfaces. Sloped ceilings and barrel vaults cause particular problems with unexpected sound transmission. Domed skylights can be amazingly noisy. (If you inherit a weird ceiling, you can add a spray-on acoustical surface, although that may do odd things to skylights.)

- Curved interior walls, lots of which function like the whispering gallery at St. Paul's. The acoustics in some small, round rooms remind one strongly of being inside an empty oil drum.
- Unusually noisy machinery that is not in separate rooms. (Some HVAC systems can be unpleasantly noisy. See chapter 33, "HVAC.")

All of these are easy to avoid.

Among basic solutions to existing acoustic problems are:

- Provide acoustic ceilings everywhere, including in particular all sloped and curved ceilings. (This is probably the most important recommendation.)
- Provide loop antennas, as specified in the ADA for meeting rooms. These are inexpensive and appear to work well, and they can be retrofitted.
- Install sound-absorbing surfaces on the back walls of meeting rooms. The usual idea is to speak from a live surface toward a dead surface.
- If meeting rooms have movable dividers, replace any that are not engineered to actually block sound.
- If the walls between study rooms fail to block sound, extend the walls from above the ceilings to the bottoms of the floors above.
- Provide supplementary sound-absorbing panels on the walls of historic library spaces with hard ceilings.

- Avoid round reading rooms if you are not a national library.
- Provide a certain amount of white noise.

When you are in doubt, there are excellent acoustic consulting engineers who can review your library's proposed plans and provide recommendations BEFORE the building is constructed. (Some libraries have hired their own acoustical engineers to review proposed designs.)

VI. Access for People with Acrophobia

Of all physical disabilities, the one most blithely ignored by library owners and designers is probably fear of heights. Even people who do not technically suffer from acrophobia can be scared to death by extreme designs. Although designers appear to avoid literally shoving people off the edge, they come pretty close, and library users complain endlessly about certain libraries.

> At a library conference, Fred and three other people shared a glass-sided elevator traveling up the edge of an atrium. All three people looked nervously out the glass walls. When they all arrived at the top floor and stepped out, the floor gave slightly underfoot, and the three people said (in unison), "I don't feel good." The elevator and floor appeared safe (the floor bounced because it was a plenum floor that housed an air distribution system), but what possible excuse is there for creeping out library users for no good reason? Any library design that causes people to say (in unison) "I don't feel good" is a bad design.

All of this is completely avoidable. Too many owners and architects love spaces that terrify many ordinary people. And all of these spaces are totally unnecessary.

Libraries that want plenum floors need to use carpeted concrete tiles suspended on steel frames, so that floors never unnerve users by bouncing underfoot.

Unfortunately, even if your written library building program forbids a handful of features that cause serious problems, you may still have to battle your owners and planners and designers to actually prevent them.

VI-A. ATRIA

Designers love atria, and visitors (as opposed to library users and staff) sometimes exclaim over them in delight. But outside of providing photos for magazine articles and architectural advertisements, they serve few useful purposes, with the possible exception of orientation.

In addition to terrifying people with fear of heights, atria cause all sorts of other problems.

- Atria are noisy. When a library has an atrium, unwanted sounds fill the building. (If the atrium has a skylight—another ill-considered design feature—the racket is likely to be even worse. And if the atrium has both a skylight and a hard-surfaced floor, things can be seriously exciting.)

- When an atrium is in the center of a building, anyone above the entry floor level has to circumnavigate the atrium.

- If the balconies around an atrium are narrow or have low walls, this terrifies people with a fear of heights.

- Atria can make it hard to arrange furniture and shelving.

- Atria are hard to light, and fixtures are hard to service. A good time to check out an existing atrium is at night. (Some library atria have light fixtures that are so expensive to maintain that libraries simply keep them turned off. Or permanently disconnected.)

- Atria are hard to heat and cool. (One of Fred's students said that her library at home had an atrium that was frigid in the winter. Every cold winter day the staff moved the service desk out of the atrium to a warmer location, but every night the maintenance staff moved it back.)

- It's easy to drop something off the balcony in an atrium.

When you are fighting off atria, people will insist that they're harmless. But they're lying. The New York University library, for example, has a huge atrium that was the site of several suicides. The university has had to spend a great deal of money erecting barricades to prevent people from continuing to leap off the balconies.

If you are in a situation where it becomes obvious that an atrium will be forced on your library no matter how loud and cogent your objections, there are a number of things you can do:

- Remember that atria can be fun to look at from below while alarming to look at from above, and figure out how to eliminate the view from above. (The world of libraries is full of great, inspiring reading rooms, but for many users the rooms are great only when the users are standing on the floor, looking up.)

- Make the balconies wide and make the barricades high and opaque. People with fear of heights need to be able to keep away from drop-offs and not be forced to peer over the edge. And if they're forced to walk close to a drop-off, it helps if they can just barely see over the edge. (Hotels with huge atria typically do this. A chest high-barricade is vastly less frightening than a waist-high barricade, and a wide balcony is a lot less frightening than a narrow one.)

- In one library Fred knows, the architects provided concrete railings at about mid-thigh height. After a major battle between the board of trustees and the architects, the architects provided major vertical extensions.

- Provide barricades that cannot be jumped without serious effort. (Unless libraries install barricade screens, the best way to eliminate atrium suicides is to never build atria in the first place.)

- Put the atrium at one end of the building, such as above an entry foyer, so that it doesn't have to be circumnavigated on upper floors, and so that users aren't forced to walk right by it on upper levels.

- Completely glass in the upper levels of the atrium, so that sounds from below don't permeate upper floors, so that no one can fall off, and so the heating and ventilating system isn't messed up.

- If the atrium has an ornamental central staircase, make the location of the alternative elevator extremely obvious. (Fred's university has a library with a large atrium and an ornamental staircase—with the elevator hidden off to the side down a completely unmarked hallway. He's always believed that the absence of a sign was intentional on the part of the designers.)

- Put light fixtures on drops for easier maintenance.

- Engineer the library so that when common sense eventually prevails it's possible to install floors in the open spaces in the atrium.

However, all of these ideas are far worse than the pleasure of having no atrium at all.

Unfortunately, atria exert an evil allure. One library Fred worked with ended up firing its architect because the architect bluntly refused to eliminate an atrium from the design.

VI-B. WALKWAYS ACROSS ATRIA

Some designers not only provide atria but then add walkways that cross the atriums. If users and staff are forced to use the walkways, this is particularly unpleasant. The Minneapolis Public Library, for example, has glass-sided walkways over an atrium, and they seriously spook some people who need to cross over.

Other people may remember the atrium walkways in the Hyatt Regency Hotel in Kansas City, which collapsed in 1981 during a social event, killing over one hundred people, and wonder about the safety of walkways in general. (The roof in the Kansas City hotel had collapsed earlier when the building was under construction, an omen of sorts.)

VI-C. GLASS RAILINGS NEXT TO DROP-OFFS

Glass railings can terrify users with acrophobia. Since glass railings serve no useful purpose, ban them in your building program and in your instructions to your designers, but be prepared for a possible battle.

VI-D. BALCONIES

Having one or two balconies is less of a problem than having a multistory atrium, but it's still a seriously bad idea.

One Illinois library has a second floor outdoor balcony off the children's department. To protect children, the library has to keep the doors to the balcony locked at all times.

VI-E. ELEVATORS WITH GLASS WALLS

In a lifetime of working in and around library buildings, Fred has never been able to figure out any functional improvement provided by glass walls on elevators. Designers may get a kick out of watching people staring fixedly at the elevator door to avoid having to stare into the abyss, but there are other sources of amusement. A modest-sized window provides users with as much information as a glass wall.

VI-F. TERRIFYING STAIRCASES

An impressive number of designer staircases scare the heck out of people who have fear of heights. Some common problems that can easily be avoided include:

- Open risers. These are amazingly popular with library designers and unpopular with library users. Ban them in your building program. (At least codes now ban open risers wide enough so that small children can fall through the openings. Unfortunately, the dangerous staircases came first and the codes second, a matter of fixing rather than anticipating problems.)
- Overly long runs of steps. If people look down and have instant visions of tumbling head over heels, staircases are too long. It's easy to have a staircase reverse direction on the way down, halfway between floors, with a comfortable landing where users can rest.
- Steps that don't run straight and flat up to the edge of the staircase and stop only when they hit the wall. Some steps stop decoratively short of the side walls. Other steps curve upward into the side walls. (Fred tripped on one at the Seattle Public Library.) You don't want any of this nonsense.
- Railings that can't be grabbed firmly. (These were banned by the ADA, but they're still all over the place. And if the ADA hadn't been passed, some designers would probably still be creating them.)
- Staircases that run at a diagonal, so that people have to move from side to side while climbing.
- Staircases with oddly shaped steps. These have been with us for far too long. Some were designed to save space, but they're all bad news.
- Floating staircases where you can walk underneath and bash your head on the underside of the staircase. (Libraries are full of staircases where the staff have had to stick all sorts of stuff under the staircase to protect users' heads. The current version of the ADA requires protective railings under floating staircases, benefitting all users.)

VI-G. "WATER FEATURES"

Because of Legionnaires' disease, "water features" are pretty much passé, but they still abound.

For many library users, having to skirt the edge of a water feature is an unpleasant experience. Remember the story of the large western public library where the mayor fell into a water feature during the grand opening. (Water features cause other problems as well. See the index.)

In your building program, it's a good thing to say "no water features," just in case people start getting ideas.

Fred knows one library that changed architects when the architect insisted on a water feature and refused to change.

VI-H. SUMMARY

Many people have a fear of heights, and for some of them acrophobia is clearly an extreme disability. There's no need in any library building to make life for these library users and staff members terrifying. When your designer exclaims, "Walking through our library will be like floating through a cloud," you need to ask yourself how many of your users and staff yearn to float through clouds while using your library.

Fred once had a conversation with an architect who said that people with a profound fear of heights would "Just have to get over it." This is far less nasty than saying that people in wheelchairs who need access to libraries should "Just get over it," but it shows a similar generosity of spirit.

Avoiding unnecessary features that disturb the many users with a serious fear of heights is easy, and it seems entirely reasonable to accommodate them.

VII. Access for People with Vertigo

Vertigo is the sensation that the world is spinning around you. Many people are subject to vertigo at one time or another, and for some it's a major medical condition. When Fred talks with people who have occasional vertigo, they tell him they never regard it as a pleasant sensation.

Some decorating schemes appear to induce unwanted vertigo. The ones that cause problems seem to usually involve wavy patterns on floors and walls that lead to sensations of the world spinning around one, but some people find a variety of bold carpet patterns generally difficult to cope with.

> A classic example was the Indianapolis airport, which had a concourse with wavy patterns in the carpet. When Fred walked down the concourse, if he looked about 20 feet in front of him, the entire floor began to move. He found it entertaining to play with the sensation, but if he had emerged from a bad flight feeling queasy, he's sure he wouldn't have enjoyed the experience.

An Illinois college has wall panels with complex, three-dimensional, embossed wavy patterns, all accented by extremely bright and direct lights that create crisp shadows on the walls. Even when Fred is just standing still, the walls still move around him. He's always thought he was immune to vertigo, but these walls make him believe he could be wrong.

Since any patterns like these serve no useful purpose outside of innovative décor, upsetting library users seems an unnecessarily high price to pay.

The rule seems an easy one: *Avoid wavy or other intrusive patterns on what should be friendly, welcoming surfaces.*

VIII. Access for People with Claustrophobia

Some people are extremely uncomfortable in small spaces, and some libraries have spaces that can cause users serious problems.

Many of these situations are examples of seriously bad design rather than sources of problems specifically for people with claustrophobia. Among the most common miserably bad concepts are dead-end shelving aisles (which are a major safety threat), study room walls that block vision but fail to block sound (failing both basic study room needs at the same time), and tiny restrooms.

IX. Access for People with Limited Senses of Direction

Some people are easily lost in labyrinthine libraries, and a few libraries are impressively labyrinthine. Some baffling libraries are historic, sometimes as a result of additions, but others are modern. People complain, for example, about being lost in the zigzag stacks of Seattle's central public library. (Years ago, one of Fred's former students sent him a postcard with a picture of the then new Seattle Public Library. She wrote, "Help, I'm a book, and no one can find me!")

When Fred was in library school at the University of Chicago, he worked at the main information desk of the historic central library building of the Chicago Public Library (now called the "Cultural Center"). The building was an artistic masterpiece, but it was so confusing that workers at the main information desk always had to give visitors driving instructions rather than simply tell them where things were.

One thing that helps improve orientation is wide vistas. When users can see where they're headed, it makes life a lot easier. Wide, flat, and open makes a happy library.

Another thing that helps is good signage, but when buildings are seriously confusing, signage may not be enough. And some directional signs in libraries are themselves confusing.

There's an extensive literature on architectural signage. Some of the suggestions that have helped Fred most in dealing with libraries include:

- Put all floor plans on north walls, since people expect floor plans to have north at the top. If posted floor plans are rotated with respect to the actual floor plans, even the most geographically gifted folks can be puzzled.

- Avoid cursive script or other artistic type fonts.

- Use high-contrast lettering.

- Have creatively minded teenage employees with extensive vocabularies read proposed signs for unfortunate second meanings not recognized by mature planners.

X. What You Can Do to Protect Your Library's Accessibility

Some of the main ways of improving library accessibility include:

- Avoid compromising with accessibility requirements to save money. If you have a historic library, face up to the cost of making changes. Historic libraries can be wonderful places, but making them friendly to all users can be expensive—sometimes more expensive than starting over with brand new buildings. We should use historic libraries because they look great, not because they are cheap.

- Recognize that buildings with multiple floors always have access problems. The solutions are always far more expensive than some people hope, and cheap solutions are almost always disasters.

- Many existing buildings proposed for conversion to libraries bring all sorts of accessibility problems with them. In addition to major problems with HVAC, floor loading, and staff supervision, there are many other issues. Frequently, owners of white elephant structures hope to make money by unloading their buildings on innocent public libraries, and they can make trouble in communities by claiming that resistance is due to the desire for "Taj Mahal" buildings rather than simple practicality. If you are faced with a situation like this, let your hired help (engineers and architects and building consultants) take the blame. That's what they're paid for, and they can often leave town at sunset.

- Don't compromise when it comes to elevators. Junky lifts and elevator substitutes of one sort or another abound, and they are all unpleasant for everyone concerned. If you can't afford to add a real elevator to your library, it's time to build a new library on one level.

- Insist that there will be NO uncontrollable direct sunlight.

- Make sure that all areas of the library will have bright, reliable, low-glare artificial light.

- Ban railings that can be climbed like ladders.

- Ban all transparent glass guard railings.

- Ban all places where users and staff are forced to walk right by drop-offs.

- Ban scary and dangerous staircases, many of which are the result of design enthusiasms.

- If you must have an atrium, never have situations where people on upper floors are forced to walk past it.

- Build on flat sites wherever possible. Sloped sites introduce access problems. Some libraries have taken advantage of sloped sites to have parking lots beneath their buildings, but many users find underground parking spooky.

- Have second handrails at child height on all staircases, and keep runs of steps short. One how-to-do-it book on library architecture by an American architect has a photo of the atrium of one of his libraries on the cover—including a monumental staircase. You can't see it in the photo, but the staircase has a kiddie gate at the top because staff members are worried that children will fall down the endless flight of steps from the second floor children's department.

- Provide enough storage space to reduce the likelihood of users and staff tripping over things that can't be stored.

- Ban places where people can be cornered. Even if you are convinced your library will be totally safe, why scare users and staff? And why take a chance on what will happen if some crazy person cuts loose.

- Ban curved walls and ceilings, especially with hard surfaces. Distracting noise problems are easy to avoid. It's mostly a matter of function vs. design.

- Avoid situations where users are forced to sit uncomfortably close together. Some libraries have tiny tables where users' legs meet unwelcomely beneath. Or tables that force strangers to sit uncomfortably close together. Some public computer areas force users to rub elbows while they work.

- Be prepared for needs not yet envisioned. Five or 10 years after your new building is constructed, you'll be doing some things very differently. If your building was designed on the premise that nothing will ever change, you'll have problems.

- Be alert to helpful spinoffs. A solution to one accessibility problem may help other users as well, just as the ADA helped people with other problems.

- Remember that lots of write-ups about new buildings are basically ignorant fluff when it comes to recognition of functionality.

XI. The Central Point of All This

Although this chapter focuses on accessibility, everything listed is just common sense. If a design concept is unessential and makes accessibility difficult, it's just a bad design.

The vast majority of cute but dysfunctional design features are completely unnecessary. For example, if you talk with staff and users, as opposed to visiting tourists, about staircases with open risers, most people's reactions range from "ugh" to "meh." But never "wow!"

XII. Snappy Rules on Accessibility

1. A glorious library that is inaccessible to people with disabilities is not a glorious library.

2. Legitimate disabilities that are not protected by statute are frequently ignored. There are lots of such disabilities, as this chapter describes.

3. There are a lot of cheap substitutes for elevators, but by and large they tend to be dreadful. If you can't afford an actual elevator, you need a one-story library at grade level.

4. Looking up at the ceiling from the floor of a three-story reading room is inspiring. Looking down at the floor from up by the ceiling is often not.

5. Atria are not always evil in libraries, but they come close enough for all practical purposes. If an atrium terrifies library users and staff with a fear of heights, it's a sign of bad library design. There's a lot of bad library design out there.

6. For every person who is blind there are probably many thousands with limited eyesight, and libraries need to take steps to serve them as well. Bright but extremely low-glare lighting is important. So is avoiding places where people with limited eyesight can trip, avoiding micro-print or cute type faces on signs, picking light sources that provide high-level color rendering and comfortable color temperatures, and having step edges that are visible while walking downstairs.

7. The Americans with Disabilities Act allows ramps, but many of them are fairly unpleasant. If you must have ramps in major thoroughfares in your library, be sure that they are (a) short, (b) indoors, and (c) wide enough for people to pass in opposite directions. But first be sure that "must have ramps" really applies.

8. While providing access for people in wheelchairs, the ADA also made life vastly easier for people with less extreme disabilities. People with walkers, canes, baby carriages, strollers, book carts, bad senses of balance, trouble climbing stairs, and other challenges all need easier access.

9. Accessible restroom stalls take a fair amount of space, but that's not a reason to make the rest of the stalls so tiny that people have to straddle the toilets to close the doors.

10. Dramatic staircases can terrify people with acrophobia, limited eyesight, uncertain balance, weak legs, and other disabilities. If you plan to indulge in a dramatic staircase, be sure that the alternative elevator is close by and extremely well labeled.

11. As with all building codes, cutting things as close as allowed by accessibility codes is not anything to brag about. Book stack aisles that are designed to meet only minimum requirements often don't work.

12. Skylights are dismal for people with limited eyesight and often bad for people with good eyesight. Your building program should say "NO SKYLIGHTS" in firm prose, and you will still need to check to be sure that your designers are not slipping any in when they think you aren't looking.

13. Correcting inaccessibility costs vastly more than preventing it in the first place. And sometimes you can't correct it. As a result of both of these problems, it often doesn't get corrected.

14. Wide, flat, and open makes a happy library.

15. Anyone who exclaims about the "Glorious Light" in a library building is probably someone who does not actually use the library.

16. Soffits in libraries can cause a wide variety of problems, although shallow soffits can sometimes break up huge expanses of flat ceilings.

17. If your library is sued over serious inaccessibility issues, you're pretty likely to lose.

18. When the author of the "Battle Hymn of the Republic" spoke of "dim and flaring lamps," she could well have been describing some libraries with recessed downlights.

19. In addition to improving accessibility, good planning can reduce occupancy costs by making library spaces more open and easier to supervise.

20. Flat sites help limit expensive and dysfunctional problems with awkward ramps and partial staircases and extra elevators.

21. Accessible libraries are usually easier to supervise and therefore less expensive to operate.

22. Elevators large enough for gurneys are more expensive but are friendly to people moving furniture, crowds of people leaving meetings, and people accompanying friends with disabilities—as well as people with disabilities.

23. If an architectural feature interferes with accessibility and provides no practical benefit to users or staff, it's a bad feature. Cute is nice, but function always comes first. And cute can be impressively expensive.

24. Photos of ramps in architectural publications always show people whizzing happily down rather than laboring up.

25. There are many suitable snappy rules in the chapters on seating, security, and restrooms.

26. Being forced to cross an atrium on a narrow walkway with glass sides is a sign that people with nasty personalities were involved in the project.

27. All adult-height tables should be accessible, since accessible tables are pleasant for all users. Forcing a user in a wheelchair to hunt for a workable table is unnecessarily unfriendly.

28. Although the ADA does not always require power-assisted entry doors, most of them are too heavy to not be powered, and many people in addition to those with official disabilities benefit.

29. When figuring clearances involving chairs, be sure to figure on occupied chairs.

30. When designing for accessibility, always involve people who actually use wheelchairs and walkers.

PART II
From Overcrowding
to Ribbon Cutting

CHAPTER 12

Surfaces and Materials

I. Introduction

I-A. EXPOSED SURFACES IN AND ON LIBRARY BUILDINGS

This chapter provides a very quick review of some basic options in construction materials, focusing in particular on their visible surfaces in library buildings.

Some construction materials have been with us for millennia. Stone walls are the great example, but brick walls have survived from the time of the Roman Empire.

Other construction materials are extremely modern. Products specifically designed to provide insulation and prevent water intrusion are far more sophisticated than those available even a few decades ago.

Some surfaces are impressively fragile. Many modern surfaces become shabby in a decade or two. They may have advantages in terms of low cost, ease of alteration or repair, acoustics, and safety, but they may lead to expensive, long-term maintenance issues. And they can look impressively crummy while they're still hanging in there.

But even traditional, strong surfaces require proper installation. A great example is brick. Bricks can last for generations, but if brick walls are not capped, rainwater gets into the mortar joints, freezes, and destroys the walls.

Other concerns with surfaces revolve around conserving energy. A variety of green materials is available, although some perform far better than others.

Modern walls are usually constructed of multiple layers of various materials, each selected to address one of the characteristics needed in the wall. But unless the materials are selected and assembled correctly, each of them is relatively useless, and many of them are fragile.

And some existing materials are dangerous. For example, some materials are toxic. Asbestos and lead are familiar problems in older buildings, but nasty chemicals can leach out of all sorts of manufactured products. And some materials are flammable.

National standards exist for many of the materials listed in this chapter. Talk with your designers and engineers.

Surfaces and materials is a huge topic, and this chapter is necessarily a once-over. But we hope it will introduce you to some of the issues involved and important questions to ask.

Additional comments on surfaces are can be found in several chapters—chapter 4, "Evaluating Library Buildings by Walking Around"; chapter 5, "Dysfunctional Designs"; chapter 16, "Remodeling and Expanding Library Buildings," and chapter 26, "Restrooms."

This chapter covers only architectural materials and surfaces. For furniture surfaces, such as countertops and tabletops, see chapter 21, "User Seating," and chapter 23, "Public Service Desks."

I-B. VOCABULARY

- *Attic stock.* Extra supplies of materials that may be difficult to match when you need them for repairs. Common materials maintained in attic stocks include acoustic ceiling tiles, ceramic floor and wall tiles, broadloom carpets, carpet tiles, floor tiles, and so on.
- *Broadloom.* Carpet in wide rolls, as opposed to carpet squares.
- *CMU.* Concrete masonry unit, which is trade talk for concrete block.
- *EIFS.* External Insulation Finishing Systems. Exterior surfacing materials made of foam plastic covered with stucco, and sometimes reinforced with fabric mesh.
- *Linoleum.* Linoleum was invented around 1860. It's a mixture of ground cork, linseed oil, resins, pigments, and other stuff on a canvas or burlap backing. Although the name may linger, today's linoleum is sheet vinyl and far more durable than the historic material.
- *Nylon.* The most durable carpet fiber. Prefer it to olefin, polyester, and acrylic. The green carpet fiber is wool, but it's expensive, and the quality can vary greatly.
- *Polyurethane foam.* Highly flammable foam used very extensively in the production of padded furniture and spray-on insulation for buildings. A cheap idea rather than a good idea. Polyurethane foam emits cyanide gas when it burns.
- *Precast.* Imitation stone made of concrete. Frequently used for repairing or expanding existing stone-clad buildings.
- *Remediation.* The removal of dangerous construction materials (such as lead or asbestos) by licensed experts.
- *Rusticated.* Said of brick or stone blocks that have surfaces carved to give the impression of natural surfaces.
- *Spalling.* Fragments of material breaking off larger chunks of various things like brick and precast. Spalling has a number of causes, but the main thing is that you don't want any of that on your library.
- *Terrazzo.* Floor covering material made of marble chips in mortar, poured into openings between brass dividers and then ground smooth. Extremely durable, but very hard and dangerously slippery when wet. A known hip breaker.

- *Tuckpointing.* Replacing deteriorating mortar joints in brick walls.

- *Vinyl.* A plastic material, PVC, or polyvinyl chloride. Huge quantities of vinyl are produced every year. Vinyl floor tile is a standard and durable product, but vinyl siding can have problems with expansion and contraction, water infiltration, fragility, fading, rattling in the wind, and just looking like plastic. Vinyl is toxic to produce and very definitely not a green product.

- *Walk-off mats.* Devices to collect water tracked into buildings, consisting of vinyl- or fabric-covered bars with pans beneath to collect water and salt. The water evaporates, and the mats are removed occasionally to remove the dried salt.

II. Health Problems

Many interior floor coverings and wall and floor finishes can be sources of health problems, especially during construction.

If you are living in a building while remodeling it, sometimes things can be controlled by keeping an airtight seal between construction areas and occupied parts of the building, but it can be difficult. Moving out during construction brings fewer complications.

Some people react extremely poorly to airborne dust from sanding drywall joints. One of the best employees in Fred's library, for example, had to resign when stray drywall dust sent her to the hospital.

Some cheap plywood used for temporary partitions exudes formaldehyde. (Some of the inexpensive trailers purchased by the federal government (FEMA) after hurricane Katrina were uninhabitable due to formaldehyde seeping out of cheap plywood. The thousands of people who were sickened by living in the trailers were awarded over $40 million in liability settlements.)

The concept of "sick building syndrome" dates from the 1970s and was named by WHO (the World Health Organization) in 1986. Among the components may have been a combination of offgassing of unhealthy chemicals (such as formaldehyde, once again) present in manufactured building materials and sealing buildings more tightly to save energy.

The situation is made far more complex by the lack of research into toxicity of many industrial products. When it comes to poisons in construction materials, this book will be out of date while it is still at the printer, and for that reason we've limited ourselves to a very few major examples.

- Lead pigments make great paint, but they're all poisonous. They were banned for indoor use in 1978, but they're all over the place in older buildings. For libraries, the main danger appears to be lead pigments chalking off or being made airborne when old finishes are sanded.

- Formaldehyde. A gas that (among many other things) is a byproduct of various types of wallboard, where the EPA now sets stringent limits. Formaldehyde is a common cause of sick building syndrome.

- Polyurethane foam, which is used extensively in upholstered furniture, is explosively flammable and emits toxic fumes (like cyanide) when it burns. Unfortunately, the chemicals added to make it less dangerously flammable are also nasty, and some used a few years ago are now forbidden.

- Many adhesives contain dangerous organic solvents, such as benzene and toluene, as well as more complex chemicals.

- Asbestos. Until asbestos was banned in the 1970s, it was everywhere. (Like lead, it worked well, except for being poisonous.) Rely on your architects to arrange suitable testing. We've run into library buildings and buildings being converted to libraries that had asbestos in vinyl asbestos floor tiles (VAT), floor tile mastic (glue), pipe lagging (insulating wrapping), Transite (cement asbestos board) liners in under-slab air ducts, drywall mud, acoustic ceiling tiles, and other unwanted places. Almost every remediation situation requires evaluation of risks and costs.

- Vinyl. Manufacturing polyvinyl chloride (the basis of vinyl tile) creates serious pollution, but that seems to be the primary problem area.

What can we do when we are planning library buildings?

- Rely on your architects and engineers to help steer you away from toxic chemicals, but always ask questions. The kind of information found in project manuals may help protect your library from unpleasant materials that are not technically illegal but are sold over the counter. If you stress to the people specifying materials for your building that you are eager to avoid potentially dangerous materials at all times, they should be able to warn you about the current state of affairs or write specifications that eliminate unhealthy construction products.

- Keep the costs of remediation in mind when planning library expansion and remodeling jobs and when evaluating the conversion of existing buildings to libraries. Dangerous materials are everywhere.

- Before you purchase—or accept as a gift—any building constructed before 1980, get professional advice. Remediation can be surprisingly expensive.

- Be slightly cynical about industry claims concerning the safety of their products. (Sometimes you can be very seriously cynical.)

- Avoid seriously overstuffed upholstered furniture in order to limit the amount of polyurethane foam in your library. Since polyurethane foam is everywhere, verify that your furniture has flame retardants and wrapping on the foam.

- If your library will have spray-on foam insulation, look up information on the toxicity and flammability of the proposed product. The most common protection separating the insulation from inhabited areas is gypsum board (plasterboard).

- After new carpet has been installed, crank up the heat to about 80 for a few days to accelerate offgassing, then air the building out thoroughly.

- If you will be using solvent-based finishes, arrange for excellent ventilation and consider sealing off the working area from the rest of the library. The psychological effect of strong odors may be a component of staff and public complaints. Give serious consideration to water-based finishes and adhesives.

- Keep up on changes reported in the press. Investigations into the properties of many materials continue, including the toxicity of common chemicals. You'll want the latest information on whether legacy materials in your building may be affecting occupants' health.

- Know your staff's individual health problems. If your staff will be around a building under construction on a daily basis, try to protect people you know may be particularly sensitive.

III. Exterior Walls

There are multiple demands placed on exterior walls, including durability and weather protection. For all practical purposes, the most durable materials are stone and brick, with buildings in both materials lasting for millennia rather than mere centuries. But a wide variety of other materials are chosen for appearance or for lower cost.

Older buildings often had masonry walls that supported the structure, but modern buildings usually have an exterior layer of brick or stone for appearance and durability, an air space, and then an inner wall of concrete block (aka concrete masonry units or CMUs). And drainage at the bottom of the air space. (Look for spacers or bits of rope protruding from the mortar right above the foundations.)

III-A. BRICK

Brick made of burnt clay is a standard architectural material in a wide variety of public and commercial buildings. Many brick buildings have been standing in America since colonial times. And there are surviving brick walls from the time of the Roman Empire.

In brick walls, individual bricks are separated and held together with mortar. Mortar is great for physical support but limited in adhesive qualities.

Bricks come in an impressive variety of materials and shapes and colors. One place to start is specifying first-class burnt clay bricks, but that's far too vague.

Standards for brick are set by the American Society for Testing and Materials (ASTM), which has many publications on masonry standards. Libraries are constructed with "face brick," where external appearance is important. Sometimes face brick is glazed. There are standards for compressive strength, size, color, density, durability, weather resistance, dimensional accuracy, chip resistance, and so on.

Finding the right brick can be difficult. Don't let yourself be rushed. More durable is always better. Having to match cheap brick is not a rewarding experience.

In years gone by, the walls of buildings were built of double layers of brick, and the ways the two layers were connected led to a significant variety of patterns, called "bonds." Exterior walls consisted of bricks laid lengthwise ("stretchers") and bricks laid crosswise ("headers") to connect the inner and outer rows of stretchers.

Today most new brick walls are a single layer of brick. An inner wall is usually constructed of concrete blocks (CMUs or Concrete Masonry Units) or metal studs and sheathing, separated from the outer brick wall by an air space for insulation. The actual structure of the building may be steel columns and beams.

Brick walls are impressively strong, but the type of brick chosen makes a serious difference, and some cute bricks won't last the way they should. Bricks are designated by grade and type. Grade SW (severe weathering) is the most durable, followed by MR (moderate weathering) and NW (interior use only). "Type" refers to mechanical tolerances. Type FBX allows a narrow variation in color ranges and sizes from brick to brick, while FBX is more common and allows greater variations.

Some older bricks were made of clay fired at low temperatures, requiring the use of lime mortar rather than concrete mortar. Unless you are working with a historic building, you don't want anything to do with soft brick that requires lime mortar. Or anything to do with taking over buildings with that sort of brick.

A library with high-quality brick walls could last for centuries if it didn't usually go out of date first.

The major maintenance concern with brick walls is deterioration of the mortar joints between the bricks. After many years, brick walls are repaired by chiseling out decaying mortar and replacing it, in a process called "tuckpointing."

The stair step cracks that appear in brick walls starting at the upper corners of windows and doors are due to inadequate foundations rather than bad brick.

One of the great challenges in construction is matching existing brick. Sometimes this is done well, but at other times the results are fairly abysmal.

Matching some historic shapes, such as the long, thin "Roman" bricks used in some early twentieth century library buildings, can be difficult. For example, Frank Lloyd Wright liked Roman brick because it emphasized the horizontal nature of his buildings, like the Robie House in Chicago, and it can be very hard to match when his buildings are repaired.

In cases where matching bricks cannot be found, one solution is to separate new and old brick walls with architectural features, such as recessed entryways or recessed windows.

III-B. NATURAL STONE

Buildings can be covered with a variety of stone, but by far the most common is limestone. Limestone has the advantages of being fairly easy to cut and extremely long-lasting. Limestone library buildings constructed a century ago often

Expanding historic buildings is frequently made difficult by problems with matching old and new brickwork. Roman bricks in this Carnegie-era building are on the left, while the new (and very different) Norman bricks are on the right.

show few signs of deterioration. Other stones are granite and marble, although they are far less commonly used than limestone. Sandstone was widely used at times in the past, but it's not as weatherproof or abrasion-proof as the other three.

Stone is usually a sheathing material. From the outside of a building, cut stone can look like the exposed portion of massive stone blocks, but it's almost always a finishing material.

Modern stone walls can be constructed like modern brick walls, with concrete block interior walls and air spaces between the concrete block walls and the outer stone walls for insulation. As with brick walls, the outer and inner walls are connected for stability. In many buildings, the actual structure is steel framing, while the stone walls provide weatherproofing and appearance.

Some buildings are constructed with "rusticated" stone, where the surfaces are carved to give the stone a natural appearance.

Other types of stone are available in addition to limestone, but be very beware. Sometimes things go terribly wrong. For example, the Standard Oil Building (now the Aon Center) in Chicago was built in 1974. At 83 floors, it was the tallest building in Chicago and fourth tallest in the world. It was covered at great expense with Italian Carrara marble sheathing. Unfortunately, the marble slabs were thin, and they warped, lifting off the metal hangers that supported them. The result was sheets of marble falling as much as 80 stories to the terrace below. After 15 years, the entire building had to be stripped and sheathed in heavier sheets of domestic granite, a three-year, $80 million project. The owners sued everyone, but the settlement terms are private.

Sandstone was popular at one time in the US, primarily because quarries were handy. But it's little used for buildings now. Sandstone is less durable than limestone or granite, and it stains. But some universities like the "generations of scholars in the halls of ivy" look that sandstone gives to staircases, because the treads quickly erode. People who work with sandstone are subject to silicosis.

Travertine is porous and can retain water. In cold climates, the freezing of trapped water leads to spalling and cracking in ever-increasing frequency, until panels fall off their supports.

III-C. PRECAST STONE

A variety of imitation stone products are available.

Precast stone is made of concrete. It's used primarily as a less expensive substitute for real stone, although in some parts of the country there are no cost savings. Thanks to color and texture control, the effect can be good, but some precast stone can disintegrate in a process called "spalling." Moisture seeps into pores in the material, freezes, and pops some of the material off. Another source of spalling is the corrosion of metal reinforcements in the concrete.

The main use of precast stone in libraries is probably for expanding historic stone buildings when the owners feel they cannot afford the cost of matching natural stone. (Check to be sure they're right.)

Standards for the industry come from the Cast Stone Institute.

There are also inexpensive pieces of imitation stone used in house construction, often rusticated and in a variety of intermixed colors. Don't.

III-D. CONCRETE

Some buildings are covered in raw concrete. This was particularly in vogue in the Brutalist era, when the honesty of exposed concrete was in fashion. Often it showed the results of the rough planks used for molds.

Unfortunately, concrete stains, it is porous, and it tends to have corners break off. Its surface may not be as tough as precast.

Some people think exposed concrete walls are seriously ugly, but others find them fashionable.

III-E. EIFS

EIFS (external insulated finish systems) is sheathing material made of sheets of foam plastic covered with products similar to stucco. Sometimes there's a mesh of netting between the foam and the stucco.

EIFS was originally developed in Europe after WWII as a way of patching damaged stone walls, and it's been used in the US since about 1970. EIFS is fragile, and it tends to trap water. Many EIFS walls soon show signs of damage. The EIFS industry has tried to address these issues by adding drainage materials and reinforcing meshes, but some cheap installations omit both.

In our opinion, EIFS is not suitable for libraries. It's a good idea to say this in your building program and repeat it to your owners and architects and engineers.

III-F. SIDING

Siding can be used on small library buildings that are constructed like houses. Usually these have overlapping strips called clapboards. The shape of the strips helps keep water from penetrating interiors.

Some libraries have vertical plank siding reminiscent of barns. They can be strikingly attractive, but they can deteriorate badly, especially if they are stained rather than painted. And they require sealants between the planks.

Painted wood is the traditional siding material most people know because of its use in houses. It requires a lot of maintenance, including

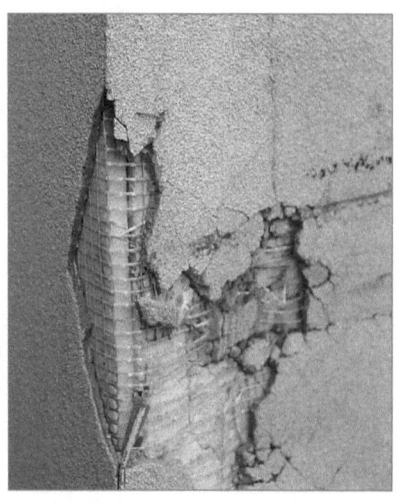

EIFS (external insulating finishing systems) can be too fragile for many situations. The first photograph shows damage from a bicycle (not really a heavy-duty weapon), while the second shows how a vulnerable corner can be disfigured despite repeated repairs. In both cases the reinforcing fiberglass mesh is visible.

frequent repainting, including attention to sealants and primers. Stains don't last as long as paint.

Alternatives to wood siding are numerous:

- *Vinyl*. Vinyl siding is extremely common in the United States, primarily as a house-covering material. It can be used on small libraries. While it does not have to be painted, it's not a particularly durable product. Vinyl has a different coefficient of thermal expansion than wood, so vinyl siding on a library needs to be loosely attached to prevent it from warping. It therefore tends to rattle in the wind, and the joints in horizontal strips of vinyl siding can be extremely obvious. Since vinyl siding tends to come in strips representing three planks of clapboard, the joints can be particularly unrealistic.

- *Aluminum*. Aluminum siding was popular for houses, but it seems to have been replaced in new construction by vinyl. We've never seen aluminum siding on libraries, but it probably exists somewhere. See section III-H. "Aluminum Composite Panels."

- *Fiber-cement*. If you like the look of wood, consider fiber-cement siding. It lasts longer, needs less maintenance, and is not food for mold. And it has a wood-like look. It's also heavier than wood or vinyl and takes more labor to install.

III-G. ARCHITECTURAL TERRACOTTA

Some older library buildings have trim detail made of terracotta—basically glazed ceramic. If a historic library has terracotta details, they may need to be duplicated when the building is expanded or when some individual pieces start disintegrating. It's possible to have matching terracotta elements manufactured, but some designers have used fiberglass, which looks about the same from the ground and is less expensive.

What looks like terracotta on some older libraries can turn out to be galvanized and painted sheet steel. Not all Carnegie-era libraries are examples of luxuriously significant architecture.

Modern terracotta tiles are used as the exterior layer (cladding layer) in multilayered exterior walls. They can be a variety of colors, thicknesses, and shapes, but are most commonly rectangular. They are more expensive, but they offer longer life, better energy performance, low maintenance costs, good impact resistance, and easy replacement.

III-H. ALUMINUM COMPOSITE PANELS (ACP)

Most contemporary use of aluminum on library buildings is as panels or composite panels. The most common are made of thin sheets of aluminum that enclose foam. The panels can be bent on the edges to create surface depth and can come in almost any color. They are relatively expensive, but they offer long life, good energy performance, low maintenance costs, impact resistance, and (depending on how they're installed) easy replacement.

III-I. PHENOLIC RESIN PANELS

Phenolic panels are made of thermosetting resins reinforced with wood fibers and are available in a variety of finish textures and colors. They have similar properties to ACM, but they're more expensive and longer lived.

IV. Roof Coverings

Roofs are another of those multilayer systems that form the exterior surface of the building. The most visible is usually the weather barrier with insulation and vapor retarders hidden underneath. As with exterior walls, the insulation is most often some sort of plastic foam. Like all foams, the insulation needs to be protected against the heat of a fire, so there is often a barrier to separate the insulation from the interior of the building. Another protection board is often laid on top of the insulation and under the weathering surface to protect it from impact damage during maintenance of the roof or roof-mounted mechanical equipment. For shingled roofs, this outer protection is often the material into which shingles are nailed. All of these layers need to be securely attached to the roof structure so that the roof cannot come apart, either in layers or as an entire assembly, in a windstorm.

Roofs come in two categories, low slope and sloped. Low slope is what people regularly refer to as flat roofs. Few roofs are truly flat, and most "flat" roofs slope at least a quarter of an inch per foot to a drain. These low slope roofs are very often a polymer membrane or built-up layers of asphalt-impregnated roofing felts. The membranes are kept in place either by stone ballast (the weight of the stone keeps the membrane tight against the underlying insulation or protection board), mechanical fasteners (screws), or adhesive.

Sloped roofs are covered with materials that are both part of the weather barrier and part of the building aesthetic. These surfaces need to be water resistant and attractive.

- Shingles, shakes, and slates are small-scale pieces of wood, asphalt, stone, or metal that are attached on top of the insulating layers of the roof assembly.

- Standing seam metal roofs come in various materials (steel, aluminum, copper, or zinc) with various lifespans and costs. Standing seam refers to the shape of the connection between adjacent pieces of metal that form the roof covering. Other joints include flat seam, rolled, batten, and t-shape profiles, each with different performance characteristics.

Before making a color choice for your roofing, always view in person an actual building with roofing of that color. The gaudiness of some shingle and metal roofs can be impressive, but not in a good sort of way. (Seeing a building in person is essential. Photographs don't help.)

The most vulnerable part of any roof is the edges. Sloped roofs with lots of interesting forms, such as dormers and domes, come with extra edges: eaves, ridges, and valleys that require extra attention to be sure that water or ice does not find its way into the building at these joints. For low-slope roofs, the edge of the roof and seams in the membrane are the weak points. With all roofs, transitions from roof to walls and penetrations through the roof (fans, access hatches, and (yuck!) skylights) are similarly vulnerable. Pieces of shaped metal (flashing) and sealants are arranged at these vulnerable points to provide multiple layers of defense against leaks.

Warranties on roofs are particularly valuable to a building owner. Make sure the design team has required the roofer to install the roof and all related flashings and penetrations in accordance with the manufacturer's requirements and recommendations. Understand the terms of your warranty and keep people off your roof!

V. Interior Walls

In most modern libraries, interior walls are constructed of gypsum board sheets (drywall) on steel studs. Most are finished with latex paint. It's a combination that lends itself to rapid assembly by skilled workers.

Drywall is plasterboard, sheets of gypsum plaster covered with heavy paper. It's a standard of the construction industry. Constructing a building interior with drywall and water-based paint is quick and inexpensive. Drywall and paint are fragile, but they're easy to repair, although new colored paint often doesn't match the original, forcing owners to repaint walls up to the nearest corner.

"Sheetrock" is a common drywall brand name.

The edges of drywall sheets are tapered to allow tape and drywall "mud" to cover the joints without sticking up.

A variety of different types of drywall are available, including drywall that is more fire resistant, moisture resistant, impact resistant, temperature resistant, and sound resistant. Some drywall is covered with fiberglass rather than paper to allow it to be plastered over.

As with almost all construction materials, there are national standards for drywall, and they should be cited in your architects' specifications for your building.

Drywall most commonly comes in four-by-eight-foot sheets, designed to be installed narrow end up to match standard eight-foot ceilings in houses. But libraries almost always need higher ceilings, and drywall is available in 4-by-12 and 4-by-16-foot dimensions.

Some libraries have made do with four-by-eight sheets, installing horizontal trim eight feet above the floor to cover the joint with upper sections of drywall. This is awkward and totally unnecessary. (If your builder tries to foist off short sheets on you, tell him that he has an unwarrantedly low opinion of you. Short sheets are for the tackier sort of fraternity house.)

Drywall is available in a variety of thicknesses, including ¼ inch, ⅜ inch, ½ inch, and ⅝ inch. Libraries will usually want ⅝-inch drywall, except when curved walls are involved, when two layers of ¼- or ⅜-inch drywall can be used by bending them into curves.

Mold-resistant drywall, often called green board, is made with a thick, wax-coated paper backing. It also comes with fiberglass mesh that resists mold growth. It's most often used in bathrooms, kitchens, and laundry rooms, and as a tile backer. (It's mold-resistant, not moisture-resistant, so it's not suitable for direct contact with water.)

Cement board comes in panels, but otherwise it's not like drywall. It provides a base for tile and stone and is used as an underlayment for countertops, walls, and floors.

For libraries, tough drywall is probably barely tough enough. Consult with your architects and engineers.

Concrete or concrete block are more durable than drywall on metal studs. Both of these are construction materials that support buildings, but some are left as exposed surfaces in storage and mechanical work areas. Or in the walls of school classrooms and hallways. In the construction trade, concrete blocks are referred to as CMUs, which stands for "concrete masonry units."

Librarians typically focus on specific needs with walls.

- Walls that block sound transmission.
- Paints that emit minimal odors while drying. It's difficult to move into a freshly painted building when the smell of the paint makes users and staff ill.
- Wall surfaces that are durable and easy to clean. The cheapest drywall and latex paint are an impressively delicate combination.

V-A. CONTROLLING SOUND TRANSMISSION AND REFLECTION

Some libraries have major problems with the transmission of sounds between rooms. Some standard things you can specify are:

- Walls that continue past suspended ceilings to the bottom of the floor or roof above. This is a standard way of keeping sound from migrating between offices or between study rooms. Fiberglass batt insulation in between the studs slows the transmission of sound.
- In the case of really noisy spaces (such as children's activity rooms), staggered stud walls are possible at only a modest increase in costs. In staggered stud walls, the plate at the bottom of the wall is slightly deeper, and the two sheets of drywall are supported by two sets of studs, eliminating the connection between the two walls that enhances sound transmission.
- Separately ducted air supplies and returns. If air ducts are not separate, they can serve as amazingly effective sound conduits between adjacent rooms.
- Sound-absorbing ceiling tiles. Tiles that absorb 90 percent of sound and simultaneously reflect 90 percent of light are available.
- Sound-absorbing wall surfaces. Many available wall surfaces absorb sound. In desperation, some libraries constructed with solid surface walls have retrofitted sound-absorbing panels, sometimes in large numbers. Because these panels are delicate, they should be located where users can't touch them.

Since these solutions are all structural, they'll be expensive to retrofit and should be in the basic specifications for your library.

V-B. TYPICAL WALL COVERING MATERIALS

V-B-1. Painted Drywall

Probably the most common wall covering in current libraries is drywall with latex paint. Unfortunately, it's also a very delicate product, one easily damaged by minor abrasion. Wooden furniture can easily knock off bits of paint. The sharp ends of rocking-chair rockers can literally cut their way through drywall. Dark paint colors help to make damage extremely obvious, and some dark-colored walls in some libraries require frequent repainting.

If durability is important, semigloss finishes are stronger than flat finishes. Oil-based paint can be tougher than latex. Enamels and other high-performance coatings are available for high-abuse areas when a more durable finish is too expensive.

In situations requiring extreme resistance to abuse, the interiors of buildings can consist of concrete block that has been sealed with epoxy and painted. This is extremely common in modern schools.

V-B-2. Plaster

Libraries' walls were traditionally plastered. It appears to be seldom done now due to labor costs, but it's far more durable than drywall.

Plaster was traditionally installed over wood lath (strips of rough-cut wood to which plaster can cling) and later metal mesh. Some was also installed over drywall, which comes in versions without paper coverings to prevent damage to the coverings from wet plaster.

Today, thin coats of plaster over impact-resistant gypsum board with fiberglass facing is available for use in high-impact areas.

V-B-3. Wood Paneling

Some libraries have wood paneling, especially in more dressed up areas.

Traditional wood paneling is actual pieces of wood. Conference rooms in major libraries are often finished this way. Raised strips of wood cover the joints between the individual wooden panels.

Inexpensive four-by-eight-foot panels with wood veneer are common, and American homes are full of them. As imitations go, they are not convincing replicas of real wood paneling.

V-B-4. Ceramic Tile

Many libraries use ceramic tile on restroom walls. Some tile is installed floor to ceiling, while other tile is on the lower parts of the walls only.

Ceramic tile comes with and without glazing. For most library situations, glazed tile is far easier to maintain, although it can be more slippery on floors.

Given the fragility of plasterboard and the frequent splashings in restrooms, floor-to-ceiling tile is a practical choice.

Very dark grout is essential in floor tile. All grout stains, but the advantage of dark grout is that we can't see the difference. (But you still have to clean and reseal the tile.)

V-C. PREVENTING DAMAGE TO WALLS

Because gypsum board and plaster walls are fragile, there are several ways of limiting damage. A couple are very historic.

In Fred's library, a user in a rocking chair slowly moved backward until the rear end of a rocker cut a long vertical gash in the drywall. The best way to prevent the damage to the wall was to get rid of the rocking chair, but far too many rocking chairs are gifts adorned with brass memorial plates and need to be prevented when they are in the early discussion phases. (For more on the many evils of rocking chairs in libraries and the uselessness of all the standard protections, see chapter 21, "User Seating.")

V-C-1. Chair Rails

Chair rails are a fine, traditional solution to the problem of chewed-up walls.

Chair rails are wooden strips mounted horizontally on walls at the correct height to prevent furniture from sliding into walls and damaging the surface.

There's a tendency to designate the height of chair rails without first checking the actual furniture planned for the library. If the backs of the library's armchairs are 32 inches above the floors and chair rails are centered at 38 inches, the chair rails won't do much of any good. So don't specify the heights of your chair rails until you've selected your furniture.

Some libraries find that when they purchase new chairs they have to install additional chair rails.

Wooden chair rails work far better if they are stained and varnished rather than painted, because painted finishes show damage far more easily.

Plastic and stainless steel bumper strips are available that do the same job as chair rails, protecting walls from adjacent furniture, collisions with book trucks, and similar mishaps. Often staff corridors are lined with plastic bumpers.

Chair rails can eliminate a lot of maintenance work. They probably aren't specified often enough.

V-C-2. Baseboards

Baseboards are another essential architectural feature hallowed by long antiquity of use. (The fact that they are sometimes called "mop boards" accentuates this.)

Today many baseboards are made of rubber, vinyl, or similar plastics. They are simply called "base" and are found everywhere. With the exception of the garage for the library van or restrooms with ceramic tile walls, you may be hard-pressed to find rooms in your library without this type of baseboard.

Vinyl baseboards have the advantage of being inexpensive, quick to glue into place, and easily replaced. While almost everyone uses simple vinyl baseboards, more ornamental ones are available. (Black vinyl baseboards make fine kick strips on service desks.)

For a more elegant look, you can always specify wooden baseboards, ranging from fairly simple boards with milled upper edges to elaborate combinations of flat wooden planks and ornamental trim pieces. Wooden baseboards need to be back primed to keep them from warping. They're also a lot harder to maintain than vinyl baseboards because they eventually need refinishing.

> Fred once inherited a library without baseboards. The architects apparently felt that baseboards are clunky, and that the crisp, baseboard-free look of library spaces would improve the appearance of the library. But the endlessly chewed-up bottom two or three inches of all the walls proved it to be a seriously bad idea.

The architectural concept for this part of a library called for no baseboards. The designers may have thought the entire effect would be tidy and modern, but it quickly became a battered mess. All sorts of traditional design features (such as baseboards and chair rails) have been around for a long time for very good reasons, and we abandon them at our risk.

Solid surface materials are available in relatively thin sheets that can be used for baseboards, corner guards, and wainscot that provides high-quality wall protection.

Baseboards are truly essential.

V-C-3. Corner Protectors

The protruding corners of walls are amazingly vulnerable to damage from furniture, book trucks, strollers, and other moving objects. Even though drywall corners may have metal L-shaped protective strips buried in the drywall mud, corners are still amazingly easy to damage.

A wide variety of metal and plastic corner protectors are available. We've had the best luck with stainless steel, but durable plastic protectors work well too.

V-C-4. Vinyl Wallpaper

Many libraries use vinyl wallpaper as a modestly priced upgrade in wall coverings. Vinyl wallpaper is far easier to wash than painted drywall. One popular place for its use is craft rooms or other places where users may spill things. Another is public library children's departments, where the combination of washability and cute artwork may work well.

Some vinyl wallpaper can be difficult to remove because traditional steaming techniques don't always work with plasticized surfaces. Talk with your architect about paper that can be easily peeled off. You can also install paper using heat-release glue.

VI. Floors

VI-A. BEARING STRENGTH

We've talked about bearing strength in floors on a number of occasions in this book, partly because it's a vital concept and because (unfortunately) some designers ignore it.

Library floors—all library floors—must be designed to carry no less than 150 pounds per square foot, live load. Outside of factories and warehouses, few buildings need to be as strong as libraries. ("Live load" means the weight of contents. The weight of the building itself is "dead load." Even extraordinarily massive buildings with huge dead loads may not have much leftover strength for heavy live loads. You'll need the opinion of structural engineers.)

Make sure your architects understand that at some future time you may decide to rearrange your library, and that you need to be able to put shelving anywhere you want. Where you will put books on opening day is only part of the story. (If you are pushed to say where books will

> In one library Fred worked with, the architect (despite all instructions) specified adequately strong floors only for that part of the building that would house books on opening day. At the ribbon cutting, Fred felt the floor shake oddly when people walked past him. When the library later had a structural engineer look at the floor system, it found it had to reinforce all the floors that did not have shelves on opening day before book shelving areas could be expanded—a lot more expensive undertaking than doing things right the first time.

go, the right answer is, "Anywhere we want." It's similar to what you say when designers ask you where you will put computers.)

Some library loads may require stronger-than-standard library floors. Fully loaded microfiche storage cabinets can be immensely heavy, as can compact shelving running on rails. In addition, compact shelving requires floors that don't flex, so the shelving won't bend the floors and run downhill. (Floor bending is called "deflection.") If you are planning compact shelving for any location other than slab-on-grade spaces, you'll need to review things with the manufacturer of the shelving and your structural engineers.

Before you coat or cover concrete with flooring, especially horizontal surfaces, you should test the concrete for moisture. These tests are primarily designed for new concrete slabs, but they can also be used on existing slabs, especially when people installing the flooring are unsure of whether a moisture and vapor barrier exists. Moisture coming out of or through the concrete can wreak havoc on floor finishes. The bubbles you may notice in floor finishes are most often the result of moisture moving up through the slab and then being trapped by the floor covering. The blame is on contractors for not waiting for the concrete floor to dry or omitting vapor barriers. If you can't stop them in time, add it to your punch list.

VI-B. FLOOR SURFACES

A wide variety of floor coverings is available. Obviously we're looking for something that simultaneously (a) is extremely comfortable underfoot, (b) wears like iron, (c) is unusually easy to clean, (d) brings an aura of beauty to our library rooms, (e) doesn't make noises when people walk on it, (f) soaks up the sounds that are bouncing around the library, (g) doesn't show dirt, (h) is not slippery when wet, (i) lends itself to easy replacement of worn-out spots, and (j) is a green product.

> If you find a floor covering that simultaneously meets all of these requirements, please contact the authors.

Most library flooring is glued down on top of poured concrete subfloor. Unfortunately, poured concrete is typically not as flat as one would wish. Sometimes self-leveling products need to be poured on low spaces before floor coverings are installed.

With the exception of terrazzo, concrete, and ceramic tile, all floor coverings are somewhat resilient and require more than just wet mopping.

Also, with the exception of terrazzo and concrete, all floor coverings require attic stock. Five or 10 years after you install your floor, you may be unable to purchase matching material, and you will be very pleased if you have some extra lying about the place.

> "Attic stock" is extra material that matches surfaces in new buildings. Common items are extra ceiling tiles, rolls of carpet, carpet squares, ceramic tile, vinyl base, rubber tile, vinyl tile, cork tile, and so on. One of the many reasons library buildings need generous amounts of storage space is the wide variety of attic stock items they may need to store. If your new building has an insanely wide variety of finishes, you'll need even more space for attic stock. Your architects may have recommendations about percentages for attic stock.

Vinyl base is usually installed after the floor covering, hiding the joint between the floor covering and the wall and protecting the bottom edge of the drywall from damage and discoloration.

If you are thinking of anything that is not an everyday product, try to view an installation or two before deciding.

There are a number of reference guides to aid in the evaluation and selection of flooring. Flooring is a highly visible surface material that receives significant wear and abuse and that impacts the safety and comfort of occupants. A broad range of criteria should be included in the evaluation.

Performance considerations include the amount and type of daily pedestrian traffic from inside and outside the building, the amount and type of "vehicular" traffic (carts, wheelchairs, desk chairs, and so on), slip resistance (see below), static resistance, impermeability, and water resistance. Other factors include exposure to moisture and change in relative humidity, sunlight through glass (UV light can cause color changes), abrasive materials (like mud and dirt), and damage due to scratches, indentations, and gouges. And the impact of maintenance materials on all of these.

Maintenance requirements should include your maintenance capabilities and expectations, frequency of maintenance required, the types of maintenance materials to be used, and their effect on the environment. For instance, there are chemicals like TSP you shouldn't wash down drains.

Installation factors include removal and disposal of materials and the treatment of subfloors, including resurfacing, leveling, toppings, insulation, underlayments, moisture barriers, and so on.

When new or innovative products are involved, always visit other libraries that use them. You never (as in NEVER) want to be the first kid on the block.

Coefficients of Friction are measures of the ability of surfaces to resist sliding or slipping. Standards require that the Static Coefficient of Friction (SCOF) be at least 0.50 or 0.42 when wet. OSHA requires 0.5 wet or dry, and the ADA requires 0.6 on flat surfaces and 0.8 on inclines or ramps, wet or dry. These standards matter because slippery floors can be extremely dangerous.

A new measure is the Dynamic Coefficient of Friction (DCOF), and we expect new standards.

VI-B-1. Broadloom Carpet

"Broadloom" carpet is carpet in rolls, typically 12 or 15 feet wide. The range of quality in broadloom carpet is huge. The best broadloom carpet is amazingly tough and strong and long-lasting, while the cheapest (and there's a whole lot of that running around) is pretty much total garbage.

The two common varieties of broadloom carpet are loop pile and cut pile. Cut pile carpet resembles carpet used in homes, while loop pile carpet consists of tight loops. A variety of pile densities may be available, and you are likely to be happier with the densest pile available. By and large, libraries prefer loop pile to cut pile because it is more durable.

Expert carpet installers can do an amazing job matching seams in broadloom carpet. Dissimilar carpets can be butted together, although variations in thickness may be apparent at the joints, and the exposed edges of the thicker carpet can deteriorate more quickly.

Because many poured concrete floors are somewhat irregular, many carpeting jobs include pouring on leveling mixtures that even out the surfaces of floors before carpeting is installed.

Carpeting can be installed on risers, such as those in children's multilevel story rooms, but strenuously avoid steps with curved edges.

Broadloom carpet in libraries is installed by gluing it down directly onto concrete. The kind of padding used in homes is unsuited for library use. The seams will split, and the weight of stacks and reading tables will permanently dent the surface of the carpet.

However, one ingenious architect Fred knows was able to pad the carpet behind a lending desk (where staff kill their feet by standing all day long). He did it by limiting the short dimension of the open space to less than 12 or 15 feet (the width of broadloom carpet) so he could install a pad while gluing down the back edge so there would be no seam to give way where the desk carpet met adjoining carpet.

Carpet is frequently used on stairs because it is quiet and tends not to be slippery. You may want plastic nosings on your steps to keep the edges from wearing out too quickly and to make the edges of the steps easier to see, especially by people walking downstairs. You'll also want to be sure that the installers get the carpet glued down perfectly flat, with no irregularities for users to catch their feet on.

Broadloom carpet lends itself to the insertion of ornamental pieces of carpet, such as animal groupings or aerial views of city streets in the carpet of public library children's departments. Check the websites of library supply houses.

Some designers create large patterns using multiple types of broadloom carpet. You may want to evaluate the intersection of these proposed patterns with the furniture layout in your library—including what the effect will be when you move the furniture around. We know of libraries where carpet patterns specified where furniture was to go, and that turned out to be a bad idea, another violation of the law of flexibility. We are also concerned that excessive numbers of seams may lead to more rapid appearance of problems.

Professionally installed broadloom carpet should be absolutely flat. We've seen bad installation jobs where carpets ended up with bubbles and wrinkles, and you want to reject them instantly.

> One library Fred worked with had carpet so badly wrinkled that it resembled a shar-pei dog. Unfortunately, the work was done by somebody's cousin, and the carpet just stayed.
>
> If you mention a bubble in your new carpet, someone may turn up with a rubber mallet, pound the bubble back down, and say, "It's fixed. Please give us the check." Always wait a few days to see if it pops up again. Fred's library once spent six months with popping bubbles before it totally rejected a carpet job and hired another firm to tear out the carpet and put in new.

Because of the wide variety in carpet quality and professionalism of installation, you may want to require in your bid specifications that the carpet vendors provide installation by their own staffs rather than subcontracting the work.

In the cheap home carpet market, lots of the installation is done by freelance workers who get the jobs from carpet firms by low bid. If you are installing carpet without the supervision of your architect, you will need to take particular pains to protect your library from substandard work.

VI-B-2. Carpet Tile (Carpet Squares)

Carpet tiles are typically about two-by-two-foot sections with adhesive designed to keep corners from lifting but at the same time making it possible to remove and replace individual tiles or to swap tiles around.

One of the great advantages of carpet tile is the ability to replace individual squares in areas where carpet wears out most quickly, such as where people stand at copy machines or in front of service desks.

Modern carpet tiles rely on patterns to conceal joints between tiles. A standard approach is to use families of tiles with a variety of similar shades to hide places where tiles have been removed and replaced. If all tiles are identical, a new tile will stand out like a sore thumb because it will be noticeably cleaner than all those around it. But if tiles tend in general to vary somewhat in brightness and color, the differences won't stand out as much.

Some maintenance staff members find the contrast between new and old tiles too extreme and instead bring older tiles out from back portions of rooms and put the new tiles in corners, where they come closer to matching the tiles less trodden upon.

Some carpet tiles have such extreme patterns that library users and librarians find them distressingly startling. Pick carefully.

Original carpet tile products were so unsatisfactory that Fred used to warn libraries against them, but modern carpet squares are often the best standard floor covering for many libraries.

While broadloom carpet is glued directly to floors, carpet tiles have a little built-in padding.

VI-B-3. Carpet Yarns

The basic varieties of carpet fiber are nylon, polypropylene (olefin), polyester, acrylic, and natural wool. The great majority of libraries use nylon. Polyester and acrylic are too fragile for library use. Wool is expensive (and the quality varies). Polypropylene does almost as well as nylon. But only almost.

Basically, unless you have the money for top-quality wool, go with nylon.

VI-B-4. Vinyl Tile

Vinyl tile remains popular, although it is not a green product. Unlike the more delicate products designed for home use, commercial vinyl tile requires waxing, stripping, rewaxing, and buffing, so it requires a fair amount of maintenance work.

Vinyl tile includes polyvinyl chloride, which is criticized by some people because manufacturing it leads to toxic byproducts.

VCT (vinyl composition tile) is a standard, modestly priced product. Individual tiles are commonly 12 by 12 inches, but some vinyl tile products now come in wood-grained strips.

Despite being discontinued in the late 1970s, VAT (vinyl asbestos tile) is still around in large quantities. A first warning sign is nine-by-nine rather than 12-by-12 tiles. As long as VAT is not crumbling, you can probably cover it up with something else, but it's more fun to know that it's not there at all. (With any building constructed before 1980, you always want to have existing vinyl floor tile tested for asbestos.)

VI-B-5. Rubber Tile

One substitute for vinyl tile is rubber tile, which is a natural product and does not require stripping, waxing, and buffing. It is also a great deal greener than vinyl.

Rubber tile is commonly used on staircase treads, particularly on service staircases. Look for rows of raised disks that resemble quarters. This pattern reduces slipperiness. If the staircase is slightly damp, water may settle between the raised quarters and leave the tops of the quarters dry.

Rubber tile is more expensive than vinyl tile but seems to be extremely sturdy and low maintenance. We've seen it in staff work areas in several libraries, and they seem to be very pleased with its performance.

Rubber tile has a more limited range of colors than vinyl tile.

VI-B-6. Cork Tile

Cork tile is a traditional, durable, and green product. Its popularity has come and gone over the years, but it has a reputation for working well.

Cork tile is made of ground cork superimposed on a base.

VI-B-7. Linoleum

Linoleum is made of linseed oil, cork dust, resins, and pigments on a cloth backing, usually burlap. Suitably for a product developed in the nineteenth century, the name comes from Latin for "flax" and "oil." It was widely used in homes for kitchen and bathroom floors, and in a variety of situations in public buildings and ships. But it went out of favor after World War II.

VI-B-8. Recycled Tires

Flooring made from recycled rubber tires is a green product and desirable for that reason. It's also fairly comfortable underfoot.

Because rubber flooring is made from old tires, it has a limited range of colors. Various varieties of speckled black are common colors. Our personal feeling is that most of the stuff is pretty ugly.

Rubber flooring can wear out in key traffic areas. One library Fred worked with had a terrible problem with endless ugly scuff marks on its new rubber flooring.

VI-B-9. Poured Epoxy

Poured epoxy is an unusually durable and chemical-resistant finish. In libraries, we see it used primarily for back room applications where spilled chemicals may be a problem, and in vehicle storage areas.

VI-B-10. Stained Concrete

Polished concrete floors are extremely durable, but they are hard on the feet of people who have to stand on them all day. Many are made in various stained colors, but the examples we see tend to have rather irregular colors. A good place to evaluate polished concrete floors is big box stores. While you're there, evaluate the floor for evenness and appearance, especially attractiveness of colors.

To the best of our knowledge, there's no attractive way to add leveling compounds to bare concrete floors, so if your floors are irregular—a frequent problem with poured concrete—you'll have to make good use of the leveling screws on your shelving and on your reading table legs.

This is pretty academic. We haven't seen many stained concrete floors in libraries.

V1-B-11. Terrazzo

Terrazzo is made of marble chips mixed with a grout-like material, cast in place, and then ground smooth when it has set. A wide variety of colors is possible, and patterns are often created by using brass bands to separate mixtures of various colors, much like champlevé work, then grinding the brass down with everything else. Terrazzo is impressively strong and water resistant. In libraries, it's frequently found where slush and snow and rain can be tracked in. It doesn't absorb moisture.

Terrazzo is widely used in entryways, but it is (a) extraordinarily hard and (b) extremely slippery when wet with tracked-in water and slush. The slipperiness of wet terrazzo leads many buildings with terrazzo entryway floors to use carpet mats. As a result, the pretty patterns in pictures of terrazzo floors in new buildings are usually obscured in everyday life with carpet mats spread out wherever users can walk.

People have slipped on wet terrazzo floors, broken their hips, and sued the libraries.

Terrazzo is a very traditional product with a long history of use in high-wear situations, such as school hallways. It's also rock hard and therefore hard on the feet. If your entire library has terrazzo floors, your staff will want to wear sneakers on the job. Our personal experience is that terrazzo seems even harder underfoot than concrete, but that may be just overactive imaginations.

V1-B-12. Bamboo

Bamboo is attractive because it is a green product with a pleasant color. The finished product is made up of many thin strips glued up edge-to-edge.

Bamboo has many uses in libraries, such as wood end panels for stacks and other kinds of trim. But bamboo is not strong enough for floors and staircases in libraries, and we've seen installations that had to be ripped out when they were still fairly new.

The quality of bamboo varies greatly. Much that was harvested when it was still green causes special problems.

VI-B-13. Hardwood

Hardwood flooring is another extremely traditional product. It can look handsome, but it strikes us as too delicate for almost all library installations. In libraries, we've seen hardwood floors in very formal reading rooms, exhibit areas, stage floors, and similar partially protected placcs.

Hardwood flooring is inherently noisy compared with more commonly used resilient floor coverings such as carpet, cork, vinyl and linoleum. A library user in spike heels crossing a hardwood floor can't be easily missed.

Hardwood flooring can vary extremely widely in quality. Once again, you'll want the advice of an architect and the ability to cite quality standards. The ASTM and ISO publish relevant standards.

Most hardwood flooring in libraries is tongue-and-groove flooring. We've seen parquet blocks used, but they gave the impression of lifting.

Standard wooden flooring is solid wood. Solid wood flooring lends itself to refinishing, with the top surface occasionally sanded down to provide an undamaged surface. Our experience has been that (a) sanding hardwood floors is a highly skilled undertaking, requiring skills that many workers don't have, and that (b) you've got perhaps two or three resurfacings before you have to replace the flooring.

The underside of hardwood flooring typically has longitudinal grooves to prevent the flooring strips from cupping or crowning.

Some inexpensive "manufactured" flooring products sold for home use are basically plywood, with a thin top layer of attractive wood glued to layers of less expensive products. These seem flimsy and totally unsuitable for use in libraries.

Hardwood can be installed over a layer of sand to enable more exact flooring heights. This is called a "floating" installation and requires expert workmanship.

Oak is the most common wood used in tongue-and-groove flooring, but hickory, maple, and other woods are available. See also the separate section on bamboo flooring (section VI-B-12).

Hardwood flooring can be a handsome but high-maintenance material.

VI-B-14. Ceramic Tile

Ceramic tile is a standard product of tremendous antiquity. It works well in restrooms, foyers, and other places where water can be frequently spilled. Unlike vinyl tile it does not need to be stripped, waxed, and buffed, but simply wet mopped or (if it's really filthy) scrubbed. The range of choices of color and surface texture is impressive.

For safety of library users and staff, ceramic tile flooring needs to have some anti-slip qualities rather than completely smooth top surfaces.

All ceramic floor tile installations need extremely dark grout. All grout stains permanently, and grout colors need to be dark enough to hide the stains. Colored grout also has a tendency to fade, so darker is better on installation day. (Maintenance firms tell us that the single hardest thing to keep clean in buildings is white grout.)

Ceramic tile is frequently used on staircases. Although bull-nosed tile is available, we've seen the lead edges chip, and you may want to have metal edges on the treads, often with inserted plastic strips. The lead edges on treads always need to be extremely visible to people walking downstairs.

The patterns and colors of ceramic change frequently, and many products are imported. For this reason, attic stock of ceramic tile is extremely important.

VI-B-15. Walk-Off Mats

Many libraries have recessed pans with fitted mats just inside their entrances. The mats have bars with spaces between that let water drain into the bottoms of the pans. When users scuff their way across the mats, salty water ends up in the pans, where the water evaporates. Periodically, the library removes the pans and scrapes up the salt. Some bars have carpet inserts and some have plastic inserts.

VI-B-16. Loose Floor Mats

Many libraries (and businesses of all sorts) place loose rug-surfaced floor mats near entries. Some of these are provided by rental services that clean the mats between uses. (Libraries that own their own mats have to have a way of cleaning them.)

Even if a library has built-in walk-off mats, users will probably track in a great deal of watery slop if the library does not use floor mats as well. In some libraries, potentially slippery areas like terrazzo floors are often completely covered by mats, making one wonder why the libraries spent the money on terrazzo in the first place.

VI-B-17. Summary

In many small and medium-sized libraries, the standard flooring materials appear to be nylon carpet tile for reading rooms and staff workrooms, ceramic tile for foyers and restrooms, vinyl tile for hallways and workrooms, and loose floor mats by the entrances to soak up extra water. You need attic stock of them all.

VII. Ceilings

For most library purposes, ceilings need to:

- Provide easy access to the tangle of equipment hidden above the surface.
- Reflect a high percentage of light for efficient use of reflected uplight.
- Absorb a high percentage of sound that strikes the ceiling.

The problems come with sloped ceilings (which may not work with acoustic ceiling tile) and with ornamental ceilings (which may not absorb sound or reflect light).

VII-A. ACOUSTIC TILE

For most libraries, the standard ceiling material is suspended acoustic tile.

Suspended acoustic tile has a number of very strong advantages:

- Providing easy access to the endless variety of MEP stuff hidden above ceilings in modern libraries, including air ducts, plumbing, electrical wiring, data cable, sprinkler piping, etc. Years ago, some buildings used plaster ceilings with access hatches, and the result was maintenance misery. With an acoustic tile ceiling, almost any section that does not include a light fixture or sprinkler head or air duct opening can be lifted out of the way, but with access hatches in drywall ceilings, extremely slender workers need to slither around in amazingly cramped circumstances.

- Sound absorption. Without acoustic ceilings, many libraries have unpleasant noise transmission and reflection. Especially in the case of sloped ceilings and barrel vaults, surfaces that don't absorb sound can be a serious pain.

- Light reflection. The best way to light libraries is to bounce light off ceilings. Brands of acoustic tile are available that combine high reflectivity with strong sound absorption.

- Generally tidy appearance, particularly with two-by-two tiles with recessed splines.

- Soffits can easily be created with ceiling tile. (But soffits in libraries are an abomination.)

A couple of major points:

- Impressive acoustic tile that absorbs 90 percent of the sound that hits it and reflects 90 percent of the light that strikes it is available.

- Regular acoustic ceiling tile can't be painted because that ruins its ability to absorb sound, but special acoustic tile is available that can be painted without ruining its acoustic qualities. We've seen libraries with sections of ceilings painted various colors, leading to dark and noisy spaces beneath—always a winning combination.

- Acoustic tile is extremely easily stained by water. Even trivial roof leaks or condensation can lead to major brown splotches on ceilings.

- Because patterns of ceiling tile come and go, and because it's so easily stained, you'll need a substantial attic stock of extra tile.

- Maintenance staff sometimes use secret marks (such as colored map pins) to indicate which acoustic tiles need to be removed for access to mechanical equipment.

VII-B. DRYWALL

Drywall ceilings are sometimes desired because they have a more finished look than acoustic tile ceilings. However, drywall ceilings are more difficult to construct, reflect sound, and severely limit access to the maze of MEP equipment above the ceilings. You don't want them.

Some spray-on treatments can help drywall ceilings absorb noise. The fuzzier the material, the better it works. (A few treatments look more like finished plaster and improve acoustics a little, but you still don't want drywall ceilings.)

The amount of equipment above ceilings is extensive, and it needs a great deal of inspection and repair to keep it going. Access hatches are available, but they require workers to slither around in amazingly tight spaces. You don't want that.

When leaks occur, moisture spreads quickly through drywall ceilings, and they're a lot harder to repair than simply replacing damaged acoustic tiles.

Just say no.

VII-C. PLASTER

Many older libraries have plaster ceilings. Plaster has the aesthetic advantage of fitting in with historic interiors. It makes elegant ceilings in great reading rooms.

Because of their hard surfaces, plaster ceilings can be impressively noisy. Spray-on materials that control the reflection of sound are available, but they eliminate the smooth look of plain plaster.

In historic libraries, equipment above the ceiling is accessed not through the ceiling but rather from above. Walking around the attic spaces of great libraries is a fascinating experience.

If roofs leak, damage to plaster ceilings can be impressive.

VII-D. WOOD

Attractive wooden ceilings have been installed in libraries. Some of the most impressive of all library ceilings are wood.

Unfortunately, especially if they are cathedral ceilings, wood ceilings tend to be noisy. If you and your designers are planning a wooden ceiling, you may want the input of an acoustical consulting engineer.

Dark wooden ceilings tend to cause lighting problems because they eliminate the ability to bounce light off ceilings, which is one of the best ways of lighting libraries. We've seen modern wooden ceilings where the architects returned to the lighting systems of a century ago—hanging fixtures to supply low levels of ambient light, plus individual light fixtures for all reading tables and shelving units. It's an expensive way to light a library, but if you can't have a brightly lighted ceiling, it may be your only option. And it can look extremely impressive.

VII-E. LINEAR SLOT AND PERFORATED ACOUSTIC CEILINGS

There are suspended ceiling systems that attempt to replicate the warm look of wood ceilings or the modern look of metal with improved acoustic performance. Some are linear strips of wood or aluminum with gaps between them that allow sound to pass between and then be absorbed by acoustic batts on surfaces above or on top of the strips. There are other systems that use perforations rather than the slots between the strips to let sound pass onto the absorbent material.

VII-F. SUMMARY

Suspended acoustic tile ceilings are the standard of the industry.

But sometimes you want something different. In this case, review the situation very carefully with everyone—your owners, architects, engineers, librarians, and building consultants—before you decide to abandon acoustic tile.

VIII. Snappy Rules on Surfaces and Materials

VIII-A. INTERIOR WALLS

1. Latex paint on cheap drywall has the strength of piecrust. You'll have to find some way to prevent furniture and book trucks from chewing everything up.

2. Chair rails are essential with drywall. Chair rail height is not an aesthetic decision. Decide on heights only after selecting your furniture, or you may end up with chairs that circumnavigate your chair rails and gouge holes in your drywall. Or end up with multiple parallel chair rails.

3. Baseboards have been around for centuries because they prevent cleaning gear from damaging the bottoms of walls. Our ancestors knew what they were doing.

4. If your library interior has lots of corners, you'll want lots of corner protectors. Especially in staff areas.

5. It's so hard to match intense paint colors that when you patch a wall you'll probably need to repaint the entire wall to both corners.

VIII-B. EXTERIOR WALLS

1. Vinyl siding can't be nailed down firmly because it has a different coefficient of expansion than the wooden walls behind it. The result is a tendency to flap. When there's a good hailstorm, vinyl siding tends to look engagingly perforated.

2. Brick walls used to hold up buildings, but when large buildings have steel frames, bricks serve primarily to provide durable, attractive exteriors.

3. There's an impressive vocabulary for bonds—various patterns of stretchers and headers in brick walls. But it's not in this book.

4. Just because brick is historic doesn't mean it always looks nice.

VIII-C. FLOORS

1. Regardless of what you'll be doing when you first move in, ALL LIBRARY FLOORS need to be strong enough to bear the weight of books.

2. If your entryway has an elegant terrazzo floor, it's possible that no one will ever see it because you'll keep it covered with carpet mats so users don't slip and fall and crack their hips.

3. Never be the first kid on the block to use a new flooring system.

4. Carpet tile is a great product. It needs pattern to hide the joints, but not TOO much pattern.

5. Solid color carpet shows every speck of crud. If your carpet is completely un-patterned, you will receive frequent and unhappy comments from your custodial staff.

6. Carpet patterns that specify the locations of specific items of furniture violate the key principle of flexibility in library design.

7. When the time comes to replace worn or damaged places in your carpet, it will no longer be in production. That's why people invented attic stock.

8. Library carpet can become impressively dirty. Home-level shampooing machines are cute but fairly helpless. Look for professional cleaning firms with heavy-duty equipment and vacuum extraction of water. And do it twice a year if you can afford it.

9. Ceramic tile and terrazzo can last for generations, but they're rock hard. All comfortable floor coverings have a limited life.

10. Some building owners opt for cheap initial flooring, hoping that budgets will be better at replacement time. Review long-term cost tradeoffs with your architects. (On the other hand, if you pick really trendy colors, you may be glad your carpet wears out quickly.)

11. If your library has a terrazzo floor, all of your staff will justifiably insist on wearing tennis shoes.

12. The less you like your carpet, the longer it will last. Fred worked with a library that had ancient avocado carpet that refused for decades to wear out.

13. Attic stock for flooring is essential. Count on the fact that you'll be unable under any circumstances to match your existing carpet or ceramic tile.

14. Ceramic tile always needs very dark grout. Don't let anyone talk you into anything else.

15. Cut-pile carpet is generally too delicate for serious library purposes.

16. The quality of carpet varies impressively. The best carpets are tough and last for years, but there are incredible quantities of total garbage available.

17. The standard carpet fiber is nylon. Lots of others are fragile or stain easily.

18. All kinds of designs are possible using a variety of carpet colors. Watch out for

designs that dictate furniture placement or for designs featuring different carpets, which tend to ravel at their exposed edges.

19. Hardwood floors can be impressive, but they require extremely expert installation, wood that can withstand library traffic, acoustic planning, and relatively high maintenance.

VIII-D. CEILINGS

1. Acoustic tile ceilings offer the great combination of enabling reflected uplight, absorbing unwanted sound, and providing easy access to all the MEP gadgetry above the ceilings. Don't sacrifice all this great stuff on an aesthetic whim.

2. If your library has dark ceilings, you'll have to provide individual lights for reading tables and shelves. It's an old-fashioned but expensive approach, with lots of areas where it's too dim to read.

3. NEVER PAINT AN ACOUSTIC TILE CEILING, for it will no longer be acoustic. If you must paint the ceiling, always stick with white. (Some specialty paints are available that supposedly do less acoustic damage.)

4. We've warned against ceilings with soffits of any kind (both perimeter soffits and soffits over service desks) in several places in this book, but they're such an abomination we're mentioning them again here.

VIII-E. ROOF COVERINGS

1. Standing seam metal roofing can be impressively brighter in real life than in small color samples. Always visit an actual building with the same brand and color of standing seam roof before you select a color. (Pictures lack the electric effect of real life and just don't work. Drive over and stand outside the actual building.)

VIII-F. GENERAL

1. When evaluating surfaces in other libraries, try to talk with those libraries' heads of maintenance.

2. Green materials are a great idea in libraries, but some can be extremely fragile. Always investigate other libraries that have been using them before specifying them yourself.

PART II
From Overcrowding
to Ribbon Cutting

CHAPTER 13

Building Codes

I. Introduction

Even if you own your site and it's paid for, there are a lot of rules that limit what you can build there or do with historic buildings.

One major area of rules is building codes. Codes may be national, statewide, or local. They are primarily concerned with issues of life safety, and many of them were originated by insurance underwriting associations. Depending on your state, there may be state electrical codes, fire codes, preservation codes, plumbing codes, accessibility codes, and so on. Local communities typically adopt codes written by national associations, such as the IBC (International Building Code), SBC (Standard Building Code), and so on.

Codes may need careful interpretation. For example, for one library Fred worked with, the engineers insisted that an energy-saving lighting option everyone—owners, library staff, and consultant—hated was absolutely required by energy codes, when it eventually turned out that another available option made everyone happy.

Remember that while saying a building "meets all applicable codes" sounds great, it actually means that "nothing in this building is so bad as to be actually illegal." Stronger floors, greater fire resistance, improved accessibility, better lighting, better plumbing, better air supplies, and better security—among many other features—are all worth carefully considering.

In many situations, as buildings increase in size, codes become more stringent. For example, library buildings need sprinkler systems when they exceed specified sizes. In situations like this, some libraries have carefully constructed buildings that are just small enough to slip under codes. Inevitably, of course, the day comes when the building needs to be expanded, and now the library has to retrofit sprinklers to the entire structure—almost certainly more difficult and expensive that installing sprinklers in the first place.

Sprinklers can at least be retrofitted, but other codes limit the amount of wood that can be used in framing, and this had led to libraries that can't be expanded without firewalls between various sections, which can create impressive functional problems.

A common zoning restriction faced by libraries is set-back requirements. Can the library be constructed right to the sidewalk, or must there be a specified open area between the library and the sidewalk?

Occasionally, libraries seek political relief from codes. Sometimes this involves shifting the zoning code definition of a proposed structure (for example, from neighborhood commercial zoning to central business zoning), but at other times it can involve challenging a specific technical requirement. Political responses can vary greatly. Zoning changes can happen, but you are likely to get absolutely nowhere challenging technical requirements.

The moral of the story is to know the rules, and to plan ahead, and do not cut corners. A high percentage of libraries are remodeled and expanded someday, especially when major funds for brand-new libraries may be limited, and expansion is undertaken instead. You don't want to make this future expansion extremely difficult or impossible.

II. Building Codes

Codes can be national, statewide, or local. It's a real tangle, one that your architects and engineers will need to sort out for you.

Building codes are usually there for good reasons. The history of American structures is full of disasters with great loss of life because of dangerous construction or criminal ignoring of rules. Many resulted in improved building codes. Some notorious examples include:

- The Iroquois Theater fire in Chicago in 1903, where 602 people died due to badly designed exits, among other things. In addition to bad design, city inspectors had been paid off to allow the theater to open before it was completed.
- The Triangle Shirtwaist factory fire in Greenwich Village in 1911, where 146 garment workers died in a building where fire exits had been chained shut.
- The Cocoanut Grove nightclub fire in New York in 1942, where 492 people died. Some exits had been welded shut to keep people from sneaking in and out, fire doors opened inward, and the front door was a revolving door. (Revolving doors are good for conserving energy, but can be fatal in fires. Modern codes have made great improvements.)
- The Our Lady of the Angels school fire in Chicago in 1958, where 95 students and teachers died. Among other things, it led to codes requiring far more fire-resistant construction and steel coat lockers instead of coats simply hanging on hooks in hallways.
- The Charleston Sofa Store fire in 2007, where nine firefighters died. It was a 17,000-square-foot building with no sprinkler system. Reports mention the incredibly inflammable nature of some modern upholstery but say little more about it. (Fred has vehement opinions about the way impressively inflammable upholstery is ignored by fire codes.)

America's more demanding codes may have helped prevent such international catastrophes as the Rana Plaza collapse in Dhaka in 2013, which led to 1,134 deaths, or the Grenfell Tower fire in London in 2017, which led to 72.

Many buildings violate codes. For example, Fred has been in libraries that were unbelievable firetraps, violating endless lists of safety codes.

Code enforcement can involve "grandfathering," where old buildings that do not meet current codes are allowed to continue in use if modifications are limited. Fred has been at meetings where architects had to point out how much could be done before the entire building was required to be brought up to current codes. Even if permitted, you may want to weigh the wisdom of leaving things as they were.

In some towns, existing buildings are larger than codes currently permit. The result can be buildings reduced to their steel frames and then rebuilt, in order to preserve the size of the structure.

Because inadequate or poorly enforced codes have led to multiple deaths, few communities are likely to compromise in any way when it comes to construction codes. Library boards that are accustomed to local willingness to discuss zoning issues are sometimes taken aback by the total refusal to even consider easing building codes.

Codes constantly change, and they never become simpler. Every time there's a major catastrophe, city officials wonder what rewrites of national or state codes will take place. (However, some catastrophes are due to willful disregard of codes—such as chaining exit doors shut to keep people from sneaking in without paying—making the issue one of enforcement rather than modified codes.)

Some buildings that initially meet codes are made illegal by owner modifications, and owners or managers need to keep an eye on things. A common example is library employees violating fire codes by adding cheap extension cords daisy-chained together rather than by requesting additional electrical outlets.

Municipal codes are basically published books written by private agencies. Municipalities adopt specific dated versions of the codes (much as some libraries adopt specific editions of Dewey). Some municipalities add additional local requirements to building codes.

Many American municipalities adopt the IBC (International Building Code). If your community has no comparable building code, you may want to suggest to your architects that they follow the IBC. (The IBC is the former BOCA—Building Officials and Code Administrators—code.)

It's important for your planners to know which editions of which codes your municipality has adopted, and what modifications to those codes it has made.

A general knowledge of code requirements is to your advantage, but you will need to rely on your architects and engineers to be sure that your building is in compliance with applicable codes. Your job is to be sure your engineers and architects are up to date on codes.

If your proposed library has a feature you don't like that's based on building codes, talk seriously with your architects and engineers. There may be a different option that achieves much of the same thing but doesn't involve altering a building code.

III. Additional Codes

In addition to building codes, a wide variety of other requirements control what can be constructed on specific pieces of property. Here are some of them, with directions to where to find them in this book.

Libraries need to be careful because not all codes agree. Sometimes different agencies enforce different codes on the same building. For example, the local building authority may enforce the IBC while the fire department or fire marshal simultaneously enforces the National Fire Protection Association (NFPA) code. The two codes may not entirely agree.

A library and its hired experts need to understand the requirements of the jurisdictions that have authority over the library's project. Usually the more restrictive codes rule. In the list that follows, some are codes and some basically just law or agreements.

- *Fire prevention codes.* The National Fire Protection Association publishes a variety of codes. Codes also cover sprinkler systems.

- *Zoning.* Zoning codes control the types of uses allowed in specific areas of land. Information on zoning is provided by local laws and planning maps. Most cities have zoning, but smaller communities may not. See chapter 9, "Site Selection."

- *Adverse possession.* Some people may have the right to use your site simply because they've been doing it for a while. This has caused serious problems for some libraries that were forced to provide access through their sites. See chapter 9, "Site Selection."

- *Covenants.* Covenants are similar to zoning, but consist of private legal agreements attached to deeds for property. Typically, covenants can be more restrictive than existing local zoning, but not less restrictive. See chapter 9, "Site Selection."

- *Accessibility codes.* Accessibility codes provide a wide range of requirements. Both national and state codes exist. They have many attributes of building codes, but they include non-structural requirements as well. See chapter 11, "Accessibility."

- *Energy codes.* A variety of codes are designed to save energy and encourage the design of energy-efficient buildings. These are included in chapter 33, "HVAC," because HVAC systems are the major consumer of energy in library buildings.

- *Plumbing codes.* The International Plumbing Code, Uniform Plumbing Code, and National Standard Plumbing Code cover different situations. See chapter 34, "Plumbing Systems."

- *Electrical codes.* The National Electrical Code. Some historic libraries have amazingly dangerous wiring. See chapter 32, "Electrical Systems."

- *LEED.* LEED stands for "Leadership in Energy and Environmental Design." Unlike building codes, LEED concepts are more like challenges, but the system has been adopted by many towns. LEED suggestions vary from year to year, which vastly complicates compliance. Because it is concerned with energy conservation, LEED is covered in chapter 33, "HVAC."

- *Preservation codes.* Many rules control what can be done with historic buildings and areas. See chapter 16, "Remodeling and Expanding Library Buildings."

In some cases, codes can have a major impact on the usability of sites, and you will need the help of your architects and engineers before committing yourself to a site. See chapter 9, "Site Selection."

The great variety of code requirements makes code compliance complex, and it can carry intense emotional baggage, ranging from resentment of loss of total free will on the part of landowners to emotional feelings on the part of enthusiasts that requirements do not go far enough. You will rely on your architects and engineers for their expertise and their knowledge of options, but be prepared to explore what options appear to exist.

IV. Snappy Rules on Building Codes

1. Beware of trying to save money by constructing library buildings that are just barely small enough to slither under code requirements. Sooner or later you'll want to expand, and the cost for upgrading the existing building can be painfully high. Sprinkler systems are bad enough, but if (for example) your building has too much wood in its construction, you may be seriously out of luck.

2. Ideally, always construct buildings that can be doubled in size and still meet current codes. This doesn't always protect you if relevant codes change before you need to expand, but it's a great start.

3. Trying to weasel out of building codes is not a good idea (as our choice of verb suggests).

4. City fathers *may* be willing to negotiate on zoning, but they'll be far less good-natured about building codes.

5. When you're faced with some sort of technical gadget for your building, the UL seal mounted on it is a comforting detail.

6. Building safety codes are almost always there for very good reasons. Don't quibble.

7. Some serious code violations—such as double-cylinder locks on the front doors of libraries—are quick and cheap to fix. If it's hard to find a good excuse for delaying, and a change could save lives, why not do it this afternoon?

8. Some of the worst losses of life have occurred in buildings where the owners purposively violated important safety codes. This is often a case for criminal prosecution rather than for altering codes.

9. Before you buy a piece of property, make sure that the applicable zoning, code requirements, and covenants allow you to construct the building you need. It's not much fun to find out that you can't build the library you need on the site you've just purchased. Get input from your architects, engineers, consulting librarian, and city officials before you commit yourself to a site.

10. Many existing buildings proposed for conversion to libraries fail to meet major building codes and are nearly impossible to correct. Never agree to any conversion without input from your architects, engineers, and consulting librarian. Codes are one of the reasons it may be cheaper to construct a new building than to remodel an older one.

11. Your architects, engineers, and city staff are your experts on building codes. Never make guesses about code coverage.

PART II
From Overcrowding
to Ribbon Cutting

CHAPTER 14

Bidding

I. Introduction

I-A. ABOUT BIDDING

Once the thousands of decisions that fill programming and design are complete, it's time to get a team in place to construct the library. For most libraries, that entails getting prices through a competitive process called "bidding." While it is typically the fifth major phase of a project (after programming, schematic design, design development, and contract documents), much of the decision making about the bidding process occurs in earlier phases. In fact, the agreement with the architect will often specify how the project will be bid and constructed.

The biggest decision, and one that should be addressed at the outset of the project, is selecting a "delivery method," which is how the project will be constructed. The allowable delivery methods and associated bidding processes for public entities are usually governed by state statutes or equivalent government regulations. Private owners have more latitude in setting the procedures by which contractors will submit bids on the work.

The traditional and most common delivery method is called "design-bid-build." Information on the project is made available to general contractors, who then submit "bids," which are the prices they will charge to complete the project as it is described.

For larger or more complex projects, many libraries use a "construction management" delivery method. Construction management firms supervise the work, and they bid it out in many small increments.

Bidding and construction requirements vary enough between the various delivery methods that the specifics can change a cost estimate, and you'll need to have made some key decisions before the schematic design estimate is prepared.

In any of the delivery methods, the specific procedures that cover the bidding process itself as well as the administrative tasks that go along with the actual construction process need to be discussed with your insurer and your attorney, who both help with risk management.

The process should begin in the design development phase and be finalized at the start of the construction documents phase to ensure that the documents clearly define "the rules of the game," and that all bidders have a clear understanding of the cost implications of those rules. Failing to do so opens the door for contractors to request additional money to cover procedures they did not anticipate in their bids.

I-B. BASIC BIDDING VOCABULARY

This list covers a number of the unfamiliar terms you will come across in bidding.

- *Add alternate.* This is an extra feature you'd like to have the choice of including in your building, and for which you want a price. Prices for individual add alternates are part of contractor's bids, and the library later chooses which ones it wants.

- *Addendum.* A written change to the instruction to bidders or to the bid documents.

- *Bid.* The price for which a contractor offers to do work. Subject to various legal restrictions, construction contracts go to the lowest responsible, responsive bidders.

- *Bid form.* A form on which the bidders state their full understanding of the project, the price for which they will complete the work in accordance with documents, and their price for any alternate bids. It is a binding agreement to enter into a contract if their bid is accepted.

- *Bonds.* Insurance to protect the owner if things go wrong during construction. Various bonds cover the decision of low bidders not to do the work after all, contractors or subcontractors going broke during construction and leaving fiscal messes behind, and situations where contractors don't pay their subcontractors, who then have the right to sue the library.

- *Construction management.* A construction method where the owner hires a firm to manage the project. The firm manages the project and hires individual contractors by low bid to do the work. Many large or complicated projects are done by CMs.

- *Contractor.* The company that agrees to provide labor, materials, and supervision needed to build the project in accordance with the contract documents.

- *Delivery.* Construction of the building.

- *Design-bid-build.* The most common construction delivery method. Architects and engineers design the library. Owners advertise for bids, and interested contractors bid the project. The bidder with the lowest responsive, responsible bid becomes the contractor and builds the library.

- *Design-build.* A delivery method wherein the bidders are contractor-architect teams.

- *Prequalification.* Evaluating potential bidders to make sure that they meet the library's qualifications before they may submit bids.

- *Prevailing wage.* State and federal laws specify minimum wages paid for various types of work. Typically, prevailing wages are equal to union scale.

- *Responsible.* Said of a bidder who meets the qualifications and requirements of the project. The qualifications requirements typically include successful experience with buildings of similar size, complexity, and cost, and the financial resources to do the work.

- *Responsive.* Said of bidders that meet (respond to) all listed requirements and can demonstrate that they have understood and included all of the work identified in the bid documents in their price.

- *Subcontractor.* A specialty contractor hired by the library's general contractor to do part of the work. General contractors are basically organizers, and most of the actual work is done by subcontractors.

- *Value engineering.* The process of evaluating construction options to determine the most cost-effective way of achieving the project's performance and quality objectives. Basically, a cost-benefit analysis. Value engineering is important to conduct early in the design process, or it may result in just purchasing cheaper materials. Value engineering is often a basic service of construction management firms.

II. Delivery Methods

"Delivery" is construction talk for the creation of the project described in the bid documents.

Two of the most used, and confused, construction roles are the construction manager and the general contractor. They both have the knowledge and experience to complete a project from start to finish. Both are involved with the hiring and overseeing of subcontractors. Both manage day-to-day work. However, there are some critical differences between the two, particularly in how money is paid out over the course of the project, owner involvement, and certifications.

II-A. DESIGN-BID-BUILD PROJECTS

In this approach, general contractors (GCs) are given or purchase copies of the construction documents, work with various specialty subcontractors (such as plumbers or electricians) to figure out the cost of materials and labor needed to complete the work described in the contract documents, and submit a bid on the project. The lowest "responsive and responsible" bidder is awarded a contract to undertake the construction.

"Responsive" and "responsible" are important terms.

- A "responsive" bidder is one who has followed all the procedural rules and submitted a complete bid within the allotted time. A complete bid is one that includes various certifications and acknowledgments, as well as prices for the various base bids and alternatives identified. It must be signed by a representative of the firm who is authorized to bind the bidder to the terms of the bid and a subsequent contract.

- A "responsible" bidder is one who is capable of doing the work. This is usually determined by checking references on projects of similar size, cost, or complexity. Most jurisdictions consider a previous project that is one-half to three-quarters of the cost or size of a project to be sufficiently similar to the project being bid to be an allowable reference.

The general contractor provides overall management, occasionally performs some of the work, and is responsible for the quality of the work and timely completion of all the work by subcontractors.

Advantages of design-bid-build:

- Simplicity. You have one point of contact. You rely on that firm to know what it is doing and to do it well.

- Single point of responsibility. Perhaps the most significant difference between a general contractor and a construction manager is who is to blame if something goes wrong. A general contractor is, by law, responsible for what is agreed upon in the building contract.

Disadvantages:

- When general contractors are in charge, owners typically do not have a say in whom the contractors assign to run the project and whom they hire as subcontractors. Because of the competitive nature of the bidding process, there is pressure on contractors to select the subcontractors with the lowest prices rather than the top reputations. This gives the subcontractors the financial incentive to cheapen the work if the bid specifications allow it.

II-B. CONSTRUCTION MANAGEMENT

A second approach has become more prevalent in the last 20 years. In this approach, the library hires a construction management firm (CM) that does work similar to that of a general contractor, but does it in a more transparent way.

There are two general approaches to contracting with a CM firm, straight construction and CM "at risk."

II-B-1. Construction Management as Advisor (CM/A)

In the advisory form of construction management, the CM acts as an agent of the owner. For this reason, it is also known as CM Agency (CM/A). The CM/A bids out each segment of the project on behalf of the owner, and the owner contracts directly with each contractor. The CM/A supervises every aspect of the work, overseeing the work of all of the subcontractors to be sure that it is completed to acceptable standards and in accordance with the construction drawings. The CM/A sorts out any difficulties, such as problems that arise with a mixture of union and non-union subcontractors.

Advantages:

- One source of comfort when dealing with a construction management firm is that the firm has no financial incentive to cheapen the product. Of course, subcontractors are selected by low bid, but the CM/A is there to fight them on the library's behalf.

- It's best to look at construction management firms as building advisors. CM/As are more often than not involved in the design phase. The owners can be as involved or uninvolved as they wish. They can work with the CM/A to pick out materials, offer design suggestions, and even supply some of the labor. The CM/A plans every phase of construction and manages subcontractors, each of whom the owner pays directly.

- Usually CM/As have many connections with subcontractors and make suggestions to the owners. Sometimes owners have specific subcontractors they want to work with.

- There is a high level of transparency related to project costs. The owners can see the costs paid by the CM/A for various items and services. If the CM/A is able to find a less expensive source of needed construction site work (fencing, plowing, cleanup, etc.), the owner saves money. With a general contractor, the GC just keeps the savings.

Disadvantages:

- A CM/A advisor ultimately is not liable for work performed, since the owner hires the subcontractors. If there are disputes during construction or after construction is complete, there could be multiple contractors to track down and engage in a resolution process. Most CM/A firms will manage this too, but it is good to understand the legal parameters and the level of direct involvement required.

- The assumption is that CM/A fees will be about the same or less than general contractor profits, leading to equivalent or lower total construction costs. But sometimes CM/A fees can be greater than the savings due to eliminating the GC.

II-B-2. Construction Management at Risk (CMAR)

The "at risk" form of construction management is a blend of the GC and CM/A approaches. In this approach, the CMAR holds the subcontracts (much as in the GC approach) but provides the preferred level of transparency found in the CM/A approach. This hybrid allows you to select the CMAR as a professional service and competitively bid out the subcontracts.

In this arrangement, the CMAR contracts directly with all of the individual contractors. The CMAR runs the entire project, coordinating the activities of all of the specialized contractors. Each specialized part of the project is bid separately, with coordination between the contractors managed by the CMAR rather than by the general contractor. The CMAR is said to be "at risk" because if the building cannot be constructed for the agreed amount, the CMAR takes a loss on the project.

The usual arrangement is that the CM/A's costs and fees are negotiated in advance. The fee is usually a percentage of the cost of construction, while the overhead costs are invoiced to the owner as they are incurred. If these costs are less than anticipated, the savings accrue to the library rather than a GC.

Advantages:

- Simplicity. You have one point of contact. You rely on that point of contact to know what they are doing and to do it well.

- Single point of responsibility. Perhaps the most significant difference between a general contractor and a construction manager is who is to blame if something goes wrong. A general contractor is by law responsible for what is agreed upon in the building contract.

- One source of comfort when dealing with a CM/A or CMAR firm is that the firm has no financial incentive to cheapen the project.

- Like CM/A firms, CMAR firms are more often than not involved in the design phase. The owners can be as involved or uninvolved as they wish to be. They can work with the CM to pick out materials, offer design suggestions, and plan out the phases of construction.

- Usually a CM has many connections with subcontractors and makes suggestions to the owner.

- There is a high level of transparency related to project costs.

Disadvantages:

- Some CMAR firms act like GCs (general contractors). You get the disadvantages of that approach with the expense of construction management.

II-B-3. Guaranteed Maximum Price (GMP)

Occasionally you will see construction management combined with Guaranteed Maximum

Price or GMP. The idea behind this is to get a fixed limit on construction costs early in the project and thereby limit the library's risk. This sounds good, but there are some problems with GMP.

- The CM is now in the same position as the contractor in a traditional design-bid-build project, because reducing costs after the GMP is established may offer financial advantage. Some agreements try to address this by allocating a sharing of savings between the library and the CM.

- Since the agreed amount of the entire project is arrived at by agreement, in advance of actual bidding, in essence the project is not undertaken by low bid. This may or may not be legal for government work where you live.

- The "price" in GMP is established in advance of completed design. Depending on how far in advance, there could be a significant amount of information yet to be developed. Most GMP projects we have experienced have numerous caveats such as "based on the information available" or a similar "out" clause that allows the CM the opportunity to revise the cost as more information is developed. As a result, the price is neither guaranteed nor is it a maximum.

II-B-4. Hiring Construction Management Firms

State law may control methods for hiring construction management firms. For example, you may be required to advertise for firms and rank order applicants. (Even if the law doesn't require this, it's a good idea.)

Hiring a construction manager is similar to hiring an architect or a consulting librarian/programmer:

- Place advertisements in suitable publications.

- Provide an RFQ with questions about the firm's past achievements. You will want to know about the variety of projects it has completed, to be sure it has done projects in your general size range. You will want to know if it has been sued, and, if so, the outcomes. You will want to know the histories of any labor disputes. You will want to know its history of bringing in projects on time. And you will want a list of completed projects with contact information.

- As with architectural firms, the specific people assigned to the project can matter. It's appropriate to ask about the person who will run the project for the CM firm and check that person's references.

- Review qualifications.

- Talk with references.

- Interview a maximum of three firms (or four if you're forced to interview a firm you wouldn't hire on a dare). Expect to meet the people who will manage your project, not their public relations staff or sales representatives.

- Select a firm.

- The process should NOT be by low bid. As with an architect, costs are important but expertise and past successes count for far more. (Your state laws for government projects may specify the equivalent of the QBS process used for selecting architects.) As with hiring architects, some states may prohibit you from asking about fees until after you have rank ordered the applicants. We think those states are very right.

What can you look for in a potential CM?

- General range of experience:
  - » Does the firm have a wide range of experience with projects?
  - » Has it done a number of projects in your size range? (You need the firm to be comfortable with projects like yours, but you don't want it to regard your project as a trivial one.)
  - » Past jobs.
- References from previous clients. Among the questions you can ask are:
  - » Did the CM estimate costs accurately? (CMs should be the real experts on construction costs.)
  - » Did things move smoothly on the job?
  - » How effectively did the CM handle change orders?
  - » Were there any union problems on the job site?
  - » Was the job site kept clean, or was it a physical mess?
  - » If you asked the firm to provide value engineering services, was it able to find ways to cut costs without just cutting quality?
  - » Did the firm maintain tight quality control? Did they keep a close eye on the work of all of the contractors and subcontractors? Were they painstakingly aware of details? Did they catch architectural errors?
  - » Did the CM attempt to self-perform? Did the CM want to use the CM's own employees for parts of the work? (This is a major conflict of interest, since it avoids bidding.)
  - » Did the firm use modern software, such as BIM?
- Possible interview questions:
  - » What unique processes do you incorporate into the process?
  - » If we called your references, what would they say about your firm?
  - » How many libraries have you built?
  - » How is your company going to make the library administration's life easy during this process?
  - » How do you handle change orders?
  - » How do you prevent schedule slippage?
  - » How do you communicate during the process?
  - » How will you protect our best interests?
  - » How do you handle adversarial or controversial situations?
  - » What challenges do you see with our project?
  - » What ideas to you have for delivering this project at a lower cost?
  - » What is your approach to managing tight sites?
  - » How do you work with government authorities?
  - » What is your approach to estimating?
  - » How do you ensure timely close-out of projects?
  - » How do you keep a job running smoothly when difficult circumstances arise?
  - » What process do you employ to screen and pre-qualify bidders?
  - » How do you ensure quality in the field?

- » How do you handle clients who are very busy both professionally and personally?
- » Give us an example of a difficult situation with a client, architect, or project, and how you handled it.
- » How do you view your role as our CM after the warranties expire?
- » How do you handle union versus non-union situations?

II-C. DESIGN-BUILD PROJECTS

Most libraries are built on the design-bid-build system or by construction management firms, but a few are design-build projects.

In a design-build project, a team consisting of a contracting firm and an architectural firm agree in advance to construct a building for a specific price.

The advantage of the design-build process is that design-bid-build projects can come in far above the architects' estimates. This may be a particular problem with signature architecture, but it can also happen in fairly modest projects, where bids can come in at two or three times the architects' estimate.

By and large, architects appear unenthusiastic about design-build projects, for it places them essentially in the role of being employees of contractors. More importantly, many jurisdictions preclude this method for public entities. The proscription is based on the architect-contractor relationship eliminating one of the checks deemed important to the public interest. In design build, the contractor has much greater control over quality and performance that, in a design-bid-build delivery method, would be the purview of the architect and owner. Chief among these is that the contractor selects the architect.

One of the problems with design-build projects is that the contractors decide on their own profits, with little the owners can do to control them. This is not as important in some building types, but for any specialized project type, the owner-architect relationship is critical and should not be replaced by a contractor-architect relationship.

From the point of view of librarians, design-build projects can be primarily glamor contests, placing vastly more emphasis on appearance than function. If the winning design turns out to need various kinds of functional tweaking, do these alterations all become high-priced change orders?

If you are interested in a possible design-build project, be sure it's legal for your project.

II-D. SELECTING A DELIVERY METHOD

Local tradition is important in determining which delivery method is most appropriate. Some parts of the country build only in one method or the other, and swimming upstream can lead to more trouble than one needs. If both methods are available, and with the exception of small or simple jobs, we think construction managers are a great idea. The underlying value is that most states allow CM services to be hired as a professional service. This allows you to assess the capabilities of the team you will be working with rather than relying on good fortune through a blind bidding process. The public's interest in low cost and level playing field are protected because the CM bids out the actual construction through the usual process of competitive bidding. Ultimately, the people you work with are the essential indicators of success. Why leave this to chance if you don't have to?

III. Getting Ready to Bid

III-A. CONSTRUCTION DOCUMENTS AND SPECIFICATIONS

Construction drawings and specifications are prepared by your architects and engineers. They are described in detail in the chapter on design.

Drawings are the basis for both bidding and construction. They provide in tremendous technical detail all of the information required to convey a design intent for your new library building or for the rooms it will occupy. ("All" is not really correct, since many additional "shop drawings" will be prepared during construction, and those are the documents from which a building is constructed.)

Sloppy construction drawings can be a nightmare for owners, for they lead to omissions, to features you didn't want, to the absence of features you want, and—expensively—to change orders. The cost problem with change orders is particularly true because so many subcontracting firms can be involved in a single change, such as adding a private restroom for the director.

For a large structure, construction drawings can be a huge roll of prints, but even the smallest library will have 20 or 30 sheets of drawings.

All construction drawings are accompanied by specification books that list applicable standards for all components of the building. National standards exist for virtually every item or construction material in your building, and by citing appropriate standards, your architects allow competitive bidding, control costs, and protect you from substitution of cheaper and lower-quality products. (Actually, contractors sometimes try to pull fast ones, but the specifications protect you.)

Even for a small building, the spec book can be an inch-thick stack of double-sided 8½-by-11-inch paper.

Because national standards exist for virtually every item or construction material in your building, most specification books can look like boiler plate. If you are interested in cost control, leveraging this standard information that applies equally to a wide variety of buildings is important. But don't be fooled: including all products that are part of an industry standard specification is in itself a considered process. Many of the products in the standard are not up to the rigorous requirements of a heavily used building like a library.

III-A-1. Cost of Labor

Bids for government work may also be affected by "prevailing wage" laws, which specify that all work will be done by workers paid not less than a specific wage. Fringe benefits may also be specified.

Prevailing wage laws go back to the federal Davis-Bacon Act of 1931, although some states had similar laws as early as the late nineteenth century. Today, many states have their own separate prevailing wage statutes in addition to federal statutes.

In many jurisdictions, prevailing wages are basically union scale. Laws may exclude a requirement for union labor, but in practice, specifying prevailing wages probably means union labor.

Early estimates should account for the cost of labor, which can be union only, prevailing wage, right to work, and so on. If you are not governed by statute or ordinance, selecting a wage rate strategy is essential in developing accurate cost estimates.

III-A-2. Value Engineering (VE)

Construction management firms often do "value engineering" for their clients. Value engineering involves analyzing the architects' plans to ask whether a very similar effect with equally high quality functionality could be achieved at a lower price by changing minor details. Frequently this will involve different engineering.

For example, a CM may point out that the curved I-beams your architect is specifying could be replaced by straight I-beams at a very substantial reduction in cost. You may want the curved I-beams, in which case you do nothing, but it could also be that they are not all that important to you. Or not important at all.

Whether it involves the CM or not, to be effective, value engineering often needs to take place early in the design process, where a simple change may bring about substantially lower costs. If value engineering waits until the end of the design process, it can result in simply substituting cheaper components rather than finding major savings by altering construction concepts or methods. There should be a value engineering exercise along with each estimate. You do not want to wait until the last minute to figure out how you are going to get bids that fit within your budget.

For this reason, if you decide to hire a CM firm, you are better doing so early in the design process.

III-A-3. Phased Construction and Interim Facilities

When libraries are expanded and remodeled, one of the major planning decisions is whether to move out during the course of construction or to do the work in phases, with the library moving contents back and forth to keep out of the way of the contractors. Typically, remaining in the building involves two-phase construction, where the library constructs a new addition, camps out in the new addition while the existing building is remodeled, and then moves back into the original building.

While many phased projects involve two phases, some have many phases, with the library endlessly moving stuff back and forth to keep out of the contractors' way.

Most projects in really large buildings end up being done in phases, for there is no practical way to move out during construction.

In general, you should expect much more attractive bids if you move out of the building during construction. From contractors' points of view, the job is much simpler. They have access to the entire building. They don't have to provide safe access for library users and staff. They can use your parking lot for their construction office and for stacking construction materials and dumpsters. They don't have to deal with complaints about noises, smells, dust, etc., from users and staff. The various trades (such as electricians, plumbers, HVAC workers, drywallers, painters, and so on) have to come only once rather than return for each successive phase.

From your point of view, the project will go substantially faster if you move out. Your staff and patrons will be spared dust, bad smells, noise (ranging from the crashes of falling objects and the whine of saws to the unfortunate choices of music on workers' radios), disruption of services, awkward access through temporary entrances, and so on.

If you do not move out, you will need to determine who controls what happens on the site. Where will library users, library staff, and construction workers park? Which doors will be open for staff and public use, and when? If there are several phases, will all of these arrangements keep changing, probably confusing library users?

Moving out also helps avoid a major problem with your HVAC system. If a library is expanded in two phases, the HVAC system for the first phase needs to be switched on at the completion of that phase so the library can operate in the new space. If remodeling of the original building requires a year, by the time the library moves back in, the standard one-year warranties will have expired on the equipment in the new addition. Subsequently, if the equipment in the new addition and the equipment in the original building fail to function properly as a single system, you're pretty much out of luck.

A solution to the HVAC problem is specifying in your construction contracts that warranties on all HVAC equipment commence at the completion of the final phase of the project, but you may have trouble obtaining this.

Moving out requires leasing temporary quarters for your library. Empty big box stores make good temporary locations if their MEP systems still function. Other libraries have rented two or three empty stores in strip malls—stores nearby each other if not actually adjacent.

Some libraries find that the available temporary spaces are too small. In this case, it's possible to put the least-used portion of the collection in storage. Most computerized lending systems can provide lists of the least used items in the collection, which can be pulled from shelves and boxed for storage.

Whatever you choose, your phasing plans need to be part of the bid specification, since the decision has such a substantial impact on contractors' costs.

III-B. ITEMS EXCLUDED FROM GENERAL BIDS

One thing that you and your architects will determine in advance is which items in your library will not be provided by your general contractor. Typically, construction bids exclude fixtures, furnishings, and equipment (FF&E).

These items are excluded because you may want tight control over some things that do not have to be carefully integrated into the construction process. For instance, some electronic systems may prove to be difficult to specify for low bids if no two have exactly the same features. In addition, for some systems, the vendor's reputation for maintenance can be vital.

IV. The Bidding Process

If you are following the traditional design-bid-build approach, your architects will normally manage the bidding process for you. If you are using a construction management firm, the CM will handle the bidding. In either case, they are doing this on your behalf and in your name. You will need to be cognizant of your state requirements as well as any policies the library has related to procurement.

With design-build projects, the bidding will be between individual contractors and the design-build team.

IV-A. PREQUALIFICATION OF BIDDERS

In many circumstances, particularly bidding situations where there are known contractors with bad reputations or inadequate experience, owners and architects may choose to "prequalify" bidders. Only bidders who have proved they can meet the owner's basic criteria are allowed to submit bids.

Your architects should handle prequalification for you. Typically it might involve checking to be sure that the contractor has undertaken projects of your scope (you don't want a tract home builder constructing a 100,000-square foot library), has an unblemished fiscal reputation, is not involved in litigation, has the necessary licenses, and so on. When advertising for bids, your architect will specify that bidders must meet certain qualifications. Obviously, these need to be objective (for example, previous experience with buildings in excess of 25,000 square feet) rather than subjective (no bad vibes among folks in town).

Instead of pre-qualification of bidders, some architects may include a list of minimum qualifications with the bid documents. As part of the approval process for low bidders, these qualifications are verified by the architects.

Although prequalification of bidders is preferable to post-bid evaluation of the lowest bidder, it is not always possible. Many jurisdictions preclude any attempts to limit the number of bidders. While pre-qualification attempts to establish who is a responsible bidder and then seek competitive bids, most jurisdictions attempt to find the lowest bid first and then determine if the apparent low bidder is in fact responsible and responsive. At that point, it is much more difficult to reject a bid, because the time available for review is limited, and because public rejection of the apparent low bidder is often followed by some form of legal action by the disappointed party.

Prequalification of bidders is essential.

IV-B. ADVERTISING FOR BIDS

When you are ready to bid a standard design-bid-build project, your architects will arrange for advertising aimed at general contractors. Laws may specify where advertisements must appear.

In days gone by, contractors interested in bidding on your project would pick up sets of drawings and specification books from the architects' office, but now these items are more likely to be sent electronically for contractors to print out in their offices. (For libraries, this saves a great deal of money, since there would be many sets of the documents, and the libraries were responsible for paying for having them reproduced.)

IV-C. PRE-BID MEETINGS AND TOURS

IV-C-1. Pre-Bid Meetings

At a time before the bids are due, the architects will schedule a pre-bid meeting where they collect questions from bidders. In order to prevent disappointed bidders from contending that other bidders were given information privately, and to help get as many well-considered bids as possible, answers clarifying the construction documents are answered after the meeting in the form of an addendum. Do not expect any answers or high drama at this meeting.

If they know what they're doing, the architects will answer all questions in writing and insist that oral answers given at the meeting or at any point in the bid process are not binding. This prevents contractors who mishear or misunderstand the architects' answers to their questions from contending at a later time that the written answers differ from those given at the meeting. The Bid Form includes space for bidders to acknowledge that they have received all addenda and that their bids are based on the information included in the addenda.

Pre-bid meetings come in two flavors: mandatory and non-mandatory. Mandatory meetings are important in complex projects or renovations. The biggest reason to get everyone there is not for the actual meeting but for the tour that follows.

IV-C-2. Tours

Particularly in the case of expansion and remodeling jobs, contractors will want to stop by the library to see the building. This is best accomplished as part of the pre-bid meeting and under the auspices of the architects or CM, who will run the meeting and tour. This is for the protection of your library staff and governing board, who can unwittingly make comments that can be misinterpreted.

Having more than one tour is a good idea because it's extremely hard to find a single tour time that all interested contractors can attend. The usual minimum number is four tours, morning and afternoon tours on two successive days.

Never offer tours outside of the publicized times. If contractors turn up unannounced at other times, tell them to call the architects or CM.

Often contractors will raise questions during tours, but librarians need to limit their responses to saying "hi" and showing contractors where things are. The importance of avoiding even a hint of favoritism is why library staff members should show bidders anything they want to see but should refrain from answering any questions except directional ones.

If you are keeping a diary of the project, you will want to note which firms toured the building and how long they spent looking at it.

IV-D. SUBSTITUTIONS AND RESOLVING CLAIMS OF "EQUIVALENCIES"

Depending on laws, government construction projects may be required to list a range of products that will be acceptable for a specific situation. For example, a bid set may list three acceptable electrical fixtures, specifying brand names and model numbers.

Problems can occur when the construction documents are required not only to list several alternate fixtures but also to state "or equivalent." This opens the door to contractors' claiming that some other product is the equivalent of the one specified by brand and model. Unfortunately, the suggested equivalents frequently fail to be equivalents. Contractors may find similar products that are being discontinued and available for far lower prices. Or they may hope to slip in less expensive products of genuinely lower quality.

Almost every week, your architects may be asked to rule on substitutions of this type. Our experience is that architects need to regard such suggestions with an extremely wary eye, usually saying "no." Unfortunately, contractors can wear architects down, and you may end up with items you really don't want.

Library staff *must* also insist on being included in all discussions of "equivalent" items. Insist on seeing cut sheets of the substitutes. Make sure that there is no difference in required maintenance. You may have to insist on seeing a sample of the item or comparing the specified and "equivalent" item side by side. If you have doubts, talk with your architects and engineers about the product.

A "cut sheet" is a catalog sheet with illustrations of items and all technical specifications.

> Fred's bad experiences in the area of equivalencies have centered on light fixtures, where easily maintained fixtures were replaced by fixtures almost impossible to service, and where fixtures supplied were out of production and could not be matched. In retrospect, he should have simply said "no" to all requests.

If a proposed substitution passes all of these reviews and is found to be truly equivalent, its acceptance must be formally acknowledged in an addendum. All addenda are issued to all contractors who have plans, so that all have the same opportunity to include the approved substitution in preparing their bids.

IV-E. ALTERNATE BIDS

Most bid documents include "add alternates." These are extra items you'd like to have if you can afford them.

A contractor competing for your job will supply a price for the basic project and then a price for each of your add alternates.

Add alternates have to be items that can be added to the structure without much redesign work. For example, you may ask for the extra cost of vinyl wallpaper as opposed to painted drywall (relatively easy), or a standing seam metal roof as opposed to asphalt singles (a bit harder because the drawings need two sets of details).

It's tempting to get carried away by asking for prices on too many add alternates, or for prices on items that are tricky to price. You don't want to drive off good contractors by giving the impression you could be a pain to work with as an owner.

Contracts with architects can require free redesign by the architect if the base total construction bid comes in over the estimate. We think this is an excellent idea. Since architects are not omnipotent or omniscient, one way that they protect themselves and the library is by designating certain non-essential parts of the project as add alternates, so that the base bid has a better chance of being within the budget.

If bidding is highly competitive and bids submitted by various contractors are very close, it is possible that the responsive, responsible low bidder may be determined by which add alternates are selected. You may want to check on the legal implications here. While many jurisdictions allow the library to select alternates in any sequence it determines to be in its interest, other agencies require that the bid documents list the sequence in which alternates will be accepted. This avoids the appearance (and possible reality) of selecting alternates as a way of determining who is designated low bidder.

It's also possible to have "deduct alternates," where contractors tell you how much less they'll charge if you deduct specific items from the contract. The general wisdom says that you'll get a lower-cost project by using add alternates, but not everyone agrees with this.

IV-F. BONDING

Bonds are insurance policies purchased by the contractor to protect owners if things go wrong financially. Since contracting can be a fiscally risky undertaking, things go wrong on a fairly frequent basis.

Since bonding companies are unwilling to insure contractors with weak reputations, requiring bonds helps protect owners from the problems inherent in rejecting companies on the basis of their bad reputations. Unfortunately, some low-cost bonding companies are sharks. Some states have rules for bonding on public projects. Ask your architects or your local government.

Requiring bonds will increase bids because it increases costs for contractors. But it's a good practice and worth the cost. We think it's important for all library projects.

If contractors object to the requirement for bid bonding, performance bonding, or payment bonding, it's a good time for your architects to suggest they may be happier working on other projects. Bonding companies have little interest in dealing with contractors with poor reputations, and by requiring bonding you help protect your library.

Some bonding companies appear to specialize in iffy contractors. The American Best Bond Companies rates bonding companies. To protect your library project, you can request a rating of 9+.

IV-F-1. Bid Bonds

Many owners—particularly the federal government—require "bid bonds" from contractors submitting bids. Bid bonds protect owners by guaranteeing that the lowest bidder will do the work rather than simply dropping out. Bid bonds guarantee that the owners will be able to obtain the work for the price of the lowest bid. If the lowest bidder is unable to do the work, the bonding company picks up the difference in cost between the lowest bid and the next lowest bid.

Bid bonding, as with other forms of bonding, also protects owners because construction firms with iffy reputations will not be able to obtain bonding from the companies that specialize in these products.

IV-F-2. Performance Bonds

Many bid documents require that contractors obtain performance bonds.

Performance bonds guarantee that the contractor will complete the agreed-upon project. If the contractor or a subcontractor goes bankrupt, the bonding company will either (1) step in and get the contractor to perform, (2) find another contractor who can complete the work, or (3) give the library the value of the remaining work to use in securing another contractor to complete the work. To be clear, the bonding company has extensive rights in these situations, and it can select the approach it deems in its best interests. There is no guarantee that there will be no extra cost to the building owner.

Although performance bonds can increase construction costs a little, they can save owners major agonies and incredible legal messes if contractors go bankrupt partway through construction.

> Bankruptcies happen a lot more often than one might imagine. For example, in both of the two construction jobs Fred was associated with in his own library, contractors went bankrupt and bonding companies had to step in. The general contractor went bankrupt in the middle of the first job and the HVAC contractor halfway through the second.

IV-F-3. Payment Bonds

Payment bonding covers situations where contractors do not pay their subcontractors, who then file mechanics' liens against the owner of the building. Bonds should cover both labor and materials.

Some protection for owners is provided by the requirement for lien waivers (see below), but there can be situations where a general contractor has collected money from the owner and abruptly goes bankrupt without paying his subcontractors.

IV-G. RECEIPT DEADLINES

As with all serious projects involving bids or quoted prices, a specific and absolute deadline is essential.

For this reason, deadlines for bids always are set at times when library staff members (or city or university or school or corporate staff members) will be present to note precisely which bids arrived on time and which arrived late. Using time/date stamps to mark bids is ideal.

This seems like overkill to many owners, but it's an important way to avoid lawsuits from disappointed bidders who contend that the winning bid actually arrived five minutes late and should have been disqualified. Since contractors tend to submit bids at the last moment, this is an important issue.

To protect your library, bid deadlines have to be enforced with brutal exactitude. The basic rule is that if a bid is due at 3:00 p.m., check the accuracy of your clocks and reject all those that arrive at 3:01 p.m. or thereafter. Ask your architects to step in if you are faced with bid deadline issues.

V. Bid Openings

Maintaining secrecy over all bids received is absolutely essential, and for this reason they are never opened or examined until after the deadline for receiving bids. The purpose of bidding is to get the best possible price, and this requires both a competitive bidding environment and ignorance on the part of all bidders concerning what the competition is up to.

Bids can be opened almost immediately after the deadline for submission. Because the contractors submitting bids want to know as soon as possible who is likely to be doing the work, scheduling an immediate bid opening can be a very good idea.

Publish bid opening times at the time that bid deadlines are announced.

Bid openings for government work are public events. Expect the contractors to have representatives present.

At bid openings, one person—probably one of your architects—opens each of the bids, reads the amounts for the base bid and each of the alternates, and checks that all required items are included. Joe usually checks for the required items first: Are the addenda acknowledged? Is the bid form signed by an authorized officer of the company? Are any required certifications acknowledged? And then he reads the prices.

All this is done without comment on which bids appear to be lowest. Everyone in the room can hear what's read, and holding off gives the owners and architects a chance to be absolutely sure that the bids are completely in compliance with requirements and to determine which add alternates will be accepted.

VI. Bid Evaluation

VI-A. BIDDING ERRORS

Typically, all bids are reasonably close together, but occasionally one is significantly lower.

Often this is the result of a mistakes by the contractors, who failed to include some important features in their cost estimates.

Since contractors' bids are legal documents, you can force the lowest bidders to build your library and lose their shirts in the process, but it will be a rotten working relationship. Underbidding may lead to sloppy work, not to mention a barrage of change order requests for trivial items that would be ignored under better circumstances.

For this reason, if the lowest bid is a great deal lower than a cluster of fairly similar bids from other contractors, the owner may choose to allow the low bidder to withdraw its bid. (This does not mean, of course, that the low bidder gets to submit another and higher bid. The bidder is simply off the hook and out of the running.)

If the project involves bid bonding and the low bidder bows out, the bonding company picks up the difference in cost between that bidder and the next lowest bidder.

VI-B. LOCAL CONTRACTORS

Many owners—especially small-town public library boards—are concerned that local contractors get local work. As a consultant, Fred is asked this question on almost every job. In most low-bid situations for public work, however, the only legal way a local general contractor can get the job is to bid lower than the out-of-town competition.

When it comes to subcontractors, general contractors will usually ask for prices from firms they know and trust. This may also make it hard for local firms to get bids if they are not known to the general contractors.

However, because they don't have to travel to the job site, local firms can often do the work for less than out-of-town firms, and a general contractor who prefers an out-of-town firm may end up losing the bid.

When a construction management firm is involved, many portions of the project are bid separately, and there may be a better chance for a small local firm to get part of the project.

VII. Alternatives to Bidding

If your library is privately owned rather than a government entity, you will probably not be required by law to hire a contractor by low bid. But you will still want competitive bidding in order to push contractors to give you the best possible prices.

Asking contractors to provide bids also prevents the project from being given to the nephew of the mayor or of the college president as a fond gift.

VIII. Awarding Contracts

Awarding construction contracts is a job for lawyers and architects and construction managers. Libraries must stand by but not try it alone. The terms of the agreements that will govern the project are another set of reviews that should be part of the design development phase of the project. Those reviews are by legal counsel and risk managers (your insurance company). We recommend that the owners or their representatives see and approve the revisions recommended by your advisors.

These approved documents should be included in the bid documents so that there is no confusion on bid day. Once the apparent low bidder has been confirmed as both responsive and responsible, and accepted by the library, the only work needed on the contract should be to fill in the detailed bid data.

Issuing the contract triggers a series of events, including the contractor securing performance and payment bonds, and beginning the administrative and startup tasks of the construction process.

IX. Snappy Rules on Bidding

1. Good bids don't happen by accident. They come from good drawings and good specifications.
2. Everything else being equal, union labor can be more technically competent than non-union labor. If prevailing wage laws mean you have to pay the same price for both, union labor can be a good idea.
3. The failure of architects to provide correct details on plans is not the contractor's fault.
4. Holding a contractor to a mistakenly low bid may lead to nothing but trouble.
5. A happy construction situation is when everyone gets along together and no one is losing money on the job.
6. Contracting is a perilous undertaking because the job goes to the lowest bidder, who then has to try to still make money.
7. Bonding can solve an amazing variety of problems that occur during bidding and construction. Avoiding bonding in the mistaken hope that you can save money is like building your new library on a really cheap floodplain location, hoping that it never gets wet.
8. When contractors are touring your building before making bids on your construction job, ask your staff to smile politely and point to requested locations, but to never answer any questions or comment on anything. Whatsoever.
9. If your library will be constructed by the design-build method, start out with an impressively detailed building program and insist that the contractor-architect team be held to it. Finding out that the design omits important features, and that adding them will raise the price, is not a happy moment.
10. One of the reasons to hire construction management firms is that when they are able to save money by cutting corners, they don't get to keep it.

PART II
From Overcrowding to Ribbon Cutting

CHAPTER 15

Construction

I. Introduction

I-A. WHAT HAPPENS DURING CONSTRUCTION

For librarians, construction is a far different experience from programming or design. The central role in this phase moves to the construction team, while the architects and owners monitor the process to see that the thousands of decisions that fill programming and design are replaced by overseeing and by watching for errors and omissions.

During major construction, the library's world can be turned upside down.

The easiest situation for library staff is when the library constructs a new building on a new site. Daily life in the library continues pretty much as usual, although administrators are frequently at the building under construction, monitoring progress and watching for problems. Or they are locked in their offices, reading endless submissions, working on construction grant reports, and keeping in touch with the architects. Or they are attending construction meetings.

If the library is being rebuilt, the library can move to a rented temporary building while construction is going on. If the building is smaller than the current library, some things go into dead storage. And the staff always work in makeshift spaces.

If the library building is being remodeled or expanded, and the library stays there while work goes on, life for librarians and library users can be a tangle. Library functions are relocated, sometimes far more often than seems necessary. Things are put into storage. Getting users safely into the building can be a challenge, and when things are being moved back and forth, sometimes the only solution is to close for a couple of weeks. If parking is limited, library users, library staff, and construction workers somehow have to all squeeze into the same parking lot. Space has to be found for construction machinery and endless piles of construction supplies. And library users and staff are subject to odd noises, temporary plywood partitions, and strange smells.

Luckily, there are firms that specialize in moving book collections without damaging books or getting them out of order, so at least the staff don't have to trot back and forth lugging endless boxes of books.

Often a new wing is built onto a library, then the library camps out in the new wing while the original building is remodeled.

Eventually, when a total of anything from nine months to a few years has passed, work is finished. The library takes over the entire building. Landscaping goes in. New parking lots are available. Once dingy things sparkle. Books and furnishings are arranged according to plans. Shelves don't overflow. Dimly lighted corners are no longer dim. Ribbons are cut. People celebrate. And normal life in the new or remodeled or expanded library begins.

I-B. A FEW COMMON CONSTRUCTION TERMS

A few terms are endlessly encountered during construction projects. All of them are defined somewhere in this chapter, but they're here for quick reference.

- **Change orders**. Agreements between the contractors and owners to change items in the original contract at specified costs.

- **Commissioning**. Testing of complex systems with a new building and educating staff in the proper operation of the systems.

- **Construction control meetings**, also known as construction progress meetings. Regularly scheduled meetings between the contractors, architects, and owners (in our case, owners are librarians, university architects, government officials, and board members) to review progress on the job, deal with problems that have emerged, and organize the next steps.

- **Construction drawings**. Drawings that are part of the package of drawings and specifications on which the contract for construction is based. This includes the bid documents and all the addenda on which the competing contractors bid. Contractors are required to follow drawings exactly or to work out issues with the architects and owners.

- **Cut sheet**. A reproduction of a catalog sheet describing, in detail, the physical characteristics of an item being installed in the library.

- **Draw**. Formally known as an "Application for Payment." A request from a contractor for payment. Architects certify that the work for which the contractor is billing the library has been completed in general conformance with the contract documents before forwarding the bill to the library for payment.

- **Ground breaking**. A ceremony to recognize the commencement of construction, although the work may have already begun or may not start for a while to come. There are speeches and snacks.

- **Lien waivers**. Documents signed by subcontractors indicating that the contractors have paid them and that they therefore cannot file fiscal claims against the library.

- **Occupancy permit**. A government-issued permit certifying that a nearly completed building is now safe to occupy.

- *Owner's rep.* Short for "owner's representative." A hired expert who assists and advises (and in certain circumstances does much of the work required of) librarians during construction. An owner's rep is a common alternative to using a construction manager.

- *Punch list.* A document prepared by the owners (library) and the architects, listing all the remaining work (and corrections) the contractors must complete before they can be paid all of the retainage.

- *Record drawing.* Drawings show specifically how buildings were constructed, including any modifications of details in construction drawings.

- *Retainage.* A percentage of each of a contractor's bills that is not paid until the project is fully completed, providing an important incentive for the contractor to stay on the job. Sometimes called "holdbacks."

- *Ribbon cutting.* A ceremony at the end of construction, usually with speeches, tours, and snacks.

- *Shop drawing.* A drawing based on the architects' construction drawings, showing how specific items will be created. A very large number of shop drawings are made during a construction project.

- *Submittal.* Materials provided by contractors to illustrate exactly how specific features will be constructed. Submittals include such items as shop drawings and cut sheets.

- *Testing.* Physical verification that construction materials and assemblies meet standards. Many of the tests are required by building codes, while others are at the discretion of the owner and architect.

II. The Contractor's Role in Construction

During construction, contractors take the lead in the process. They coordinate the work of many subcontractors, suppliers, and manufacturers, adapt their efforts to the weather, ensure a safe construction site, and do all of this under the watchful gaze (or belligerent stare) of the architects, construction managers, owners, public, and press. For the contractors, there are tremendous financial risks associated with meeting the schedule and cost requirements of the contract.

The contractors must:

- Report to the architects any issues they discover in the course of their work. However, the contractors are not required to know the contract documents, and they are not required to know if the documents comply with applicable laws.

- Supervise and direct the work, using their best skills and attention. Contractors must employ competent superintendents and necessary assistants to be on site during the performance of the work.

- Take responsibility for, and have control over, construction means, methods, techniques, sequences, and procedures, and for coordinating all portions of the work.

- Be responsible for the acts and omissions of the contractors' employees, subcontractors and their agents and employees, and other persons or entities performing portions of the work.

- Enforce strict discipline and good order among the contractors' employees and other persons carrying out the work. The contractor shall not permit employment of unfit persons or persons not properly skilled in tasks assigned to them.

- Warrant that materials and equipment furnished under the contract will be of good quality and new, conform to the requirements of the contract documents, and be free from defects.

Because of these responsibilities, contractors are given extensive authority over the project. This authority is to be respected by all parties (including architect and owner) so as not to hinder the efforts of the contractor or transfer responsibility (liability) from the contractor to themselves.

III. The Architect's Role in Construction

One of the major responsibilities of your architectural firm will be construction administration. Construction administration is not the same thing as construction management. Your architects are not responsible for providing daily supervision of the project, which is the job of the general contractor or the construction management firm.

However, the architect is customarily responsible for:

- Being present at all construction coordination meetings to maintain communications with the contractors and subcontractors.
- Receiving and approving "shop drawings." Shop drawings are detailed drawings showing exactly how a piece of work will be accomplished. Construction drawings are not intended to be sufficiently detailed to be fabrication or installation drawings, and shop drawings are the means by which contractors and manufacturers provide the extra information needed to build the project. Architects are expected to review and approve shop drawings for selected products and systems to be certain that the contractor understands the intent of the architectural and engineering documents. The contractor is responsible for the details. Owners should require a complete set of drawings for the library's files, in each case showing that the architect and contractor (and construction manager, if you have one) approved the drawing. (Some people feel that this is serious overkill, but it will help you know what's going on and that all parties are on top of things.) Shop drawings are also helpful for future maintenance and alterations.
- Monitoring the work to make sure that the contractors' work is in general conformance with the plans and specifications. (The architect does not verify that the contractor is following the plans and specifications exactly.)
- Dealing with situations where the work to be done turns out not to match the intent of the construction documents. This can happen fairly often. For example, Joe made a roofing contractor replace a new roof twice in a row because the contractor did the job "his way" rather than the way it was described in the drawings and specifications.
- Receiving and approving periodic bills (sometimes called construction "draws" but technically known as "applications for payment") from contractors. For all bills, the architects determine whether the contractors have actually completed the work before authorizing payment.
- Receiving at each draw and monitoring lien waivers, legal documents that certify

that the contractors have been paying their subcontractors.

- Monitoring contractor compliance with the requirements of local authorities, to be sure that all inspections and permits are properly undertaken.
- At the end of the project, verifying the contractor's "punch list" of items to be completed before the contractors' retainage (holdbacks) are paid. This often results in the architect preparing the punch list directly.

IV. The Librarian's Role in Construction

Librarians can play a more active role in construction than the books suggest, and the result can be a better building. The key is to find the balance between active observation and quality control on the one hand and counterproductive meddling on the other. One of the hardest things for librarians and architects alike is to acknowledge the responsibilities that contractors have during construction and the control they need to meet those obligations.

IV-A. VISIT THE JOB SITE

For librarians, it's worthwhile walking through the construction zone almost every day. Ask for a white hard hat (denoting an important personage) and try to keep an eye on things. If nothing else, just be visible. If you see problems, bring them up in construction meetings rather than attempting to deal directly with workers. This is important—do not break the communications protocols set for the project. Better yet, bring the matters to the attention of your architect or CM—make them be the bad guy. If you see a major problem, call the architects immediately. Posterity loves an alert and intrepid owner.

You can learn a lot by unobtrusively observing workers. Are things being done in a sloppy manner? Is there trash lying around everywhere? What do you hear people saying? (If you're around all the time, people may almost forget you're there.)

Maintain a friendly relationship with workers. Learn their names and greet them. But don't tell them what to do or slow them down with irrelevant conversation. If you bring snacks, let the general contractor or construction administrator decide how to distribute them.

If you have seen work you don't like in other libraries, now is not the time to set quality standards. That is part of the contract documents phase. What you can do is make clear from the beginning what you expect from your contractor and subcontractors to meet these standards, and that things that don't measure up will show up in the punch list process. Good contractors know it is easier and more profitable to do things right the first time and easier to fix problems right away than to wait for the punch list. Bad contractors will try to wait you out, just hoping you'll forget or be so worn down that they can get away with less than required. Active observation lets them know early that they have met their match.

For example, floor boxes for electrical outlets set in concrete floors are frequently twisted out of square. If you want them in dead-straight lines, make this clear from day one. Your electrical contractor will be annoyed, but he'll have trouble arguing that sloppy is fine. The time to bring this up is before boxes are laid out. If you miss that, double-check before the concrete is poured. Once things are "set in concrete" it will be harder to get things fixed.

Placement of items in walls—electrical outlets, fire alarms, thermostats, HVAC grills, and so on—is frequently somewhat vague in construction drawings. If you have plans for shelving or a bulletin board on a wall, you may know exactly where you want the outlets and other devices to be located. As soon as the steel studs go up, have your contractor use a marking pen to note the exact location of each item on the raw concrete floor. (Most items will be at standard heights, but there is room for a lot of sideways slop if you aren't extremely specific.) After all the locations are marked, walk through the building with the contractor and architect to make sure that everyone is on the same page.

You may also find that walls are located slightly off where they belong. If a filing cabinet will be located in a narrow alcove, check to be sure that the alcove will be wide enough. If shelving needs to fit between a door and a wall, check to be sure that the door isn't half an inch too close to the wall. The precise location of steel stud is easy to tweak when it first goes up, and that's the time to check.

Don't be put off if people say you're "fussy." Everyone else gets to leave the building when construction is complete. You and your users and staff do not. The repetitive impact of poor construction over the life of the building can be frustrating, expensive, or both. Getting everything right should be the responsibility of all but often comes down to one. It may need to be you.

To be fair, this is not an invitation to insist on carte blanche changes to the project. The cost of the project was determined by what was included in the bidding documents. That covers quantities and quality. You should get everything you paid for, but you are not entitled to any more.

At the end of the project, attend the punch list site visits and prepare your own punch list. Work with your architect to be sure that your items are included on the official list.

IV-B. ATTEND CONSTRUCTION MEETINGS

As the owner or administrator of the building, you will want to be sure that you are in the loop so that decisions do not occur without your knowledge and consent. Plan to have two library staff members assigned to attend all meetings between your architects and contractors, so that at least one of the staff can always be present. In many instances, the owner (in the person of the library director or designee) joins their architect, owner's representative, construction manager, or consulting librarian at meetings and is a direct participant.

Some believe that library staff need to attend all of these. Accompanying the library staff may be designated members of governing boards or building specialists from parent organizations. In any case, there are industry standard rules at play in these meetings, and the participants must be familiar with and committed to respecting these rules. Free-for-alls serve no one's interest.

IV-C. REVIEW SUBMITTALS

Another focus of the library's efforts will include reviews of submittals from the contracting team to show that they do understand the intent of the design. There are large numbers of "shop drawings" and other submittals that provide details on specific items, and libraries need to know what's going on with these as well.

Despite all efforts, things don't always go according to plan. There will always be change orders, situations where there are errors in drawings or where there turn out to be hidden problems with existing buildings. Contractors may ignore the construction drawings or simply make mistakes, and architects may have to make them rip things out and do them over. Or contractors may make mistakes and offer owners cash in lieu of ripping things out and doing them over. Contractors or subcontractors may go bankrupt partway through the job, and bonding companies may have to step in to protect the library from loss. Some feature of the library may come as a horrible surprise to the owners, who did not recognize it in the construction documents and decide to spend the money to change it immediately. The library will need to be aware of these situations as they arise and be an active participant in the resolution of each.

Construction is a long process. A quick remodeling job may take only a few months, but the construction of a straightforward frame-on-slab building can take close to a year. And a complex, two-phase expansion and remodeling job may take two or three years.

Along the way are important public ceremonies such as ground breaking and ribbon cutting that acknowledge key contributors and keep users informed on progress. These are usually organized by library staff, foundation offices, PR offices, and other groups that do not report to the architects or contractors.

As mentioned in the chapter on design, it's always a good idea to keep a diary of the project, with dated entries on meetings, decisions, problems, weather delays, and so on. If problems lead to finger pointing, having a record of your understanding of what happened when and why can be useful.

V. Coordination and Quality Control

V-A. CONSTRUCTION COORDINATION MEETINGS

All construction projects have frequent construction coordination meetings, which are usually held by the contractor or construction manager. For larger projects, these meetings will be weekly, and for small projects probably biweekly.

The main purpose of these meetings is to make sure that everyone is aware of the state of the project and the times at which each of the subcontractors needs to be ready to do its work to keep the project moving along on schedule. Because a lot of contracting work is of the "we-can't-do-X-until-Y-is-done" variety, the inability of a critical subcontractor to appear on time can mess up the project schedule. For example, the electricians may not be able to install electrical conduit until the steel studs are in place, the drywallers won't be able to work until all of the wiring conduit is in place, and the painters can't work until the drywall is installed.

The construction coordination meeting will be led by the general contractor or construction management firm and attended by representatives of the subcontractors, the architectural firm, and the library.

At most construction coordination meetings, the various subcontractors will review the status of their work. The review of progress is helpful, but the essential benefit of these meetings is the looking ahead to upcoming work. These are often termed "look ahead" and are intended to make the quality expectations as well as the interconnected nature of various systems within the building clear to all the trade on site in the coming timeframe. This is the opportunity to talk about those floor box locations.

In Fred's opinion, having the project architect serve as construction administrator leads to a more coordinated approach where fewer things slip through the cracks.

If the library has hired an owner's representative, that person will be present at all meetings as well. A few libraries ask their consulting librarians to be present at construction coordination meetings.

The bid documents should have a detailed agenda for typical meetings as well as kick-off meetings for major phases of building systems. Follow the agendas to make sure that important issues do not go unnoticed until it is too late.

The general contractor or construction management firm will prepare charts showing when they expect each of the interdependent steps of a project to take place. If you don't get one at each meeting, exercise your constitutional rights to raise hell.

You need to control the people who turn up for construction coordination meetings. They should not be media events, and you don't want so many members of your governing board turning up that applicable open meetings acts apply. You also don't want members of the general public, some of whom may turn up because they want to argue with your experts. Your contractor has control over who can come onto an active construction site. Do not invite people without the contractor's permission.

V-B. VERIFICATION THAT CONSTRUCTION MATCHES DRAWINGS AND SPECIFICATIONS

One of the major jobs of the architect is making sure that the construction is in accordance with the drawings and specifications.

Even a small library building is an amazingly complex undertaking, and there will be thousands of details for architects to check against the drawings. One of the signs of a good architect is a rigorous verification process that includes multiple methods of review to determine whether construction is in accordance with drawings.

It is important to note that this does not mean that the architect is providing constant verification or certifying 100 percent conformance with the documents. The contractor does that at the end of the project.

Some of this verification process consists of making sure that the dimensions of the building match the drawings, that various materials pass tests proving conformance with specific standards, that flashings and roofing have been installed correctly, and that all MEP (mechanical, electrical, and plumbing) systems are installed and operating correctly.

Owners assist with this by visiting the building frequently and raising questions with the architects or construction manager if things appear to be incorrect, but they should not deal directly with workers or subcontractors.

V-B-1. Shop Drawings (Submittals)

In most cases, not all construction details appear on architects' construction drawings. Additional drawings with extensive additional construction details are prepared by contractors and submitted to architects for approval. The drawings and other pieces of literature—cut sheets, product data sheets, and material samples—are collectively known as "submittals."

Each submittal should be stamped by the contractor or the CM to indicate that they have carefully reviewed the submittal, find it consistent with the intent of the drawings, have reviewed it with the other trades whose work is impacted by that submittal (think about the electrical contractor who has to run power to big pieces of HVAC equipment), and that the work described by the submittal will not interfere with other aspects of the project. This is a big deal. The CM or the general contractor is being paid for this level of coordination. The lack of a stamp is a red flag. The presence of a stamp is no guarantee that the needed coordination has been completed, but it's a start.

The architect will distribute the submittal to other participants whose review is needed. Most often this is the engineering team and the owner. A specific period of time, established in the bidding and construction documents, is allowed for these reviews. Comments are collected, verified, reconciled if necessary, and then integrated into the returned submittal.

If you want to be part of the review process, you will need to abide by the timeframe set out for the project. Delays in returning submittals are frequently used as the basis for claims by the general contractor or subcontractors for additional money. (Some architects have a reputation for falling behind on approval of shop drawings—and of simply initialing drawings without careful review. The same is true of contractors. And some librarians get caught trying to simultaneously run the library and review sizeable stacks of submittals.) Having a set of approved submittals and a log of when they were received and when they were returned helps protect the library. You will find that most contractors, CMs, and architects maintain submittal logs. This is the clearest indication of how frequently the processing of submittals becomes a point of contention.

Even if you do not want to be an active participant in the submittal review process, as a librarian you want to keep track of these "shop drawings." While many are merely technical, others involve decisions on details that may matter significantly to the library owners and staff. Protect your library by insisting on receiving copies of all approved shop drawings—all with the contractor or CM and architect indications of review and approval—for inclusion in the library's permanent files on the project.

Shop drawings also provide essential information when the time comes to modify buildings.

> Many architects may suggest that libraries planning to keep copies of all shop drawings is overkill. We think that it can never hurt, and that it's good to be seen keeping an eye on everything. You can still be selective, but when in any doubt keep everything.

V-B-2. Testing

Review of submittals is a proactive means of assuring conformance with the project documents, but it does not mean that follow-through occurs. Testing is a means by which performance can be certified. Many tests are required by building codes and are there in acknowledgement of the limitations of visual inspection. Materials such as concrete, mortar, and sealants are all tested to be sure that they have the strength and other attributes required. Some tests, such as those of welds or bolt tightening, are used to verify installation as well as materials. Installation is a key aspect of most buildings. It is becoming more important as wall assemblies, mechanical systems, and electrical systems become more complicated.

As with other verification steps, testing is usually conducted on a representative number of samples rather than on literally every bolt. For example, one concrete test per mixer load is representative of all of the concrete in that load. (If you see a row of what look like Pringles cans, that's concrete testing going on.)

As with submittals, test results are reviewed by the architectural and engineering teams. Copies of the results and the CM, architect, and engineers review comments are supplied to the owner.

Time is also essential in testing. Some tests, such as concrete, require seven- and 28-day timeframes. Others, such as soil compaction tests, are hard to replicate if they were missed in the normal sequence of activities. The scheduled discussion in each coordination meeting should include the timing of testing and the reporting of results.

Who does the testing is also important. While most testing entities are independent (not owned by the construction company or the library), we think it is a cleaner line of responsibility if the testing agency is hired directly by the owner, usually with the assistance of the architect or the CM. The cost of this testing should appear as a line item in budgets and cost estimates to be sure there are no surprises.

V-B-3. Commissioning

Commissioning is a specialized form of testing. Electrical and mechanical systems are exceptionally complex and require multilayered software and hardware integration to functional properly. (Any parent involved with preparation of toys on Christmas Eve knows the understatement of the phrase "some assembly required.") There is no way of looking at all of the components that make up a building's HVAC system and knowing if it will function properly. The commissioning process runs the system through a series of typical, seasonal, and emergency situations to verify that everything has been assembled correctly and that the software that operates the system is free of errors. The software testing component cannot be overstressed. While generally similar to those in other libraries, individual systems are literally unique to each building's design and operation. It is a significant undertaking to get this right, and it is no place to simply trust the HVAC contractor.

Proof of operation is provided by a commissioning agent. This is someone who did not work on the design or installation of the system and is therefore independent. We do want to note that in some instances, this person may work for the engineer or installer, but was not involved in the project in any way up to this point. Some projects need the assurance of a truly independent commissioning agent, in which case a firm separate from both the engineers and installers should be engaged.

The extent to which systems are commissioned can vary. Most building codes establish a set of parameters that constitute a minimum level of verification. This is most often driven by a combination of health concerns (fresh air) and energy conservation. More elaborate testing is needed to support the pursuit of various green building certificates.

Budgeting for the testing, the services of the commissioning agent, and the time required of the contractor to assist the commissioning agent is another of those line items in early estimates. It should also be part of your discussions with the architect when negotiating a contract, and again prior to the schematic design estimates.

V-C. RESOLVING ERRORS

Occasionally, contractors will make major errors and suggest a cash settlement in lieu of correcting the errors. If architects are primarily in a hurry to get things done, unholy alliances of architects and contractors can form in opposition to the library.

This happened with Fred's first building consulting job, decades ago. Fred specified a network of electrical and data conduit in the concrete floor slab to permit the flexible location of computers and other equipment. When this kind of work is done, the conduit for the wiring is first supported in place and the concrete slab is then poured around it. Unfortunately, the contractor got concrete into the open ends of the conduits, making it impossible to use many of them for wiring. Faced with the major cost of ripping out the floor slab and conduit and starting over, the contractor offered the library a small cash settlement instead, and the architects encouraged the library board to take the settlement. Which it did. Because the building had a cathedral ceiling, power poles were not an alternative for power and data. So the library ended up with a tremendous loss of long-term flexibility, all for a small payment from the contractor.

What disturbed Fred most was that he was never asked or told about this until long after it was too late, and that the architects were complicit in the situation, encouraging the board not to fall behind on their schedule (using up the architects' time and delaying their final payment in the process).

To balance this, something went wrong in another of Fred's library projects, where the library board president was head of quality control for a large factory. Even through the architects—the same architects, as a matter of fact—encouraged him to take a (minor) settlement for a serious omission, he refused to budge until the work was redone according to specifications.

V-D. CODE INSPECTIONS AND OCCUPANCY PERMITS

At key points during construction, the work will be inspected by code enforcement officials, typically employees of local government.

For example, when wiring is complete but drywall has not been installed, electrical inspectors will go through the building making sure that the wiring has been done in accordance with local codes.

Building inspectors have the authority to stop construction until a problem has been addressed.

Note that these inspections do not determine whether outlets have been omitted, but only that those installed have been done properly from a life safety viewpoint. Code inspection, therefore, does not substitute for the architects' determination that everything called for in the construction documents is present and properly done.

When the building is complete, local government will issue an "occupancy permit," allowing the library to use the building. At the time the permit is issued, minor things may remain to be done, but key safety items (for example, hand railings and outlet cover plates) will all be in place.

V-E. SUBSTANTIAL COMPLETION AND PUNCH LISTS

No one is happy at this point in construction. Contractors wanted this to occur much sooner, so that they had access to the retainage and could stop being responsible for insurance and other costs. Librarians want into their buildings, but they don't want to release retainage or take over insurance.

There is a multistep process that protects (and frustrates) everyone involved.

- When the contractor considers that the work is substantially complete, the contractor is supposed to prepare and submit to the architect a comprehensive list of items to be completed or corrected prior to final payment. (However, failure to include an item on such list does not alter the responsibility of the contractor to complete all work in accordance with the contract documents.)

- When they receive the contractor's list, the architects inspect the project to determine whether, in fact, the work is substantially complete. If the architects' inspection discloses any item that is not sufficiently complete, the contractor must complete or correct such item upon notification by the architect. The contractor must then submit a request for another inspection by the architect to determine substantial completion. Once all the work meets this standard, the architect can issue the "Certificate of Substantial Completion."

- The Certificate of Substantial Completion establishes the date at which the owner is once again responsible for security, maintenance, heat, utilities, damage to the work, and insurance. It also fixes the time within which the contractor shall finish all items on the list accompanying the certificate. Warranties required by the contract documents commence on the date of Substantial Completion.

- The Certificate of Substantial Completion is then submitted to the owner and contractor for their written acceptance of responsibilities assigned to them in the certificate. Upon such acceptance and consent of the bonding company (surety), the owner shall make payment of retainage applying to the completed work. That payment can be reduced for work that is incomplete or not in accordance with the requirements of the contract documents.

The lists described are called "punch lists," and the process of preparing them is called "punching," as in, "We punched the first floor wiring last week."

Final punch lists are notoriously unwelcome to contractors. They're finished with the buildings, ready to pack up and be paid, and suddenly the owners give them what they regard as picky lists of unreasonable complaints. Frequently punch lists involve bringing back all the trades involved in the project, so the cost and nuisance for the contractor may be considerable. If your social relationship with your general contractor has been warm and wonderful, the punch list may cool things off.

Like contractors, architects are also ready to wrap things up and get on to the next project, and their punch lists may occasionally be perfunctory. Because of this, punch listing is one area where you may want to bring back your programmer (building consultant) or hire an independent outside expert. If you have an owner's representative, university architect, or company architect, that person may provide constant quality oversight.

Depending on your architects, your punch list may be much more detailed than theirs. This does not mean you have done a bad thing.

It's important to do punch listing before you've moved anything into your library. Many of the problems in final punch lists are concerned with minor dings and scrapes, and if you've been doing anything inside the building except walking gently through, your contractors may contend that everything was great when they left, and that any damage was due to clumsy librarians. Because latex paint on drywall is impressively fragile, it's easy to cause unintentional damage, and your contractors may be right.

Punch listing requires a systematic approach. Make lists of things to inspect, then check them one by one in definable areas of the building. If you have big areas to check—such as ceilings or walls—you can "paint" the surface with your eyes, sweeping them systematically back and forth to cover an area. Some things to look for are:

- Dents, scrapes, and lumps in paint. (If you want to be really demanding on dents, go in at night with a flashlight and hold it flat against the wall, making even minor irregularities in the finish stand out like the Mountains of the Moon.)
- Rough surfaces. Check in particular painted windowsills, where construction dust can settle in wet paint.
- Damaged ceiling tiles. Acoustic tiles in suspended ceilings are fragile, and workers sometimes leave them in chipped or stained condition.
- Sloppy trim. If moldings are crooked or meet badly at corners, if there are wide gaps between trim and the adjacent surfaces, if there are gaps where pieces of trim are supposed to meet snugly, all of these should be corrected.
- Bad carpet seams or wrinkles.
- Electrical switches and receptacles that don't work properly. Watch for substitutions of cheaper products (for example, regular receptacles substituted for child-proof (tamper-proof) receptacles). It's easy to buy an outlet tester and send a low-paid employee to test every outlet in the building.
- Crooked electrical fixtures, outlets, switches, and so on.
- Restroom floor drains that don't drain properly. Try pouring water on the floor a few feet from the drain and see what happens.
- Restroom fixtures that don't function properly. Automatic faucets should operate when hands get generally near them. Automatic toilets should flush consistently and enthusiastically. Automatic towel dispensers and hand dryers should not require you to repeatedly wave your hands about trying to get them to work. If these gadgets don't work perfectly at punch listing time, they almost certainly will not improve with age and experience. Don't be lenient with them.
- Faulty fixtures and equipment provided as part of the contract. Test everything, particularly automatic switches, which can easily fail to work correctly.
- Motion detector lighting (if you are unfortunate enough to have it) that activates only after people have entered the area in question and that turns off too eagerly. Door motion should activate restroom motion detectors.

- Items out of plumb. Crooked walls, skewed windows, and so on, are best if you note them immediately rather than waiting for the final punch list, but if that's the first time you spot something, bring it up.
- Damaged brickwork or stonework. For instance, look for chips in bricks and chips or saw cut marks on stonework.
- HVAC systems are so complex that you will want to hire an expert to check them out. This is called "commissioning," and it is invaluable. Fred once paid an expert about $10,000 at the end of a construction project and found out in turn that about $60,000 in work had been left undone or incorrectly done. In situations like this, make sure that your expert is totally separate from the firms doing the work.

Ideally, you will maintain good communications with your contractors throughout the project, letting them know in construction coordination meetings what type of work you expect.

Occasionally, local architects and contractors appear to tacitly agree that problems very visible to the library staff simply don't exist. If this happens to your library, you will probably have to be a complete pill to protect yourself.

> One library Fred knows found that the architects, engineers, contractors, and city inspectors were all local and all buddies and all blithely insisted that major problems simply didn't exist. The library had to hire an out-of-state engineering firm with a nationwide reputation and with enough professional clout to get past the good-old-boy blockade.

One of the most serious errors a library can make is not sticking by its guns at punch list time. Although your building will come with a one-year "correction period," getting things corrected is infinitely easier when you're sitting on someone's money.

Punch lists need to be in print and fully detailed. If you tend to pick nits, you have just the right sort of mind for punch listing. Software is available for documenting punch lists, including photographs of all problems.

Frequently your contractors will contest some of the items in your punch list. If so, offer to walk through the library with them and review each item.

> Fred had this happen once. When he offered to meet with the contractor and remove any unreasonable item from the list, the contractor replied that the point wasn't unreasonable items but simply too many items. Things were somewhat tense after that.

Running through all the items in a punch list can take months or sometimes even years. This is totally unacceptable. No Certificate of Substantial Completion would ever allow such a timeframe. There are measures available to move things along.

Throughout the process, you may be under continuous pressure to release nearly all of the holdback money. Your contractors will contend, for example, that you are sitting on $100,000 of their money while the total remaining work is perhaps $5,000, and that this would be a good time to pay all but the $5,000. However, if you do this, you are unlikely to ever see your contractors again. The thing that keeps contractors coming back is the leverage of the $100,000. You are not allowed to be arbitrary here. The amounts withheld can include the costs of going out to find someone who will complete the work should the contractor refuse to complete the contract. This is often more expensive because it involves startup, overhead, and warranty costs for the replacement contractor that were built into the original contractor's price. The proper response is always to assure your contractors that you are very eager to release the entire retainage, that you hope the small amount of work can be completed quickly, but that you are prepared to take other measures if they do not complete the work within the timeframe identified in the Certificate of Substantial Completion.

For those who miss the sense of power, there's one more list. Once the final punch list is completed and the contractor is paid out, more things can be discovered. These are still the obligation of the contractor. As you discover additional items, add them to a new list. Some of them may be warrant issues, others incomplete work. In either case, bring them to the attention of the CM or contractor.

As the owner, you can help in the punch list process by keeping an eye on the building as it goes up and bringing up things that appear to be wrong. If you maintain a diary of the project with specific, dated entries, make notes as to whether and when your observations are addressed. As the project nears completion, review the items that never did get resolved. This provides a source of items for your punch list.

VI. Money

VI-A. DRAWS, LIEN WAIVERS, AND RETAINAGE

On most construction projects, the general contractor and subcontractors will submit monthly applications for payment, informally called "draws," which are bills for work completed to date.

One major responsibility of the architect is to make sure that the work for which bills are submitted has actually been completed, and that all of the participating subcontractors have been paid by the general contractor for their previous work.

Problems can occur in several areas. For example, if a construction firm is running short of cash, it may start billing for work that is almost—but not quite—finished. Architects quickly learn which firms jump the gun, just as they (very) occasionally learn which firms have to be prodded to submit bills.

Any contractor who does requested work and does not receive payment may file a "mechanic's lien" on the completed building. The problem sometimes occurs when a general contractor collects money for work by subcontractors but does not pay them. As part of the construction administration process, therefore, architects require that the general contractor provide "waivers of lien" from each of the subcontractors, certifying that they have been paid and that they therefore waive the legal right to submit mechanics' liens on the building. During the course of the project, lien waivers can amount to a substantial amount of paper. (As mentioned above, payment bonds also protect owners in these situations.)

One way in which librarians involved in construction projects can be of assistance is to watch for trucks with the names of possible subcontractors and be sure that the architects know about these firms, keeping notes in project diaries.

As soon as the library pays for any part of the work, it now owns that section of the building. To protect the library from liability and losses connected with that section, the library purchases "builder's risk insurance." Because losses are more likely during construction than after the building is occupied (think cutting torches), builder's risk insurance is more expensive than everyday insurance on library buildings.

By contractual arrangement, owners hold back a specific portion—typically 5 to 10 percent—of each draw, for payment at the time the building is completed and accepted and all punch list items have been corrected. The entire amount withheld is called "retainage." By the end of the project, this can be a very substantial amount of money, and it some cases (again by arrangement) this may be reduced to something like 5 percent when the project is nearly done. Some contractors constantly angle for payment of retainage before work is completed, and owners need to stand extraordinarily firm.

VI-B. CHANGE ORDERS

Change orders are agreements between owners and contractors to add or alter items in the contract for an additional charge.

Change orders inevitably cost more than if the item had been part of the original contract. Prices for the original contract are arrived at by low bid, where the contractor is in competition with other contractors in order to get the job. But the price of change orders is set by negotiation, leading to prices much less advantageous to the owners.

You are also required to respect the construction process. Things do not happen overnight, and a last-minute change on paper does not always result in a "next day" change on the construction site. Your CM or architect can help you understand both the timelines and the costs involved.

Change orders become necessary for a variety of reasons:

- Architects make mistakes. Drawings are inconsistent, necessary items are omitted, or incorrect features are specified. For example, the ceiling of a room may be too low for the compact shelving scheduled to be installed there, resulting in the need to raise the suspended ceiling grid and alter the location of sprinkler piping.

- Unexpected conditions are encountered. This happens frequently in remodeling jobs. For example, a wall believed to have no wiring turns out when it is opened to have electric lines that need to be relocated before a door can be installed. Since contractors were told they would not have to relocate wiring in order to install the door, the extra cost of moving the wires leads to a change order.

- Owners change their minds. Owners read about new features they would like to have in their libraries, they change their minds once they see what something actually looks like, or they find they have extra money and decide to improve some feature of the building. Occasionally, owners misread the construction drawings, are surprised and disappointed when they see what's actually constructed, and then pay extra to have it changed.

Architects whose projects are characteristically accompanied by vast numbers of change orders do not develop good reputations. Since it's impossible to draw up anything as complex as building plans without making mistakes, a few architectural errors are par for the course. But endless change orders mean sloppy designing, drawing, or coordinating. (Supposedly, contractors who know an architectural firm's reputation for excessive change orders will submit lower bids on the presumption that they'll make up their losses in change orders.)

Expecting that any set of architectural drawings is completely correct is unreasonable, for even a small building may involve tens of thousands of details, and the cost of getting everything absolutely consistent is too high. For new construction, change orders due to architectural errors shouldn't be much more than 3 percent of construction costs.

Unexpected conditions are always encountered, but better examination of existing buildings can prevent some of them.

Fickle owners are responsible for the results of changing their minds. Architects, however, can take time to be sure that owners realize what they're actually getting.

Change orders are one of the many reasons that all construction budgets include contingency lines. Typically, these are 5 percent for new construction. For remodeling and expansion, contingency lines may be 10 percent, since the chance of discovering unexpected conditions is much higher.

Contractors who seriously underbid projects are notorious for constantly demanding change orders.

It's extremely important that all change orders be documented. Your relationships with your architects need to specify who is authorized to agree to change orders (it's the owner and the contractor), and that change orders must always be in writing, not simply conversations between the architects and contractors. All change orders must include specific prices and any adjustments to the time allowed to the contractor to complete the work. (This is another good place to keep a diary of action taken on the project.)

VII. Recurring Tasks

VII-A. RECORD DRAWINGS

One of the routine tasks that needs to be checked every month, as part of a construction meeting or review of an application for payment (draw), is verification that the contractors are keeping an accurate record of what is being installed and where. In combination with the submittal, "record" or "as-built" drawings will be essential for the maintenance, repair, and future modification of the building. Much of the detailed knowledge is lost if it is not immediately put to paper as items are installed. Contractors who claim they can wait until the end of the project are wrong. Many projects include requirement for automatic reductions in payments to contractors if the record drawings are not current as of the date of the application for payment.

VII-B. CONSTRUCTION SITE MAINTENANCE

Your contractor or construction manager will need to clarify who is responsible for removing construction trash and debris. Construction sites can become dangerously cluttered almost overnight, and you don't want accidents for workers or owners. If you see trash everywhere on the construction site, this is a good subject to bring up at a construction coordination meeting.

Your contractor or construction manager will also need to establish job site security, particularly overnight. Construction sites have expensive tools and supplies lying around.

Most construction sites have temporary fencing of some kind with controlled gates for entry of workers. (If you have a mixture of union and non-union workers, you may have to have two gates.) Fencing can also control blowing trash.

Remember that as you pay off the building during construction, the responsibility for insurance rests with the library rather than with the builder. See section III-D "Builder's Risk Insurance" in chapter 36.

VIII. Contract Close-out

In their haste to move on to the next project or get into their building, contractors and owners are both tempted to rush through an important set of project end tasks. Architects may also be exhausted at this point and just want to be done. Do not succumb to this temptation.

VIII-A. TRAINING

By the end of your project, you should know how much of your maintenance will be handled by your staff and how much will be covered by service agreements with outside vendors. If the work will be done by library staff or by a parent organization, training is all the more important.

Before training begins, major building system components and software should be tested and commissioned, so that all procedures can be properly demonstrated to your team. Manuals and parts lists should be distributed in advance. Training itself should go through routine processes such as startup, shutdown, and emergency shutdown.

Many projects require staff to pass a comprehensive test in order for the contractor to be considered to have provided adequate training. This is not just a box to check. Your staff may be as reluctant to participate in this level of training as the contractor is to provide it. Stick by your guns.

Make sure your project includes a requirement that a video be made of the training. People forget details, and you're bound to have new staff from time to time.

VIII-B. WARRANTIES

Warranties should be organized. Include any obligations of the owner (many roof warranties, for example, require a log of who went on the roof and for what reason). Include contact information for both the manufacturer and the installer. Don't assume this information will be all available later when you need it. Check now. With the Certificate of Substantial Completion, you become responsible for contacting installers or suppliers for warranty work.

VIII-C. RECORD DRAWINGS

This is the time for a detailed review of the record drawings, record specifications, and record submittals. If there were any items that seem odd over the course of the project, any changes to the work, and major substitutions, check the record drawings to be certain that the documents match reality.

It's also important that owners receive all the instruction sheets that come with equipment installed by the contractors. Since many workers understand how many things work before they even unpack them, owners need to remind contractors that they want all the sheets.

IX. Post-occupancy Inspection

In the construction industry, the standard warranty period is one year. After that, you are generally on your own. Thankfully, many parts of the building do not revert to this default but are covered under specific manufacturers' warranties for individual components of your building—such as roof, windows, and mechanical systems, for example—and these are typically much longer than one year.

Warranties are useful, but only as good as the company behind them. Look for long-lived and reputable manufacturers during the selection process. Remember that as the building component ages, the warranty covers less—you do not get a free air conditioner at the end of 20 years under your warranty. Remember also that product warranties do not necessarily cover installation. And finally, do not think of warranties as a substitute for completing work remaining after substantial completion.

To take advantage of your warranty, you need to keep careful track of problems during the first year of occupancy. Frequently, owners and architects get together about 10 months after buildings are completed to work up lists of items that should be corrected under the terms of the contractor's warranty.

It helps if you remind your staff to let you know during the first year about anything that appears to be wrong.

X. Public Events during and after Construction

X-A. INTRODUCTION

One of the really fun things in library construction is ceremonies—brief shining moments of hope and victory and widespread congratulations in between barrages of plaster dust, crashing of falling objects, strongly scented glues and finishes, workers' radios, and who knows what else.

Ceremonial construction events serve many purposes:

- They provide newsworthy events.
- They keep your community focused on your progress. Because construction of a major library can take two or three years, you may need to have something of note happen not only at the start and at the finish, but also while you are underway.
- They satisfy community curiosity about what's going on behind the construction fences. Looking through peepholes in fences is less satisfying than one might expect.
- They provide opportunities to thank all of those whose support made the project possible, including granting agencies, individual and corporate donors, administrations (university, city, school, hospital, and so on), and politicians.
- They provide opportunities for prospective donors (who never thought the project would get off the ground but have had their minds change by seeing things actually under construction) to reconsider making serious donations.
- They allow the public to recognize all the local people who have done the work: library

and university and school board members, fundraising groups, and so on.

- They provide opportunities to note the achievements of the hired guns, including library staff members, employees of parent organizations, architects, contractors, consulting librarians, and construction workers.

Ceremonies involving buildings require extra planning in advance. Be sure to consider:

- What will you do if it rains?
- Can speakers be heard?
- Will speeches bore listeners to death? Ceremonies are better shorter than longer. (Try to avoid speakers who have reputations for never shutting up. It's always possible to point out people, speak briefly about them, ask them to wave to the crowd, and then move on.)
- Will you have copious treats?
- Is your event schedule compatible with somewhat uncertain construction timetables? When contractors are at work, you can't tell them to stop for 10 days or to do 10 weeks' work in two weeks because of a scheduled event.
- If there is earth to turn, will you have loosened it first?
- Will you recognize everyone who expects to be recognized?
- Have you invited all the politicians, even those who gave you no help at all? After all, they may help you another day.
- Have you prepared fact sheets for the media? (However, despite your best efforts to give everyone all the names and numbers and dates, someone will still get it all wrong.)
- Have you involved cute children?
- Do you have a competent person in charge to plan your events? Disorganized events can be embarrassments.
- Have you checked out all of your technical equipment in advance? It's embarrassing if the big day arrives only to have the PA system shrieking and howling or the flagpole have a permanently jammed pulley, and have 300 people watching while the folks in charge struggle to get things working.

X-B. AT THE BEGINNING

X-B-1. Ground Breakings

Ground breakings are times of hope and glory. After many years of space planning and design and fundraising and bidding, things are actually underway.

The major problem with ground breakings is that they are out of doors and there is really nothing to see yet. But there are lots of other things to keep in mind.

- Schedule ground breakings for nice weather. Basically, April through October in temperate parts of the country. Since you want to get as much work as possible done before winter, spring ground breakings are a practical idea from the construction viewpoint as well as the pleasant weather viewpoint.
- Ground breakings are not the actual start of construction. You can work around being either early or late.
- Invite all the politicians, whether or not they helped. Library ground breakings are great political photo ops, and you never know when they'll pay you back. (Library buildings are the kind of positive projects

that lots of politicians love to be seen hanging around with.)

- Invite all the support groups—foundations, donors, friends, staff, boards, councils, faculty senates, library employees, and all of the rest.

- Invite all the hired types—architects, engineers, consulting librarians, contractors, surveyors, and other specialists.

- Make sure the media are there. Announce in advance. A good way to remind them is to call the day before, just to be sure that you have "prepared everything they need."

- Have a fact sheet ready for the media. Reporters need names, numbers, schedules, and other information.

- Have your own photographer. There's no such thing as taking too many pictures.

- Have public handouts listing all the participants and supporters. List all of your donors, right down to those who gave five dollars. Print lots of copies. (Keeping precise track of donations is a job for a precise person. Omitting a donor from a list can lead to years of unhappy memories.)

- Have a pavilion or other shelter available. If rain comes unexpectedly, it's too late to plan quickly for alternative action.

- Have places for elderly donors to sit. Preferably under the pavilion.

- Have a PA system. Some crucial speaker will have a voice that can barely be heard in a small clothes closet, and very few people can talk loudly enough to be heard out of doors.

- Have renderings of the building-to-be on display somewhere. Your architects will supply them. Have extra copies for the press. Have releases assuring the press that they have the right to reproduce the drawings, just in case they hadn't thought of doing so.

- If you're still raising money for furnishings or opening-day collections or mortgage retirement, let people know. People who won't give to vaguely promised projects may be positively motivated by signs of actual work.

- When in doubt, be brief. You can be just as joyous in 15 minutes as in an hour. You may need to remind speakers in advance of your intent to keep things moving.

- Provide food. There are probably some kinds of happy events that are not improved by food, but we are not aware of them.

- Consider some kind of souvenirs of the occasion.

- Loosen the earth in advance. An elderly donor struggling helplessly to turn a spoonful of earth is not an auspicious sign.

- Ask your contractor about fancy shovels. Most have a supply, often chrome plated. If they don't, spray some brand new garden spades with gold paint.

- Let everyone have a chance with a shovel. Take lots of pictures.

- Involve cute children, who are far more photogenic than politicians, members of governing boards, or hired professionals. (One library Fred worked with featured a small boy who gave the building fund six months of his allowance and was a hit.)

X-B-2. Laying Cornerstones

A cornerstone is an ornamental stone block set fairly close to the ground where two exterior walls of the building meet. The block may be inscribed with the date and with whatever else the owners want to see there.

Many cornerstones have hollow cores with boxes of documents and other memorabilia, for recovery at some unspecified future time—perhaps when further construction makes the relocation of the cornerstone necessary—or just to provide a good excuse for looking inside. In this respect, cornerstones serve something of the function of time capsules, but without the recommended opening date. (When ancient cornerstones are opened, people often find that water has intruded and spoiled the contents. This is one of the advantages of indoor time capsules.)

The name comes from the idea that the cornerstone is a basic supporting element in the structure, sort of like the keystone of an arch (even though the arch would collapse with the removal of any individual stone). As a result of the implication of essential underlying support, "cornerstone" is a popular element in names of many organizations.

Most modern cornerstones are really date stones and simply display the date of the building.

X-C. MID-PROJECT EVENTS

X-C-1. Signing Beams

Some projects include a ceremony where library governors, staff, construction workers, and others all sign a steel beam. This can be the final beam, which is signed before it is lifted into place. Or it can be a beam that has already been installed but is within reach of people standing on the floor. In some cases, people sign columns rather than beams.

The presumption is that the signed beam will be hidden by later finishes. You may be tempted make a permanent display of your signed beam, but many are fairly ugly.

Beams intended for signing can be painted white in advance, or they can just be primed steel and signed with white or yellow pens.

Since the beam may be covered up later, extensive photography is important.

X-C-2. Topping Out

"Topping out" is a traditional ceremony that focuses on construction workers. It customarily involves mounting a fir tree on the very top beam of the building when the beam is installed. If the building has no top beam, the ceremony may revolve around a ridgepole, the last roofing piece, the last brick, or some other element. Obviously, topping out takes place long before the ribbon is cut, for much of the curtain wall construction, window installation, MEP equipment, and interior work may remain to be done.

Sometimes the beam is painted white and signed by all the workers and staff and owners and others before it is hoisted into place. (See the section X-C-1, "Signing Beams.")

In addition to a fir tree, the top beam may also be decorated by an American flag. In some parts of the country, the tree is omitted if any construction workers died from accidents during the project.

Frequently the contractor or owner will treat the construction workers to a meal as part of the ceremony.

Topping out is a traditional ceremony focusing on the construction workers, but on many projects it becomes a media event as well, with owners seizing the opportunity to report to the community on the status of the project.

As with all ceremonies, public relations opportunities abound. If you decide to make a big deal of the ceremony, be sure that every suitable person is invited—public library or school board members, university officials, political supporters, donors, foundation members, all sorts of members of the press, library employees, and so on.

But the meal may be limited to the workers. Sometimes (for example) it is served on a newly poured floor in an upper area of the building not yet open to the general public. Medieval topping-out ceremonies supposedly included alcohol, but you may want to think about liability issues before trying that route.

The main point is that the focus of topping out is on construction workers, who deserve the attention.

X-C-3. Phase I Completion Events

Some phased projects involve constructing an addition to the library, camping out in the addition while the original library is remodeled, and then moving back into the original library.

When the new addition to the library opens, it's possible to hold an event recognizing the newly completed work. This obviously depends on the size of the new addition. For example, if a library is tripled in size, the new addition is a very significant achievement.

One possible ceremony is having tours the first days the new addition to the library is open.

Sometimes when libraries camp out in new additions, however, the result is a crowded and very much half-finished space, and visitors may need help envisioning what's still to come. Or you may want to wait for the final ribbon cutting.

X-C-4. Tours of the Work in Progress

Some libraries prevail upon their contractors to allow tours of construction sites before the work is finished. These may be for staff, members or governing boards, media, and other people who want to see how the work is progressing. Often staff members are particularly curious about new spaces. However, you have to have permission for tours, and you have to have appropriate insurance coverage.

Tours are difficult for safety reasons. Until staircases and hand railings have been installed, access to upper floors of the building will be by ladder, and neither the library nor the construction firm will be happy about the risk of injuries. Tours are difficult to conduct until construction workers have left the site for the day, which means late afternoons or weekends.

While some contractors maintain very clean sites, there are always construction materials lying about for people to trip over.

In general, tours of buildings under construction are a really bad idea for large groups.

Most visitors will have trouble envisioning how things will look when the work is completed, anyway. A stretch of bare concrete floor with steel studs and wiring conduit and suspended ceiling grids without acoustic tile and with air ducts and sprinkler pipes lurking above tells more about the inner workings of the structure than about how it will look when it's finished. For this reason, tours when the building is nearly finished may be more useful.

If visitors have to wear hard hats and goggles while touring the building, they may find the whole experience more empowering. You can always do it when things are about 98 percent complete and still have the same fun.

X-D. PROJECT-END CELEBRATIONS

X-D-1. Construction Plaques

There are a lot of decisions in this area:

- Every new library needs one or more plaques by the front door to recognize all the right people. Determining who the right people are is more complicated.

- For public libraries, plaques usually list the name of the library, the date of completion of construction, board members, library director, architect, contractor, and programmer. If you had a construction grant, you may be required to list it on the plaque.

- Private academic libraries will need the university board of trustees and president, but public universities may also need the names of state officials, recognition of construction grants, and so on. Be sure to check on required wording.

- If the library had a single, major donor, that person's name will usually appear on the plaque.

- If you have a lot to say, it's fine to have more than one plaque.

> One of Fred's libraries took years to plan and build. A plaque listed all board members who had been associated with the project since the beginning of planning. Their names filled a large plaque all by themselves, but the people deserved to be mentioned.

> This sounds silly, but there are some amazing howlers out there. One city had to remake a major stone monument in front of its new city hall because it referred to the women on the city council as "aldermen."

- Some architects find consulting librarians annoyingly independent and will not want to share plaque space with them. Tough.

- Getting names right is complicated, but one wrong name on a bronze plaque is an expensive mistake. Insist on receiving draft versions of everything and have lots of people read them. Including teenagers with raunchy senses of humor, who may see troublesome second meanings where more sober adults do not.

- Time capsules are trite, and most have painfully boring contents. Fight both tendencies. Ask yourself what kind of stuff would be fun to discover inside a just-opened 50-year-old time capsule. Old toys are more fun than old lists of old people. Any digital media will probably be too old to read.

X-D-2. Donor Recognition Plaques

All sorts of donor recognition plaques are available commercially. Many are designed for adding extra names over the years, but some libraries create final plaques at the time the building is completed.

Lots of libraries recognize major donations by mounting individual letters on walls. Unfortunately, major problems occur when then have to repaint the walls or relocate the letters. Be sure your letters are engineered for easy removal and reinstallation. (Some are.)

Here's a plaque for a completely imaginary public library:

THE WILLIAMSTOWN PUBLIC LIBRARY
2025

[The date is usually the date of the ribbon cutting]

BOARD *of* TRUSTEES

[Names of board members go here. The problem is whether you list current trustees only, or whether you list all trustees that were involved since the beginning of the project. If a couple of board officers who inspired and led the project end their terms three months before the ribbon cutting, you don't want to omit their names. But if you include their names, you then need a consistent way of dealing with the names of other former board members.]

DIRECTOR

[If you changed directors in mid-stream, will you list both of them? Who goes first? If an associate director played a major role, do you list that name too?]

JOHNSON AND WILLIAMS | *Architects*
WILLIAMS AND JOHNSON | *Contractor*
WILLIAM JOHNSON | *Consulting Librarian*

[Up until now, things are pretty standard. Depending on the situation, you may want to list donors, local government officials, a second architectural firm, grant agencies that require they be listed, university boards of trustees, government officials, and so on. Sometimes two plaques are needed to cram everyone in.]

[One of Fred's libraries took years to plan and build. A plaque listed all board members who had been associated with the project since the beginning of planning. The names filled a plaque all by themselves, but the people deserved to be mentioned.]

Your fundraisers will need to figure out what level of donation results in what level of recognition. It's tremendously important to be absolutely consistent. See chapter 19, "Building Costs" and chapter 20, "Funding."

X-D-3. Donor Receptions

Many libraries have special receptions for the donors who contributed to the project. Sometimes these are evening events with special food, wine, and so on.

Receptions provide time for more personal attention to donors. If a ribbon cutting is a mob scene, you may not have the chance you want to take time to talk with each major supporter of the project.

However, don't let a donor reception become the major celebration or a substitute for a ribbon cutting. The vast number of members of the community need to be welcomed as well.

X-D-4. Ribbon Cuttings

Ribbon cuttings are fun. Have a great time, but prepare for common problems.

- Some libraries have grand openings with people seeing the library for the first time, but they're tricky to bring off. Like retail stores, you may want to have a "soft opening" and unveil something like recognition plaques at the grand opening.
- Be prepared for things not being entirely done. Furnishings frequently arrive late. Some furniture manufacturers swear that everything's nearly ready to ship while they haven't even begun production. Somewhere there'll be a missing ceiling tile with wires hanging down.
- Punch lists are almost never resolved in time for ribbon cuttings. But there's so much to see in a new building that we hope that lots of people won't notice failings.
- Publicize the ribbon cutting full blast.
- Just in case something goes wrong with construction, it's probably a bad idea to pick the date months in advance.
- Invite all the people you invited to the ground breaking: politicians, donors, boards, foundations, faculty senates, friends groups, students, employees, hired experts, and the rest. Omitting people is a far greater sin than inviting too many, so invitations are vital. Back them up with mass emails.
- Make sure the media are there, although ribbon cuttings are reliable sources of media activity because they are good photo ops.
- Print booklets listing everyone, particularly all donors and volunteers and supporters. No donation is too small for recognition.
- Keep speechmaking short. People want to see the building. But take time to thank everyone. It takes only seconds to say, "Our great architects are here," and ask them to wave. (At one ribbon cutting, Fred was told he had "120 seconds," which told him they really knew what they were doing.)
- Be sure that a speaker points out the functional features of the building. Everyone can see the handsome architectural features, but they may not be aware of how well things work.
- Schedule ribbon cuttings for nice weather, both to allow people to congregate out of doors and to allow people from out of town to attend the occasion.
- Hold ribbon cuttings on convenient days— basically Saturday or Sunday at 2:00 p.m. A Thursday evening ribbon cutting is anti-social.
- You may want a special event for donors, but the main event should be for everyone.
- Hold most of the event inside the building rather than keeping everyone hanging around outside in the rain. Unless it's a seriously lovely day, traipse in first and cut the ribbon second.
- If necessary, the ends of the ribbon can be hand-held rather than anchored to the building.
- Some people use huge prop shears for ribbon cutting.
- With proper staging, 20 people can cut one ribbon at the same moment. It's fun to watch 20 bits of ribbon fall to the ground at the same time. (Make sure your 20 pairs of shears are all sharp.)
- Even if everything takes place indoors, you'll still need a PA system.

- Take endless photographs.

- Try to have the donor recognition plaques installed in time for the ribbon cutting. For some donors from out of town, this may be their main visit to the library, and it's a great time to have the maximum number of people see the plaques.

- When you put up donor recognition items, consider how you will repaint the walls on which they are mounted. Individual letters look great on walls until repainting day arrives, when you'll want them easy to remove and replace.

- Have staff present to give tours or to introduce people to what goes on in their departments. Write lists of key points for them to make, rather than just leaving everything to chance.

- If you need money for extra stuff, have information available. (One library Fred worked with had booklets with maps of the building showing each piece of needed furniture, with prices marked on each needed object. It worked.)

- Feed people. Even if it's just candy corn and circus peanuts (although you can almost certainly do better).

- If you can afford it, spend money on an opening day collection to make the shelves sparkle. (Some ill-advised public libraries, however, have pitched out all their older books to make their shelves seriously sparkle, making citizens wonder why they bothered to build a new library in the first place.)

- People may want to see the back rooms, but probably more out of general curiosity than an overwhelming interest in library staff functions. Most people want to see things they will use personally, and this does not include tech services, staff lunchrooms, panel rooms, water rooms, loading docks, or storage.

- During a grand opening, people will try every available door. If you don't want visitors wandering in, keep doors locked.

- When you cut the ribbon, the library is brand new. Outside of things that didn't turn up on time or punch list problems, the building will never look better.

XI. Snappy Rules on Construction

1. A badly constructed building is a pain forever. Or until it falls down, whichever comes first.

2. Everything else being equal, union labor is more technically competent than non-union labor. If prevailing wage laws mean you have to pay the same price for both, union labor can be a particularly good idea.

3. Punch listing tries the previously warm social relationships between owners and contractors.

4. The failure of architects to provide correct details on plans is not the contractors' fault.

5. Contractors and construction managers tell workers what to do. Owners do not.

6. In some parts of the U.S., no workers turn up on the first day of deer season or trout season.

7. If you want to provide cookies for the workers, talk with the contractors. A large crew taking time off work to line up for cookies in mid-morning can cost

a contractor hundreds of dollars in lost production.

8. Someone from the library staff needs to be present at all construction coordination meetings. Directors may have to delegate their favorite activities while construction is underway.

9. If you know you will be a real stickler on a certain area, tell people up front. (Fred insisted that all electrical boxes in the floor be square and in exact rows. He was never popular with the electricians, but the result was a lot less sloppy looking than most jobs of that kind.)

10. If the contractor messes up, be extraordinarily wary of accepting cash in lieu of corrected work. You have a right to a building that works the way it is supposed to, and it's easy to bargain away proper performance for far too little money. If your architects encourage you to accept a cash settlement, always talk to your owner's rep (if you have one) and your consulting librarian.

11. It's a good thing if the project architect or a person with similar responsibilities is the person the architectural firm sends to attend the construction coordination meetings.

12. If you have named categories for various sizes of donations to your project, be careful how you name them. "Supermen" and "Sharecroppers" are probably not good choices.

13. Short public ceremonies followed by extensive socializing, extensive tours or explorations, and extensive eating make everyone happy.

14. If your designers want to mount individual letters on walls, ask them how the letters can be removed for repainting the walls 10 years from now. (Latex paint on drywall has the durability of piecrust, and you *will* have to repaint.)

15. If you decide to have a cash bar at public events, you'll need dram shop insurance, which the press may find entertaining to report.

16. It's almost impossible to have everything completed in time for your ribbon cutting. Luckily, you will be far more aware of what's missing or wrong than will the people seeing the building for the first time, and incomplete details may not register. (Furniture is notoriously late, and punch lists may linger longer than they should.)

17. It's hard to find the right place between having two few public ceremonies and having so many ceremonies that the press and bloggers start having fun at your expense.

18. At public events, what people want to hear is probably more important than what you want to tell them.

19. Settle in advance what kinds of advertising from designers and contractors and other participants can be posted on the construction site.

20. A few libraries are able to time things so that the first time the public enters the library is at the ribbon cutting. But it's tricky to pull off. Exact timing is hard to predict far enough in advance, and it's usually better to have a soft opening and then celebrate a little later when the furniture has actually arrived.

PART II
From Overcrowding to Ribbon Cutting

CHAPTER 16

Remodeling and Expanding Library Buildings

I. Introduction

This chapter deals with the special problems encountered in remodeling and expanding existing library buildings.

One of the most satisfying undertakings in library design can be the expansion and remodeling of historic libraries. When owners walk into projects with a firm idea of functional needs and the special challenges of dealing with existing buildings, the results can be outstanding.

However, although the logic of preservation and conservation leads to strong public interest in the reuse of existing structures, the costs can be extremely high, and the results can be extremely disappointing from a functional viewpoint. If, in addition, the historical qualities of the original structure are compromised or ruined, not much is gained by reuse.

If you are considering expanding an existing library, one absolute prerequisite is a completed building program, one written on the basis of functional needs, not existing spaces. If you have a program, you can constantly use it as a yardstick to determine whether proposed modifications and additions provide the spaces you actually need. Without a program, you are likely to provide features because you can, rather than because you need them.

While remodeling and expanding existing libraries can be a positive experience, converting existing non-library structures to libraries is often a perilous and ill-advised undertaking. See chapter 17, "Converting Non-Library Buildings to Public Libraries."

See also chapter 9, "Site Selection"; chapter 11, "Accessibility"; chapter 22, "Collection Storage and Display"; chapter 31, "Lighting"; chapter 32, "Electrical Systems"; chapter 33, "HVAC"; and chapter 34, "Plumbing Systems."

II. Comparative Costs

It's extremely easy to underestimate the cost of remodeling and modernizing an existing library building. If a building needs a new HVAC system, new wiring, new roof, new lighting, new plumbing, a sprinkler system, abatement of asbestos and lead paint, provision of accessibility, and substantial other work to bring it into compliance with building codes, the necessary work can cost easily as much as new construction—and sometimes substantially more.

In addition, the increased space taken up by air ducts, larger restrooms, legal clearances between furnishings, removal of historic but inaccessible book stacks, retrofitting of electrical outlets and data conduit, addition of an elevator, and provision of additional staircases required to meet safety codes means that the existing building will almost certainly hold substantially less after remodeling. This means that remodeling historic libraries without simultaneously expanding them is unlikely to be successful unless the libraries have a great deal of currently unused space.

One of the problems that accompanies possible remodeling and expansion is public pressure. Even if your building is clearly unworkable, few people will believe that reworking it involves throwing good money after bad.

When you are considering remodeling and expansion, you will need:

- A written building program listing the spaces you need when you are finished—not those spaces you think you can create by conversion of existing spaces. Existing spaces will have to be considered later, but they should not affect your initial description of what constitutes a suitable building for your library. All of us who live in existing buildings are constantly thinking of ways they might be tweaked to improve things, and it's hard to suppress these ideas and think instead of everything we actually need. To protect yourself in situations like this, always make sure that your program is designed to be equally suitable for either remodeling or new construction. Or use the "tornado" approach and pretend that a windstorm has completely eliminated your current building, and only then list what you need.

- The opinions of architects and engineers on the physical condition of your current building and its suitability for expansion. This kind of analysis can be complex. The unfortunate thing is that even if your building is only 10 or 20 years old, it may still be unsuited for expansion.

- A thorough review of the available expansion site, including its size and any physical limitations. Without a suitable site, any thought of expansion is doomed.

- A schematic design prepared by your architects showing how your building can be expanded and remodeled to meet the needs specified in your building program.

- A review by your consulting librarian of your architect's design for expansion and remodeling, to be sure that there are no resulting functional problems.

- A solid cost estimate for the project, prepared by people who have experience with old buildings.

- For comparison, your architects' estimate of the cost of starting over with a completely new building.

- And a review of your options the next time you run out of space.

> Estimates for the cost of remodeling and expanding historic buildings can be extraordinarily inaccurate. One Illinois Carnegie library found its lowest bid was three times the architects' estimate.

If discussions about the need to start over on a new site get ugly, it's important to let your hired professionals—your architects, engineers, and programmer—take the flak. Remember the basic rule: the library should always deliver any good news, and hired professionals should deliver the bad news. The professionals will probably be more believable, but the important thing is that they can leave town at the end of the meeting.

III. Problems with the Reuse and Expansion of Existing Library Buildings

III-A. CHANGING BUILDING CODES

Unless your library is very new, it can easily be out of conformance with existing building codes. As long as you don't change it much, it may be considered to be "grandfathered" as an existing building. And in some cases there are exceptions to codes for historic buildings. But if you carry out significant expansion or remodeling, you may be required to bring it up to code. And by not bringing it up to code, however you are able to arrange this, you are making your building less safe and effective.

Determining what you can and can't do is a technical undertaking that will require conversations between your architects (and engineers) and local code enforcement officials.

Inevitably there are gray areas. Officials may be willing to bend on zoning, but asking that building code matters be waived is not welcome. (Sometimes historic buildings may be allowed to vary from codes, while more recent buildings of less architectural significance may not.)

III-B. NEW CODE CATEGORIES RESULTING FROM EXPANSION

Many building code requirements vary with the size of the structure.

You may find, for example, that your building is perfectly legal as a 10,000-square-foot structure but no longer legal as part of a 30,000-square-foot structure.

This can frequently happen if the construction materials in your building are inappropriate for a larger structure. For example, existing wooden structural components may not meet local fire codes for significantly larger buildings.

If this is the case, it's possible that you may not be allowed to expand your building. Or you may be required to construct what amounts to two separate buildings with a narrow opening between them, equipped with doors that close automatically in case of fire. A narrow opening between two sections of the building may work well if each section is the right size to meet the one of the major spaces listed in your building program. But if the resulting spaces don't match your program, you may find it difficult or impossible to develop the functional spaces you need. And if a department is divided into two essentially separate spaces, this may introduce expensive problems with staff oversight.

Another frequent requirement when buildings expand is the addition of a sprinkler system. The IBC (International Building Code), for example, specifies that any library over 12,000 square feet must have a sprinkler system. Libraries have been intentionally built just under 12,000 square feet in order to avoid this requirement, but when the time comes to expand, they are faced with the additional complexity of retrofitting sprinkler systems to buildings that may never have been intended to have them.

Be sure your architects determine what this situation is before you make any public announcements about your plans.

III-C. ASBESTOS AND OTHER POLLUTANTS

Almost any building constructed before about 1980 is likely to contain asbestos and lead-based paint.

Outside of its health risks, asbestos is a great material. It makes good pipe insulation, strengthens materials like vinyl floor tile and plaster, absorbs sound, and does many other desirable things.

But you still don't want it, and in many cases you will have to have it removed (remediated) during construction. (Even if you plan to tear your old library down and build a new one on the site, you will still have to remediate the asbestos.)

Actually, asbestos that is not in danger of being dispersed in the air can sometimes be left in place. A good example is vinyl asbestos floor tile (VAT) that is intact and not crumbling and will be covered by new material.

You are most likely to find asbestos in pipe lagging (insulation), vinyl asbestos floor tile (always suspect the worst of nine-by-nine inch tile), tile mastic (the glue that attaches tile to the floor), fireproof enclosures, some under-slab air ducts (look for concrete asbestos board called Transite), acoustic ceiling tile, and some drywall and joint compounds. Asbestos was banned for construction in various stages during the 1970s.

Lead paint was banned in interiors in 1978. As with asbestos, lead paint was great except for its poisonous qualities. If it's stable and not attached to crumbling surfaces and not powdering off, it may not be a major problem. But it can be nasty if you need to modify things. For example, sanding wood that has been painted with lead paint leads to airborne lead dust.

A number of poisonous metallic compounds have been used in paint. The most common are lead pigments (red lead, white lead, chrome yellow, chrome orange, chrome green), cadmium pigments (shades of red, orange, and yellow), vermillion, Paris green, and so on. Lead pigments are by far the most common.

As part of remodeling a building constructed before about 1980, you will need to have it assessed for lead and asbestos. Architects can recommend firms to do this work or arrange to have it done.

III-D. BEARING WALLS

"Bearing walls" are walls that hold up a building.

If your library has load-bearing walls, it will be far more difficult to open up larger spaces. While it's almost always possible to create openings, it can be expensive and may even require strengthening foundations if the remaining portions of walls are carrying more concentrated weight than the footings below them were intended to support.

One of the standard solutions when expanding historic libraries is to convert existing windows to doors, because the lintels over the windows are already in place. Cutting out a section of wall to essentially lower the windowsill to the floor may have little or no impact on the structure of a building and therefore be a relatively inexpensive alteration.

The expansion of old buildings with small rooms and bearing walls can lead to larger structures that are labyrinths, with too many rooms and too many invisible corners to supervise.

Many historic small libraries of the Carnegie era have front reading rooms and back offices or stacks. If the offices all have bearing walls, it may be difficult to open up the back of the existing library. And the artistic character of the formal reading rooms may be hurt if they are enlarged. If a new wing is added at the rear of a library of this type, the old offices may create a wasp waist between the original reading rooms and new public spaces at the back of the building. The danger in such a situation is that the original reading rooms may become forgotten adjuncts, spaces down the hall and around the corner. And they may be hard to supervise.

III-E. HVAC

Many historic buildings do not have the ductwork necessary for modern heating, ventilating, and air conditioning systems. This is particularly true of Carnegie-era buildings, which were built with radiators but without cooling systems.

If a historic library has two floors—a main floor and a basement—it may be fairly easy to add ductwork to heat and cool the main floor because many old buildings have substantial attic spaces that provide sufficient room for ducts.

The basement is another matter. If a library has two floors plus a basement, there will be no attic space available for ductwork to provide air to the main floor. Hanging ductwork from a historic ceiling is an abomination, so the only option may be installing ducts in the basement. But that leads to air grills in the floor, and they get in the way of furniture placement.

Whether or not they must house ductwork for the floor above, basements in old libraries are often a serious problem for modern HVAC systems. If a basement has an eight-foot ceiling, for example, the addition of ceiling-mounted ductwork will make basement spaces too low for occupants. However, sometimes it's possible to install perimeter ducts that leave the center of the basement usable.

Many historic library buildings are also energy hogs. Solid masonry walls have no insulation value, nor do single-pane windows. Rooms with high ceilings are more expensive to heat than those with lower ceilings. The lack of entry foyers can expose users and staff to blasting winter winds. If old skylights still exist, they can waste heat in the winter and waste cooling in the summer—in addition to bringing in unwanted glare by day and dark by night.

Unfortunately, ill-considered responses to the energy problem can ruin attractive buildings. Some historic windows have been replaced with modern windows with different muntin patterns, essentially ruining the historic appearance of the building. Some libraries have added cheap aluminum storm windows, which are ugly but at least do not result in the destruction of the original windows. Handsome ceilings with elegant cornices have been hidden by suspended acoustic tile ceilings. Awkward foyers have been added to the front of historic buildings to block winter winds.

Although it's more expensive, existing small-pane windows with single glazing can be replaced by double-pane windows that look essentially identical.

If high ceilings lead to a concentration of heat, paddle fans that suit the era of the building can often be installed.

III-F. ELECTRICAL WIRING

Old libraries can have extraordinarily tangled wiring, frequently cobbled together over many years and sometimes in spectacular non-compliance with even rudimentary building codes.

It's still possible to find old libraries with working knob and tube wiring, often with its original insulation happily cracking off.

Knob and tube wiring uses ceramic tubes to separate wires from wood when they pass through structural members, and ceramic knobs to support wires away from wood and other surfaces. The system was generally used from about 1880 through the 1930s. Because wires were held away from surfaces, they radiated heat well. But by separating positive and negative wires, the system led to greater magnetic fields around wires and electronic problems. And knob and tube systems do not have ground wires. Insurance companies may not want to insure your library if it has knob and tube wiring, and some building codes may ban it. Regardless, you don't want it in your library.

Because historic buildings often have solid masonry walls, it's tempting to add new wiring by attaching metal conduit to the surface of the walls. Unfortunately, the result can be extraordinarily ugly. If you care enough to preserve and expand your historic library, you should care enough to hide the new wiring.

When remodeling historic libraries, designers need to bury new electrical conduits as much as possible, although it's tempting to save money by surface mounting ugly electrical conduit on the walls. In the top picture, the three electrical items were installed by chiseling through the plaster (and the brick beneath), installing the conduit, and then covering the conduit with new plaster. In the second picture, the conduit emerges to pass over the historic dark marble baseboard because the designers were concerned about possibly ruining the baseboard if they tried to remove it and reinstall it.

The attractive way to add wiring is to channel through the plaster (and sometimes part of the masonry beneath) to provide space to bury electrical conduit in the walls.

If you are remodeling and expanding a historic library, it may already have a variety of unsightly exposed electrical conduit, added piecemeal over the years as occasional new outlets or light fixtures were needed. A major remodeling job is a great time to get rid of the mess.

III-G. WINDOWS

One of the most important sources of character in historic buildings is their windows. The dimensions of the frames and muntins, and the number and proportions of the windowpanes, play a critical role in the appearance and aesthetics of historic libraries.

One of the worst things that has been done to historic buildings is replacing historic windows with modern windows that do not match the originals. Removing small pane windows, for example, and replacing them with large sheets of glass, can alter the appearance of a building destructively.

If modern aluminum sash windows are used to replace original steel sash windows, the result is likely to be unfortunate. For reasons of strength, aluminum windows will probably have bulkier muntins than steel windows, and even if the pattern of window panes is similar, the new windows will look distinctly different.

Obviously, the best thing is to leave historic windows in place, but they often have serious problems. Old wooden windows may be rotting out. And windows may have been destructively modified in the past. They may be totally uninsulated or equipped with ugly storm windows.

The best solution may be to use photographs of the original building to create custom-made, insulated windows that match the originals as closely as possible.

Historic skylights can be covered over and lit electrically, or they can be provided with translucent protective covers, as in the 2008 restoration of the Tiffany skylights at the Chicago Public Library Cultural Center.

If your library is subject to the oversight of a historic preservation agency, it will probably pay special attention to what you plan to do with your existing windows.

III-H. CHEAP OR FRAGILE CONSTRUCTION MATERIALS

It's fun to believe that historic buildings were always well built, but that can be far from the truth.

Lots of historic libraries have wooden floors rather than concrete floors.

Many Carnegie libraries have cornices that resemble stone balustrades but are actually made of painted sheet steel. If this material is rusting out, or if more is needed, details of this kind can usually be matched in fiberglass or similar materials.

One of the most attractive features of classical library buildings is architectural terracotta, ornamental details made of glazed ceramic material. Eventually, some terracotta develops major crazing and cracks and has to be replaced. Other terracotta simply needs matching on additions. While replacement terracotta is available, the cost can be significant, and some architects have been very successful at matching historic terracotta details by making molds from the originals and using them to produce replicas from materials like fiberglass.

III-I. POOR FUNCTIONAL LOCATIONS

Some otherwise great library buildings find that with the passage of time, the building is no longer in a functional location.

This seems particularly true for public libraries, which can interact strongly with their neighborhoods. If all of the retail stores around the library have closed and relocated to preferred areas, the library loses much of the synergy that occurs between libraries and commercial neighbors. If the houses that surrounded the library are replaced by industries, or if cheap bars have been established close to the library, it may be time to move away rather than undertake major remodeling.

If a library has a functional location, it may need extra land not only to expand its building but also to add off-street parking.

III-J. MATCHING HISTORIC EXTERIORS

Many library expansions involve matching exterior finishes.

- *Brickwork*. Matching exterior brickwork is a special problem, since many types of brick used a century ago are not easily available. For example, the slender Roman bricks with thin horizontal mortar joints that are sometimes found in late-nineteenth- and early twentieth-century buildings are particularly hard to match. Taking the time to thoroughly investigate brick sources is important, and the rush to select brick quickly may lead to gross mismatching that grates on the eyes forever. One standard approach to satisfactory expansions of historic buildings is to never place new and old bricks directly adjacent to each other. If two areas of brick are separated by a new architectural element perhaps 10 to 20 feet wide, it's much harder to tell that the two types of brick don't quite match.

- *Stonework*. Limestone can sometimes be matched, and it may even be available from the same quarry that provided the original stone. A greater problem than matching stone can be matching the carving on the stone. The work can still be done, but the cost can be higher than libraries can afford.

- *Windows*. Another problem with historic buildings is that windowsills are often too high to allow users to see the outside world. A century ago, the main function of windows in libraries was to provide natural light, and book shelving was frequently located along perimeter walls beneath windows. However, library users today often want to read in locations that let them see the outside world pass by. Larger windows also make it easier for passers-by to see what's going on inside the library. In our opinion, constructing additions with windows that match those in the original buildings but have lower sills does not destroy the historic look of the buildings, particularly if the tops of the new and old windows all align, the framing elements match, the muntin patterns are as identical as possible, and the widths of the new and old windows match.

  As a side note, shelving mounted on exterior walls tends to conflict with seating, with users seated at adjacent tables sometimes blocking access to shelving. To prevent this problem, the unoccupied ends of tables need to face the shelving.

- *Architectural styles*. Opinions differ strongly on whether historic buildings

In this library, the architectural design of the expanded building (below) didn't actually match the existing building (left), which wasn't very interesting but instead made visual reference to favorite architecture in the community. It was a tremendously popular idea.

SOURCE: ENGBERG ANDERSON

should have matching additions or have distinctly different modern additions. The argument against matching additions is that the building exemplifies the intent of the original architects, and any addition should be obviously an addition, a structure that no one will assume was part of the original architects' vision for the building. We find this contention a silly one, something that bothers primarily design professionals who are either historical purists or offended by the prospect of imitating an older building style. Usually everyone else, particularly the users of the building and the residents of the area it serves, is happy with a matching or very similar addition.

One of the problems with totally unmatched modern additions to historic buildings is that they age badly. When the new addition is constructed, the building consists of a historic library and a cute modern wing, and the two function comfortably together. But after 30 years, when styles for contemporary architecture have changed, the building consists of a historic library and a painfully dated addition. (Not unlike an antebellum mansion with avocado shag carpet.)

Admittedly, some historic buildings have oddly matched sections built at different times in different styles. Hampton Court palace provides an example. But why take a chance? Your architect may also contend that matching an original look is impossible because it will be too expensive. This can be the case, but one suspects that the real motive may be a desire to make an original design statement rather than be derivative. To save money, original looks can be matched in somewhat simplified form, skipping for example the most expensive stonework details.

We are convinced that being talked into an unmatched addition to a historic building is almost always a terrible mistake. The words "talked into" are the right ones. In every case we've seen, the owners are talked into an ill-considered and unmatched addition by the architects.

However, a lot of additions are to non-historic buildings, and many of them have exteriors that are probably better off not matched. Always explore options, including completely remaking the image of the library. Joe and Fred worked on an addition to an impressively bland library, transforming it into an updated Prairie Style building that fit into its residential neighborhood and provided a far more welcoming identity for the library.

> An example of miserable failure in integrating an addition is provided by a large American academic library. The library was expanded in the late 1960s by a large and completely unmatched addition to the original historic library. The new addition was connected to the original library only by a basement tunnel and an out-of-the-way link into the back of a small departmental library. The fact that the new addition was impressively dysfunctional and partially inaccessible didn't improve things.

III-K. ADJACENT LAND

In many cases, the ability to expand a library building is hampered or prevented by the lack of adjacent land.

- Some libraries have been built on sites too small to support expansion. This is one of the worst mistakes that can be made in library planning. At the time a new library is built, it seems huge—a building that will last forever. But in 10 or 20 years, the library is packed solid. Library collections—particularly university library collections—grow remorselessly. When campuses add new programs, substantial new collections may suddenly be required. Public libraries introduce new services, services that were never anticipated when the library was designed, and the services need new spaces. When a public library finally constructs a new building after many years of forced weeding, collections may grow surprisingly quickly.

  Needing to expand a library when the available space is too small leads to hard decisions. Libraries cobble on crowded additions. They try to build upward, which is almost always impossible or badly advised. They put high-density storage units miles away rather than next door, where books can be accessed quickly. Or they delay and delay before finally cutting their losses and starting over on new sites.

- Other libraries have had expansion space, but they sold it or gave it away. On a scale of bad planning from plus 10 (great planning) to 0 (seriously awful planning), this rates about a minus 10.

  On crowded campuses, somebody always wants the empty space by the library. Protecting it for long-term library expansion can be a major political problem, with avid departments oinkingly coveting the prime central land surrounding the library. Unfortunately, once land is lost to the library, it is almost certainly gone forever. Part of the problem on campuses is that library planning is a very long-range undertaking.

Holding empty expansion land for half a century or more may be difficult.

Public libraries sometimes purchase large sites and immediately sell off some of the space to raise construction money. Inevitably, when the library needs to expand, the space it sold off is no longer available, or available only at an unaffordable price.

> One public library with which Fred worked bought a large site in an excellent location—substantially larger, in fact, than the library would ever need. The Board of Trustees considered selling off a back section of the site for home sites, but luckily it decided to wait. Within months, the state department of transportation took a third of the site for highway relocation, leaving the library with exactly the space it needed—but no more.

- Changes in zoning may make a library's current site too small. A good example is the requirement that libraries detain water runoff. At the time the building was constructed, on-site water retention may not have been required, but when the time to expand arrives, the library may find out that new zoning requirements have made most of its available land required for ponds. (There may be solutions to the problem. Existing structures may be grandfathered in, with only land being converted from turf to building requiring retention ponds. In that case, if the library demolishes an existing nearby building to construct a library addition, the net decrease in turf may be small. In some communities, green roofs also count as turf rather than building.)

The moral of all this is a simple one:

- Never let the land you own around your library go, particularly for a short-term (and often minor) cash infusion.
- Never let available land next to your library slip through your fingers. You may not need it for 10 or 20 or 50 or more years, but when the day comes, you'll be ready.
- Someone will always contend that with the coming of electronic books, libraries will never need to expand again. Often these people have axes to grind (they hate taxes or covet your land), and libraries need to combat them vigorously. There are no doubt libraries out there that are awash in unneeded space, but they are probably few.
- Pay particular attention to proposed developments near your library building. Chapter 9, "Site Selection," contains information on the types of neighbors that are likely to undermine the functions of your library.
- On campuses, fight all attempts to convert empty land around your library to non-library purposes.

III-L. ACCESSIBILITY

Any library built before the passage of the Americans with Disabilities Act or similar state statutes may have serious problems with accessibility.

Libraries are full of steps, ranging from essential staircases for movement between floors to irrelevant steps introduced because the designer thought they were cute. All of these have to be overcome.

Many libraries also have inadequate clearances to allow wheelchair traffic. These can range from narrow doorways to narrow stacks, cramped restrooms, and other common problems, and they have to be corrected as well.

Vast numbers of other needs are discussed in chapter 11, "Accessibility."

III-M. HISTORIC ENTRANCES

A large number of historic libraries have entrances that do not meet modern requirements for accessibility for people with disabilities.

There are no quick and easy solutions.

Many people will suggest adding an entrance ramp, but unless the difference in height is a foot or so, the ramp will be endless. Remember that moving two feet vertically requires a ramp a minimum of 24 feet long. An exterior ramp will be miserable or impossible to negotiate in the rain or in the winter, and it will make a significant contribution to the architectural destruction of the building.

Even worse is an unenclosed exterior ramp leading to a basement entrance, because sooner or later the drain at the foot of the ramp will clog or back up, and rainwater will flood the basement. And there's something insulting about being routed through the basement.

The only practical solution to access the vast majority of historic libraries is to provide a second entrance at grade level, with an elevator inside that can transport people to the various original levels of the library. Usually entrances of this type are on one side of the building, and the elevators are often where the original building and new addition meet.

Larger historic libraries usually have multiple elevators, one to move people from street level to the main floor, where they can pass through a security checkpoint, and then additional elevators to move people between floors.

It's important that entrances to new parts of buildings be at grade level, with movement between floors all internal. As a bad example of poor design, when one Illinois public library was expanded, the architect added a huge new exterior staircase, supplemented by a ramp down to the basement level. The results were miserable. The staircase faced northwest and was covered with ice all winter, forcing the library to rope it off for weeks at a time. The exterior ramp down into the basement channeled rainwater into the building, leading to frequent floods. The fact that the library had two new exterior entrances forced it to provide two lending desks. With a single, grade-level entrance, a library can arrange to have all users pass a single desk before being transported between floors, but this library found it impossible, and the result was having to staff two desks at times of the week when one would have been sufficient. The addition of self-check equipment can make the situation even worse.

Once a new entrance has been provided, it's tempting to take the historic entrance out of service. Watching two doors is expensive, and the original entrance may be poorly sheltered from winter weather.

Unfortunately, a major architectural message of historic buildings is frequently "this way in." If historic doors are taken out of service, the building may lose essential navigational clarity.

If you are forced to take a front door out of service, one thing to do is to convert it to an emergency exit but otherwise mothball it, leaving it strictly alone, so it can be used as an entrance once again if times change.

III-N. ROOM ARRANGEMENTS THAT DEFY EXPANSION

Some room layouts make expansion nearly impossible. For instance, some libraries feature central entry halls with narrow wings extending in three directions, leaving no places to attach additions.

III-O. BASEMENTS IN EXPANDED HISTORIC BUILDINGS

Most basements in historic library buildings have low ceilings, severely limiting the use of basement spaces.

When these buildings are expanded, the best solution to the problem is to build a large addition at grade level with a grade level entrance, mothball the historic entrance to the original library, provide an elevator between the original library and the new wing, put all the heavily used areas of the library in the new addition, use the main floor of the original historic library for elegant reading, and use the basement of the original library for storage.

If the original building is large, it's also possible to drop the level of the basement floors in the new additions to provide adequate ceiling height. The change in level may be only a couple of feet, so elevator service may not be essential to both basement levels, or the elevator can be equipped with doors on both sides and positioned to serve both basement levels.

If staffing is limited, use basements for services that don't require constant supervision. Common uses include meeting rooms, restrooms (although there may be supervision problems there as well), storage, equipment rooms, workrooms, and so on.

IV. Phasing Expansion Projects

When libraries need to expand, one major decision is whether to stay in the building during expansion work or to move out temporarily.

If the library continues to provide service in its building during expansion and remodeling, the result is a "phased" construction project.

A simple phased project may begin with the construction of a new wing. When construction is complete, the library may camp out in the new wing while the existing library is remodeled. Then the library moves back into the remodeled space.

Some projects involve more than two phases, and planning them becomes reminiscent of planning complex military campaigns.

With really large buildings, phasing may be the only practical option, but it always deserves careful evaluation and review.

IV-A. ADVANTAGES OF PHASED CONSTRUCTION

The main advantage of phased projects is that libraries don't have to move out during construction.

And that's about it.

IV-B. PROBLEMS WITH PHASING

Phasing a project introduces a number of problems:

- *Extended construction time.* Phasing a major construction job can more or less double the time required for the project.

- **Lack of space for staging construction.** Construction companies need space for their construction trailers, for parking for workers, and for piling construction materials. A common way to provide this space is to cannibalize the library's parking lot, leaving staff and patrons no place to park during construction. If your library has trees you want to preserve, you will need to take special and very firm steps to keep contractors from piling construction materials around the trees—and very likely killing them.

- **Discomfort for patrons and staff.** If you are trying to operate a library while construction is going on behind a plywood partition, you can expect to be subjected to a constant barrage of the sounds of masonry drills, falling objects, loud conversations, and workers' radios, which they will turn up loud enough to be heard over the drills and falling objects. There will also be bad smells. Because of construction, you may also have problems getting patrons and staff in and out of the building. Entrances will vary as the project continues. Temporary staff parking and even patron parking may need to be blocks away, particularly if the contractor needs your parking lot for a construction trailer, construction materials, dumpsters, etc. Construction dust will inevitably make its way into the inhabited part of the library, making some staff members and users ill.

- **Phasing and good design.** The better integrated the new and old sections of the building are, the greater your problems are likely to be. If the new addition is almost totally separate from the original building, phasing may be easier, but the resulting building is likely to be somewhat dysfunctional, with essentially two libraries where one would be better.

- **Higher bids.** Phased projects cost more. Contractors don't like to have owners and users underfoot, and they will spend more money bringing all the trades back at least a second time. If they have to work slowly due to phased construction, they will worry more about inflation and increase their bids accordingly. Because of this, bids for single phase work will almost certainly be lower. For smaller libraries, it may be cheaper to move out during construction, even with the extra costs renting temporary space, setting up temporary networks, and hiring commercial movers. Your architects or construction management firm may be able to help with comparative cost estimates for one-phase and two-phase work.

- **Problems with warranties on equipment.** Extended construction can lead to major problems with HVAC equipment. Because the equipment in the new addition may have to function together with new equipment added to the original building, you won't know if they work properly together until the project is completely done. The problem is that you will need to turn the equipment on in the new addition while you are camping out there. If a year passes during the second phase (remodeling the original building), by the time the project is completely finished, the one-year warranties on the Phase I equipment will have expired. If the total system doesn't work right when the project is done, you will have trouble because half of the equipment will already be out of warranty. This sounds like a minor point, but it's not. Modern HVAC systems are extraordinarily complex and expensive. In a library construction job, the cost of HVAC may be 25 percent of total construction cost. Commissioning the system (making sure that everything works correctly and that the library staff members know how to operate the system) is a major undertaking. You will not be happy if, when HVAC components in the Phase I part of the job don't work right when the total project is over, the contractor informs you that the Phase I part is now out of warranty, and that it was working just fine when he turned it over to you 15 months earlier. One solution to this is to have your agreement with your contractor provide that the warranty on the HVAC system will commence at the completion of the final phase of construction, but because equipment warranties may all run just one year, you may have trouble obtaining this requirement.

- ***Additional moves***. If you move out during construction, you'll move just twice, but if you phase construction you may have to move a number of times.

IV-C. SO WHY PHASE YOUR PROJECT?

- No space available for temporary housing for the library. If you are faced with the absence of a space large enough to house your library temporarily, it may be a lot better to put part of your collection in dead storage for a year than to try to live in a building under construction. Any automated lending system should be able to give you a list of the least-used items in the collection.

- Pay as you go. Some owners want to extend the project time to match cash flow. If this is important to you, phased construction may help. But it's important to be aware of the extra costs that accompany phased construction. When all is said and done, pay-as-you-go construction may actually be a bad fiscal choice.

- You have a really large building. Small public libraries and school libraries and special libraries are all better off clearing out, but a large academic or public library may have no choice except phasing the project and living with the mess. But be sure to explore issues carefully. There are large central libraries that operated temporarily out of storefronts and still managed to achieve three-quarters of their typical circulation.

- Timing can help a phased project. Some academic and school libraries have started construction at the end of a spring semester, worked through the next academic year, and wrapped things up by the end of the following summer semester, being closed for one academic year and two summers.

V. Snappy Rules on Remodeling and Expanding Library Buildings

1. Remodeling always costs more than 99 percent of what the world expects.

2. Written building programs for expanding existing buildings should always be written without regard to existing structures. One good approach to dealing with staff and users and owners is the "tornado" approach, asking what they would need if the building were destroyed and they had to begin completely over.

3. Matching historic construction materials can be nearly impossible, but experienced architects can do a lot to conceal the differences between new and old, often by separating them physically. (This is important. Some additions to historic buildings feature horribly unmatched bricks. And once you have those bricks, you have to share them with generations yet unborn.)

4. Remodeling and expanding a historic library is difficult. Trying to merge it with a second historic building is seriously scary, but the concept has an evil appeal to the inexperienced. Always say "no!" Loudly.

5. Once they've been expanded, historic buildings frequently have too many floors and too many rooms, with resulting implications for access, supervision, and numerous elevators and staircases.

6. Retrofitting wiring, plumbing, and (particularly) air ducts may require serious surgery. Dropping historic ceilings to conceal air ducts is not an acceptable aesthetic compromise. Adding air ducts to a basement may be impossible because the ceiling is too low. And if you can add basement air ducts, you may be tempted to have air grills in the floor of the main level of the library, something that librarians usually hate.

7. Trying to get along with inadequate electrical outlets is not an acceptable functional compromise.

8. Expanding a historic library will frequently mean maintaining a historic but inaccessible entrance, in addition to at least one modern entrance. If you can't afford to watch the historic entrance, you can mothball it by converting it (reversibly) to an emergency exit.

9. The walls of most historic libraries are uninsulated, and you probably won't be able to do anything about it. In a day of concerns over energy wastage, that's an important consideration.

10. Older libraries typically have bearing walls, which make remodeling and expansion far more difficult and may force you to have dysfunctional room sizes.

11. Moving people between floors requires real elevators. Ramps don't work, and lifts of one sort or another are (at best) only marginally civilized.

12. Be considerate of aesthetics when reassigning spaces. Converting historic reading rooms to book stacks (which happens) is nasty.

13. Most surviving plans for older libraries are at best inexact. Record drawings from the original construction may not exist, and there may be no records of subsequent alterations. In a firm sort of way, discourage your owners and architects from relying exclusively on old drawings.

14. Remodeling is far more complicated than new construction, and your architects will need increased payment to compensate them.

15. Excavating next to the footings of old library buildings can be tricky. Experienced architects will plan transitions in ways that eliminate expensive reinforcement of original footings. For example, the floors of new additions can be cantilevered to keep from adding stress to original buildings.

16. The great and evil temptation in dealing with historic buildings is to construct what you can have rather than what you need.

17. When someone says excitedly, "We could put an X here" or "We could use this room for a Y," always ask yourself whether you actually need an X or a Y. Often you need something else instead.

18. If your historic building needs new lighting, new wiring, a new HVAC system, and new plumbing, just fixing those can be 40 percent of the cost of a brand new

building. And sometimes the results will be second rate anyway.

19. Some self-appointed historic preservation enthusiasts have big plans for other people's money. Ask yourself whether you can afford to be one of those other people. Or suggest that the preservationists help fund the project.

20. A bargain building in a bad location is a bad building. A beautiful building in a bad location is pretty bad as well.

21. Changing window muntin patterns in historic buildings is often unattractive. And state historical preservation agencies may ban it.

22. A contemporary addition to a historic building will sometimes—with the passage of time—become a painfully dated addition to a historic building, the architectural equivalent of glass brick in Mt. Vernon.

23. The decision to expand an old building can lead to destructively tossing out needs listed in the building program, often without full discussion by everyone involved in the project.

24. If your historic library has already been expanded once, a lot of the problems listed here may already have been solved. Or you may just be living with them.

25. Remodeling projects can lead to lots of expensive change orders because unexpected complications are discovered only when historic walls are opened.

26. Despite all the problems, a remodeled and expanded library can be a resounding success and a focus of community pride. Just be careful. Have lots of expansion space, both for this time and the next. And have lots of money.

PART II
From Overcrowding
to Ribbon Cutting

CHAPTER 17

Converting Non-library Buildings to Public Libraries

I. Introduction

This chapter deals with the conversion of non-library buildings to public libraries. It also applies conversions to other kinds of libraries, but proposed conversions to public libraries appear to be by far the most common.

The first and most central and important point in this chapter is to be extraordinarily careful when considering conversions. Always assume the worst, and never say "yes" to any proposed conversion project without the input of architects, engineers, and consulting librarians—all three rather than just one. Read all of the many warnings in this chapter. And never, as in NEVER, just go out and buy an old building.

When a community needs a new public library building, people frequently suggest the conversion of existing (usually vacant) structures to a new library. Occasionally these are structures that can be converted to good public libraries, but much more frequently they would make terrible libraries. The situations are often complicated by extreme political pressures, and libraries need to be prepared to explain to their communities why or why not conversions are good ideas.

As with all such situations, if your library has to deliver unwelcome news, always let your hired experts do it, especially if they can go home to other towns at the end of the meeting.

In all conversion situations, one of the major problems involves the building shaping the library rather than the library shaping the building. If too many of the basic functional needs of libraries are compromised by limitations imposed by existing spaces, the result is at best dysfunction and at worst an amazing waste of money.

When possible conversions loom on the horizon, libraries need to be prepared. Among the most important things libraries can do is have building programs ready and waiting. By the time a conversion is proposed (or occasionally simply announced) it may be too late to begin planning. It's also important for libraries to have an architect selected ahead of time, particularly if you are subject to laws (such as QBS—Qualifications Based Selection—laws) that prescribe a time-consuming process.

Converting non-library spaces to libraries has a lot in common with remodeling and expanding existing libraries, but it's a far more perilous undertaking. Many of the proposed spaces may lack many of the basic needs of libraries, such as ceilings high enough for reflected uplighting, sufficient power supplies, working HVAC systems, workable configurations of spaces, desirable natural light, good sight lines, sufficient floor strength, flexibility of design, accessibility, and the many other special needs that set libraries apart from other buildings. Unfortunately, citizens and planners and owners of unoccupied buildings are frequently smugly confident while lacking even the foggiest ideas of how libraries operate.

See also chapter 3, "The Basic Configuration of Successful Library Spaces," and chapter 16, "Remodeling and Expanding Library Buildings."

II. Rationales for Conversions

There are good and bad reasons for converting existing spaces to libraries rather than starting over.

II-A. GOOD REASONS FOR CONVERSIONS

It's important to be extremely objective when presented with an existing building. There are few (if any) perfect sites and structures, so everything involves compromises.

- *Location.* Sometimes the best locations already have buildings, and some of these buildings may be delightful and easy to convert. Others, however, may be nondescript, difficult to convert, and useless as libraries, or politically impossible to remove. But location always matters most.

- *Existing parking.* If a building has an existing parking lot in good repair, the library is spared the cost of constructing a new lot.

- *Existing utility hookups.* The cost of bringing water, natural gas, electric power, data, sanitary sewers, and storm sewers to a new site can be very high. If everything is already in place, conversions will be less expensive. Of course, if you have to relocate all the utilities as part of conversion, conversions can be painfully expensive. And the age of the utilities matters.

> Fred worked with a library that purchased a site with all utility hookups in place and a parking lot constructed, but with no actual building to limit the library's options. But this wonderful opportunity happened just once in his consulting career.

- *Modern buildings available for conversion.* A building constructed after about 1990 is more likely to be accessible to users with disabilities and not suffer from asbestos, lead paint, or other problems that will be extremely expensive to overcome. But good luck finding buildings this new.

- *Buildings that are in good shape and fairly easy to convert.* The best examples are probably modern big box stores, particularly if their MEP systems are in good condition and generally suited to library use. ("MEP" is mechanical, electrical, and plumbing. "Mechanical" in turn is HVAC—heating, ventilating, and air conditioning.)

But "generally suited to library use" doesn't mean you won't have to spend money on conversion.

- *Political necessity.* In some cases, a city may announce that money will be available if and only if the library converts a specific building to a new library. This version of Hobson's choice sounds grim, but it may be that such a conversion is actually in character for the community, and things may work out well. Joe has worked with a number of libraries on "necessary" conversions that turned out to be sources of local pride. And Fred admires them too.

- *If a building is available at no cost,* that makes conversion more attractive, but successful conversions can cost as much or more than building new.

II-B. AND (OF COURSE) BAD REASONS FOR CONVERSIONS

Although some buildings can easily be converted, many conversion jobs make no economic sense.

One frequent rationale proposed for conversion jobs is saving money. Few people, however, have any concept of how much it costs to convert an old building to a library, but they eagerly (and sometimes aggressively) promote a bad idea.

Things can get particularly nasty when the owner of a building (or real estate salespeople) see big profits to be made in palming off a white elephant on the public library and hence on the taxpayers. The nation abounds in buildings that are standing vacant for very good reasons.

Library owners need to keep reminding people that almost all conversions will involve constructing new restrooms, replacing existing lighting, adding electrical outlets, upgrading or replacing HVAC systems, adding an elevator if the building is on more than one level, providing new plumbing in staff work areas and lunchrooms, removing unwanted partitions, strengthening floors, adding new floor coverings, adding windows, improving insulation, and so on.

The structure proposed for conversion must have both expansion space and off-street parking space.

Libraries have more specific space needs than many other types of buildings, and non-experts can't be allowed to insist they know far more about libraries than they actually do. It's perfectly fair in public meetings to inquire about the credentials of people promoting stupid ideas. Or protect yourself and have your consultant ask.

- *Many towns have landmark structures that are standing vacant.* Citizens are always scouting about for possible conversions. Some of these buildings are vacant for very good reason, and converting them to libraries makes no rational sense.

- *Many existing available buildings are structural nightmares,* with endless lists of features that will cause libraries nothing but grief. ALWAYS have your architects, engineers, and building consultant check things out before you start praising offers enthusiastically.

- *Some proposed conversions may come with unacceptable limitations.* The donors of the building must have no rights of any kind over the subsequent use of the property. The library needs full title to the building, including the site, allowing it to make any changes it wants and to sell off the building and site and move on at any time it wants.

Any proposed limitations must be total deal killers.

III. Common Problems in Conversions

III-A. POOR NATURAL LIGHT AND INSUFFICIENT WINDOWS

Modern public libraries need windows for light and for openness. Libraries typically place reading tables and chairs next to windows, where users can see the outside world while they work.

Unfortunately, many existing commercial buildings proposed for conversion to public libraries have almost no windows. This may meet retail sales needs, but libraries need windows on all sides. If the commercial building in question is part of a row of structures, adding more windows may be impossible. And skylights—one of the True Evils in Library Design—are not an answer.

III-B. UNWANTED PARTITIONS AND FLOORS

Libraries tend to consist of large open spaces, both for readers and for collection storage.

Libraries of less than 30,000 or 40,000 square feet tend to work far better if they are on one floor at grade level, to simplify floor loading problems and to avoid the permanent costs of elevators and of staff to supervise additional levels.

Any structure that features unwanted but immovable partitions or unnecessary levels is one to avoid.

III-C. BAD LOCATIONS

Bad locations for public libraries abound. Chapter 9, "Site Selection," provides a great deal of information on what constitutes good and bad sites.

The quick, easy measure is to ask whether library users would want to go there in general, and whether the location is compatible with their daily travel patterns.

A bad location for a nice store is a bad location for a nice library.

III-D. OBSOLETE OR NONEXISTENT AIR CONDITIONING

A library without air conditioning is a miserable library. Unfortunately, adding HVAC systems to ancient buildings can be extraordinarily expensive, especially when there are no air ducts or there is insufficient space between floors to install them.

Window air conditioners are friendly warning signs of structures you probably want nothing to do with.

Even if a building has an HVAC system, it may be out of date or simply worn out. HVAC equipment is expensive, and its expected life is about 20 years.

III-E. INSUFFICIENT FLOOR STRENGTH

Many proposed conversions simply ignore the problem of weak floors. With the exception of warehouses and factories, few existing buildings have the strength in upper floors to carry the weight of books.

Existing slab-on-grade construction will probably be strong enough for books, although a structural engineer will need to verify this. But upper floors are in almost all cases insufficiently strong. Among those floors that are usually not strong enough are church floors, regardless of how massive the pews appear to be.

One solution to weak floors is to use lower shelving units and wider stack aisles, but this will require more floor space, and the floor space projections in your building program will have to be increased.

Some floors can perhaps be reinforced, but the supporting columns and column footings will need to be capable of handling the extra weight. In many cases, providing the extra strength may be more expensive than starting over.

III-F. LACK OF UTILITIES

Older buildings may lack essential utilities. As part of evaluating the potential of an existing structure, check for the provision of natural gas, electric power, water, telephone, data, sanitary sewer, and storm sewer. And be sure that if they are there, they are of large enough size to support modern library operations.

A building heated by propane rather than natural gas will be extraordinarily expensive to operate, and the inability to supply natural gas should be an automatic deal killer in a town that has natural gas available elsewhere.

On the other hand, many existing buildings will have all necessary utilities already connected, eliminating what can be the very high cost of extending utilities to a new building.

You'll need engineers to check the quality of utility provision and the condition of the connections. For example, if the building's water supply is provided by a lead pipe, you'll have to rip it out and replace it.

III-G. LACK OF EXPANSION SPACE

An existing structure that completely occupies its site may be a very poor choice for conversion to a library, unless the building is substantially larger than the space specified in the library's building program.

When some large buildings are converted to libraries, not all the available space may be needed immediately. The available space stands empty or is used for storage until it is needed at a later time.

Unfortunately, there have been cases where the extra space was converted to a non-library purpose rather than kept in reserve, eliminating any possibility of long-term expansion.

Even worse than lack of expansion space is lack of sufficient space even on opening day. Moving into an undersized building is an extraordinarily ill-considered choice.

III-H. ACCESSIBILITY PROBLEMS

Many older buildings are inaccessible to users with disabilities, and the extra cost of providing the necessary restrooms and elevators and entrances may be greater than the value of the converted building.

In general, attempting to convert a building constructed before the Americans with Disabilities Act and never modified to provide accessibility may make very little sense.

See chapter 11, "Accessibility."

III-I. PARKING PROBLEMS

When you are considering a building for conversion to a library, parking is a major consideration. Looking at a specific building, always ask:

- Where will users and staff park? People who are pushing for a specific conversion project may claim that parking is not an issue, but they are wrong. On a lovely spring morning, a few users may decide to walk to the library. Kids may stop at the library on their way home from school. But most users drive most of the time. The failure to provide good parking may lead to the failure of the entire library.

- Will the library control parking, or will it be at the mercy of other owners or agencies? It's hard to know where, but at any specific time somewhere, someone has a brilliant community development plan that involves eliminating library parking.

- Will the front door of the library face the parking lot, or will the parking lot be behind the library? If the lot is behind the library, users will insist on two entrances, one facing the street and one behind the library facing the parking lot. And this violates one of the primary rules of library design. Unless the two entrances lead to a shared hallway, with a single door from the hallway to the library, it will take extra staff to supervise both entrances. Forever.

Convenient parking looms large in citizen evaluations of community services, and any situation that leads to inconvenient parking will alienate users.

Don't underestimate public library parking needs. As a first quick estimate, a public library parking lot needs to have the same square footage as the library. This means that a two-story library with a 25,000-square-foot footprint will need about a 50,000-square-foot parking lot. If the library will house major public meeting spaces, or if there is no overflow parking on an adjacent street, its parking lot may need to be even larger.

Zoning ordinances will help define minimum parking requirements and the amount of space needed to fit the library on a site.

III-J. BEARING WALLS

Bearing walls are walls that hold up a building, as opposed to curtain walls, which simply fill the spaces between support columns.

Older buildings with bearing walls rather than curtain walls may prove to be extremely difficult to convert because interior walls cannot be removed to create larger spaces without significant expenditure. If the building proposed for conversion has bearing walls, and you don't want to spend a great deal of money replacing bearing walls with footings, columns, and beams, you need to be sure that the spaces you need already exist. Having to work with a number of small spaces when a library needs a single larger space is a mess.

If you are attempting to expand an old building, you may need to be careful about not digging too close to the existing footings. You'll need the input of an architect and a structural engineer.

III-K. BASEMENTS

Old basements are a lot less useful than many people imagine. Century-old retail structures may even have dirt-floored basements. Humidity in old basements may be so high that almost nothing can be stored there. The presence of a basement may also indicate that the main floor is not strong enough to support the weight of books.

Occasionally, main floors with wooden joists can be strengthened by putting props under the joists, but it's a pretty makeshift approach if you're converting a building to a library. Slab-on-grade construction is a lot more useful in libraries.

III-L. CHEAP CONSTRUCTION

Some commercial buildings are built to minimum standards, and the prices may be attractive because the buildings are pretty much junk. Buildings sheathed in sheet steel, for example, may have a relatively short life before rust begins to eat away at the sheathing. Similarly, EIFS is a sheathing material with an uncertain long-term reputation. There may be little or no insulation. HVAC systems may be primitive. Wiring may be minimal. Floor slabs may even be of substandard quality.

We've looked at a number of strip malls proposed for library use, and some of them had extraordinarily flimsy construction, with exterior walls made of two-by-fours and no fire walls between units. Renting space for a branch in a building like this may be okay, but you don't want to own it.

If a building looks cheap to you, it probably is. But even if it looks great, you need the opinions of your architect and structural engineer.

III-M. CODE COMPLIANCE PROBLEMS

Building codes change constantly, and the older a building is the more likely it is to be seriously out of compliance. Even relatively new construction may not be adequate. If the building was not a library before, it will almost certainly need updates to meet building codes. For example, energy conservation codes may require more roof or wall insulation, newer equipment, or a more advanced control system.

As long as changes to a building are minimal, remodeling may take place without bringing a building up to code, but with significant changes it may suddenly become necessary to make radical upgrades. You may have to add a sprinkler system, provide all-new electrical service, introduce automatic fire doors, provide an elevator, add fireproof staircases, construct new and larger restrooms, and who knows what else.

If you want to provide an addition to a building, you may need to add fire doors between the old and new areas, leading to problems with awkwardly divided spaces.

This is a particularly good reason to have architects, engineers, and programmers size up a building before you decide it can be converted to a library.

III-N. ASBESTOS, LEAD PAINT, AND OTHER HAZARDOUS MATERIALS

Any structure built before the late 1970s may be awash in asbestos and lead paint, and no matter when the building was constructed the soil may have serious contaminants. Before you agree to any reuse of an older building, you need to have qualified experts check for these and estimate the cost of remediation. Mold is a concern, as are mercury, chromium, radon, certain complex hydrocarbons, and a host of other chemicals.

III-O. CONVERTING HISTORIC STRUCTURES

It's hard to convert non-library structures to libraries, but it's even harder if the structures have historic significance. Unless a building has spaces and windows and ceilings and floors and accessibility that already match those in your program, you may find yourself in a situation where reworking the structure to serve as a library is nearly impossible and frighteningly expensive.

If you do commit to converting a historic structure, you may have to deal with a wide variety of additional pressures. Historic preservation committees and agencies will demand that you seek their approval. Self-appointed local groups may want to step in.

Why might a library decide to convert a historic non-library structure to a library? First, there may be no other good place to build. Second, large amounts of money may be available if and only if the library agrees to repurpose a historic building. ("Large" is a keyword here. If you don't tremble with embarrassingly ill-concealed anticipation when you hear the amount, it's probably not enough.)

And third, of course, historic buildings are often worth saving and may possibly become functional libraries as well.

III-P. BUILDINGS "DESIGNED FOR ADDING AN EXTRA FLOOR"

Owners of one-story commercial buildings frequently assure prospective buyers that their buildings were designed to allow an extra floor to be added. Your reaction should always be:

- Friendly disbelief. Many people constructing buildings originally considered providing the stronger footings and columns necessary to support a second floor, but they abandoned the idea when they learned how much extra it would cost. Thirty years later, they remember talking about a second floor but forget that the idea of a stronger structure was abandoned. If you're serious about the building and the second floor matters, you'll need a structural engineer to check things out. Remember that even surviving drawings may not be accurate.

- Suspicion that—even if the columns and footings for a second floor were installed—they may not have been designed to carry the weight of a library. A second floor perfectly fine for office use can be completely unacceptable for library use.

- Questioning whether an extra floor would be better than a larger main floor. A 10,000-square-foot main floor is vastly better than two 5,000-square-foot separate floors, for with a single floor you will avoid the high (and continuing) cost of an elevator, the cost of staircases, the fact that it's much more expensive to build an upper floor strong enough to hold books than it is to house books on a floor slab, and (probably worst of all) the high cost of supervising an extra floor.

All in all, the only good reason to build upward rather than outward is that (a) you are desperate for more space, (b) there's absolutely no way to expand the footprint of your building, and (c) no one will let you move somewhere else.

III-Q. INSUFFICIENT ELECTRICAL WIRING AND OUTLETS

Retrofitting electrical outlets to buildings can be difficult, and buildings converted to libraries may end up with far too few outlets. Modern libraries need electrical outlets everywhere, not just in places where power will be needed on opening day. The cost of providing sufficient power may substantially increase the cost of converting a non-library building to a library.

Adding outlets to slab-on-grade buildings requires saw cutting floors, inserting outlet boxes and conduit, and filling in around the new conduit. Because of the cost, libraries may end up with power poles instead. Power poles connect to the ceiling grid and are screwed to the floor. Although they work, they are ugly and inflexible and fragile.

Some old buildings still have knob and tube wiring. Not only will you have to replace it all, but it's a friendly warning sign of other hidden bad news.

III-R. UNWORKABLE LIGHTING

Library lighting needs tend to be very specific, and most conversions require complete replacement of lighting systems.

A possible exception is some big box stores with modern lighting that may be bright and even enough to meet library needs.

Since people have to look nearly straight upward in libraries to view top shelves, harsh downlighting is unworkable. One way to test the light in a building is to look straight upward at the ceiling. If it blinds you anywhere, you'll need different lighting.

III-S. LOW CEILINGS

The absolute minimum ceiling height for libraries is 10 feet, and 11 or 12 feet is better.

Light fixtures for reflected uplighting need to hang at least two feet below the ceiling. Allowing eight feet for clearance, this means 10 feet.

Sprinkler heads usually need to be up to three feet above the tops of the book shelving. With seven foot shelving, this also means 10 feet.

III-T. THE HIGH COST OF CONVERSIONS

Probably the single greatest problem with conversions is unexpectedly high costs. Remodeling and modernizing an old building can easily cost as much as starting over, and if the result is less efficient to operate than a new building, the higher costs can continue for the life of the structure.

It's extremely easy to underestimate the cost of remodeling and modernizing an existing building. If a building needs an all-new HVAC system, all-new wiring, all-new plumbing, a sprinkler system, abatement of asbestos and lead paint, the addition of an elevator, removal of interior partitions, addition of windows, addition of code-compliant exit staircases, and other miscellaneous code compliance work—and many older buildings need all of these—it can easily cost as much as or more than new construction—and cost far more to operate than a new building of similar size.

Architectural fees are also likely to be higher for conversions than for new construction, since architects have to learn all about an existing building. They also have to prepare two full sets of plans, one for demolishing features you need to eliminate and the second for adding new features.

If you have a choice between converting an existing two-story building and constructing a new one-story building of the same total square footage, the one-story building will be far less expensive to operate.

Local citizens are unlikely to believe the high cost of conversions. Libraries will need to rely on their architects and engineers and programmers to provide a realistic idea of what kind of money will need to be spent.

However, some architects can be equally ignorant. Fred knows one remodeling and expansion project where the architect's estimate was one-third of the lowest bid.

IV. Types of Buildings Often Suggested for Conversion to Libraries

This section reviews some of the building types that are frequently suggested for conversion to libraries.

IV-A. SCHOOLS

Abandoned school buildings are frequently proposed as locations for public libraries.

Empty school buildings abound. Unfortunately, most have been abandoned for very good reason because they have outlived their natural life or were badly designed to begin with. Local residents have probably been speculating for years on how these buildings can be recycled, but that doesn't mean they'll make workable libraries.

Most old schools will fail to meet a wide variety of building codes. Schools dating back to the 1970s or before may be awash in asbestos and lead paint. Most will have accessibility problems, perhaps requiring the addition of elevators. Most will be badly insulated. Despite the stability of schools, floors will probably not be strong enough to carry the weight of books.

Schools are often not in good public library locations. Schools are typically built in residential areas away from local businesses, but the best location for a public library is a good location for a retail business.

Parking lots around old high schools may be reasonably adequate for library use, but grade schools and middle/junior high schools may have only enough parking spaces for the faculty.

If a town that needs a new public library has an old school building, people will inevitably propose that the school will be a great place for a new library. Unfortunately, with rare exceptions, they are spectacularly wrong.

About the only space in an old school building that is large enough to be converted to a workable library is the gymnasium. Classrooms are no good for most library purposes. Gyms can be converted to attractive and functional libraries, but that presumes that the gym is large enough for all those library functions that need to be in a single, open space or can be expanded on the same level. In a small public library, for example, the service desk, adult area, and children's area all need to be in a single room. If a balcony has to be added to a gymnasium to provide essential floor space, the library will be at a disadvantage forever. If the elevator is in a different part of the building, there will be a second (and probably unsupervised) library entrance leading directly to the balcony, violating the basic single-entrance rule.

An even larger question is, once the gym is converted to a library, what happens to the rest of the school building? The last thing a library needs is to be part of an otherwise abandoned building.

However, historic schools can be popular with local citizens, and if voters approve the substantial necessary funding, impressive libraries can result.

IV-B. BANKS

Some communities have successfully converted bank buildings to public libraries.

Some banks appear to be more strongly constructed than many other commercial buildings, and they may be capable of carrying the weight of books without extra reinforcement. But always assume they aren't strong enough and have an engineer check.

Modern banks will usually be at grade level. Older banks may have steps up to the front door, and you do not want them.

Most bank conversions are faced with what to do with old vaults. Vaults are strongly built and will probably be too expensive to remove. In the conversions we have seen, most vaults have been used for storage or office space. Obsolete vault doors may make interesting reminders of the buildings' history, but you'll at least have to disable the locking mechanisms and install some kind of bolted-on flanges on the floor that prevent the doors from swinging.

Most banks will have far more small interior spaces than libraries need, and part of the evaluation of a possible bank conversion will involve checking to see how easily partitions can be removed.

Many banks have drive-through service windows. In small banks, these are frequently on back walls so that staff at a service counter can simply turn around to assist customers at the windows. It might be possible to convert bank service windows to book pickup windows, but drive-up service windows in libraries are not always successful because library users sometimes treat them not only as places to pick up held books but also as short-order windows, where library users can request items that are not on hold but have to be searched and retrieved from throughout the library by staff members while the customer waits.

One of the appeals of converting banks is that they may have been maintained in better repair than many other structures.

IV-C. DEPARTMENT STORES

Some communities have converted abandoned department stores to public libraries. Since the rise of big box stores and shopping centers, department stores have tended to become available for other uses.

Because department stores may have been focal points of traditional city centers, there may be warm memories among older citizens and strong political interest in conversions. If a community cannot find alternate uses for a major department store now standing vacant, sooner or later someone will think "library!"

Department store conversions may be aided by existing elevators, eliminating the high cost of retrofitting new elevators.

Department stores typically do not have floors strong enough to carry library loads. If a department store has a basement, perhaps only the basement is strong enough for book stacks. In order to reduce loads, it may be necessary to use shorter shelving units and space them more widely apart, significantly increasing the amount of space necessary to store a given number of books.

Lack of floor strength may be one of the greatest challenges in converting department stores to libraries. However, some libraries like the idea of 66-inch-high shelving and four-foot aisles because of the improved browsing possible.

Older department stores may have the windows libraries need, but if windows were removed at some time in the past to provide wall space for merchandise display, the library may be faced with a choice between spending the money to install replacement windows or having to live in what feels like a basement.

In addition, most department stores have too many floors. Instead of a wide, single-level space, a store may have several floors. If the resulting library has more floors than the library needs, supervision may be extremely expensive.

IV-D. STRIP MALLS

Strip malls have been proposed as public library locations.

There are some possible advantages. Strip malls may be in highly visible locations, and placing public libraries next door to retail stores is good for both.

But there are a number of potential problems.

Strip malls come and go. A dying strip mall is no place for a public library, and one sees dying strip malls everywhere.

Just as good commercial neighbors can be of great benefit to libraries (and libraries of great benefit to the nearby businesses in strip malls), businesses can change quickly. Because libraries in strip malls are right on top of the other businesses, if the clothing stores, paint stores, toy stores, and bookstores are quickly replaced by liquor stores, tobacco shops, video gambling parlors, and bars, the effectiveness of the libraries' locations can be quickly changed.

As speculative commercial structures, strip malls may be very cheaply constructed and quickly thrown up. If someone is proposing an existing strip mall as a location, it helps if you can see one of the units under construction and have your architects and engineers check things out. Code requirements for libraries are very different from code requirements for retail spaces, and if libraries move in they will have to upgrade the building to meet more demanding codes.

Some strip malls do not have firewalls between stores. As a result, a fire that starts in one store can quickly spread to adjacent stores through the attics of the stores.

Because buildings in strip malls share common walls, there is no possibility of adding additional windows on the sides of the stores.

Expansion is probably impossible without acquiring an adjacent unit, and fire codes may make it impossible to join two units together.

As with old stores on courthouse squares, retail spaces in strip malls may be too deep and narrow for good library service.

The best uses of strip mall spaces are probably locations for branch libraries or temporary locations while main libraries are being rebuilt.

IV-E. BIG BOX STORES

Of all the projects converting non-library buildings to libraries, conversions of big box stores are among the most successful. In addition to being practical, at least one has won an ALA interior design award.

Modern big box stores have a number of advantages:

- Grade-level entries.
- Single floors, eliminating the need for elevators and staircases and reducing the number of staff required for supervision.
- Concrete slab-on-grade floors, making it easy to carry the weight of books. (But always have an engineer check to be sure the slab will handle the load.)
- High ceilings, making lighting far easier.
- Modern wiring.

Because of their high ceilings and lack of permanent partitions, big box stores lend themselves particularly well to conversion to libraries. The contrast can be striking.

SOURCE: ENGBERG ANDERSON

- Post and beam construction, meaning that there are few if any interior partitions that cannot easily be removed.
- Large parking lots, typically as close as possible to the public entrance. Modern designers know that parking lots need to be in front of buildings, not behind them, and you are most likely to find this arrangement in big box stores.
- Utilities connected. Most big box stores will have electric, natural gas, water, sanitary sewer, storm sewer, and data connections already in place.

There are also some potential problems:

- Virtually no windows. How easily windows can be retrofitted will depend on the type of construction. And the evil allure of skylights may always lurk around the corner.
- Potentially undesirable locations. Libraries need stores where chains built lovely buildings but then went bankrupt, not where stores moved out because the locations were far from ideal.
- Cheap construction. If a big box store was designed with a 20-year service life in mind, it won't be a happy choice for a library.

Big box stores were designed to meet the retail needs of modern populations, and these have a lot in common with the library needs of modern populations. Which makes the entire conversion project a lot easier.

Since big box stores are economically constructed, however, you will need engineers and architects to evaluate the condition of a building you are considering. It may just be worn out.

IV-F. HISTORIC STORES ON COURTHOUSE SQUARES

Although this section says "courthouse squares," it applies to all historic retail spaces that are deep and narrow and trapped between adjacent buildings.

Former stores on courthouse squares have sometimes been converted to public libraries. While locations adjacent to retail businesses are very functional, there are large numbers of challenges in conversions of this type.

- Former stores tend to be narrow and deep spaces. This is a bad configuration for public libraries. Users have to thread their way through successive areas of the library. If the adult department is in the front of the store, children must walk through the adult area to reach the children's area, with consequent implications for disturbing adult readers. If the children's area is in the front of the store, all adults must walk through the children's area—a possible security risk. Fitting in meeting rooms can be difficult, because a store may be so narrow that it is wide enough only for the meeting room and a hallway to bypass it. Service desks will probably be located half-way to the back of the store, between the children's and adult areas, making it difficult for staff to see the front entrance and greet arriving users. Public libraries work better if users enter the center of the wide side of the building.
- Former stores typically have small shop windows in front and perhaps alley windows at the rear, but no side windows due to adjacent buildings. If the former store is narrow and deep, this means a general absence of natural light. Skylights—one of the Great Evils in library architecture—are not a solution.

- The appeal of courthouse squares comes in part from unbroken lines of facades facing the squares on all sides. Maintaining these lines of storefronts is not compatible with library functional design.

- If an old store has partitions, they may be in unsuitable locations and difficult to remove for structural reasons. Although the library may need partitions for a meeting room, restrooms, and staff workroom, existing partitions are unlikely to be in the right places.

- Historic stores will probably have wood joist floors that are not strong enough to support the weight of books. However, if one-story stores have unused basements, existing wood joists can possibly be propped from below to strengthen them. (Metal bar joists, by contrast, are far more difficult to strengthen.)

- Old historic stores may be approaching the limit of their reasonable life. They may have antiquated MEP systems. Few buildings will have restrooms suitable for library use. Wiring may be ancient. Just replacing all of these components may cost half as much as starting over with a new building.

- An old store building may have a couple of parking spaces on the street in front and more off an alley at the rear of the structure. Users may want to park in the alley and enter the library through the back door, a major violation of the single-public-entrance rule.

- If the library needs additional parking, it will have to go behind the library, making the double-entrance problem a lot worse.

- If the building has a second floor, that will introduce a wide variety of problems. Ideally, it can be just used for storage. Using a second floor for public services means an elevator and staircases (including new exit staircases) that meet fire codes, second floor staff (an extraordinarily and permanent expense if the staff would not be needed in a single-story library of the same total size), supporting an insufficiently strong floor when there is no space for props below, dealing with what may be very low second-story ceilings, and so on.

- Some old retail spaces are a step or two above sidewalk level, introducing access problems. Sidewalks have been regraded to provide entry ramps, but it's not a great solution. Among other things, it can lead to incredibly high curbs by the ramp.

- Often the main reason people want to convert an old retail space to a library is that business around the courthouse square is dying, and they hope that the presence of a library can revive it. Basically, this means using the library as a cat's paw. The same features that make businesses want to relocate will also make the library wish it had never gone there.

Even if a courthouse square building of this type is available to the library at no charge, it will be very far from "free." Unfortunately, political pressure to accept gifts of old buildings can be strong, with persistent advocacy from people who have no real idea how libraries work.

Some libraries have been created by purchasing a number of adjacent historic retail structures, opening up archways between the buildings, and converting the resulting spaces to a library. The library occupies the entire combined main floor with a single entrance. The upper floors stand vacant or are rented out, with their own separate entrances from the street. The wider building front seems to work well, but all the stores will need floors at the same level and accessible from the front sidewalk with no steps or ramps, and the library will need to make arrangements for parking that is accessible from the new front door.

If the presence of the library on the courthouse square is essential, another solution is to obtain a row of commercial buildings (including a corner structure), demolish them all, and build a new library facing the courthouse. Even then there are likely to be parking problems. If a parking lot is constructed behind the library, there will be pressure from users to enter the library both through a door facing the courthouse and through a back door facing the parking lot. This violates the one-entrance rule, and you won't like it.

All in all, attempting to convert ancient retail spaces to public libraries is likely to be extremely expensive, especially if upper floors or basements are used, and the resulting structures are highly unlikely to be satisfactory.

IV-G. CHURCHES

Some churches have been converted to libraries.

Generally, this involves converting the sanctuary of the church to the main area of the library. Churches usually have a number of smaller rooms, including Sunday school rooms and small meeting rooms. If the church has a fellowship hall, it may be large enough to use as a multifunction room, but the remaining rooms may be large enough only for offices and storage. Support spaces in churches may also be located in extremely awkward places, such as separate wings.

One advantage of converting sanctuaries to libraries is that the ceilings are frequently high enough for good lighting.

Another advantage can be good natural light. Many churches have big windows.

The easiest sanctuaries to convert are modern ones built at grade level on concrete floors. Fred worked on one small town library where the board came in at night and removed a front platform and baptismal tank, added better lighting, patched the front carpet, and then moved in, all for very little cost.

Some churches have sloped sanctuary floors, and these are impossible for conversion to libraries.

If the church is not a modern structure with concrete floors, always assume that sanctuary floors are not strong enough. Some people insist that a floor that can carry the weight of heavy pews will surely be strong enough to carry the weight of books, but they are wrong. Or, more accurately, WRONG.

If the sanctuary has religious symbols they should probably be removed. This is easy with most decorations, but a shame if there are strongly religious stained-glass windows.

As with all conversions, modern structures with concrete floor slabs, grade-level entrances, and curtain walls are the easiest to work with.

IV-H. HOUSES

A number of small town public libraries have been located in converted residences. Although some are charming, there are inevitable challenges.

- Making the floors of houses accessible to users with disabilities can be extremely expensive. If the main floor is more than a foot or two above grade, the result may be a virtually endless entry ramp. Even then, libraries may be limited to main floors for everything except storage. The other solution is an elevator, which is a very expensive device.

- Older houses may be badly insulated, with single-pane windows and uninsulated walls. Unless it's done with care, replacing the windows of a historic house with modern windows may damage the historic appearance of the building.

- Floors may not be strong enough to hold books. It may be possible to strengthen wooden floor beams with props if there's an unused basement below where the props can be placed, but that doesn't work with upper floors.

- Most houses consist of many small rooms, which may lead to supervision problems and to collections awkwardly divided between rooms. Because partitions between rooms may be bearing walls, opening up larger spaces may be extremely difficult. And it may also spoil the historic architecture of the home.

Houses of the mansion variety may have considerable charm, but they may also be serious white elephants.

IV-I. AUTOMOBILE SALES ROOMS

Some communities have converted former auto sales facilities into public libraries.

Auto sales rooms have the advantage of strong floors (but double-check, because books are heavier than cars). They frequently have open floor plans, single levels, and large show windows.

But you will still have to deal with all of the other conversion issues—lighting, wiring, HVAC, restrooms, and the rest. And it's hard to find uses for old grease racks in a modern library.

IV-J. ABANDONED GOVERNMENT BUILDINGS

Some communities have converted former government structures to public libraries.

Sometimes this can be very successful. A town in Illinois, for example, converted a former Air Force base bowling alley to a public library, but the bowling alley was no ordinary bowling alley. It was a huge and sturdy structure with high ceilings and no bearing columns to get in the way.

Lots of former government buildings are cut up into many offices, and these are bad choices for conversion to libraries. An old city hall, for example, may have a council chamber surrounded by a rabbit warren of offices. A fire station may have a large and high-ceilinged first floor equipment room, with a second floor filled with small rooms and with no elevator access.

Former city garages may offer lots of wide-open spaces and good parking, but public works garages may not be in suitable locations for public libraries.

Our experience is that old city buildings were often abandoned for good reason. New buildings were constructed because the old ones were seriously inadequate. The old buildings may be awash in asbestos and lead paint. Parking may be inadequate for public library service.

Even worse, cities may run old buildings into the ground once new buildings are underway. If maintenance stops for the last year, there may not be much left, certainly not enough to make the conversion to a public library economically sensible.

V. Summary

Converting non-library buildings to public libraries is done all the time.

Sometimes everything works out beautifully, but on other occasions the library ends up spending far more on a reworked but dysfunctional building than it would spend on a brand new building, and in addition is saddled with higher operating costs for the life of the building.

How do you keep out of trouble?

- First, always have a building program in hand, one that lists in detail what spaces you need when the project is done. As soon as people start talking about conversion and there's no existing program, "What we could do with this space?" takes over from "What spaces do we need?"

- Next, have a good idea of what kinds of buildings lend themselves to conversion. Many of the basic issues are covered in this chapter. Remember that the ADA came along in 1990 and that buildings built before the late 1970s may be full of asbestos and lead paint. Buildings constructed before 1990 are a gamble, and you are unlikely to be offered buildings that new.

- Remember that HVAC machinery has an expected life of about 20 years. And it's expensive to replace.

- Be sure that there is space for expansion of services and sufficient off-street parking. Many proposed conversions lack both.

- Be sure you will have total ownership of the property.

When people pressure you to accept or purchase an existing building, always get help before saying "yes." Because the pressure you face will frequently be political, outside help is particularly important. The help you will need includes:

- A written building program listing all the spaces you need when you are finished. Sometimes a building will be so unsuitable for reuse that your consultant's opinion may be enough to stop things.

- An architect with wide library experience to help you evaluate the building to be sure that it is in good condition and can be converted to a functional, modern library at a reasonable cost. In many cases, a quick examination by your architect will lead to the rejection of the proposed conversion project.

- Engineers to evaluate the structure of the building, the condition of MEP services, any hidden threats (such as asbestos), the ease of opening up internal spaces, any difficulties involving accessibility, and other issues.

- If the project passes initial checking, your programmers, architects, and engineers will need to review as a group the ability of the building to meet all specified functional needs.

- If the conversion looks feasible, your architects will need to develop a cost estimate. This is a dangerous area, particularly when it comes to remodeling. There may be pressure on your architect to lowball costs. In all cases of this type, your architects and other experts will need to report on both conversion costs and the likely cost of building a similar structure from scratch.

Rejecting a proposed conversion job may be unpopular with your community. This is one area where your hired outside experts will prove their worth. They can deliver the bad news and then return home to distant communities where their annoyed neighbors cannot snarl at them at the supermarket.

If all of this chapter sounds negative, it's because there are so many pitfalls in conversion projects.

Luckily, there are some examples of really excellent libraries constructed by converting other buildings, so it's a matter of caution rather than outright rejection. In general, fairly new buildings in good condition with wide-open spaces, high ceilings, good windows, concrete slab floors, high-quality construction, space for expansion, sufficient parking, and histories of good maintenance seem to offer the best possibilities.

VI. Snappy Rules on Converting Non-library Buildings to Public Libraries

1. Owners who can't unload vacant buildings often have special epiphanies about what wonderful libraries they'll make.

2. Big, open, one-story spaces with high ceilings tend to make workable libraries. Complex, multistory spaces with low ceilings tend to make seriously bad libraries.

3. NEVER buy an existing building or agree to a conversion job without the help of a consulting librarian (a programmer), architects who have had serious experience with functional library design, and engineers to check the quality of the structure.

4. Any existing floor that is not slab-on-grade construction is unlikely to hold the weight of books.

5. The cost of converting an existing building can be vastly higher than most people want to believe. The right price to pay for a building to be converted to a library is often free—and even that may be a bad fiscal deal.

6. Unfortunately, there's often no such thing as a "free" building, and lots of "free" buildings can end up costing more than starting over from scratch.

7. When a building is standing vacant, there is likely to be a very good reason. Or many very good reasons.

8. Be very afraid of proposed conversions that would involve your library sharing space with another agency. Anyone with a key to your library must report to the library director.

9. The cost of an unnecessary second floor can be extraordinary—and an extraordinary waste.

10. As shopping patterns have changed, American cities are full of abandoned downtown department stores. Converting them to libraries is not a job for institutions with limited construction funds or limited operating budgets.

11. Converting retail buildings to libraries will usually require adding a lot of windows. Find out the cost implications before agreeing to anything.

12. Political pressures to convert amazingly unsuitable structures to public libraries can be intense and sometimes amazingly nasty. Get professional help before you agree to anything, and let your professional helpers take the blame.

13. With the exception of rented space for branches, public libraries need to own their buildings, including full titles to the sites. Always avoid situations where the library does not have permanent and clear title to the property. A number of libraries are in situations where the property will revert to someone else if the library ever moves out. This leads to wretched messes, and you don't want anything to do with it.

14. Never trust anyone's offhand estimate of conversion costs. People can be wrong by a factor or five or 10 and feel no guilt afterward.

15. Always be wary of proposed conversions, and sometimes be very afraid.

16. Converting a building that has no expansion space and no off-street parking space involves making two impressively major errors at the same time.

17. Age matters. Buildings constructed before 1980 are likely to be EPA nightmares. Buildings constructed before 1990 may not meet accessibility codes, and lots of those constructed after 1990 may not either.

18. Just because buildings look huge and massive, that doesn't mean their floors will support the weight of books. (In the engineering trade, the huge and massive part concerns "dead load," and floor strength concerns "live load." Some historic buildings are barely able to hold themselves up, let alone hold any extra weight of contents.)

19. Libraries do well in good commercial locations, not destitute commercial locations.

20. Good libraries are wide, flat, and open, while a lot of historic buildings are tall, narrow, and all cut up.

21. Converting a non-library building to a library can be impressively more expensive than most people anticipate. And involve far more functional compromises than most people expect.

PART II
From Overcrowding to Ribbon Cutting

CHAPTER 18

Shared Buildings

I. Introduction

This chapter was motivated primarily by complaints from librarians, and for that reason it's somewhat scattershot. It includes everything from excellent ideas to truly awful ideas, plus a lot of stuff that can work or cause trouble depending on how things are organized and governed.

Unfortunately, a lot of the interest in shared library buildings appears to be generated by hoping to save money rather than to improve library services, and the push seems to come primarily from people other than librarians or library users. University libraries may have completely irrelevant campus agencies shoved into their buildings. Public libraries may be located in other people's buildings or merged into other people's libraries. School libraries may share spaces with unpleasantly irrelevant functions. Libraries may be expected to contribute fiscally to buildings that can evict them at pleasure in the future. And library meeting rooms may be regarded as the property of agencies other than the library.

When people are proposing shared facilities, always talk directly with the librarians who are doing the sharing, and be prepared to totally ignore the people who are promoting the ideas.

The benefits of shared spaces tend to be:

- Making more intensive use of expensive and underutilized facilities, such as very large meeting rooms that go days without use.

- Constructing a variety of public service spaces in close proximity to each other, leading to greater public awareness of available services, more convenient access, or simultaneous use of a variety of different services by members of the same family.

- Making efficient use of limited available sites in areas of high-density construction.

Unfortunately, shared spaces in buildings can lead to an extensive variety of serious problems:

- Shared buildings are frequently intended not to improve services but to cut costs, and the cost cutting often involves saving money by cutting the quality of services. For instance, the promoters of shared spaces may contend that two very dissimilar libraries can be combined, using only the space and staff previously used by just one of the two libraries, and that everything will be great. This is why the Bronx cheer was invented.

- In many shared buildings, libraries face serious security problems. Once people are inside the shared building, they may have access to all of the library's collections and electronic equipment, whether or not the library is even open.

- School shootings can make schools unwilling to allow the general public into their libraries, having a major impact on the idea of combined school and public libraries.

- When libraries share buildings with other agencies, often the activities of those agencies make life difficult for library users and staff. Too many libraries located in city-owned buildings are in spaces not designed to separate the sounds (and smells) of non-library use from the library. The library ceilings may be lower than 10 feet, and the libraries may be hidden in basements, where the floors are strong enough for books. But if a sump pump goes bad, the library may be the soggy victim.

- On some occasions, the agency sharing the building with the library assumes that it is in charge of the library and can help itself to anything it wants. Even when agreements not to do this are in writing, it can still happen.

- When two types of libraries are combined, they may not function well together. They can face security issues, which have been a major issue in combined school and public libraries. They may find that a good location for one of the libraries is a bad location for the other. One group of users may not work well with the other group. And there may be parking problems.

- Libraries sharing space may end up being expected to contribute construction money to buildings to which they will have no rights. And they may be expected to leave at the convenience of another agency.

- When two libraries are combined, the needs of users, and the necessary collections and staff, may be so dissimilar that no space or personnel are saved.

- If two libraries occupy a space that belongs to only one library, the non-owning library is in an amazingly vulnerable position.

- In many cases, multiuser buildings were not designed to meet library needs but simply involve a library moving into an inappropriate but empty space.

- Often the victims of badly designed shared spaces are public libraries, which can be expected to move into unsuitable locations.

- If a shared library has two groups of employees, and one is paid significantly better than the other, the libraries have to know how they will sort this out. If the result is increasing the pay of the more poorly paid group, what are the budgetary implications? If the library increasing pay is a branch of a larger system, how will this affect pay for employees in the rest of the system? If the shared library was created on the premise that total staff salary costs will be cut, how will changes in pay affect the library with the better pay?

- The problems with shared buildings often appear to be as much administrative as architectural.

The easy way to do things is to never have libraries share buildings with any other agency. With the exception of school and special libraries, which are relatively small spaces in large buildings with the same owner, this is often the case. But even school and special libraries have problems, frequently involving bad security. For example, school libraries may be bizarrely designed to serve as pathways to other parts of school buildings. A school or special library may be on two levels, with access to the second levels from outside the library. If the library cannot afford a staffed security gate to the second level, all access control is ended. School libraries are often located next door to extremely noisy neighbors. Physicians may have 24-hour access to hospital libraries and leave them unlocked.

The major exceptions to this prohibition are:

- Agencies that provide student services maintaining service points in academic libraries. Students who are new to campus may find the library a major center of campus-wide orientation.
- Multifunction community agencies joining together to take advantage of the juxtaposition of services rather than attempt to save money.
- Branch libraries on the main floors of urban buildings in areas where space is at a premium and where the buildings are designed specifically to separate the libraries from other functions.

A major problem occurs in academic libraries that are designed to share elevators with adjacent academic departments. If academic libraries have open book stacks, shared elevators end all collection security. Unfortunately, some university administrators see no problem there. Or they think (wrongly) that there is some ingenious way around the problem. But there is no way around the problem. Shared elevators are always a disaster.

Sometimes the easy way is not the best way. Preventing the problems that occur as a result of shared buildings is easy. Just don't do it. But the people who are blinded by visions of saving money are frequently unaware of the problems that result from badly planned mergers. Understanding user needs, operational practices, maintenance, and the proper balance between independent and collaborative use of space requires more planning than just thinking through entry, internal access, security, and maintenance. Behind much of this is the need for a clear understanding of the finances involved. This too needs to be worked out in detail for a number of scenarios. Unfortunately, many of the shared spaces in libraries appear to be the result of attempts to save money rather than to provide improved functions. And as a result they frequently lead to serious problems.

The most successful shared spaces result from attempts to improve functions, not to save money. If you can avoid all of the problems listed in this chapter, the improved functions of some types of shared facilities can have real benefits to a variety of direct and indirect users as well as the institutions or communities served by the shared facilities.

But the general rule always must be: When people suggest merged services, always say no.

II. Types of Shared Facilities

All sorts of functions and spaces can be shared, though some of them are to the dismay of the libraries and library users involved.

II-A. COMBINING TYPES OF LIBRARIES

II-A-1. Combined School and Public Libraries

For a while, there was a vogue for combined school and public libraries. Supporters of the concept assured people that this was the wave of the future, and that soon large numbers of public libraries would be in school buildings.

The concept brought a number of architectural and organizational challenges:

- Good school library locations are generally different from good public library locations. With combined facilities, public libraries end up in school buildings, and the general public often has clearly second-choice locations.

  A major exception may involve a group of small towns sharing a single consolidated school building that includes a shared school and public library.

- Combined school and public libraries need their own outside entrances, to keep out-of-school adults from wandering through school hallways. Inside the school, there needs to be some way of permitting students to enter the rest of the school while preventing non-students from doing so. One approach is to design a library that is adjacent to the school rather than combined with the school, one that can be entered only from outside the school building.

- Combined school and public libraries can have separate hours for non-school-student users, but this is a major compromise with good public library service. For example, the library may be open to the general public from 4:00 to 8:00 p.m. on weekdays, or perhaps on weekends. From the point of view of public library users, this is very awkward, but it may help solve school concerns about mixing students with the general public.

- Parking for public library users needs to be available directly outside the entrance to a shared library. And it needs to be kept free for library users, not filled by high school students at 8:00 a.m.

- Accommodations for many users have to be added to school library spaces, including in particular for young children, but also for senior citizens that do not want to share spaces with teenagers. This means the addition of a variety of new spaces not otherwise necessary for school libraries.

- When classes are taking place in the library—as they do in many school libraries—how will that affect non-student users? If two classes attend a single event in the library, the students may occupy up to 60 seats in the center of the library.

- To what degree do the school library and public library collections duplicate each other, thereby saving total shelf space?

- The limitations placed on school library collections do not apply to public libraries, and some way needs to be found to house collections deemed unsuited for school students. This means either separate physical spaces for unsuitable books, or unacceptably censored adult public library collections. (Envisioning how one would identify and house a collection of adults-only books in a combined library is entertaining in a rotten-library-service sort of way.)

- All users need access to restrooms, but some school restrooms may be unacceptable to non-students. Envision the reactions of older public library users when faced with toilet stalls without doors.

- Many schools are concerned about allowing public patrons into the school for safety reasons. Even if the library is architecturally separate from the school, supervisors may feel that the two functions are still dangerously intertwined. Or they may not want to be faced with any accusations of fostering inappropriate activities.

- If the public library owns a specific area of the combined library space, what will happen when school security issues arise?

In the long run, of course, school shootings have often made combined school and public libraries untenable. There are no easy workarounds.

II-A-2. Combined Public and Academic Libraries

There have been many suggestions that money can be saved by combining academic and public libraries, especially in small town universities and colleges.

Unfortunately, combined libraries pose a variety of challenges, and it seems highly unlikely that any money can be saved without compromising public or academic library service.

Among the very many challenges are:

- How will study spaces for college students be integrated with seating for children and teenagers?

- Is public library computer use compatible with academic library computer use?

- Where will public library users park? How will campuses with their characteristic parking problems cope with this need?

- What kind of extra spaces will be needed to provide for children and their parents and caregivers?

- What will happen when public library users hit on students?

- Where will all the shared collections of very different materials go? Public libraries have a wide range of materials not found in many academic libraries, such as books for children or teenagers, or large collections of adult fiction. If academic collections (such as law or medical books) need to be completely separate from children's collections (such as picture books), how will space or staffing be saved?

One exception may be colleges with education schools that can make use of the popular books for children and adults.

- When exam time approaches and the library is packed to the gills with students, how will the library serve both academic and public users?

- Will academic librarians be comfortable helping children and non-student adults find the materials they want?

The public libraries in academic library buildings that Fred has talked with were all hoping for separate locations.

II-B. COMBINED COMMUNITY CENTERS THAT INCLUDE PUBLIC LIBRARIES

Famous examples of shared community cultural buildings exist. For example, the historic Carnegie Institute in Pittsburgh combines a library, a natural history museum, an art museum, and a recital hall. It is a national landmark. But it wasn't built on the cheap, the various functions can be completely separated, and all of the uses are cultural.

In more recent times, a number of towns have constructed community centers that include a wide variety of functions, including community theaters, concert halls, gymnasiums, swimming pools, event spaces, meal spaces, and libraries. These centers can be great, but participating libraries may need to take strong precautions.

- First, libraries must have their own architects and engineers. They can match the external design of the centers, but only the libraries' own employees know how libraries work, and they must not be overridden by people who are both ignorant and confident.

- Libraries need to make sure the units that share the building with the library have their own necessary facilities. For example, the library needs to assure that its restrooms or reading areas are not patronized all day long by people freshly dripping from the swimming pool or shouting about the basketball game just finished.

- Libraries need to be able to determine their own access hours, with opening and closing times not dictated by the designs of the centers. This may require entry vestibules that lead both to the library and to the rest of the community center.

- Libraries cannot ever be passageways to other areas of the building. And separate functions may need to have separate HVAC systems from libraries.

- The noisiest functions in the community centers (such as gymnasiums) need to be as far as possible from the quietest functions (such as quiet reading areas).

- And all public libraries that are not branch libraries need to be expandable.

All of this is helped by preemptive programming. When community planners come to the library with their concepts for shared facilities, it helps a great deal if the library has a list of its needs and the resulting spaces ready, preventing outside agencies from assuming they can single-handedly dictate the size and functions of the library.

II-C. SHARED MEETING SPACES

Public library meeting rooms are often used by cities or other government agencies, and academic libraries may have meeting spaces that are used for general university purposes as well as library purposes. School libraries can be used for classes, and conference rooms in special libraries can be used for corporate purposes. While there can usually be workable arrangements involving shared meeting spaces, sometimes problems occur.

To make shared meeting rooms work well:

- Meeting spaces have to be genuinely underutilized. Merely hoping that one room will be enough for two organizations is not enough. If a new meeting room generates far more use than expected, and library meetings alone could keep it busy all week, there need to be plans for an additional meeting room.

- Parent organizations cannot deal with unanticipated use levels by simply stepping in and taking over meeting spaces, and this needs to be spelled out in advance.

- A shared meeting room must be in the library. One of the functions of library programs is to bring people into the library building, and if a program is held in a different building, this important function is lost. In addition, some family members may attend an event in the library meeting space while others are using other library services.

- Shared meeting spaces need to be completely separable from the rest of the library. Use of the meeting spaces and associated restrooms should give people no access to secure areas of libraries. The usual way to accomplish this is to have the meeting spaces and restrooms directly accessible from the library's entry foyer.

- The library needs to have prior experience with scheduling heavily used meeting spaces and juggling the demands of many users. And there need to be strong agreements preventing one agency (such as the mayor's office) from preempting meeting room use at the last minute.

- Scheduling of shared library meeting rooms must always be done by the library itself, never by the city or the university or the school district office.

As the list above indicates, issues involving shared meeting spaces are often more administrative than architectural. Unfortunately, community uses of shared meeting spaces have made it nearly impossible for some libraries to function.

II-D. ACADEMIC LIBRARY BUILDINGS THAT INCLUDE OTHER ACADEMIC AGENCIES

II-D-1. Student Service Facilities

Some universities have library buildings that provide space for units that are not part of the library.

This can work extremely well. Libraries are great places for agencies that issue student IDs or that help students with their laptops. Getting ID services while registering for library cards is a great idea, and having computer services and library services under one roof works very well, becoming a form of one-stop shopping.

Typically these combinations require that libraries have long hours, so that the ID and computer services are never open when the libraries are closed. In some cases, both of these services report to the director of the library.

II-D-2. Irrelevant Facilities

The problems occur when the agencies tucked into academic library buildings have no connection with the library except helping themselves to available space, and when they don't have their own exterior doors and restrooms.

The obvious thing to do is to make such agencies totally independent architecturally, and then lock the doors between the agencies and the adjacent libraries with locks to which only the director of the library has a key. Or even better, just wall up the doors.

Otherwise there can be amazing messes. If the academic dean of arts and sciences has an office in the library, the dean will insist on having keys to the building. In turn, the dean will provide keys to grad assistants, and the grad assistants will share the keys with their fraternity brothers or sorority sisters. And the library will have no security whatsoever.

Situations exactly like these have arisen in academic libraries, and we have heard many unhappy stories from academic libraries. Directors need to be alert and in charge.

II-E. PUBLIC LIBRARIES IN SHARED GOVERNMENT BUILDINGS

Libraries in government buildings have had trouble with government employees feeling that they can simply take over the library, including simply letting people in without permission of the library.

For example, if your public library is a room in the city hall, the staff in the mayor's office may decide that they have the right to unlock the library to let their teenagers and friends play games in the library when the library is closed.

Other activities in government buildings can make life miserable for libraries. For example, if the meeting room is above the library and the village schedules noisy events or community fish dinners, what happens to library services? If your library will be in a government building with no odor-blocking or footfall-stifling systems, you need an iron-clad no-fish and no-thumping agreement before you budge. But you may not be able to enforce it.

The main challenge is providing adequate architectural separation of functions. If the areas of the building have adequate noise and air handling separation, a lot of things are possible. But far too many libraries in situations like this appear to have been included as afterthoughts rather than planned from the beginning.

The crucial difference appears to be the involvement of the library's own architect. And a programmer if the library has no staff member who can do the job.

II-F. SHARED FACILITIES IN SINGLE BUILDINGS

Some problems with shared buildings occur when university or school or city planners decide they can save money by having equipment serve more than two agencies in a single building.

II-F-1. Shared Elevators and Staircases

One major source of amazingly serious problems with shared spaces is shared elevators. Since elevators are expensive (or extremely expensive), someone will invariably try to work out ingenious ways of having a single elevator serve both a library and an adjacent classroom or office building. Unfortunately, despite the proud assertions of university or other administrators, this never works. EVER. Unless the upper floors of the library consist exclusively of departmental libraries with lockable doors, each with a staff of its own, people can take the elevator to an upper floor, help themselves to armloads of books, and then leave through the common exit on the main floor.

Putting a library exit control point on the main floor won't help, since a thief can exit the elevator at any floor except the main floor, walk downstairs, and leave through an entrance on the non-library side of the building.

Any university or municipal administrator who wants a shared elevator needs to explain in a public meeting attended by hordes of rabid library staff members, library architects, and consulting librarians why this will cause no trouble.

In similar fashion, some school libraries have second floors. Such libraries never have their own elevators, and access to the upper levels is therefore from outside the library, through a usually unstaffed door. This means that anyone using the library can walk out the second-story door with any wanted books or equipment, making any attempt at library security a joke.

II-F-2. Libraries as Passageways and Atria

Libraries must never serve as passageways between non-library spaces.

Some school libraries have been designed to double as passageways through schools. One gets the impression that the idea was a gimmick instituted by school administrators or architects without consultation with librarians.

School libraries are libraries, not corridors. The results of this kind of planning can be endless racket in the libraries, impossibility of holding class meetings, and loss of materials and equipment.

Some schools have even created atria by opening the ceilings of libraries to corridors above, combining the many benefits of unpleasant noise transmission, objects dropped into the library, and athletic students demonstrating how they can get into the library from the floor above. None of which support good library service. Or even seriously mediocre library service.

This situation appears to be part of the endless architectural search for vindicating innovations.

Always shout "No!" when people talk about libraries as passageways.

II-G. PUBLIC LIBRARIES IN RESIDENTIAL OR COMMERCIAL BUILDINGS

Joe has worked with communities that have constructed buildings with libraries on the main floor and commercial office or apartment spaces above, and his observations from these experiences point out some of the many needs that must be met to make these projects successful.

Often projects of this type involve working with developers who may or may not understand the needs of public libraries. It may be easiest for libraries to start with the needs of retail spaces—which developers understand—and then progress to the special needs of libraries.

- Libraries are considered assembly spaces in most building codes. They need fire-rated separation from residential spaces, commercial spaces, or parking areas in the building.

- Libraries have a wide range of noise levels. The quiet activities don't need to hear what's going on in apartment 2B. And the noisy activities don't need to generate endless complaints from the homeowners' association. There needs to be good acoustic separation between the library and the other users above, below, or alongside.

- Housing has a lot of plumbing, and much of it may need to pass through the library. Libraries need to limit the locations where this occurs. This is an added cost to the building but essential to the library. Any water passing through the library's space also needs to be in insulated pipes. Not all running water sounds relaxing.

- Leaks happen. And with a lot of apartments, a lot of leaks happen. A water barrier at the level above the library can intercept a lot of water before it can become a library

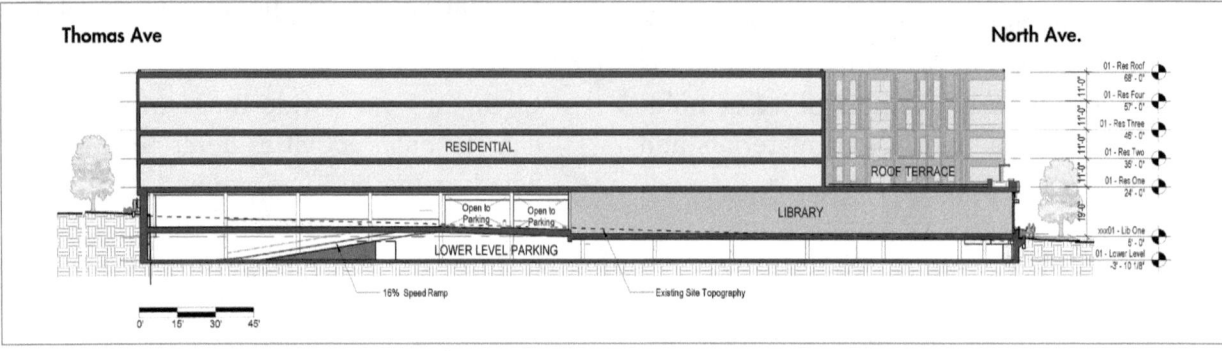
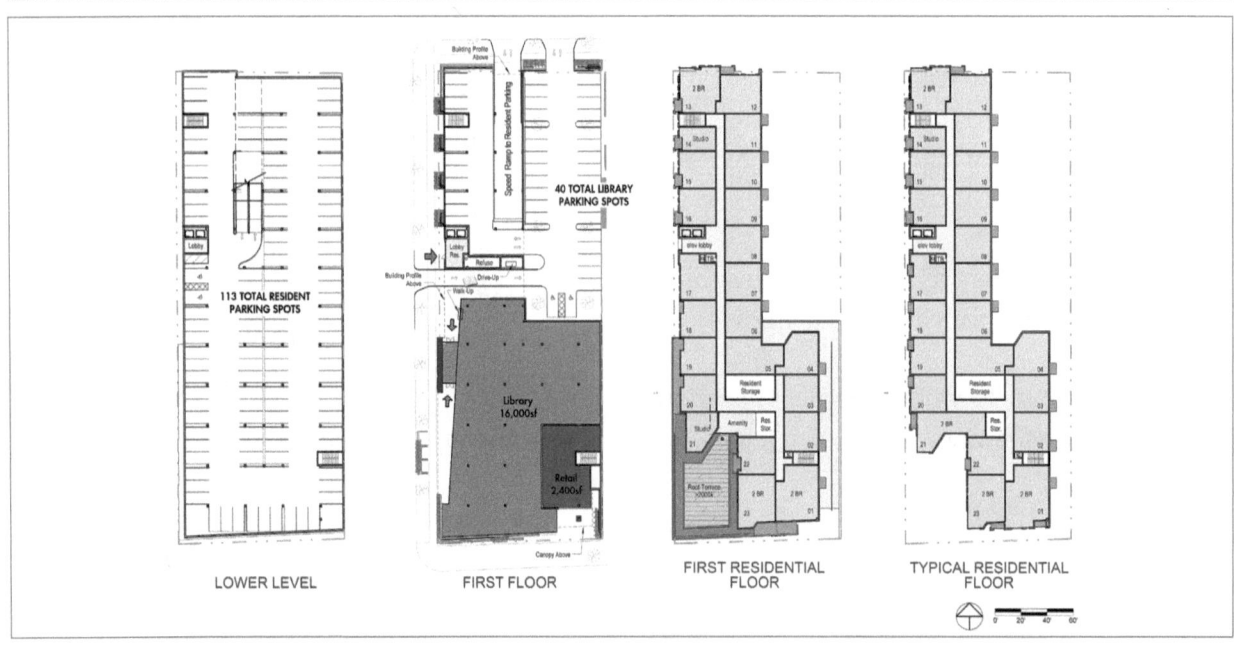

[Left] Shared buildings lend themselves especially to public library branches, where long-term library expansion is not essential.

This building designed by Joe's firm illustrates some of the important attributes, including higher ceilings for the library than for the apartments above, separate parking for the library and apartments, totally separate access to the library and apartments, library location completely at grade level, and commercial space beside the library.

Not visible in the illustrations is the extreme physical separation of the library and apartment sections, with different column locations and with strong sound barriers between the library and the apartments. It's a great way to use scarce land, but attempting to do it on the cheap will lead to many miseries.

SOURCE: ENGBERG ANDERSON

problem. This also adds to the cost of construction.

- Libraries need large structural bays (the space between support columns). The apartments above the library may have load-bearing internal and perimeter walls, which means some sort of shift in structural system is needed between the library and the apartments. And this means more construction cost.

- If a joint-use building is constructed on a library's site, who will pay the extra structural costs involved? If the community or developer are the major benefactors, should the library be expected to provide more than the airspace, with the cost of new construction paid entirely by the city or developer? Will people expect the library to pay rent? Who will pay for long-term maintenance? The library will need legal representation, bearing in mind that many of the parties involved—developers or city councils or even library trustees—may be impressively unscrupulous and not have the library's interests in mind.

Some of the possibilities here are reminiscent of the many agencies that thought they could profit mightily from the site of New York's Grand Central Station.

- What are the implications for library service if the building is privately owned, and what are the implications for long-term maintenance if the building is government owned?

- If space is at a premium and the new structure is constructed on the library's previous site, what will the library do if it's expected to pay rent? (Fred thinks it should be rent free forever, but that may not be realistic.)

- What will happen if the library runs out of space? If it's a branch of a public library, things can always be shifted to the main library. But if the space described here is the main library, the library may have no expansion options whatsoever.

III. Things You Can Do

While we can wish that combined functions in libraries would lead to mutual benefits, to better outcomes for all at lower costs, that appears all too often to not be the case.

The very limited benefits of combined services seem to be:

- Convenient juxtapositions. Some services benefit users through adjacency. This can involve placing student ID services or laptop assistance services in academic libraries. Or public services like libraries, civic auditoriums, and swimming pools being placed close to each other.

- Exposure to new services. People can stumble over unexpected services while using other services in the same building. Libraries hope that people attending events in library auditoriums will get to know the library at the same time.
- More efficient use of extremely limited ground space by stacking housing or offices on top of libraries. Doing so requires architects who really know what they are doing. There may be major problems sorting out the interests of the building proprietors and the library. The overhead housing or offices may turn out to be bad neighbors, especially due to sounds of water, footsteps, or other noises. If the library is not the owner of the building, it may find itself in a financial mess, faced with high long-term rents. And if the library runs out of space it may have no expansion options. (It sounds like a recipe for branches rather than central libraries.)
- And that's about it.

The claimed reasons for sharing that make no sense include:

- People who propose shared spaces often appear to believe that totally new services can be added to existing libraries with no increase in space or staff. This may sometimes be possibly true. But it's amazingly unlikely. We save money by doing less.
- Sharing spaces that can be used by more than one agency. Shared meeting spaces are a good example. Sharing may sometimes work, but conflicts over usage priorities can be a major problem. If a library has to cancel an event because another agency suddenly needs the space, sharing was a stupid idea.
- Supposed cost savings. No matter what is said in public, this may be the major motivation for the combined services idea. Check out suggestions very carefully, for the alleged savings may not stand up to careful analysis, may make library use unpleasant for various kinds of users, may severely threaten library security, or may leave the library with no expansion options.

The big challenges concern:

- If the perceived benefit is cost savings, do the math. Sometime cost savings are an unstated goal but the underlying motivation for the shared project. Check out suggestions very carefully, for the alleged savings may not stand up to careful analysis. The project may cost less only because it diminishes the quality of service, cutting space, reducing collections, reducing staff services, making library use unpleasant, severely threatening library security, or preventing long-term expansion.
- If the advertised benefit is accommodating new services that are made possible by shared space (basically, eliminating duplication of services), go through a use analysis for both entities to see whether their space and time needs are compatible or in conflict.
- Understand the motivations of your proposed neighbors in the building and the motivations of the decision makers involved.
- Finding places for combined agencies in crowded campuses or crowded cities. Sometimes the proposed combined library is even presumed to take up no more space than the single-purpose library it replaces.
- Outright theft of other agencies' space. People may propose adding collections or user groups or irrelevant offices to a library building without adding any extra space.

- Good fences make good neighbors. It's essential to:
  - » Maintain security for library collections and equipment.
  - » Provide spaces, collections, and staff that meet actual needs of different types of libraries that may have almost nothing in common.
  - » Provide and protect convenient parking for all types of users.
  - » Maintain absolute library control over any spaces that are part of the library or accessible through the library.
  - » Keep adjacent non-library functions from making life difficult for library users. Library ceilings must not echo with footsteps from overhead. HVAC systems must not share unwanted aromas from non-library spaces.
  - » Protect dissimilar groups of library users from one another.
  - » Prevent non-library groups from preempting library meeting spaces.
  - » Make sure that all mechanical functions, such as HVAC systems, are compatible with shared buildings.
  - » Provide spaces and staff that meet actual needs of different types of libraries that may have almost nothing in common.

When shared spaces are proposed, here are some basic things to clarify in advance. Always in writing:

- Will each agency own its share of the building?
- Will you be expected to spend your library's money on structures you won't own? (Grant agencies are very aware of this issue and almost certainly won't pay for shared facilities for which the library receiving the grant does not have a clear title.)
- What will you do if the library or other agency whose space you are sharing dumps you?
- If two libraries are combined, will each library have its own staff, or will they share staff? If you share staff, how will the staff hired by the other library feel about your library and your library users? If you are in a shared school and public library, will the librarians regard themselves as teachers rather than as librarians? What impact will different pay scales have?
- What kind of remodeling will take place? Who will determine the details and who will pay for it?
- What will happen if you run out of space? What are your options? If your library is a branch library it may not be a major problem, but if your library is a central library, anticipate major and insoluble problems.
- If you merge with another library, how will you handle shared collection development? Where will the book budget come from and who will make purchasing decisions? What will you do if your partner library is handling acquisitions and your users are unhappy? In combined school and public libraries, how will the public library deal with situations where some materials in the collection are regarded as unsuited for students of school age?
- Who will pay for building maintenance, improvements, and repairs if the library doesn't own the building? What will happen if the owner wants to upgrade the appearance of the building, but the library is satisfied with the current look and doesn't

have the remodeling money? What will happen if the library wants to upgrade its share of the building at its expense? Will it now own part of the building, since it has paid for it? Will the owner immediately raise the library's annual financial contribution?

- What will you do if the owning agency suddenly changes the rules? For example, suppose your library is the public library in a shared school and public library, the school abruptly limits public use to evenings and weekends, and the parents of young children are outraged?

- What will you do if the owning agency suddenly announces it will start charging you large and unexpected rent? This happens.

- If a developer is involved in the project, expect to invest a great deal in legal fees to protect yourself.

- What will you do if your partner agency's noisy or smelly activities make it nearly impossible to run your library? (Think again of folk dancing at the fish dinner in the room over the library.)

- What are your options when the agency that owns the building completely takes over control of the shared meeting space, making it impossible for you to plan programs?

- If your library owns the building, what will you do when you find your partner agency is looking for free service and free space rather than a chance for cooperative services?

- If your university demands that your library share an elevator with an adjacent classroom building, and the result is impressively new levels of book theft, what will the university do?

- How much administrative time will coping with all of these new shared use situations consume?

- Will the parent agency expect to dictate your architecture?

- What will you do if people sharing your building demand access to your library after regular hours? Or just help themselves?

The many stories we have heard about problems with shared spaces suggest that eternal alertness—and sometimes seriously crabby alertness—is required of library administrators.

IV. Snappy Rules on Shared Buildings

1. All of the evil stories in this chapter of co-operative spaces run awry are true. So do not dismiss them lightly, saying, "Ho Ho! That would never happen here." Because they all too easily could.

2. Get all agreements in writing in legal detail, even (or perhaps especially) if people assure you that's not necessary.

3. Unless every individual space in your library building is behind locking doors, doors that are unlocked only when library staff are present, everything in this chapter applies to your library. Often painfully.

4. Directors need to be extremely wary of anyone who wants to plan anything for their libraries without them present. (This happens all the time, so don't let anyone accuse you of paranoia when you bring this up.)

5. Shared elevators never work. Ever. Or more specifically EVER. Despite what a

university administrator or mayor and architect meeting in private decide will be great. Always say "no" early and loudly. A shared elevator is like a stacks pass given freely to anyone off the street.

6. Probably the single most successful shared space arrangement is university ID agencies and laptop maintenance services in university library lobbies.

7. If the library in a multipurpose building will receive free housing for a few years and then have to start paying rent, run away as quickly as possible. The library has to own its floor.

8. Shared meeting rooms inside the library must be controlled by the library, and non-library users must be required to provide long-advance notice of any changes. Your puppet show scheduled three months ago must always outrank the mayor's press conference scheduled yesterday afternoon, even if that comes as a terrible surprise to the mayor's secretary.

9. Shared library spaces and shared meeting rooms require access to restrooms. Be sure you know how this will work. If your shared school and public library doesn't have its own restrooms, users will have to have access to adjacent school restrooms. Schools can't block them for security reasons, and the school restrooms will need to be acceptable to out-of-school adults. Including having doors on the toilet stalls. And when your library is closed, absolutely no one may use your library restrooms.

10. Use your own written building program to test whether the shared space will meet your needs.

11. If your library is in the basement of the village hall, any non-librarian who opens the door when the library is closed must set off public alarm sirens loud enough to wake the dead. And no village function must ever take place inside the library unless the library staff are present.

12. In a college or university library, all offices or workspaces in the building must be part of the library or there as a planned and relevant combined service. Irrelevant campus agencies must learn to stay away.

13. For any new shared-use building or remodeling project, the library must have its own architect, engineer, and library space consultant.

14. Public libraries in shared-use buildings need to be in buildings that were engineered for this purpose. Simply moving a library into an empty space may be pretty much a disaster, as the fish dinner and floor thumping stories indicate.

15. Outside of the fact that they both need bookshelves, tables, a service desk, and staff, two libraries of different types may have absolutely nothing in common. And despite the avid hopes of anti-tax fanatics, they may have no possibility whatsoever of being combined to save money without massive cuts in quality.

16. If a shared multifunction community building has a library and a swimming pool, know how the design of the building will enable you to keep people in sopping wet bathing suits out of the library.

17. How will your library be protected fiscally? If the library does not own its building, how will the library's investment be protected? There's nothing wrong with fierce

legal contracts, but if someone else owns the building, will bringing suit be worth it?

18. If your public library occupies the first floor of a commercial building constructed on the site of your previous library, what will you do if the owners of the building suddenly announce that you will now pay rent? Protect your library from this by rigid contracts before you sign anything or let them have your building.

19. If you have a library that serves a variety of groups, will the shared location be convenient for all users? Or will some users feel welcomed while others feel they are barely tolerated intruders?

20. If you are in a shared building, know what you'll do when you run out of space.

21. Because books are heavy, there may be pressure to put the library portion of a shared building in the basement. Two of the main features of basements are the lack of natural light and the presence of unwanted water. Always say no.

22. Be prepared for what you will do if you are the public-library half of a shared school and public library, and the school abruptly announces that for security reasons having members of the public in a school building is no longer allowed.

23. Anyone who wants a totally irrelevant office in your library but does not report to you directly must be prevented from doing so by all available means, even if the means are both immoral and illegal.

24. The easy rule is, never share any part of your building with any other agency without thorough review with your library staff and owners. And with your architects, engineers, and library space consultants present at all meetings. And with thoroughly formalized relationships worked out with your lawyers, covering money and ownership and protocols.

25. Many of the sharing ideas we hear about involve dumping a public library into some other library's space or shoving irrelevant services into academic libraries. Neither of these ideas reflects the desire to improve library service.

26. We suspect the vast majority of libraries in shared buildings are unhappy with the idea of merging. If you don't feel that sharing will be good specifically for your library, always say "no."

27. Merging dissimilar libraries doesn't save money unless it involves major service cuts.

PART II
From Overcrowding
to Ribbon Cutting

CHAPTER 19

Building Costs

I. Introduction

I-A. BUILDING COSTS ARE NEVER MINOR

Buildings are expensive.

This chapter reviews the various expenses involved in the design and construction of library buildings. It also discusses the tradeoffs between initial expenditure and long-term operating costs.

In general, public libraries may be most on their own when it comes to money. Most special and school libraries are components of larger buildings. Academic libraries usually have the benefit of campus planning and fundraising offices, although universities may have their own priorities, and they may have decided which wealthy donors will be approached for which projects, sometimes leaving needy libraries waiting endlessly in the wings.

Always talk about project costs, which can be substantially higher than construction costs.

And operating costs will almost always increase after buildings are expanded or built.

In general, there's a tendency to underestimate both project and operating costs. Architects may quote "construction costs" to library boards, not explaining from the start that total project costs can easily be 40 percent higher. Library owners may not anticipate increases in operating costs that will accompany new or expanded buildings, or they may not evaluate designs with regard to implications for long-term operating costs. Well-meaning local citizens may claim that total project costs will be vastly lower than reality. Cost estimating is so challenging that even experienced architects, who know more about this sort of thing than ordinary mortals, tend to seek out cost estimating firms.

The distinction between construction costs and project costs is amazingly important. Project costs include a wide range of essential expenditures, including site acquisition, architectural and engineering fees, site development, FF&E, utility connections, paving, landscaping, detention basins, and many others. Whenever people cite a cost for your building, always stop everything immediately and ask whether they are talking about construction costs or project costs. If they are citing construction costs only, ask them to come back later with a genuinely helpful number, which means project costs. If they say they don't have that number yet, ask them to provide an estimate and come back later. There are few things less fun than realizing at the last minute that your library building project will cost 40 percent more than you have anticipated.

For information on coming up with the money, see chapter 20, "Funding." For more information on costs, see chapter 7, "Building Programs"; chapter 9, "Site Selection"; chapter 10, "Design"; chapter 14, "Bidding"; chapter 15, "Construction"; chapter 16, "Remodeling and Expanding Library Buildings"; and chapter 17, "Converting Non-library Buildings to Public Libraries." And from one point of view, all the chapters in this book.

I-B. VOCABULARY ON BUILDING COSTS

- *Construction cost*. The cost of erecting the building. Actually building a library costs far more, for construction costs omit professional fees, site acquisition, furnishings, utility connections, paving, landscaping, site engineering, detention basins, and other costs.
- *Contingencies*. Extra money set aside for unexpected (but inevitable) extra expenditures.
- *Escalation*. Increases in total project cost due to inflation.
- *FF&E*. Furniture, fixtures, and equipment. These items are almost always not part of the construction cost and are not included in the general contractor's bid.
- *Project cost*. The total cost of providing the completed library.
- *Utilities*. All of the essential services that will need to be connected to your building, including electricity, data, telephone, water, gas, storm sewers, and sanitary sewers.

II. Capital Costs

Capital costs are all of the one-time expenditures required to construct a library building. They include the costs of land, construction, professional fees, FF&E (furnishings, fixtures, and equipment), site development (utility connections, paving, landscaping, etc.), and other costs.

II-A. PROJECTING BUILDING COSTS PRIOR TO DESIGN

Anticipating costs is less simple than some people suggest, particularly when projects involve remodeling.

Some people want to establish project costs in advance, often before planning has taken place. Sometimes they simply pick cost figures out of midair. When these figures prove to be unrealistically low, unfortunate confrontations occur. This is an extraordinarily bad process. Even when huge bequests are involved, expenditures are usually not absolutely fixed.

Our experience is that library building costs often involve a degree of negotiation. A library develops a building program, hires an architect, creates a schematic design, and then evaluates likely costs. At that point, everyone reviews the project and sorts out costs and benefits. Commonly, the program is cut somewhat to reduce costs, and the owners come to grips with the fact that things are still going to be more expensive than they had hoped.

II-B. ESTIMATING

The first edition of this book said, "One of our architect friends always says 'estimate early and estimate often.'" The "architect friend" was Joe.

Before you begin the fundraising process, you need to have a fairly good idea of what funds you will need to complete the project. Unfortunately, all long-term estimates need to be taken with a grain of salt because estimates are only estimates. In making estimates, your hired experts are projecting into the future. Assumptions are being made on the future costs of materials, land, labor, borrowing, and whether construction will be in a boom or bust cycle.

Never do your own estimating. Unless you are a professional in the area of building design and construction, leave the entire enterprise to hired experts. Particularly avoid informal but aggressive requests for estimates from local governments, university administrations, and other agencies, since the figures you come up with today may return to haunt you later.

The failure to estimate accurately leads to endless troubles. This seems to be a particular problem with some big-name architects, who tend to have no realistic grip on costs and to enmesh their clients in horrendous cost overruns.

Because cost estimating is so vital, some architectural firms employ outside cost estimators. In addition to specializing in this process, cost estimating firms are more likely to be uninvolved emotionally and thus will not optimistically guess-a-bit-too-low-and-hope-for-the-best.

When plans are preliminary and vague, cost estimates are of necessity rather general. But as projects move from schematic design through design development to bid documents, the increasingly specific detail enables more accurate estimates.

Some professional publications provide extremely general information on likely costs. (A good example is Means.) For example, you can look up the likely cost per square foot of a library in a specific part of the country built to various levels of quality. It's easy to be overly optimistic when using publications of this sort, so take the cost figures with a grain of salt. Libraries can erroneously assume, for example, that their high-end plans are actually low-end plans and low-ball costs accordingly.

While using published cost figures may work for informal discussions, an architect or construction manager with experience building libraries in your area will provide far more accurate cost projections.

Cost estimates involve a number of items:

- ***Construction cost estimates***. Construction costs are the costs of building the actual structure. Since project costs will always be significantly higher, insist that your planners and designers always speak in terms of estimated total project costs, NEVER construction costs. If they say they don't have enough information yet to estimate project costs, tell them to estimate as well as they can for the time being, and put it in print.

- ***Project cost estimates***. As opposed to construction costs, project costs include parking lots, driveways, sidewalks, utility connections, landscaping, professional fees, FF&E (fixtures, furnishings, and equipment), water detention, and so on. These can add 40 or 50 percent to the total cost of a project.

- *Site acquisition costs*. Usually the site is acquired before projects begin, but some public libraries obtain options on their proposed sites and purchase the sites if and only if their tax referendums pass and they obtain sufficient funding for the entire project.

- *Allowances for contingencies*. All cost estimates include allowances for unexpected construction costs. Commonly this is 5 percent for new construction and 10 percent for remodeling and expansion, but other percentages are possible. Unexpected costs can come from many places, including changes in materials costs, unknown underground conditions, changes in labor contracts, and so on.

- *Allowances for escalation*. If a project will not be bid out for a year or more after the estimate is prepared, the estimate must include cost increases due to inflation. Materials and labor will almost certainly increase in costs. If building codes also change, escalation can be even greater.

- *Add and deduct alternates*. In order to prepare for bids being higher or lower than expected, projects usually separate out some elements for separate bids. If the base bids are attractive, the owners may decide to add one or more of the extra items to the project. If the bids are too high, the owners may select deduct alternates or decide against any or all of the add alternates. Alternates are attractive to owners because the prices are arrived at by bidding rather than negotiation, which always costs more. Examples of add alternates might include sidewalks with pavers rather than concrete, better roofing such as standing-seam metal, or completing interior spaces originally planned to be left unfinished.

- **FF&E** (*furniture, fixtures, and equipment*). These items are usually not part of construction contracts, but libraries need to be able to purchase them. Among other things, FF&E includes all of the shelving in the library, which can be a major item for research libraries.

- *Moving*. Relocating books safely while keeping them in order can be a big job. If the library moves out and then back in, or if it puts a significant portion of its collection in storage during construction, moving can be complex and expensive.

- *Temporary housing*. Unless a parent agency has a building available at no charge, some libraries may have to budget for rent.

- *Collections*. Public libraries in particular are inclined to purchase new books to fill out their shelves on opening day.

II-C. COMPONENTS OF BUILDING COSTS

II-C-1. Site Acquisition

Site acquisition costs are primarily an issue for public and academic libraries. Most school and special libraries are located within buildings that are a responsibility of larger units.

In cases of congested areas, such as cities and urban university campuses, the cost of real estate can be a major component of total library building project costs. In some urban situations, the cost of sites can be double or more the cost of construction.

In all cases, never (as in NEVER) purchase a site without a written building program and the assistance of an architect and an engineer. Among other things, you need to be sure that:

- *The site is actually large enough* for the building, parking, driveways, sidewalks, landscaping, water detention, and long-term expansion. Many non-professionals seriously underestimate necessary site sizes—and some of them do so very aggressively.

- *The site is buildable*. There can be all sorts of hidden problems, including soil (such as peat) that won't hold the weight of a library, pollution (which is why old filling station sites stand vacant forever), floodplains or high water tables, underground obstacles (such as sewers), distance from utilities, street access, and so on.

- *There are no zoning or code problems*. Once you hire architects, one of the first things they do is get to know the folks at the city who implement zoning and code requirements. Some code and zoning enforcement is pretty standard, but other requirements like historic preservation can vary widely from community to community or from neighborhood to neighborhood. It's also important to have an idea about what sorts of changes in zoning or codes are likely to come along.

- *The site permits a building entrance facing south—or at worst east*. North- and west-facing entrances lead to problems with ice on sidewalks, stairs, and ramps, and with winter winds buffeting users and staff whenever outside doorways are opened. If you have no choice when it comes to a northwest entrance, be sure your plans and cost estimate reflect that reality.

Architectural firms evaluate sites on an everyday basis. Always utilize their expertise. Also ask your building consultants. (As the saying goes, "Do not do this at home.")

And never buy an old building to convert to a library without vast amounts of technical advice from your architects, engineers, and building consultants.

In many cases, libraries in need of sites run into owners of white elephant buildings who decide that their long-vacant structures would be perfect for libraries. This is an interesting but perilous situation. Make use of your out-of-town experts, who will be far more immune to local political pressures and will not have to worry about being confronted at the grocery store.

II-C-2. Construction

Construction is expensive. Unless site costs are immense, construction will be the single most significant cost in creating your new library building.

If you will be using a construction management firm, be sure you hire them shortly after you hire your architects so you can take advantage of their abilities to estimate costs and to conduct value engineering studies—suggesting how changes in design can diminish construction costs without diminishing functionality.

II-C-3. Utilities

Libraries require access to a wide range of utilities, including natural gas, electric power, water, data, telephone, sanitary sewers, and storm sewers.

If utilities are not available at the library site, the extra cost of bringing them to the site (or just rerouting them around your building) can become a major component of total project costs.

If key utilities cannot be brought to the library site at all, that can have a major impact on long-term operating costs. Relying on propane rather than natural gas to heat a building, for example, can vastly increase heating costs. Forever. The absence of storm sewers can lead to problems with flooding and may make it particularly important that the library occupy high ground.

II-C-4. Site Development

Site development includes all those things that have to be done to the land surrounding the library. The list can be considerable and can be strongly affected by zoning and codes.

- *Parking lots.* If you have a 40,000-square-foot public library, a good guess is that you'll need a 40,000-square-foot parking lot. And if there's no available overflow parking or you have unusually large meeting rooms, you may need even more. By the time your designers have worked out how to build parking lots that will drain properly (and therefore not be covered with ice in winter) and not crack the first time someone drives a truck onto them, this can be a major investment.

- *Driveways.* Driveways can be complex, particularly when libraries include places where users with disabilities can arrive easily, loading docks, drive-through book returns, and discreetly hidden sites for dumpsters.

- *Sidewalks.* One of the major criticisms of some new libraries is that—in an effort to save money on paving—pedestrians and vehicles share the same pavement. Another is sidewalks that curve artistically, encouraging users to take shortcuts across lawns.

- *Utility connections.* Bringing utilities from the street to the building is typically a site cost, not a construction cost. The absence of convenient utility connections can have a major impact not only on costs but also on building design.

- *Utility relocation.* Some sites have buried utilities that will need to be relocated before construction starts. Sewers can provide special problems.

- *Ornamental stuff, such as fountains, statuary, etc.* (Librarians by and large dislike fountains because they have images of users falling in. This seems paranoid, except that users do fall in.)

- *Detention and retention basins.* Many zoning ordinances require detention basins to control the speed of water runoff. (Retention basins are permanent ponds that serve similar functions.)

- *Landscaping.* As a professional group, landscapers tend to resent the fact that—when money is tight at the end of a project—landscaping is often the first thing to go. Owners also recognize that you can easily add landscaping later but that expanding the building later is a major expense.

II-C-5. Furniture, Fixtures, and Equipment (FF&E)

In addition to the cost of site, utility connections, and construction, most libraries need to purchase furnishings, fixtures, and equipment. These costs are not included in architects' estimates of construction costs, and in many cases they are not part of general bids on the project.

If you follow the advice in this book and avoid built-in furniture wherever possible, this will lower the base bid on your project (because built-ins will be excluded) and raise your furniture costs.

Some of the common items in this category include:

- Shelving and other collection storage equipment.
- Service desks (we strongly prefer modular furniture to built-ins).
- Reading tables and chairs.
- Office furniture.
- Meeting room furnishings.
- Computer systems.
- Automated book handling equipment.
- Anti-theft systems.
- Video surveillance and other security equipment.
- Audiovisual equipment.
- Interactive learning materials.
- Relocating or reconfiguring existing furnishings.

Your architects will need to provide a reasonable estimate of your costs for FF&E. If you need to review each item of furniture to decide whether it will be replaced, refurbished, or reused as is, it can become a significant job. (The interior designers in some architectural firms are gifted at this.)

II-C-6. Moving

Moving libraries can be expensive, and these costs need to be included in building cost estimates.

Because books are numerous and heavy and need to be kept in order, relocating collections can be a major undertaking.

If a library constructs a new building, moving can be a straightforward process. When a library does its own moving, a librarian oversees packing books at one end, including careful numbering of boxes so that collections don't end up in mysterious disorder on the new shelves. Staff or volunteers or commercial movers transport the boxes to the new library, where a receiving librarian makes sure the books go back on shelves in the right order and with the planned extra space on each shelf.

Ranges of shelves in the new library need to be marked in advance to be sure that the old collection and the new shelving work out right.

Some libraries make great use of volunteers, especially when there are students old enough to tote boxes of books.

Moving all of the library furnishings is another job, but at least it's pretty much like any furniture moving job.

Some professional moving firms specialize in relocating library collections. They can be expensive, but the savings in work and planning can be significant.

If either the library being abandoned or the temporary housing are not accessible, moving can be a great deal more work.

In the case of remodeling and expansion jobs, collections can end up being moved twice, first into the new wing of the library, and then partly back into the original building after it has been remodeled.

II-C-7. Temporary Housing

Many libraries need to rent temporary housing during construction, and these costs also need to be estimated.

II-C-8. Opening Day Collections for Public Libraries

Many public libraries purchase "opening day collections" to help fill the empty shelves with sparkly new books.

Library book jobbers are accustomed to meeting needs for such collections. They can supply books pre-processed and provide necessary database information. In the stresses of remodeling and moving, few tech services departments can handle the stress of large numbers of new books, so the services of jobbers are vital. If you'll be placing a large order, negotiate a good discount.

One serious pitfall involves discarding worn-looking books to make the shelves really glisten on opening day. Some of your users won't appreciate the fact that the depth they found in your collections in the past is no longer there.

II-C-9. Professional Fees

Your total project cost will include a number of professional fees.

- *Consultants*. Programming fees charged by library building consultants tend to be modest, and they come very early in the project. You will also want your consultants to review your schematic designs and construction drawings from the point of view of experienced librarians, but that as well comes long before ground breaking. At this point, any additional consultant services will probably be the result of unanticipated problems, where finding the best solutions may require a joint conference of the owners, architects, engineers, and librarians.

- *Architecture and interior design*. The range of services provided by architects is impressively large (see the chapters on design, bidding, and construction) and fees can be about 10 percent of construction costs—and more if your project consists primarily of very tricky remodeling. Most architectural fees include structural, electrical, HVAC, plumbing, and other engineering, but there may also be charges from lighting, acoustic, and other consultants. Make sure which extra fees are not included in your contract with your architects before you sign.

- *Construction management*. Increasingly, libraries use construction management firms to substitute for general contractors in the delivery of major projects. The general belief is that the cost of the two approaches is roughly similar, but ask around your area.

- *Surveys*. You may need to have your site surveyed to verify its exact boundaries, topography, utility locations, easements, and many other things.

- *Some engineering fees* are excluded from architectural fees. You may be billed separately, for example, for soil testing, geotechnical engineering, and environmental testing.

- *Permitting*. Building permits involve a great deal of work by municipal employees and can be expensive. Permit fees can also be a major source of cash for cities. As benign public institutions, libraries should always attempt to have these fees waived.

- *Fundraising*. If you hire a professional fundraiser or provide staff for a library foundation office, costs will be involved. If your library is tax-supported, you may be limited by law in how you use public money for these costs; check with your attorney.

- ***Testing and commissioning*** are quality assurance processes required by building and energy codes. Fees for independent testing agencies and commissioning agents can be significant.

II-D. ESTIMATE EARLY, ESTIMATE OFTEN

Estimating is not a one-time event. Ideally, open discussion about costs, budgets, and programs occurs on the first day of design work. Quality, quantity, and cost are tightly linked, and resolving differences between estimated costs and available funds is constantly part of the design phase of the project. Any time someone at a meeting says "wouldn't it be nice if?" or "could we?" design and cost issues come up again.

To be successful, you have to know your goals and resources. And be aware of tradeoffs. Copper roofs and granite walls are nice, but you don't want to purchase them at the cost of a working heating and cooling system. If you want as much space as you can get and are willing to add extra features later, say so. If you need to have a two-phase project, be sure your program and planning reflect that. See chapter 7, "Building Programs"; chapter 9, "Site Selection"; and chapter 10, "Design."

III. Anticipating Operating Costs

Even with well-designed spaces and the best possible equipment, operating the new library can be a lot more expensive than operating the old one.

Two-thirds of the cost of operating a library can be salaries. Any structural decision that leads to fewer staff can pay for itself quickly. By contrast, complex designs that may save a little money up front can be fiscal long-term disasters if they require extra staff just to keep an eye on things, even at times when no service to users is required. Basic strategies for controlling staff costs without compromising on quality of service include:

- Avoiding unnecessary partitions. It's a lot easier to watch big, open spaces than nooks and crannies.

- Keeping walls of study rooms and quiet reading rooms transparent for easy staff oversight. (A small window is not a transparent wall.)

- Keeping restroom entrances visible to library staff.

- Maintaining single building entrances, because all security gates must be staffed.

- Using generally horizontal rather than vertical building designs, because moving people between floors is expensive and all floors have to be staffed.

- Avoiding complex mechanical gimmicks that promise high long-term maintenance costs.

- Remembering that vast expanses of glass are expensive to clean and can increase energy costs.

A larger building means larger areas to clean. It usually means more restroom fixtures. It means more light fixtures (and sometimes, in badly designed buildings, a huge variety of different lamps). It may mean new and dramatically high spaces, with all the extra maintenance they require. It will almost certainly mean more glass to clean.

Modern HVAC systems are often far more efficient than the older systems they replace, and libraries may find the cost of heating and cooling per square foot of space is significantly less, even if the size of the new building means an increase in total energy costs.

While most buildings come with at least one-year warranties from contractors, and some components like roofs and windows have longer warranties, repairs and upkeep begin almost immediately. Even if the first year is nearly free, with everything both brand new and covered by warranties, soon things change. Latex paint on drywall is fragile and may need to be repaired almost as soon as the building is opened. Some light sources fail, although modern LED fixtures can have long lives. Attic stocks of frequently damaged items like acoustic ceiling tile can run out, and matching replacements may not be available. Carpet has to be cleaned once or twice a year, and it will eventually wear out, although carpet tile from attic stock can replace quickly worn areas like floors in front of service desks and copy machines. Some modern devices have a short working life; for example, while old-fashioned electric switches may go for many decades, sensors used for automatic switching may fail in a few years. Many systems and equipment have annual upkeep costs and maintenance costs. Elevators, HVAC systems, book handling systems, and others may have substantial annual maintenance costs.

In the long run, major construction items wear out. HVAC equipment is expensive and is considered old after 20 years. Roofs can go for decades, but eventually need to be replaced. Double-pane windows can leak and fog up and have to be replaced.

Because some libraries find it easier to find construction funds than operating funds, they adopt a strategy of buying all sorts of automated equipment up front, hoping that it will save on staff costs in years to come. A typical example is highly automated lending systems. The problem with this approach, of course, is maintenance overhead on expensive equipment and eventual replacement.

If you don't know what it will cost to maintain complex equipment, a first guess is 10 percent of purchase price per year.

The issue of operating costs arises in particular for public libraries in states that require separate referendums for construction funds and for operating funds. If the voters are willing to spend money for construction but not for operations, libraries can find themselves in fiscal hot water: the new building is finished but the old operating budget is all that they have. For this reason, good planning calls for buildings that require staff to do the necessary work but not to supervise overly complex structures.

IV. Anticipating Capital Renewal and Replacement Costs

Many architectural firms can create documents projecting upkeep and maintenance costs, including long-term replacement of key architectural components. Having this kind of information at hand is useful and can help avoid situations where predictable repairs have not been planned for.

This is an extra service at extra cost and not part of standard contracts with architects. Among the costs libraries can anticipate are:

- Staffing, which can increase due to building size, new departments, and increased use
- Repairs due to everyday wear and tear
- Cleaning

- Redecorating
- Maintenance of mechanical equipment, such as HVAC equipment
- Replacement of worn furnishings and floor coverings
- Remodeling to add new services that emerge in the field

V. Snappy Rules on Building Costs

1. The single most important construction material is money. (This is not an original remark, but we can't find a source.)

2. Unless you do this kind of thing all the time, you'll suffer from instant sticker shock. If you are not shocked, your estimate is probably too low.

3. If you hire a world-famous architect, you'll probably get a lot less library than you pay for and have a lot higher operating costs than you hope for.

4. Always think in terms of project cost, never in terms of construction cost. And make sure that all your hired help does the same. (Unfortunately, some architects never mention project costs until it's too late to reduce total expenditures by eliminating flashy concepts.)

5. Remodeling is almost always more expensive than either your critics or your supporters expect.

6. Before you undertake remodeling, always ask your architects to estimate what it would cost to simply start over. Sometimes there isn't a vast difference, and sometimes starting over is cheaper, with lower operating costs to boot. Always do the math.

7. Some people suggest you begin with your project cost and design a building that can be built for that cost. This is almost always backward thinking. It works only if you begin with a realistic project cost rather than with a hopeful lowball guess. (Lots of proposed project costs are hopeful lowball guesses, and some are insanely lowball guesses.)

8. We much prefer starting with needs, estimating costs, asking whether you can afford them, and only if and when you decide it's too expensive, compromising on needs.

9. Today's terabyte is yesterday's megabyte. Don't let building size alone scare you.

10. Preparing building programs and hiring architects can take a surprising amount of time and cost surprisingly little up front. It's a lot easier to have a program completed and an architect waiting in the wings than to suddenly have to rush madly about.

11. Never build a library on land to which you do not hold a completely clear title. (Government construction grants may require this, demonstrating that these governments really know what they're doing.)

12. You can't get through any funding for a new library building without hearing "the book is dead." Be prepared to point out how packed your library is and that computers are not the ultimate solution to educating the youth of America. But don't expect to convert everyone.

13. Any project larger than a woodshed will be called a Taj Mahal and a monument to the inflated egos of members of managing boards. It's good to have people ready to point out the actual modesty of your plans.

14. Know what you'll do if you end up with the larger library of tomorrow but yesterday's operating budget.

15. Local non-experts are frequently eager to estimate construction and remodeling costs on your behalf. Run away quickly.

16. Quality includes functionality, durability, and aesthetics. A really nice building that is really big is going to be really expensive.

17. A new building needs less maintenance than an old building. At least at first.

18. Kids grow up faster than you think, and buildings wear out faster than you think. Start planning right away.

PART II
From Overcrowding to Ribbon Cutting

CHAPTER 20

Funding

I. Introduction

Money is the single most important construction material.

Sometimes things are wonderful:

- Wealthy donors who love libraries drop in on college presidents bearing large checks.
- Two or three new factories are constructed in a public library's taxing jurisdiction, and the resulting increase in property tax cash flow is inspiring.
- Totally unexpected bequests brighten otherwise gloomy November afternoons.
- You have a referendum to issue bonds for a new library building and 80 percent of your voters support it.

But because money is almost always an emotional issue, emotions can run high while buildings are being planned, financed, constructed, and operated. We don't have any data, but we've run into a number of situations that involved annoyed people.

Some everyday problems involve:

- Local governments try to redirect library construction funds to other projects. Here's where library foundations can earn their keep, since they are totally independent of local governments and can simply say "No."
- Major donors attempt to impose dysfunctional design ideas on projects. A few libraries have had to simply turn down gifts.
- Belligerent anti-tax groups make life miserable for everyone involved. Abuse of freedom-of-information acts can be spectacular.
- Local library boards lose their nerve and are unwilling to even *ask* their neighbors to support projects.
- Whether or not a university library has independent access to funds, the university may insist on determining the library's construction priority.
- Local agencies or university units with no funding (and no chance whatever of funding) attempt to merge themselves physically with libraries. Unfortunately, the last

things libraries need is non-library agencies hanging out in their buildings.

- Some libraries can get funding for construction but not for operations. This is why wide-open spaces and wonderful sight lines are so important. By opening up sight lines designers can reduce the number of staff necessary in a building. If your library gets a larger building but the same operating budget, you have to be able to cope somehow.

Luckily, almost all of these complications are surmountable. At least, by reading this chapter you'll be forewarned (and sometimes forearmed).

II. Sources of Money

II-A. MONEY ON HAND

Some projects can be funded with cash on hand. Some smaller projects such as special libraries, school libraries that are not part of large projects, departmental libraries in universities, and public library branches may be modest enough to be paid simply out of pocket. Some industrial communities with large tax bases have also paid for new central libraries.

When projects are small enough to be paid for with cash on hand, preemptive (or perhaps "proactive") programming becomes particularly important. If the library's needs are well-known and in print and are sitting around administrative offices, this may help prevent off-hand conversion planning from taking place without input from the library staff.

Many special libraries are corporate and part of corporate budgets. These special libraries may find themselves under pressure from other agencies within the business that also need better or more advantageously located spaces. If the libraries' needs are on file, it may give the libraries advantages over other corporate agencies that complain but aren't as well organized.

II-B. SAVINGS SET ASIDE FROM OPERATING FUNDS

Depending on how funds are handled, some libraries are able to set aside surplus (or carefully hoarded) funds to meet long-term remodeling needs. For instance, libraries may set aside funds for occasional "refreshing" to update specific areas or to repurpose spaces that are no longer relevant to the libraries' needs.

Public libraries tend to be the most frugal of all local government bodies and the most likely to have money in the bank. Often they have enough to at least pay for remodeling or to hire programmers and architects to carry out initial plans.

Unfortunately, the result of money in the bank can be other governmental bodies casting greedy eyes on library savings, with consequent reduction in availability of construction funds. For example, anti-tax types have sometimes demanded that library funds set aside for construction be redirected to reducing annual operating costs, thereby reducing tax levies.

II-C. REFERENDUMS AND BOND ISSUES

Many public libraries and school libraries are built with money from bond referendums, although some states allow bond issues without referendums under specific circumstances.

A bond is a private loan to a government body, authorizing taxes to be levied over a number of years to retire the loan. Usually the bond issue specifies the number of payments and the amount of each payment. If the assessed value of taxable land in the jurisdiction increases more than anticipated, this may lead to the bonds being retired before the expected number of years has passed, which makes everyone happy.

The library's parent organization will need professional assistance with developing legal language for the issue that appears on the ballots, for merchandising the bonds (selling the bonds to investors), and so on. All of these things require professional legal and technical assistance. Laws regarding issuing bonds are complex and vary from state to state, so individual prior experience of non-experts cannot be relied on.

Timing of referendums is important. Fundraising consultants may be able to help. And because the successful passage of bond referendums is essential to their income, banks that market bonds to investors frequently provide expert advice to libraries on holding successful bond referendums. (Banks that specialize in this work are typically not paid until they merchandise the bonds.)

Government bonds can be attractive to investors because income from the bonds can be exempt from federal taxes and sometimes exempt from state taxes. In addition, most governments are good for the money because they are backed by taxable real estate. (But a few governments are bad risks, as some fiscal meltdowns in recent years demonstrated. Leave any concerns in this area to the agency marketing your bonds.)

Because income from bonds can be tax-exempt, libraries that issue bonds can offer lower rates of interest and still be attractive to investors.

All libraries need legal advice on the roles they can play in bond referendums. As a typical example, public funds cannot be used to influence the outcome of an election. Your lawyers will insist that paid staff members cannot be advocates for the bond issue, and that library money cannot be used for production of promotional materials advocating "yes" votes. Public money can typically be used to provide neutral information about the proposed election, but people and materials advocating positive votes must be strictly independent of public funding and paid for by library foundations, friends groups, or other non-government support groups.

Depend on your lawyers and bankers all along the way. They can tell you how to get issues on the ballot, how to word issues, what to do next if your issue passes, how to legally select a firm to market your bonds, and what other special steps you need to take to be sure that everything is done in painfully accurate compliance with the law.

In some states, the total indebtedness of political jurisdictions is limited by law to a relatively small fraction of total assessed property value, and this can lead to the creation of multiple overlapping jurisdictions in order to (for example) be able to build new schools and libraries and fire houses at the same time. Know what your local situation is before you progress too far with planning.

II-D. BEQUESTS

Some libraries are constructed with large bequests. Other, smaller bequests are enough to fund a part of a library, with donor recognition based on named features of the building, such as meeting rooms.

Some bequests carry requirements with them, including specific uses of the money. For example, a donor who knows how governmental units tend to operate may specify that the money be spent for new construction rather than for remodeling or repairs.

> Remodeling and repairs can constitute a major portion of the cost of library expansion projects, and to some donors, this part of the work may seem similar to pouring money down a rat hole. It's not a rat hole at all, but it's much more fun to envision the Johnson Wing of the new library than the Johnson HVAC replacement project. And because the library may have to find the money to fix the HVAC system regardless, the limitation of the donation to new construction may increase the net construction money available to the library.

A bequest large enough for an entire building may specify the design of the library, the name of the library, or pretty much anything else that the donor wants. Some requirements may not be legally enforceable, but that's why we have library lawyers.

Many bequests are totally unexpected, but others are the result of long-term cultivation of donors by library fundraisers. Because bequests can have an immense impact on library buildings, libraries should at least make their needs known. Offices of attorneys who specialize in estate work may welcome information on library needs. (Some professional fundraisers talk about long-planned bequests as "maturing," when the donors die, but that seems somewhat tacky.)

Large bequests can lead to sudden projects in campuses and communities that never anticipated constructing handsome new library buildings.

Some bequests may have time limits attached, of the "If you don't break ground or complete the building by a certain date, the money will be taken away from you and given to a home for cats" nature. If these time limits are realistic, there is time for essential steps in programming, design, and construction. If enough money is involved, work can go surprisingly quickly, but it means that university or public library boards of trustees or other authorities can't dawdle.

A bequest can also lead to an attempt by a local government to take tax money away from a library to compensate for the bequest, thereby undermining the intent of the donor. A well-written bequest will anticipate this kind of buccaneer approach to local government. So will having the bequest come to a private 501(c)(3) foundation rather than directly to the library.

Often bequests will not be large enough to construct a new building, but they can have a powerful effect in motivating bond referendums or reallocation of university assets, particularly if they are for one purpose only and have a time limit for taking action before the offer is withdrawn.

> We've seen one-time state incentive grants for public library construction that motivated otherwise extremely anti-tax communities to vote for new projects.

Stories abound of bequests given for specific purposes but simply redirected by the agency that received them. We suspect that libraries would never do that sort of thing, but there are a lot of non-libraries out there that might succumb to temptation. It's hard to imagine that misdirecting a bequest helps with future bequests.

II-E. MORTGAGES

Laws on the use of mortgages for construction of government-owned libraries will vary from state to state. Sometimes mortgages cannot be used at all, but in other cases at least a specific portion of the project can legally be supported by a mortgage.

The problem with mortgages is that they need to be paid off from operating funds or from ongoing fundraising. If your library has seriously ample—if not almost excessive—annual cash flow, a mortgage may be usable.

In our experience, mortgages have been used not for major funding but rather for last-minute extra cash when projects run somewhat over budget.

As with all mortgages, be sure your arrangement with the lending agency allows you to retire yours at any time with absolutely no penalty for paying in advance of scheduled payments. You may also want to build into the mortgage language that prevents the lending agency from selling your mortgage to another lending agency.

You will probably have no trouble finding a bank happy to provide a mortgage, particularly if your library is supported by authorized taxes on real estate.

II-F. FUNDRAISING

With the exception of some special and school libraries, most library construction projects involve fundraising, even when libraries are also supported by bonds, grants, massive donations, or other sources of funding.

If you have a public library, citizens may sometimes respond far more positively to requests for donations than to bond referendums, especially in times or places where anti-tax sentiments are strong.

II-F-1. Fundraising Consultants

In some libraries, fundraising campaigns are managed by library employees or by university employees. But expecting directors of small public libraries to find the extra time to take on fundraising in addition to their usual management responsibilities can be extraordinarily unreasonable.

Some libraries hire fundraising consultants. Depending on needs, consultants can perform such services as:

- Estimating the amount of money that can be raised. The accuracy of such projections can vary. For example, Fred's library raised several times the amount its consultant estimated.

- Managing campaigns, including solicitations for donations, donor recognition, donor social events, and other functions. A campaign manager may play a major role in the wide variety of special events described in the chapter on construction.

- Preparing grant applications.

People hired to raise money need to be extraordinarily well organized and socially gracious. Thanking of donors must be meticulous. Checks must not go astray. The voice on the phone must be warm and welcoming. The fundraiser's office must be clean and attractive but not imply any significant outlay of funds for overhead.

If you are considering hiring a fundraising consultant, one good place to begin is talking with other libraries. Because library fundraising is a highly specialized area, you may also want to consider people who have worked on similar government or cultural projects.

It also needs to be clear from the start that fundraising consultants are paid agreed-upon fees and NEVER a percentage of the funds raised. Paying a fundraiser a percentage is regarded as extremely unethical, and you don't want anything to do with anyone who suggests it.

II-F-2. Capital Campaigns

When planning projects, some libraries hold capital campaigns, in which they attempt to raise the needed funds in a period of a few years or less. These apply particularly to public libraries, which will probably not have the ongoing fundraising efforts that characterize colleges and universities.

Many campaigns begin with planning studies, which typically identify amounts that can probably be raised, what aspects of the project will be most appealing to donors, and which community leaders might participate. Work on planning studies also helps make communities more aware of library needs.

Because most campaigns involve identifying which potential donors have how much money and how they can be convinced to donate to the projects, publicly funded libraries that are subject to open meetings acts or to freedom of information act requests are in a very awkward position, because these conversations can't be carried out in public. This is another reason to set up a 501(c)(3) foundation where fundraising can legally be discussed in privacy.

A fundraising campaign is often carried out by a team. Remember that people who are selected for their ability to give money and ask others to give money must not be expected to do any clerical work.

II-F-3. Lead Gifts

Typically, campaigns begin with quiet solicitation of "lead gifts," significant donations that help launch campaigns and provide the majority of funds. Big gifts are essential. One runs into various numbers, but a common claim is that 10 percent of the donors may give 90 percent of the funds. Another common presumption in fundraising campaigns is that out of even hundreds of donors, the top donor may provide 10 percent of the total funds and the next two donors an additional 15 percent. Perhaps 45 additional donors provide the following 65 percent, and all of the other donors combined no more than 10 percent. So despite the good feelings that widespread support engenders, a relative handful of major gifts provides the majority of funds.

Book sales and bake sales are socially rewarding occasions and make everyone feel like part of the project, but the money that they raise is relatively insignificant.

All solicitation of major donors is in person, and the selection of who will make the request for funds is particularly important. The traditional approach is to ask who—of all possible people—the possible donor will have the greatest trouble turning down.

Large donors are usually a great thing, but problems can arise:

- Some donors want to take over the design of the project, including determining the functions of the library. This puts the university or public library in a bind, and some have had to turn down money because of the unacceptable strings attached.

- Some donors insist on a particular architectural firm. This can be just fine, but if the architects are (a) very ego driven and (b) feel that the owners have little say in what they do, since they're really working for the donor, the owners can lose control of the functional aspects of the project.

- People with dysfunctional designs in mind have sometimes claimed that this is what the donors want. It's frustrating for universities or cities to find out after the fact that the donors never said any such thing. Beware if mayors or university administrators or architects attempt to separate you socially from the donors.

All campaigns need careful follow-up work to be sure all the funds are collected, that all donors are thanked, and that public recognition—such as naming opportunities—goes off without errors.

As noted in the next section, most serious public library fundraising campaigns require a 501(c)(3) foundation. Colleges and universities should already have fundraising units with this or similar status. Public libraries that don't have foundations should probably set them up in advance.

II-F-4. Making the "Ask"

In all fundraising—particularly raising funds for significant gifts—which person makes the appeal matters a great deal. One of the things members of foundations do (in private, since they are not government bodies) is ask themselves who are the right people to ask for money and who are the right people to do the asking. Obviously, the caller should be the one person in the world to whom the would-be donor will have the greatest difficulty saying "no." Callers do better if they themselves are donors, because people being asked for money are likely to ask, "How much are *you* giving?"

As a result of their qualifications as people who can make large donations and have friends who can make large donations, members of foundation boards are likely to have very limited responsibilities—basically writing a check and making a few calls. All the organizing and record-keeping work is done by foundation staff.

Because they are often selected because they have substantial personal wealth, most foundation board members can be very different from friends of the library members. Friends of the library are typically working groups, not people with big bank accounts. Occasionally this is a socially touchy area. One solution is to have, for example, the president of the friends of the library be an *ex officio* member of the foundation board.

II-F-5. Record Keeping

All fundraising foundations need staff members to do the work of arranging mailings and correspondence, setting up social events, keeping painfully careful track of donors and donations, and being the smiling face of the foundation whenever people call. Expecting people who were appointed to the foundation board because of their ability to donate and ask for donations to also keep track of organizational details is inappropriate.

Some library foundations keep the shopping list for naming opportunities private, but others simply post it in the library and report good results.

Keeping track of all donations is of vital importance. Even extremely minor errors can cause serious problems, and a few donors with seriously hurt feelings can jeopardize a fundraising campaign.

II-F-6. Donor Recognition

Finding good ways to recognize donors is important. Most donors are extraordinarily public-spirited, but few of us are made happy by total anonymity.

Many libraries seize upon "naming opportunities" as a way of recognizing major gifts. This requires careful advance planning by the agency raising funds, which needs to determine in advance what individual items will cost. Planning ahead will lead to costs that are internally consistent, so that a small conference room and the main university reading room don't carry the same price tags.

The result of this kind of planning can be a shopping list of features, each with a price attached. People asking prospective donors for money will start high and then work their way down the list to items the donors can pay for.

Planning in advance this way helps prevent situations where naming opportunities take place in an unplanned, free-for-all atmosphere, frequently resulting in either annoying inconsistencies or in donations so low that the library runs out of naming opportunities long before making an actual dent in its costs.

One thing planners will have to ask themselves is the relationship between the size of the donation and the actual cost of the space. If (for example) a building is projected to have a project cost of $300 per square foot, should the naming of a 1,000-square-foot meeting room require a donation of $300,000?

One question all owners need to ask themselves in advance is what it will cost to actually change the name of the library. To have "Hazelton Library" replace "Jamestown University Library" should require a substantial donation, far more than the "Hazelton Wing of the Jamestown University Library."

In addition to library names and building names, libraries typically offer naming opportunities for departments (children's, Slavic languages), meeting rooms (auditoriums, classrooms), reading rooms (massive reading rooms, quiet reading rooms), special features (study rooms, library cafés), and so on.

Of course, lots of essential library spaces don't lend themselves to donor names. Few people want to be remembered as the sponsors of hallways or restrooms.

Sometimes donors make substantial gifts and don't really care about naming, and others may not want their names mentioned at all. The important thing is honoring the wishes of the donor.

II-F-7. Recognizing Smaller Donations

In addition to named buildings and spaces, libraries need ways to recognize what may be hundreds of individual donations. A wide variety of plaques are available commercially, some with individual tags that can be inscribed as gifts continue to come in.

Some libraries have raised funds through the sale of inscribed paving bricks that are used to create patios or other features. There are a couple of important points:

- Be sure you know what it will cost to have an inscribed paver made and installed before you settle on prices. Fred worked with one library that priced pavers so inexpensively that it made no money whatsoever on the project—although the pleasure of seeing one's name on the patio had goodwill value.

- Be sure you have an index to paver locations. If you have a patio with 200 pavers, donors will come to a service desk inside the library and complain that their pavers are not there, when in reality it's just hard to find them.

Every once in a while, a library will receive an unexpected late gift when the building is already planned and under construction. The foundation board needs to have contingency plans.

Be careful about putting donor plaques on items that can be damaged. In the case of reading tables, for example, a library can mount a plaque on the wall saying "Ten of the tables in this room were made possible by donations from the following..." By not identifying who gave what tables, the library spares itself dealing with an unhappy donor whose personal table has been vandalized in some way. As long as a few of the tables were paid for from general library funds, libraries can maintain the happy fiction that the damaged tables were paid for by the library, not by donors.

The chapter on construction includes a list of possible social events for donors. There are a lot of great possibilities. (Two to avoid are events with cash bars—which means dram shop insurance—and final ribbon cuttings held for donors only.)

The important thing is to find ways to recognize all donors, regardless of donation size.

II-G. 501(c)(3) FOUNDATIONS

All kinds of private groups can raise money for library construction. However, there may be strict legal limits on how much they can raise and hold, depending on their federal tax status.

The most common legal status for fundraising groups—such as library foundations—is 501(c)(3) tax-exempt status. This status allows groups to raise substantial sums of money and to hold it until the time comes to spend it. 501(c)(3) foundations are under the supervision and control of the IRS.

501(c)(3) status is available to not-for-profit organizations with a variety of purposes, such as charitable, educational, religious, scientific, and so on. Libraries fit neatly into the educational category.

To obtain 501(c)(3) status, you will need the assistance of an attorney to help set up a foundation that meets IRS requirements for tax-exempt, not-for-profit status and to file the necessary application. Once formed, the foundation must follow record-keeping and reporting requirements.

The federally certified tax-exempt status of 501(c)(3) organizations is essential to fundraising. Some organizations and businesses will probably refuse to donate funds if you do not have a 501(c)(3) foundation.

Foundations and other groups of this type are independent by law and are not controlled by library boards, city councils, university administrations, etc. There's always a danger, of course, that the board of the foundation may disagree on how money is to be spent, but there appears to be a greater benefit in the fact that local politicians or university administrations cannot loot the assets of the foundation. If a mayor, for example, congratulates the foundation on its fundraising and proposes that local government can now cut its support of a project accordingly, the foundation board can simply say "No" in a way that a local public library board could probably not do because foundations can be totally separate from local government. (We don't have data on the frequency of politicians' attempts to loot foundations, but we've both seen it happen.)

Foundations also have the benefit of being able to hold private meetings, without which their speculations on who can give what would be impossible.

Colleges and universities have their own foundations that can take over fundraising responsibilities, but individual academic libraries can have their own foundations.

Laws controlling 501(c)(3) foundations require that foundations provide for the disposition of funds if the foundations choose to disband. This comes up because some libraries find little use for their foundations once funds have been raised, buildings have been constructed, ribbons have been cut, and donor receptions have been held. Our personal feeling is that it can be surprisingly few years before serious fundraising needs to take place again, and having the foundation in place can be a good idea.

II-H. GRANTS

Depending on political and business climates, grants can be a major source of construction funds.

Many construction grants for libraries are government grants, but privately funded foundations also have grant funds available. In particular, consider approaching companies that do business in your community.

Many government grants are competitive, which means that your library will need to make a more impressive application than other libraries in your state.

As with all grants, pay attention to required items. Typical grant applications may require:

- Written building programs.
- Schematic designs. (Remember that it's *essential* that schematic designs include furniture layouts. A library floor plan without placement of furniture is basically an empty square.)
- Cost estimates (which should accompany schematic designs). Good cost estimates are vital for grant applications. (Know your architect's reputation for accurate estimating, and check with your construction management firm if you are using one.)

> Fred knows a public library where the architect's estimate was about one-third of the actual low bid. The library was awarded a state construction grant, and by the time the project was bid, the state had irrevocably committed the funds. Things were eventually sorted out when the library was able to locate the extra money, but it was an amazing political mess. In addition, the higher cost of the project threw the project into a different grant category requiring extra documentation and planning documents from the library. To make things worse, after all the tangles had been surmounted, the resulting building was a functional disaster.

- Project narratives, explaining the need for the project.

- For government grants, sign-offs from specific government agencies. For example, a state grant may require a sign-off from the state's historic preservation agency.

- Demonstrations that proposed projects meet minimum state standards for libraries. Depending on the state, standards that affect schematic designs may include collection sizes, seating, accessibility, etc.

- Except for some challenge grants, where the announcement of the grant is intended to spur donations and referendums, certification that local matching funds have already been raised. (Some applications even require photocopies of bank records to prove that local funds are in place.) In many cases, nothing messes up agencies administering government grants more than libraries that receive grants and then admit they don't have their share of the money.

- Certification that the library has clear title to its site.

> Public libraries occasionally are constructed on sites to which they have rights only as long as they occupy their buildings. This can lead to extraordinarily bad situations where the library doesn't want to spend money on its building because the building really belongs to another agency. It's a lot like the problems with tenant houses on farms.

- Letters of support may be useful. (A letter from a powerful local politician may be just what you need, or it may just annoy a committee of librarians. Just ask around.)

- If the grant application permits them, photographs of your existing library may be a powerful addition, particularly if you can provide images depicting an honest and hard-working library coping bravely while encumbered with a neatly maintained but painfully obsolete structure.

All of these things take time. A good building program can be developed in a couple of months, but for a public library, working that fast may require a long board meeting every week. Three or four months is a much more practical aim. If your state has a QBS law for public buildings, hiring an architect may also take a couple of months. It's hard to develop a schematic design in less than three or four months after the completion of a building program. And sign-offs from overworked government agencies can take longer than one wishes.

Because all of this work can take half a year or more, it can be hard to complete everything in the time between the announcement of a grant program and the due date for applications. This is another reason for doing the low-cost part of the work—preparing a building program and selecting an architect—well in advance.

Corporate grants for library construction will typically require far less documentation than government grants, but they will almost certainly require strong local financial support and a 501(c)(3) foundation to guarantee to donor corporations that their grants are tax deductible. You will probably want to start with industries associated with your community, but persistence sometimes pays off in unexpected ways. A board member of a public library with which Fred worked sent serious inquiries to a couple hundred corporations and eventually turned up a major grant. (He was retired and found the whole process an entertaining challenge.)

For libraries expanding their historic Carnegie buildings, it can be disheartening to recognize that the Carnegie Corporation's major grant programs for totally free buildings ended about 1915.

As with all grants, clarity and completeness of applications are vital. If the grant application form lists 15 numbered items, a good application lists all 15, labelled and numbered and in the same order, so overworked employees or grant committee members can do a quick conformance check to be sure all required items are present.

Deadlines for government grants are usually ironclad. It's fun to drive your application to your state library on due date and run into folks from a dozen other libraries who are there for the same reason.

The terms of some grants may include specific wording for recognition of the grant. For instance, a plaque somewhere in the building may need to say something like, "This construction project was made possible in part by a grant of [program name] funds made possible by the following [government agency, corporation, political person]." If there's a politician you don't like in the group, keep it to yourself, remembering that recognition is a miniscule price to pay for substantial financial assistance.

II-I. SPECIAL APPROPRIATIONS

America being America, sometimes the best way to get money for construction involves pure politics. As with private fundraising, knowing whom to ask and when and how to ask is important. Often, special appropriations occur as riders on bills.

From politicians' point of view, libraries have the advantage of being a lot less expensive than interstate exits and providing far better photo ops.

If emergency money is running around after a catastrophe, get yours for your library.

III. Snappy Rules on Funding

1. The single most important construction material is money. (This is not an original remark, but we can't find a source.)

2. Unless you do this kind of thing all the time, you'll suffer from instant sticker shock.

3. There are no new Andrew Carnegies providing libraries for all. For most libraries, this means finding your own money, although wonderful individual donors come along.

4. When it comes to bond referendums, making sure that your friends vote works a lot better than trying to convert your enemies.

5. Firms that market bonds sometimes have staff members who study voter behavior and can advise you on the timing of referendums.

6. If your state allows mortgages on government-owned libraries, that may be a quick way to deal with sudden cost overruns.

7. You have only one chance with naming opportunities. Plan first and negotiate second. All too often, libraries initially give

things away too cheaply and find themselves trapped.

8. Thank everyone. For some donors, $100 was a greater stretch than $100,000 for other donors.

9. For most citizens, a new public library is a lot more important than a new city hall or a new public works garage. This annoys city government folks, but they'll have to get over it.

10. Donors would rather pay for a new college library (think shining city on the hill) than a new dormitory (think restrooms on Friday nights). This is probably why dormitories are often named after early college presidents.

11. Before you start mounting donor-recognition letters directly on drywall, ask yourself how you'll repaint the wall. (Some systems for mounting letters allow the letters to be removed when it's time to repaint.)

12. Campuses may have priority listings for capital projects. In the wrong fiscal climate, libraries can hover indefinitely at number two or three.

13. Grant applications tend to expect local matching funds.

14. When you have money, move right along. Construction costs tend to increase faster than the value of money in the bank.

15. Applications for government construction grants may lead to the required involvement of additional government agencies. This may not be fun.

16. Some donors come equipped not only with money (good) but with weird structural ideas they want to inflict on you (bad). Some want to pay only part of the cost of the building but still get to inflict their unfortunate ideas on you. It hurts to say "no" to money, but sometimes that's the only sane option.

17. For public libraries, know the spirit of your community. Some angrily anti-tax people can be amazingly generous when asked for voluntary donations.

18. People reading grant applications may have backbreaking jobs. Make their lives easier by writing clearly, by helping them match their questions to your answers, and by including all the required support documents in the right order.

19. Bake sales and book sales are fun and make everyone feel involved and appreciated, but they don't bring in much money. Construction projects rely on seriously big bucks from a more limited range of sources.

20. Legitimate fundraising consultants always work for agreed fees or hourly salaries and never (as in NEVER) for a percentage of funds raised.

PART III

Essential Spaces All Libraries Need

PART III
Essential Spaces All Libraries Need

CHAPTER 21

User Seating

I. Introduction

I-A. ABOUT USER SEATING

Most libraries provide seating for their users.

Over the years, we've run into a handful of people who feel that library users should come to the library, get their books, and go home. But this is hard to justify, given that the people who are paying for the libraries want to sit there and read there and socialize there.

Some users are driven away by lack of adequate seating. In one public library Fred was working with, he saw groups of teenagers stop by after school, see that there was no seating anywhere, and leave. (This library had one reading table and one conference table that doubled as a board table and a computer table, so it filled quickly.)

Many libraries have obsolete seating. It's pretty easy to chuck it out if it's old and battered and ugly. But it's a lot harder if it's historic (even if it's awkward and ugly and inaccessible) or if it's fairly new (but dysfunctional). Getting rid of bad seating is important, but it can be politically difficult. One way is to just put it in storage until people have forgotten about it, and then discretely eliminate it.

Over the years, libraries have made bad decisions on seating.

- Some have purchased armchairs so large that people who sit up against the backs of the chairs end up with their legs sticking straight out like those of four-year-olds in adult chairs.

- Some have purchased armchairs so low that almost no one who gets in can get back out again.

- One public library in Illinois had its armchairs upholstered in imitation suede, which absorbed body oils like a magnet and had to be replaced within months.

- Some libraries install sofas, only to find that the two major uses of sofas in libraries are sleeping and necking, neither of which corresponds closely with most long-range plans.

- Some libraries have purchased discount store seating and had it fall apart in a few months. Or less.

- Some libraries purchase seating upholstered in garish colors du jour, only to find that the colors scream passé long before the upholstery wears out.

- Some libraries have purchased side chairs for reading tables, only to find that the chairs tore carpet to shreds. Sled bases or casters help.

- Some libraries have let their architects design chairs without trying out a preliminary version for comfort.

The list of snappy rules at the end of this chapter is a fairly long one because the world of library administration abounds in shared stories about unfortunate user seating.

At one public library with which Fred worked, the president of the board spoke out firmly against user seating, although users attending the meeting wanted more. She contended that people should pick up their books at the library and then read them at home. She also spoke out against popular materials. When a young mother attending the meeting complained about the absence of picture books for young children, the board president pointed out that the library had just purchased the McGraw Hill Encyclopedia of Science and Technology. The mother didn't ask the obvious question—Who's paying the taxes around here?—but she was clearly thinking it. And the board president retired.

Luckily, there's lots of really great seating out there.

Some libraries pick out and order their own seating, while others rely on their architects and interior designers for help.

Library conferences usually have booths by furniture firms. Even if you have no immediate need, it's good to be familiar with what's out there. Try things out. Collect catalogs. If you're immersed in planning, ask companies for binders (collections of brochures in monster three-ring binders).

In addition to traditional wooden tables and chairs, there's a wide variety of less formal furniture available from firms that specialize in equipping offices and schools.

Although there's a lot to say about furniture, as far as we're concerned, the most important things are:

- Buy strong. Home strong is not library strong.

- Chipboard (aka particleboard) is not library strong. Chipboard is a mixture of sawdust and glue. Always avoid it. (One magic phrase for solid tabletop construction is "lumber core.")

- Always sit in chairs at least 15 minutes before selecting them.

- If your architects want to design your chairs, never just say "yes." Have one made up to their design and try it out extensively. Based on prior experience, we'd say that the chances of it being seriously comfortable are pretty low.

- Buy soft seating that is not too low, not too deep from front to back, not too soft, and not too hard to climb out of. And wide enough.

- Buy tables that are accessible to users with disabilities. This means 27 inches leg clearance, which in turn means no aprons. (Aprons are vertical boards attached to the undersides of tabletops and connecting the table legs. They strengthen cheap tops and provide a flimsy connection to table legs.)

- Don't buy round tables except for coffee shops. A library plan with a large group of round tables is a rotten plan. "Large group" means any number over two.

- Buy tables with 110-volt electrical outlets—and ideally with powered USB ports—on top. (Who knows, even toddlers may need electrical outlets on their tabletops any day now.)

- Make sure that multi-person tables provide enough space for individual users. A rectangular tabletop space 18 by 30 inches per person is absolutely minimal with four-person tables. (That's the space provided by a three-by-five-foot table.)

- Buy from manufacturers rather than from office supply firms or furniture retailers.

- Buy tables that are rectangular and have chairs on only two sides. Never agree to rectangular tables with chairs on all four sides, round tables, or strangely shaped tables.

- Keep away from as much excessively padded upholstery as possible, particularly overstuffed seating. Most padding is made of polyurethane foam, which is extremely flammable. Extensive padding harbors infestations of all sorts. And user comfort does not require massive amounts of padding.

- Avoid fabric upholstery whenever you can, and use vinyl to make cleanup easier. Also investigate hard plastics. Despite the name, these can be quite comfortable. And they are really easy to maintain.

I-B. FURNITURE VOCABULARY

It helps to know some basic vocabulary in chair design:

- ***Apron***. The horizontal boards that connect the style to the front legs and support the seat.

- ***COM***. Short for "customer's own materials," as in situations where libraries provide the upholstery fabric to the furniture firm.

- ***Corner bracket***. The diagonal brace that connects the aprons to the styles. This joint is the most vulnerable to damage and is often a metal-to-metal joint in chairs designed for library users.

- ***Parsons Design tables***. These consist of flat tops with legs on all four corners, no aprons, and no cross beams connecting the legs. The name comes from a design school. Accessibility was not the original motivation, but the tables work really well.

- ***Rail***. The horizontal board that connects the two styles.

- ***Splat***. The vertical flat board in between the styles that provides a smooth surface for people to lean back against.

- ***Stretchers***. The boards that connect the styles and the legs, or the two front legs, below the level of the seat.

- ***Style***. The upright post at the rear of the chair.

- ***Top rail***. Horizontal board at the top of the back of the chair, connecting the top ends of the two styles.

II. How Much User Seating?

One major decision when buildings are planned involves the quantities and types of seating. Since seating takes a lot of space (one three-by-five foot reading table with four chairs occupies about the same space as 1,000 books), the estimated square footages in building programs are strongly dependent on numbers of tables and chairs. (A three-by-five-foot reading table is the smallest possible four-chair table for people older than about seven years.)

What are some sources of information and ideas?

- Published standards.
- Current overcrowding in your library, and your estimate of the additional seating required to alleviate it. (This is always dangerous, because new library buildings can generate greatly increased user space demand.)
- Seating in similar institutions.
- Expected growth in college enrollment or public library service populations.
- New seating ideas that strike librarians as exciting, such as collaborative study spaces.

Specify furniture very precisely in your building program. For example, "10 reading tables" could lead to almost anything. A better specification might be: "Ten three-by-five-foot reading tables, each with two chairs on each of the two long sides and no chairs at the ends."

Some other desirable building requirements include:

- Electrical outlets in the center of each table, with enough sockets for four people to plug in their laptop computers at the same time.
- Tabletops with lumber cores, with high-pressure laminates on both sides. Chipboard will not be used for any table components.
- Rectangular table lamps running the length of each table, designed to cast bright and even light on the entire tabletop.
- Tables without aprons. (Aprons are vertical boards below tabletops that connect the tops of the table legs and support the tabletops.)
- Tabletops will be about 29 inches above the floor, and clearances beneath the tops will be 27 inches. Legs will be a minimum of 30 inches apart. All of this meets ADA requirements. (The ADA allows tabletops up to 34 inches above the floor, but heights of over 29 inches are generally uncomfortable. (Many historical library tables are too high to be comfortable.)
- Table legs held in place by metal-to-metal connections, with metal plates bolted to tabletops and steel posts inside the legs. Screws running diagonally through angled corner plates into wooden legs are flimsy and will not be used.
- Table legs without crossbeams at the ends of the tables. It should be easy for users to pull extra chairs up to the table ends.
- The glides on the ends of the table legs will screw in and out to adjust for irregularities in the floor.

Some library owners and library designers try to cram too much seating into too little space. Some do it by converting larger tables to smaller tables while keeping the same number of chairs. Some convert rectangular tables to round tables, which can be crammed more closely together (but are no good for serious work). Some place tables too closely together, violating ADA clearances.

> One architect Fred worked with changed the schematic design by taking out a six-foot section of shelving in a stack unit and drawing in a reading table. Unfortunately, it wouldn't have worked. With 42-inch aisles and two-foot-deep shelving units, the total space opened up between the two rows of shelves would be nine feet. However, a small reading table takes up three feet for the tabletop, about six feet for seated readers, and another seven or eight feet for people to get past the seated readers and get at the books on the shelves. All of this leads to a table needing 16 or 17 feet of space. Trying to cram it into a nine-foot opening requires seriously sloppy arithmetic.

III. How Library Furniture Is Ordered

III-A. INVENTORIES OF EXISTING FURNITURE

Unless you intend to chuck everything out and buy all new, you will end up inventorying your available furniture and deciding what will be reused and what will be discarded.

Often this inventory is done by the architect's interior designers. A careful study will identify all existing furniture and indicate where each piece will go in the new or expanded library building—or whether it will be tossed out.

If your library has pieces of furniture you want to retain at all costs, or items you hate and never want to see again, this is a good time to discuss things with your interior designer.

If cash is tight, it's better to make do for a year or two with old furniture, since it's easier to find the cash later for new furniture than to try to stretch the building a little.

III-B. SELECTING NEW FURNITURE

Furniture is bid separately rather than provided by the general contractor, so it will not be part of your construction bid.

Rely on your interior designer whenever possible. If not, there are sales reps who can deal with factories on your behalf. Nonetheless, verify everything. In particular, you want to make sure that all selected furniture is comfortable, which means obtaining samples from manufacturers.

A lot of good library furniture is built to order, so you can't delay ordering until your building is nearly finished. In fact, furniture is notorious for not turning up on time for ribbon cuttings.

> An architect told Fred about a library project where none of the furniture was delivered in time for the grand opening. The architect called the company every few days and was always assured that the furniture was almost ready to ship. But at the time of the grand opening, the factory had not even begun to start building it.

Because good-quality library furniture is built to order, most libraries obtain it directly from the manufacturer or from a manufacturer's representative. (Little stuff, like computer tables, can be an exception.)

Don't miss opportunities to see furniture on display and try it out. Manufacturers often have booths at major library conferences, in showrooms, or at design centers. This can be useful especially for office furniture. Talk with your interior designers.

If you'll be ordering a lot of furniture, particularly chairs, ask the makers to send you samples of the items you like for you to try for comfort. Our experience has been that manufacturers are less happy to send samples than in days gone by, but it doesn't hurt to ask. Because samples are intended for evaluation of comfort and structure, colors and finishes of samples are basically whatever the manufacturer has lying around. A second problem can involve getting manufacturers to remove their samples in a timely fashion after the library has made a decision.

Cheap furniture won't survive library use. A library table should be strong enough to drag down Main Street or across the main quad on one leg without the leg joint loosening.

> Many years ago, a staff member in Fred's library bought a handful of ultra-cheap footstools at a discount furniture store. In a few weeks nearly all had completely disintegrated, as in nothing left but a few worn-out shreds of fabric and some bits and pieces of chipboard.

IV. Tables

IV-A. CONFIGURATIONS

Tables are available in a wide variety of configurations:

- Single-user tables. Single-user tables need to be a minimum of three feet wide, but they work better when they're four feet wide, particularly in academic libraries, because the combination of a laptop, open book, and notepad takes up more than three feet.

- Carrels. Carrels are single-user tables with vertical panels like short walls on three sides to provide a degree of privacy. Carrels in academic libraries need to be four feet wide, just as with single-user tables. Our experience has been that carrels with raised barricades work well in academic libraries but not in public libraries. In both academic and public libraries, "pods" are taking over as more versatile furniture options that have many of the features sought in carrels. Manufacturers have photographs of pods on the internet. For example, see the Steelcase "Brody" system.

- Square tables for two users. Square tables need to be three-by-three feet or larger, with chairs on only two sides. One thing that goes wrong with furniture layouts is architects trying to save space by putting four chairs at a two-person table, one on each of the four sides, resulting in each user's space being a small triangle. Watch for this in schematic designs and stamp it out quickly.

- Rectangular tables for four users. These call for two chairs on each of the long sides, not one chair on each of the four sides. The absolute minimum size for a four-person table for adults is three-by-five feet, but lots of four-person tables are larger, particularly in academic and research libraries. Among other things, the COVID epidemic has made more widely spaced chairs desirable. Many people question the need for four-person tables, but we think four-person tables are important. Most adults prefer to sit one per table, but single users at four-person tables have more room to spread out than they would at one- or two-person tables, making four-person tables more attractive. When every four-person table in the room has a single occupant, a second person will usually sit down at a diagonal corner from the first occupant. Teenagers, on the other hand, make great use of four-person tables. They enjoy sitting four to a table, and they often drag over extra chairs from adjacent tables to create five- or six-person tables. (This is one reason why cross beams connecting table legs at the ends of tables are a seriously bad idea.)

- Rectangular tables with dividers. Academic libraries sometimes purchase large reading tables with low dividers (perhaps three inches high) to define user spaces. Four-by-six feet is probably a minimum tabletop size.

- Round tables for two or more users. Round tables are intended for socializing, for drinking coffee, or perhaps for reading novels or magazines, but not for work. Among other things, round tables have no working surfaces. Users need to be able to spread things out in front of themselves, and with round tables, things that are spread out to the left or right simply fall on the floor. Designers frequently draw in round tables where libraries have specified rectangular tables, either because they look cute or because they allow more tables to be crammed into a limited space. Be prepared to reject (firmly) all round tables that are not in coffee shops or social areas, and forbid them in your written building program.

- Index tables. In the heyday of the *Reader's Guide to Periodical Literature* and other long sets of books that people consulted as a group, libraries purchased huge tables with double-faced two-shelf dividers down the center. One could use surviving examples for spread-out reading spaces or as computer tables or as Lego tables in children's departments, but old index tables are basically massive and ungainly museum pieces.

- Custom computer tables. Computer tables come in a variety of non-rectangular shapes. A common shape is hexagons, with user chairs on six sides and all of the computer wires funneled through the center of the table to simplify wiring. However, it can be hard to arrange hexagonal tables effectively, and readers can feel crowded. Computer tables also come in unusual shapes with lobes for individual computers. For users who need space for books and papers beside their computers, these appear not to provide what people need, but we've never really studied them.

- Machine tables for computers. Unlike wooden single-person tables, machine tables can be specifically designed for computers, with wire management troughs to keep wires from dangling. Many libraries purchase machine tables from firms specializing in furniture for offices and schools rather than from wood furniture firms.

- Game tables. Game tables often have chessboard or backgammon patterns printed on their high-pressure laminate surfaces. The tables look neat and educated, but checkers and chess may be extremely unusual activities in most libraries. Tables that are compatible with computer games and miscellaneous board games make a lot more sense.

- Tables for very young children. These can include toddler-height tables for preschoolers and primary-height tables for lower grades.

When designers suggest tables other than rectangular tables with chairs on two sides, always check to see the actual working space available to individual users. A good way to do this is to make a sketch of the top of the table and then indicate surface space available to each person at the table by drawing dotted lines on the tabletop. If the lines end up diagonal and the work areas triangular, pick a different table design.

IV-B. ESSENTIAL REQUIREMENTS

Library reading tables should have a variety of features

- No aprons. Aprons are vertical boards located under the tops of tables. Inexpensive tables have metal plates (or strips of wood) installed diagonally between aprons at the corners of the tables. Diagonal bolts connect the plates to the table legs. Unfortunately, tables built this way aren't strong enough for library use. While cheap tables with aprons are usually flimsy, massive tables with aprons can be extremely difficult to use, for the thickness of the aprons either leaves no room for users to get their legs under the tables or raises the tabletops to uncomfortable heights.

- Adequate leg clearance. Tables for use by adults should have at least 27 inches of leg clearance, as required for use by people with disabilities.

- Tops about 29 inches high.

- Adequately large tops. Four-person tables in public and school libraries need to be an absolute minimum of three by five feet, and tables in academic and research libraries can be four by six or four by seven feet.

- Adequate space between tables. Tables need to be far enough apart so that users can walk between tables comfortably when all the chairs are occupied and users are not pulled up neatly to the tables. Or are not sufficiently slender to do so. In the days of COVID, extra space will be welcome.

- Durable tops. Although some beautiful library tables are available with wooden tops, they're expensive and may prove to be high maintenance. Lots of libraries appear to prefer tops made of high-pressure laminates, which are not strong enough for lending desk tops but seem to work well on reading tables.

- Edge banding is sometimes used to keep laminate tops from chipping. On wooden tables with lumber cores, this can be a strip of wood, but on some tables the edge bands can be plastic resins cast in place. Wooden edge banding tends to need very occasional refinishing.

- Matching laminates on the undersides of tabletops, to prevent the tops from warping with changes in humidity.

- Tabletops that are neither black nor white, both of which cause eyestrain. Colors like birch or pale gray appear to work best.

- No chipboard tops. Chipboard is a mixture of sawdust and glue. The phrase "built for the ages" does not apply.

- Electrical outlets. All reading room tables for adult and young adult use (except game tables) require electrical outlets, ideally in the center of the top. Some tables have outlets hidden beneath the tops; in a computer age this seems to be a triumph of aesthetics over function. Tabletop reading lamps can have electrical outlets built into their bases.

- No beams connecting the legs. Students using library tables may want to pull extra chairs up to the ends of the tables. If the legs

Shiny tabletops lead to distracting reflections of ceiling fixtures. Glass is particularly undesirable, but so are white surfaces of any kind, which can be unpleasantly bright. Tabletops and service desktops need to be of gentle hues, neither black nor white.

are connected by beams, this doesn't work. (In well-engineered tables, beams between the legs are cute rather than functional.)

- Legs at the corners of the tops rather than inset. Inset legs get in users' way and provide no compensating benefits. And to meet ADA, legs need to be at least 30 inches apart.

- Legs on all four corners rather than pedestal legs. Tables with corner legs are a lot more stable than tables with pedestal legs (center legs), and pedestal legs get in the way of human legs. Our strong feeling is that pedestal legs are a bad idea. Square tables with single pedestal legs offer opportunities for upset. And they may have ADA issues.

- Adjustable glides at the bottom of legs. If glides screw in and out, they can be adjusted to compensate for unevenness in floors. (More concrete floors are uneven than one would expect.)

- Very large wooden tables, such as leftover index tables, may have additional steel stiffeners mounted on the undersides of the tables, running down the centers of the tables.

- Large reading rooms sometimes have long tables lined with chairs on both sides. (Or shorter tables butted together end to end, providing a similar effect.) Outside of requiring a little more walking around, they seem to look and work just as well as two- or four-person tables, and they save some floor space. They tend to look particularly elegant with rows of reading lamps on their tops.

- Some research libraries have long, single-sided tables, arranged in parallel rows so that all readers face the same way rather than staring at each other across the tabletops. We've seen these mainly in European libraries.

Many historic reading tables are unsuited for modern library use because they have uncomfortably high working surfaces and aprons too deep for accessibility. If they are also dramatic in appearance and admired by local folks, you may have a problem. Some libraries have converted tables of this type to display areas for new books and other materials. Others have simply sold them at auction or put them in storage until they're forgotten.

IV-C. OPTIONS

A handful of options are available:

- **Table lamps.** Some libraries add table lamps mostly for romantic atmosphere, but in other libraries (particularly those with historic dark ceilings) table lamps may be essential. The main tricks with table lamps are:

    » Bolt them down.

    » Make sure that they cast light on the entire tabletop. This is most easily done with straight fixtures that run the length of the tabletop. If you would rather have round fixtures, get hold of a couple of identical fixtures and experiment to see if they cast light in useful places. A couple of round circles of light in the center of the tabletop won't help readers much.

    » See if you can find lamps with electrical outlets in their bases, which may limit the amount of clutter on your tabletops.

    » Check with your engineers concerning electrical codes. Can you have a table with a pigtail lead connected to a floor socket below?

- **Privacy panels.** Many carrels for single readers have raised panels on three sides. Selecting panels high enough to provide a feeling of privacy without appealing to a reader's sense of claustrophobia may take a little research. Some libraries have done well with translucent privacy panels.

As this historic fixture shows, lamp fixtures on reading tables can be elegant and welcoming. However, some work well while others provide no useful light. If you are planning tables with lamps, always obtain a sample lamp in advance and try it out in an otherwise dark room. (If your tabletop lamps have electrical outlets, your users will be even more happy.)

- **Wire management troughs.** Some more modern tables are available with wire management arrangements to conceal the worst of the dangling wires.

- **Provisions for laptop security.** See what systems are available to protect library users' laptops during restroom breaks. We've seen locking cabinets at the back of user workspaces where laptops can be shoved back and locked in without being turned off, but things change constantly.

IV-D. ADAPTATIONS BASED ON THE AGE OF USERS

There are some adaptations based on the ages of users:

- Some furniture companies offer slightly shorter versions of adult tables with slightly shorter chairs for use by older children. Our experience has been that these are not different enough from adult tables to justify their existence. Unless the children's and adult tables are visibly very different, they tend to get intermixed, with some tables too low for adult chairs and others too high for children's chairs.

- A variety of special seating for preschool children and for children in lower grades is available, often with fanciful designs cut into the chair backs by laser cutters. The catalogs and websites of furniture manufacturers are full of examples. Libraries typically purchase children's tables and chairs at two heights, primary tables for suitable for perhaps ages five through seven, and toddler height tables for younger children.

- Some libraries have purchased stools for children. If you do, avoid three-legged stools, which tend to tip over.

- For over a century, children's libraries have purchased slope-top reading tables with lips to keep books from sliding off. The general idea is that large picture books can be laid flat on the tabletops while kids read them. We both tried them out when we were small children and found them unpleasant places to sit, so you don't want to hear our opinions, which remain extraordinarily negative. Despite our opinions, slope-top tables still turn up in new public libraries with grim regularity, but when we visit libraries we see them used for displays rather than reading. If you think we're wrong, please let us know. In the meantime, we suggest you avoid them. Slope-top tables seem to come equipped with backless benches more often than with chairs.

- Seating for infants. Many parents arrive in children's departments with several children ranging in age from a few months to perhaps sixth grade. The youngest children may be too small for even toddler tables, but a wide range of printed carpets is available that can be inserted flush in broadloom carpet or carpet squares.

V. Chairs

V-A. SOFT SEATING

Almost all libraries try to provide comfortable seating, particularly for people who want to read without taking notes.

As many libraries become destinations as well as book warehouses, comfortable seating is even more important.

V-A-1. Armchairs

For adults, the most workable soft seating is armchairs.

Armchairs come in a wide variety of styles. Because library furniture is usually made to order, almost any upholstery is possible. Furniture manufacturers will offer their own range of fabrics, but they will also use fabrics purchased by their customers. ("COM" stands for "customer's own materials" in the trade.)

Many armchairs are too deep from front to back. It's no fun to slide back into the rear of a chair, bracing your back against the back of the chair, only to find that your feet stick out straight, like a three-year-old on the family sofa.

In addition to being too deep, many armchairs are too low for library use. Your octogenarian users will need to arise from armchairs without assistance. Having to roll out of a low armchair onto the floor, then struggle to get to your feet, is not a heartwarming experience.

If armchairs have heavily padded arms, it's hard for users to put their weight on the arms to emerge from the chairs. And upholstery on the arms of chairs can wear out quickly and get dirty even more quickly.

One source of good armchairs for libraries is companies that make waiting room furniture for medical offices. Often they offer both regular widths and slightly wider widths for more comfortable reading. Unlike some overstuffed armchairs, waiting room style chairs are high enough to allow people to get back up again, and they have wooden arms because clinics don't like shabby arms any more than libraries do, and because inflexible wooden arms are easier to use to lever oneself out of a chair.

An increasing need in America is the need for truly wide chairs. A manufacturer of high-quality wooden furniture told Fred that bariatric chairs were a great new area for sales. If you've visited a doctor's examining room recently, you may be impressed at the width of some of the chairs provided for patients. Libraries may need to provide ultra-wide chairs as well.

Some libraries have had trouble with users dragging armchairs around so that they serve as footstools. You can fight this by making armchairs heavy and hard to move or by not putting two armchairs close together. You can also buy footstools, although they may tend to get in the way.

V-A-2. Loveseats

Loveseats seem ideally suited for parents and children to sit together in children's departments. And they're too short for adults to nap on.

When equipped with wooden arms, loveseats don't take up a huge amount of space.

Buy institutional furniture. There is no theoretical upper limit to the number of teenagers who can occupy a chair.

V-A-3. Sofas

Sofas look attractive and homey, but as a general rule they cause problems in libraries. Often serious problems.

In children's departments, they're almost always too long. A parent with one or two children can fit comfortably into a loveseat.

In areas for adults, sofas are a problem because users who don't know each other well don't want to share. One person sits alone at one end of the sofa, while the rest of the sofa is empty and wastes floor space.

V-A-4. Rocking Chairs

Librarians disagree on the subject of rocking chairs.

Fred thinks that rocking chairs in libraries are seriously evil. Libraries tend to put rocking chairs in children's departments, where the fingers of toddlers are constantly at risk.

> Fred knew a children's librarian who was forced to tell stories to children while seated in a rocking chair given by a donor so important that the chair could not be replaced with something sane. She said she spent the entire time frozen in place, terrified to move because children were gathered tightly about her with their fingers right by the rockers.

The other problem Fred found with rocking chairs was their tendency to creep backward in use. One library user in Fred's library slowly backed the chair into a wall, whereupon the back tip of one of the rockers ended up cutting a six-inch vertical slot right through the drywall.

By contrast, other library administrators found rocking chairs benign and harmless. The things that dismayed Fred never happened, users enjoyed rocking alone or with their children, and all was well.

Either way, local groups love presenting gift rocking chairs with brass gift plates to libraries. If you are like many librarians, you will be gratified, and if you are like Fred, you'll probably be stuck with more of that sort of thing than you want, because staff members accept the gifts without clearing things with administrators.

V-A-5. Problems with Soft Seating

Soft seating is important, but libraries have occasional problems with it. Lots of the problems are avoidable with adequate planning.

- Flammability. As mentioned in several places in this book, most upholstered furniture made in the US has polyurethane foam padding. Unfortunately, polyurethane form is impressively flammable, and it exudes unpleasant chemicals like cyanide when it burns. To meet flammability standards like the now defunct CAL 133, flame-retardants were sometimes added, but they can also exude nasty chemicals. The moral seems to be that libraries should avoid seriously overstuffed furniture. (To be realistic, libraries have lots of flammable materials that produce noxious chemicals when they burn. It's another argument for sprinkler systems.)

- Worn-out arms. Upholstered arms in soft seating tend to wear out quickly, and libraries do a lot better when their armchairs have wooden arms, or at least wooden inserts at the points of greatest wear.

- Excessive depth. Some soft seating is so deep from front to back that people can't sit with their backs against the backs of the seats without their legs sticking straight out in front of them, much in the manner of toddlers on living room chairs. (This is one reason you want to try out chairs before purchasing them.)

- Excessive general bulk. Some armchairs are impressively huge, with massive stuffed arms, 18-inch thick backs, and an amazing ratio of total bulk to actual sitting space. They make a statement, but we're not sure what kind. If you decide you want huge armchairs in your library, increase the minimum estimated space per chair in your building program. And think about all that flammable stuffing.

- Overly soft arms. It's much easier to arise from an armchair if it has firm wooden arms.

- Overly low seats. This is yet another reason you want to try out chairs before purchasing them.

- Infestations and urine. Libraries have had to destroy soft seating that became infested with bedbugs, or that was urinated upon or into. (Although one hates to sell college and law libraries short, it appears to be a public library problem.)

> One librarian Fred knows vowed to never buy another computer chair for public use that wasn't totally washable—basically a molded plastic seat with metal legs. (She never explained why people with bedbugs appeared to be particularly drawn to computer chairs, but that's where the bedbugs turned up in her library.) Other libraries try to fight part of the cleanliness problem by using plastic upholstery that is less easily ruined and easier to wash.

V-B. CHAIRS FOR SEATING AT TABLES

"Side chairs" (chairs intended for seating at tables) are available in a variety of options:

- Often you have a choice of chairs with arms or without arms. If you're interested in chairs with arms, have several people of different heights and diameters check them out.

- If the arms on your side chairs won't slide under the tabletops, you'll have a lot of empty chairs sticking out into aisles. Since cleaners often put chairs upside down on tabletops when they are cleaning floors, if you select chairs with arms, you may want to be sure the arms allow the chairs to be placed legs-up on tabletops without falling off or blocking aisles.

- Importance of strong joints. It must be possible to tip back and forth on chairs all day long without causing any damage. No cheap chairs (and few expensive chairs for home use) can withstand this.

- Two-position chairs. Chairs are available with bases that allow users to sit straight upright or tilt backward a specific amount. Apparently younger users like them, but older adults like Fred panic when the chairs start to tilt back (even though he has tried a lot of them and has never flipped over backward).

- Four separate legs vs. sled bases. Some side chairs have two wooden pieces that connect the bottoms of the legs on each side of the chair. They provide extra strength and may limit carpet damage.

- Casters. Some libraries equip the chairs at their reading tables with casters to make it easier for users to slide chairs in and out from under tables and to limit damage to carpets, particularly tearing carpets up at

An architectural firm specified these bucket seat chairs for a library conference room without ever trying one out. Although the chairs were from a big-name manufacturer, they were a disaster. The library staff concluded that the intent was to select chairs so painfully uncomfortable that meetings would last as short a time as possible. Sooner or later, everyone found alternative seating, and the chairs migrated throughout the building, ending up being contributed to a dumpster.

the seams. Chairs with casters are common in places like dining rooms of retirement centers.

- Padding choices. Typical options include padded or solid seats and padded or solid backs. Padding is more comfortable if your library is not panicked about dirt and/or bugs.
- Smooth or spindle backs. Some good-looking chairs are available with spindle backs, like Windsor chairs. Try them out first for comfort.

As with all chairs, trial sitting is vital. No matter lovely or historic or modern a chair looks, if it hurts to sit on it, it's a failure as a chair. If the chair has a spindle back, are the spindles comfortable to lean against, or do you find yourself wondering about the availability of pads that can be tied on?

If you're equipping a library with identical chairs, furniture vendors will lend you examples. Remember that no matter how cute it is, if it isn't comfortable, it's not "cute" in the deeper and more philosophical sense of the word "cute." Go for comfortable.

V-C. PADDED BENCHES

Libraries occasionally have small padded benches for users.

Some are just places to sit and rest a moment, away from regular tables and chairs. It there's a long hike between seating areas, users may appreciate intermediate seats.

One use of benches is to provide places for parents and children to sit together at computer workstations. (Or for two kids playing computer games together.)

Another place for benches is lobbies, for people waiting to be picked up.

V-D. BOOTHS

Some public libraries have installed diner-style booths, particularly for teenagers.

Diner booths have some advantages. They encourage a feeling of group support and privacy (even though if the booths are viewed end on, library staff can see every toe wiggle). Four-person diner booths can take up somewhat less floor space than four-person reading tables.

Some libraries have used a combination of free-standing tables and free-standing bench seats with high backs that can be arranged to create diner booths, with the knowledge that if fashions change, it's easy to rearrange the furniture.

V-E. WINDOW SEATS

Many public libraries have window seats. Window seats are welcoming and easy to build. Basically, they're just upholstered benches located beside windows, or in the embrasures where windows are located.

Problems with window seats occur when storage is provided inside the benches, with seats that lift up for access. Unfortunately, users

This attractive bay window includes a window seat for children, an armchair for an adult, and an unusually delicate light fixture that provides strong uplighting.

(particularly kids) can lift up the seats and then drop them, where they slam on other people's fingers or startle nearby readers with crashing noises.

Our preference is to not bother with trying to provide storage in window seats. If you can't resist, provide access through sliding panels on the fronts rather than from above. (See chapter 22 on "Collection Storage and Display.")

V-F. NOVELTY SEATING FOR CHILDREN

Some companies offer a wide variety of colorful seating units for children, snug places to sit and read where parents don't really fit. One company with a large catalog is Gressco.

Other libraries purchase backyard buildings in molded plastic, sometimes changing them seasonally.

Many libraries purchase stools for children and young adults. Be wary. Three-legged stools are far too tipsy for library use. High stools for use at counters seem hard to justify: lots of people don't like them, and they seem not to confer any benefit.

All sorts of unusual new chair designs turn up every year. Many furniture companies display them in their booths at library conferences because they attract attention. This is a good place to sit on one. Page in a leisurely fashion through the catalogs available in the booth while you see if your body is happy with the sitting experience.

V-G. FLAMMABILITY STANDARDS

Current federal flammability standards for upholstered furniture appear in the 16 CFR (Code of Federal Regulations) part 1640. The standards are in the U.S. CPSC (Consumer Products Safety Commission) Requirements for Upholstered Furniture Flammability.

As of June 25, 2022, all furniture must carry labels about its compliance with these standards.

Old furniture that has been reupholstered for sale must also be labeled.

Nonetheless, federal standards do not guarantee that furniture is not flammable, and in our opinion, avoiding large quantities of polyurethane foam—which means avoiding most overstuffed furniture in your library—is always a good idea for a variety of reasons.

VI. Placement of User Seating in Library Buildings

VI-A. ADEQUATE CLEARANCES

While some libraries have furniture comfortably spaced, too many libraries have inadequate clearances between furnishings.

- Sometimes inadequate clearances are a result of designers paring down the spaces listed in building programs. A first way to check for troubles of this type is to ask your architects to provide for each department or major area in the library a list comparing the programmed and designed spaces for each area of the building. If your owners and designers don't want to do this, expect to find trouble. Frankly, a lot of building programs don't allow a lot of extra space, so cuts can quickly become problems.

- No one who uses a wheelchair should find any aisles too narrow or any tables too low.

- Some designers faced with space limitations start changing the dimensions of furnishings, particularly reading tables, or by adding extra chairs to tables that are already sufficiently small. Make very clear in your building program what minimum sizes of tables you want in terms of the dimensions of the tops, and make sure that things don't change on you. Watch out for rectangular tables suddenly becoming round or for chairs suddenly appearing at the ends of rectangular tables.

- The area allocated for each table has to include floor space required for the table, seated readers, and the aisle space between and around occupied tables. Watch in particular for adequate aisle space.

- Sometimes administrative powers—such as school principals or superintendents—suggest library spaces that are simply too small to hold the necessary furniture. Your architects should step forward and announce that things won't work. But if they won't do it, you'll have to. Or better yet, get your building consultant to do it, since having your consultant fired is a lot better than having yourself fired.

VI-B. SEATING NEXT TO SHELVING

Never place seating so that chairs—particularly chairs at reading tables—back up against shelving.

No seated user should ever block access to adjacent shelving or seating. Comfortable clearances are about four feet. If a user seated at a table occupies three feet of space, the total space from the edge of the table to the nearest fixed object needs to be about seven feet. If we allow three feet for each user and a four-foot aisle, the space between the tops of adjacent tables with user seating should ideally be at least 10 feet.

Having chairs backing up toward bookshelves is often an extraordinarily bad idea because designers do not allow enough space for both readers at tables and people looking for books on shelves. One still finds it in century-old Carnegie-era buildings, where it's a source of serious dysfunction. But the designers of some modern libraries have experimented with the use of shelving to separate reading tables, simultaneously creating chairs that block access to shelves and endless small sections of shelving where call number order is a total mystery.

If seated readers block access to shelving, users looking for books have to ask seated readers to move. It's hard to find anything really nice to say about the idea of having seated readers blocking access to shelving, so building programs need to ban the concept in firm terms.

VI-C. SEATING BY WINDOWS

Generally speaking, people like daylight and books don't. If your library has a limited number of windows, you can deal with both books and readers by making sure that there are armchairs or reading tables by all of your windows.

We can't say this too often, because the problem turns up eternally. All exterior windows that face any direction except due north still need adjustable blinds, so the mere fact that there are no nearby books doesn't end the need for controlling direct sunlight. Of all areas where architects and librarians end up in conflicts, the failure by architects to control direct sunshine is one of the most common.

VI-D. MOVABLE SEATING

The vogue for information commons and flexible seating places even more stress on essential flexibility.

If students or other users are going to (a) rearrange the furniture and (b) nevertheless use their laptops, you'll need:

- Even, all-purpose lighting. The closer your space comes to an evenly lighted ceiling, the fewer problems you will have with glare and shadows. Occasional rectangular light fixtures won't do the job unless the ceiling is far higher than in most library reading areas. In our experience, what works best is 100 percent uplight fixtures with ceilings an absolute minimum of 10 feet high. Eleven or 12 feet works better.

- Electrical outlets all over the place. Talk with your designers and electrical engineers about what's available and meets codes. We assume that a floor grid of totally flush outlets a minimum of 10 by 10 by 10 feet is important in all public service and staff work areas, but in areas with movable seating this may be insufficient.

- Furniture on casters.

Sometimes it's hard to tell what's a fad and what's a trend, but information commons have been around for a while, and they may be a genuine trend.

VI-E. SEATING WITHOUT USERS' BACKS TO THE ROOM

In general, people don't like sitting with their backs to the room, especially when clearances are tight and other people are standing or walking right behind them. Even in an environment as pleasant and warmly sociable as a library, people don't like the feeling of unseen strangers brushing up against their backs.

This is one of the downsides of placing computer workstations on countertops along walls, especially if there's not much clearance between the countertops and other furnishings.

> Fred knows one library where the designers provided seats for computer users at a central counter that encircled a staff work area. The idea was that users would sit with their backs to the rest of the library, and that the library staff could reach them all to provide help. Unfortunately, users hated sitting at the counters, and the library ended up using the counters for storage. The repurposing was impressively evident.

The main advantage of computers on wall-mounted counters, of course, is they make it easy for staff to keep an eye on users' web use practices. But that seems a high price to pay if your users are all uncomfortable.

Instead of providing what amounts to a single, long table against a wall, consider setting a number of single-user-sized tables perpendicular to the wall. Now users at the tables have a shoulder to the room behind them rather than sitting with their backs to the action.

In general, tables are almost always better than counters because it's easy to move tables, while relocating counters can take major surgery. As this book says endlessly, it's almost always better to solve functional problems with furniture than with built-in stuff.

VII. Snappy Rules on User Seating

1. Few things are better than sitting in a comfortable chair by a window in a library, reading a new book, drinking coffee, and watching the world go by. All of this is possible in any library, with the possible exception of rare book rooms and archives, which take a dim view of both coffee and sunlight.

2. The only good way to serve all of your users all of the time is to make all tables for all adults accessible to people with disabilities.

3. With the possible exception of small children, all users need easy access to electrical outlets.

4. Beware of built-in stuff. Don't send architecture to solve furniture problems.

5. Library users don't like sitting facing walls with unseen people walking closely behind them. Things are a lot more comfortable if you rotate desk surfaces 90 degrees, with users' shoulders facing passers-by.

6. Many impressive historic library tables are unsuited for current library use. Sell them for a good price.

7. Even the sturdiest of library users need to use restrooms occasionally. Make provisions for the security of their laptops while they are away.

8. If a group of carrels looks like a swastika when seen from above, the fact that it twirls the wrong way will not palliate the offense.

9. Since the coming of universal laptops, study carrels need to be four feet wide.

10. You don't want sofas in your public library. Children and their parents can do well with small loveseats with wooden arms or with padded window seats. Adults who don't know each other won't share sofas; sofas in areas for adults simply create opportunities for sleeping and necking.

11. Older users have trouble getting out of low-slung soft seating.

12. Round tables are for conversation and for relaxed reading, not for work. Beware (as in be very afraid and extremely uncooperative) when your owners or designers start converting the rectangular tables in your building program to round tables.

13. Standard library tables are rectangular, with two chairs on each of the long sides. If your designers try to convert them to square tables with chairs on all four sides, stop them. If they try to convert them to round tables, take more serious action.

14. All tables need electrical outlets boldly installed in the centers, not hidden away discretely out of sight on the ends.

15. If your college dormitories are noisy and crowded, you'll need more study space in your library. Know what you'll do if 75 percent of your student body tries to crowd into the library during exam week. (If your public library is near a college, you may have experienced study-space overflow at exam times.)

16. Most upholstered furniture is padded with polyurethane foam, which is seriously evil stuff when it comes to fires. Flame-retardant chemicals are available but are nasty. So far, the score on polyurethane foam appears to be furniture industry 100, federal safety standards 0. (If you don't worry

about fire, think of the life forms lurking in the upholstered crevices.)

17. A current vogue is study areas with movable furniture. This means electrical outlets everywhere. When your designers ask, "Where will you put computers?" the answer is always, "Anywhere we want."

18. To check user space allocations on reading tables, draw dotted lines on sketches of the tabletops to show who gets what space. Any tables that end up with diagonals need to be rejected as possible purchases.

19. Users need to move comfortably between reading tables when all the chairs are occupied. Some owners and designers don't leave enough space. Check on everything, and show the drawings to your staff and building consultants. Ask your architects to have their schematic designs show all tables with chairs pulled out the way they would be when occupied.

20. Lamps on reading tables are a great idea. Even if the light isn't essential, it feels warm and comfortable. Rectangular lamps that run the length of tables are more functional. Round lamps are more attractive, but too many don't shed much of any light on readers' books. Experiment with sample fixtures before ordering a roomful.

21. Square reading tables are for a maximum of two users. Laptops with open screens provide helpful barricades between two users facing each other.

22. Library users tilt their chairs when reading. Yelling at kids won't help, so buy chairs that can take it.

23. Never place reading tables so that users can block access to shelving. The ends of tables that don't have chairs should face the shelving.

24. Never buy a chair until you've spent at least 15 minutes sitting on it.

25. If your designers want to create custom-made chairs for your library, be extremely wary. Insist on trying out samples that you can actually sit on, and compare them with standard industry products for comfort. Or just say "No" to your designers and buy standard seating.

26. If you visit a library and see that all the users seated at the reading tables are resting on their elbows rather than leaning back in their chairs, there's a good chance the library has lousy chairs.

27. Junior-sized tables for public libraries are available about one inch shorter than adult-sized tables. Avoid them, for the difference is inconsequential, and the usual outcome is the junior- and adult-sized tables and chairs simply getting intermixed.

28. Armchairs in libraries need wooden arms. Upholstered arms turn filthy overnight and threadbare after a few months. And the padding just adds more flammability to the library.

29. With the exception of folks playing video games, computer users need elbow room for books and papers.

30. Since users like light and books don't, put reading tables and armchairs by windows.

31. Posed promotional photos from the architecture and furniture industries sometimes show library users reading happily in direct sunlight. Yeah, right.

32. If each area of your library is assigned its own individual furniture color scheme,

you'll soon have piebald mixtures as you start regrouping furnishings.

33. Tables for use with several computers, such as hexagonal tables, offer the advantage of feeding a lot of wiring through a single opening in the floor. But the workspaces for individual users can be pretty cramped.

34. You can almost always have your upholstered furniture made up with your own fabrics. ("COM," as in "customer's own material," is a good phrase to know.)

35. Most good quality wooden library furniture is made to order, so don't expect to select from available stock. Production will take several months.

36. When you're selecting upholstery fabrics, look at swatches from at least a dozen feet away. Some fabrics with attractive up-close detail look muddy from a distance.

37. You can always buy some of your furniture later, but you can't build your library undersized and make it a little bigger later. And some generous people may offer to pay for extra furniture once they see the building actually going up.

38. The most fragile joints on a chair are the ones between the vertical posts at the rear (styles) and the horizontal supports of the seats (aprons). Good library furniture makers reinforce these joints on wooden chairs with metal-to-metal connectors.

39. Furniture manufacturers are notorious for being late. Lots of library grand openings take place with substitute furniture.

40. Never buy a chair with fewer than four legs. No matter how cute they look in the catalog, or how cute they sound in the vendor's booth at a library conference, or how cute they sound in your designers' descriptions, all three-legged chairs and stools tip over. When your users are abruptly dumped on the floor, you are unlikely to be happy.

41. Some of the most uncomfortable library seating we've ever encountered was custom-designed by architects. Always have a single chair built to your architects' design and then try it out extensively. Or just save time and money and say "No."

42. Buy strong. There is no theoretical upper limit to the number of teenagers that can occupy an armchair.

43. Always avoid architecturally mounted task lighting. If users move their chairs, you want the light to be just as good wherever they move them.

44. Ungainly historic reading tables can make interesting display units, but nine-tenths of your tables need to be actually usable.

45. Americans are getting more ample, and available seating reflects this. For example, wider versions of chairs can be user-friendly and easy to exit. The code word is "bariatric."

PART III
Essential Spaces All Libraries Need

CHAPTER 22

Collection Storage and Display

I. Introduction

Selecting the best shelving is an important decision because of the significant cost and the impressive longevity of the product. Steel shelving made in the nineteenth century is still in use in American libraries.

Because high-quality shelving will last the life of a building, decisions are forever. Trendy colors, for example, vastly outlast their popularity.

Even though shelving will occupy only part of a library, all library floors need to be strong enough to handle at least the weight of standard shelving—150 pounds per square foot. The tricky planning part comes when we use storage systems that require stronger and more rigid floors—including compact shelving and microfiche cabinets. The easy thing is to put these on a slab-on-grade floor, but sometimes they need to be on upper floors. Your engineers and shelving manufacturers will need to work together to be sure there are no problems.

Back in the days when books were scarce and precious, shelving could line the walls of libraries. But even the tiniest modern libraries have parallel rows of shelves with aisles for access.

Shelving mounted flat on walls is attractive, but the ends of reading tables need to face the shelving. If the sides of tables with chairs face shelving, users push their chairs back and block access to the shelving. Old Carnegie-era libraries tend to have serious problems with this, but some modern designers still try to lay out furnishings that way.

High-quality cantilever steel shelving is the standard of the library industry. Old wood shelving can be handsome, but for most librarians it tends to be a serious pain.

Much of collection storage equipment is at least partially inaccessible to users with disabilities. It probably represents the major area of access problems in libraries because of the quantities of space involved, and this book does not have an answer.

In addition to covering the basics of shelving, this chapter also mentions some of the standard ways non-book materials are stored.

Selecting stack aisle width is one of the most important decisions in library design. To avoid having building columns end up in the middle of stack aisles, leading to all sorts of awkward shelf placement and wasted space, the on-centers structural column spacing of library buildings needs to be a multiple of the on-centers column spacing of book shelving units.

II. Steel Cantilever Shelving

The standard of the library industry is steel cantilever shelving with decorative end panels. Except for situations where seriously ornamental shelving is required, we believe that anything else is a serious mistake.

Cantilever shelving has center columns with shelves that hook onto the columns. The name comes from the fact that individual shelves are cantilevered out from the central column. Typically, a shelving unit consists of a rectangular inner frame, feet that extend from the frame to support the unit and keep it from tipping, and individual shelves hooked onto the vertical members of the frame.

The two main varieties of cantilever shelving are starter-adder shelving and welded frame shelving.

With starter-adder shelving, the columns and spreaders are separate pieces. In a range of shelving, the first unit (the "starter") consists of two columns separated by two spreaders. Additional units ("adders") are each created with a single column and two spreaders.

With welded frame shelving, each unit consists of a rectangular welded frame. Multiple units are simply bolted together.

The easy way to check what you have in your library is to look at the uprights. If they are about four by four inches with no center seam, you have starter-adder shelving. If the uprights are about four by four inches and have a vertical division down the center, you have welded-frame shelving.

When people enter a library, they want to see books and staff. This bookstore has book shelving almost immediately inside the entry doors. A staff desk is close by but not visible in this photograph.

II-A. ADVANTAGES OF STEEL CANTILEVER SHELVING

Steel cantilever shelving is fairly easy to assemble, much like working with an Erector or Meccano set.

Cantilever shelving has leveling screws, often at the ends of the transverse feet. Leveling screws are important because poured concrete floors are seldom as flat as we would like them to be. If you relocate cantilever shelving, you will probably need to readjust the leveling screws. In fact, because floors are uneven, you may find that if the screws are adjusted for a different part of the floor, when you relocate shelving, things will be worse than having no leveling screws at all until you readjust the screws.

One of the advantages of cantilever shelving is that moving firms with hydraulic stack lifters can relocate whole ranges of fully loaded shelving. If you are recarpeting your library, not having to unload, disassemble, reassemble, and reload shelves can save you vast amounts of money in staff time.

When the time comes to recarpet, many libraries that chose not to purchase cantilever shelving end up cutting the old carpet around the edges of each shelving unit, leaving the old carpet under each unit, and simply replacing the carpet in the aisles. Among many other things, this makes relocating any shelving unit by even a fraction of an inch an unfortunate undertaking.

Cantilever steel shelving has the advantage of being capable of being repeatedly disassembled and reassembled. Welded frame shelving in particular is compatible with this treatment. With starter-adder shelving, however, the spreaders (cross bars that connect the vertical posts) may loosen eventually after many disassemblies and reassemblies.

II-B. SPECIFYING STEEL CANTILEVER SHELVING

About half-a-dozen US firms manufacture cantilever steel shelving. The products can be remarkably similar, to the point where shelves by one company may be possibly compatible with posts made by another. But never count on it.

One way to tell brands apart is by the vertical ends of individual shelves, which tend to have individual patterns.

The thickness of sheet steel is measured by "gauge." Somewhat counterintuitively, the smaller the number, the thicker the metal. However, we think the best way to compare shelving is in terms of mils, thousandths of an inch. Always inquire about the mils of components. The feet of shelving units will probably be the thickest, followed by columns, and then by actual shelves.

Many architects specify shelving the way they specify lighting fixtures, listing a preferred item and a couple of acceptable alternatives. Be careful to specify brand if your library has existing shelving it needs to match.

II-B-1. Paint

Standard finishes on high-quality steel shelving are electrostatically applied powder paint that is fused in place. For this reason, you can't repaint steel shelving unless you have someone who can apply powder paint in what amounts to a factory setting. Spray-on finishes, such as those in auto body shops, won't do. The abrasion on steel shelving is too great, and automotive-style paint will soon begin to rub off.

Because powder paint is extremely tough and permanent, and because repainting is difficult, libraries often sell off shelving in unwanted colors rather than trying to repaint it.

> Fred worked with a library in a town that actually had a powder paint factory. The factory's gift to the new building was repainting all of the library's steel shelving, which until that moment had been in a variety of varied and significantly obsolete decorator colors.

The point of all of this is that you don't want shelving in funny colors. ("Funny colors" includes trendy colors.) It's easy and cheap to repaint walls or change carpet, but changing shelving colors is another story.

The best shelving colors are those that are light enough not to show dust, light enough to not soak up all the available light, dark enough not to show every fingerprint, and neutral enough not to fight any future color decisions. We prefer pale gray.

II-B-2. Standard Dimensions: Heights

Cantilever steel shelving is available in a variety of heights. If you order a lot, you can have pretty much anything you want, but there are advantages to selecting standard heights, because you can order a few more sections without paying a fortune for a special order.

For adults, the standard shelving heights are seven feet (84 inches) and seven feet, six inches (90 inches). Many people find 90-inch shelving uncomfortably high, and 84-inch shelving is probably the more popular, with 72-inch and 60-inch gaining in use.

If you're stuck with 90-inch shelving units you don't really want, you can of course just attach the top shelves a little lower than the column heights allow. The spreaders between the posts will always stick up too far, but if you don't have unusually low ceilings, about all the difference it makes is a somewhat awkward appearance.

Since cantilever shelving operates in a fashion similar to Erector sets, you can often replace individual components you don't like with new pieces from the same manufacturer. For example, with welded-frame shelving, you can buy a new welded frame of a different height but use all the other components over again, including the individual shelves, feet, and front kick strip. (But verify this with the manufacturer.)

Lower shelving is used for children's materials, and you may be required to use lower shelving for accessibility reasons for reference books and current magazines. Check with your architect or state library or attorney.

For children's picture books, many catalogs recommend 42-inch-high shelving, but it's too low for three shelves vertically. If you use 48-inch shelving, three shelves of picture books will fit.

Many libraries use 60-inch-high shelving for children's books for upper grades, basically chapter books and junior nonfiction. With 84-inch shelving, there's room for seven shelves vertically of adult fiction and six shelves of adult nonfiction.

You can actually use seven shelves vertically for adult nonfiction, but you'll end up with a lot more oversized books. If oversized books are shelved in a different part of the building, most users will never find them. It's also possible to store oversized books flat on the bottom shelf, but this means dedicating a lot of shelves to the purpose, and this will in turn affect your space projections for shelving. And users may still not find the oversize books when they're just a few shelves down. Areas of the collection that run extensively to oversize books—such as art books—usually end up with only five shelves vertically.

With all these basic arrangements and notable variations, it is important to balance any recommendations on the number of shelves vertically based on your circumstances. Available floor space (a euphemism for available money), collection sizes, lending rates, and the need for a balanced use of space will be library-specific. Always experiment on a small scale with your own collection before ordering large quantities of shelving.

Staff members of new library buildings frequently leave the top and bottom shelves empty, so that six or seven shelves vertically begins its life as effectively four or five shelves vertically, with the remaining two shelves available for long-term collection growth. Short users, people in wheelchairs, and those with creaky knees all appreciate not having to deal with high and low shelves.

Some librarians worry that the public will criticize new libraries for wasting space with empty shelves, but most people understand the concept of room for growth.

II-B-3. Standard Dimensions: Depths

The individual shelves that hook onto the support frame come in a variety of depths.

When selecting shelving, it's important to realize that shelving comes in actual and "nominal" depths. For example, if you want shelving 11 inches deep, you may need to order nominal 12-inch deep shelving. Once again, check carefully with your vendor.

The nominal 12-inch deep description is based on the premise that there is a gap at the back of the shelf, corresponding to the thickness of the support column. The manufacturer takes credit for the open air at the back of the individual shelves. For example, with a nominal 10-inch deep shelf, the two-inch space between shelves where they are separated by support columns gets credited to the actual shelves, with each actual nine-inch shelf getting credited for an extra inch.

Most cantilever shelving uses 11-inch (nominal 12-inch) deep shelving for bottom shelves. This covers the cross feet that support the frames and the filler piece that connects the ends of the feet and fills the gap between the bottom shelf and the floor. Depending on needs, upper shelves in the unit may be either nine inches (nominal 10 inches) deep or 11 inches (nominal 12 inches) deep.

Shelving can be purchased with shorter base feet and shallower shelves. We've seen libraries with cantilever steel shelving as shallow as five inches (nominal six inches) or seven inches (nominal eight inches). Unfortunately, this often results in books sticking out over the fronts of the shelves.

On those rare occasions where books are all of the same depth (such as pocket-sized paperbacks) libraries have put blocks at the rear of shelves to keep all of the books aligned neatly at the front of the shelves. (One library Fred knows uses lengths of two-by-four lumber for pocket-sized paperbacks, which turned out to be just the right dimension.)

Shelving depths are usually described in terms of the upper shelves and the base shelves. For example, nominal 10-inch shelves with a nominal 12-inch base shelf is usually described as 10 over 12. If the shelves are all nominal 12-inch, it's described as 12 over 12.

Shelving shallower than nominal 10 inches is a bad idea, and base shelves should be nominal 12 inches deep. By using shallower base shelves, double-faced shelving units can be less than the standard two feet deep, but the space is skimpy, the units are less stable, and the saving in floor space is very modest. The libraries we've visited that have such shallow shelving don't like it.

II-B-4. Standard Dimensions: Widths

Virtually all cantilever steel shelving is sold in units three feet wide, and there are large libraries with many thousands of essentially identical units.

Occasionally, libraries will order narrower units to fit very specific situations. Because these are specialized and seldom sold, they tend to be more expensive than standard three-foot-wide units.

II-B-5. Bookends

Most cantilever shelving is available with some devices to keep books from tipping over on the shelves.

Companies may offer standard steel bookends, typically painted to match the shelving and perhaps with anti-skid bases, such as cork.

Some shelving is available with slots that run the length of the shelving, with bookends that slide in the slots. Some very small books may want to fall into the slots, but in general they appear to work fairly well.

Other shelving comes with sliding wire book supports that run in the folded-over bottom edges of the shelves above. By squeezing the front and back wires together, library staff can slide the supports snugly up to the last book on the shelf. If you want to have a support like this on the top shelf, you'll need a canopy over the top shelf. Check with the vendor to make sure this works.

Libraries often are concerned about the possibility of slender bookends damaging books that are forced carelessly into the bookends. Some people call this "knifing." Purchasing bookends that have wide front edges helps.

Our personal preference from years of personal experience putting books away is that the sliding wire supports are the easiest to use and the least likely to fall on the floor.

II-B-6. Accessories for Cantilever Steel Shelving

All sorts of accessories are available for cantilever steel shelving.

- *Lips* (*backstops*) to prevent books from falling off the back of individual shelves into the gap between front and rear shelves, vanishing into the murky depths at the bottom of shelving units. Some of these are simply pieces of metal bent upward at the back of the shelves, while others are separate pieces that are held in place between the shelves and the support columns.

- *Hinged tilting shelves* for periodicals. Shelving of this kind is designed to display the current issue vertically. By flipping up the display shelves, users can access stacks of earlier issues on flat shelves beneath the tilt shelves. Tilt shelves allow current issues to be in display binders, which is important if the library does not lend them. If you buy tilt shelving, be sure that the tilting shelves lock open. Shelves that just depend on balance tend to drop down on the hands (or heads) of people looking for back issues. There's nothing more annoying than having to hold a tilt shelf up with your shoulder while you use two hands to sort through the magazines underneath. Unfortunately, in our experience, tilt shelves are the only components of cantilever steel shelving that tend to go bad.

- *Flip bins* that hook onto cantilever shelving support columns. The most attractive ones pull out like drawers, to allow users to flip through materials like CDs that are too thin to shelve like books. Be careful to be sure how many items the bins you select will actually hold and still allow easy flipping.

- *End panels or end caps*. The ends of cantilever steel shelving units tend to look pretty industrial, and many libraries add end panels. For large stack areas, manufacturers will offer steel end panels painted to match the shelving. They may also provide simple panels covered in high-pressure laminates. For browsing or for open stacks, many libraries create custom-designed wooden end panels. Some have panels of laser-cut steel.

- *Decorative wooden end panels* are frequently designed by architects to accompany the general interior look of the library. You can also specify them yourself. You will need to consider:

    » Veneer. What kind of wood do you want? Do you want slip matching or book matching? (Book matching can look neat, but if the front and back of the veneer takes stain differently, you can end up with zebra striped end panels.) You will need to specify veneer thickness.

Although this is a door rather than an end panel, it illustrates the problems that can occur while staining book-matched veneers. Avoid unwanted stripes by specifying slip-matching or by specifying that adjacent veneers will show no signs of different staining.

    » Edges. Veneer is too fragile to run right up to the edge of end panels, and you will need some kind of solid wood banding to prevent damage to the sides and top. Anything thinner than half an inch is probably too thin. Some manufacturers have equipment that will do automatic edge band application, and you may want to ask around to see how thick the banding can be before manufacturers have to do it all by hand.

    » Kick blocks. The bases of end panels are subject to more abuse, and edge banding will probably not be sufficient to prevent damage. One possibility is solid wood end blocks three or four inches high and the same thickness as the panel.

» Finishes. Many clear finishes are too fragile. Other finishes are so inflexible that they can separate from the wood beneath if the finishes are bumped, leaving little white spots. (A lot of companies use pre-catalyzed lacquer. You can specify a "coin test" for the finished product, consisting of dragging a coin over the finish to make sure it doesn't separate from the wood below.)

» Inside material for the end panels. Usually this will be some kind of manufactured board. The section of board for each end panel is veneered, fitted with edge bands and kick blocks, stained, and finished. The quality of manufactured board can vary from impressively strong and permanent to total crap. Get help from someone who knows current products.

» Remember that aisle width is measured at the narrowest point in the aisle, which is probably the distance between the two end panels, unless you have an oblong book sticking out.

» End panels sometimes have slat-wall inserts to allow books to be displayed on the ends of shelving units. If you are ordering slat-wall end panels, be sure that the slats are lined with metal channels to prevent chipping the wooden edges of the slat openings. Plastic brackets are available from library supply firms for use with slat wall end panels. Be sure the front of the bracket (away from the end panel) is lower than the back, so the books slip down to the front and tilt backward. (Some brackets are designed in such a way that books slip to the back of the brackets and tilt forward, making it hard to see the covers.)

- **Canopies.** Canopies are steel or wooden tops that go over the top bookshelves. With low shelving, such as that in children's departments, they provide places to display books or other objects. With high shelving, canopies shield books from dust, but they prevent the occasional extra-tall book from sticking up slightly above the top of the shelving unit, and they can block light and make the aisles feel darker. For areas like children's departments in public libraries, canopies are often custom made to match end panels.

- **Divider shelves.** Individual shelves are available with high backs and with slots in the backs and shelves. Flat metal sheets fit into the slots and provide dividers to keep materials from tipping over.

- **Bottom shelves** that angle upward, making the spines of the lowest books easier to read.

II-C. COMPACT SHELVING

Compact shelving consists of ranges of shelving running on rails. It's tremendously popular with large academic collections, with archival collections open only to library staff, and for other situations where a relatively small number of people are using a large amount of shelving.

With compact shelving, one aisle provides access to perhaps 10 or 20 ranges of shelving, with the ranges moving back and forth to open up aisles where they are needed. Compact shelving permits far more efficient use of space.

Occasionally, libraries use compact shelving in ill-considered places. If you are planning a small or medium-sized public library, a small college library, or an undergrad library, you may find that compact shelving is a seriously bad idea. Users become annoyed if their access to a specific area of the collection is made impossible because other users are browsing in different aisles. And you may not want teenagers in your public library horsing around with compact shelving.

The two common varieties of compact shelving are "mechanical assist" and "power driven." Mechanical-assist shelving has hand cranks. Inside the end panel is gearing to make the shelving easier to move. (And requiring correspondingly more cranking to get somewhere). Typically the mechanism involves the equivalent of sprocket wheels and bicycle chains. It's usually possible to move an impressive number of ranges at the same time.

Librarians tell us that it's important to get mechanical-assist shelving that can be repaired by popping off the front of the end panel rather than having to unload books from behind the back side of the end panel.

Power-driven shelving uses electric motors to move the shelving back and forth. One advantage of power-driven shelving is that it comes with safety switches to prevent people trapped in aisles from being compressed in unpleasant ways. (Mechanical-assist shelving can simply keep squeezing as long as someone is turning the crank, another reason you don't want seventh-graders using compact shelving.)

Power-driven shelving can take a long time to get operating correctly, and some has controls that are impressively non-intuitive. If you are considering a brand of power-driven shelving, talk with directors of libraries that have the same brand. Or talk with users.

Archivists have told us they much prefer mechanical-assist to power-driven shelving.

Be sure to plan for the extra height of movable shelving. Rails are no more than an inch high, but the carriages that run on the rails are several inches high, and the steel cantilever shelving ranges are mounted on the carriages. Check with the designer of your sprinkler system to be sure that there's adequate clearance between the tops of the compact shelves and the sprinkler heads. Eighteen inches appears to be an absolute minimum clearance, but larger clearances result in less expensive sprinkler heads.

And be sure to plan for the extra weight. Converting from fixed shelving ranges to compact shelving can significantly increase the weight of fully loaded shelving per square feet, and if you don't plan in advance, floors may not be strong enough.

The weight of compact shelving can also cause floors to bend. The official name for this in building design is "deflection." If your floors bend, your compact shelving will want to roll downhill to the lowest point on the track, probably halfway between support columns.

For all of these technical reasons, you need to talk with technical reps of compact shelving manufacturers and with your structural engineers if you are considering a compact shelving installation.

Because compact shelving involves constantly relocating aisles, lighting for compact shelving consists of strip lighting fixtures installed end-to-end, perpendicular to the shelving aisles. No matter which aisle is opened, lights will be located above the open aisle.

III. Alternatives to Cantilever Steel Shelving

III-A. SHELVING WITH END-SUPPORTED SHELVES

One great feature of cantilever-style shelving is that the weight of the books holds everything tightly together. The books on individual shelves maintain the tightness of the joint between the flat surfaces and ends of the shelves, and in turn the weight of the books on the assembled shelf units keeps the connection between the shelves and the support columns tight. If components of the shelving shift, nothing falls down.

By contrast, in cheap shelving units, the individual shelves are often supported by the end panels. The shelf ends rest on pegs or clips extending from the end panels, or the shelves are slipped into slots in the end panels. In either case, if the end panel shifts a half inch or so, the end of a shelf may no longer be supported, and the shelf can simply fall.

> Fred once broke a rib when a handful of heavily loaded shelves in a cheap shelving unit fell on him, so he knows whereof he whines.

Some shelving with end-supported shelves uses metal tracks mounted vertically on the end panels, with metal clips that snap into holes in the tracks. On the better shelving of this type, the tracks are inset into the end panels, but on really cheap shelving, the tracks may be simply screwed to the surfaces of the end panels. As a result, books can catch on the tracks as the books are slid in and out of the shelving, tearing the bindings or dust jackets.

Steel shelving units with slide-in shelves are sometimes made of metal scarcely thicker than tin-can metal.

> Fred once inherited a children's department with shelving of this quality, and it would collapse without even being touched. Nothing is more fun than being in the library after hours and hearing unexpected crashes in the next aisle.

Although some physically attractive shelving is made with end-supported shelves, particularly shelving with heavy wooden end panels and painted steel shelves, we think it's a poor choice, even though it looks more attractive than cantilever shelving. (We see it most often in school libraries and in very small public libraries, where we suspect librarians may not have much input on decisions.)

III-B. WOOD SHELVING

Although steel end panels are available for cantilever shelving, most libraries have ornamental wooden end panels for use in public areas. This gives the libraries the strength and effectiveness of cantilever shelving with the attractiveness of wood.

Shelving made completely of wood seems to be a different matter. The libraries of the nineteenth century had access to first growth timber, but modern wood is a less sturdy product.

> Fred once consulted with a library that had wooden shelves that tended to sag. Every few months, the library would unload sagging shelves, flip individual shelves over so that they humped rather than sagged, and then reload them.

Good wooden shelving is also expensive, far more expensive than cantilever shelving.

Cheap wooden shelving may consist of chipboard covered with vinyl paper with wood-grain patterns. The problem is that chipboard varies from fairly durable to material that breaks as easily as soda crackers.

III-C. NON-LIBRARY SHELVING

Because good shelving is expensive, some libraries have experimented with other kinds, such as retail shelving, that are not designed for book storage. Most of these experiments are pretty awful.

Fred worked with one library that had shelving designed for use in hardware stores. The units were only about five feet high, they had no ends to keep books from falling over, and the shelves stepped inward as they moved up. As a result, the library could hold only about two-thirds of the books that could have been held by standard 84-inch shelving, and because the individual units had no ends, books were shelved in endlessly long rows, with bookends only at the end of each row of shelving units. Since a row of units was about 30 feet long, that meant a great deal of running back and forth by library users hunting for books.

The easy rule is: never purchase shelving not specifically designed for books.

IV. Shelving Placement

IV-A. ALL LIBRARY FLOORS NEED TO BE STRONG ENOUGH FOR BOOKS

Floor strength is vital and non-negotiable. Regardless of initial intent, libraries need to be able to store and display books anywhere they want, and buildings must be compatible with retrospective rearrangement.

> In the case of one public library, the architect ignored the program's requirement that all floors be strong enough to carry the weight of books. When the time came to add additional shelving, the library had a structural engineer check the floors, and only those areas designated for books on opening day were strong enough. As a result, the library had to re-engineer about half of its floor area, a tremendous waste of money.

Floor loading capacity is a major problem with repurposing non-library spaces. With the exception of slab-on-grade floors, few non-library spaces can hold the weight of books. See chapter 17 on "Converting Non-Library Buildings to Public Libraries."

IV-B. BE CAREFUL WITH PERIMETER SHELVING

Historic libraries often have walls lined with books. For reading rooms in great university libraries or the front rooms of Carnegie-era libraries, the effect is scholarly and elegant.

But perimeter shelving causes problems.

First, if a room has perimeter shelving, all adjacent reading tables need to be arranged with the ends that have no chairs facing the shelving. If the table sides with chairs face the shelving, readers will push their chairs back and block access to the shelving. This appears to be a particular problem in historic public library buildings. Historic university library reading rooms appear to more often have rows of tables running perpendicular to the perimeter shelving.

A second problem with perimeter shelving is that it has historically been installed on walls beneath high set windows. In the days when windows in libraries were intended primarily to bring in daylight, this was a great idea, but in many modern libraries users want to see the outside world while they work.

Another problem with perimeter shelving is that architects are tempted to set up perimeter soffits, often with recessed downlights and sometimes with the undersides of the soffits painted dark colors. The result is spotty light on the books located on the perimeter shelving. (When your architects mention perimeter soffits, assure them that you want crown molding instead. It's far more elegant, and it doesn't screw up your lighting.)

All in all, perimeter shelving belongs in historic reading rooms, but it's not a great idea in modern libraries.

IV-C. RANGES OF SHELVES BELONG IN PARALLEL ROWS

A handful of libraries have arranged shelving in radiating rows, something like the spokes of a wheel. This happens more than you would think and appears to have been done mainly because (1) architects selected non-rectangular interior spaces as a design concept, and (2) librarians like the idea of sitting at a single desk and looking down every aisle with a simple rotation of their head (an idea borrowed from the panopticon prisons of the nineteenth century).

The results of this approach range from disastrous to merely an extraordinarily serious annoyance.

If ranges of shelving are not parallel, space is inevitably wasted, with aisles wider than necessary as they radiate outward. Sometimes the situation is so extreme that partial ranges are tucked into the widest spaces between shelves.

A major university library has circular stack towers. In an attempt to make better use of the spaces, the spoke-like stack ranges consist of alternating full ranges, 1/3 ranges, 2/3 ranges, 1/3 ranges, and then full ranges again. Even then, a lot of space is wasted at the outer ends of the ranges, and the aisles in the inner ends are too narrow to comply with ADA requirements.

Other libraries attempting to fit stacks into circular spaces have provided breaks resulting in aisles that jog every few shelving units. This limits visibility and complicates provision of continuous call numbers.

The basic rule is that purposely creating non-rectangular spaces for shelving is an absurd idea. If people on your project bring up the idea, deal with them rapidly and severely.

IV-D. ABSOLUTELY NO DEAD-END STACK AISLES—EVER

One serious mistake libraries make when space is tight is to create dead-end stack aisles. Dead-end aisles seem to occur when libraries are out of space and decide to fill the gaps between ends of shelving ranges and walls by adding one more shelving unit to each range.

The problem with dead-end aisles is that users can be trapped or cornered at the ends of aisles. Unless the aisles are at least four feet wide, users who are blocked in aisles by other users have to ask the other users to vacate the aisles so they can get out. Even with really wide aisles, squeezing past another user is embarrassing. Or worse, a user may feel unsafe or uncomfortable in this situation. The only acceptable solution is to have no dead-end aisles whatsoever.

IV-E. AISLES ORIENTED FOR BEST PRACTICAL STAFF OVERSIGHT

Staff oversight of shelving areas can be improved by orienting shelving so that staff at service desks have the best possible view down shelving aisles.

The usual way is to place shelving so that the end panels face service desks. It's a lot easier for staff members at service desks to walk back and forth a few feet, looking down all of the shelving aisles, than to walk the entire length of a block of shelving to see into each aisle.

Some libraries have set up blocks of shelving on the diagonal to improve staff oversight. This seems to work well, although it requires a little more floor space. Aisles must be parallel.

An extraordinarily dreadful idea that occasionally reemerges is radiating shelving aisles laid out like the spokes of a wheel, with a service desk located where the aisles converge. See the section IV-C in this chapter for more information on the importance of parallel shelving units.

IV-F. ELECTRICAL OUTLETS EVERYWHERE

Except for major book stacks intended to remain unchanged for generations, shelving areas need recessed electrical outlets, ideally in flush-topped floor boxes. Libraries are always moving stuff around, and what's a shelving area today may suddenly become a reading or computer area tomorrow. Retrofitting the necessary electrical outlets is never as satisfactory, since the usual way is to core drill through the floor slab, and the result is an outlet raised at least a quarter of an inch above the floor slab. If the floor is slab-on-grade construction, things are even worse, since trenching through concrete slabs to retrofit electrical conduit is a major fiscal undertaking.

Some libraries install light fixtures mounted directly on shelving units. If power isn't available through the floors, the only other source is unsightly electrical conduit running up to the ceiling.

IV-G. UNBROKEN CALL-NUMBER RANGES

When a user comes to the end of a shelving range, and the last call number is somewhere in the middle of the Dewey or LC call number range, it should be obvious where the call number sequence continues.

The need for simplicity is one of a large number of major arguments against locating shelving in a number of small spaces.

> We saw a proposed architectural plan for a small college library that divided the collection among dozens of separate small rooms, not out of necessity but because the architect liked having dozens of separate small rooms. And all the rooms were to have opaque walls, providing huge numbers of spaces where people could be attacked. This is a spectacularly stupid idea.

Continuity of call numbers is one of the problems that emerges when shelving ranges are set at right angles to each other. How things continue from one range to the next can be mysterious. When ranges of shelving are set up in parallel rows, it's tempting to have the rows end not by a wall, but instead to have an additional single-sided range flat against the wall, but libraries that arrange things that way have to be sure that the contents of the extra range are clear to users.

Obviously, call number ranges cannot be continuous in libraries with stack decks. Ideally, numbers would start at the top deck and work down to the bottom, but with huge collections this is often impossible due to the cost of rearranging large collections. While major segments have continuous call numbers, these segments are not always in order.

Occasionally, expanded libraries will have historic library rooms with odd bits and pieces of shelving. One solution is to use these rooms for whatever sections of the collection will fit, possibly new books, current magazines, or some other inherently small collection. The other approach, of course, is to use relatively small historic rooms exclusively for seating rather than shelving.

IV-H. LIGHTING STACK AISLES

Permanently mounted lighting only works if shelving is also permanently mounted. Permanent shelving is typical of research libraries, academic libraries, and large public libraries.

Light fixtures can be installed over the aisles in stack units. Typically, these fixtures are installed end-to-end. To prevent the books at the top of shelving units from being far more brightly illuminated than those at the bottom, library fixtures are available that distribute the light more evenly. Be sure to review with the manufacturer how much variation in aisle width the fixtures can handle, or borrow a light fixture and experiment.

Lights parallel to aisles can also be mounted on shelving ranges. Typically, lights are mounted on alternate ranges of shelving, with arms that stick out from both sides of a range to support rows of lights over both aisles.

Other lighting schemes presume that aisles may be relocated occasionally. One way to do this is to set up rows of fixtures perpendicular to the book aisles, so that there are always light fixtures over every aisle and aisles can be shifted to make them farther apart or closer together.

Many light fixtures in the book stacks of large libraries have some sort of mechanism for turning off the lights when no one is in the aisle. You can use:

- Simple manual light switches. These presuppose proper human behavior, something in which automatic switch fanciers may not believe.

- Push buttons that turn lights on, with timers to turn them off again. These are annoying when they go off too soon, forcing users to return to the beginnings of aisles. And if users finish very quickly, they may want to find a way to turn the lights off when they leave.

- Motion sensors. These can be amazingly annoying to users who tend to stand still while looking at books.

- Pressure sensors in the floors of stack aisles. This approach offers the advantages of having lights always go out as soon as users leave the aisles, combined with *never* having lights go off when users are in the aisles. It seems to be the best of the currently available options.

Cross aisles will need to have lights on all the time, in order to (among other things) not plunge stacks into annoying darkness.

We think that automatic switching of lighting on the shelving of smaller libraries can be a very poor idea, especially if the automatic switching turns everything off rather than reducing the lighting level to perhaps half regular levels.

The selection of light levels is always a battle between those who want to use libraries for reading and those who are concerned primarily with energy savings. Light falling on the spines of books (as measured pointing outward, horizontally to the floor) shouldn't ever be less than about 20 foot-candles on the bottom rows. Vertical light, for users checking the contents of books, should be at least 50 foot-candles.

One public library has LED lights on the end panels in the stacks. Unfortunately, none of the light from the LEDs falls on the spines of the books.

IV-I. STACK AISLE WIDTHS

As indicated in the introduction to this chapter, selecting stack aisle width is one of the single most important decisions in planning library buildings.

Because selected aisle width can have a strong impact on column spacing, libraries need to designate aisle width during the programming phases of their projects. Basically, the center-to-center distance between building support columns needs to be a multiple of the center-to-center distance between book shelving columns. If this is not done, building support columns end up in the middle of aisles.

Accessibility requirements include minimum legal aisle widths. The ADA (Americans with Disabilities Act) requires minimum widths of 36 inches and recommends 42 inches. Individual states, however, may require wider aisles.

Aisles are measured at their narrowest points. Sometimes this is between the end panels at the end of ranges, and sometimes it's where books stick out into the aisle. At any rate, even if your steel shelving is all perfectly legal, your effective aisle width may not be acceptable.

It's also difficult to lay out aisles so exactly that they are genuinely parallel. If you're aiming at 36-inch aisles, one may end up 36 ½ inches wide while the next one is 35 ½ inches wide. Being legal on the average is not enough, since every individual aisle will need to be legal.

The moral is to never crowd minimum standards. If your minimum legal width is 36 inches and space is tight, you'll probably need 38 or 39 inches to stay out of trouble. But that's still pretty narrow.

IV-J. CROSS AISLES

Since most aisles are too narrow for users to pass each other, all shelving arrangements need cross aisles. The main decision is how many connected shelves a library should have before a cross aisle becomes necessary. If a first user needs access to a book and the aisle is blocked by a second user, the first user needs to circumnavigate the second user and come in from the opposite end of the aisle. Obviously, aisle segments need to be short enough so that third users aren't involved.

Our experience in public libraries has been that a cross aisle after about every seven attached shelving units is about right. Small college libraries will probably do all right with about the same spacing.

The number of cross aisles required in large academic libraries may be fewer. Because circumstances can vary widely, the best approach may be to hang out in your current book stacks for a while to get an idea of how frequently users find their way blocked by other users.

Cross aisles need to be at least four feet wide, and you may want wider aisles to make access comfortable for users in wheelchairs.

IV-K. SEISMIC ISSUES

Most double-faced shelving simply sits on the floor, but in areas with seismic activity some kind of stabilization is required. From the point of view of mechanical advantage, hanging onto the tops of the posts makes vastly better sense than bolting the feet of shelving units to the floor.

Protecting book stacks from tipping over during earthquakes is vital but beyond the scope of this book. Talk with your architects, engineers, and shelving suppliers.

IV-L. MULTI-DECK SHELVING SUPPORTED BY SHELVING COLUMNS

Many (if not most) early stack units used the vertical columns in the shelving units to hold up more than one level of shelving ranges. Walkways in the upper levels were supported by the columns.

Some early stack units had translucent glass floors to allow light from below to seep up through the glass and illuminate the spines of books in the bottom rows of shelving units. Interestingly, relatively few of these glass floor sections broke, and nineteenth century stacks with glass floors are still in use.

Many libraries with multi-deck shelving units have retrofitted boards between the walkways and the adjacent bottom shelves. According to popular explanations, this was to (a) prevent books from falling from one level to the level below, (b) combat feelings of acrophobia on the part of users who didn't really want to look down to lower levels right next to where they were standing, and (c) keep guys from trying to look upward through the gaps between walkways and shelves to see up girls' dresses.

Some multi-deck shelving units have been built with steel gratings for floors. This is not a sign of functional design. Imagine the problems for people in high-heeled shoes or using wheelchairs. And the fun of wondering if people are trying to look up your skirt from below.

The old multi-deck shelving systems we have seen are impressively inaccessible to users with disabilities. They are probably also fire risks, since with open spaces between floors and shelving units, fire could race upward, and there's no vertical space for sprinkler systems.

The old multi-deck shelving units had narrow aisles, very low ceilings, narrow staircases, and occasional extra tight places. When these units are removed and the space reused, the result is vastly less shelving.

Some manufacturers of cantilever steel shelving may still offer multi-deck equipment. In our experience, this kind of equipment tends to be inaccessible to people with disabilities and awkward and a fire hazard. *If you have it, you don't want it. If you don't have it, you really don't want it.*

IV-M. MARKING THE CONTENTS OF SHELVING RANGES

End panels on shelving ranges need small signs to indicate the contents of the ranges. Traditionally, these were holders for three-by-five-inch cards, although larger holders allow end signs that are more easy to read.

Until the coming of attractive computer printer output, libraries had endless problems keeping range content labels up to date and attractive. Libraries were full of labels crudely altered with markers. Some companies merchandized ingenious shelf-marking signs with movable plastic letters, much like Lego bricks.

Today, range markers are easy to maintain. Plastic label holders are available with transparent plastic fronts and slots for computer printout, and keeping things up to date is easy. The main challenge is keeping up with changes.

Labels change because sections of collections do not remain the same forever. New subject areas arise or old subject areas shrink, and both lead to shifting call number ranges.

Over the years, libraries have experimented with a variety of range contents indicators, and librarians have learned things in the process. Fonts used in range indicators need to be extremely legible rather than artistic, and contrast between lettering and background needs to be substantial—basically black lettering on white backgrounds. We know of one library that had signs with artistic script lettering done in dark gray on a light gray background, and users had to peer closely at the signs as they attempted to make them out. Permanent range indicators (such as the floor mats at the end of the aisles in the Seattle Public Library) seem like a recipe for eventual irrelevance (or forced sign-based weeding).

Overly specific call numbers may also lead to signs that are continually out of date. It doesn't cause problems if libraries shorten the call numbers on signs slightly. Users can easily check a shelf on each side of the end panel to see where the exact call number break actually occurs this year.

IV-N. SHELVING ON CASTERS

Some libraries use shelving on casters to allow the rearrangement of spaces for various reasons, most often to accommodate large programs. This has been more common in children's libraries, but it can be found in adult libraries as well. Some planning issues include:

- Weight. Even if they are on casters, shelving units are heavy.

- Stability. When you push units around, you do not want to have to worry about tipping them over. A 60-inch or lower A-frame will probably have enough stability, but taller units will not.

- Available space. Just putting things on casters does not guarantee flexibility. Where will you put the mobile shelving while you use the floor space for something else? If your shelving is inaccessible when you move it, how will you reconcile additional program space with loss of access to the collection?

Although this works, it strikes us as a desperate measure in the face of the lack of necessary program space.

IV-O. CURVED SHELVING

In recent years, a number of libraries or library designers have installed curved shelving, especially for display areas.

Individual shelving units that are manufactured to be curved are a genuine disaster. Books are rectangular, and trying to fit them into spaces that are shallower at the back than at the front is a terrible idea. If anyone ever suggests this, shout "No" in a particularly unfriendly voice.

Rows of shelving units can be arranged in curves. This can look very attractive, and the shelves hold books well, but the triangular open spaces between the ends of adjacent shelving units may be difficult to deal with. If the shelving units are double-sided, the triangular openings on the convex side can be fairly wide. If the shelving units are single-sided, they will need some kind of bracing to prevent them from falling over.

V. Other Types of Storage

V-A. FLIP BINS

Flip bins are useful for extremely slender publications with spines that are difficult to read if the items are shelved like regular books. Some prime candidates are CDs, 33 rpm records, children's picture books, and graded readers in public libraries.

Librarians tell us that the impact of using flip bins on the borrowing of picture books is powerful, but some library staff oppose the idea because the books are more difficult to keep in order. Our feeling is that user enthusiasm (measured in vastly increased lending) trumps staff inconvenience, but not everyone agrees.

Unlike cantilever steel shelving, flip bins do not always have standard dimensions. Your interior designer should be able to help you calculate capacities and required square footages for a product you select.

Flip bins for children's picture books lead to impressive increases in borrowing, but some librarians complain that they lead to more books out of order.

SOURCE: ENGBERG ANDERSON

Remember that a flip bin can hold only part of its capacity if users are going to flip comfortably through the contents of the bin.

V-B. SPINNERS

Some libraries store books on spinner racks, basically central posts with attached pockets or with additional spinners at the end of extension rods. Although somewhat larger pockets are available, small pockets usually mean rack-sized paperbacks.

Spinner racks may offer a cheerful and less daunting alternative to masses of seven-foot shelving. Spinner racks with transparent plastic pockets also allow users to see the front covers of a lot of paperbacks. Considering that paperback publishers can spend as much on the cover as on the contents, this allows library users to appreciate the art.

The small pockets in spinners may keep paperbacks from falling out as easily as paperbacks on regular shelving.

In general, spinner racks are high-maintenance objects from the point of view of those putting books away. Because the pockets are small, putting a book back in the right place can involve moving a lot of books around forward or backward to create space in the right place.

Because spinner racks have so many pockets, it can be hard for users to figure out the filing order.

Spinner racks can be easy to tip over. (One major library supply firm sold good-looking spinner racks with four plastic spinners on the end of arms that stuck out from the central column. When the spinner racks tipped over, the plastic spinners often broke, frequently enough that the supply firm catalogs listed replacement spinners. Library basements used to have abandoned spinner racks with all of the plastic spinners broken and discarded.)

Enthusiasm for spinner racks seems to come and go. They're probably most commonly used as racks for paperback fiction, where keeping things in proper order may be of less importance to library staff.

Our experience with spinner racks as library directors has not been positive. Or to put it more technically, seriously awful.

V-C. ATLAS CASES

Atlas cases are furniture units designed to store atlases and provide surfaces where atlases can be opened and read. They're important because many atlases will not fit on standard shelving.

Atlas cases are usually intended for users to stand up while consulting atlases. The top of the case will be sloped slightly, with a lip at the bottom to prevent atlases from sliding off while being consulted. Shelves beneath the top have space for storing additional atlases. Some shelves pull out on rollers to make it easier to retrieve atlases.

Some libraries have tried to cope with atlases by creating wide surfaces consisting of aligned shelves on both sides of ranges of double-faced shelving units. This creates a flat space about 24 inches deep and 34 inches wide. Although this technically works, it leaves it up to users to locate the atlases, pull them off the shelving units, and haul them to a nearby flat surface to view them.

Because maps don't lend themselves well to digital substitutes (except for wayfinding), atlas cases will probably remain standard items.

Atlas cases need enough free floor space for users to stand and to pull out shelves. See chapter 7, "Building Programs."

V-D. MAP CASES

Map cases consist of stacks of large, flat drawers, typically in units consisting of five drawers. Drawers usually have sheets of fabric attached to the back of the drawers and designed to clamp to the inside of the drawer fronts to hold loose maps in place and prevent them from curling up and being caught in the drawers.

Important features of map cases include double-extension suspension systems in drawers so that drawers are relatively easy to pull out. Good-quality map cases will have mechanisms like those found in filing cabinets to prevent more than one drawer from being opened at a time and overbalancing the unit. (Being squashed by a map case that tilts and falls is probably an unpleasant fate.)

In some map libraries, cases are stacked so high that users must stand on stools to access maps in the top drawers.

Most map cases available today are made of enameled steel. As with other steel products, libraries are probably better off purchasing all cases in a standard light gray color because they'll go with everything and can be moved from area to area of the library without creating odd patches of unmatched colors.

As with atlas cases, map cases take up a fair amount of room because the drawers have to be pulled fully out for users to retrieve individual maps. See chapter 7, "Building Programs."

V-E. DICTIONARY STANDS

Dictionary stands were developed because unabridged dictionaries are too large for ordinary shelving and require flat surfaces for consulting. Most stands are made of wood and designed for users to consult while standing. Dictionary stands have sloped tops with small ledges at the front to keep dictionaries from sliding off.

The tops of dictionary stands are intended for single dictionaries, but shelves below the top hold additional dictionaries. As long as copies of *Webster's New International Dictionary*, Second Edition, survive, libraries will probably want stands to hold them.

> Joe worked with a library to test the effectiveness of various aspects of merchandising (display) concepts. Surprisingly, they found that if you put your dictionaries and thesauri on face-out shelves, even at the end of a pathway through your building, they will circulate.

V-F. MICROFILM AND MICROFICHE CABINETS

The future of microforms may be something less than forever, but libraries still have large collections.

Microfilm is still used extensively for newspapers and census records. Fiche is used for journals and other publications.

Microfilm cabinets will store either 16mm or 35mm microfilm. A standard cabinet from a firm like Russ Bassett will hold over 500 rolls of 35mm film, and you can buy an extra cabinet that balances on top of the main cabinet to hold another 200 or so rolls.

Because fiche can be packed so closely together, a fiche cabinet can hold 125,000 individual fiche and may weigh 300 pounds per square foot when fully loaded. If you will be installing a number of fiche cabinets, ask your engineers and the cabinet manufacturer to be sure that your floors will be strong enough to support the cabinets.

Basic requirements for film and fiche cabinets include:

- Ball-bearing double extension hardware on all drawers.
- Locking mechanisms designed to prevent more than one drawer from being opened

at the same time. (Nothing's so much fun as opening too many microfilm cabinet drawers at the same time and having the entire thing fall over on top of you.)

- Powder paint finish in some innocuous color like light gray. (Strangely enough, the same color we recommend for cantilever steel shelving.)
- Label holders on all drawers.

Film and fiche cabinets are available in a variety of sizes, ranging from desktop units to floor-standing units with additional units on top with drawers that pull out like shelves. If your cabinets will be used for local newspapers, you may never actually throw any away, so plan for expansion.

V-G. DISPLAY SHELVES

V-G-1. Low-Density Shelving for Intensive Browsing

While steel cantilever shelving is the standard of the industry, there are circumstances where it's too compact.

A good example is new book shelving in public libraries. Some libraries have used 84-inch steel shelving for new books, and the results have been ugly encounters between users trying to see new books at the same time.

One standard substitute has been wooden A-frame shelving with three or four shelves vertically on each side. The shelves are all at a comfortable height for browsing, and because the shelves all tilt inward, it's easy to arrange books spine out or cover out as crowding permits. Multiple copies of popular titles, for example, are easy to display cover out.

V-G-2. Novelty Displays for Children's Books

Children's books lend themselves to novelty display units. Check manufacturers' catalogs and websites.

Our main concern is that it's easy to get carried away, substituting variety shelving for standard steel shelving.

VI. Super High-Density Storage

High-density storage is based on warehousing principles, with bins of books lifted by machinery and tucked into tall storage shelving units, often mounted on rails. Some are lifted by forklift trucks and others by cranes running on tracks.

The great advantage of many super high-density storage systems is their use of standard warehousing machinery rather than machinery developed for a vastly smaller library market.

Super high density storage is a separate and highly specialized area, one that we regard as beyond the scope of this book. A specialized literature exists, but if your library is planning super high-density storage you will need to visit other libraries.

Our main comment is that super high-density storage adjacent to main library buildings is infinitely superior to super high-density storage in another county. When library users request books, having the books in their hands in 10 or 15 minutes is a vastly better way to serve them than making them wait two or three days.

VII. Estimating Required Space for Collection Storage

"Estimating" the required space for collection storage is very much a matter of estimating. Needed space depends on aisle width, number of cross aisles, number of shelves vertically, average size of books, and other issues.

For basic information on space estimating for shelving, see chapter 7, "Building Programs."

VIII. Snappy Rules on Collection Storage and Display

1. Every area of a library needs to be strong enough to bear the weight of books. Flimsy floors are not a good way to save money. Question your architects specifically on this subject, for some have failed to make floors uniformly strong while not informing their clients of the decision.

2. One of the first and most vital decisions in library planning is stack aisle width, because it determines structural column spacing.

3. Don't *ever* buy cheap shelving. Steel cantilever shelving is the standard of the library world, and if you buy anything flimsier you will end up throwing it out. Or (more likely) wishing you could.

4. High-quality steel shelving can last a century, but it's extremely difficult to repaint. This tells us why bright orange or vivid purple is such a seriously bad color choice.

5. No matter how short your library is of space, never (as in NEVER, under penalty of being cornered in the 800s by a faceless fiend) have book aisles with dead ends.

6. All shelving aisles need indicators listing what's stored in the aisles. This changes frequently, so permanent markings are a dumb idea. Modern location signs have plastic fronts and accept computer printout, which makes things easy to alter.

7. To the intense chagrin of some designers, end panel indicators you can actually read and are easy to change are far more important than indicators that provide aesthetic gratification.

8. Shelving for one type of item does best in continuous ranges. Dividing it up into lots of separate chunks in separate spaces is A Very Seriously Bad Thing.

9. Shelving needs to be in parallel rows. Some libraries have arranged shelving like the spokes of a wheel, and this proved to be a Wretched Idea.

10. If you arrange shelving around the walls of a room, know how you will prevent people sitting at tables from blocking access to the shelves.

11. It's hard to shelve books in spinners, because there are so many small pockets. Spinners also tend to tip over in the presence of enthusiastic teenagers, who may be uninterested in putting all the spilled books back in order. And spinners tend to break when they tip. The easy rule is, "Never (ever) use spinners."

12. Cheap wooden shelving tends to sag, resulting in annual flipping. Libraries unload individual shelves, turn them bottom side up, and then reload them. If the end panels on cheap wooden shelving flex, the individual shelves also tend to fall. You will not like cheap wooden shelving.

13. If you're desperate for shelving and can't afford it, look around for libraries that are remodeling and have old shelving to dispose of. If you get it really cheaply, you can replace it without guilt when you have money (and pass it on to another desperate library).

14. We think the right price to pay for shelving that is not steel cantilever shelving is free, but the world is not always a perfect place.

15. Compact shelving places unusual loads on buildings. Your structural engineers will need to consult with the shelving manufacturers before the construction drawings are prepared.

16. In bygone days, the support columns in cantilever shelving were used to hold additional decks of shelving. If you are forced to consider something like this, check on code implications, especially for fire suppression and for accessibility for users with disabilities.

17. Some libraries purchase shelving that is difficult to move and then recarpet by cutting around the shelves and replacing just what's exposed.

18. Know how cantilever steel shelving is specified before ordering any.

19. When as a library user you're trotting along a range of shelves and they end at 327.8, it should be extremely clear where to find 327.9.

20. All book stacks require cross aisles to allow users to bypass each other. We think a cross aisle after about every seven shelving units works out about best, but your experience may vary.

21. There's always some new odd-ball collection format you'll want to store in your library. Hope for stuff that fits on standard bookshelves.

22. Cantilever steel shelving is an add-on system, and you can count on having to add on some day. Generally, it's not really practical to purchase lots of attic stock. When the time comes to match shelving, you will appreciate having shelving that's made in the US and can be matched.

23. Canopies are closed tops for shelving units. They're great on low shelving units, where they can be used for displays, but on high shelving the main thing they do is make things darker.

24. Shelves supported by clips on the end panels, supported by pins sticking out of end panels, or slipped into slots in the end panels, have a tendency to fall, dumping books on the place (or persons) beneath. Never use end panels to support your shelves.

25. Due to the weight of loaded shelving, any library with floors that cannot hold at least 150 pounds per square foot is an incredibly foolish idea.

26. Rows of shelving units can be arranged in curves, but there are design challenges. Individual shelving units that are curved are things you never (ever) want in your library.

27. Lighting in book storage areas needs to illuminate the fronts of the books on the shelves. There are examples of lighting the tops or ends of books instead, and they do not speak well of their designers.

28. Storage and display for a "library of things" depends entirely on your things.

PART III
Essential Spaces All Libraries Need

CHAPTER 23

Public Service Desks

I. About Public Service Desks

Functional service desks are a vital aspect of library design. Many staff members assigned to public duties spend the majority of their time at service desks, and badly designed desks can be a source of serious problems.

Libraries perform many services at public desks. An important part of the planning is deciding which services will be performed at which desks. While libraries such as small public libraries, school libraries, special libraries, and academic department libraries may have single desks, a large library may have a dozen or more separate desks, each with its own group of responsibilities.

Some of the basic needs that face service desk design include:

- Never let monumentality replace functionality. Too many service desks make architectural statements at the expense of practicality. For example, bizarre shapes like wild curves lead to impressive fronts and cramped staff areas behind. One of the jobs facing library administrators involved with building projects is preventing unworkably monumental desks.

- Maintain essential flexibility. Service desks need to be flexible, because library functions constantly change. It's tempting to assume that we've been changing for decades, but now all of that's over, and we know where we're headed. Unfortunately, we don't know where we're headed, and if we can't modify our service desks we're likely to be out of date in a matter of months. Desks need to be modular. They need to be capable of rearrangement, relocation, enlargement, shrinkage, separation, and combination with other desks. And there must never be overhead soffits that match the configuration of the desks below.

- Encourage staff to greet library users as they arrive.

- Provide individual staff workstations large enough for all the specialized equipment that may come along.

- Provide essential durability. Service desks receive a lot of wear. The tops of inexpensive lending desks frequently have their laminate patterns partly worn off. This is why libraries need to be extremely careful when purchasing ready-made desks from catalogs.

- Maintain proper lighting, including banning all recessed downlights and other lights that shine downward. Service desks are working areas, and staff and public need to be able to see everything going on. Light fixtures that match the configuration of the desks below are a major source of inflexibility.

- Never equip desktops with white (or very light) or black (or very dark) surfaces, both of which cause terrible eyestrain for users and staff.

- Keep staff occupied between customers. Because user needs vary in unpredictable ways, most service desks need off-desk spaces where staff can work on projects between helping library visitors. If libraries don't have desks that facilitate work, staff members may just sit idle when no users are present.

- Facilitate staff supervision. Among other duties, all service desks provide staff essential oversight. Architectural details that block lines of sight are sources of serious trouble. Some desks have raised barricades with narrow apertures where staff can peer out; they look weird as well as limiting oversight.

- Avoid staff tendencies to prefer back room seating to public desk seating. This may happen especially because staff are alone at service desks but can be in a far more pleasant situation (although partially out of the way) seated in a group.

- Provide essential adjacent support spaces. Service desks may require off-desk staff workspaces, off-desk storage spaces, public shelving for held books, outdoor book return and book pickup facilities, storage spaces for high-theft collections, book return and sorting spaces, and many other features in addition to the actual desks.

- Provide extensive electric wiring and data connections. Library service desks need tremendous technical support, and things can change every few years.

- Provide functional connections to automated book handling systems. Too many systems that move books between floors (occasionally dropping a few en route) have no space for the addition of an extra return slot.

- Maintain rectangular configurations. Unless the curves are impressively gentle, all service desks need to be rectangular.

- Meet all accessibility requirements. All service desks need at least one service point that meets all ADA requirements. Public and school libraries need service desks at convenient heights for children.

- Make clear to the public which areas of the desks are for staff only.

- Do not offer library users attractive shortcuts through staff spaces.

- Review options involving seats for users. Many reference desks have user seats, but seats at lending desks appear little used. Luckily, if chairs don't work, you can always remove them.

- Equip desks with drawers and cabinets. All drawers need to have full-suspension, double-extension hardware and have light-colored interiors that don't conceal the contents.

- Provide staff security. Desks must never provide spaces where staff members can be cornered. Desk designs need to make clear which spaces are for staff only. And desks need to be deep enough so that strange users can't reach across and try to grab the staff.

- Provide desktops that are pleasant to rest your hands on. Beware of elegant but chilly cut stone.
- Provide enough floor space on both sides of desks. Users and staff both need to be able to pass by each other without crowding.
- Provide service desks that are nowhere near "water features." (Better yet, provide nothing whatsoever that is near a "water feature.")

Library staff and administrators play critical roles in the design of service desks because they know how libraries work, where libraries are likely to be headed, and how staff need to be made available for public assistance. The opinions of library staff and library building consultants must always outweigh the opinions of library owners and library architects.

If you are a librarian, always remember that librarians know more about library service desks and their functions and pitfalls than architects, campus planners, interior designers, school principals, mayors, library boards, city councils, superintendents of schools, university presidents, provosts, corporate officials, and all manner of other people. Plan in advance, make your needs painfully clear, and be totally unmovable.

If you are not a librarian, leave the decisions up to librarians or learn amazingly fast.

II. Typical Functions of Public Service Desks

Libraries use public service desks for many fundamental functions. Among these are:

- Greeting library users
- Lending books and other things, including checking books (and other things) in and out, issuing borrowers' cards, collecting charges for late books, and other familiar functions
- Receiving returned items
- Providing reference services (answering factual questions)
- Providing reader guidance (advice on selecting fiction)
- Selling beverages and snacks and library T-shirts (and collecting charges on late books)
- Assisting users with collection access
- Computer assistance
- Providing information on an amazing variety of topics
- Dealing with interlibrary loan requests
- Supervising of adjacent spaces and maintaining library security
- Controlling entrances and exits (including checking user identification in limited-access libraries, such as those in private universities)
- Providing access to sequestered collections (including deliveries from remote storage)
- Providing held books, including interlibrary loan items
- Serving as telephone switchboards

- Providing assistance with mail and delivery services
- Registering for library events
- Staff workspaces

In small libraries, all of these services may be provided from a single desk for efficient use of staff, while large libraries may have a number of service desks. In almost all cases, however, some or many of the functions listed above will be combined in single desks.

The functions of service desks are frequently in flux. Traditional reference is replaced by computer assistance, sometimes combining desks in the process. Lending desks shrink as self-check workstations multiply. Information desks are created, shifting duties from lending, or information desks are abandoned and their functions returned to lending. Reference and reader guidance functions are separated or combined. Staff members in some libraries are cross-trained, resulting in fewer and more general purpose desks, while staff members in other libraries develop greater specializations, resulting in more desks.

All of these changes make the monumental, inflexible desks that many designers installed in the past an increasingly bad idea. Although designers may find them uninteresting, modular desks that can be expanded, shrunk, rearranged, and relocated are probably least likely to become obsolete long before they wear out.

III. Placement of Public Service Desks

In general, public service desks function best when they face users entering the library or a department of the library. Staff members at such desks are best positioned to greet users, answer questions, and keep an eye on things.

- The ideal physical arrangement for an area with a service desk is to place the entrance to the area in the broad side of a wall, with the desk set back from the entrance, facing the entrance.
- Many libraries have T-shaped circulation pathways in such spaces. A pathway from the entrance leads to the desk, and a cross pathway running the length of the space to the right and left of the service desk provides access to all the areas in the space. If access to all key elements in the space is provided by the two pathways, the result is basically a "main street" concept.
- In any library open to the general public, each architecturally separate area (such as a floor or a very large reading room) will benefit strongly from the presence of a service desk that can also provide supervision. Glass walls greatly improve the ability of service desks to supervise adjacent areas.
- Because desks are expensive to staff, planning for the most effective and efficient placement of service desks is extremely important.
- If there are two desks on a floor, the one serving the greater number of users should be closest to the point where people arrive on that floor.
- All public non-emergency exits need to be staffed, whether or not they have book theft

detection systems. Much of the challenge of service desk placement in libraries lies in making sure that desks provide exit control in addition to meeting other needs.

- If you have more than one service desk on a floor, it's great for safety if the staff members of the two desks can see each other.

IV. Evaluating Proposed Public Service Desks

Here are some things you can look for in service desks. Even a simple floor plan gives you many opportunities to verify functions.

- Evaluate sight lines. What areas of the library are invisible to staff members at service desks? How could you rearrange shelving, convert opaque walls to transparent walls, or make other changes to improve sight lines? Are service desks immediately visible to users entering major areas of the building? Some designers are tempted to arrange shelving like the spokes of a wheel, radiating outward from a central service desk, so that a staff member seated at the desk has simultaneous views of all aisles. Although it sounds tempting, this concept has led to extraordinarily bad space utilization, extreme difficulty in figuring out call number sequences, inaccessibility for people with disabilities, poor lighting, and many other serious problems. Say "no" swiftly and firmly the first time you hear this idea suggested.

> Good shelving is strictly parallel shelving. Radiating aisles are always evil.

- Make sure that the plans take maximum advantage of your limited number of staffed service points.

- Make sure that columns do not block access to any service desk. A library Fred worked on has a column so close to the lending desk that it essentially divides the desk into two separate desks.

- Make sure that service desks that will be staffed at all times are close to all security gates. The people planning or governing your library may not want to face the fact that *security gates are worthless if not closely supervised*. But that's the way it is.

- Evaluate book transport systems carefully. What effect will they have on long-term flexibility? Do they have areas that will be hard to reach if books fall off? If a system can't handle the numbers of books in your busier library, is it easy to add additional capacity?

Once a service desk is constructed, it may be a generation or more before your library can justify the cost of major alteration or even replacement. As with all planning, the time to check everything out is before the big expenditures begin.

V. Types of Public Service Desks

V-A. LENDING DESKS

Lending desks are found in almost all libraries, with the exception of some special libraries or research libraries that do not lend any materials. In a small library, lending is often only one of many functions provided by an all-purpose public service desk.

Because lending desks can be focal points of mass movements of materials, they require far more planning than other kinds of desks for functional layouts and for position in relation to such building functions as public entrances, delivery entrances, sorting operations, and so on.

V-A-1. Lending Desk Functions

The major functions of lending desks include:

- Checking out library materials.

- Providing access to self-check workstations.

- Exit control. Remember that staff members need to be within 15 feet or so of security gates, a fact ignored by many designers.

- Checking library materials back in. Wherever items are checked in, you will need floor space for bins of materials waiting to be checked in and for carts where materials are placed once checked in.

- Some libraries have provided two separate lending desks, one for checkout and a second for check-in, but these lost the advantage of staff checking materials in when between customers.

- Greeting library users. One of the extremely negative aspects of completely self-service lending is the loss of this important social contact.

> Sooner or later, almost every library hires a lending staff member who shouldn't be inflicted on library users. Library users can remember bad experiences with that sort of turkey for decades. Transferring ill-tempered staff members to technical services to get them away from library users is tempting but nevertheless A Seriously Bad Idea compared to Not Hiring Them in the First Place.

- Issuing borrowers' cards.

- Supervising the entrance to the library or department.

- Dealing with holds, interlibrary loans, and items retrieved from storage. Wherever holds and interlibrary loan items will be stored, libraries need to plan space for suitable shelving. To keep lending areas neat, some libraries have placed shelving for holds and interlibrary loans in back rooms, but the result is a great deal of time wasted by staff running back and forth to fetch them. Public self-service shelves can work well, but they're a problem if some books go on public shelves and others on backroom shelves.

- Serving as a library telephone switchboard. (Some libraries deal with incoming calls by installing automatic telephone-answering equipment, an astoundingly popular service.)

- Providing a place to sequester high-theft items.

- Providing reserve reading functions in academic libraries. In years gone by, separate reserve reading rooms with separate staffs were common in academic libraries. Although modern electronic reserves have made this function largely obsolete, copyright restrictions may result in hard-copy reserves never entirely disappearing.

V-A-2. Lending Desk Placement

Unless a library has a separately staffed security gate, it will almost certainly depend on lending desk staff to supervise users coming and going from the library.

To function effectively, security gates need to be close to service desks.

Some library owners and designers assume that an extra entrance can be left unstaffed, and any problems prevented by the installation of a security gate. But this doesn't work. Or, more bluntly, THIS DOES NOT WORK. When people want you to add extra public entrances to your library, always point out the staffing cost implications. The extra costs of extra entrances can certainly be worth it, but everyone has to know that there are extra costs.

Some libraries have used sales counters, such as coffee shops, to supervise extra entrances, but coffee shops—particularly in public libraries—have a high rate of business failure, and one can't count on them providing this function forever (or even after the morning coffee rush). If you are considering using a coffee service to supervise an exit, you'll need to plan how you'll staff the counter while coffee shop staff members are on breaks, let alone what you'll do when the shop folds.

V-A-3. Lending Desk Staff Spaces

Because lending desks are work areas, they need space for library staff, book carts, and return book bins.

If books are returned through slots in the lending desk, there will be receiving bins on casters under the desk. Desks lower than the standard 40 inches are too low for receiving bins. Often, books are checked in directly from a receiving bin, and this may necessitate two bins for each return slot. As bins fill, staff members pull them out to check materials in, replacing each full bin with an empty bin.

Most lending areas require shelving for storage of various parts of the collection, including holds, interlibrary loans, high theft items, and (as noted above) reserve items. There are also such miscellaneous functions as lost and found, storage of frequently needed supplies, and so on.

V-A-4. Lending Workrooms

Lending workrooms need to be directly behind lending desks to handle the constant flow of materials. Materials checked in have to be sorted (usually onto book carts) and reshelved. Incoming interlibrary loan materials have to be received and checked in, and users have to be notified. Returned materials that have holds need to be taken out of the flow of materials and set aside, and users have to be notified. Materials needed to fill interlibrary loan requests from other libraries have to be processed after they have been located on library shelves. Supervisory staff members need to have workspaces close to desks for oversight.

Building programs need to pay close attention to spaces required in lending workrooms. Features that require space vary greatly. In some libraries, lending workrooms are the primary staff workrooms, while in other libraries they are highly specialized. Possible lending-oriented space needs include:

- Desks (or offices) for supervisory staff.
- Workstations for checking in returned materials.
- Workspaces for volunteers.
- System printers for staff computers.
- Places where staff can telephone users out of earshot of other users.
- Floor space for carts loaded with returned materials.
- Shelving for supplies needed on a daily basis.
- Shelving for lost and found items.

- Shelving for incoming interlibrary loan books and for books on hold.
- Shelving for materials set aside for repairs.
- Filing cabinets for lending records.
- Worktables for unpacking shipments.
- Floor space for bins or totes used for incoming and outgoing interlibrary loans.
- Places to wrap and unwrap interlibrary loans sent by mail or delivery service.
- Safes for cash receipts. Small safes are available that bolt to the floor and have slots in the top for deposit of cash receipts.
- Card files for registration cards.
- Coat storage for staff.
- Lockers for staff purses or backpacks. Remember that you need a locker for each worker. Many young people who work as pages may carry backpacks where they keep wallets. For security, lockers need to be large enough for backpacks. Half-height school hallway lockers work well.
- Windows to the lending desk, so staff in the workroom can help keep an eye on the desk.
- Bulletin boards for staff information.
- Sinks for hand washing, which is important to staff members dealing with users who appear to be ill or who turn in surprisingly sticky books.

If check-in operations are carried out in a lending workroom, there will be less space needed behind the lending desk but at least a corresponding additional space in the workroom.

Many libraries provide private offices for heads of lending departments because of the large number of people who need to be hired, supervised, and evaluated.

V-A-5. Seated vs. Standing-Height Lending Desks

Lending desks can be constructed for staff to either sit or stand.

All desks need at least one area at seated height to comply with ADA requirements. The ADA permits heights from 28 to 34 inches. However, most office desks are about 29 or 30 inches high, and something similar may be the most comfortable for users and staff.

The ADA also requires at least 27 inches of clearance under desks, so if you opt for a 30-inch high desk, you will have only three inches available for the thickness of the desktop. And because not all wheelchairs will fit, there needs to be space for library users to take a side approach to desks.

Another possibility is adjustable height desks, which provide ergonomic benefits as well as flexibility.

V-A-6. Provisions for Book Return

Many lending desks have slots for book return, with receiving bins under the desk.

Bins are available from a variety of commercial sources. Some have bottoms that sink as the bins fill with books, while others simply have cloth bags to receive the books.

Some libraries provide separate return slots for books and for non-print materials, usually on the presumption that the weight of a large book falling on a recording may have an evil result.

Often these slots work very well, but there are a couple of potential design problems:

- A slot with a receiving bin needs to be in a full-height counter, 39 or 40 inches high.

- Return slots need to be in places where library users checking out materials and users returning materials are not forced to occupy the same turf.

- The openings at return slots have to be large enough to make the return of most items possible, while small enough to prevent people from reaching through slots to retrieve recently returned items.

- The chutes that lead returned books from return slots to receiving bins will probably have to bridge over raceways for wires.

Whether or not you have slots, you will need to be prepared for people simply handing materials across the counter. Your staff will need a convenient and close place to put these materials. (Your staff can always refuse to accept materials and direct users to the return slots, but calling this a less than friendly gesture is an altogether too positive view of the situation.)

A common practice is to separate return slots completely from lending desks. Some libraries have slots just inside entryways, leading either to receiving closets or directly to staff workrooms.

There are a couple of downsides to return slots in remote locations:

- If your library limits quantities on certain types of materials, people may arrive at the library, drop materials in the slot, and pick out new ones, only to discover that they can't borrow them because the old ones haven't been checked in yet. One easy way to cope is to set operating rules for computerized lending systems at double the number of items that may officially be checked out. If the limit on an item is officially four, the system may be set to allow eight, so that four items recently dropped off but not yet checked in don't prevent a user from borrowing four new ones.

- People returning items to slots hidden from the view of the staff may be more likely to include dead squirrels, ice cream cones, half-consumed beer bottles, and even incendiaries. Any book return slot that is not close to staff members must lead to a fire-resistant receiving closet with fire-suppression devices and alarms.

- Library staff will have to haul returned items much farther.

V-A-7. Desks with Off-Desk Workspaces

To make this work arrangement possible, libraries can place separate work counters behind desks. Counters of this type have to be placed so staff members standing there are facing users approaching the desk.

Some libraries have counters behind desks that force staff members to face the wall, with their backs to library users. Because these counters take up less space than counters where staff members face library users, architects frequently draw them that way, ignoring the necessity of staff facing users. You will need to be constantly alert to prevent counters from being designed this way.

V-A-8. Visual Barricades on the User Sides of Lending Desks

Lending desks are frequently designed with visual barricades to hide materials stacked on the desk and to prevent users from messing with computer wiring. Sometimes these are partial barricades, with staff members located in strategic gaps, while others run the entire length of the desks. Library supply catalogs are full of desks with front barricades. We feel strongly that these are bad ideas.

However, seated height service desks need modesty panels for the benefit of all parties.

V-A-9. Queuing Space

Desks need space for users to queue up for service. This is common at lending desks, but on busy days, queues can form at reference desks and computer help desks. Users can line up for individual staff members, but many libraries provide consolidated waiting lines.

The advantage of a single queue is that no one "picks the wrong line" and ends up behind a user who is prepared to argue all afternoon over a two-cent late fee.

> We realize that two-cent late fees disappeared with the Harding administration, but it's more fun to say "two-cent late fee" than "two-dollar late fee."

Consolidated queues require floor space. They also require some way for users to understand where the line begins and ends. To accomplish this, some libraries have elaborate structures built of metal bars, all reminiscent of devices to encourage cows to return to the correct barn. Unfortunately, structures like this are extremely awkward during low-traffic times, as one can notice in airports. They can also consume a great deal of floor space.

Our experience has been that about all one needs to do is to define the front of the line clearly. Sometimes all that it takes is a single sign saying, "Wait here for service."

V-A-10. Sorting Rooms

Many libraries maintain sorting rooms where recently returned books are sorted prior to being reshelved.

Although this sounds like a very logical function, in practice people reshelving books fall behind on their work, and sorting rooms frequently consist of mounds of materials. Books that fall into categories of materials that are hard to reshelve may be passed over by staff in favor of easy tasks like reshelving mystery stories, leaving more challenging books to vanish into layers of bibliographic permacrud, perhaps not emerging for weeks.

In the meantime, if online lending systems inform users that these books are on the shelf, the result is expensive reference staff rooting helplessly around sorting rooms, just in case the missing books are there.

By contrast, public sorting shelves tend to stay neater because failure to keep up is too obvious.

Having been there, we think public sorting shelves (also functioning as "recently returned" shelves) greatly reduce staffing costs and improve the quality of library service.

V-A-11. Automated Book-Handling Systems

If you think your library may convert to an automated book handling system, talk to vendors about space needs.

Sorters can take a lot of space, particularly if you want to be able to switch full and empty bins.

Some libraries have installed book-handling systems with an insufficient number of return slots. It will help you a lot if the structure of your building allows the installation of additional return slots.

Some libraries have installed book-handling systems that transport books between floors. Be sure to work out with your vendor how this will take place, and what you will do if books fall off the transport system.

Librarians with automated book handling systems joke about "sorter bin envy," but it will help if you have space to extend your sorting system if you turn out to need additional bins.

If you want outside book return slots, you will have to decide whether they will feed directly to the sorter equipment—and how your system will handle the very large quantities of materials that can be returned overnight or during a holiday weekend.

V-A-12. Drive-up Book Returns with Receiving Rooms

Most libraries need some provision for return of materials while the library is closed.

Many libraries have slots leading into rooms with receiving bins.

One main problem with these arrangements is that people put incendiaries into slots and set buildings on fire. The Danforth, Connecticut, library was set on fire in 1996, but it happens elsewhere. A small-town library Fred worked with was nearly burned down when someone shoved a flaming object through a mail slot that served as a book return.

The solution to the problem is to always have book return slots lead to fire-resistant receiving spaces. Losing the contents of the book return closet is a lot less annoying than losing the entire building.

One problem with book return slots is that vehicles come in many different heights. A slot that is at a convenient height for a Hummer won't be at a good height for a Miata. Installing slots at two different heights is possible, but you need to be sure that the lower slot has enough clearance in the receiving room for a receiving bin on casters.

Drive-up book returns need one-way driveways, so that drivers can lean out their windows to drop books into the slots.

Drive-up book returns also need fairly generous driveways that allow cars to straighten out and sidle up to the slots. Frequently, driveways are too short, with tight curves leading to short sections of straight wall. As a result, drivers cannot pull up closely enough to the return slots.

You may have arguments with your designers about driveways leading to book returns. The designers may insist that the driveways are just fine, when in reality almost no one can make them work.

Whether or not you have a drive-up external book return, you'll need a walk-up return. It's possible that one return can serve both purposes, but having pedestrians and cars share the same area is always tricky.

Because of technical problems with drive-up returns, some libraries have considered return slots with three-minute parking spaces beside them.

Book returns are a problem during holiday weekends because they usually need to be emptied a number of times over a weekend.

Some libraries remove receiving bins during holidays and just put a mattress on the floor, so that staff will not have to stop by the library several times a day to empty the bins. (If the door to the room swings inward, overflowing books may get in the way of door swing.)

Depending on design, some book returns can be impressively noisy.

Because of the noise associated with drive-up book returns, we need to be careful where they are located in buildings. Probably the worst places are rooms adjacent to program rooms. Sometimes the falling of books can be heard in the program rooms, and sometimes staff members have to trudge through program rooms when events are taking place, in order to empty book returns.

The easy solution is to always have access to book returns from service corridors and not from public spaces.

Some companies make fire-containing returns with metal chutes leading directly from the exterior slots to enclosed steel receiving bins. However, these returns can make an incredible amount of noise, and it's not fun to watch users and staff leaping convulsively every time a book is returned.

The morals of this section are:

- Users expect to find after-hours book returns at all libraries.
- Book returns that lead directly into library buildings can offer a serious threat of fire.
- Driveways for drive-up book returns have to have curves gentle enough to allow drivers to actually pull up next to the return slots.
- Different vehicles require different heights of book returns.
- Both pedestrians and drivers need return slots.
- Book returns are inherently noisy, and the receiving bins need to be kept away from user and staff functions.

V-A-13. External Book Return Bins

Rather than deal with book return slots, many libraries purchase curbside book return bins.

One of the great advantages of freestanding return bins is that fire cannot spread from the bin to the rest of the library.

As with return slots in buildings, curbside bins require arrangements where bins are on the drivers' sides of cars. This can mean a one-way driveway, which works well, or bins perched on medians in streets, which leads to difficulties with cars stopping in fast lanes and with staff members unloading bins in traffic.

Bins are typically available in more than one height, but even then, drivers complain that they are too high or too low.

Bins are usually available in carbon steel and stainless steel. Our experience is that stainless steel is a lot more expensive up front, but that carbon steel can rust out in a couple of seasons.

Protecting return bins from collisions with cars is always a challenge. Typically, libraries create bollards consisting of six-inch steel pipe filled with concrete. The necessity of bollards is indicated by the amount of colored automobile enamel that rubs off on them.

With well-designed bins, the top sections with the return slots can be separated from the base sections with the access doors, allowing the return slots and access doors to face in whatever direction is best for the library.

V-A-14. Exterior Book Pickups

Some libraries install exterior book pickup boxes. Typically, these resemble banks of large personal PO boxes. Library staff members check out requested items to users and put them in boxes, which are open at the rear for staff access. A keypad next to the array of boxes allows users to enter code numbers. When users enter code numbers, the appropriate boxes pop open. And when users take the books and close the boxes, the access number is canceled.

Libraries that installed these systems assumed that they would be used for after-hours book pickup, but the primary users proved to be people for whom it would be awkward to come into the library, such as parents with children in car seats or elderly couples where one of the two could not be left alone in the car.

Early book pickup boxes were suitable for inside locations only, but modern ones are weatherproof. The main thing that goes wrong is ice forming in the openings between the doors and the frames.

Libraries have told us that wind tends to whistle through exterior pickup boxes, and that the boxes need to be serviced from a hallway or service area rather than from a staff area.

V-A-15. Lending Service Windows

More and more libraries have drive-up service windows. Easy access to a call button, and simple staffing models help both patron satisfaction and operational budgets. A bit of education is needed so that patrons know they can pick up only items previously placed on hold.

Some libraries have told us that users tend to treat lending service windows like McDonald's, not just picking up held items but assuming they can drive up and place a subject request on the order of "I'd like four books on the War of 1812."

Anyone who had drive-up service during the pandemic can attest to its utility in such circumstances.

V-A-16. Additional Lending Desk Spaces

Lending desks are frequently located in high-traffic areas. In a well-designed small public library, the desk faces the entrance and separates the children's department from the adult and young adult departments. (Nothing repels a young adult faster than finding YA books shelved with children's books.) Locations of this type mean that lending desks need a substantial amount of extra elbowroom. People moving from the entrance to library departments will pass by the desk, as well people traveling between departments.

In addition, libraries tend to locate other features next to lending desks because this is a convenient location. For example, you may need:

- Security gates. Magnetic security systems require a space of at least three feet between the security gates and a door. Architects who don't realize this have created libraries where the doors to the lobby have to be locked open in order to prevent proximity to door hardware from setting off alarms. See chapter 35, "Security," for a more extensive discussion of security gates.

- Self-check equipment. If your library will have self-check equipment, the best place for it is close to the lending desk. Self-check workstations can take a surprising amount of space, not because the stations are huge but because of the floor space for users using the self-check stations and other users queuing up for their turns. And users may need staff assistance while attempting to use self-check equipment.

- Spaces for public photocopiers. Many people come to libraries specifically to copy items that are not part of the libraries' collections. From their point of view, a location right inside the entrance is optimal. Remember that public photocopiers always require small tables where users can put materials they are copying, plus floor space for people waiting to use the machines. Copiers never become less complex, and public photocopiers need to be located near friendly library staff, who will routinely be called up to untangle electronic puzzles.

- Spaces for coin-operated fax machines. Fax devices take up less space than photocopiers, but the planning issues are the same.

- New book displays. In some libraries, new book displays are part of lending departments. Shelving that is heavily used, such as shelving for books and book sale books, requires extra space for people to stand. A-frame units with only three or four shelves vertically are available for new books.

- Used book sale displays. Even libraries that have occasional monster book sales may find that a small used-book display unit near the lending desk generates a surprising amount of cash over the course of a year. Some libraries have shelving, while others have decorative carts or other types of furniture. If your library will have used book sale shelves by your lending desk, remember that you will need storage space for books used to restock the shelves. Interestingly, used book displays encourage honesty. Some libraries attach coin boxes and find they result in greater payments per book.

- Displays of recently returned books. Some public libraries put recently returned books out where users can browse through them, while others specialize in rapid reshelving. Both approaches can be vastly better than sorting rooms.

- Spaces for small displays. The areas around lending desks are one of the great places for displays of books of extremely current interest.

- Areas to sort incoming and outgoing interlibrary loan traffic. If a library receives interlibrary loan materials in bins or totes, it will need floor space to stack these while materials are being processed. This will be particularly true in branch systems or in libraries with reciprocal borrowing agreements. Similarly, if libraries have a lot of outgoing materials, they may need floor space for as many bins as there are delivery routes.

The main point of providing this long list of possibilities is to emphasize that what looks like generous space around a planned lending desk may sometimes be unrealistically small.

V-B. REFERENCE AND READER GUIDANCE DESKS

While in smaller libraries—particularly public libraries, school libraries, and academic department libraries—all services may be provided from a single desk, middle-sized and large libraries usually have reference desks.

In reality, of course, the term "reference desk" is increasingly a misnomer. Reference service has changed in major ways since the advent of library automation, to the point where library professional staff members revel happily when asked the very occasional actual, genuine reference question that lends itself to traditional reference techniques.

V-B-1. Reference Desk Functions

Professional staff members at reference desks provide a wide range of services, including:

- Traditional reference service. Old-fashioned reference questions still continue to be asked, even if there are not enough of them to justify a single-function reference desk.
- Reader guidance. Many public libraries provide reader guidance, helping users find books—particularly fiction—that they will enjoy reading. A few libraries have separate desks for reference and reader guidance, in some cases only a few feet apart. Sometimes two desks look like serious overkill, but if a public library's adult fiction and nonfiction collections are on separate floors, a separate reader guidance desk on the fiction floor may make sense. Separate reader guidance desks may also be useful if libraries have completely separate staff for the two functions.
- Computer assistance. One of the main functions of reference desks is computer assistance. People who a decade ago might have asked a question about (for example) Afghanistan, now come to the desk and plaintively say, "I just looked up 'Afghanistan' on Google, and I got 17 million hits. Now what do I do?" If you visit libraries with separate reference and computer help desks, you may see the reference desk standing idle while users are lined up in droves at the computer help desks. We are convinced that having separate reference and computer help desks makes very little sense either functionally or economically.
- Supervision. Most reference desks are also responsible for supervising the departments they serve.

V-B-2. Reference Desk Heights

The majority of reference desks appear to be seated-height ones, but this can vary with the needs and preferences of the library.

Remember that to meet the requirements of the ADA, you will need one section of the desk no more than 34 inches high, with knee space at least 27 inches high underneath. However, 34 inches is too high for seated staff and users, and too low for standing staff and users, and 30 inches works a lot better.

V-B-3. Determining the Number of Service Points at a Reference Desk

When you are planning a reference desk, you may be adding additional functions, and you may therefore need additional spaces for staff.

In addition, many service desks provide occasional seating for volunteers. At the time of summer reading club registration in public library children's departments, for example, the reference desks may have two or three times the usual number of people.

V-B-4. Implications of the "Roving Librarian" Concept

Many libraries have been planning roving librarians, staff members not tied to a desk but rather out on the floor assisting users.

While this appears to be a very successful idea, unless professional librarians are willing to wear colorful vests in the fashion of employees at some big box stores, they can be extremely difficult to find.

> Fred saw a reference desk in a Dutch library that consisted of a high stool, a computer on a tiny shelf, and a post with a little round sign at the top with an "i" for "information." He also waited by the desk for 10 or 15 minutes, hoping to ask the librarian a question, but eventually gave up because he couldn't tell who the librarian was, where the librarian was, or even *if* the librarian was.

V-B-5. Reference Desk Placement

Because reference desks usually have an important secondary function of overseeing library interior space, the strategic placement of reference desks is important.

It's also important that reference desks be immediately visible to people entering a public service department.

In modern libraries, public-use computers tend to require the most staff assistance, and they need to be as close as possible to reference desks. In addition, giving some of the engaging materials available on the Internet (with or without filtering), placing public Internet computers where library staff can see the screens is useful. (Obviously this doesn't apply to libraries with separate reference and computer help desks.)

Reference desks also need to be close to reference collections, but in many cases these collections are shrinking or totally gone, often being replaced by additional computer workstations. This is one of many reasons why it is so important for libraries to have (a) multifunction lighting and (b) access to electrical power and data conduit everywhere.

V-B-6. Storage at Reference Desks

Compared with lending desks, reference desks require relatively little storage space.

Many libraries have traditionally had "ready reference" collections of books that reference librarians used almost daily, but these may be largely gone.

Some libraries hold materials for readers at reference desks. For example, a librarian in a public library may select books for a schoolteacher and hold them until the teacher arrives at the library and can review the materials with the librarian. If your library provides this type of service, you will need additional storage space at your reference desks.

Other materials stored at reference desks typically need drawers. Frequently these materials consist of standard forms and office supplies (which users constantly ask to borrow).

V-C. DESKS FOR ENTRANCE AND EXIT CONTROL

Some large libraries have staffed desks at their entrances that have no function other than security. Typically, a staff member there checks the identification of people entering the library and monitors adjacent security gates for those exiting the building.

Desks of this type are especially common in private academic and research libraries that limit entrance to the library to their own students and faculty, or that want to identify users.

For a private university, national or state library, or similar limited access institution, such desks may be essential, but the person who works there may spend a lot of time sitting.

V-D. INFORMATION DESKS

A few libraries have separate desks that take over the functions of greeting users, providing orientation and information on library programs and events, and similar activities.

We have the impression that staff members at information desks are often short of things to do, and that these desks may be vulnerable when budgets become tight. The lending desks—which traditionally performed general greeting and orientation functions—take the functions back from the information desk staff.

It may be possible to staff information desks only during peak hours. We envision problems, however, in attempting to train users to try the information desk first and then (if and only if the desk is closed) turn to the lending desk. One possibility is portable desks that can be placed out of sight when not in use.

V-E. MULTIFUNCTION DESKS

Almost all public service desks in libraries perform multiple functions, but the assortment can vary from desk to desk and from library to library. In larger libraries with multiple desks, duties are occasionally rearranged and regrouped. Most desks are responsible for assisting users and keeping an eye on things, but after that almost anything can happen.

Because of the variations in staff duties, it's sometimes hard to decide what to call a service desk. Some libraries experiment with more accurate names, only to find that users are confused.

> One library changed the sign over the reference desk from "Reference Desk" to "Ask a Librarian." It struck us as a brilliant name, but they later changed it to "Ask a Librarian / Reference Desk."

VI. Public Service Desks and Security for Staff

Public service desks are generally very safe places, but there are many things libraries can do to make their staff members more secure. For more ideas, see chapter 35, "Security."

- Always design desks so that there are at least two ways out from behind. If some threatening person comes behind the desk, the staff member there has an easy exit.

- If you have a video-based security system, place cameras to record the faces of users (rather than of the staff).

- Consider panic buttons. Panic buttons should be connected to annunciators in a couple of key places, such as administrative offices and main lending desks. Panic buttons can also be linked directly to alarm services.

- Pay close attention to line-of-sight supervision. If staff at desks can see staff at other nearby desks, it's much easier to keep an eye on things. Always avoid unnecessary opaque partitions. Blocking sound works just fine with glass partitions.

- Provide enough space to allow staff at desks to step backward if someone reaches across.

An extra couple of inches of depth in desktops can make a major difference.

- Consider enclosing desks with barricades with swinging doors. (Swinging doors can also be a real pain. Be sure doors have mechanisms to allow them to latch open, and be sure they have single swinging panels rather than double panels, since trying to push a book truck through an opening with two swinging panels requires an abnormal number of arms.)

VII. Common Problems in the Design of Public Service Desks

Historically, there have been many functional problems with service desks. Some of the most common are listed below.

VII-A. MONUMENTALITY

Some service desks are ungainly and inflexible because they were designed as architectural icons rather than as functional furniture.

One can understand the desire of architects to create something dramatic and memorable with service desks. Functional modern libraries tend to consist of large open spaces that offer disappointingly few opportunities for architectural design, and designing a desk can be really satisfying. As a result, service desks are sometimes built with dramatic illumination, brushed steel fronts, sweeping curves, flickering colored lights, water features, elaborate soffits, and so on. Some of these details are fun, while others are at best engagingly dysfunctional.

Service desks cause particular problems when they are round or semicircular, because essential contents don't fit well into curves. Drawers are almost impossible to install. While the desks are immense from the outside, they have very little space for the staff within. If a circulation desk is round, working with essential book bins and book carts may be nearly impossible. (Historic libraries frequently had round lending desks, demonstrating the historic longevity of bad ideas.)

VII-B. INFLEXIBILITY

Many service desks have been constructed under the ill-advised presumption that technology and library procedures and public needs will never change.

Circular service desks are frequently very attractive, but there's not much staff space inside. It also is a great deal more difficult to install storage shelves and drawers.

Small, round service desks look attractive from the front, but they provide amazingly little interior space for staff to stand, plus awkward storage space.

A large number of service desks, for example, have matching soffits with inset task lighting. If the soffit matches the configuration of the desk exactly, the desk can never be enlarged, shrunk, or relocated without the expense of tearing out or heavily modifying the soffit. Or having the relocation of the desk apparent to all who approach it.

Typically, soffits over service desks have recessed downlights. Can lights (circular recessed downlights) provide what is probably the worst light one can find in a library, joyously combining uneven illumination, rigidity, unpleasant shadows, and glare.

Moving or relocating soffits can be a particular problem in libraries with sprinkler systems, because individual sprinkler heads may be located on the surfaces of the soffits, forcing alteration of the sprinkler piping if the soffit is altered.

Other desks may have ornamental pendant lights, bright lamps in small glass globes. You don't want them either.

While this is a handsome service desk, the lighting structure above means that reconfiguring or relocating it will involve major surgery—or leave everything looking unusually awkward. Always shout "No" when designers suggest matching soffits or other fixed structures over service desks.

Service desks can be constructed to function at both standing and seated heights. If you are planning these for accessibility, check with your architects about current requirements, such as user legroom below countertops.

SOURCE: ENGBERG ANDERSON

VII-B-1. Modular Desks

Due to changes in library technology and services, service desks are more practical if they are modular, but too few desks are designed this way.

Desks are also more flexible if they are installed on top of carpet, so they can be relocated if necessary.

It's possible that freestanding desks might occasionally creep in use, but the libraries with modular desks tell us they have no problems.

If your library has modular service desks, it will be vastly easier to enlarge or shrink them. For example, vast increases in lending may make it necessary to add additional service points. Or wholesale conversion to self-check equipment may make it possible to reduce the size of a lending desk.

As library functions change, service desks sometimes need to be relocated. If a desk is modular, moving it can be easy, but if it's a monument, or it has a matching soffit or special lights, relocating it may cost more than a library can reasonably afford.

Some libraries find that staff space behind service desks is simply too small, and that desks have to be relocated accordingly.

Modular desks can consist of units that simply bolt together. Moving the desks requires unbolting the units, disconnecting the wiring, shoving the desks around, and bolting them back together.

Some libraries have constructed service desks from office system components, with similar gains in flexibility. If not elegance.

For a modular desk to be successful, both ends of every section need to be finished, so no matter how components are rearranged, there are no raw ends exposed.

VII-B-2. Movable Desks

In addition to using modular desk construction, libraries can ensure flexibility by avoiding architectural features that determine exactly how large a desk can be and where it must be located.

Some of the undesirable features that lead to inflexibility of desk location include:

- Matching soffits.
- Special downlights installed to match the location of the desk.

In addition to inflexibility, of course, most downlights create unpleasant glare. People who make the mistake of looking up are blinded by concentrated light, and the concentrated sources of light create unpleasant veiling reflections. In addition, harsh downlights cast strong shadows, which aren't a happy thing at any service desk.

VII-C. FRAGILE DESKTOP SURFACES

Planning the tops of service desks, particularly lending desks, require the attention of staff and careful discussion. You will want to review durability, reflectivity, color, ease of adding openings for wiring, and comfort to the touch.

A number of materials are unsuited for service desktops because they are too fragile. This is particularly true of lending desktops, which are subjected to a great deal of friction as books are slid back and forth.

- A common example of insufficiently durable materials is ordinary high-pressure laminates. If the pattern is wearing off your lending desktop, consider replacing the high-pressure laminate with any one of a number of similar but more durable products, such as solid-core laminate or acrylic polymers, where the color goes through the material rather than just being printed on the surface.
- Wooden desktops are also too fragile. This is particularly true with modern wood, which is less durable that the wood used in some century-old desktops.
- Some libraries have used glass or transparent plastic to protect the surfaces of service desks, and these are almost always a mistake. There are two potential problems. First, many such surfaces are shiny, subjecting the eyes of users and staff to annoying reflections, particularly reflections of overhead light sources. Second, of course, glass breaks, and transparent plastic soon becomes scratched and cloudy and basically ugly.

Some of the most common materials used for successful desktops are acrylic polymers (Corian is a common trade name) and stone. Both are sufficiently durable to withstand the constant friction at lending desks, in part because the color goes all the way through.

- We prefer acrylic polymers because they are warm to the touch, can easily be drilled for grommet holes, and come in an immense variety of colors. And they don't chip.
- Stone is more elegant than acrylic polymers, much more expensive, and much colder to the touch. Some stone is porous and needs to be sealed periodically. And unlike acrylic polymers, it can chip.

Because most libraries add electronic equipment to service desks over the years, it should be possible to add additional grommets (openings for wiring) to the top of the desks. Desktops that are nearly impossible to drill may be a mistake for this reason.

Selecting colors for service desktops is a matter of function as well as aesthetics, so do not simply delegate the decision to a designer. In general, colors with middle values work best. Very dark colors soak up a lot of light, and the contrast between white paper and a dark desktop may lead to eyestrain. White desktops reflect too much light and may therefore lead to eyestrain.

Reference desktops receive slightly less abuse, but they are still subject to vastly more wear than reading tables, where standard laminates are usually sufficiently strong.

VII-D. PERSISTENCE OF OBSOLETE DESKS DUE TO SENTIMENT

If you have a historic library with a painfully obsolete desk, users may insist that it remain in service because they remember it from their childhoods.

Unfortunately, many of the beloved desks in historic libraries are semi-circular, with the characteristic total lack of staff space within. Most are also far too small. Many have tops that are made of fragile materials (such as wood), and many are equipped with obsolete features (such as recesses for circulation card tubs).

Sometimes you can expand and remodel a desk like this, but it's probably better to find a politically acceptable way to repurpose it (or even to tuck it behind the furnace).

VII-E. FORTRESS DESKS

Some service desks have all the warmth and welcome of a castle parapet. Vertical panels form barricades on the front of the desk that hide the staff. Sometimes the barricades have narrow openings through which staff can peer cautiously into the outside world, much as defenders peered through the sawtooth crenellations on the walls of medieval castles. On other desks the barricades are continuous, with the staff nearly invisible behind.

Many of the inexpensive desks in library supply catalogs have barricades, and enough desks are designed this way to make a fast review of functional issues worthwhile.

Why you might think a fortress desk is a Good Thing . . .

- The great advantage of fortress desks is that the barricades in front conceal debris piled on desktops. If staff members at a lending desk are checking in magazines or doing other work between users, the desk will look neater if their work is largely concealed.

- Fortress desks with crenellations may help clarify the location of service points. Users will know that they are most likely to be helped where there are openings in the walls.

- The protective panels in fortress desks may keep library users—especially small children—from playing with exposed computer and telephone wires. Most wires of this type are vulnerable because they travel at least a few inches across desktops before vanishing into grommet holes.

And why you might find fortress desks A Bad Thing . . .

- Fortress desks may limit the ability of desk staff to oversee the library. To the extent that staff members are hidden behind barricades, they may not be able to see what's going on.

- Fortress desks may encourage mess. If everything on the desktop is visible, staff members may tend to be neater.

- Fortress desks interfere with a sense of warm greeting for library users. If library staff members appear hidden away, users may feel less welcome.

- Fortress desks with crenellations can exude a kind of medieval feeling, with library staff peering nervously through defensive opening.

- Lending desks that have fortress fronts without crenellations force staff members who are checking books in and out to hand them to users over the top of the barricade rather than simply sliding the books across the desk. This means that every transaction forces staff members to extend heavy objects at arms' length. We assume there may be health implications.

- If barricades are continuous but counters are seated height, users may peer awkwardly over the barricades to see the staff seated below.

- If library technology changes, the more complex construction of fortress desks may lead to more frequent needs for expensive remodeling.

One attractive alternative to barricades is the use of heavy panels of patterned glass directly behind the desktop computer monitors, to hide wiring and keep children from playing with it. Panels of this type are far less intrusive and off-putting than actual barricades, and they lend themselves to easy alteration if desk uses change.

VII-F. OBSOLETE FEATURES STILL FOUND IN LENDING DESKS

Almost all service desks will change function over the years, and libraries need to plan for changes in usage. Unfortunately, many desks are designed or sold with features that are both inflexible and soon obsolete.

A good example of obsolete design is lending desks with recessed openings in their tops for card tubs that held book cards or "transaction cards." Book cards were used repeatedly, but transaction cards were generated for each transaction and discarded when books were returned.

Manual lending systems of this type were a royal pain, and once electronic lending systems actually started working well, librarians abandoned card-based systems joyously.

While small libraries may still use card tubs, most of the tubs have been made obsolete by

Years ago, lending desks often had recesses for the tubs that held the lending records—either book cards or transaction slips. The recesses survive in some old lending desks, creating more awkwardness than assistance and stressing the importance of flexibility in all desk design.

automation. Libraries with lending desks with cutouts for card tubs are then required to rebuild their desks or come up with creative uses for large rectangular recesses in what should be smooth desktops.

> Librarians who are nostalgic for card tubs probably have more cuticles than they really need.
>
> Actually, few librarians miss card tubs. In Fred's library, long ago, a little girl leaned over the children's department card tubs and threw up. Since all the information on the location of all the books in use was in the card tubs, the staff couldn't just toss the cards out. So the staff member with the least seniority ended up hosing off the cards. And then went home sick.

We've seen a number of brand new school libraries with service desks with openings for nonexistent card tubs.

VII-G. SOFFITS AND BAD LIGHTING

An unfortunate but popular design feature for service desks is to build matching soffits over them and install can lights in the soffits. The result is inflexibility, harsh lighting, glare off shiny surfaces, unpleasant shadows, and spotty illumination. Always say "No!"

VII-H. BAD ACOUSTICS

Service desks are potentially noisy places for conversations, telephones, computers, and miscellaneous machinery. Lending desks in particular tend to radiate noise.

Unfortunately, lending desks are frequently located in inherently noisy areas. If a lending desk is located in an atrium with a ceramic tile floor and a skylight, the result will be an extraordinary amount of racket. And if the atrium is open to upper floors of the library, the entire building may be permeated with amplified noises of lending.

VIII. Library Supply Company Service Desks

Some standard library supply firms offer components for service desks.

The good point about these is that they encourage flexibility of design. By purchasing a variety of components and bolting them together, the library has the ability to rearrange components, add additional sections, or relocate the entire desk.

Some limitations include:

- If the tops are made of high-pressure laminate, they will be too fragile to function well for lending. On lending desks in particular, the colors and patterns on the tops will soon wear through. Solid-core laminate and acrylic polymers are strong enough for library use. Be sure to specify strong materials when you order desks.

- Sometimes individual modules have ornamental ends so that there are no raw ends visible when components are rearranged. However, if these ends stick up above the desktop, the result may be a service desk with low dividers every two or three feet. But that's a lot better than raw, exposed ends.

IX. Snappy Rules on Public Service Desks

1. A service desk is a service desk, not a monument.

2. The chance that any service desk will provide the same functions decade after decade is about the same as the chance that your lovely new computer will last you 50 years.

3. Most service desks need occasional rearrangement, relocation, readjustment, and repurposing. Inflexibility of construction is not a virtue. Chant the word *modular* when speaking with your designers.

4. A matching soffit with recessed downlights over a service desk ensures a strong and happy combination of inflexibility and glare. And potentially high cost to eliminate, due to having to relocate sprinkler piping when you remove the soffit. Always say "no" to all soffits, "no" to all recessed downlights, and "no" to all other lights that don't point upward and reflect off ceilings.

5. When service desks are being designed, always seek detailed input from the people who use them. All of these people have been employed in libraries. Few (if any) desk designers have been employed in libraries.

6. Almost all service desks in libraries perform multiple functions, one of which is always supervision. An overcomplicated building design that requires separate service desks simply for supervision may lead to fiscal unhappiness.

7. Staff members at service desks should face users entering the space, not be hidden around a corner or behind a partition, and not be working at a counter facing a wall.

8. Lending desktops suffer amazing abrasion. Cute but fragile materials will soon not be cute. Standard high-pressure laminates are cute but fragile. So is wood.

9. A crenellated service desk front that resembles a castle parapet makes the staff members behind it look like they expect users to act like Viking raiders.

10. Roving librarians are a user-friendly idea, but if they're not at their desks, how will users ever recognize them or find them? Or even know they exist?

11. Curved service desks can look massive from the outside but have almost no staff space inside.

12. A public service desk is no better than the people who staff it. If your employees are unfriendly, no architectural elegance will compensate.

13. You don't want library users behind service desks. Make it structurally clear which areas are "behind."

14. All exterior windows that face any direction except north (including monitor windows, clearstory windows, and skylights) need shades. Nothing handicaps a service desk faster than an ornamental window high above the floor that admits uncontrolled direct sunlight and blinds the staff at the desk. Readers who are blinded by the sun can move to a different part of the library, but staff members are stuck at the desk. (This is a very common problem, and we are not making it up.)

15. If you have a local cabinet firm construct a service desk for your library, remind them

to think in terms of modular furniture rather than kitchen cabinets.

16. If you have two service desks on a floor, it's good for security if the staff at one desk can see the staff at the other desk.

17. If you have two service desks on a floor, it's convenient if the busier desk is closer to the elevator and stairs.

18. Service desks need to have tops with medium hues. Both black and white tops are a serious mistake.

PART III
Essential Spaces All Libraries Need

CHAPTER 24

Program, Activity, and Study Rooms

I. Introduction

The great majority of libraries include one or more special rooms for public programs, meetings, classes, tutoring, and quiet study.

Frequently these rooms serve a wider purpose than the narrow function of the library. Academic libraries have classrooms and seminar rooms and faculty studies. Public libraries have rooms for library-sponsored programs, community programs, children's crafts and stories, committee and board meetings, and tutoring. Special libraries have rooms for confidential meetings of organizational staff. School libraries have rooms for study groups.

Most program and study rooms are intended to control noise, either protecting users from the noise of the rest of the library, preventing users of the rooms from disturbing the rest of the library, or providing security for closed meetings. In large meeting rooms, the ability to hear performers or other presentations becomes an important issue. Because of these concerns, the acoustics of program and study rooms is an important consideration.

Heating ventilating and air conditioning of program and study rooms is challenging because many rooms alternate between empty and crowded. Many librarians complain that the program and study rooms in their buildings are either too hot or too cold, and either stuffy or drafty. Because of the widely varying demands of these rooms for temperature control and air supply, they cannot be simply piggy-backed on the air circulation and controls of large adjacent spaces. Even in tiny libraries, meeting rooms need separate thermostats.

Many program rooms have security issues. Parent institutions may essentially take over program rooms. Faculty studies in academic library book stacks may raise supervision issues. Study rooms in public libraries should be glass boxes but are often not. Multipurpose meeting rooms need secure storage areas but may not have them.

All sorts of program rooms offer great naming opportunities during fundraising for library construction. The fact that the library will announce endless future meetings taking place in the "Thompson Room" makes the donation especially attractive.

This chapter begins with a review of general planning issues that affect most program and study rooms, then discusses individual types of rooms and their special needs. Our intent is to avoid duplication of material, but inevitably some concepts are mentioned in both of these sections.

II. General Features of Typical Rooms

II-A. RECTANGULAR ROOM CONFIGURATION

The right floor shape for almost all meeting rooms is a simple rectangle with the front of the room narrower than the sides. This approach provides the best possible viewing of projected material, since viewers to extreme sides of a screen see distorted and frequently dim images. It also provides the best sight lines.

Unfortunately, many meeting rooms are built in odd shapes. Among those we have seen are:

- Banana-shaped meeting rooms, where people at one end cannot see people at the other.
- Meeting rooms with oddly irregular floor plans, which prevent logical arrangement of seating or tables. For example, there are meeting rooms with abrupt triangular projections or with unexpected curves. None of these improve functions.
- Trapezoid-shaped meeting rooms where rows of chairs get shorter or longer as one progresses from front to rear.
- L-shaped meeting rooms, where a speaker visible to everyone in the room has to stand in one corner of the room, at the bend of the L. Under these circumstances, speakers have to speak in two different directions, and a projection screen at the center has to be viewed at about a 45-degree angle by most of the people in the room.

Most of the odd floor shapes we have seen were a result of gimmicky exterior designs rather than of functional necessity, but occasionally they were the result of difficult expansion projects.

If your designers propose anything other than a simple rectangle, it's time to challenge the concept.

II-B. DETERMINING ROOM CAPACITIES

A major problem in planning program and study rooms is determining the number of people each room should be designed to hold.

In situations where individual public school classes will use rooms, standard class sizes are used as a guide. Pessimists will want to provide extra seating on the presumption that in years to come, some schools will find themselves under financial pressures and increase class sizes. Rooms may also need to be able to handle two classes at the same time.

Academic meeting rooms can vary widely in size, providing space for anything from seminar groups to rooms seating hundreds of people. The room size chosen can be driven both by library needs and campus-wide needs.

In public libraries, the sizes of multifunction meeting rooms often depend on both library program needs and the availability of alternate meeting spaces in the community. In a small town, for example, the library may possibly provide the only good and accessible group meeting space in the community, and community-wide needs may drive the size of the public library meeting room.

Conference rooms are often found in academic libraries, public libraries, and special libraries. Often they are designed to hold groups of limited size, with the understanding that under unusual circumstances (for example, one hundred angry citizens attending a public library board meeting) meetings will have to be relocated to other spaces.

II-C. REQUIRED ROOM SPACES

This section covers meeting rooms of all types except formal auditoriums. Rooms for serious dramatic or musical performances may require a large amount of support space, and planning the total required square footage for support spaces of this type is beyond the scope of our book.

- *Audience*. Calculating the space required for a multifunction meeting room is fairly straightforward. As a first estimate, assume that the area for seating users in chairs requires about 10 square feet per person, while seating at tables requires at least 25. If all the furniture is removed from a room, an amazing number of children can sit on the floor, perhaps one child for every six square feet.

- *Performers*. Meeting rooms often require extra space for performers. This can vary from perhaps 100 square feet at the front of the room to permanent or portable stages or platforms. Depending on the kinds of performances expected, libraries can provide dressing rooms, green rooms (off-stage spaces for performers, with direct access to stages), back passageways allowing performers to cross the stage unseen, storage for scenery and props, sound and light booths, and so on.

- *Furniture storage closets*. Assuming stack chairs on dollies and folding plastic tables (or flip-top tables on casters), your furniture storeroom may be about 10 percent as large as the room itself. But it's important to have your architects calculate closet space needs for you when the room is designed, to be sure that everything can be put away. Furniture storage closets work much better if they are wide rather than deep. You don't want to have to empty an entire closet to get at something tucked in the back. A wide shallow closet with double (or even more) doors is a lot easier to use.

- *Coat storage*. Many libraries feel that coat storage areas are little used and choose to omit them from their plans. If you want coat rods in alcoves at the back of the room, a good space estimate is alcoves 2.5 feet deep and one coat every three inches. Other methods of storing coats include hooks along walls and coat racks on casters.

- *Kitchenettes*. Meeting room kitchenettes vary from a counter behind closed doors to full, walk-in kitchens.

- *Audiovisual equipment closets*. If members of the public are allowed to set up furniture (or forced to if the room is free), you will want to keep your AV equipment in a separate locking closet. The same is true if the meeting room serves as a classroom.

- *A variety of special storage spaces*, including:
  » Closets for maker space equipment.
  » Program equipment storage closets, particularly for children's programs.

- » Storage closets for book sale books. If your Friends of the Library group holds sales in the meeting room, you will want the boxes of books to be stacked nearby. It's much easier to move boxes of books one by one to the meeting room between book sales than to move them there all at once from other parts of the library when the sale time arrives

- » Storage closets for groups that use the room on a regular basis and leave their equipment there. Many meeting rooms, particularly those in small-town public libraries, are used routinely by scout groups, clubs, elections, etc., and we have seen a variety of provisions for storage.

The proper configuration of storage closets may affect room space. Workable storage closets are wide and shallow rather than narrow and deep, and the required double doors may prevent movable furniture from being placed close to walls.

With the possible exception of large, formal auditoriums, most meeting rooms in most libraries are probably too small. In many years of consulting, Fred has never had libraries complain that their meeting rooms were too large—even when he thought the rooms were amazingly big.

Regardless of formulas, there needs to be enough space to walk comfortably around people seated on chairs or at conference tables without rubbing against walls. In far too many conference rooms, people have too little room to squeeze past occupied chairs.

If the conference room will be lined with side chairs, there needs to be space between the edge of the table and the wall for people seated at the conference table, people seated in side chairs, and people walking between the two rows of chairs. This means anything from eight feet or more of space. If the conference room is designed to be converted from chairs around a table to rows of chairs, there will need to be a substantial extra closet to hold the sections of a modular conference table when the room is set up with rows of chairs, or to hold extra chairs when the room is set up as a conference room. Convertible conference rooms also require chairs of normal proportions rather than immense swivel chairs.

If the role of the conference room is to be an impressive place, that can mean substantially more square footage.

II-D. LOCATING ROOMS IN BUILDINGS

Almost all library program rooms—including auditoriums, classrooms, multifunction rooms, and conference rooms—work better when they can be used when the rest of the library is closed. This enables programs to continue after closing time, classes to be scheduled at times when the library is closed, and board meetings to continue after the rest of the library closes.

Codes often require that at least half the occupants have access to emergency exits that allow them to exit the way they came in.

This kind of flexibility is particularly important in small public libraries with limited hours, but any library that closes at 9:00 p.m. and has a meeting room not accessed directly from an entry vestibule may be forced to end library programs prematurely and to kick out community groups before people are ready to leave.

If classrooms are buried in the middle of academic libraries, particularly in areas to which the library may someday want to limit access, any attempts by the college or university to schedule classes there can lead to problems.

In all cases, the easy way to separate meeting rooms from the rest of the library is to make them directly accessible from entry foyers. This has become a standard approach to library design.

Foyers that provide access to meeting rooms also need to provide access to restrooms. (There are additional benefits to locating restrooms off entry foyers, because for libraries with book security systems, materials that have not been checked out cannot be taken into restrooms.)

To prevent security problems in these situations, staff members at lending desks should have direct sight lines through the foyer and out the front door of the library, so they can see who is entering the library and entering the restrooms and program rooms.

II-E. FURNISHINGS

The comments on furnishings in this section apply in particular to multifunction meeting rooms, conference rooms, seminar rooms, and classrooms. For notes on seating in quiet reading rooms, study rooms, children's craft and story rooms, and multilevel children's story rooms, please see the relevant parts of this chapter.

- *Stacking chairs*. By far the best seating for multifunction meeting rooms is provided by stacking chairs. As with all chairs, when the time comes to select stacking chairs, ask manufacturers for samples and have a number of people try them out. Remember that most chairs feel pretty decent when people first sit down, and their failings become apparent only after 15 minutes or so. All stack chairs need dollies. When selecting stacking chairs, always make sure that there are no sharp places on the frames that will scratch the backs of adjacent chairs in the stack. For example, a tubular frame with a joint at the top may leave extremely visible scratches on the front sides of the chair backs. Stacking chairs are available with either molded plastic seats and backs or upholstered seats and backs, with corresponding tradeoffs between comfort and ease of cleaning. Stacking chairs are also available with plastic mesh seats and backs that provide comfort and unusually light weight.

- *Armchairs on casters*. These can be extremely comfortable, but if they are not designed to stack you will need to increase the sizes of your furniture storage closets.

- *Traditional folding chairs*. These are miserable to set up and take down, and they are extremely hard to store. Avoid them.

- *Conference room chairs*. A wide variety of conference room seating is available, ranging from comfortable swivel chairs that might be used for administrators' desks to high-backed and imposing chairs that suggest corporate boardrooms of a pompous variety. In terms of actual comfort, high backs contribute very little, since most people want support in the lumbar region—the small of the back. So to us, the decision appears to be mainly one of desired message. Remember that pretentious chairs can excite snide comments from local critics. If the conference room is planned to be flexible, with a modular table that can be stored, the chairs selected will affect the amount of storage required. Ideally, the chairs will be of modest size.

- *Folding tables*. Many meeting rooms are supplied with folding tables. When specifying tables, remember to require enough tables to take care of table-intensive situations, such as book sales. The worst kind of tables are the heavy folding tables with metal legs and frames and tops made of laminate-covered chip board. Setting up tables like these is a job for a couple of strong people, who will quickly tire of the metal edges of the frames cutting into their hands and want heavy leather gloves. Similar tables are available with molded plastic tops. These weigh much less than the tables described above, and they don't have sharp edges. If folding tables are six feet long rather than the traditional eight, they will be lighter, and they can be carried vertically through doorways, which are typically six feet, eight inches to seven feet high. Standard folding tables used in most meeting rooms are two feet, six inches from front to back. Narrower ones are available for situations where the members of an audience need a place to write while they all face a speaker or projection screen. Tables of this type can be set up in pairs if the library requires deeper tables.

- *Tables on wheels.* Another option is tables on wheels with tops that flip up vertically for storage. These have the advantage of never having to be picked up. Typically tables on wheels will have locking casters and tops that latch into position. With the tops flipped up for storage, tables of this type usually can be nested together for more compact storage. The great thing is that one small person can easily set up a flip-top table with casters, something that is not true of other table types.

- *Conference and seminar room tables.* Large conference tables are extremely expensive and amazingly inflexible. They are also extremely heavy and awkward—if not impossible—to relocate. If removed from the conference room, they are almost impossible to store. For this reason, unless it is important that the conference room be really impressive, you will want to consider modular tables. Modular tables also provide extra flexibility. If the table can be folded up and stored in an adjacent closet, a conference room can be temporarily reconfigured as a small meeting room. The closet can hold the extra chairs when the table is in use. A conference room that seats 16 around a table should probably seat about 32 in rows of chairs with the table dismantled and put in a closet. Remember that this kind of flexibility requires practical chairs rather than the monstrous swivel chairs provided in some pompous conference rooms.

- *Furniture storage.* Your architects will need to make sure that the furniture storage closets can hold all of the scheduled items. Schematic design drawings should indicate how this storage will work, including all placement of furniture in storage. As with all storage closets, you need to make very clear that no other functions will intrude into closets. Nothing is more frustrating than finding some item of technical equipment has been added to your furniture storage closet at the last minute, and that it will no longer hold all of your furniture. (This can happen.) Closets for furniture storage need to be wide and shallow rather than narrow and deep, so that people setting up furnishings aren't forced to drag half a dozen dollies of stack chairs out of the way to get at a large folding table at the back.

II-F. LIGHTING

II-F-1. Natural Lighting

Windows in meeting rooms are a mixed blessing because they require blackout shades, and meeting rooms that will be used for projected images may be better off without windows.

We have seen a number of libraries that had windows at the front of their meeting rooms, behind the speakers. Usually this appears to be due to the exterior design of the building. Luckily, blackout shades to prevent glare behind presenters are available, but why have windows there at all?

II-F-2. Artificial Lighting

As with almost all areas in libraries, the best way to light meeting rooms is to bounce the light off the ceiling. This is particularly true in rooms that are intended to be multifunctional, which includes all meeting rooms mentioned here except formal auditoriums, formal conference rooms, and faculty studies.

The ideal level of illumination in meeting rooms varies widely. Some groups (such as stamp collectors' clubs) require fairly bright lighting, at least 60 foot-candles, while audiences at musical performances may require only low levels of light.

Although many existing meeting rooms have fluorescent lighting, all new meeting rooms will want LED lighting, often specifically designed for variable brightness. (Not all dimmable LED lighting works equally well. You will need the assistance of an experienced lighting designer.)

Some rooms benefit from supplementary downlight systems for situations where class members need to take notes while viewing projected material. Downlights can illuminate flat writing surfaces and lecturers' notes while not interfering with projection.

In meeting rooms used for performances or classes, lighting needs to be zoned, with the front or performance end of the room capable of being brighter or darker than the rest of the room.

In planning lighting systems in program and meeting rooms, it's important to avoid situations where pendant uplight fixtures can interfere with projection paths from ceiling-mounted projectors.

One extremely unpleasant (but unfortunately popular) lighting concept is perimeter soffits with inset downlights. Although this design causes fewer problems in meeting rooms than it does in other library spaces, it's still an impressively bad idea. The use of perimeter soffits with recessed downlights results in odd patterns of light and dark on walls, direct glare from overly concentrated light sources, dark room perimeters, and sometimes low vertical clearances under the soffits. Crown moldings offer a far better way to ornament the junctions between walls and ceilings without screwing up lighting.

See chapter 31, "Lighting."

II-G. ACOUSTICS

Acoustical planning is of major importance in all types of program and study rooms. Unfortunately, there are many libraries with problems in this area.

II-G-1. Unwanted Sound Transmission

Preventing the unwanted transmission of sound between adjacent program rooms or between program rooms and the rest of the library is important whether the rooms in question are huge meeting rooms or small seminar rooms or tiny study rooms.

While sound transmission can be merely annoying in most situations, it can be a very serious problem in others. Consider, for example, a medical library that needs to keep conversations between physicians private, or a law library where members of the firm are having a confidential meeting concerning a case.

Some easy ways of limiting sound transmission include:

- Extending and insulating partitions between rooms vertically to the bottom of the floor above or the underside of the roof rather than simply ending them at ceiling level, and only after that installing suspended ceilings.

> For years, Fred attended monthly meetings in a library building where the suspended ceiling had been installed before the partitions between rooms were installed. When he visited the men's restroom next to the main meeting room, he could see an eighth inch of light at the top of the partition. He could also hear every word spoken in the meeting room with crystal clarity, giving him uneasy fears of reciprocity.

- Providing separately ducted air supplies and returns for all rooms rather than using louvers in the doors. Some libraries have study rooms with air supplies but no returns. Apparently, the designers assumed that air would find its way under the edge of the doors and from there to a central return duct. Air can also be returned through louvers in doors. Unfortunately, louvers in doors transmit sound particularly easily. Louvers in doors are a cheap tract-house-quality substitute for ducted air returns and have no place in a library.

- Avoiding connecting doors between meeting rooms. The small spaces around closed doors, particularly at the bottom, make it easy for sounds to carry between rooms.

- Providing door seals. One way to limit sound transmission through doors is with flexible seals that function much like weather stripping.

> Fred worked with one library that had an ordinary door between the board room and the multifunction program room. Board meetings conducted at the same time as children's programs were always interesting.

- Using sound absorbing panels that can be mounted like pictures on walls. Fred visited one library program room where the concrete walls had been covered virtually edge to edge with sound-absorbing panels.

- Keeping internal book return bins far from meeting rooms. (In fact, far from anything except rear service halls for library staff.)

- Limiting sound transmission by using double-stud (staggered-stud) walls. In walls of this type, drywall in one room is attached to one set of studs, while drywall in the adjacent room is attached to the other set. This prevents vibrations of the drywall in one room being transmitted directly to the drywall in the other room. Wood-framed apartment buildings often use this kind of construction between apartments. In libraries, it may be helpful in the walls separating story and craft rooms from adjacent quiet areas.

If you are concerned that the proposed designs for your program rooms will lead to acoustic problems, particularly if your designers do not want to follow the ideas above, consider hiring an acoustic engineer. Few architectural firms have acoustic engineers on staff, and most do not propose to hire them for anything smaller than formal auditoriums, but a number of librarians have insisted on them and benefitted from doing so.

II-G-2. Movable Room Dividers

Many program rooms have movable dividers designed to separate a large room into two smaller rooms. Dividers that function well are expensive, but they are cheaper than building multiple rooms of different sizes.

While the best room dividers work well, cheap room dividers usually perform poorly. Unfortunately, a great many existing program rooms have cheap dividers. Groups using rooms with cheap dividers are usually very much aware of what's happening in the adjoining space.

Although cheap room dividers usually perform poorly, with sounds bleeding through the dividers, they're still expensive.

For acoustic control, there needs to be an acoustic partition continuing the divider above the ceiling, reaching up to the underside of the roof or to the bottom of the floor above. And the divider needs to have a bellows or similar device at the bottom that fills the opening between the bottom of the divider and the floor, once the divider is in place.

To keep dividers from sagging, dividers need to be supported by strong beams. When you work with your design team, mention your concern with "deflection" (sagging) due to the "dynamic load component" (the added force that results from the motion of the individual panels of the divider).

Unfortunately, large numbers of meeting rooms in new libraries appear to be built with cheap dividers. Directors tend to speak highly of them, but staff members less emotionally involved in the building projects and more frequently involved using the rooms often admit that their dividers don't work well.

Some librarians also report that their dividers are difficult to operate. Occasionally staff members even get trapped between sections of movable dividers and have to call for help.

Some dividers can be unattractive. Their presence alters the otherwise symmetrical look of meeting rooms. Some dividers stick out into rooms even when the dividers are open. And dividers that fit into pockets that have doors to conceal the open dividers affect ceiling designs, interrupting crown moldings or other details.

Dividers can complicate projection systems. A digital projector and screen suitable for a large meeting room may be in a poor location when the room is divided. One possible outcome is three projectors and three screens—one set for occasions when the entire room is in use, and the two separate sets for occasions when the room is divided.

Dividers can also make it difficult to take room reservations because of the size options. A group that reserves a half-size room, for example, can deny space to another group that needs a full-size room.

Some librarians complain that it can be almost impossible to locate repair parts for movable dividers.

Movable room dividers may require additional entrances and exits to program rooms, and they can alter the arrangements of kitchenettes.

Fred and Joe disagree to some degree about room dividers. Joe recommends that you examine your meeting needs and your construction budget and use this information to compare strategies. Fred recommends that you simply put your money into an extra, small meeting room rather than try to use a movable divider in your larger meeting room.

> Nothing relieves a boring string quartet more than the happy voices of children playing video games on the other side of the room divider.

II-G-3. Room Acoustics

In our opinion, all general-purpose program, activity, and study rooms need flat acoustic ceilings and rear walls that absorb sound.

Although some program rooms are built with washable floors, most are carpeted. In addition to feeling far more welcoming, carpet helps control noise.

Children's program and craft rooms, however, are almost always constructed with tile floors (vinyl or rubber) to allow messes to be cleaned up. To provide places for children to sit during story hours, the libraries purchase area rugs, carpet squares, or pillows. As a result of having hard floor surfaces, story and craft rooms particularly need acoustic ceilings.

Formal auditoriums require analysis by acoustical engineers and are not covered in this book.

In addition to movable interior room dividers, meeting spaces can have entire walls that open.
SOURCE: ENGBERG ANDERSON

II-H. HVAC

The heating, ventilating, and air conditioning demands of all sorts of meeting rooms are extreme.

Typically, rooms of this type are either empty or packed with people. Since people arrive and depart abruptly, HVAC systems have to be able to respond to changing needs unusually quickly.

The problem, of course, is that people exude large quantities of heat, moisture, and carbon dioxide. A meeting room without a highly responsive HVAC system soon becomes oppressively warm and humid, and excessive CO_2 and humidity buildup can make audiences extremely uncomfortable. Modern systems have CO_2 and moisture sensors, but they still have to adapt quickly.

Many library employees are unhappy with unresponsive meeting room HVAC systems. They report that rooms are frigid when empty or lightly occupied and quickly unpleasant when programs take place.

Of all mechanical systems in libraries, HVAC systems are by far the most complex. Be sure to include air-handling needs for meeting rooms in your building program statements.

II-I. COAT STORAGE

Although many people using meeting rooms just drape their coats over the backs of their chairs, all meeting rooms larger than study rooms need at least some kind of way to hang up a few coats. Stack chairs are generally too small and aisles between seats too narrow to accommodate coats draped over the backs of all the chairs. Coats draped on the chairs around a conference table are clumsy and get in the way. On rainy days, wet winter coats can bring the exciting aroma of wet dog to the event.

Without provision for coat storage, children's coats end up piled everywhere on the floor, and adults either pile them on tables or end up wearing them (in rooms that often become too warm when they are filled with people).

II-I-A. Coat Hooks or Pegs

One simple method of storing coats is coat hooks or pegs mounted along walls, particularly at the back of the room. To avoid people impaling themselves on hooks, you can specify hooks or pegs with wide faces.

If you have a row of pegs on a wall, consider providing a shelf above for other possessions. (Since people will pile books and other heavy objects on shelves, they need to be unusually strong. Be sure your architects provide for the extra strength by installing blocking in the walls rather than relying on toggle bolts through the drywall.)

You may want pegs at staggered heights, for use by both children and adults.

When you specify hooks or pegs, make sure they are not made of cast zinc. Zinc castings are notoriously breakable. (Fred visited a library with a long row of coat hooks in a children's department. Virtually all had broken off at various lengths, leaving impressively sharp edges, all at about children's eye level.)

II-I-B. Coat Bars

Perhaps a neater way to store coats is on hangers on bars. If the bars are inset in alcoves, it may also help keep rooms looking less cluttered.

In inexpensive house construction, many closets are two feet deep, but coats don't fit in closets that shallow. A minimum depth of two feet, six inches works a lot better. (Many metal coat rod holders are engineered for two-foot-deep closets. If you use them, you'll need to find a way to hold the backs of the holders away from the back wall of the closet.)

> Some coat bars come with permanently mounted coat hangers that cannot be removed from the bars. These are about as popular with library users as automated telephone answering gear.

There needs to be a couple of inches of space between the top of hanger bars and any shelves above them.

II-I-C. Movable Coat Racks

Coat racks on casters are a standard item in some meeting situations. In many meeting rooms they tend to be too small and too messy, but they have the advantage of being movable, and they can be stored out of sight when not needed. If you have a place to store them.

II-I-D. Locations

Because hanging coats are not as decorative as one might hope, some architects find ways to avoid having them on display in meeting rooms. One method is to place coat bars in a short entryway to the meeting room. If you have coat bars in alcoves, you can add doors, making them in essence extremely broad coat closets.

II-J. WIRING

Most program rooms need a great deal of wiring, and they are likely to need more rather than less as the years pass.

The inexpensive way to provide wiring is to do so during construction. Retrofitting outlets in walls is expensive, and adding outlets for floors that are slab-on-grade is painfully expensive.

Unfortunately, libraries abound in meeting rooms with inadequate wiring. Just a few years ago, for example, Fred gave a talk in the meeting room of a brand new library and had to find a 50-foot extension cord to plug in his projector.

The comments in this section do not apply to formal auditoriums.

II-J-1. Electrical Outlets and Circuits

All program rooms, study rooms, and quiet reading rooms need electrical outlets every four or five feet on all the walls.

Rooms also need outlets in a grid in the floor, probably about a ten-by-ten-foot grid. Be sure to insist in your printed specifications to your architects that all outlets be completely flush with the floor, so tables and chairs can be positioned anywhere and people never trip.

Since many meeting room users have laptop computers, many program and study rooms need very frequent electrical outlets to prevent users from trailing their laptop cords across walkways.

Conference tabletops also need electrical outlets for laptops.

To envision the stress than can be placed on meeting room wiring, imagine a large computer class using laptops, all of which need to be plugged in while keeping the floor free of wires that people can trip over.

Kitchenettes in meeting rooms require a number of separate circuits for times when users will bring several heated serving dishes they want to use at the same time. Unfortunately, many meeting room kitchenettes have far too few circuits, leading to seriously dangerous practices like stringing daisy-chained extension cords down hallways to access extra circuits in other rooms.

II-J-2. Wireless Signals

All modern program and study rooms require strong Wi-Fi signals.

Given the reliability of wireless transmission, you may decide that you do not need a great deal of data conduit in your program and study rooms, but hard-wired connections via Ethernet jacks provide better service. In addition, you will need ways to connect laptops and computers to your ceiling-mounted digital projector.

Whether or not you use laptops in your meeting room, speakers may require strong wireless signals to present their programs.

And who knows what's coming in another 10 or 20 years. Although wireless signals have made some data wiring obsolete, the best time to install data conduit is before the drywall goes up and the floor slab is poured.

II-K. AUDIOVISUAL EQUIPMENT

Modern meeting and conference rooms are expected to be compatible with a wide variety of electronic equipment. Among other things, they need some sort of video display, either large-format monitors or projection screens with ceiling-mounted digital projectors, audio amplification systems, strong wireless signals, compatibility with items like whiteboards, and the flexibility to deal with unforeseen technological changes.

The problem with planning audiovisual (AV) equipment for libraries is the tremendous rate of technological obsolescence. A good library building may remain in use for a century or more. Compared to this sturdy longevity, projection and amplification equipment has the lifespan of a gnat. (There are some of us who remember how recently we were still creating projection rooms with special windows for 16mm projectors. Those who have no memories of this can just enjoy their youth.)

So first and foremost, assume frequent updating of equipment.

II-K-1. Projection Equipment

Properly selecting and locating projection equipment can be challenging. Some people are very competent at this, and others are not. To verify your design, try to find an AV firm that specializes in audio-video installations.

If you mount your video projector on a drop, things will look neat and tidy, but there's a good chance it will end up in the wrong place with regard to the projection screen when you buy a new projector. If the projector is simply mounted on the ceiling, it will be easier to relocate. (A "drop" is a section of the ceiling that is lowered by an electric motor and provides a platform for a projector. Some require about two feet of clearance above the ceiling. Check with your AV specialists before the construction drawings are finalized. Be sure they coordinate the projector placement with the layout of suspended light fixtures.)

To limit damage to projection screens from mishandling (and the predictable failure of the clutch mechanisms that keep screens open) you may prefer electrically driven screens with key switches.

Many video projectors come with zoom lenses, but they don't zoom very much.

Projection technology can change rapidly, and constructing spaces that assume certain technologies can be a problem. Lantern slide projectors and 16mm projectors are basically museum artifacts, and most separate projection rooms are no longer built. Very large, high-resolution video monitors are replacing projectors and screens in some libraries. Available equipment will change by the time this book is published, and you will want to explore current options before making decisions.

II-K-2. Amplification Equipment

All meeting rooms of any size need sound systems for playing video and audio recordings.

Sound systems are also necessary for amplifying the voices of speakers. We all have mental images of strong-voiced speakers and acute young ears, but programs can also feature the feeble-voiced speaking to the partially-deaf.

Be sure your sound system is suitable for both voice and music.

Accessibility codes require broadcast gear that functions with individual amplification units. Most of these require loop antennas linked to the room's PA system. There are four main types of Assistive Listening System (ALS), each with different installation and maintenance costs.

- *Radio Frequency*. This system requires a receiver and head phones. This system has a more economical first cost but the receivers need to be maintained. Additionally, several systems located in different meeting spaces could have single overlap. This is great low cost system for single meeting space buildings.

- *Infrared* (**IR**). This system requires a receiver and head phones. This system has a more economical first cost but the receivers need to be maintained. Additionally, the receiver needs direct line of sight to the IR broadcaster (technology similar to a TV remote). This system does not have any overlay with adjacent systems and is a great low-cost option.

- *Ground Loop*. This system requires an antenna to be installed in the floor. The antenna broadcasts the signal directly to an individual's hearing aid device. Additional equipment is not required. This system has a high initial cost but lower maintenance cost over time. This system can be retro-fitted to a space, but is best when installed during construction.

- *Phone Application*. A newer technology broadcasts the signal over the buildings wireless network and can be received on an individual's smart phone through the use of proprietary application. This system has a high upfront cost and could have limitations for young and older users who do not have a smart phone.

Remember that audio amplification is not just for the totally deaf. As with physical access, where libraries serve users with walkers and strollers, many users simply have failing hearing.

II-K-3. Video Recording

You may need to be able to record or broadcast events taking place in meeting rooms. Public library board meetings, classes that have both in-person and remote attendance, and other functions may require this ability.

II-K-4. Security

The cost of electronic apparatus in a well-equipped meeting or conference room can be impressive. Depending on anticipated use, there may need to be extra security provisions. For portable equipment, a locking closet may be the best solution.

II-L. STORAGE CLOSETS

One of the most frequent errors in program and meeting room design is the failure to provide essential storage closets. Depending on their purposes, program rooms need storage spaces for furniture, electronic equipment, children's program and craft supplies, book sale books, materials used by cooperating clubs or agencies, materials used by various academic classes, and so on.

Amazingly, some large program rooms in new and expensive libraries have no storage closets at all.

As an example of the importance of storage closets in meeting rooms, public library children's departments can be forced to haul program supplies hundreds of feet for each program, when the supplies could be simply left locked in a meeting room closet.

Storage spaces need to be separate closets that can be locked individually.

All closets work better if they are broad and shallow than if they are narrow and deep. Having to haul out stacks of stuff to get at something at the back of the closet improves no one's mood. Large closets need at least double doors.

The absence of storage closets diminishes the actual capacity of meeting rooms. A room designed to hold 60 people seated in rows theater-style won't be able to do so if tables, AV equipment on carts, and other items are piled around the edges.

Stacks of unused furniture and equipment in meeting rooms look impressively unprofessional. Librarians may eventually get used to this disarray, much as people eventually fail to note the moving cartons that have been piled in one corner of the living room for a few years, but the first impression outsiders receive is of slovenly disarray.

> Somewhere there is probably a program room with excess storage space, but we have never seen it.

Closet doors are easily damaged. Because of this, the lead edges of all closet doors need to have metal protectors.

All but the smallest closets need lighting. Fixtures need to be protected from collisions with furniture and other objects.

A serious architectural misdemeanor involves using program room storage closets to house irrelevant mechanical and electrical equipment. Include strong words in your program forbidding this practice, and watch your construction drawings for last-minute violations of this necessary requirement.

See chapter 22, "Collection Storage and Display."

II-L-1. Furniture Storage Closets

All multifunction meeting rooms need furniture storage closets, as do almost all specialized meeting rooms.

Although you can estimate the size of your furniture closet at about 10 percent of actual meeting room space, it's important to have your architect verify this by figuring out the space required for the actual furniture you select. For example, flip-top tables on wheels may take up more space than simple folding tables, and extras like portable stage sections can require a substantial amount of extra space. Insist that the floor plans in your schematic designs include drawings of all the tables and chairs placed in your furniture closets.

Even conference rooms can benefit from furniture storage closets. For example, if libraries use modular conference tables that can be folded up and stored, conference rooms can be reconfigured as meeting rooms with chairs in rows. But doing so requires space to store the extra chairs when the room is set up conference fashion and the conference table sections when the room is set up with chairs. It also requires smaller chairs (which can be just as comfortable as massive swivel chairs).

II-L-2. Audiovisual Storage Closets

Many program rooms—including in particular multifunction program rooms, conference rooms, and classrooms—need space for the secure storage of expensive AV equipment.

They also need space for computer racks to hold projection and amplification equipment.

Separate closets are important here to protect expensive and delicate equipment from being bumped by (for example) furniture, and to allow people using your room to set up their own furniture without mucking about with your equipment.

See also section II-L-7, "Closets for 'Maker Space' Equipment."

II-L-3. Program and Craft Supplies Closets

Probably the most frequent use of public library meeting rooms by departments of the libraries is for children's programs, and almost every public library multifunction room needs closet space for children's program supplies.

Far too many libraries are designed without such closets, forcing children's staff members to waste vast amounts of time hauling materials between children's departments and meeting rooms.

The failure to provide storage closets for children's program supplies in meeting rooms doesn't save space, for the same material will have to be stored somewhere else.

Unlike most other storage closets, children's supply closets need shelving. As with all storage areas, this is one possible place to use obsolete but sturdy shelving when buildings are expanded or replaced. (Think of how much happier you'll be when your old mauve steel shelving is hidden inside a storage closet.)

Children's supply closets also need floor space for such bulky objects as puppet theaters.

In the best of all worlds, a children's program closet will be directly accessible from both the meeting room and the children's craft and story rooms, or from the craft and story room and the children's staff workroom.

II-L-4. Book Sale Closets

One of the most aggressive consumers of library space is book sales run by volunteer groups. Librarians always hesitate to cross volunteer groups because support groups are so important, but some groups have taken over vast amounts of floor space for book sale activities, frequently providing more space for individual books than the potential sales prices of the books justify. In some libraries, volunteer groups have actually maintained stack units in which customers can browse for used books.

We think a much more efficient model is to sell used books either in kiosks by lending desks and/or at periodic major book sales in program rooms.

To support the latter, libraries need book sale storage closets directly adjacent to meeting rooms. It's far easier to move boxes of books to the storage closet one at a time between sales, and then pull them all out in one fell swoop when the sale time arrives, than it is to store them far from the meeting room and have to transport them all at one time to the site of the sale. (If you worry about the space it will take to store boxed books by your meeting room, it will cost about the same amount to store them anywhere else in the building.)

Book sale storerooms need to be large enough to hold cartoons of books stacked no more than five feet high.

II-L-5. Computer Storage Closets

One group of important but sometimes underutilized library spaces is computer classrooms. They perform a vital function, but in some libraries they stand idle much of the time.

One approach to avoiding the high cost of little-used computer classrooms is to build them adjacent to groups of public computers, installing sliding glass walls that allow the classroom computers to be used for general purposes when classes are not taking place.

Another possibility is to set up classrooms only when needed. A multifunction meeting room can be set up as a computer classroom with laptop computers. A large number of floor outlets will be needed, but a strong wireless signal should work.

A meeting room designed to serve as a computer classroom will probably need a storage closet for a laptop charging rack and for a movable teaching station.

II-L-6. Closets for Cooperating Groups

Many libraries work with groups that use program spaces on a regular basis and need a place to store equipment and supplies.

In public libraries, groups like the Boy Scouts and Girl Scouts may meet in the library and need space for banners, flags, and program materials. Hobby groups may have equipment that is difficult to transport. If the library serves as a polling place, it may need a closet for voting booths and other equipment.

In academic libraries, equipment needed for specific courses may need to be stored in meeting rooms.

However, the possibility of providing storage for outside groups can be a door that libraries would prefer not to open. Once a group has a storage closet in your meeting room (a) you'll never get rid of their stuff, even if they never actually use it, and (b) all sorts of other groups will want to store their stuff in your library as well.

II-L-7. Closets for "Maker Space" Equipment

At the time this book was written, public libraries were extremely enthusiastic about maker spaces, rooms provided with a variety of equipment for audio and video production work, 3-D printers, and other equipment aimed primarily at young adult users. Complex maker spaces may include small production studios with acoustic separation.

The problem with any spaces designed for young adult purposes is that they stand idle when teenagers are in school.

Some libraries have dealt with this problem by using multifunction meeting rooms for maker spaces, setting up equipment as needed, particularly after school. Given the cost of the equipment, separate storage closets are ideal, although closets for general projection and program equipment can also be used to house maker space equipment. However, shared closets presume that only library staff will set up equipment.

II-M. KITCHENETTES

A variety of program spaces—particularly the multifunction meeting rooms found in many public libraries—benefit from having small kitchenettes with sinks, refrigerators, and counter space for making coffee.

In small program and conference rooms, these can be no more than simple alcoves (with or without doors), with no actual floor space inside the kitchenette, but larger program rooms often have walk-in kitchenettes.

If you provide a kitchenette, be sure that the sink has enough clearance to allow a coffee urn to be filled. This means a high goose-neck faucet and perhaps a deeper than normal sink. There's nothing more frustrating for people making coffee than to have to hunt to find a janitor's mop sink to fill a coffee urn or have to find a small sauce pan to ladle water into the urn.

> No matter how small the meeting or conference room, you don't want a toy sink. Fred worked with a library where the conference room sink was about four inches deep and a foot square. When he asked about problems with the building, the sink was almost the first thing the staff and board mentioned.

Fred thinks that providing stoves or microwaves in public meeting room kitchenettes is generally a bad idea and frequently an extraordinarily bad idea. These greatly increase the chance of users starting fires, and keeping them clean may prove to be less entertaining than one might hope. Sooner or later, someone will heat up something that puts out an unpleasant smell. Depending on local zoning codes, cooktops may require extremely expensive commercial range hoods with fire-suppression systems.

Many libraries store their hospitality gear in their meeting room kitchenettes. For this reason, it's a good idea to provide locks on all cabinet doors and drawers.

If you have a larger walk-in kitchen used for community dining events, you may want a pass-through window for food service.

You will also need to make provisions for trash disposal, both in the kitchenette itself and in the main program room space.

This library meeting room includes a serious kitchen. The first picture shows the space set up as a service counter, and the second as a teaching kitchen. The third shows a crowd attending a neighborhood dinner prepared on site. A movable wall can block off access to the entire kitchen when the meeting room is used for other purposes. Note the commercial range hood over the stove. Planning for meeting room kitchens (as opposed to sinks and refrigerators) includes controlling who has access to the equipment and who is responsible for cleaning and maintenance.

SOURCE: ENGBERG ANDERSON

Kitchenettes may also need to meet health codes. On campuses, there may be an agency responsible for kitchen specifications. Public libraries can check with local governments.

Many meeting room kitchenettes have an inadequate number of electrical circuits. Even a small kitchenette in a small meeting room in a small library will need five or six separate 20-amp circuits, or users with electrically heated devices like coffee urns, Dutch ovens, and toasters will constantly trip electrical circuit breakers. A large kitchen used for community dinners may need a dozen or more separate circuits. The result of an insufficient number of electrical circuits may be people daisy-chaining cheap extension cords together to access outlets on different circuits somewhere down the hall. Fire marshals take an extraordinarily dim view of this.

Joe has worked with a number of libraries with impressive kitchens that support everything up to and including preparation of food for sale. Most of these kitchens are similar to teaching or demonstration kitchens, including features like three or four compartment sinks; grease traps; lots of stainless steel surfaces; easily washed and sanitized wall, floor, and ceiling surfaces; refrigeration equipment; sanitizing dishwashing equipment; and ranges with industrial-scale hoods complete with fire suppression. These areas need to be arranged so that they can be closed off from the rest of the program room, providing essential security and the ability to use the kitchen and the program room simultaneously for separate events.

Large kitchens of this type require special plans for long-term maintenance, ideally in partnership with other agencies. They can support a variety of popular events, including community dinners and training events.

II-N. FLOOR COVERINGS

This section contains brief comments on the use of floor coverings in meeting rooms. For a far more extensive discussion, see chapter 12, "Surfaces and Materials."

II-N-1. Carpet

Most modern program and study rooms have carpeted floors. Carpeting soaks up excess noise. It's comfortable to walk on. And it looks less brutally institutional than other floor-covering options.

Traditionally, libraries used broadloom carpet for meeting room floors. However, the improvements in carpet squares in recent years make them a preferred alternative. One of the advantages of carpet squares is the ability to replace one that becomes badly stained through (for example) beverage mishaps.

II-N-2. Resilient Flooring

Resilient flooring is smooth flooring that flexes slightly and is more comfortable to stand on than concrete.

Some meeting rooms have vinyl or rubber tile floors. Both are less soft underfoot than carpet, but more comfortable than ceramic tile or concrete. They are easy to wash, but they are cold and noisy. And the necessity of occasional stripping and rewaxing of vinyl tile floors means more maintenance than one might like.

With the exception of children's craft rooms, where washability is essential, we don't see many reasons to use VCT (vinyl composite tile) or rubber tile floors.

II-N-3. Concrete

A few harshly modernist libraries have concrete floors. Concrete floors create the welcome aura of (at best) a cheap big box store and (at worst) an ancient basement.

Staining and sealing concrete makes it look a little better. But not much. Staining and sealing don't soak up reverberation or the noise of footfalls. Stain typically doesn't take evenly. And staining and sealing don't make concrete any softer underfoot.

And it has unpleasant acoustics.

II-N-4. Stains

One of the easiest ways to avoid permanent stains in carpets is to ban all red and purple beverages.

> The indelible nature of red food coloring is no doubt greatly to the credit of American industry, but you still don't want it in your library.

II-N-5. Tarps

Some libraries that have messy art or craft projects in their meeting rooms protect the floors with tarps. If so, they need storage space for tarps when they are not in use, as well as bins on casters large enough for tarps.

However, tarps can lead to tripping hazards and accessibility problems.

II-O. CEILING HEIGHT

Meeting rooms need ceilings high enough to allow audiences seated in chairs to see projected images over the heads of the people in front of them. Even in fairly small meeting rooms, this usually means a minimum ceiling height of about 12 feet.

Many meeting rooms have built-in raised platforms or folding platform sections to raise performers off the floor so people in the back row can see something over the heads of the people in front of them, and this means higher ceilings.

The best way to light meeting rooms is with reflected uplight. Because these fixtures must hang down a minimum of two feet from the ceiling, this also adds to ceiling height requirements.

Conference rooms seating a dozen or so people around a table can get by with slightly lower ceilings because people frequently sit on both sides of a long table, looking at a projection screen at the end of the room. However, conference rooms of this type are most flexible if they are set up so their large tables can also be stowed and chairs arranged in rows. In this case, people using the room may have to see over each other's heads.

Because meeting room ceilings in a library often need to be higher than the ceilings in the rest of the building, a number of libraries have made their meeting rooms separate wings rather than raise all the ceilings on a floor to a far greater height than otherwise needed.

Meeting rooms also benefit from having no occupied spaces above because that results in fewer bearing columns getting in the way of seating and viewing.

When you are working with your architects on plans for a meeting room, a lengthwise cross-section drawing of the meeting room will help you evaluate whether the ceiling is high enough.

II-P. ACCESSIBILITY

All meeting rooms should be accessible to users with disabilities.

As with many other construction situations, making new meeting rooms accessible is easy, but bringing older ones up to code can be difficult.

Auditoriums with sloped floors need open spaces for wheelchairs. Review specific requirements with your architects.

Other meeting rooms with flat floors just need enough elbow room to maneuver wheelchairs. Check the clearances in particular in small study rooms, which need to be large enough for the assigned table and for one or more wheelchairs. (This is another argument for having all furnishings movable.)

The major problem in large meeting rooms involves raised stages. If you have a stage, it will need to be accessible, including both permanent stages and folding stage platforms. In practice, this means either a ramp from the floor of the room to the stage, a mechanical lift, or access at stage height from some other space in the library.

II-Q. SECURITY

This chapter touches on meeting and study room security in a number of places. To summarize briefly:

- Arrange buildings to permit after-hours access to program rooms and classrooms without allowing people into the library proper.

- To provide staff oversight of multifunction rooms—particularly in public libraries—install internal windows with Venetian blinds between program rooms and service desks.

- Study rooms need to be terrariums, with three glass walls extending from a foot or less above the floor to at least seven feet from the floor. The interiors of *all* study rooms should be visible to staff members seated at service desks. (For some reason, architects tend to resist this. Be insistent.)

- Emergency exits from program rooms MUST lead directly outside the library, NEVER to other areas of the building. If this is not the case, a parent organization that takes over a program room may end up allowing people to wander all over the library when it is closed.

- Provide separate storage closets for furniture and for expensive computer and AV gear. All storage closets should lock.

- All cabinets and drawers in meeting rooms should lock.

- An insufficient number of electrical circuits in kitchenettes is a fire risk as well as a general nuisance.

- Even if codes do not require a second exit from a meeting room, you may still want one because it gives people an extra way out in case of emergencies. As mentioned above, it must lead out of doors and never into another area of the library.

- A wall telephone may provide an extra way to call 911.

III. Types of Program, Activity, and Study Rooms

This section reviews the range of program and study rooms found in typical libraries and comments on their special needs. The section is divided into auditoriums, classrooms, multipurpose rooms and community rooms, conference and seminar rooms, quiet reading rooms, study rooms, children's craft and story rooms, multilevel children's reading rooms, and faculty studies.

Information on general needs common to several types of program and study rooms appears earlier in section II. Unfortunately, it has proved to be difficult to eliminate all duplication between sections II and III.

III-A. AUDITORIUMS

Auditoriums with fixed seating and sloping floors are found primarily in large libraries because of their expense and limited flexibility. Depending on their equipment, auditoriums are used for lectures, musical performances, and dramatic presentations.

In academic libraries, auditoriums may be created primarily to meet wider campus needs. In this case, the auditorium does not reflect library needs as much as a campus shortage of large classroom spaces.

In public libraries, spaces of this type are generally limited to large central buildings of city libraries, but some medium-sized and even small buildings have formal auditoriums with sloped floors.

Unlike many other types of library program and study spaces listed here, auditoriums are fairly inflexible.

Auditoriums have a number of significant advantages when it comes to visibility. By comparison, a performer in a multifunction meeting room can be hard for audience members to see if the heads of other people in the audience get in the way.

Some major planning issues involving auditoriums include:

- Does your library really need a space of this type? Does your library hold enough large classes or formal presentations to justify an expensive space with limited flexibility? Are there other spaces in your city or on your campus that already meet this specific need?

- If you have a large space of this type, will your parent institution take it over? Having library spaces scheduled by outside agencies can lead to difficult planning and even security problems.

- Do you want a space that will support theatrical performances? Possible support components may include a proscenium arch, curtains, cyclorama, fly loft, lighting and audio equipment, dressing rooms, green room, spaces for set construction and storage, prop storage, and so on. These will require advice from a professional designer of spaces for dramatic performances.

- Do you plan musical performances? Will you have special storage needs, such as space for a piano? Will you need an orchestra pit?

- Is the space designed to serve primarily as a large lecture hall? In this case, support spaces will be far simpler.

- Will you need projection equipment and a screen? This will require professional advice on equipment.

- Acoustic specifications will require professional analysis by an acoustical consulting engineer.

- Where will the auditorium be located within the building? It will need to be usable after regular library hours, which often means that the auditorium must be accessible from the entry foyer or lobby.

- Sloped auditoriums can introduce complicated accessibility issues. You will need the advice of an experienced architect.

- Are you prepared to provide sufficient restrooms? With auditoriums come intermission rushes not found with other types of library program and study spaces. In particular, women's restrooms may need to have far more toilets than men's restrooms.

- Your architect will need to be sure that your facility meets all applicable ADA and state accessibility requirements, both for audience seating and for performer access to the stage. If you have no accessible access to backstage, you will need a ramp in the auditorium. Unfortunately, ramps take up a lot of space. More importantly, although ramps meet the letter of the law, traversing a long ramp in a wheelchair is hard work. For example, the ramp up to a four-foot-high stage will be over 50 feet long.

- If you need lighting that can be brought slowly from total dark to light, you will need LED lighting specifically designed for that purpose.

III-B. CLASSROOMS

Although classes are often held in public libraries, academic and school libraries are probably more likely to construct rooms specifically designed to function as classrooms.

Most educational institutions will have campus standards for classroom design and equipment. Even if these do not apply to the classroom planned for your library, they will be a good source of technical requirements.

Most new classrooms are designed to support a wide range of technologies, and these should be incorporated in library classrooms.

One danger of incorporating technology is the rapidity of change. Whatever libraries install now will be obsolete in a decade. This means paying extra attention to details that will be difficult to alter once the classroom has been built. Among the most important are electrical circuits and data conduit. Trying to envision the unexpected future is difficult, but librarians can console themselves in the knowledge that there appear to be few libraries anywhere with too many electrical outlets, too many electrical circuits, or too many communications jacks.

Among the issues affecting classroom design are:

- Who will determine the use of the classroom? For example, if you want a classroom for library instruction classes, will your institution allow you to schedule it to meet your own needs, or will it become part of an institutional pool of classrooms?

- If the classroom is buried in the library, what are the implications for security? What will happen, for example, if the parent institution decides to schedule classes when the library is closed? What will happen if the classroom is accessible through the stacks and you wish to limit stack access? What will happen if the classroom is attached to your rare book room? (The main moral here is, never put classrooms in the back recesses of libraries. Direct access from the entry foyer is always an important thing. Or construct a library with huge numbers of lockable doors.)

- How will you protect high-tech gear in your classroom? At the very least, classrooms need locking closets.

- What kind of seating will you provide? Writing tablet chairs (chairs with folding writing areas) are probably the most flexible, but tablets have to be strong enough to withstand people sitting on them. See chapter 21, "User Seating."

- How much seating will you need? The capacities of many classrooms are set by institutional policy, and this will affect the size of any classrooms in your library. The guiding principle, however, should be the special needs of the library. If your library needs a room to seat 20, bowing to university pressure to convert it to a room to seat 60 may result in a classroom that no longer meets your needs.

- Will you need other furnishings, such as folding tables?

- How much flexibility do you need? Ideally, almost nothing in the classroom with the exception of high-tech lecterns will be fastened down.

Although it's always possible to argue with the administration when your classroom is scheduled for what you regard as inappropriate use, things are a lot easier if the design of the building prevents classroom takeovers from causing problems in the rest of the library.

Given the uncertainties of classroom use, therefore, we think it's extremely important that any classrooms be accessible when the rest of the library is closed.

III-C. MULTIPURPOSE ROOMS AND COMMUNITY ROOMS

Many libraries—particularly public libraries—construct multifunction meeting rooms designed to accommodate a wide range of functions and events. Rooms of this type are typically rectangular, with level floors and with ceilings high enough for projected images.

In designing rooms of this kind, maximum flexibility of function is clearly a primary concern.

Many multifunction rooms in public libraries are used both for library-sponsored events and for events sponsored by community groups, and security for library equipment is therefore a major concern.

Many of the planning issues that affect multifunction program rooms appear in section II, above, but some special ones are listed here.

III-C-1. Seating Capacity

In public libraries, multifunction meeting rooms are usually constructed large enough to house all but the most extraordinary programs. (Every library can remember a program when attendance was triple that of any other program before or since, but most libraries cannot afford to construct space adequate for such extremely unusual events.)

In planning new buildings, however, libraries with currently undersized program rooms can be led astray by the fact that the small size of existing rooms has artificially constrained program attendance, and that past attendance may not be a good indicator of future audience sizes.

Most public library multifunction meeting rooms are designed to serve as community meeting spaces when not needed for library programs, and likely audience size at community meetings can also influence meeting room size. If a library figures that a 100-person capacity will meet the needs of library programs, there may be good reasons to make the room larger if there are a number of groups in town that need 125-person spaces.

In our experience, errors in planning meeting room capacity are almost always in the direction of planning too small.

The situation is made worse by what we think is a tendency to overestimate how many people can fit comfortably into a multifunction meeting room. See section II-C, "Calculating Required Space."

Some state public library standards may specify minimum meeting room sizes, but we haven't seen them. In the absence of standards, make sure that your meeting room is genuinely large enough to meet your needs.

If large community meeting rooms are available near a public library, the library can base the size of its rooms on space needs of library events only. But making the room so small that the library has to hold many of its programs in other places undermines one of the purposes of programs, which is to bring people into the library, and to provide a place for some family members to attend events while others are elsewhere in the library. In addition, nearby meeting rooms in other buildings may cease to be available in the future.

Movable room dividers are frequently recommended for multifunction meeting rooms. See section II-R, "Movable Room Dividers."

III-C-2. Provisions for Performers

Many multifunction meeting rooms need to accommodate a variety of performers. Among the things that can be provided are:

- Floor space. The simplest way to accommodate performers is to have sufficient floor space. Because some performers use a lot of space and others use very little, the lack of a fixed performance space increases the flexibility of the room.

- Ceiling clearance. Be sure your ceiling is high enough to provide adequate vertical clearance for performers, particularly if you have a stage or portable platforms. Remember that both adjustable lighting for performers and suspended uplights will hang down at least two feet below the ceiling.

- Stages. Stages are useful because they elevate performers enough so that they can be seen over the heads of people in the audience. Stages also must be accessible, which means a ramp or lift.

  Some libraries purchase folding stage sections (platforms about four by eight feet with folding legs, designed to be butted together). However, stage sections are extremely heavy. It will require at least two strong people to set them up and extra space to store them when they are not in use. And you will still need to make them accessible. See chapter 11, "Accessibility."

- Pianos. If your multifunction room has good acoustics (and it should) it will be in demand for small musical performances. It's a good idea to have enough space for a baby grand piano, in case someone decides to give you one. For security, you can be sure the keyboard cover locks, and you can also buy protective blankets that lock into place. (Since people tend to use pianos as tabletops, covers are important.) You will probably also want a piano trolley—a carriage with locking casters that will allow you to move the piano easily. Unfortunately, dragging pianos around a lot can throw them out of tune.

- Lecterns. A lectern is a stand that holds notes at a convenient height and provides a structure behind which speakers can position themselves. Many speakers feel naked without a lectern. If you don't have a PA system, lecterns with built-in sound systems are available. Lots of conference centers have lecterns with the name of the center emblazoned on the front where it will be picked up by cameras. Your library can do so too. But you may wish it didn't when the news media photograph speakers with extremist positions.

III-D. CONFERENCE AND SEMINAR ROOMS

Many libraries have conference and seminar rooms.

Conference rooms serve a variety of functions. In public libraries, they usually serve as boardrooms. Often these rooms have a table large enough to seat the board of trustees and director, plus side chairs for library department heads, members of the press and public, and the library secretary.

In academic libraries, rooms of this type may serve primarily for seminar groups or for groups that need access to nearby portions of the library's collections.

Conference rooms in special libraries may be used by student groups, planning groups, groups working on projects, and so on. Occasionally these groups may need real privacy, especially in law and medicine.

III-D-1. Range of Functions

Planning conference rooms requires a preliminary review of all of the expected functions of the room. As usual, getting things in print helps to clarify what kind of structure and equipment a conference room will need.

The usual expectation is that conference rooms will serve groups that need to sit around a table, including governing boards, library staff, students, and so on. Planning for group use requires a decision on seating capacity. How large a group will be accommodated? Will everyone sit around a single table, or will some people sit in side chairs? Will the side chairs line the walls flanking the table, or will they be in rows at one end of the room? (To us, chairs lining the walls suggests overflow seating, while rows of chairs at one end of the room suggests a distinction between board and audience.)

A major decision in public libraries is whether the conference room will be made available to the general public when it is not being used for library functions. If the room will be open for community use, it will need much better protection for electronic equipment. And it will need to be accessible from the entry vestibule.

III-D-2. Location in the Building

A couple of factors affect the location of conference rooms:

- Will the room need to be accessed when the rest of the library is closed?
- Does the room need to be near the library's administrative offices?
- Does the room need to be adjacent to any specific portion of the collection?

Due to the requirements of open meetings acts, public libraries often need to make board meetings accessible to the press and general public. If the board meets in a conference room buried in an administrative area of the library, the building planners will need to decide how the general public will get to the meeting. How will the library prevent users from wandering into other administrative areas once office staff members have left for the day? And how will building-wide security be maintained if the board meeting continues past regular library opening hours?

For all of these reasons, public libraries need to make conference rooms accessible from entry foyers. The downside is that all administrative materials for the meeting will need to be transferred from the administrative offices to the conference room.

One could perhaps assume that the board of trustees will always meet when the library is open, but the life of a building is long. Trustees reserve the right to change their minds, and if a hot topic emerges, a library that seldom has any outsiders attend board meetings may find itself with 100 or more people trying to crowd into the board room.

III-D-3. Staff Oversight

If conference rooms will be used by non-library staff, there may be a need for staff oversight. As usual, the best way to accomplish this is to have an interior window with a Venetian blind on the conference room side of the window.

III-D-4. Ownership

With all conference and seminar rooms, there is always a possibility that a parent institution may decide to take over the room.

If a university or city government takes over a meeting room, the library needs to be able to maintain security while the parent organization is using the room.

The most important point is designing rooms that can be accessed directly from the library foyer, to make sure that users of the room cannot enter the rest of the library when the library is closed.

III-E. QUIET READING ROOMS

Quiet reading rooms are particularly common in academic libraries and public libraries.

Academic reading rooms can be real showplaces, often with special browsing collections, hardwood floors, Persian rugs, and a variety of soft seating.

As public libraries have become busy, crowded places, they have lost their traditional silence. Where once a scholarly hush hovered over the books, accompanied by somber bindings (no overstimulating Mylar dust jacket covers), newspapers on split rods, and sober readers, now there is the constant chatter of staff and visitors, ringing of telephones, beeping of computers, and gurgling of coffee brewers.

In response to the fact that most libraries are no longer quiet places, many public libraries have constructed quiet reading rooms. Typically, these provide isolated housing for reading tables and armchairs, but do not contain computer workstations or other noise generators. Libraries can also ban laptops in rooms like this, but it may be a hard ban to enforce unless the library can block Wi-Fi.

> There are straightforward ways to block Wi-Fi. The principle is that of a Faraday cage. Metallic wallpaper is available, as are paints with a high metal content. Or you can luck out and move into the old x-ray suite and find that the lead lining the walls does a fine job. If you block Wi-Fi, you'll probably block cell phone signals as well, and that may make your room especially desirable.

Here are some design issues and suggestions for quiet reading rooms:

- Quiet reading rooms often offer the opportunity to create elegant spaces. Many quiet reading rooms are low-key showplaces. They may have fireplaces, tables with mounted reading lamps, and area rugs.

- Because of their panache, quiet reading rooms offer major naming opportunities for fundraising campaigns. Having one's name over the door of an elegant reading room is a lot more gratifying that having one's name over the door of a staff restroom.

- Quiet reading rooms in public libraries require visual oversight. Because few of these rooms are staffed, there needs to be provision for staff members at service desks to keep a general eye on what's happening in quiet reading rooms. A typical way is through the use of interior windows. As with study rooms, quiet reading rooms can be designed to provide quiet without visual secrecy.

- Although users of quiet reading rooms frequently are reading current magazines and newspapers, shelving these materials in the rooms leads to problems. Users selecting magazines and newspapers annoy readers who came to the rooms seeking relative silence. It works a lot better to locate magazines and newspapers directly outside the entrances to quiet reading rooms.

- However, browsing collections in academic library reading rooms are common. (Some are full of seldom-read great books.)

- Typical furnishings might include anything from one to four four-person reading tables and four to perhaps 16 armchairs. Smaller tables—such as two-person tables or carrels—can be used as well, but they may look more utilitarian than the library wants.

- When it comes to noise, many quiet reading rooms are almost self-policing. Users seeking solitude glare angrily at those who choose to conduct conversations.

- To emphasize their intent, some libraries label quiet reading rooms "silent reading rooms." We find the name more chastising than we like, but to each his or her own. Opinions differ.

- Quiet reading rooms can be alcoves rather than actual rooms. If both ceilings and floors have proper acoustic surfaces, just the interposition of stacks between the alcove and the noisier areas of the library may be enough to block sound. Some quiet reading areas are also separated from noisier areas by freestanding fireplaces or by low partitions. One possible cost advantage of quiet reading alcoves is simplified HVAC. A quiet reading room needs its own thermostat, air supply ducts, and return air ducts. These may not be essential in reading alcoves.

- As with all spaces in libraries, uses may vary over the years. For this reason, if you plan donor recognition through a plaque or lettering, you may want to speak in generalities. For example, "The Johnson Reading Room" may be a better long-term bet than "The Johnson Reading Room for Eastern European Journals in Nuclear Physics." A simple "The Johnson Room" is even less limiting.

III-F. STUDY ROOMS

Many libraries have study rooms, small rooms for groups of perhaps four to eight people. Study rooms are used for quiet reading, student group projects, small group meetings, tutoring, test taking, gaming, listening to recordings, and other purposes.

In some ways, study rooms are similar to very small conference rooms.

III-F-1. Three Vital Features of Study Rooms

Study rooms have three vital features, and the vast majority of study rooms fail in at least one area:

- *Extremely good visibility*, to provide both safety for users and oversight for staff. Study rooms need glass walls not only on their entry sides but also between study rooms. Many study rooms have cute little windows instead of glass walls, and that's nothing you want.

- *Extremely good sound control*, to protect users of adjacent rooms from distracting noises and to allow users to have confidential conversations. In far too many study rooms, it's too easy to hear conversations or noises next door.

- ***Extremely good air handling***, to protect users from bad air. Too many study rooms have to be aired out between users.

All of this should be completely obvious, but it's amazing how many librarians complain of one or more of these problems with their library study rooms. And how plans for new libraries can show the problems the moment you look at them.

III-F-2. Supervision

Oversight of study rooms is particularly important. Librarians in public libraries constantly tell us that they have to be careful who they assign to what study rooms, and they occasionally give study rooms that are extremely difficult to supervise descriptive nicknames like "the sex room."

The main trick in designing successful study rooms is to regard them as terrariums. People using study rooms need to be visible from all angles, and the users of all study rooms should be completely visible from service desks. If a number of study rooms are in a row, they may need to be separated by glass walls, so that librarians can see through the entire row like a shotgun house.

Our experience is that some people have a strange aversion to creating study rooms that are easy to supervise, and that libraries abound in study rooms that cause problems. To avoid these problems, you will need to pay very close attention to the proposed design of study rooms in your library. Check the lines of sight from service desks, and then consider how lines of sight will work if you relocate the desks. Insist that you want glass walls rather than windows and get really crabby if your designers don't listen to you. (Codes will require a horizontal mullion in a glass wall. This is fine.)

The last thing your staff should have to do is pace back and forth outside study rooms, peering into each one to make sure that no evil deeds are afoot.

Actually, glass-box study rooms have another real advantage for users. Study rooms are small spaces, and if the walls are mostly opaque, the rooms tend to feel oppressively small.

III-F-3. Furnishings

For group projects, tutoring, and similar functions, tables can be either in the center of study rooms or pushed up against one wall. Tables against walls allow equipment to be plugged in without wires trailing across floors to encourage tripping.

Built-in counters are a great deal less flexible than movable tables and strike us as a very poor idea.

Rather than purchase large tables for study rooms, we prefer to use one or more standard three-by-five-foot reading room tables. If a longer table is needed, two reading tables can be pushed together end-to-end.

People using study rooms often group five or six people around a four-person table. For this reason, tables with cross beams between the legs at the end of the table are a bad idea.

If you have a study room with a solid wall, it helps to have electrical outlets on the wall above tabletop height, allowing users to push a table up against the wall and plug in laptops without having to crawl under the table. It's a good place for a quad box.

This picture from the inside of a children's craft and story room shows good architectural planning. Windows allow staff to keep an eye on the room. And instead of using cast zinc coat hooks, which tend to break, leaving extremely sharp edges, the designers specified steel hooks, which can bend but not break off. (Some librarians prefer craft and story rooms with high windows that allow parents to see in without distracting the children in the room.)

III-F-4. Movable Walls

Some libraries have installed movable walls between study rooms, allowing two rooms to serve as one larger room, but the walls need to be of high quality to control noise between rooms. And because movable walls are opaque, they limit staff oversight.

Instead of providing movable walls, consider one or two larger study rooms.

III-F-5. Locking Doors

You will need to decide whether you want to lock the doors of your study rooms when they are not in use. To meet safety codes, if doors can be locked, they will need an exit device on the inside arranged so that users cannot be locked in.

III-F-6. Family Computer Rooms

One interesting use of study rooms is to provide a place where a parent with small children can work at a computer while keeping an eye on the children—and containing their noise. It's easy to convert a regular study room to this purpose, and with modern laptops one could improvise the entire arrangement, encouraging parents to pick out books and toys from the children's department, check out a laptop, and then bring kids and toys and laptop to the assigned study room.

III-G. CHILDREN'S CRAFT AND STORY ROOMS

Children's craft and story rooms in public libraries are probably the most specialized program spaces found in libraries, and for this reason we have included a large amount of special detail.

Although rooms can be constructed for crafts or stories only, many children's librarians like to provide programs that include both activities. Typically these start with a story—when children can best concentrate—and then progress to a craft.

Use of craft and story rooms is usually limited to events produced by library staff during hours suitable for children, so the rooms do not need to be accessible when the rest of the library building is closed. Some libraries, however, let outside groups use their craft and story rooms, and for this reason locking storage closets, cabinets, and drawers are important.

Providing a separate craft and story room keeps the mess associated with crafts out of the library's multifunction program rooms. Spilled glue, glitter, and gingerbread house frosting fall on washable floors instead of being walked into meeting room carpet.

III-G-1. Location

Most craft and story rooms will not be made available to the general public, and they do not need to be accessible when the library is closed.

Most librarians want craft and story rooms to be directly accessible from children's departments, so that children leaving the rooms after programs find themselves back in the children's department rather than leaving the library. If a craft and story room is at the back of a children's department, children leaving the room will walk through the entire department on their way out, selecting books in the process.

As noted under security, some librarians worry about strangers peering into craft and story rooms. This is another reason for placing these rooms at the back of departments, where non-parents will be far more noticeable.

III-G-2. Sizes

Most craft and story rooms are for relatively small groups. Capacities vary with the size of group the children's department staff members are happy with. In our experience, it's usually between 20 and 30 children.

A room for 20 children will need floor space for 20 children to listen to a story, plus enough additional floor space for 20 children doing crafts at tables. And in most cases additional seating for parents.

The room will be far more flexible if it's possible to set it up in a variety of ways, including (a) floor space for stories plus tables for crafts, (b) tables put away, with rows of chairs filling the room, and (c) the room entirely empty, for children to sit on the floor for stories.

When figuring out the space required for a craft and story room, be sure to find out whether the library intends to have parents attend the programs, since this can require additional floor space.

III-G-3. Décor

Some story rooms have been created with elaborately painted backdrops for storytellers. Some of these backdrops are even movable like stage flats.

These can be charming, but they need to be fairly timeless and flexible. A good argument can be made for pinnable walls that lend themselves to frequent redecoration.

Because children rub against the walls and spill craft supplies, craft and story rooms are great places for washable wall coverings like vinyl wallpaper.

III-G-4. Floor Coverings

Some story rooms are built with a carpeted area for stories and a larger area with vinyl or rubber tile for crafts.

Other libraries tile the entire room and use portable carpet sections or area rugs for children sitting on the floor. This strikes us as the most flexible option.

With children sitting directly on a tile floor, some libraries install radiant heating in the floor slab.

III-G-5. Sinks and Cabinets

Because crafts are messy (especially library crafts, it seems) all craft and story rooms need running water. Usually architects provide what amounts to a kitchen counter with sink and cabinets.

The problem is providing a way for very small children to wash their hands. Some installations have a slide-out step by the sink, while others have sinks at two levels. Slide-out steps are really clever, but some librarians worry about children falling off or the steps moving when children are standing on them.

Cabinets can be both above and below the countertop. Everything needs to lock. As with other built-in furniture, drawers work a lot better with ball-bearing, double-extension hardware.

II-G-6. Storage

Children's departments need a surprising amount of space for storage of program supplies, and a closet off the craft and story room is a convenient place. If the closet is large enough, it can also be used for storing furniture, so the craft and story room can be cleared completely, or tables can be put away and the entire room filled with rows of chairs.

If the library's multifunction meeting room and its craft and story room are on the same floor, it's sometimes possible to have the program supplies storeroom accessible from both program rooms. In other situations, the storeroom can be located between the craft and story room and the departmental offices.

III-G-7. Windows

Because of video or puppet presentations in craft and story rooms, it is sometimes necessary to darken the rooms. For this reason, exterior windows can be a problem if they do not have effective blackout shades.

Skylights in craft and story rooms may sound exciting but they are basically disasters. They reflect sound, the racket of rain falling on skylights can make it difficult to hear storytellers, the glare during the day interferes with programs, the dark ceilings at night are depressing, and sooner or later the skylights leak.

Many librarians are uncertain about first floor exterior windows leading to craft and story rooms because of the potential for odd people hanging around outside.

In general, librarians who tell stories like story rooms without windows leading to the rest of the library because activities visible through the windows distract the children. In many cases, however, parents inside the library want to be able to see into story rooms to be sure their children are getting along all right. One possible solution is to have a few windows at the right height for parents to see in but too high above the floor for children to see out.

II-G-8. Lighting

Because of the variety of activities in craft and story rooms, we think providing lighting options is important.

For general craft work, reflected uplighting should work well. Dimmers will allow the general lighting to be darker during stories than during crafts.

The area where the storyteller sits may be a good place for some track lighting with dimmer switches.

As with multifunction meeting rooms, craft and story rooms are not good places for night lights that cannot be switched off. Fred visited one library where the staff had taped dark paper over the meeting room fixture that stayed on at all times.

III-G-9. Acoustics

In general, craft and story rooms are small enough not to need any special acoustic treatments. However, with tile floors, ceilings must be covered with sound-absorbing material.

Fred visited a library with a story room shaped like a high cylinder. The staff told him the room echoed like an empty oil drum until the library retrofitted extensive acoustic wall and ceiling panels. Remember that concave curved walls with hard surfaces in a small room are usually an acoustic disaster.

III-G-10. Adjacent Children's Restrooms

Many children's librarians want a restroom attached to the craft and story room or just outside the door. It speaks well of children's librarians that small children are so mesmerized by programs that they delay restroom visits until the very last second. Mothers faced with emergencies may appreciate not having to sprint the length of the library holding a small child on the verge of explosion.

III-G-11. Public Use of Craft and Story Rooms

Some libraries permit public use of craft and story rooms, either for potentially messy occasions like private birthday parties or for overflow when other meeting rooms in the library are all in use.

If a library lets outside groups use its craft and story room, it will particularly need to have a room with locks on everything, including all storage closets, cabinets, and drawers. It will need to protect permanently mounted equipment. And it will need some way of keeping an eye on things from a service desk.

Allowing private birthday parties to be held in library spaces strikes us as a singularly bad idea, but we're old and crabby. And we have also seen the horrible messes they make.

III-H. MULTILEVEL CHILDREN'S STORY STRUCTURES

Lots of public libraries have multilevel structures on which children can sit to hear stories. Some are in separate rooms, while others may be in corners of large rooms. There are right and wrong ways to build these.

Among other things, always remember that your staff may change their minds. Risers that can be easily reconfigured or even bodily ripped out have some significant advantages for long-term occupancy.

All multilevel story structures must be accessible to users with disabilities.

Here are some things to avoid:

III-H-1. Avoid Story Hour Risers Made of Concrete

Flexibility of internal space means libraries occasionally want to rearrange risers or eliminate them entirely. Having to bring in a jackhammer to rearrange a story hour room is no fun.

In addition, concrete platforms are inherently cold and hard.

III-H-2. Avoid Wooden Story Hour Risers that Echo

There's nothing like broad steps to encourage jumping, and the resulting hollow thumping will be unwelcome.

One good way to prevent thumping is to do what stage set designers do to keep the ghost of Hamlet's father's footsteps from echoing hollowly as he morosely treads the supposedly stone battlements of Elsinore. Glue Homasote—a compressed paper material that muffles vibrations—to the *undersides* of the plywood platforms of the risers.

Architects are sometimes puzzled by this technique and want to put the Homasote on the tops of the risers, but it's too soft for that purpose. Check your final construction drawings carefully to verify that it's actually underneath.

III-H-3. Avoid Bare Wooden Risers

Bare wooden risers are uncomfortable and splintery.

Cheap painted wood looks ratty after a few months of use. Stained and varnished oak is expensive, and available sizes of wood may limit your options.

Always use carpet.

III-H-4. Avoid Risers in Strange Configurations

The design and layout of story hour risers brings out unfortunate creativity in some designers. When you check your proposed design, watch out for:

- Curved risers. These look cute, but it's extremely difficult to carpet them neatly. Fred's library had a story room with curved risers. The shapes were cute, but attempting to carpet them properly defeated one of the best carpet firms in the area and led to unhappy confrontations between the carpet layers and the library staff.

- Illogical riser heights. Risers should (a) permit all children to see the storyteller and (b) not have height variations that can lead to unpleasant falls. The risers in some story hour rooms are at more-or-less artistically random heights. Check your construction drawings, and when in serious doubt ask your architect to cobble up a shirt cardboard model.

III-H-5. Avoid Story Hour Pits

Even worse than badly designed story hour risers are story hour pits.

Ask the librarian who has fallen into one.

III-I. MAKER SPACES

Maker spaces are rooms or groups of rooms designed to provide access to creative equipment, primarily for teenaged public library users.

Equipment found in maker spaces can include a wide variety of computer-driven devices, 3-D printers, sewing machines, video game systems, and whatever new technology your imagination can think up.

Many maker spaces also include separate sound-insulated rooms designed to serve as recording or video studios.

Maker spaces became popular earlier in this century and are now found in a wide variety of public library buildings. Some are improvised—basically a variety of equipment set up in a room—while others are purpose built and sophisticated.

Whether maker spaces are a passing fad or a long-term trend, they still deserve coverage.

III-J. FACULTY STUDIES

Many university libraries have faculty studies in the stacks.

Typically, these appear to be anything from 50 to 125 square feet. Furnishings may include a desk, shelves, and a chair for visitors. Many studies are on the perimeter of stacks, in order to provide daylight for the users. If studies include filing cabinets, staff inspections for books that have not been checked out (see below) get a lot more complicated.

By and large, faculty studies appear to be a royal pain from the library administration viewpoint.

First, faculty may want access to their studies when the library is closed, and this has to be prevented aggressively. Once faculty start asking for keys to the library, the result would be chaos.

And second, faculty also tend to take books from the shelves and put them in their studies without checking them out, forcing library staff to routinely inspect faculty studies for books not checked out. Libraries with faculty studies have to make clear that the studies can be inspected at any time, but it still represents a potentially massive waste of library staff time.

Faculty studies also need windows on the library side as well as the outside window side. The last thing libraries need is (claimed) invisible assaults in faculty studies.

If faculty studies have keys, the library needs master keys and specific authority to check studies at any time.

IV. Private Use of Program, Activity, and Study Rooms

If you plan to allow outside groups to use your meeting room, it's important to establish all of your policies before word of the new meeting spaces gets out in the community. Usually this means before the building is announced.

Most of this applies specifically to public libraries because their activities are not limited by ownership of spaces, but one can envision issues arising in school libraries or on campuses with student groups.

The policies for private use of meeting rooms need to cover an impressive range of issues:

- Will certain types of groups be exempt from rental charges? (This is a dangerous area, but if you charge for use of your meeting room by outside groups, some groups will claim that the nature of their undertakings means they should not have to pay.)

- Will rooms be available for commercial uses, such as promotional and sales events? Will this have an impact on rental charges?

- Will you require that private groups using meeting rooms make clear in all of their advertising that the library is not a sponsor of their program?

- How long in advance will the library accept meeting room reservations?

- Must all outside groups have business addresses in the library's service area? Must private users live in the service area?

- Will rooms be available for private parties, such as children's birthday parties?

> Fred's library did not allow private parties. A mother who complained about this policy demanded to speak with the director, saying, "I don't want that awful mess in my home!" Fred was tempted to say, "Thanks a lot for wanting to leave your awful mess in the library," but instead he just repeated the policy, trying not to sound totally toneless.

- Will groups bear the cost of major damages, such as spilling red beverages on the carpet (resulting in new carpet, since red dyes are a splendid example of American know-how and never come out)?

- What happens if the library's parent organization tries to preempt a group that has reserved the room?

- Will the library allow buying and selling in its meeting room?

- May groups using your meeting room deny access to non-members?

- Will the library allow groups to use meeting rooms when the rest of the library is closed? What kind of extra charge will be made to cover the cost of having staff present to secure the building when the group is through?

- May groups charge admission?

- Will groups be allowed to use the library's AV equipment? What will the library do if specific groups predictably demand that library staff drop whatever they're doing to help the groups use the equipment?

> Fred's library had a group that was so demanding that the library eventually had to refuse all use of AV equipment by outside groups.

- Will the library allow catered meals?

- Will the library require security deposits? If it requires them from only specific groups, is it opening the door to claims of discriminatory treatment?

- Will library staff set up furniture for groups? If so, how will it charge? Or will groups be required to set up their own furniture?

- What groups will qualify for use of kitchen space? If they are expected to do their own cleanup, how will standards be enforced?

Remember that use of meeting rooms is controlled by the general time, place, and manner concept. Attempting to accept or refuse groups on the basis of the intellectual content of their undertakings can lead to serious legal unhappiness on the part of the library.

V. Snappy Rules on Program, Activity, and Study Rooms

1. All program rooms need storage closets for furniture and program supplies. Having to pile materials around the edge of a room is always a mess.

2. Outside of study rooms, quiet reading rooms, and craft and story rooms, most program rooms need to be usable when the rest of the library is closed. This

means that program rooms (and the accompanying restrooms) must be directly accessible from the entry foyer.

3. Good movable room dividers are expensive. Cheap dividers do a bad job of acoustical separation and are hard to repair.

4. Never put a window without extremely serious shades behind where performers will stand. Or don't put it there at all.

5. Acoustic isolation is important. If you can hear everything that's going on in the meeting room when you're in the restroom next door, imagine reciprocity. This means separately ducted air supplies and returns, plus walls that continue past the suspended ceiling to the bottom of the floor above. Cheap movable room dividers fail badly when it comes to acoustics.

6. Meeting rooms need flexible and controllable lighting. Motion detectors are not part of lighting of this kind.

7. Complex lighting and AV control systems with many pre-set options are acceptable only when you have to train an extremely limited number of people to use them.

8. Some traditional formulas for guesstimating meeting room size are seriously inadequate.

9. Funny-shaped meeting rooms are less amusing than one might hope. Nature loves rectangles.

10. Meeting rooms need a lot more electrical outlets than many planners want to put there.

11. Kitchenettes in meeting rooms need large numbers of separate 20-amp electrical circuits, particularly if they are used for serious food service.

12. Very few libraries complain that their meeting rooms are too large.

13. No matter how small the library, each meeting room and study room requires its own thermostat.

14. HVAC systems for meeting rooms need to be able to respond fast. When 60 overheated Cub Scouts or 100 enthusiastic undergraduates tumble abruptly into your meeting room, the HVAC system needs to cope with a lot of excess heat, carbon dioxide, and moisture. Many systems don't.

15. Unless you have a large and pompous library, conference rooms with large and pompous conference tables and with large and pompous chairs tend to look silly.

16. Few public libraries complain that they have too many study rooms, but most of them complain that they have too few.

17. Meeting room storage closets are not for irrelevant equipment, including fire-suppression gear, electrical gear, HVAC equipment, and so on. Make this clear in your building program, watch your construction drawings like a hawk, and tear your designers to shreds if they ignore you.

18. Be careful that parent agencies like universities or city governments don't take over control of your program rooms. And arrange your library spaces so there won't be serious security problems when your parent agencies show that they can override you and take over anyway.

19. Study rooms need to be terrariums—soundproof glass boxes that can be supervised from every possible angle. Some designers will attempt to substitute small windows for your floor-to-ceiling glass walls, have some study rooms without glass walls facing service desks, or have

opaque walls between study rooms. You will need to stop this sort of thing quickly and firmly.

20. Having a windowless YA study room is a bad idea and may become known to your staff as "the sex room." You do not want to have to have staff monitor it to ensure young adults are using the room for its intended use—to study—and not for other purposes.

21. Storage closets, cabinets, and drawers in program and meeting rooms all need to lock.

22. Funny-shaped meeting rooms are less amusing than one might hope.

23. If cooperating groups have arranged access to your meeting room kitchen, what will you do if your library comes to regret the kitchen? What if they contributed to the cost of the kitchen?

PART III
**Essential Spaces
All Libraries Need**

CHAPTER 25

Display and Exhibit Areas

I. Introduction

A large percentage of libraries appear to have at least modest spaces devoted to displays and exhibits.

Most libraries have some sort of objects on permanent display.

- Perhaps the most common are oil paintings (or reproductions) of founders. America's surviving Carnegie libraries usually have framed portraits of Carnegie (even though he apparently didn't like the idea and charged the libraries for the portraits).
- Many libraries have significant historic objects.
- And they have all sorts of artworks.

And most libraries are set up for temporary displays that are changed every few weeks or months:

- Floor space for traveling exhibits that some libraries book months or even years in advance. Some are funded by corporate or government grants.
- Display cases, ranging from massive units to hole-in-the-wall display cases in public library children's departments.
- Wall space for art displays.
- Some libraries have historical museum components, with permanent or rotating displays of local artifacts.

As with meeting room use, libraries benefit from policies concerning displays. The problem is when displays become freedom of speech issues.

Libraries may also reach the point where people with professional museum training may be needed.

All displays have security and insurance implications, especially for the potential loss of valuable (or at least valued) materials.

Displays are pretty straightforward, but there are good and bad ways of doing things. Some are summarized in this chapter.

> Maintaining a suspicious attitude toward displays can be useful. For example, about 50 years ago, a major public library agreed to display the works of a local artist. The artist showed the library a couple of innocuous examples, but when the day came to hang the exhibit, virtually every painting was a vibrant rendering of the male organ. This was in the 1960s, a far more censorious time. Although the library had advertised the exhibit extensively, it panicked and said "No," whereupon the artist took his story of censorship to the press. The library realized it had been had, but the press had a great time taking the library apart without mentioning the actual issues.
>
> In most cases, accepting an exhibit sight-unseen is more likely to result in something bland rather than something hair-raising. For example, Fred's library once had a display of artistic potholders. The staff members that arranged the exhibit expected creative gauntlets shaped like fish or perhaps alligators or bunnies, but the exhibit turned out to be about 200 identical square potholders of the kind made in Girl Scout camp by weaving elastic loops together. When puzzled library users inquired what this was all about, the staff smiled brightly and said "Potholders!"

II. Open Exhibit Areas

Many traveling exhibits require only open floor space and effective lighting.

Our experience has been that traveling exhibits come around so seldom that it's better to simply rearrange furniture when the time comes, rather than have an area that's awkwardly vacant most of the time.

One advantage of the shadowless indirect lighting mentioned in chapter 31, "Lighting," is that it is typically compatible with traveling exhibits, making placing exhibits in unplanned areas far easier.

> Fred once cleared out an entire reading room for a display of working models of Leonardo machines that arrived in a semi-trailer. It was fine. Library users found different places to sit, and everyone seemed to enjoy seeing the feeling of newness that occurs when old familiar things get moved around. No one made invidious comparisons with the way grocery stores rearrange stock to force customers to look at everything in the store.

III. Display Cases

Library supply and furniture catalogs often include display cases, and some may meet your needs.

You can also have display cases custom built. Before you turn your cabinet makers or architects loose to design your display cases, however, you need to have very carefully written specifications.

As a general rule of thumb, horizontal (tabletop) display cases are commonly used for displays of printed books and drawings, while vertical (wall-mounted) cases are used for artifacts and framed materials.

For some special items, display cases have to be custom made. For example, Audubon elephant folios need special cases that support the folios at suitably tilted viewing angles.

What features do display cases need?

- Movability. Most display cases work best if they are movable furniture.

- The only cases we've seen that have to be built in are small, brightly lighted "jewel box" cases for children's collections, built into walls at child height.

- Easy access to contents. Although this seems fairly obvious, we've seen a number of architect-designed display cases with major sections of glass that were fixed in place. To set up displays, library staff had to crawl into display cases to reach the areas behind the fixed glass panels.

- Light-colored interiors—usually light, neutral colors like cream. Too many display cases have dark interiors, leading to displays that look like openings into dark cellars. Displays should glow.

- Displays above waist level. Some libraries have been equipped with cases that start at ankle level, but no adult wants to bend double to see a display. (Children's display cases, of course, need to be at child height.)

- Glass in front or on three sides.

- In vertical display cases, easily movable shelves. Shelves need to be quarter-inch plate glass, tempered glass, or laminated glass. (We saw one library with half-inch glass shelves, which most of the staff found too heavy to handle.) One good way of supporting shelves is to use shelf bracket support strips slightly inset into the back of display cases. Keeping the strips inset allows flat artwork to be displayed bridging the support strips when the shelf brackets are removed. Most bracket systems have brackets with a variety of depths, and glass shelves can be made to fit more than one size of bracket.

- Pinnable backs. The inside backs of display cases have to accommodate materials pinned to the backs. Heavy hopsacking fabric over a pinnable board works well.

> One shouldn't have to mention this, but you need to remind your designers that "pinnable" means some kind of surface that accepts pushpins and straight pins. Fred inherited an architect-designed display unit with a back that consisted of 1/16 inch of cork over heavy plywood, resulting in a surface into which pushpins could be driven only with a hammer, usually leading them to break. Of a number of ill-advised architect-designed items for the building, it was the first one to be thrown away.

- Bright, low-glare lighting. Lighting for display cases is easy to design so it doesn't shine directly into viewers' eyes. To avoid reflections, things are easier if lights are inside the cases. If a room has a number of display cases, track-mounted LED lights can work well. For horizontal display cases with glass tops, external lighting has to be designed to avoid annoying reflections on the tops of the cases.

The best lighting for display cases is LED since there is little heat buildup. Never get talked into incandescent lighting, particularly quartz halogen lighting, which can be miserably hot and quickly burn out in an enclosed display case. And the high heat can't be desirable for the items on display.

- Security. All display cases need to have locks. In addition, libraries that display items that don't belong to them need to carry exhibit floater insurance or get waivers from their exhibitors.

- Horizontal display cases usually resemble glass boxes mounted on top of reading tables. The boxes have four low glass sides (perhaps a foot to 18 inches high) and flat glass tops. Usually the tops swing open on piano hinges, and they may have movable braces to hold the tops open while displays are being arranged.

Here are specifications that appear in several of Fred's building programs for an eight-foot-wide, wall-mounted display case:

"A wall-mounted display case 8 feet wide and 7 feet high, with a glassed-in front from 3 to 7 feet high. The case should be 16 inches deep, with glass on ends to match the front. The back of the case should be pinnable and covered with a durable, coarsely-woven, fairly light colored cloth. Shelf bracket strips should be mounted on the inside back of the case, with the strips set below the pinnable surface to allow large items to be pinned across the bracket strips. The color of the bracket strips and brackets should match the color of the fabric back of the case. Movable ¼" plate glass shelves about 6 inches and 12 inches deep should be provided to fit the brackets selected. The case will have locking glass doors in front, and all sections of glass on the front of the case will be movable."

IV. Wall Spaces for Hanging Artworks

Many libraries have sections of wall set aside for exhibits of artwork.

A variety of systems are available for temporary exhibits. Many resemble old-fashioned picture rail installations, except the artworks are suspended on rods hanging from the rail rather than by picture wires. The top and bottom clamps need to be adjustable to hold the artworks. (Not all hooks fit all picture rails, so buy everything from the same supplier.)

Artworks for temporary loan are widely available. Talk with local artists, with art galleries that show the work of local artists, with community art leagues, and with university art and architecture departments. Some libraries have annual shows for various groups.

V. Pinnable Surfaces

Many libraries rely on bulletin boards for temporary displays. The main problem is keeping them filled. Elementary school teachers complain about the tyranny of bulletin boards, and librarians can too. Nothing is less fun that an administrator telling you that your holiday bulletin board is overdue when you are up to your gills in summer reading programs.

One possibility that comes without bulletin-board tyranny is pinnable wall surfaces. Large cloth-covered panels are available to mount on

> One small town library Fred worked with served as an after-school study center for the children from the K-4 school down the block. The kids came to the library about 3:30 p.m. and worked there for an hour or two until the many working parents came to pick them up. Some days the pinnable walls were covered with "A" papers done in the library.

walls. You can stick things anywhere you want, which gives you a lot more space for wild creativity than a bulletin board, and when the pinnable surfaces are empty they look like colored wall sections rather than empty bulletin boards.

VI. Security Issues

Issues of security are especially important for loaned items that the library does not own. Despite the library's best intents, things can go wrong, ranging from pilferage to fires.

One easy way is to refuse to exhibit anything to which the owner attaches a value. But one can imagine many owners refusing to waive all rights to their display items.

Another possibility is to purchase an exhibit floater policy. Such a policy will probably have a deductible amount and provide coverage limits for items not specifically scheduled (listed individually with agreed-amount valuations). But it may be enough to satisfy people lending material to the library.

VII. Permanent Works of Art

Many libraries have permanent works of art. Some may be of great age, commissioned at the time the building was built or donated soon thereafter.

Permanent works of art need labels of some kind, typically explaining the origins of the works and their significance to the library.

It's easier to deal with insurance on permanent works of art. First, they belong to the library, so no angry owner will be involved if something

> Fred's library had niches with busts of Longfellow and Lincoln flanking the inside of the front entrance. Everyone recognized Lincoln, but essentially no one (not even in a university community) recognized Longfellow. So Fred had labels made. He had one made for Lincoln, but for Longfellow he ordered half a dozen, with additional names such as Kelvin and Marx and Darwin. Every week or so he switched the label under the Longfellow bust. Fred thought this was serious fun, but no one (as in no one) shared his opinion. Since he had no other use for the extra labels, Fred tucked them away in the back of a desk drawer. Thirty years later, while he was retiring and cleaning out his desk, he stumbled across the extra labels and found he still had no other use for them.

goes awry. And second, because they are the permanent property of the library, arranging for insurance is easier.

Occasionally libraries want to deaccession works of art and sell them for cash. In these cases, public relations can be very touchy, just as they are when valuable items in the book collection are cashed in. The main suggestion that occurs to us is to talk things over extensively in private before making any announcements.

VIII. Exterior Displays

Libraries occasionally have outdoor sculptures.

For a long time there was a vogue for bronze figures, typically life-sized children or adults seated on benches, reading, or just enjoying the view. The figures provided a human scale to the exterior of the library, and frequently library users would pose for photos beside them. Entire catalogs of figures were available. We get the impression that life-size bronze sculptures have probably run their course, but we could be wrong.

Some libraries commission custom sculptures. Fred's library had a tortoise and hare (with intervening books) sculpted on site from a 20-ton block of limestone. The artist (who grew up locally) was hard at work (and covered with white dust) for about six weeks, which made the whole thing a lot more fun than trucking in one of a number of identical casts by an artist no one knows.

IX. Combined Libraries and Museums

Some libraries and museums are combined in one building.

There are classic examples such as The Carnegie in Pittsburgh, which includes a public library, a concert hall, and a natural history museum.

For most libraries, combining a library with a museum brings up serious questions of ownership and control. In Fred's one experience, the existing library shared space with a museum, and there were tensions. When a new library was constructed, the library board assumed total control of the museum, including ownership of all its collections. Museum employees reported to the director of the library. All went well as a result, but anything less than total library ownership and control would probably have led to problems. (Until the mayor announced the terms of the merger, the museum staff ignored the entire programming process.)

The moral is the same one that faces libraries in all sorts of circumstances: Ideally, anything in the library building has to belong to the library, and anyone who works in the library building has to report to the director of the library.

X. Policies on Displays and Exhibits

All libraries benefit from written policies on displays and exhibits.

Among the things you may want to include are:

- Is ownership of permanent exhibits absolute? Are all permanent exhibits the property of the library? Do the library's governors have the right to keep or dispose of them as they see fit? What level of approval is required for permanent exhibits?

- What will you do when temporary exhibits have unexpected political overtones? If your staff has arranged for an exhibit that turns out to be extremely offensive to some of your users, what will you do?

> This may sound like excessive worry, but over the decades, Fred's library had many objections from all ends of the political spectrum—a couple of them totally unanticipated.

- What are the limits on library liability? If a temporary exhibit is damaged, then what? Do traveling exhibits come with insurance, or is the library expected to obtain coverage? Do you want waivers of liability? (And if you insist on waivers, will anyone put anything on display in your library?)

- Do you have any recourse if the charming sculpture installed by the Friends of the

Library in 1972 seems embarrassingly insensitive in 2024?

- Do you want a policy to never accept permanent works of art? Or to require that permanent works of art be approved at campus or library board level before being accepted?

XI. Snappy Rules on Display and Exhibit Areas

1. Beware of open-ended acceptance of temporary displays. Insist on approving all objects by seeing them in advance. For major displays, approve everything that will appear before even announcing the display.

2. Beware of providing permanent exhibit space for things you don't own, because it can lead to turf disputes. If it goes on permanent display, it has to belong to the library.

3. Museums and their technology are a world of their own. For anything major, get technical assistance.

4. Many architects love to design display cases but don't do it well. When you see an unusual display case in a library, ask the staff who have to maintain it how they like it.

5. Items displayed permanently in the library should be owned by the library. If the library wants to sell a painting, it should have the right to sell the painting, bearing in mind that local folks may take strong exception to the idea.

6. If you take a tour of a library building, and the tour consists entirely of pointing out works of art, you should have questions about priorities.

7. Libraries that want permanent art displays need to organize donor trusts to pick up the costs. And they need to find a way to occasionally say "No" to proposed objects. (Things can get awkward when the husband of the president of the library foundation creates truly ugly art that he wants to see on permanent display in the library.)

8. All sorts of elaborate multipart sculptures hang on wires in library atriums. They can be fun, but budget for dusting.

9. Many artworks on display require explanatory labels. If you have an oil painting of the first president of the university, or a photograph of the board of trustees that created your public library in 1874, you need to point out who they are.

10. The nice thing about local art as opposed to art from catalogs is that people are far less hypercritical when they know the artist personally.

11. Small, brightly lighted "jewel box" display cases set into the wall at child height are amazingly popular. If children bring their own displays, all the library staff have to do is unlock the case and dust off the shelves on exhibit changing day. But custodians sometimes object to having to clean nose grease off the glass every morning.

12. Nobody likes viewing displays below waist level. Children like low display cases because they have low waists.

13. Movable display cases are sometimes a lot more useful than fixed display cases. Think "furniture" rather than "building."

PART III
**Essential Spaces
All Libraries Need**

CHAPTER 26

Restrooms

I. Introduction

With the exception of libraries that consist of a couple of rooms in larger buildings—such as school libraries or special libraries—all libraries need restrooms.

Many librarians wish this were not the case, because restrooms cause problems vastly in excess of the space they occupy.

Although not all problems with restrooms can be eliminated by good design, restrooms in a well-planned building can keep both library users and library staff far happier.

No one who spends years working on library buildings can escape without a fund of stories of Restrooms from Hell. Over the years we have seen:

- Library restrooms where gentlemen at the urinals are all on full display whenever the doors are opened.
- Library restrooms without floor drains. Although this may sound trivial, think about the pleasure of cleaning up major messes using only a bucket and mop. (There are also library restrooms that have floor drains, but where spilled liquids flow into back corners of the rooms rather than into the drains.)
- Libraries with restrooms for women but not for men.
- Libraries where the only restrooms are accessed through the directors' offices.
- Library restrooms without even rudimentary sound insulation. If restroom users can hear every word spoken in nearby rooms, they are left with the unnerving potential of reciprocity.
- Library restrooms with motion-detector lighting systems that plunge users into total darkness. Fred visited one library where the women's restroom had a stall out of range of the motion detectors. Women trapped in the stall when the lights went out could not turn the lights back on with any amount of arm waving.
- Library restrooms with motion-detector lighting systems that require users to walk

two or three steps into pitch dark rooms before the lights go on.

- Library restrooms that open directly into inappropriate public areas, such as reading rooms and program rooms.

- Buildings where the restrooms for men have a sufficient number of fixtures, but where women need to stand in line. Concert halls and stadiums provide constant examples.

- Libraries where the staff are forced to share restrooms with extraordinarily unsavory members of the public.

- Restrooms with diaper changing tables but no receptacles for dirty diapers.

- Restrooms with insufficient (or even non-existent) exhaust fans, resulting in nearby spaces that defy both description and occupation.

- Restrooms where users can lock themselves in and enjoy complete privacy while they set wastebaskets on fire, add creative decorations, or do other fun things.

- Staff restrooms that lead directly into staff lunchrooms, with resulting unhappiness for both the staff eating lunch and the staff using the restrooms. (An amazing number of these exist.)

When reviewing proposed floor plans, pay particular attention to sight lines. In most cases, good sight lines make good libraries, but in some instances they really don't. This photo was taken by balancing a camera on a public library's romance fiction shelving, where readers can easily be treated to unwanted views of the men's room in action. (With rooms designed for more than one user, it always helps to imagine how things would work if the entry doors were simply removed.)

- Restrooms with entry doors that swing inward but without paper towels to protect freshly washed hands from having to grab handles previously used by the great non-hand-washing masses. (An amazing number of these—both the doors and the masses—exist.)
- Restrooms with stalls so miniaturized that users have to straddle toilets just to close the doors.
- Restroom stalls without coat hooks.
- Restrooms with fancy soap dispensers that break during the first week but are never replaced.
- Restrooms in locations so secret that library staff members spend more time giving directions to the restrooms than in checking out materials, answering reference questions, and providing computer assistance.

All of these problems are easy to prevent by advance planning, but many are difficult or impossible to cure once buildings are constructed. Be sure your building program includes very specific requirements for restrooms, and then review the architectural drawings with a fine-toothed comb. Just because you say you want something doesn't mean you'll get it.

Remember that fixtures and equipment that are just fine in private homes can be disastrously inadequate in public buildings, and that the judgment of laymen may not be helpful. Always consult with your custodians.

The authors of the book of Leviticus were fond of the word "abomination." It's a good word for describing badly designed library restrooms.

Luckily, there are also really good library restroom stories. Our favorite involves an Illinois public library that began a century ago as a ladies' restroom in a town that had no downtown public restrooms for women. The group that founded the restroom included an anteroom with places to sit and a few things to read. And it just grew.

II. Building Codes

In many cases, state and local building codes will establish base rules for restroom design in public buildings. In addition, the Americans with Disabilities Act has a great deal to say about restroom design.

Codes may specify the minimum number of fixtures, whether lighting must be activated by motion sensors, whether restrooms have floor drains, the presence of nearby mop sinks, and other items.

However, codes provide only minimum legal requirements, and you will want to specify many additional features. For example, toilet stalls can be made more accessible to users with disabilities by exceeding the bare minimums set by the ADA and some state codes.

In the past, codes were notorious for not providing an adequate number of fixtures for women, but some codes may now require twice as many fixtures for women as for men.

Some building codes seem to call for significantly more toilets and washbasins than you may expect. This is usually an acknowledgment that libraries are places where large numbers of people can congregate, often for events of one type or another. In the past, the vast majority of the space in libraries was dedicated to book and material storage rather than user seating, and the number of fixtures needed might have been fewer. Current codes are more in tune with libraries constantly changing the balance of space use—often to include more space for people and less space for "stuff." You will be happy that the codes do require significant numbers of fixtures as your use levels increase.

Codes can be surprisingly lenient on restroom locations. Some buildings have floors with no restrooms. Others have women's restrooms and men's restrooms on alternate floors, which must complicate hunting for a restroom in a hurry.

Kiddie toilets don't count as toilets in the eyes of building codes, and they are probably different from what most children have at home anyway. If you add kiddie toilets to your library, you'll have even more toilets rather than substituting kiddie toilets for full-sized toilets.

One architect friend claims that codes can sometimes be interpreted to result in buildings that would consist mostly of restrooms. You can probably have too much of a good thing.

See also chapter 11, "Accessibility."

III. Fixtures and Equipment

III-A. TOILETS

All public restrooms need wall-mounted rather than floor-mounted toilets, and most staff restrooms can benefit greatly from them.

Wall-mounted toilets simplify maintenance because there is no joint between the base of the toilet and the floor. With wall-mounted toilets, people cleaning restrooms can simply mop the entire area.

Due to concerns about obese people breaking wall-mounted toilets off walls, some institutions (such as clinics) have added support braces to the front of wall-mounted toilets. But most places haven't.

Although codes may allow you to install flush-tank toilets, you will deeply regret doing so. Flush-tank toilets are extremely high-maintenance devices, and in public restrooms this means serious trouble with cranky flush mechanisms. By contrast, flush valves are amazingly durable and low-maintenance devices that can perform for decades with little attention.

Flush-tank toilets also have removable lids, tempting people to hide things within, or simply to drop and break the lids.

Automatic flush toilets are widely recommended, but not everyone is thrilled with them. When they work, they're great, but if they don't flush properly the result is human misery. If a washbasin operated by electric eye doesn't work properly, you can always move to the next washbasin. But when a toilet operated by electric eye doesn't work properly, it's *too late* when you find out. If you have automatic flush toilets, be sure the valves have manual push buttons.

> People may assure you that modern automatic toilets never cause problems, but we've seen far too many examples to the contrary. In one major library we visited, signs in every restroom advised users to hold their hands over the electric eyes a minimum of 20 seconds in order to flush the toilets.

Flush-valve toilets have a great deal more flushing power than tank toilets do, making it at least somewhat less likely that small children can plug up the entire system by flushing clothes or other objects down the toilets, or that adults can plug everything up by attempting to flush paper towels.

Once you have tank toilets installed, it's extremely difficult to convert to flush-valve toilets, so don't assume you can start with tank toilets and convert later. The water supply pipes leading to flush-valve toilets are substantially larger than those for tank toilets, and they emerge from the wall in different places. To replace tank toilets with flush-valve toilets can mean tearing up large chunks of a building's plumbing system, as well as ceramic wall tiles, to install larger feed pipes.

Flush-valve toilets require reasonable water pressure. In some small towns, local water pressure may be inadequate to operate flush-valve toilets, especially at the top of the hill. Your architects or engineers can determine whether water pressure is adequate.

If you have tank toilets and are driven crazy by kids plugging them up, you can purchase replacement tank toilets that have power-assist flushing mechanisms. The mechanisms are impressively noisy, but they offer a way to improve flushing without putting in all new plumbing.

> We aren't exaggerating the noise of power-assist mechanisms. Fred's library replaced some children's tank toilets with power-assist toilets. In the first couple of days after the new toilets were installed, a mother flushed the toilet while sitting on it herself. Her shriek was audible throughout an entire floor of the library.

Wall-mounted toilets require space in the wall behind the toilets to house the brackets that

> The problems of children plugging up plumbing are also not exaggerated. In Fred's library, a small child flushed his clothes down a toilet, plugging up the library's entire drain system and flooding a freshly recarpeted auditorium. Talk with your designers about drain pipes that discourage clogs.

support the toilets. Look for this space when you review your schematic designs and construction drawings. If there's no open space behind the wall, you're not getting wall-mounted toilets.

Toilet seats need to be elongated ones, not the tiny circles found in some older houses, and they need to have open fronts. (Seats with open fronts are also called split seats.)

The main rules for toilets are:

- Always use wall-mounted toilets.
- Always use flush-valve toilets (unless your community has insufficient water pressure).
- Always use elongated toilets with split seats.
- Be sure that stalls are sufficiently large.
- Be sure that automatic flush toilets have supplementary manual controls.
- Be sure you have enough toilets.
- Don't expect to buy library-quality toilets at a discount home supply store.

III-B. STALL ENCLOSURES

Unless you plan to shoot a World War II barracks comedy, all toilets must have stalls. The minimum size of the handicapped accessible toilets will be determined by codes, but other stalls are frequently made uncomfortably small.

- Be sure all of the stalls in your restrooms are adequately large. Too many restrooms have one large, accessible stall, accompanied by a number of additional stalls too small for anyone over about six years of age. In some stalls, the door swings barely clear the front edges of the toilets, and users almost have to straddle toilets in order to close the doors. Stalls not intended to meet accessibility regulations need to be big enough for human beings. In our opinion, this means stalls a minimum of 42 inches wide, with door swings that clear the front edges of toilets by a minimum of 18 inches. Double-check your drawings for adequately large stalls.

  Special equipment in stalls, such as fold-down infant seats, can lead to larger required stall dimensions.

- Make sure the stall doors have strong hooks. Nothing is more frustrating than toilet stalls that provide no places to hang coats, but such stalls are everywhere. Make sure that the doors on the stalls are strong enough to carry the weight of heavy coats and even backpacks. Two hooks are a lot better than one. Imagine a user burdened with a coat, blazer, book bag, and purse, none of which she wants to put on the floor. Hooks made of cast zinc are brittle and frequently break in use, so always specify hooks made of steel or of resilient alloys like brass.

- Talk with your architects about graffiti-resistant surfaces. Some stalls are engineered for use in schools and other high-graffiti locations.

- A variety of commercial toilet paper dispensers is available. Most are specifically concerned with ways to prevent stalls from running out of paper during a single day. Other libraries have trouble with theft of toilet paper, but we hear about this more from overseas libraries than from libraries in the United States. Variations in dispenser design include standard single-roll holders, side-by-side roll holders, drop-down holders where a second roll descends when the first one is used up, and huge diameter rolls. Single-sheet dispensers are also available. Some units provide both holders for two rolls plus sanitary napkin disposal containers.

III-C. URINALS

In addition to toilets, all men's rooms require urinals, and they may be specified by the building codes that apply to your library.

Urinals do a great deal to limit mess. Users are much less likely to miss the fixture and splatter on the floor or on the rim of the toilet. And some gentlemen have never been trained to lift toilet seats before urinating from a standing position.

Although old-fashioned urinals were frequently massive devices mounted on the floor, most modern ones are more compact and wall mounted.

Urinals in some European restrooms have images of flies imbedded in the enamel, to give users something to aim at, and the practice has now spread to the US. Not only does this improve neatness, but it also turns a visit to the restroom into a sporting event.

Since flushing urinals use a substantial amount of water, some buildings have installed waterless urinals. The receiving area in waterless urinals consists of water with a layer of oil intended to allow urine to pass through but to block odors. As urine enters the water below the oil, overflow goes down the drain. Waterless urinals have mixed reviews. They require a great deal of maintenance, and odors can creep through the oil. If people innocently pour liquids (such as coffee) into waterless urinals, this causes serious maintenance problems.

III-D. WASHBASINS

The second major component of restrooms is places to wash hands.

All restrooms require washbasins, and all building codes for public buildings should require them.

Unlike toilets, washbasins lend themselves to electric eye activation without the potential for embarrassing problems when mechanisms don't work. In addition, users of public restrooms appreciate being able to wash their hands without having to touch potentially filthy faucet handles.

If you have manual faucets, be sure that they have bat handles that can be operated with a wrist. Round faucet handles are particularly off-putting, since they must be grabbed by the fingertips, the very items we are trying to keep clean.

Getting newly installed electric eye faucets to operate properly may require expert attention. As part of punch listing, therefore, try out all the restroom faucets in your building and demand that they work without forcing users to hold their hands in extremely specific places. (Almost everyone has had the frustrating experience of moving one's hands back and forth endlessly under a faucet, trying fruitlessly to get it to work.)

Many washbasins are wall-mounted. *As with wall-mounted toilets, wall-mounted washbasins will simplify floor cleaning, but they also need to be strong enough to support the weight of people standing on them.* Restroom users in libraries have been known to stand on washbasins to lift ceiling tiles and hide personal objects above the ceilings, and the result can be basins broken off walls. One library Fred worked with had a basin broken off the wall almost immediately after the ribbon cutting.

III-E. SOAP DISPENSERS

Something as simple as dispensing liquid soap shouldn't require much discussion, but in reality, things often go awry.

Most soap dispensers are wall-mounted boxes. However, one popular modern design for liquid soap dispensers consists of devices mounted on countertops beside sinks. An arm from the dispenser extends over the sink, and the top of the mounting is a plunger that dispenses liquid soap when pressed.

The main problem with dispensers of liquid soap is that, sooner or later, they all tend to corrode internally and stop working. America's public restrooms are full of sinks with elegant plunger-type dispensers that no longer work, and with fancy stainless wall-mounted dispensers that also no longer work, and both have been supplemented with wall-mounted disposable dispensers, or even with the kind of plastic bottles with plunger tops designed for home use. The old plunger devices sit unused, tempting users to whale away at them without results, or they've been removed, leaving raw holes in the countertops.

What can you do?

- Expect to replace your permanently mounted soap dispensers on a regular basis, hoping that when the time comes you can match the spaces required by your current dispensers. With gadgetry supplied by low bid, this plan may represent the triumph of optimism over experience.

- Use disposable soap dispensers. Most janitorial supply companies can supply these at little or no charge to their customers. Dispensers are mounted on walls or mirrors with double-sided tape and are filled with plastic bags of liquid soap. Because the dispensing tube is part of the bag, the dispenser has no built-in tubes to corrode shut. And if the dispenser breaks, the janitorial firm can give you a new one.

One ongoing problem with soap dispensers is dripping liquid soap on the floor. Unfortunately, with separate washbasins it's hard to avoid this because the ADA requires that mirrors virtually touch the top of washbasins, and there's no space between the bottom of mirrors and the tops of sinks for soap dispensers. One solution is to mount disposable soap dispensers directly on the mirrors, where soap will drip on the sink rather than the floor.

Soap dispensers operated by electric eye are now available, making it unnecessary for users to touch what may be dirty surfaces. These are attractive devices from the point of view of good public service. Whether or not they have the same clogging problems as older permanent dispensers we don't know.

III-F. HAND DRYING

Many libraries end up deciding between forced-air hand dryers and paper towels, although there

Sooner or later, almost all restroom soap dispensers stop working. If the original dispensers were mounted in holes in the countertop, most libraries simply add a disposable plastic dispenser to a nearby wall or mirror. (Some libraries remove the nonworking countertop dispensers, leaving round holes in the countertops.)

are probably no rules saying you have to choose just one.

Users clearly prefer paper towels, but paper towels lead to greater maintenance costs. If your library has paper towel dispensers, you will be faced with:

- Running out of towels in the middle of the day, when custodial staff members may not be around. One partial solution to this is always having two dispensers or having both dispensers and dryers.

- Large quantities of used paper towels. Used paper towels add up quickly. Cute receptacles, such as the neat little bins incorporated in combination towel dispensers and trash bins that are fitted flush into walls, can fill up and overflow in minutes. Unless you want to service restrooms many times a day, you'll need a serious container for paper towels.

- Paper towels on the floor by the door. If your library has restroom doors that open inward, users will (for extraordinarily good reasons) wash their hands and then use a paper towel to open the door, because they don't want to grasp dirty door handles with freshly washed hands. If you are stuck with a library with restroom doors that open inward, you'll need an extra wastebasket right by the door.
- Occasional paper towels flushed down toilets. This appears to be a particular problem in single-user restrooms, which have other bad attributes as well.

Many libraries install paper towel dispensers with motion sensors. Each time users wave their hands in front of a dispenser, another section of toweling emerges. One of the great things about these is that they lessen the chance of having to touch what may be a dirty dispenser with freshly washed hands. As with other automatic gadgets, you may want to have two dispensers, in case one is empty or otherwise temporarily out of service. And you'll want to be extremely demanding at punch listing time. *Lots of motion sensor towel dispensers don't work well, and you need to be painfully insistent on perfect performance.*

The alternative to paper towels is hand dryers. Users may dislike them, but they require less frequent janitorial service.

Dryers can be controlled by push buttons or electric eyes.

Some older hand dryers relied too much on heat and not enough on air movement. The least satisfactory devices combined high heat with limited airflow, burning the hands without drying them.

The trouble with hand dryers is similar to the trouble with electric razors. When razors have blades, people shave until they're through. With electric razors, people shave until they get bored and give up.

One useful innovation that eliminates the boredom factor is high-velocity hand dryers that actually do the job. Of course, they also make an amazing racket, potentially eliminating from libraries the doorless restrooms developed for airports. Another reason of the many reasons to have restrooms leading to foyers or other open non-library spaces is to avoid bothering library users with the roar of the dryers.

If at all possible, insist on trying out a working model of your hand dryers before you authorize their installation, judging effectiveness and noise. We see a lot of bad examples in government buildings, perhaps the result of contractors claiming "equivalencies."

III-G. MIRRORS

All restrooms need mirrors.

Most have mirrors directly over the washbasins, but you may benefit from an additional mirror or two.

Check your restroom floor plans carefully to be sure that mirrors are not visible from outside the restrooms when the doors are open. Many restrooms provide an amazing view of the activities within, all reflected in the mirrors over the sinks.

Be sure that the lighting by the mirrors lights the fronts of people's faces as well as the tops of their heads. There are restrooms where the tops of people's heads are blazingly illuminated while their faces are in deep (but not romantic) shadow. People use mirrors to check their appearances, and they need light to do so.

III-H. SHELVES

Many restrooms have shelves where people can place objects while they are using the restrooms. A common place is above the sinks and below the mirrors, but there may not be space. Shelves can also be located between mirrors.

III-I. FEMININE HYGIENE PRODUCTS

Women's restrooms need dispensers for feminine hygiene products. Typically, these can be mounted on a wall in the main area of the restroom, where people will be less tempted to break into them for the paltry amount of change they contain, and where a single dispenser can be equally accessible to all users. Or just be civilized, forget about the small change, and make the products free.

Depending on the effectiveness of your waste plumbing system, you may want containers mounted on the walls of stalls for the disposal of these products. Remember that feminine hygiene products are medical waste, and their handling and disposal is subject to concerns about blood-borne pathogens.

III-J. HYPODERMIC NEEDLES

The most common medical waste in restrooms (if you don't count feminine hygiene products) is used insulin syringes. "Sharps" containers for disposal of syringes are usually bolted to walls somewhere near the sinks, since people taking insulin will probably use sink tops as shelves.

III-K. VENTILATION

Exhaust fans are essential to restroom design. No matter how lovely your restroom décor or how elegant your fixtures, inadequate ventilation will spoil everyone's appreciation.

Most fans are located at the farthest point from the entry door to reduce the chance of any bad smells being detected outside the entrances to the restrooms.

Minimum restroom ventilation requirements are specified by codes, but you may want to exceed the minimum.

III-L. MOP BASINS

To prevent custodians from rinsing out mops in toilets, most codes require a mop basin (floor sink) on any floor that has a toilet.

Mop basins need to be in mop closets (aka janitors' closets). Simply putting mop basins inside restrooms is a really bad idea. They're ugly, and who knows how they'll be abused.

Mop closets are often located near restrooms to consolidate plumbing. However, mop closets that are accessed *through* restrooms are a bad idea because there are problems if the mopper is a different gender from the restroom users. (Don't assume that this will be okay because floors will be mopped only when the library is closed, or because all moppers will be male.)

IV. Accommodations for Children and Infants

IV-A. CHILDREN'S RESTROOMS

All larger public libraries need separate restrooms for children, particularly when children's departments and adult departments are on separate floors.

As with adult restrooms, children's restrooms can suffer from vandalism and other problems. Small boys in particular occasionally lock themselves into restrooms and create mayhem.

The best way to prevent vandalism is to never have restrooms with locking doors. Even if a restroom has only one toilet, the toilet can be in a stall, making a locking door to the restroom unnecessary.

Miniature restroom fixtures are available, but we are not taken with them. Most kids manage well with adult-sized fixtures. If they can do it at home, why not at the library as well?

Regardless of fixture size, toilet stalls in children's restrooms must be generously proportioned because they often must simultaneously hold both a child and the parent helping the child.

See also section IV-C, "Infant Seats."

IV-B. CHANGING TABLES

Virtually all libraries need changing tables. Although your library may in theory serve only adults, unless you card infants at the door, sooner or later one of them will slither in and promptly need changing. No matter how you feel about all of this, the experience of having a parent change an impressively dirty diaper on top of a reading table will provide positive thoughts about the utility—not to mention pleasantness—of having changing tables in your restrooms.

Both men's and women's restrooms need changing tables. If you assume that only women have infants requiring changing, you will at the very least be branded as a troglodyte.

Do not make the mistake of placing changing tables in toilet stalls. In some libraries, the changing tables are in the accessible stalls, leading to the very real possibility of users in wheelchairs and users with infants needing to occupy the same turf.

Changing tables can be fixed to a wall, or they can fold down. Commercially available folding tables are designed to be cleaned, but if your architects invent their own fixed tables, be sure the tables are easy to clean.

There needs to be some source of wet wipes or other ways of cleaning off infants.

Be sure you have a receptacle for dirty diapers. It needs to be located right beside the changing table and marked more boldly than you would really think necessary. If the lid is opened by a foot pedal and is equipped with a deodorizer, everyone will be happier. The last thing you need is people flushing disposable diapers down the toilets.

IV-C. INFANT SEATS

Infant seats are fold-down, wall-mounted seats with restraining straps to keep infants secure while parents are using restrooms. Few parents want to balance infants on their laps while using the toilet, and the options of placing infants on dirty restroom floors or handing them off to strangers are equally icky. Infant seats are inexpensive and take very little space when folded up.

IV-D. RESTROOMS BY STORY AND CRAFT ROOMS

Many children's librarians note the extreme utility of having at least one small unisex restroom located adjacent to story and craft rooms.

Enchanted by the engaging events in story and craft rooms, children delay mentioning their needs until there are only seconds to spare. For parents, the idea of having to sprint across the entire library carrying a four-year-old time bomb is not a happy one.

V. Family Restrooms

Many libraries include family restrooms, a name that belies the wide range of user comfort these rooms offer. These provide a place for parents to assist children, adults to assist grandparents, better accommodation of larger mobility devices (even accessible restrooms can be decidedly difficult to navigate), and they are gender neutral.

For some reason, some libraries keep such restrooms locked and ask users to request keys. This seems annoying at best and repressive at worst.

VI. Size and Locations of Restrooms

VI-A. NUMBER OF FIXTURES

Plumbing codes may dictate the minimum number of toilets for your library. If your state does not have codes specifying minimum numbers of fixtures, you can ask your architects to check the codes of other states.

As we noted at the beginning of this chapter, you may feel that your plumbing code requires more fixtures than your library actually needs. Others feel that there simply are not enough fixtures to meet demand. We encourage you to review expected use levels and consider providing more toilets for women than for men. This is particularly important if you anticipate major rushes to use restrooms, such as times when large numbers of people are leaving events at the same time.

VI-B. LOCATIONS

Most libraries—even very small ones—provide at least two restrooms, one for women and one for men. If you want a single unisex restroom, your architect will determine if that is legal in your area.

Small public libraries benefit from restrooms that are accessible from foyers. If a library's meeting rooms and restrooms are both accessible from its entry foyer, the door between the foyer and the rest of the library can be locked and meetings can take place when the rest of the library is closed.

Placing restrooms outside a library's theft-control security gates also helps prevent users from taking library materials into restrooms without first checking the materials out. This arrangement can greatly reduce the number of materials left in unusable condition in restrooms.

No restrooms should lead directly to reading rooms, meeting rooms, staff workrooms, staff lunchrooms, and so on. Unfortunately, restrooms of all of these types exist in abundance.

Placing restrooms in the same location on each floor makes it easier for people to find restrooms, and stacking restrooms this way also simplifies plumbing, but it should work best in large libraries with similar services on several floors, not in libraries serving a variety of users, such as adults, children, meeting room users, and so on, where it becomes important to place restrooms adjacent to specific services.

Having women's restrooms and men's restrooms on alternating floors is done, but we're not sure it's done wisely.

From the point of view of both staff oversight and efficient use of fixtures, it's easier to have fewer and larger restrooms than many small ones.

All entrances to public restrooms should be visible from library staff service points.

When restroom doors are open, baffle walls should prevent views of the insides of the rooms. Far too many restrooms provide passers-by with views of all the men at the urinals when the doors open. Views of stall doors are not quite so unwelcome, but they are still inappropriate. If restrooms provide passers-by with a view of sinks, the reflections in the mirrors over the sinks may provide views of the urinals and stall doors.

Avoiding restrooms that provide views of this kind is easy, but they unfortunately exist everywhere, including in new and expensive buildings that could have been properly designed. When you are checking over your library designs, always inspect the restroom drawings for inappropriate sight lines.

Some public restrooms in libraries are in such secret locations that no one can find them without assistance. We've even seen some library restrooms that are located in hallways accessed through unmarked doors.

> One library we visited has not only invisible restroom doors but also an agreement with the designer that the library will not install any additional signage. The real blame for this lies with the owners who were foolish enough to give their designers this kind of power after the building was completed.

Library staff members grouse endlessly about giving directions to restrooms. Some of this is unreasonable kvetching, but it helps if restroom locations are reasonably obvious.

When you are evaluating your schematic designs and construction drawings, ask yourself whether users will be able to find the restrooms.

VI-C. STAFF RESTROOMS

Most library staff members strongly dislike sharing toilet facilities with library users, and it is reasonable and proper to provide separate restrooms for library staff members. In the case of a small library, a single unisex staff restroom is probably sufficient, although unisex restrooms may not count toward the minimum number of fixtures specified in some plumbing codes.

One of the most serious but common errors in the creation of staff restrooms is to have them directly accessible from staff lunchrooms. We've seen many libraries where staff members having lunch are actually treated to views of toilets through open restroom doors. It's hard to imagine wanting to eat lunch three feet from a toilet, or wanting to use a toilet three feet from where one's co-workers are eating lunch, but buildings are designed that way all the time.

VI-D. IMPLICATIONS FOR EXPANSION

If you are planning a two-phase library, you will almost certainly want to be sure that the restrooms built for the first phase will be sufficient to serve the expanded building.

If you have to add extra restroom capacity when you expand your building, you may end up trying to cram extra toilets into rooms not designed to hold them or be faced with the far greater cost and loss of flexibility that accompanies having to construct additional restrooms.

Extra restrooms will cost more than larger restrooms, and they can lead to situations where users dash from restroom to restroom trying to find a free stall.

Extra restrooms are also far more likely to end up in awkward places, like directly off reading rooms.

VI-E. GENDER-NEUTRAL RESTROOMS

Increasingly, libraries want to accommodate transgender and gender-nonconforming users. While a growing number of libraries throughout the nation have incorporated gender-neutral facilities, some libraries do not yet offer them, and designs are still in transition.

Here are some possibilities:

- Have gender-neutral restrooms with reasonably private stalls.
- Do the way Europeans have done and regard gender-neutral restrooms with ordinary stalls as providing sufficient privacy.
- Retain current men's and women's restrooms, but update signage and make all toilet accommodations private, including stalls for urinals.
- Create small, single-user, non-gendered restrooms.
- To improve security, avoid doors. Consider providing restrooms with zigzag entrances like airport restrooms.
- One issue with single-user, unisex restrooms is whether to include urinals in all restrooms. Urinals result in far less mess. Many fast-food restaurants are moving to this approach.
- Repurpose family restrooms as gender-neutral restrooms.

VII. Security

VII-A. STAFF OVERSIGHT

One of the best ways to limit problems with restrooms is to have restroom doors visible from staff workstations.

In public libraries with restrooms and meeting rooms accessible from entry foyers, it's easy for staff to observe people entering and leaving restrooms.

Some libraries that have problems with vandalism in restrooms have restroom doors that are kept locked at all times and unlocked by push buttons at service desks.

It's also possible to have keys at service desks, but keeping an eye on keys can be a real nuisance. Keys usually have to have huge blocks of wood or other objects attached to prevent users from wandering off with them. And who wants to handle potentially dirty wooden blocks all day long?

VII-B. SINGLE-USER RESTROOMS

One major source of security problems in library restrooms is single-user restrooms with doors that lock. If individuals can lock themselves in, there's more possibility for trouble.

To prevent this, with the exception of staff restrooms, no restroom doors should have locks, and necessary privacy should be provided by stalls. Providing a stall in a single-user restroom takes somewhat more space, but the reduction in vandalism can be impressive.

Consequently, all public restrooms need baffle walls to prevent people standing outside from viewing the inside of restrooms in action.

VII-C. DOORLESS RESTROOMS

Some libraries have doorless restrooms of the style used in airports. While these provide sufficient privacy, they discourage vandalism because people using them receive no advance warning when someone else enters.

Doorless restrooms let more sound escape, but so do regular restrooms when the doors are open. As long as the restrooms are reached from hallways or foyers, things seem to work well.

Ideally, doorless restrooms with zigzag entries will be designed so that doors can be retrofitted later if necessary. This requires attention to clearances, wall construction, and air supplies during initial restroom planning.

VII-D. VIDEO SURVEILLANCE

One way to fight vandalism in restrooms is with video surveillance. Although cameras in restrooms are obviously inappropriate, cameras can be located to permit identification of people leaving restrooms.

VII-E. RESTROOMS AS TORNADO SHELTERS

Libraries in areas prone to tornados frequently include restrooms that can serve as tornado shelters, with concrete walls and ceilings. A small frame-on-slab library is unlikely to withstand a major windstorm, but if the restrooms have concrete walls and ceilings, people can take shelter there.

Restrooms have the advantage of being the only rooms in libraries that are never used for storage. Library staff members are always hunting for places to put stuff, which all libraries have in generous quantities. If any room except a restroom is designed to serve as a tornado shelter, people arriving there may find it full of puppets and used paperbacks and miscellaneous shelving components—and unable to serve as a shelter.

By locating restrooms directly off entry foyers, libraries make their tornado shelters available to people using meeting rooms after regular library hours, as well as to users diving off the street seeking shelter.

Obviously, restrooms designed as shelters cannot have windows and cannot be doorless.

> This sounds like a silly observation, but one library Fred worked with relocated its tornado shelters from the restrooms to the library proper—where they could not be accessed after regular hours—in a room that ended up filled with furniture, all to preserve a translucent glass window in one of the restrooms.

VIII. Lighting

VIII-A. MOTION SENSORS

Energy codes may require that your restrooms have lighting operated by motion sensors. If this is the case, you will have to deal with two serious potential problems.

First, motion sensors need to operate the moment the restroom door starts to open and not require users to grope their way into a dark space. This may require a separate detector on the ceiling, not a cheap one combined with a light switch. (If the restroom has cheap detectors, users will reach inside the dark room and attempt to turn on the light switch, usually messing up the setting of the sensor.)

Second, there must be no way that anyone in a stall can fail to be detected and plunged into total darkness. Motion-sensing technology may eventually prevent this, but until then, always provide a dim level of 24/7 night lighting—even if it's just one or two foot-candles—in all public restrooms.

> This is not an imaginary problem. There are library restrooms where no amount of hand-waving in specific stalls will turn the lights back on.

Because restrooms usually have no windows, being in a restroom when the lights go out is a little like being in an unlighted limestone cave. Few non-cavers will appreciate the experience.

Some libraries are so antagonized by the functions of motion detectors in restrooms that they quietly replace them with light switches.

VIII-B. MANUALLY SWITCHED LIGHTING

If your restrooms have manual light switches, you will need a way to prevent people leaving restrooms from turning off the lights, leaving other people in the dark without even a slight hope of waving their arms around to bring the lights back on. (This can happen accidentally, or kids can get a kick out of leaving each other trapped in pitch-dark restrooms.)

A standard way to prevent this kind of misery is to use key switches that require a special tool to turn the lights off and on.

VIII-C. LIGHT DISTRIBUTION

People using washbasins need to be able to see their reflections in the mirrors over the basins to check hair, makeup, and so on. If the light provided is harshly vertical, this doesn't work.

There also needs to be at least a minimum amount of light in toilet stalls. The lower the restroom ceiling, the harder this is to achieve from a limited number of light fixtures.

IX. Planning for Maintenance

IX-A. FLOOR COVERINGS

Although some restrooms have resilient flooring such as vinyl tile, by far the most practical floor covering is ceramic tile.

Unlike ceramic tile, vinyl tile is sufficiently porous to be hard to keep clean in restroom situations, and it can wear quickly in places users always stand. And moisture may eventually lead vinyl tile to lift and curl and separate.

To work properly in restrooms, ceramic tile needs:

- A surface rough enough to prevent the tile from being slippery when wet. Installing polished stone flooring or terrazzo in a public restroom provides a great opportunity to test your liability insurance coverage.
- Very dark (never pastel) grout. Trying to keeping white grout clean is essentially impossible, the bane of cleaning firms everywhere. (Dark grout is, of course, no easier to clean than white grout, but with dark grout the stains don't show.) *We cannot emphasize this point too strongly.* If you have white or light-colored grout, you will come to hate white or light-colored grout with true passion.

IX-B. FLOOR DRAINS

Regardless of building code requirements, all restrooms need floor drains.

Due to construction errors, some floor drains don't work properly. As part of your punch list process, pour buckets of water on your restroom floors to make sure that water flows toward the drains rather than away from them. If the floor drain in a restroom with a ceramic tile floor installed over concrete doesn't drain properly, both the tile and the concrete beneath will probably need to be replaced. This is another time to be firm with your punch list.

IX-C. WALL COVERINGS

The best wall covering in restrooms is ceramic tile.

Unlike floor tile, it can be smooth, but dark grout may still be important, not only to hide stains but also to prevent creative people—frustrated by the way that glazed ceramic tile rejects ballpoint pen ink and marking pens—from writing messages on the white grout.

The best approach is to install floor-to-ceiling tile. However, some libraries have tile wainscots, with painted drywall above.

IX-D. GRAFFITI

Restrooms have for generations been favorite places for inventive graffiti.

Glazed ceramic surfaces help, because almost any markings can be washed off. So do stainless steel toilet partitions. Dark grout eliminates the possibility of writing colorful observations on the grout when the tile resists decoration.

Locking single-person restrooms are particularly appealing places because they provide users with the time to write leisurely graffiti.

X. Snappy Rules on Restrooms

1. The fact that this chapter has a large number of snappy rules tells something about the perils of restroom design.

2. If your library will have meetings that large numbers of people leave at the same time, you will need more women's toilets than men's toilets. (Even concert halls and sports arenas sometimes fail to do this.)

3. A poorly ventilated restroom is a seriously unlovely object.

4. Always use flush-valve toilets unless your community suffers from low water pressure. You can't start with tank toilets now and switch to flush-valve toilets later, so take the plunge.

5. Always check sight lines into restrooms on your floor plans. One way is to ask if your restrooms would still be sufficiently private if the entry doors were removed.

6. Remember that if people can see the mirrors from outside the door, they can probably see everything from outside the door.

7. Owners may like hand dryers, but users prefer towels. You can have both.

8. Unless your building successfully bans infants, your restrooms will need changing tables. And receptacles for dirty diapers. (Very few buildings successfully ban infants.)

9. If your washbasins aren't strong enough to bear the weight of adults, sooner or later someone will break one off the wall.

10. Even in tiny libraries, staff do not want to share restrooms with library users. Unless you've spent your life working in libraries, you have no right to regard this as an unreasonable attitude.

11. Restrooms must never open directly into reading rooms, program rooms, or staff lunchrooms. Don't get yourself into a situation where expanding your library will require additional restrooms in unacceptable places.

12. It's easier to control restrooms if the doors are visible from staff workstations. Video cameras recording people entering and leaving restrooms also help.

13. When deciding whether to use automatic fixtures, ask yourself how awkward things will be if a fixture fails to operate as promised.

14. Users with freshly washed hands do not want to grab dirty door handles when they leave restrooms. If your restroom doors do not swing outward, you will need wastebaskets for paper towels right by the exit doors. (If your doors swing inward and you have only hand dryers, your users will speak ill of you.)

15. As part of the punch list process, always make sure that all your restroom gadgets work properly. Check automatic faucets and toilets. Check floor drains. Check soap dispensers. Check hand dryers and automatic towel dispensers. Check exhaust fans. Check that motion detectors don't require people to actually enter the room to turn the lights on, and that lights don't go out too quickly. Check to be sure that the motion detectors work in all of the stalls. And never, NEVER pay your holdback until everything works perfectly.

16. If your area is prone to tornados, tornado-proof restrooms are a great idea. Especially in one-story buildings, where people

can't take shelter under a strong upper floor. (Unlike other sorts of storm shelters, restrooms are almost never used for storage, and people diving for cover can expect to find the floors clear.)

17. The only suitable restroom floor covering is anti-slip ceramic tile with very dark grout. White grout is impossible to keep clean. Vinyl tile is hard to maintain and tends to come loose. Shiny ceramic tile is excitingly slippery when wet.

18. Cheap fixtures are a lack of joy forever. Or until they quickly die in service. Fixtures designed for home use are often cheap fixtures.

19. Be sure all of your toilet stalls are large enough for actual human beings. Surprisingly, a great many are not.

20. A toilet stall without two sturdy hooks for coats, purses, book bags, jackets, and coats is an unhelpful toilet stall.

21. Sooner or later, all soap dispensers fail. Have a plan.

22. Picturesque, antique restrooms are probably less fun than picturesque, antique reading rooms.

23. If you are constructing a two-phase building, make your Phase I restrooms large enough to meet Phase II code requirements, or you may end up with extra restrooms added during Phase II construction in seriously unfortunate locations.

24. Wall-mounted toilets allow far easier maintenance. The joint where a floor-mounted toilet meets the floor is always dirty.

25. Faucet handles are probably among the dirtiest objects in public restrooms. Get electric-eye operated faucets or get faucets with bat handles than can be operated by the wrist.

26. Gender-neutral restrooms are here to stay. Plan accordingly.

27. No decent lighting system plunges restroom users into darkness or forces them to grope their way into pitch dark restrooms.

28. Try to observe recommended fixtures in action before you specify them.

PART III
Essential Spaces All Libraries Need

CHAPTER 27
Staff Workrooms

I. Introduction

Most libraries have overcrowded staff workrooms, and many libraries have too few workrooms.

On some occasions this is no doubt the result of librarians who are pack rats, but we suspect that it is more often due to the fact that staff workrooms are almost always inadequate to begin with.

One way to fight this is to make sure that the written building program for your library includes adequate staff workspaces not only for opening day but also for just as long as you expect the library to continue in use without expansion.

II. General Considerations for Staff Workrooms

Staff workrooms are an essential part of all libraries.

All libraries larger than broom closets require staff workrooms. Staff need space to spread out work and leave it undisturbed while helping library users. Supervisors need spaces where they can talk with their staff members privately. All sorts of special activities require special equipment and places to spread it out. And many materials handled by library staff members require secure storage.

Throughout this book, we've called these areas "workrooms" rather than "offices." The word "office" conjures up an image of spaciousness and luxury that is alien to virtually all library employees.

II-A. WORKROOM SIZES

When groups of non-librarians that supervise libraries have to cut planned building sizes, the two things they seem to cut first are staff workspaces and storage spaces. Both can be amazingly bad decisions.

The people who know what kind of workspaces they need are the staff who work there. It's easy for remote employers to develop standard workspace sizes (and they probably go with standard because it's easy to do so), but planning workspaces means working with individual staff members. Many library tasks require very specific pieces of equipment, plus elbowroom for the people who operate the equipment, and the actual staff who work there know this best. It doesn't have to be in a private room, but necessary equipment needs to go somewhere.

Some universities may have standard office sizes based on rank. These don't work with library workspaces, no matter how even-handed they seem. (Imagine a graphic artist with the title of "instructor" trying to fit a scanner and folder and storage for a wide variety of paper sizes into a 125-square-foot workroom.)

Far too many libraries plan new shelving to meet decades of growth but construct workspaces only for current staff. This qualifies as seriously bad planning, but some libraries are adamant. Sooner or later, however, libraries hire additional staff, who have to work somewhere.

As the years go by, libraries tend to add new specialties more rapidly than they eliminate old ones, and the long-term pressures for expanded workspaces inevitably continue.

Some libraries reduce needed staff workspaces by outsourcing functions, but others reverse the situation by bringing outsourced functions back home again.

One of the issues in planning workspaces is envisioning the future. Another issue is what you will do if you are wrong and construct too little space.

As a matter of practice in all libraries, all workrooms need to meet all codes for accessibility by people with disabilities. Planning workrooms that are too small from the beginning is a violation of accessibility.

II-B. WORKROOM ARRANGEMENT AND ADJACENCIES

No staff workroom should be a public passageway. (It shouldn't be necessary to say this, but it keeps happening.)

If you have a group of administrative workrooms, it may help to put human relations near the front if a lot of visitors are job applicants.

Planning about workroom adjacencies appears to mainly affect small libraries that have to decide when to have an all-purpose staff workroom and when to have separate departmental workrooms. One way of looking at the situation may be to ask whether departments are separate rooms.

In most libraries, staff workrooms are in logical places, but every once in a while there's a workroom for departmental library staff located far from the actual departmental library.

From the selfish management point of view, that's a lot of expensive staff time wasted running back and forth between the workroom and the library. From the employee point of view, it's a total pain in the neck.

II-C. WINDOWS TO THE REST OF THE LIBRARY

A window with a Venetian blind between the workroom and the adjacent public area of the library is an important feature, one that is reasonably priced upfront but extremely expensive to retrofit.

Windows between staff workrooms and the public areas of the library provide great opportunities for staff oversight at no additional cost to the library.

Staff members who like privacy can just keep the blinds closed. We think that windows of this type are also very important for library directors and supervisors, who may be uneasy about overly private meetings with employees or visitors of the opposite sex.

In some libraries there's a constant tendency of staff members to close their blinds between their workrooms and the associated public areas, followed by administrators reopening the blinds.

II-D. PRIVACY

Unless there's a need for privacy, go with group work areas. This means that supervisors need private workrooms because they need to have confidential conversations, bookkeepers need private workrooms because they have financial records, personnel officers need private workrooms because they have confidential files, and rare book catalogers can't leave rare books just lying around . . . BUT most other staff can be in shared work areas. All sorts of office system furniture is available, from traditional cubes to various multifunction units. And a group work area lends itself to the kind of shared worktable that can be used for staff meetings, spread-out projects, and staff social events.

Some businesses have tried putting everyone in group workrooms and then providing spaces that can be used for private conversations. Unfortunately, this makes it painfully clear when an employee is going to get a stern talking to, because everyone sees the supervisor and employee heading off for one of the private conversation spaces. We talked with people who work in environments like this, and they aren't happy.

II-E. MODULAR FURNISHINGS

Unless specific furnishings require running water, prefer modular furniture to built-ins. Staff members often want to rearrange their workspaces, and there's no reason they shouldn't. As with all library work areas, this means soft, even, all-purpose lighting and lots (as in LOTS) of electrical outlets at above tabletop height on walls and all over the floor.

Built-in furnishings violate the core principle of library design: flexibility.

II-F. LIGHTING

Workrooms benefit from natural light. This is one more reason why upper floors are preferable to basements. (Other reasons include the fact that basements are nearly as expensive as upper floors, basements tend to be damp, and sooner or later many basements end up flooded. As a friend in the insurance business says, "Basements are places you put things you really don't want.")

One traditional trick for providing natural lighting for workrooms buried in the interior of buildings is "borrowed light." High interior windows in these workrooms lead to adjacent rooms that have natural light.

Artificial lighting in workrooms needs to be bright but low-glare. The kind of allover lighting that works in public reading areas should also be effective in most workrooms. The usual formula is between 70 and 100 percent uplighting, 60 foot-candles of illumination on horizontal surfaces at desktop, and at least 30 foot-candles on vertical surfaces. We think that 100 percent uplighting is best because it avoids glare.

For rooms used for special functions like filming books, extensive light control will be essential, and windows of any kind may cause serious problems.

Workrooms also need controllable natural light. This means (in particular) no skylights, but also movable blinds on all exterior glass surfaces that don't face straight north. (Many designers and planners are enamored of windows that cannot be fitted with blinds, so be prepared to say "No!")

Many workrooms benefit from interior glass areas facing adjacent areas of the library, both for security of workroom staff and for extra staff oversight of public areas. The time to install interior glass is when you are constructing your building; adding windows later can be extraordinarily expensive. (If you don't need the window right now, keep the blind closed, knowing that you'll rejoice if you need the window later and it's already there.)

(Fred inherited an office with a one-piece plastic skylight. The worktable under the skylight was too bright by day and too dark by night. And one day the skylight blew off, reducing Fred's stacks of working papers to entertaining chaos. The total experience did not enhance his love of skylights.)

II-G. WIRING

The main secret of wiring for workrooms is to have lots of electrical outlets on both walls and floors. It's particularly frustrating to find that the office system furniture you have selected blocks access to the only electrical outlet on that wall. (We've seen libraries tackle expensive new office system equipment with saber saws, just to get access to outlets.)

Unless the workroom is intended to be a showplace for an administrator, electrical outlets work a lot better above tabletop height, so that staff members do not have to crawl under furniture in order to plug in pieces of equipment. In addition, some workrooms end up with machinery lined up edge-to-edge all the way around the room, and it's impossible to plug things in without high outlets.

When you're looking at the electrical drawings for your new library, outlets that are 36 inches above the floor should be marked "+ 36."

If you plan data conduit as well as 110-volt service, you can install dual-conduit wire mold that allows both sets of wires in the same enclosure.

II-H. WATER

With the exception of some private workrooms, all library workrooms need running water and sinks.

The main point is to be sure that sinks are specified in your building program, since retrofitting a sink is a seriously expensive undertaking. As usual, sinks need to be deep enough to allow something relatively serious to be filled. The kind of toy sinks called "bar sinks" may be suitable for playhouses, but they will make workroom occupants unhappy.

Sinks need to be located in fixed counters, but all other work surfaces should be movable furniture to allow long-term flexibility.

II-I. RESTROOMS

It's hard to imagine a library employee who would not rejoice in a private restroom. But many of us who have been directors would be a little hesitant to bring up the idea.

We suspect that most libraries limit themselves to staff restrooms. The main point is that shared staff restrooms should always be accessed from a staff hallway and not from a staff workroom, a lunchroom, or a public area of the library.

II-J. CLOTHES WASHERS AND DRYERS

Clothes washing equipment is important in children's department workrooms, where staff otherwise have to haul puppets, dress-up clothes, and similar stuff home with them. Washers and dryers have to be installed up front, because connections are complex (220-volt power for dryers, exhaust vents, water supplies, and drains) and very difficult to install after the fact.

II-K. STORAGE

Many library workspaces involve storage as well as actual work areas. Storage in the workroom is more convenient than storage down the hall and around the corner and up three steps. Since libraries often pay their staff by the hour, not having people constantly running back and forth to fetch things and put them back is worth money.

II-L. VENTILATION

Acoustics and fresh air are important. In general, all staff workrooms need to be inherently quiet and well ventilated, with consideration to the level of crowding. Large workrooms with cube farms need particularly careful consideration of partition heights and surfaces, provision of fresh air, and lack of unwanted shadows in individual cubes. Some workrooms need extra ventilation, particularly graphic arts rooms. Some preservation equipment also needs extra ventilation.

Ventilation is simple to provide during construction but may be extremely expensive to retrofit. Be sure to specify special ventilation requirements in your building program and check your construction drawings to be sure your architects provided it.

Group workrooms may have more people per square foot than other areas of the library, and that may require better ventilation.

II-M. TEMPERATURE CONTROL

To be effective, all workrooms require independent temperature controls. Trying to make a single thermostat (and associated temperature control equipment) do double duty for two separate rooms is an amazingly awful idea, but we occasionally find things set up that way. Inevitably, the people in the workroom without the thermostat will be impressively uncomfortable. (The alternative of a space heater is a great way to start a fire.)

Office system furniture needs adequate clearance between the tops of the partitions and the ceiling above, to allow adequate air circulation.

Some group workrooms are large enough to need more than one temperature control zone, especially when one far end of a room is on an outside wall with windows.

III. Individual Workrooms

At least some employees will need individual workrooms.

> Fred actually had a corner "office" in his library, but it sounds better than it was in real life, for it was in a corner of the basement with one high window that led to a light well with a steel grating.

Library directors have a lot of individual opinions about ideal workspaces, and a well-written building program will enumerate these.

In our experience, some directors are particularly wary about extra features in their own workrooms. They push strongly for good staff workspaces, but are hesitant to request anything for themselves. As a result, programmers need to arrive with a long list of possible features and be sure that directors don't sell themselves (and those who follow them and use the same workrooms) short.

Other single-person workrooms common in libraries include workrooms for deputy directors, department heads, bookkeepers, office managers, personnel managers, and any other staff members who need to be able to have private conversations, particularly staff evaluations, or work with confidential documents.

Individual workrooms can be located in all sorts of places. Some library directors want their workrooms where they can see everyone entering the building—and everyone entering the building can see the directors. Other directors want somewhat more protection, if for no other reason than they have to get some work done once in a while.

Lots of director's workrooms are reached through secretarial spaces, so that office managers or other workers can greet people who are looking for the director. If the outer rooms have a couple of armchairs and a coffee table, that gives visitors a place to sit while waiting to see the director. Other director's workrooms are one of two or more workrooms leading off a common lobby, with perhaps office managers and bookkeepers in the other workrooms.

Administrators' workrooms serve important roles in establishing or maintaining the identity of the library. As such, they need open wall space for their diplomas and certificates and (we assume in the case of your library) a wide range of awards. Director's workrooms and seating areas for visitors awaiting appointments are great places for this kind of wall area and displays that convey the status of the library.

We've seen a few situations where director's workrooms were passages to other parts of the library, and these arrangements were a terrible mistake.

> In one library Fred worked with, the only restroom in the building was reached by walking through the director's workroom, which people did about every five minutes all day long. When the new library was constructed, the director wanted the most remote room in the entire building. In addition to access through a door in a back corner of the staff workroom, it had a second door leading directly outside.

The best location for workrooms for department heads is adjacent to the multiuser staff workrooms of the departments.

Some workers who are multitaskers may need to spread more than one project out at the same time rather than constantly picking up one project before returning to the other. And wasting a lot of expensive staff time in the process.

> All directors have problems with where to put their framed stuff when they retire and have to clear out their workrooms. Fred used the basement stairs. John Moorman, co-author of the first edition, lacked basement space and threw his away. Fred thought this was a rush to judgment.

IV. Workroom Furnishings

This section of the chapter consists of a list of possible furnishings and equipment in staff workrooms.

When in doubt, avoid built-in anything. Outside of counters with running water, nothing needs to be custom built or fastened down. Moving furniture in or out is a lot cheaper than changing a built-in item. A wide variety of modular office system units including desks, filing drawers, and overhead storage bins is available, but individual furniture items may do a better job of meeting the needs of individual staff members.

Flexibility is particularly important when staff change. The new resident of a workroom may want to change from a seated-height to a standing-height desk, or from a low chair to a high chair, or to a large rubber ball. If it's just a matter of rearranging furniture, life is easy.

As the snappy rule says, "Never send architecture to do furniture's work."

IV-A. WORK SURFACES

IV-A-1. Desks

Many staff members with individual workrooms have desks that serve both as workspaces and as spaces for meeting with people. Some modular office system desks are designed to provide two separate surfaces, a desk (perhaps with storage bins above) and a wide L that provides a surface between visitors and the staff member.

Some directors want very much to have separate furniture for working and for meeting with people. As a result, some directors have installed small, separate conference tables for meeting with visitors. Others have worktables for doing paperwork and use their desks for meeting with people.

Most desks have two pedestals, each with a file drawer and a shallower drawer. If the desk has a computer L, the L may replace the drawers on one of the pedestals.

Some desks have shallow pencil drawers between the knee hole and desktop, but these can cramp the available legroom.

Lots of directors don't want really pompous executive desks in their own workrooms, but sometimes they inherit desks that are uncomfortably grand. It's hard to toss out expensive furniture, and it's also annoying to have to explain to every visitor that your predecessor picked it out. It's even more awkward if the desk is so big you can't circumnavigate it.

Luckily, a huge range of more modest wooden desks is available and suitable for library directors.

For many staff members, high-quality steel desks are a happy choice.

There is increasing demand for desks with adjustable heights. Some staff members want standard desks, some like desks with elevated chairs, some prefer to work while standing, and some like to vary things during the day. Movable furniture is essential. And given these variable preferences, equipping most workrooms with adjustable furniture may be worthwhile.

All desks need modesty panels. We see catalog illustrations of minimalist desks that are little more than tables, but we expect that few staff members want to have their legs on display that way. (Modesty appears to be a good option for everyday libraries, and most libraries are everyday libraries.)

Many separate desks are accompanied by credenzas. A credenza is a low cabinet behind a desk. The idea is that the top will provide space for (hopefully) neat storage, while the cabinets and drawers provide extra storage space. Often credenzas are pieces of furniture that match the desk and make a set. We've heard a number of library directors laugh about what they store in their credenzas, sometimes using the term "crudenza."

IV-A-2. Modular Office System Workstations

Modular office system workstations (also called systems furnishings) are particularly important when a number of staff need to share a workroom. Workstations can be rearranged, and they usually make very efficient use of space. Many have overhead storage bins, shelving, built-in lighting, file drawers, locking desk drawers (for purses), and other features.

Some large staff workrooms have masses of identical modular workstations in rows, a kind of Levittown effect.

The websites of office furniture firms are awash in modular office system workstations. This appears to be an excellent time to work with your interior designer. But be sure that staff who work in offices aren't overruled without reasons.

IV-A-3. Worktables

Many staff group workrooms have shared worktables for staff tasks, including packing and unpacking shipments, working on sprawly projects, and similar things. In some workrooms, staff use these tables for occasional group meetings by clearing the tabletops.

IV-B. SEATING

IV-B-1. Workroom Chairs

The main thing with chairs is comfort. It's a shame to spend three hours seated at work, only to find that an ill-conceived chair has led to temporarily frozen knee joints, making it embarrassing when you plan to leap to your feet to greet a visitor and instead lurch to your feet. The wrong chair can also lead to horrible back

> When Fred arrived as a library director in the mid-1970s, he found a dozen new conference room chairs that had been selected by an interior designer and purchased without being tested. They were from a very big-name manufacturer of office furniture, but they were molded plastic bucket seats with no possible adjustments, and they were impressively painful to use. Fred's staff contended the chairs had been carefully selected to keep staff meetings short. One librarian said she hated bucket seats because she had a "different-sized bucket."

fatigue. As with all chairs, sitting is the only true way to evaluate them.

The best workroom chairs have a lot of adjustments, and some have a maze of levers beneath to allow rearrangement for individual comfort.

One approach to workroom chair selection is to let individual employees try out the available samples and pick what they like best.

Trying to save money on workroom chairs may be extremely shortsighted.

IV-B-2. Visitor Seating

All workrooms for individual staff members need chairs for visitors. Sometimes there are a couple of chairs facing the staff member's desk, while other library staff want several chairs or small conference tables.

The usual problem with conference tables in staff workrooms is trying to cram too much table into too little space, forcing people to crawl over each other to get to the corner chair. A small conference table needs at least 25 to 30 square feet per chair. Check your schematic design carefully to be sure that office tables have enough space. There needs to be at least five feet between the edge of the table and the wall.

In some director's workrooms, the conference table doubles as a working surface when visitors aren't present.

Also consider the alternative or addition of a shared conference room amid a group of staff workrooms. There's nothing better than thanking a sales rep, then getting up, leaving the conference room, and going back to your own workroom.

IV-C. OPEN FLOOR SPACE

Many individual staff workstations need space for book trucks. You need to make clear to your designers that almost every workspace needs floor space for one or more book trucks, and that space for all of the trucks cannot be concentrated at one end of a workroom.

Some libraries also need to plan for unexpected arrivals of materials that have to go somewhere, but ideally in the appropriate offices. A nearly total lack of open floor space can represent a major challenge.

IV-D. STORAGE

IV-D-1. Storage Cabinets

Some administrative workrooms have storage cabinets, particularly for administrators who tend to store individual projects in separate piles of paper. A lot of administrators make due with standard steel cantilever shelving with separate stacks of papers, but enclosed cabinets are friendly things that lead to long-term neatness.

As administrators, John always had a neat desk and Fred always had stacks of papers. Fred should have had a cabinet for stacks of papers, but he always used open shelving instead. Visitors averted their eyes.

Locking storage cabinets are extremely useful in group workrooms, particularly when high-theft items are involved.

IV-D-2. Shelving

Most staff workspaces need shelving of some kind. Modular workstations almost always include some shelving, but many workrooms also include separate shelving. Typically, it's wall-mounted, single-faced shelving. Unless the need to show off is great, standard cantilever steel library shelving works very well. If you use the same color of shelving you have in the rest of the building, it's a lot easier to interchange parts.

It's easy to underestimate the need for storage shelving in staff workrooms. Administrators can have large book collections and stacks of papers they want to store flat for easy access. Library supplies need to be stored somewhere, and libraries need to plan spaces for colored paper, printer cartridges, boxes of rubber bands, and other space-consuming stuff. Technical services workrooms need shelving for all sorts of materials in process, as well as wide varieties of supplies.

Copier paper has to be stored somewhere, usually in boxes stacked on the floor. Some libraries keep the stacks of cartons in staff workrooms, while others keep them by a delivery dock. Decide which you prefer and include your decision in your building program.

Some libraries create separate, secure rooms for office supplies and keep careful track of who takes what. Others use an honor system.

Standard steel cantilever shelving works best for workrooms.

IV-D-3. File Storage

Almost all staff workspaces need filing cabinets. The main choices are between vertical and lateral cabinets, width of drawers (letter or legal, with legal a lot more useful), number of drawers vertically (five is as high as things usually go), and length of drawers in the case of lateral cabinets. Quality is essential, and that means avoiding discount office supply stores. Cabinets need double-extension drawer hardware and standard library paint colors to allow rearrangement. Ideally, you won't be able to pull out all the drawers at the same time and tip the cabinet over on top of yourself. Locks can be useful, particularly with personnel files. Key locks are a lot better than plunger locks, since they keep people from locking themselves out accidentally.

If you've ever found yourself locked out on the front stoop on Sunday morning in your bathrobe because the front door has a night latch rather than a dead bolt and you have no key in your bathrobe pocket, you'll appreciate why plunger locks on filing cabinets are a threat to civilized world order.

IV-D-4. Storage Cabinets for Loose Papers

Some library directors who need to meet with visitors in their offices arrange to have high shelving areas with doors, providing space for hiding stacks of working papers when visitors arrive. Cabinets like these can have shelves about a foot deep and double doors about six or seven feet high.

IV-D-5. Secure Storage

Library staff workrooms have lots of materials that need secure storage. Common things are personnel records, fiscal records, and expensive or rare materials. Any plan for staff workstations needs to include information on how security will be maintained.

IV-D-6. Coat and Purse Storage

Coat storage can range from a hook on the back of the door to a coat tree to a piece of trim on the wall with several coat hooks to a private coat closet. If you opt for the coat tree approach, make sure that there's space for it on your schematic design, and expect to have it tip over once in a while. Remember that cheap coat hooks made of cast zinc usually break, while steel and brass hooks don't.

For accessibility reasons, you may want coat hooks and coat bars at both accessible and standard heights. Long coats on accessible hangers drag on the floor, and standard height hangers are too high to meet accessibility requirements.

In shared workrooms, libraries need to provide a way for staff members to lock up their valuables. Basically, storage needs to be provided for anyone who does not have a personal desk or workstation with locking drawers. If you provide lockers, be sure they're large enough for workers who carry their wallets in backpacks. If they toss their backpacks in the corner of a workroom, sooner or later something will vanish. Half-height school hallway lockers have worked well for libraries.

IV-E. EQUIPMENT

IV-E-1. Printers

Every workroom needs a printer.

In group workrooms, printers are typically shared, but needs can vary. There are advantages to personal printers in group workrooms, particularly for staff members who load printers with adhesive labels, only to find someone printing a stack of letters onto the labels. Modern printers that require codes to release print orders save supervisors doing staff evaluations from hitting "print" and then racing madly to next-door printers.

IV-E-2. Telephones

Every workroom needs at least one telephone. Even if you initially plan lots of sharing, keep your options open for the day when staff get tired of racing across large rooms to answer the only phone. Know what you'll do if the sole phone connection turns out to be in an awkward place.

When programmers write building programs, they need to specify a telephone at every workspace. Some libraries can delay the actual phone, but failing to provide necessary wiring is painfully shortsighted.

IV-E-3. Paper Shredders

Library workrooms need paper shredders or easy access to nearby paper shredders. Paper shredders tend to fit neatly under tabletops, but include them in the list of workroom features in your program, and be sure you specify adequate vertical clearance under any furniture.

Staff members who deal with quantities of secure documents, especially in human relations, may need their own shredders in their own workrooms. Shredders are cheap.

IV-E-4. Refrigerators

Some people move dormitory-sized refrigerators into their workrooms. Often these are personal property rather than library owned.

The downsides of small private refrigerators are that food can be forgotten in them and that they can be amazing energy hogs. They also encourage staff to eat lunches in their workrooms (walking peanut butter into the carpet) and to avoid socializing in shared staff lunchrooms.

> The president of the Friends of the Library group in Fred's library hid book sale receipts into the freezer compartment of the little refrigerator Fred had brought from home and tucked under the worktable in his workroom. She contended this was the origin of the expression "cold cash."

IV-E-5. Bulletin Boards

Every staff workroom needs at least one bulletin board or whiteboard.

Many administrators like to post reminders of projects with deadlines in their personal workrooms. It's easiest to keep track if one can see the reminders when seated at the desk.

All group workrooms need bulletin boards for staff notices, for posting legally required notices, and for posting reminders of projects and due dates. Obviously, locations near entries work best.

IV-F. SPACES WITH SHARED EQUIPMENT

Groups of adjacent workrooms can sometimes share equipment. Some libraries have set up shared areas with such things as a counter and sink, photocopier, paper shredder, coffee pot, fax, paper cutter, safe, and other equipment for group use.

A good place for shared equipment is a large area connecting a number of staff workrooms. But perhaps not the area where people sit while waiting to meet with the director.

V. Staff Conference Rooms

Many libraries have small conference rooms adjacent to administrative workrooms. Depending on room size and needs, they can be used for library staff meetings, library board committee meetings, meetings with vendors, interviewing job applicants, ad hoc staff problem-solving meetings, and so on.

Some public libraries have tried to use staff conference rooms for full board meetings, but it's usually a bad idea. For full board meetings, a conference room needs to be large enough to house the entire board, the library director and the library department heads, members of the press, and members of the general public. Most staff conference rooms are far too small. In addition, staff conference rooms are often tucked into groups of staff workrooms rather than located with the library's other public meeting rooms, and escorting large numbers of people into staff areas of the library is an awkward undertaking.

Rooms used for board meetings also need to be accessible when the rest of the library is closed. By contrast, to be convenient for staff use, administrative conference rooms need to be located with the rest of administrative workrooms rather than near the main entrance.

Staff conference rooms are a great place for meetings with vendors, since the staff can end the meeting by simply saying "Thank you so much" and leaving the room. Prying vendors out of your personal workroom can take a lot more time.

Some libraries make their staff conference rooms available for public use on evenings and weekends. This requires extremely careful planning in order to completely separate staff and public functions and be sure that the public has no access to secure areas of the library. If the conference room is buried in the middle of a group of staff workrooms, making it available to library users is a seriously bad idea.

Unless you are a world-famous private library, avoid the temptation to purchase pompous conference room tables and pompous conference room chairs. (Pompous tables are horribly unwieldly, and some conference rooms are literally constructed around them. Pompous chairs are no more comfortable than many ordinary chairs with low backs. Tax-supported libraries that purchase pompous tables and chairs leave themselves open to the jibes of bloggers as well.)

Some useful features for a staff conference room might include:

- Modular conference table with comfortable but reasonable chairs.

- Counter with a sink and space for a coffeemaker. Sinks need to be real sinks, deep enough to allow a coffeemaker to be filled. So-called bar sinks don't work. The counter will need electrical outlets on at least two circuits, to allow a coffeemaker and a second power-hungry device to be operated simultaneously. If the counter has cabinets or drawers, all of them should lock. Cabinets should be made of plywood, with no chipboard components. Drawers should have ball-bearing double-extension hardware.

- Telephone. If the general public will ever use the conference room, the phone needs to unplug. Speakerphones are useful in conference rooms, but you'll need to be sure they're compatible with your phone system.

- Projection equipment. For staff training and other purposes, you may need a digital projector and a screen, but new equipment appears every year or so, and by the time this book actually appears there will be endless varieties of new gadgetry. You will need to have places to keep this stuff where you don't stumble over it when circumnavigating the room.

- Coat hooks. A row of hooks on a wall may be the best approach. Be sure to specify hooks made of brass or steel—never cast zinc, which has a tendency to break, leaving sharp edges.

When you are evaluating schematic designs for staff conference rooms, check clearances carefully. Lots of conference rooms are so small that it's almost impossible to squeeze past people seated at the table. Even carefully estimated space needs can prove to be inadequate if conference tables are too large. (We suggest that tables larger than three by five feet or at most four by six feet be modular. Massive conference-size tables may sound neat, but they are always a major pain. With emphasis on the "major." You don't want to build your building around a massive table.)

VI. Specialized Workrooms

VI-A. GRAPHIC ARTS

The amount of space required for graphic arts depends very much on the equipment to be housed. Since it's hard to predict in advance, extra space is a good idea. Large pieces of equipment like plotters can take up a lot of space.

It's a good idea to assume you will eventually add extra staff. If your graphic arts space is barely large enough for one person, you are likely to regret the situation.

You may also end up with publicity staff and a graphic arts staff sharing the same workroom. You'll need space for both.

Among the things your graphic arts workroom may need are:

- Computer workstations. Graphic arts are increasingly digital, and most artists will spend most of their time at computers.

- Drafting tables. Although graphic arts work is increasingly digital, people still need to draw, to lay out artwork, and so on.
- Flat worktables for assembling projects and laying out materials.
- Printers, especially color laser printers.
- Plotters for printing on wide rolls of paper, especially for posters.
- Paper cutters.
- Paper folders.
- Laminators. (Some laminators are huge. Others exude unpleasant smells, emphasizing the need for good ventilation.)
- Enclosed spray booths with exhaust fans. Keep the length of exhaust vent as short as possible, for you will need to clean it out now and then, particularly if your graphic artists use spray glue. (Your library's spray booth can be the envy of visiting graphic arts librarians, particularly because spray booths can be hard to retrofit.)
- Wall-sized bulletin boards for large artwork in development, such as temporary murals for special events.
- Storage space for paper, printed posters, artwork, printer cartridges, and other materials on shelves, filing cabinets, map files, and other equipment.
- Excellent, negative ventilation. Aromas from graphic arts should be drawn into the ventilation system rather than blasted out the workroom door whenever it's open. It's not as serious a situation as restrooms, but it's still important. Even if you plan to install a spray booth, specify extra-strong exhaust fans.
- Flexible, low-glare lighting. Graphic arts workrooms need high-quality lighting similar to that under which the artwork will be viewed, especially in terms of CRI (color rendering index) and K (color temperature). If the library has spaces with distinctively different lighting, graphic arts may need to make versions of the same artwork with different colors. In addition, artists may need a variety of light levels. For example, some artists like to work in fairly dim light when they are using computer workstations. And as in other areas of libraries, highly direct lighting is a bad idea. See chapter 31, "Lighting."

It's essential to enumerate the equipment you expect to house to be sure that your graphic arts workroom will be sufficiently large. Some graphic arts rooms are so small that equipment spills over into adjacent hallways or other workrooms.

Libraries may use a mixture of in-house equipment and farmed-out work, depending on costs and benefits. The real cost of taking artwork to be (for example) folded may be more a matter of the cost of library staff time running to and fro than of the investment in the equipment.

> Fred knows a library where the graphic arts workroom included a ping-pong table. He has always assumed the table was used for assembling large projects or displays, but there may be a far more interesting story.

VI-B. TECHNICAL SERVICES

The term "technical services" dates back to the days when academic libraries divided their functions administratively into "public services" and "technical services."

The most common functions performed in technical services are:

- Placing orders for new materials, including standing orders for materials shipped on a regular basis.
- Receiving new materials.
- Cataloging of new materials and (usually) entry into online catalogs.
- Processing new materials, including adding labeling, bar codes, anti-theft devices, Mylar dust jacket covers, special storage containers, and so on.
- Mending, cleaning, and repairing circulating materials.
- Dealing with donated materials.
- Deleting weeded materials from online catalogs.
- Storing materials awaiting processing.
- Providing suitable security for rare and expensive items.
- Transporting processed materials for shelving.
- And other functions, depending on the library.

Each of these activities needs different work and storage spaces and different supplies, and programmers need to work extensively with departmental staff to determine the types of workspaces and equipment needed.

In a very small library, all technical services functions may be performed by a single staff member, but in a large library, technical services can occupy a great deal of space, either in one very large room or a number of smaller spaces.

> In one of the first libraries for which Fred prepared a building program, the space he estimated for the staff workroom was cut so extremely by the owners and designers that the catalogers had to balance books on their laps while cataloging them.

Some common needs of technical services workrooms include:

- Running water (the only built-in furniture in the department). All sinks need to be deep, with high goose-neck faucets. Sink tops need to be large enough for equipment that needs access to water.
- Flat work surfaces.
- Computer workstations.
- Wall shelving for arriving books, departing books, gift books, supplies, and all manner of other things. In some libraries, every tech services workstation needs a surprising amount of individually assigned shelving in addition to general departmental shelving. When planning technical services, enumerate all of the types of materials that need to be stored, including what kind of space they require.
- Filing cabinets for financial records, order records, and correspondence with vendors.
- Secure storage. This may include locking cabinets, locking filing cabinets, locking closets, or even separate rooms for specialized items. (Rare book rooms and archives may need separate technical services work areas.)
- Work tables for opening shipments and similar jobs.
- Floor space for more book trucks than your designers expect. Be sure your designers

provide book truck space at individual workstations, as well as storage areas for groups of book trucks. And it takes space to maneuver book trucks. Some staff members in tech services have desks surrounded by book trucks. Floor plans that show all the book trucks in a massive cluster along one wall don't work.

- Bright, low-glare, all-purpose lighting. Architecturally mounted task lighting is unsuitable because it is difficult to relocate furniture.

- Vast numbers of electrical outlets, including floor outlets where there's any wild chance you might actually need them.

- A minimum of obstructions, to allow easy rearrangement of furnishings as needs change.

- Depending on staff needs, either wide-open spaces or cubes.

- Separate workrooms for department heads and possibly other staff who deal with private information, such as staff evaluations, negotiations with vendors, and so on. Because of HVAC requirements, separate workrooms are expensive, and libraries need to evaluate the competing needs for privacy vs. lower-cost construction and maintenance.

- Storage and workspaces for unusual non-book collections. Some can require a substantial amount of space.

- Floor space for deliveries and other unprocessed materials.

- Heated or chilled containers for shipments from parts of the world that tend to have bugs, or for returned materials that may have been infested locally.

Locations for technical services departments:

- Convenient to delivery doors.

- Not hogging prime space. With a convenient freight elevator, a tech services department on an upper floor can still be essentially right next to a delivery door.

- Convenient to storage facilities, such as storerooms for unprocessed books. (Research libraries are notorious for treasure troves of unprocessed materials, but some small libraries can seriously hold their own.)

The people in your library who know most about how technical services operate in space are the people who work in technical services. Never leave them out of discussions.

VI-C. CHILDREN'S DEPARTMENTS

Children's departments tend to have amazing quantities of stuff, and their workrooms reflect this. Some things to consider including are:

- Sinks for washing hands (after dealing with oozy children), washing gooey material off books, and so on. Sinks need to be deep and with high, goose-neck faucets to allow containers to be filled. (We have no idea what kind of containers, but we know children's librarians, and the containers will come along.)

Remember that retrofitting a sink to a workroom is a very expensive undertaking, so include it in your written building program and make sure it doesn't quietly vanish.

- Washers and dryers for puppets, dress-up clothes, and similar shared materials. If space is an issue, consider stacked washers and dryers designed for apartment use. The main thing is to get the water supply, drain, power supply (often 220 volts, something you otherwise wouldn't have in a workroom), and dryer vent installed when construction is taking place, because you will probably not be able to do so later.

In the age of bedbugs, washing puppets and plush toys on a regular basis is a particularly worthwhile undertaking.

- Storage for posters and similar large, flat objects. Some libraries use map cases, while others have vertical slots beneath standing-height work surfaces.
- Space for die-cutting machines and racks for storing dies. If your library plans to let the general public use its die-cutting equipment, you may need to create a neutral space available to both library users and library staff.
- Space for kits in all sorts of plastic tubs, usually on steel library shelving.
- Extra space for storing things that non-children's librarians might not anticipate.

> Fred's children's department had a plastic wading pool and a hula hoop used for making giant soap bubbles. You can't tuck either one into an everyday storage cabinet.

- Windows with Venetian blinds facing the public areas of the department, to allow staff members to keep an eye on things while they are working. (Our experience is that children's staff are not always thrilled with this idea, but that it works well.)
- Space for an accumulation of summer reading club prizes, no two of which were intended to be stored on the same kind of shelf.
- Extra work surfaces. Children's staff members are always making things, and forcing them to do so on public reading tables is not a good thing. (If you work around children with scissors, sooner or later someone will run with them.)
- Storage for seasonal books, such as Christmas books, that may be brought out only at certain times of year.
- Storage for storytelling collections, materials that need to be handy but are not intended to be lent on a regular basis.

> In Fred's home town, the public library was governed by a committee of the school board. Each fall, each grade school teacher was consequently allowed to take one chest of books from the public library for nine months' classroom use. To prevent every children's book purchased in the previous 25 years from vanishing, starting in July the children's department staff stored all the books purchased in the last 25 years in a back corner of the furnace room, bringing the books back out only after chest-filling time was over. Even if the department had had a good storeroom, the furnace room may have been better, since—like the arrival of the Spanish Inquisition—no one expects all the new children's books to be lurking behind the furnace.

- Craft supplies. It's amazing how much expensive space boxes of toilet paper tubes can occupy.
- Unusual equipment. Film-strip projectors are probably all gone now, but we can confidently expect other things to turn up.

- Children's departments with more than a couple of staff members need a private workroom for the department head, who will need to evaluate staff and to meet with concerned parents.

One of the greatest sources of tension between children's librarians and library administrators is storage. Some administrators feel that if children's department storage were not limited, nothing would ever leave the department from generation to generation. Children's librarians in turn hate throwing out useful programming materials. Finding the proper balance can verge on Solomonic.

VI-D. RARE BOOK DEPARTMENTS

Rare book departments can have wide varieties of specialized equipment. But figuring space needs for devices like Hinman Collators is beyond the scope of this book.

VII. Workspaces in Otherwise Public Areas

Many library staff members work at public service desks when they are between requests for help from library users.

If it's a matter of selecting books, this is usually compatible with working at a service desk, but other tasks (such as processing books) may take too much space or involve too much mess.

A standard approach in small libraries is to create a work counter behind the service desk, a place where staff members can work out of the way of library users but simultaneously keep an eye on the library and leave their work when users approach the desk.

To work effectively, work counters need to be arranged so that staff members seated or standing there are facing the public areas of the library rather than having their backs turned to the service desks and to the users approaching the desks. With work counters facing library users, library staff members can work on off-desk tasks while simultaneously keeping an eye on the rest of the library and watching for users needing help. With this kind of arrangement, there needs to be two places for library staff to sit or stand—one behind the main service counter and the second behind the work counter. Both spaces need space for staff chairs, book carts, and so on.

Our experience has been that counters of this type never occur to most architects, who almost always draw work counters facing the wall, so that staff have their backs turned to users and to the spaces they need to supervise. Make clear in your building program how you want things arranged, and even then expect to make your architects redraw things.

Behind-the-service-desk work counters need low front barricades to hide the mess but not interfere with librarians' oversight of public areas. About six inches or so is fine.

A work counter of this type needs enough length for open counter space as well as a computer, printer, and phone.

VIII. Required Workroom Sizes

Of the making of workrooms there is no end, and the staff who will be working there are your best guide to needs.

As usual, space estimating is great, but the final proof is the architect's schematic drawing. The ability of a workroom to hold the necessary furniture can depend greatly on the general proportions of the room, and a drawing is a great way to test things out. (As we've said endlessly in this book, a schematic design that does not indicate furniture placement is worthless.)

Remember that sketches can also mislead. In Fred's library, an alcove intended for a filing cabinet failed because it turned out about half an inch too narrow in real life. The building program should have specified what needed to fit into the space rather than the dimensions of the space.

Furniture types can make a big difference in the layout of workroom furniture. For example, vertical filing cabinets and lateral filing cabinets need very different spaces.

Workrooms that are not strictly rectangular will make less efficient use of space. A workroom estimated to need 150 square feet may need 175 or more if the room is L-shaped. And substantially more if the room has the severe misfortune to be triangular or curved.

The absolute minimum size for an individual workroom is 125 to 150 square feet. In our opinion, anything less than 150 square feet is a seriously bad idea.

However, some libraries with very limited space have created professional staff workrooms with shared equipment and about 50 square feet of space for each staff member. This gives each person a small working surface, a chair, overhead shelving, and a couple of file drawers. It's terribly crowded, but it's better than no workspace at all.

IX. Snappy Rules on Staff Workrooms

1. Always say "workrooms" or "workspaces" rather than "offices." The word "office" antagonizes anti-tax crazies and tight-fisted administrations, and the number of librarians with the sort of luxury corner offices envisioned by their critics can be counted on the fingers of one foot.

2. Beware of universities that have standard workroom sizes based on academic rank. No busy cataloger or graphic artist can work in an "instructor" level space without overflowing into adjacent areas. If your university's space standards refer to "offices," this may be another good reason to call yours "workrooms."

3. Workrooms need windows with Venetian blinds to adjoining workrooms or public spaces. It's a lot easier to close a Venetian blind when you want serious privacy than to install a new window when you seriously need to see out or to be seen.

4. Lots of administrators are happiest with separate stacks of loose papers for each project. Our job is to figure out ways to make this possible, not to suggest behavior modification. One approach is to hide the stacks in cabinets with shelves and with doors that close.

5. The great thing about meeting with sales people in a conference room rather than your personal workroom is that when the time comes you can just say "Thank you," get up, and leave.

6. We don't have any statistically reliable research data, but our impression is that the great majority of library staff workrooms are far too small, and that a lot are like the

steamship stateroom scene in the Marx Brothers' *A Night at the Opera*. ("Is it my imagination, or is it getting crowded in here?")

7. If you plan your new building for 30 years of collection growth but no staff growth, the fact that workers eventually end up sitting on each others' laps shouldn't come as much of a surprise.

8. Library workrooms need more electrical outlets than lots of planners expect, and they need them in places that are easy to reach. Except for dressy workrooms (the kind occupied by administrators, who are expected to look nice for visitors), outlets above countertop height are a friendly gesture to library staff.

9. Every group workroom needs a sink. Not a toy sink like a bar sink, but a seriously sized sink with a high gooseneck faucet.

10. When people are waiting to see the director, where will they sit?

11. Good places for departmental storerooms are spaces right next door to the relevant staff workrooms. A number of public libraries have children's storerooms located between the children's staff workroom and the craft and story room, with convenient access from both directions.

12. If the library director has to pile working papers on chairs originally intended for visitors, that's one warning sign of an undersized workroom.

13. If you want a small conference table in your director's workroom, provide enough space. Too many conference tables in small workrooms require users to crawl over each other to reach the chairs.

14. Outside of counters with sinks, none of the furniture in workrooms needs to be built in. And it shouldn't be. Never send architecture to solve furniture problems.

15. Every workroom needs at least one telephone (or whatever communication device is in use at that time). After that it's a question of how much you expect people to jump up and dash across the room to answer the phone. Put in phone connections in advance for every workstation, just in case staff grow seriously tired of dashing.

16. Catalogers faced with built-in work counters have ended up balancing books on their laps while they cataloged them. Beware of cute but tiny built-in workspaces.

17. Every workroom needs a thermostat and individual temperature control. If two separate workrooms share a thermostat, the staff members in the room without the thermostat are likely to be very unhappy for very good reasons.

18. Good shapes for staff workrooms are simple rectangles. Curved walls and diagonal walls cause serious problems, as do L-shaped spaces. All funny-shaped spaces do a bad job of housing furniture. Functional trumps cute.

19. Most workrooms are short of storage space. When in doubt, provide extra floor space for shelving and filing cabinets and for cabinets with doors that close.

20. Departmental staff workrooms need to be immediately adjacent to their departments. (This sounds like an unnecessary remark, but unfortunately it's not.)

21. Be careful when making workrooms passageways to other workrooms, and never make them passageways to public areas.

22. Multi-person workrooms are a lot cheaper per person and a lot more flexible than single-person workrooms. If a staff member does not require privacy or does not deal with materials requiring security, a single-person workroom may be a major waste of money.

23. A multi-person workroom may have a lot of people crammed into a relatively small space and still need to meet ventilation standards.

24. When library directors can't keep their offices neat, the cure is not to fire the directors but to improve hiding places for their loose papers.

25. Weird room geometry can turn a workable area into a worthless space. Any room that is not a rectangle can qualify as "weird," and rooms that are round, oval, banana-shaped, triangular, L-shaped, and other strange shapes can often qualify as "worthless." The patron spirits of library buildings all like 90-degree corners.

26. Saving money by cutting staff workspaces often doesn't.

PART III
Essential Spaces All Libraries Need

CHAPTER 28
Staff Facilities

I. Introduction

In addition to staff workspaces, all libraries need support spaces for their staff members, including lunchrooms, restrooms, lactation spaces, mailboxes, and places to store personal belongings.

Often these spaces are a last thought, and sometimes they are nearly forgotten. Frequently they are too small, and sometimes they have major design flaws.

Of all the errors and omissions in staff spaces, the worst is having staff restrooms accessed directly from staff lunchrooms. This happens all the time. Clearly we do not learn from other people's grossness.

> Teachers tell us the problem with library staff restrooms is also common in faculty lounges in schools.

There are a few other important features too often omitted from staff spaces:

- Enough electrical circuits in staff kitchenettes.
- Exhaust fans in all staff lunchrooms.
- Garbage disposals in the sinks of all staff kitchenettes.
- Sufficiently large sinks in staff kitchenettes (tiny bar sinks are not "sufficiently large" for almost any purpose in libraries).
- Access for staff with disabilities to all staff areas.
- Spaces for both noisy and quiet users.
- Lactation spaces.
- Mailboxes large enough to hold sheets of paper laid flat rather than rolled up.
- Safe places for staff purse storage, including for people who keep their purses in backpacks.

II. Staff Lunchrooms

II-A. FUNCTIONS

Every library needs a place where staff members can eat lunch and relax when they are off duty.

In some very small libraries, staff members are on duty through the lunch hour and end up eating their lunches at a service desk or a reading table. This can work, but it may be socially awkward if the library does not allow its users to eat in the reading rooms.

Most staff lunchrooms provide a variety of functions. We call them "lunchrooms," but they are also places for coffee breaks, places for staff social events and shared food, places to lie down briefly when feeling bad, places for socializing, and places for retirement parties.

By definition, staff lunchrooms are spaces for staff, not for library users, and library staff members can be extremely protective of their spaces. One serious mistake library administrators can make is letting people who are not library staff make use of staff lunchrooms.

If your library absolutely must have a stove, the staff lunchroom is a good place for it. But stoves bring many potential problems. They require special ventilation and special fire-protection systems. The addition of a stove can mean that a staff lunchroom becomes a "kitchen" under building codes, and health department rules then kick in, requiring lots of special equipment and plumbing, such as three-drain sinks and grease traps. You can try calling the room a "kitchenette" but codes may overrule your choice of names.

If your kitchen meets codes, you could put the same equipment in a kitchen attached to a public meeting room, but then you are faced with all of the potential messes made by the general public.

One of the reasons staff lunchrooms are important is that libraries tend to have some low-paid staff members—such as book shelving staff—who cannot afford to eat out, in addition to many staff who prefer to spend their money in other ways. Occasionally there are members of governing bodies who don't understand this and tend to argue, "I go out for lunch every day. Why do we have to provide an expensive lunchroom for the library staff?" Someone needs to take such people gently aside and explain how the other 80 percent lives.

II-B. LOCATIONS

In many ways, staff facilities can be put wherever they'll fit, usually somewhere off the beaten path.

Lunchrooms are more pleasant for the staff if they are accessed through staff hallways, where library users can't peer interestedly into staff spaces every time the door opens. The same kind of privacy can be provided with a jog in the entryway, so that when the door opens, staff can't be seen eating their lunches.

Lunchrooms are a lot better off with windows.

Staff restrooms also work well when they are accessible and visible only from staff areas of the library, so users don't end up saying, "I don't see why *everyone* can't use that restroom."

The single most important point about staff restrooms is that STAFF RESTROOMS SHOULD NEVER OPEN DIRECTLY INTO STAFF LUNCHROOMS. Although this prohibition seems obvious, the country is awash with library staff lunchrooms where people eat their lunch directly next to sanitary fixtures. Since this unfortunate design pattern is well established—or the result of endless independent invention—librarians working on building plans need to include vigorous prohibitions in building programs and follow up with eagle-eyed oversight as floor plans emerge.

Many smaller libraries have places where staff eat lunch in the corners of staff workrooms. This has some practical advantages, particularly with shared water supplies. The main trick in providing this kind of space for staff lunches is to put the lunch table(s) where library users can't see them. Some libraries have alcoves or doglegs at the back of workrooms to provide a place for staff lunches. Others have used shelving units to block the view.

Staff coat and purse storage could be in staff lunchrooms, but staff corridors or large staff workrooms seem far better places. Why have a winter coat smell of fish TV dinners?

II-C. FOOD PREPARATION AND SERVING

II-C-1. Microwaves, Coffeemakers, and Other Countertop Equipment

Most staff rooms provide microwave ovens. For many libraries, a single microwave is not enough, especially when a number of people are trying to prepare lunch at the same time. Microwaves are cheap; the main planning issue is sufficient counter space and enough electrical circuits.

Some libraries also have toaster ovens, coffeemakers, and other countertop equipment in their staff lunchrooms. As with all other equipment, the main thing these require is counter space, extra electrical circuits, and exhaust fans. And there may be code requirements.

II-C-2. Stoves

Some library staff rooms have kitchen stoves, especially if there is a tradition of group eating. Stoves can be great, but there are some major implications:

- Building codes may lead to your kitchenette becoming a commercial-grade kitchen, with many resulting extra costs for plumbing and equipment.

- The chance of fire is greatly enhanced with stovetop cooking. Open flames are a lot more trouble-prone than microwave ovens. Hence the more demanding codes.

- While microwaves can be messy, stoves can be Seriously Messy, especially when large numbers of people share them. Someone both patient and particular will need to keep the stove clean.

- You may want a range hood with an exhaust fan. These are standard items, but they require exhaust vents.

- Depending on your local building codes, you may need to install a commercial range hood over your stove. Commercial range hoods have fire-suppression equipment and are extremely expensive, enough to make people reconsider stoves entirely, if they haven't done so already.

If you must have a stove in your library, the staff lunchroom is a better place than a meeting room kitchenette. But you still want to discuss it carefully with your architects and engineers, asking whether "no stove whatsoever" isn't really the better decision.

Given available stoves, you may also have problems with accessibility.

II-C-3. Refrigerators

Staff lunchrooms require refrigerators for the storage of lunches. Since food associated with children's programs or with staff social events may also need to be refrigerated, most libraries need at least one full-sized refrigerator in addition to the refrigerators in meeting room kitchenettes.

Ice dispensers set into refrigerator doors may seem like a frippery, but they get around the problem of staff unloading shared ice cube trays with their bare hands. Microbes on ice cubes will probably not be killed by freezing. (If your owners raise cost issues, you can suggest that if a refrigerator ice dispenser in a library with staff health coverage prevents even a week of staff paid sick leave due to illness, it may pay for itself.)

II-C-4. Dishwashers

Dishwashers may sound like silly luxuries, but they have the advantage of being capable of disinfecting dishes.

In many libraries, staff share dishes and tableware, washing everything with bare hands in tepid water. As in the case of handling ice with bare hands, this is a great way to share microbes. If scalding shared dishes prevents disease transmission, it's both a humane thing to do and (for those of more purely mercenary motives) a way of saving money on paid sick leave costs.

Dishwashers require electric power, water, and drains, and they don't lend themselves to easy retrofitting. Even if you think you don't want one, you may be ahead roughing in the space where a dishwasher can go if you change your mind.

II-C-5. Counters and Sinks

All staff lunchrooms need sinks. Deep sinks with high gooseneck faucets allow staff to fill large containers like coffee urns without having to bail water with a saucepan or go hunting for a mop sink. Single-drainer sinks are probably sufficient for libraries that do not do home-style dishwashing, but review your needs with your staff. (We think home-style dishwashing is a seriously bad idea, as noted above under "dishwashers.")

Provide garbage disposal units in your staff room sinks. Some staff members are meticulous about putting all food scraps in the garbage, but others just dump foodstuffs in the sink and eventually clog the drain.

Remember that countertops need to be accessible, which means no more than 34 inches high.

> Library staff rooms abound in signs warning staff that there are no garbage disposal units and asking staff not to put garbage in the sinks. As far as we can tell, these signs are the result of bad experiences.

II-C-6. Cabinets and Drawers

All lunchrooms need storage for both permanent and throw-away cooking and eating equipment. Standard kitchen cabinets and drawers work well. A counter long enough to hold a variety of microwaves and other appliances will have plenty of space for under-counter drawers and cabinets.

Be sure that all drawers in base cabinets have ball-bearing double-extension hardware, or you will have staff struggling to drag them open and shove them shut, and either losing objects in the back or dumping the contents of drawers on the floor when they pull the drawers out too far.

You may also want cabinets above countertops, but be careful about clearances. And remember that over-counter cabinets are inaccessible to staff members in wheelchairs. Cabinets that come too close to microwaves and other countertop appliances are a pain.

Counters and cabinets and drawers need to be constructed of furniture grade plywood, never of chipboard. Cheap chipboard cabinets are sold in discount furnishing stores. Even if they're okay for home use, you don't want them in your library.

All drawers and cabinets need white interiors so that contents do not vanish into the murk.

II-C-7. Buffet Shelves

Library staffs frequently bring a wide variety of snacks, especially for staff social events. Putting them on lunch tables leaves no place to eat.

One response to this problem is to install a buffet shelf at a comfortable height for self-service. For accessibility, this means no more than 34 inches high.

As with service counters, buffet shelves need multiple circuits for electrically heated serving equipment.

II-C-8. Plumbing Connections and Electrical Circuits

Like all kitchens, staff lunchrooms need a lot of plumbing and power.

Sinks, dishwashers, and refrigerators with automatic ice makers need water supplies and drains, limiting your ability to move them around or to add them later.

Some electrical equipment may require 220-volt power supplies, particularly stoves.

A lot of the 110-volt items used in library lunchrooms are power hogs because they use electricity to generate heat. Many of these gadgets may need separate circuits. Imagine a staff holiday dinner with two microwave ovens, a Dutch oven, a toaster, a toaster oven, and a coffeemaker in simultaneous use and the resulting need for six separate 20-amp circuits, plus those for the regular appliances.

As with meeting room kitchenettes, many library staff rooms have far too few separate circuits. Nothing is more fun than blowing breakers and having to figure out which appliances you won't use. Trying to hook up appliances by running extension cords from other rooms in the library is awkward, and if your fire marshals see you doing it they will be strongly tempted to hyperventilate.

II-C-9. Exhaust Fans

It shouldn't be necessary to mention this, but architects have created staff lunchrooms without exhaust fans. Sooner or later, everyone regrets this omission. Mostly sooner.

Some aromas can fill a library quickly. One main culprit is microwave popcorn abandoned to cook while its owners leave the room for just a quick moment and fail to return in time. Another is TV dinners featuring fish.

II-C-10. Accessibility

Be sure that all of your staff food preparation and serving facilities are accessible. Countertops, stovetops, and buffet shelves need to be no more than 34 inches high.

There's no way of making high cabinets over countertops accessible, but you can provide alternative storage.

II-D. SEATING

While round tables are generally anathema in reading areas in libraries, they seem to do well in staff lunchrooms. In part, this is due to the fact that round tables are for conversation and rectangular tables for work.

Some staff groups play cards on their lunch hours. Folding card tables and chairs take up a modest amount of storage space and are easy to set up and put away. But be sure you have space for them when they are set up and in use.

All staff lunchrooms need armchairs, places where staff can relax. Some amazingly tacky old armchairs are remarkably popular in staff rooms.

And staff lunchrooms need sofas. Many people use their breaks for catnaps, and the absence of sofas makes this difficult. Just as we try to discourage sofas where our users can sprawl on them, we want to take good care of our sprawling staff.

Estimating quantities of furnishings is tricky. Many library staff stay in the building all day long. This is balanced by staggered lunch hours, where half the staff are on desk service while the other half are at lunch. Some staff members like sitting four to a table, while others are stressed out and want to sit alone. Some staff groups coordinate their lunch hours so they can play games. Libraries will vary, but it seems reasonable that the staff lunchroom should be able to seat a quarter to a third of the staff. However, your experience with your library is a far better guide.

II-E. VENDING MACHINES

Some library staff lunchrooms provide snack closets on the honor system. This works particularly well when outsiders cannot sneak into the staff room.

Other lunchrooms have vending machines, usually serviced by an outside vendor.

If you are part of a larger organization, your vending machines may come from vendors who have negotiated with the parent institution. Some campuses, for example, have "pouring rights" agreements with soda firms.

Be sure to allocate space for vending machines. Some are monsters.

And remember to provide electrical supplies, water supplies, and drain lines for vending machinery.

Many vending machines have pictorial plastic fronts with brilliant illumination, apparently intended to make machines visible for miles through night and fog. All of these machines have brilliant light sources behind their plastic fronts, and you can simply disconnect the lights, making visiting your staff lunchroom a far more gracious and welcoming experience.

II-F. COMPUTER WORKSTATIONS

Some staff lunchrooms provide one or two computer workstations for use by staff members who have no office computers and want to check their email on breaks.

Workstations of this type take little space. If you allocate 30 square feet per workstation, you should be in good shape.

However, with the nearly universal ownership of cell phones, computer workstations may be far less in demand among your staff. Ask them.

II-G. BULLETIN BOARDS

State laws can require that a variety of legal notices be posted for staff. Bulletin boards in staff room areas are a good place. Check to see how much space you'll need to meet legal requirements.

Many staff rooms also provide bulletin boards for photographs of staff members and for notices of staff events.

II-H. SECLUDED SPACES

Many staff rooms provide separate spaces for staff who are feeling ill and wish to lie down. Often these are no more complicated than a separate room with a recliner and a Venetian blind on the window.

II-I. LACTATION ROOMS

Libraries of any size need to provide lactation rooms rather than relegating users to nearby storerooms or restrooms. Usually lactation rooms are close to lunchrooms.

Lactation rooms need pleasant lighting and decor, comfortable seating, small refrigerators, sinks, and shelves for equipment, with everything meeting ADA requirements. The rooms need door latches that indicate clearly on the outside when rooms are occupied, to spare users the disturbing sounds of people trying to open the doors. And the rooms need to be large enough to make users not feel they are locked in small closets.

II-J. DÉCOR

Staff lunchrooms need to be light and cheerful and welcoming and comfortable.

Unfortunately, this is not always the case. In 1974, for example, Fred inherited a library with a brand new staff room with one bright orange wall, three battleship gray walls, and no windows. When the staff immediately painted the gray walls white, the designers were dismayed. The orange wall lasted a few years and then magically turned white as well.

II-K. ENTERTAINMENT

Given the extreme opinions expressed on the media today, library staff rooms may want to ban television sets and radios entirely, or limit them to innocuous broadcasts. For example, there are medical clinic waiting rooms with television sets permanently tuned to house remodeling channels.

If you provide a TV set, you will also need to make provisions for staff whose lunches may be spoiled by forced television viewing, and that means a quiet second lunchroom.

III. Staff Restrooms

In all but the very tiniest libraries, staff members should not be expected to share toilets with library users. If library users leave the public toilets in grotty shape, a staff member who is scheduled to be in the library for the next seven hours can't just decide to go home and use the facilities there. (If you are a non-librarian, you are not entitled to argue against staff toilets, although you can always ask librarians in a very non-opinion-telegraphing way how they feel about the issue.)

If your library is a small one and has accessible toilets, you may want to provide only a small restroom for your staff, but it's a lot more considerate not to force a disabled staff member to use the public toilet that all the other staff get to avoid.

Chapter 26, "Restrooms," covers many of the basics of good library design. Among the things you will want in your staff restrooms are:

- Compliance with accessibility codes.
- Wall-mounted flush-valve toilets, which greatly reduce maintenance.

> One of Fred's head custodians said he spent far more time repairing the staff room flush-tank toilets than the public flush-valve toilets, despite far heavier use of the public toilets and presumably far greater abuse.

- Electric eye-operated washbasin faucets. (Imagine how filthy a washbasin faucet handle can be! Even when it's just librarians using the washbasin. If you can't have an electric eye, get bat-handled faucets that can be operated with a wrist.)
- Ceramic tile floors with dark grout and floor drains.
- Provision for safe disposal of potential sources of blood-borne pathogens, such as sanitary napkins.
- Provision for safe disposal of used hypodermic syringes, typically a sharps container mounted on the wall.
- Dual coat hooks (not made of cast zinc) on the toilet stall doors.
- Sensor-operated lights that do not force people to grope their way into dark restrooms in order to turn on the lights.
- Effective exhaust fans.

If staff restrooms are single-user restrooms, you may find that unisex restrooms provide for more efficient use, with staff members simply taking any restroom not in use. Depending on applicable plumbing codes, however, unisex restrooms may not count if you are struggling to meet codes for minimum numbers of toilets or lavatories in your building. Check with your architects. (If a code requires a minimum number of toilets for each gender, you can always label single-user staff restrooms M and F and then then just ignore the signs once the building has received its occupancy permit.)

As mentioned several times elsewhere in this book because things are so often arranged badly, staff restrooms should be accessed from staff corridors, never directly from areas where staff are eating lunch.

IV. Staff Coat and Purse Storage

Coat and purse storage is not much of a problem for that rarified group of staff who are assigned private workrooms with personal keys, but for everyone else it's an issue.

IV-A. COAT STORAGE

Many private staff workrooms are equipped with coat hooks on the back of the doors, with hooks mounted on wooden supports on the walls, with short coat rods projecting from the walls (with coat hangers), or even with coat closets. (The list attempts to depict ever-increasing costs, but we may be wrong.)

Shared workspaces can have either individually assigned coat storage or shared storage. With shared storage, the idea is that the entire staff are almost never present at the same time, and that the number of coat-storage sites can be smaller than the number of staff members.

In a very small library, all staff coats may be stored in a single place, but libraries with offices and departments may want decentralized storage.

Some coat storage options for shared workspaces include:

- Hooks on wooden beams mounted on walls.
- Coat rods projecting from the walls, with coat hangers.
- Coat trees.
- Hallway lockers of the kind found in school buildings.
- Various combined coat-and-purse storage units, with stacks of purse lockers supporting a coat bar between the stacks (and often a row of purse lockers above the stacks of lockers and connecting the stacks).
- Coat closets. With more than a small staff sharing a closet, you may find that it may have to be double-width with double doors. (Remember what a tangle the front hall coat closets are in many homes.)

Along with coat storage goes storage of boots and galoshes dripping with salt-laden slush. You can purchase plastic floor trays. You can make the floor beneath coat-storage areas ceramic tile rather than carpet. And there are probably many other ways.

Most of the methods listed above do not provide protection from theft. If you are concerned about theft, you may have to rely on lockers with padlocks.

You are likely to encounter a couple of common problems with coat storage:

- Accessible-height coat hooks and rods are important, but they are too low for many coats. You'll need both heights.
- Cheap coat hooks made of cast zinc tend to break. Steel and brass do not.
- Many coat bars do not extend far enough from the wall, making it particularly hard to store coats on hangers. This can be a problem storing indoor garments, so imagine trying to hang up a jumbo parka. (Standard metal supports for coat rods in home closets have this problem and need to be shimmed out from the back walls of closets.)

IV-B. PURSE STORAGE

Many libraries need to pay special attention to problems with theft from purses. For example, library users (no doubt feeling the sense of security that accompanies libraries) leave their purses on reading tables while they wander off into the stacks, returning only to find that billfolds are surprisingly missing.

While staff areas are usually far more secure than reading tables, thefts nonetheless occur.

One common solution is the provision of purse lockers, small lockers about a foot or 14 inches square provided in stacks four or five lockers high. Each locker has a hasp for a padlock. Because of the padlocks, you will need a separate locker for every employee. (Actually getting employees to lock up their purses is far harder than purchasing the lockers, so things still vanish now and then.)

A major security problem results from the popularity of backpacks. Many employees will keep billfolds in backpacks that are too large to fit into purse lockers. Although they sometimes remove the billfolds and lock them up, at other times they just toss the backpacks into a convenient corner.

One solution is to purchase larger lockers. School hallway lockers, for example, are available in half-height versions, with lockers stacked two high, and these should be large enough for backpacks.

The library will need to decide whether it wants to provide padlocks or ask employees to bring their own. Providing library padlocks has a couple of advantages. First, all the lockers will actually have padlocks. And second, when staff resign their library positions and leave town, you won't have to use a bolt cutter to remove their padlocks from their lockers, since you can have a list of all padlock combinations.

V. Staff Mailboxes

All libraries with more than a couple of employees need a bank of staff mailboxes.

It may be tempting to assume that mailboxes will be replaced by electronic communication, but there's always something that's easier to distribute in hard copy. Or impossible to distribute electronically, like printed books.

A few points are important:

- With the exception of very large buildings, it's easiest to put all the staff mailboxes in one location. Often this turns out to be in or near the staff lunchroom, since this is likely to be the most convenient location for

The designers for this library provided pigeonholes rather than 10-inch-wide flat openings for staff mail. As a result, everything distributed to staff members had to be rolled up first, and large items couldn't be distributed at all. The people who had to use the pigeonholes were not happy.

staff members. As with shared lunchrooms, mailboxes in a single location help staff get to know people from other departments of the library.

- Mailboxes need name label holders so that assignments can be altered as staff members come and go. It's probably annoying for staff to find their mailboxes moving mysteriously around in the night, but if the mailboxes get seriously out of alphabetical order, things soon become impressively muddled. Some libraries group mailboxes by department or rank to avoid having to move all the name labels whenever a new person arrives.

- Mailboxes need to be large enough to allow the distribution of memos and other materials without having to fold them or roll them up. This means boxes about 10 inches wide and perhaps 14 inches deep. (Some libraries have been equipped with banks of pigeonholes, making distribution of anything larger than flashlight batteries a real pain.)

- Some staff members will use their mailboxes for storage of personal objects, and libraries need some policies for dealing with this. Sometimes mailboxes get so crowded there's no room left for mail. Sometimes staff store food in their mailboxes, presenting problems similar to old lunches lurking in the backs of staff refrigerators, but offering opportunities for even more rapid deterioration.

- You may need extra mailboxes in addition to those for staff members. For example, public libraries may want mailboxes for board members and for key volunteers, such as Friends of the Library.

- Plan ahead. Having a few mailboxes too many is a lot less annoying than having a few mailboxes too few.

VI. Staff Bike Storage and Showers

In some libraries, everyone bikes to work. In other libraries, the thought that people might bike to work is regarded as reasonably bizarre.

If staff members bike to work, they need a secure place to stash their bikes. It's better to prepare for this in advance than to be surprised later when everyone is stumbling over staff bikes in an entryway or in the staff lunchroom.

A few libraries provide showers, so that the sweaty staff who bike to work can make themselves sweet before greeting library users. Showers take little space and may be hard to retrofit, and you're certainly better off just including one in your plans than trying to add it later. Besides, some non-bikers may want to shower also.

If you have showers, staff may want lockers to hold their working clothes overnight and their biking gear during the day.

> We don't think many library directors are given to ordering staff members to the showers, but it creates an entertaining image.

VII. Snappy Rules on Staff Facilities

1. A staff lunchroom without a powerful exhaust fan is not as gross as a staff restroom without an exhaust fan, but the general principle is the same. Trust your architects, but always ask to be shown where all the fans are on the plans. (Think fish TV dinners and burnt microwave popcorn.)

2. Staff toilets located directly next to staff lunch areas are depressingly prevalent and one of the most easily avoided library design idiocies. Toilets next to eating areas are extraordinarily gross for all parties involved, both the lunch eaters and the toilet users. Watch for them carefully on your floor plans, for they spring up like unwanted fungi, just when you thought you had disinfected everything.

3. Sooner or later, staff members will feel ill and want to lie down for a few minutes rather than simply go home. They deserve something friendlier than the floor.

4. Check your local building codes before you plan to have a stove in your staff room kitchen. A commercial range hood can cost as much as a modest automobile.

5. Staff lunchrooms are havens for employees stressed out by exuberant participants in story time and library computer labs.

No matter how welcoming and warm these staff people may be, they do not want to be on public display while eating lunch.

6. There is no such thing as too many 20-amp circuits in a staff lunchroom. (In both staff lunchrooms and meeting room kitchenettes, owners and designers usually provide far too few separate circuits. No one is sure why, but there it is. Even if your owners and designers are really great folks, they still may not provide enough circuits.)

7. You do not want any public functions intruding into your staff lunchroom, including receiving bins for book returns.

8. Staff members feel strongly about having staff toilets. If you have never worked in a library, you have no right to suggest that staff use the public toilets instead of having their own facilities.

9. Libraries need to provide pleasant lactation spaces for their staff. Sending people down to a loading dock or a storeroom with camp stools is not acceptable.

10. When your staff bike to work, where will they put their bikes?

11. A single staff member whose hobby is making desserts can turn a library staff room from a Barren Wasteland into a Promised Land.

12. Staff mailboxes need to be large enough for 8½-by-14-inch handouts. Pigeonholes are not acceptable and will drive your handout distributors crazy.

13. A staff room sink without a garbage disposal is not a seriously lovely object.

14. Be careful about trying to cram too much furniture into a small staff room. Staff members in wheelchairs deserve to use the room.

15. Stoves can cause many problems. Read section I, "Introduction," and section II, "Staff Lunchrooms," from this chapter if you are seriously tempted to add a stove.

16. In case insistent repetition helps, NEVER, NEVER have a staff toilet directly accessible from a staff lunchroom. It seems to happen in libraries everywhere, and it's an amazingly avoidable yet deeply offensive screwup.

PART III
Essential Spaces All Libraries Need

CHAPTER 29
Storerooms

I. Introduction

Storage sounds like a boring and unexciting topic to those whose jobs don't depend on finding workable places to put things. For the rest of us, storage is an endlessly compelling topic.

The story of this chapter is a simple one.

- Most libraries have far too little storage space.

- Because of this, library staff members can waste a lot of expensive time hunting for places to put things and hunting for things that have been put somewhere or other.

- Storage spaces need to be the right size and in the right locations, but in many libraries, storage space is in awkward or inconvenient locations. The same staff members who waste time hunting for places to put things also waste time toting things from where they are stored to where they are used, or in figuring out where to store one set of furniture when the storage space is already full of the furniture that will replace it.

- Some storage spaces are badly designed architecturally, making them unnecessarily hard to use, inefficient, or even completely useless.

- Good storage space is always at risk. Owners reject storage space during the programming process. Librarians underestimate the space they actually need. Architects cannibalize storage space during the design process. Library departments steal each other's storage space. Non-library agencies try to take over library storage space for their own illegitimate purposes.

- Overcrowded storage is sometimes the result of bad housekeeping or pathological hoarding, but it's far more often the result of simply not having enough space.

- We suspect that most libraries have inadequate storage space because owners don't want to spend the money, architects don't find storage space any fun, and librarians underestimate.

- A few libraries may have too much storage space, tempting them to hang onto things that might really be discarded. But we think they're in the tiny minority. What we see more often is libraries with good stuff stacked everywhere due to lack of storage space.

- Some libraries actually toss out important materials, such as unique local history documents, simply because there's no storage space left.
- By and large, the only people who know what storage space libraries actually need are practicing librarians and library building consultants, although some owners who do extensive volunteering in libraries also understand. Everyone else needs to let librarians do the talking.

It could probably be proved with facts and figures that, just as people feel personally underpaid while everyone around them is overpaid, lots of people think they personally have far too little storage space, while by contrast other people and agencies and departments have more than they really need. But that's probably a standard reaction to universally inadequate space.

[Left] John Moorman once ran a library that had been converted from a department store. Because the building was larger than the library needed, the library ended up with a 35,000-square-foot storeroom. The vast majority of libraries are designed with seriously inadequate storage space, and John was the envy of his fellow directors.

[Right] The architects of this library designed this small room to serve as the workroom for all of the staff of a public library (including the library director and technical services). It was also intended to serve as a staff lunchroom and a storeroom. It failed amazingly (not to mention astoundingly and spectacularly), and the library had to wall off one end of the building to provide workable space.

Our experience has been that providing enough storage space in library buildings is a real challenge. The storage spaces libraries specify in their building programs often end up smaller or made to do double duty. As a result, librarians need to keep close protective eyes on storerooms throughout the entire space planning and design process.

Equally challenging on some occasions is trying to figure out whether an object really deserves space in your library or whether the fact that the puppet stage that hasn't been used since 1968 is really telling us something.

II. Locations of Storage Places

Storerooms need to be in places that are convenient for library staff members who need to store books and papers and supplies and equipment and general library miscellanea. The following sections review some of the possibilities.

While some library storage spaces are carefully planned, vast numbers of other storage spaces are created because it's possible to squirrel things away in corners that are hard to use for other purposes. Unfortunately, the result of this thinking is dysfunctional storerooms in dysfunctional places. Instead of being large enough and easy to use, and located where library staff need them, storage spaces are tucked into damp corners of basements or into all sorts of illegal (or at least extremely unsuitable) places, such as HVAC spaces, mechanical equipment rooms, stairwells, electrical panel rooms, and many others.

When it comes to access to storage, frequency of use really matters. Storage for something

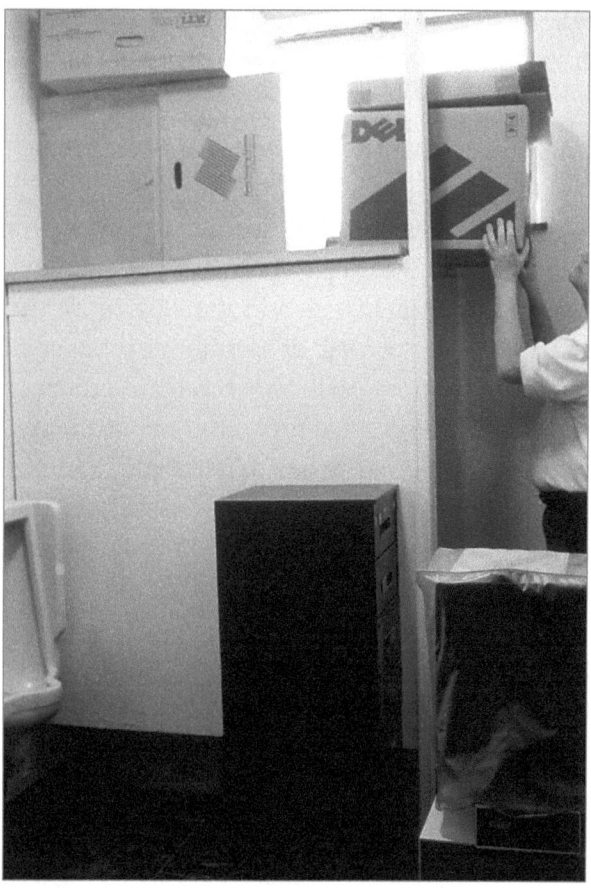

Desperate needs for storage space lead to desperate solutions. In this library, staff members put a sheet of plywood on top of a staff workroom toilet stall to provide a space for computer boxes.

used only once every couple of years may not require convenient access, but libraries have many situations where staff members waste large amounts of time fetching and carrying frequently used items to and from distant storerooms, and that means wasted operating funds.

The obvious rule is that storage spaces need to be constructed for that purpose, frequently using space that could be used for other purposes. The tradeoffs are tempting, but going without essential storage spaces can be as dysfunctional as trying to cut corners on power, light, fresh air, and other likeable things.

III. Assigned Storage Spaces

All library departments need storage space.

Assigned departmental storage space has a number of advantages. It can be convenient to departmental staff workrooms. Because the space belongs to that department alone, contents can be more easily protected. And the fact that storage areas are protected departmental spaces means that other departments cannot poach space and simply transfer their excess objects to your storage space, hoping that no one will notice.

Some common items requiring assigned storage are:

- *Books and other materials*, including items that need to be sequestered due to potential theft, items awaiting processing, items in closed stacks, items being considered for withdrawal, and so on. Some academic libraries have truly impressive stocks of unprocessed books. Some academic and public libraries have devices to heat or freeze incoming gift books or books from overseas, in order to pre-emptively eliminate six-legged wildlife. And some have to store wet books.

- *Business records*, particularly records stored next to administrative workrooms. Think of personnel and financial records, correspondence, minutes of meetings, rolls of building plans, and the vast amounts of other paper that need to be kept somewhere. An important consideration is always records that require security.

- *Office supplies*, not only stuff for graphic arts and other staff workrooms but also supplies used throughout buildings, such as copier paper. The level of security libraries require for office supplies can vary and affect locations.

  For example, some libraries just stack boxes of copier paper in staff entry areas, letting departments help themselves, while other libraries keep the boxes under lock and key. Your library's policies may dictate the architecture of storage arrangements.

- *Program equipment and supplies*, particularly for public library children's departments and for school libraries. Children's departments can have impressive quantities of craft supplies, summer reading club prizes, and similar things. Unfortunately, school librarians can wake up on Monday morning to discover that 20 new pieces of classroom equipment on carts have appeared magically over the weekend and are now occupying essential floor space in their libraries.

  Decades ago, school libraries were clogged with rows of 16mm projectors on carts, and with each new instructional device the tradition can be repeated. To some school administrators, the library is clearly the school's storeroom. One thing you might do is require space for classroom equipment in your building program and then see what guarantees administrators make if they reject the idea.

- *Furniture*, particularly furniture that needs to be stored away when not in use, such as meeting room furniture. Far too many meeting rooms have furniture not used during programs piled around their walls because storage closets are inadequate. Libraries also need to store furniture awaiting assembly, furniture awaiting repair, or historic furniture that is not usable but too beloved to sell off. Unfortunately, essential furniture storage closets are sometimes either inadequate or nonexistent.

- **Book sale books.** Friends of the library groups that hold occasional book sales need places to stash books for the next sale.

- **Technical services supplies.** These can be in storerooms, although many departments seem to prefer open shelving for easy access.

- **Custodial supplies** that need to be kept locked up, including lightbulbs, tools (which tend to vanish if they're not kept under lock and key), cleaning solutions, paint, cleaning supply carts, mop basins, vacuum cleaners, rug shampoo equipment, lawnmowers, snowblowers, salt for sidewalks, gardening equipment, and so on.

- **Attic stock.** All new libraries have supplies of ceiling tile, floor tile, carpet squares, broadloom carpet, extra lighting elements, and other items needed to replace things that fail in use. "Attic stock" is important because it's often impossible to match things even a few years after the library goes up. And it can take up an impressive amount of space.

Be very explicit in your building program about storage closets, and then watch to be sure that . . .

- Storage closets don't magically shrink during the design process. Or magically vanish entirely.

- Closets that must be separate for security purposes are not merged.

- Department storerooms are not merged. The result of unwanted merger can be staff of two departments squabbling over who gets the space, or merged storerooms that are no longer in a good location for some of the users.

- Storage closets don't mysteriously relocate themselves to awkward places.

- All storage areas are accessible. Storerooms that need to be accessed by ladders or staircases or tunnels are unworthy.

- All ceilings in storage closets are comfortable standing height—at least seven feet.

- Storage closets are well lighted, with shields to protect light fixtures from collisions with objects being stored, and with convenient light switches.

- Unscheduled items don't migrate into storage closets planned for other purposes, such as mechanical gear that prevents the use of the closets for storage.

A lot can go wrong at both the programming and the construction drawing stages, and you'll want to keep a wary eye open. It helps to remind your owners and architects that no changes can be made to storerooms without consultation with the library staff, resulting in a written and signed memo of the decision.

Occasionally, library departments want unreasonable amounts of storage space. Determining that the spaces are unreasonable is a job for practicing librarians and programmers, not for owners or architects.

IV. Meeting and Program Room Storage Spaces

For some reason, meeting and program rooms frequently have seriously inadequate storage spaces.

It should be easy to clear all furniture out of a meeting or program room and store it in attached closets. Nothing says bad planning more loudly than a program room with unused furniture piled around the walls.

Program rooms usually need separate closets because libraries need to control access to the contents. Common closet spaces include:

- ***Furnishings***, including tables, chairs, lecterns, and so on. Furnishings require separate closets because libraries may want users to set up their own furniture but not have access to other stored items. Building programs need to specify the items that will be stored in furniture closets and *require that the owners and architects make sure that all of the specified items will actually fit into the furniture closets*. This is important, because owners try to cut corners and architects occasionally fail to make sure things will fit. During the construction drawings phase of your design, make sure your architects have taken time to calculate things. Once the building is built and the furniture purchased, if things don't fit, it's too late. Remember that when you hold an event that doesn't require any tables or chairs, ALL of the furniture needs to fit into the furniture closet.

  The space required for meeting room furniture storage depends heavily on the actual furniture. Are stack chairs easy to lift and to stack? How high are people expected to lift the chairs? Are the chairs on casters and unsuitable for stacking? How heavy are the tables? Do the tabletops flip upward for storage? Are the tables on casters? Does access to furniture at the back of the storage space require emptying the front of the space? To use a technical term, is there wiggle room?

- ***Program equipment and supplies***. Many program rooms have associated electronic equipment, ranging from monitors on carts to server racks to places to connect to ceiling-mounted projectors. In some public libraries, meeting rooms are designed to be set up as "maker spaces" from time to time, and storage space for all of the associated equipment needs to be provided. When it comes to children's departments, it's easy to underestimate the space that program supplies can occupy, particularly if the departments have large puppet stages and similar objects.

- ***Book sale books***. If your Friends of the Library group holds book sales in your program room, you'll want an attached storeroom for boxed books. Storerooms can be filled a box at a time over the months, but when the time comes for a sale, your Friends will want to open closet doors and simply pull the books out. If book sale books are stored in some distant part of the building, setting up a sale will be a serious pain and probably require hiring a crew to move all of the books at once. Your Friends group will also need a space for receiving and sorting and boxing books. And easy access to the library dumpster for those occasions when boxes of donated books turn out to be awash in mildew.

- ***Equipment that belongs to outside groups***. Some libraries have permanent relationships with outside groups that require storage space, often separate locking closets for each group. Among those we've seen in public libraries are voting booths and scout equipment. If you are considering letting outside groups use library storage closets, however, remember that you will almost certainly never get the space back, even if you have a great need for it. Saying, "Sorry, but no" up front is probably several thousand times easier than saying, "Sorry, but you'll have to move out" later.

- ***Kitchenettes***. Many program rooms have kitchenettes. Storage is usually provided with cupboards and drawers. All drawers need ball-bearing, double-extension hardware, and all drawers and cabinets need locks, but a single key formula for all drawers and cabinets will keep things far less complicated. Cabinets and drawers need to be made of furniture-grade plywood with no chipboard components. The interiors of cabinets and drawers need to be very light colored so that objects do not vanish into the gloom. Open shelves make it easier to find things, but they invite public discovery and rearrangement of contents.

The configuration of storage spaces is important. Closets for furniture, equipment, program supplies and book sale books need to be wide and shallow rather than narrow and deep. Double doors are a lot better than single doors. Furniture closets in particular need doors with steel edges to prevent them from being damaged by people moving furniture in and out.

One of the banes of meeting and program rooms is monster conference tables. If there's no separate conference room, make sure that conference tables are modular, and that there's a place to stash them out of sight. (Unless the scions of the great merchant families of the United States serve on your boards, modest conference tables are just fine.)

Our experience has been that storage closets in meeting rooms are almost always too few and too small. The result is furniture piled around the edges of rooms because it won't fit in the furniture closet, program supplies awkwardly transferred from other parts of the building for every program, book sale books hauled from remote storage spaces, and electronic equipment in a jumble in undersized closets.

V. Mechanical Equipment Storage Spaces

Libraries need to store all sorts of stuff in addition to books, technical equipment, furnishings, and program supplies.

V-A. OUTDOOR EQUIPMENT

Public libraries often need space for outdoor equipment, including lawn mowers, snowblowers, salt for sidewalks, gardening equipment, hoses, fertilizer, lawn furniture, and so on.

Codes typically require that gasoline-powered equipment and fuel be in spaces that can be accessed directly from out of doors. There may be additional requirements in your jurisdiction. Verify things with your architects.

In the winter, you ideally use photovoltaic panels to heat a glycol solution that you pump through your walkways, but if you don't have that, you need sidewalk salt stored in closets right next to entries. Particularly if your entries don't face south.

> In Fred's library, the architects lowered the ceiling in an area designed for ladder storage in the construction drawings, apparently because some junior member of the firm saw no reason for a high ceiling and simply deleted it without talking with the client or the project architect. Fred spotted the change only when the ceiling grid started to go in. It did not improve his mood.

V-B. LADDERS

Public and academic libraries need to store required ladders and lifts. List these in your building program and then double-check your construction drawings. There's a constant tendency to omit ladder storage from libraries. But ladders have to go somewhere, and parent organizations (such as universities) may have no interest in hauling ladders around to individual buildings.

Lots of libraries also struggle with ladders stored in such cramped spaces that it takes amazing contortions to bring them out for use.

V-C. HVAC SUPPLIES

HVAC equipment has necessary supplies that will need to be stored somewhere, typically in the corner of an equipment room. A common item is stacks of disposable air filters. Be sure you enumerate what you'll need to store and mention this in your building program. Your HVAC engineers can help you determine what you'll need to store.

In some very critical situations, libraries may need to keep replacement HVAC machinery in stock, so that there are no long delays in obtaining replacement parts.

V-D. VEHICLE STORAGE

If your library has vehicles, you will probably want garage space. This introduces a whole range of technical requirements and possibilities. Will you have enough elbowroom to load vans and bookmobiles? Will the bookmobile collection be located directly adjacent to the garage space? What provisions will you have to move books into the bookmobile without climbing the entry steps with endless small handfuls of books? Will

Every library needs a place to store ladders. This historic library had no place for ladders and ended up chaining them to a railing next to its historic main entry. The word "unsightly" was invented to cover situations like this.

you want to wash vehicles in your garage? Will you want a concrete floor or some type of poured epoxy finish? What kind of air exchange will you need?

Garage design in public buildings is a huge topic requiring extensive input from your architects and engineers.

VI. Describing Storage Spaces in Building Programs

Storage spaces are easy to describe in building programs. Be sure to specify:

- ***Minimum size of each storage space in total square feet.*** It's usually wise to estimate generously, since stuff in storage gets bigger when the closet doors are closed and nobody is watching.

- **Adjacencies**. Administrative records, for example, need to be adjacent to administrative workrooms, not in some other location where they happen to fit. Children's program gear needs to be next to program rooms or next to departmental workrooms.

- **Configuration**. Most storage closets are far better wide and shallow than narrow and deep. Double doors are better than single doors. A rectangular storage closet holds more per square foot than an oddly configured storage closet. Adjacent storage closets should not be connected inside unless they are described in the building program as a single closet. Some of the most vicious storage closets in library buildings are long and narrow and accessed from one end.

- **Clearances**. In addition to holding items, storerooms have to allow access, and they frequently need to allow individual items to be removed and returned. This may take more aisle space than provided in initial designs, since no one wants to completely unload and then repack a storage room just to get at a single item at the back.

- **Ceiling heights**. Crawlspaces under staircases can make impressively rotten storage closets. Specify that spaces under ceilings less than seven feet high will not be counted as meeting a programmed space requirement.

- **Minimum contents**. After listing square footages, you may still want to instruct architects to make sure that specified items will fit in the allotted spaces, particularly if the items will vary in size depending on architectural choices. For instance, you can specify that the listed filing cabinets will actually fit into the designed space, and require a drawing. Or you can specify that the tables and chairs and other furniture listed for a program room must fit into the allocated storerooms. *And work with your architects to make sure that things actually fit.*

- **No extra equipment.** Equipment that has nothing to do with the storage functions of the space. You will want to specify that building systems equipment will not intrude on storage spaces. Then watch construction drawings like a hawk to be sure this doesn't happen. If a piece of HVAC equipment is suddenly added to an auditorium furniture storeroom, the room needs to be enlarged rather than leaving the library staff trying to figure out how to make a suddenly unworkable situation work.

- **Unalterable dimensions**. If you have worked out how specific numbers of filing cabinets and feet of shelving will fit into a storeroom of specific length and width, be sure your dimensions allow extra space for the lack of precision in some wall placement. Allow an extra couple of inches of space. And be sure your architects don't change the proportions of the room on the mistaken assumption that all that matters is total square feet. It may be better to simply list the sizes of the items that have to fit into the room and ask the architects to provide a measured drawing of the room with all the items in place.

- **Access**. A wide and shallow storeroom with double doors will be far easier to use than a narrow and deep storeroom with a single door. Specify your needs in your building program and then check to be sure you're getting what you specified.

- **Furnishings**. Storage spaces are great places to use old book shelving units made surplus by expansion or new construction. They are also great places to use the high-quality (but bright orange or avocado) steel shelving your library purchased in 1970.

- **Flexibility**. If your meeting room furniture storage closet is too tightly configured, you may find it impossible to store slightly different furniture. You also don't want to be forced to have a diagram that shows the only way the meeting room furniture will fit.

- **Durability**. Storerooms can be battered through frequent use and through dragging things in and out. Door edges need steel reinforcements, to prevent chipping. Interiors of furniture storage closets need the equivalent of chair rails, frequently at multiple heights.

- **Lighting**. All but the tiniest storerooms need lighting and light switches. Light fixtures need to be designed not to be damaged by objects being moved about.

During the programming phase of your project, try to review all the stuff you'll need to store, either chucking it out or making provisions for it. If your storage area will require special equipment (such as locked steel cabinets for high-theft materials), you'll want to list them so your architects can make sure they'll fit.

Frequently, owners will more or less blow off storage spaces, and you'll need to keep a close eye on things, both at the schematic design phase, when it's tempting to use space for more visible purposes, and at the construction document phase, when architects may feel the need to cram something in somewhere at the last minute and be tempted to cannibalize storage space.

Pay particular attention to things your parent organization may decide to inflict on you after the fact. This seems to occur on a regular basis with some school libraries, so the programming phase is a good time to watch for new things and to pin the school administration down—if not planning extra space just on general principles.

To protect yourself from strange objects taking over your storage space, consider including in the description of each storage space wording something like the following: "This storage closet will be used only for the listed purpose. No additional equipment or functions will be added to the space unless it is correspondingly enlarged."

VII. Protecting Storage Spaces from Looters Who Covet Your Space

We've mentioned throughout this book that storage space is almost never adequate and that it can easily be taken from you while your back is turned.

During the design process, architects can reduce square footages for storage without mentioning it to you, change configurations of storerooms so that contents no longer fit, relocate storage to less convenient parts of the building, and combine individual storerooms (thereby reducing security and convenience).

In addition . . .

- University or high school administrators can come scouting around for storage space and seize upon yours. Some high schools even convert library user space to equipment storage.

- Other school and academic departments can attempt to move their stuff into your storerooms.

- Medical and law and industrial libraries may find that confidential organization records suddenly appear in their storerooms, perhaps even with the locks changed.

- Storerooms may be combined with non-storage functions to the detriment of storage. If a drive-through book return receiving bin is added to a storeroom, for example, there will be all sorts of safety and access and noise-control implications.

Protecting necessary storage requires eternal vigilance, including realistically large projections of needed space in building programs, careful oversight during design to be sure that programmed spaces are provided, and making sure that extra things aren't crammed into your storage space when your back is turned. Keep an eye on construction documents, where spaces in the original schematic designs can be suddenly altered.

You can also be sure that your current departmental storerooms always look clean and neat but packed to the gills, discouraging people who are scouting around for extra space or considering challenging your needs.

VIII. Snappy Rules on Storerooms

1. Few libraries have ever built enough storage space on purpose.

2. The minute you plan an important storeroom, someone will scheme to put something else into it.

3. Ladders and lifts and other awkwardly shaped gadgets need to go somewhere. Usually in your building. Be sure your building program and your building plans include the spaces.

4. Describe all of your necessary storage spaces in your building program, and even then be prepared to fight to get them (and retain them).

5. If a gadget runs on gasoline, you'll need a door leading directly from the storeroom to the outside world. Or you may even need a separate building. Ask your architects and engineers to double-check applicable codes.

6. If your building will have light fixtures with 75 different bulbs, imagine the storeroom you'll need in order to have a stock of each type. (Not to mention the cost of purchasing supplies of 75 different bulbs.) Before you build an immense lightbulb storeroom, you probably need to rethink your lighting strategy.

7. Review your construction drawings with an eagle eye, for it's there that evil forces will suddenly appear, robbing you of your storage space. Practice saying, "Get that @#$% out of my storeroom" in the tone of voice even middle-school students don't customarily elicit.

8. Never assume that campus maintenance services will bring their ladders with them when they come to service your library.

9. You'd be impressed by how much storage space a 50-year backlog of uncatalogued agricultural monographs in 50 assorted languages can occupy. Or the morgue of your local newspaper. Plan for it.

10. Attic stock is vital and can consume an impressive amount of storage space. Don't get caught short-square-footed.

11. The name "attic stock" sounds cozy and old-fashioned, but few libraries have actual empty attics that can be used for storage. Think of all the physical strength,

heating and cooling, accessibility, fire protection, and other legal requirements. And if your attic was not engineered for storage, think of all the excitement when the trusses start to give way.

12. Public library children's departments can make use of any amount of storage space available. One of the tough jobs of library directors is deciding where things are getting out of hand and have to stop.

13. School libraries are prone to having shared classroom equipment abruptly dumped on them. If someone turns up Monday morning with 30 bulky electronic gadgets on tall carts, you need someplace to put them that does not involve your main library room or staff workroom. When your library space is first being planned, protecting a space for equipment-yet-to-come may require a stern attitude and creative labeling. Consider asking the administration for a written statement about whether the library should plan space for this kind of equipment, or whether it will be going somewhere else in the school.

14. Program and meeting rooms need separate storage closets for movable furniture, electronic equipment, book sale books, equipment owned by outside groups, and other kinds of separately owned stuff. It's easy for double doors to closets to completely line an entire long side of a meeting room. And even that may not be enough.

15. Program room storage closets need to be located adjacent to program rooms, because that's where the stuff in them is used. Dragging stuff from all over the library to a program room every time you have a program is a royal pain. An avoidable pain if you plan first, watch things like a hawk, and stand your ground.

16. Storage closets work infinitely better if they are wide and shallow rather than narrow and deep. A closet with a double door works a lot better than a closet with a single door. Keep a special eye out for proposed designs of closets under staircases. Once the ceiling slopes down to below seven feet, the space is pretty much worthless. And fire codes will take a singularly dim view of storing stuff in staircases.

17. Every floor that has a toilet is required by code to have a usable floor sink (aka mop basin). The same room that houses the mop basin can often provide storage space for service carts, vacuum cleaners, carpet shampooers, and other custodial stuff.

18. Few things excite owners and architects much less than storage spaces. Keep an eye on what's proposed, in case your specified storage spaces slowly disappear as plans are revised.

19. A storeroom without a storage policy is trouble just over the horizon. If you run a law library, a medical library, or an industrial library, be prepared for the possibility that someone will want to store confidential documents there. It helps to sort things out with the administration in advance, so you don't suddenly find your library storage areas converted to corporate secure storage and your own stuff piled out in the hall.

20. A long, narrow storeroom entered from one end is a pain forever.

21. If an outside book return slot leads into a storeroom, make sure that (a) the storeroom is designed to contain a fire and (b) you can get at the receiving bin without moving all sorts of debris out of the way and (c) the noise of falling books does

not echo through occupied spaces nearby and (d) the storeroom is not accessed through a meeting room.

22. Never miss an opportunity to specify lots of locking storage cabinets and drawers. Great places are public service desks, technical services departments, kitchenettes in meeting rooms and in staff lunchrooms, and counter areas in children's craft and story rooms. Then figure out how you'll keep track of the keys. The best way is to have a group of adjacent drawers or cupboards use the same key.

23. Doors to storerooms need metal edges. Those without metal edges often are battered almost beyond recognition.

24. The backyards of endless numbers of small public libraries have kit-built garden sheds, not because the staff are avid gardeners but because the buildings were designed without much of any storage space.

25. A school library is not a storeroom for irrelevant equipment.

26. If you have to choose, storerooms are more useful than water features. And innocent, unsuspecting people almost never fall into storerooms.

27. All of the unlikely problems in this chapter and in the list of snappy rules are based on actual real-life occurrences. So beware.

PART IV

Technical Issues

PART IV
Technical Issues

CHAPTER 30

Elevators, Staircases, Railings, and Ramps

I. Introduction

A vast number of ill-considered building designs involve unsuitable methods of moving between levels, with many problems associated with cheap elevator substitutes, with dysfunctional staircases, with uncomfortable handrails, and with unpleasant ramps. This chapter lists a lot of the problems that occur, but new ones come along on a regular basis.

Moving people between floors in a library should be a simple, straightforward, safe undertaking, but it all too often goes awry. Too many staircases are dangerous (or at least frightening), and too many inexpensive elevator substitutes are unpleasant or even dangerous. Parents who have children in strollers have a terrible time with steps. For lots of people who have wheelchairs, canes, and walkers, elevators are essential. Other people just don't like steps. Icy steps in the bleak midwinter are a menace. Exterior ramps to front entrances are a pain at all times of year, but seriously nasty in the rain or snow, and indoor ramps are only marginally better. Carrying furniture or boxes of books up or downstairs is a pain. Herding three or four children upstairs is a lot harder than just shooing them into an elevator, keeping their fingers out of the door, and pressing "up." And if the elevator is too small for a family—parent, strollers, and children on foot—does the library expect the parent to make two trips, leaving children alone at both floors while doing so?

The easiest way to cope with this situation is by just building one-story buildings at grade level. If a sufficiently large site is available, any building less than 40,000 or so square feet can easily be constructed this way—avoiding the high cost of elevators and staircases, avoiding the abuse of users and staff with acrophobia, avoiding people falling on staircases, avoiding users struggling up ramps in the rain or snow, avoiding hiring extra staff to watch extra floors, avoiding the excitement of wondering when the basement will flood, avoiding the high cost of constructing upper floors strong enough to hold books when a concrete slab on the ground will do it easily, and avoiding other bad things.

But in crowded communities, large sites may not be available. And sooner or later, even when large sites are available, lots of buildings need extra floors.

If a building has more than one level, the easy thing to do is to avoid converting the connections between the levels into hazards. Unfortunately, all too often the urge to make an architectural statement overwhelms the basics of moving between levels, although there are plenty of ways to make architectural statements that do not involve dizziness. Staircases need to be safe and relatively enclosed, not exciting and soaring monuments. Floating staircases in the middle of atria are a seriously overworked architectural cliché, but they refuse to go away, terrifying library users on a regular basis. Staircases that combine steps with reading or shelving areas are amazingly bad ideas.

Many historic library buildings are just plain inaccessible and need to be updated. Unless the building has a single floor that's only a foot or two above grade level, the only solution is an elevator. And creative remodeling.

> Joe converted a historic building with 17 different levels into a library with two levels, and others have done likewise.

II. Elevators

If you have a library with more than one floor, or with a floor that is not close to grade level, you need a mechanical way to move users from outside the library to the inside of the library, and to move them between floors.

For all except single-story libraries at or very near grade level, elevators are an essential component—expensive but essential. Any library with more than one floor must have an elevator.

One of the main problems associated with elevators involves cheap substitutions. Elevators need to open into entry lobbies, not into outside walls at the back of libraries. They need to be large enough for users, including users with wheelchairs and friends. They need to have automatic doors. And for any change in elevation of more than a foot or two, ramps are not an acceptable alternative to elevators.

One of the difficulties in dealing with historic library buildings is that almost all of them need elevators. Historic library buildings can be great, but making them work is not free.

II-A. ELEVATOR TERMINOLOGY

There are a handful of terms that are heavily used in this chapter and in the construction of buildings. Many involve very specific building code requirements.

- ***Car***. The small compartment in which elevator users ride.

- ***Conveyance***. A mechanical device that moves people between floors or down long corridors. Some architectural cost estimates include an allowance for "conveyances." (Steps and ramps are not "conveyances" because they involve no mechanisms.)

- ***Dumbwaiter***. A car for moving books and other objects, but not people.

- ***Electric traction elevator***. With traction elevators, cabs are raised and lowered by steel ropes or belts on a pulley system. Unlike hydraulic elevators, which are limited to about four floors, traction elevators can rise to many floors. Because they use counterweights, they save energy compared with hydraulic elevators, but they are far more expensive to install.

- *Escalator.* A power-driven staircase. The advantage is the ability of escalators to move large numbers of people with no waiting for the next available car. Escalators are probably found only in the largest of library buildings. Escalators cannot replace elevators because escalators are mechanically assisted staircases, with no space for wheelchairs, walkers, gurneys, strollers, book trucks, and people with uncertain senses of balance.
- *Gate.* Another name for an elevator door.
- *Hoistway.* The elevator shaft.
- *Hydraulic elevator.* A hydraulic elevator is somewhat like a hydraulic piston lift in a service station. They are far simpler to install than traction elevators, but they are limited to about four floors.
- *Leveling zone.* The acceptable range of alignments between the floor of the elevator cab and the floor of the building.
- *Lift.* A lower-cost substitute for an elevator, almost always completely unsuitable for libraries.
- *People mover.* A device that assists people faced with long corridors, moving them horizontally. Some of the most commonly encountered are in airports. In libraries, they appear to be very uncommon.
- *Traction elevator.* See *electric traction elevator.*

See also chapter 3, "The Basic Configuration of Successful Library Spaces"; chapter 11, "Accessibility"; and chapter 16, "Remodeling and Expanding Library Buildings."

II-B. REAL ELEVATORS

The civilized way to move people between floors is with elevators, and most codes simply require them. However, there are a lot of old multistory library buildings out there that have no elevators and desperately need to be modernized.

A standard way of dealing with two-level, Carnegie-era libraries is to install an elevator with doors on two sides. One door opens at ground level and the door on the other side opens at various floor levels in the library—basement, main floor, and sometimes additional floors.

The problem with elevators like these is that they can compromise collection security. Unless there is a staffed desk at ground level, or desks at the exits of each floor, users can sometimes leave the library without passing by any service desk.

To deal with this problem, larger historic libraries have provided one elevator to lift people from the entry to the main floor. After passing through security gates, library users can then use a second elevator that connects all the floors of the library. This balances the needs for access, service, collection security, and human safety.

Elevators are available in a variety of sizes. If you are installing a brand new one in a new elevator shaft, ask your designers about accommodation for people in motorized wheelchairs, attendants for people in manual wheelchairs, parents with large strollers, day care groups with only two teachers, people moving furniture, emergency workers moving people on gurneys, and other users requiring open space. Ask how you will handle the crush at the end of special events if your meeting rooms aren't at grade level and many people have children in strollers. And if you have parents with children in strollers waiting to board the elevator, will there be enough floor space for them to wait?

Almost all elevators that move up to about 60 feet vertically are based on the operating principle of grease racks. The elevator is guided through the shaft along greased rails, while a hydraulic piston lifts the elevator cab from floor to floor. The cabs in taller elevators are lifted by cables.

Hydraulic elevators have a number of advantages:

- They are quick to install.
- They are less expensive to install and maintain than are electric traction elevators.
- With custom cabs, they can move heavy weights.
- No access to the top of the shaft is required from outside the building.

Hydraulic elevators also have disadvantages:

- They are limited to fairly low buildings, about 60 feet high.
- They are relatively slow, about 50 feet per minute at the low end, and up to a typical speed of 150 feet per minute, generally at the maximum end of typical applications.
- They have larger power requirements than electric traction elevators.

Electric traction elevators are standard for taller buildings or where speed is essential. Their advantages include:

- Workability in all but fairly low buildings.
- Smaller motors.

Electric traction elevators also have disadvantages:

- Greater expense to build and maintain.
- Longer installation time.
- Outside access required to the top of the hoistway, which means that the library roof cannot enclose the top opening.

II-C. ELEVATOR OPTIONS

Many codes and other rules affect the installation and operation of elevators. Rely on your architects and engineers to be sure your elevators are completely up to code.

When you are considering elevator options, include performance and maintenance in your considerations.

- If you have a video security system, do you want a camera in the elevator? (Getting security people and elevator people to work happily together may take work, but you can do it.)
- Do your local emergency services have any special requirements? For example, an elevator large enough for a gurney makes things a great deal easier in times of troubles. (Having to tilt seriously ill people on stretchers up on end to fit them into small elevators is not very friendly.)

> An elevator in Fred's library had a sign beside an indicator light on the fire control panel that said, "When flashing, exit elevator." He felt that this was the kind of behavior the library was actually trying to discourage.

- How does the elevator respond in case of emergencies? Does it automatically carry passengers to the entry-level floor, where the doors open and controls are then limited to emergency personnel? Or do signs simply warn users not to use the elevator in case of emergency? To what degree are your options limited by codes?

- Does your elevator meet special control requirements for use by firefighters?

- What mechanisms are included to prevent doors from closing on people? Elevators have electric eyes to detect the presence of people in the path of closing doors. Electric eyes need to be at a variety of heights to detect adults, children, and pets.

- Is your elevator large enough to meet predictable long-term needs? Talk with your architects and engineers about size vs. cost decisions. And the amazing cost of making an existing elevator larger.

- Is your building large enough to require a second elevator? If you have only one elcvator, what will you do whcn it's out of service?

- If your first floor is above grade level, do you have an elevator to move people between grade level and the main floor? If you have to move people more than a foot or so vertically, a ramp is an uncivilized idea. If the ramp is out of doors, it's an impressively uncivilized idea. If it's out of doors and more than perhaps eight feet long, it's disgustingly uncivilized. And if it's out of doors AND over eight feet long AND too narrow for people to pass in opposite directions, it's a criminal and disgustingly uncivilized idea.

- Are all of the controls on your elevator at heights accessible to users with disabilities? Modern codes require this.

- If you have a large meeting room that is not on your main floor, what kind of elevators will you need to handle a large number of people leaving at the same time? (Even if viewers arrive one-by-one, they tend to leave as a mob.)

- Will people who avoid your floating staircases because of their acrophobia appreciate your exciting glass-walled elevators?

- Will some people with claustrophobia have trouble being in small elevator cars?

- What kind of alarm mechanisms will you have in your elevators?

A few things can go wrong with elevators once they have been installed. Luckily, most of them are minor, but some can lead to serious problems. Among things that cause problems in libraries are elevators that stall between floors, elevator doors that close too quickly, elevator doors that repeatedly open and close, and elevators that stop when they are not aligned with outside floors but have doors that open anyway.

> This happened once in Fred's library. A staff member in a wheelchair didn't see the misalignment, rolled into the open elevator door, fell down into the elevator car, tipped over, and broke a leg. Fred's words to the elevator company cannot be shared in this nice book. See the definition of "leveling zone."

Despite all sorts of fictional fears, modern elevators don't suddenly plummet down their shafts. Elevators that serve only a few stories are hydraulic, basically multistory grease racks.

If the hydraulic systems spring leaks, the cars simply sink slowly. If higher elevators are hoisted by cables, releasing the tension on the cables engages brakes that rub against the guide rails, and the elevators slide down slowly.

By law, elevators require regular maintenance and inspection.

Scheduled inspections are performed by local authorities, with inspection certificates posted in elevators. (Some owners get around the problem of occasional vandalism of posted certificates by having signs indicating where in the building the certificates can be inspected.)

You will want a maintenance contract on your elevator, especially for those exciting times when someone is caught between floors in a stalled elevator and starting to hyperventilate. When you are selecting an elevator, always inquire about local maintenance and any extra charges for after-hours calls when people are trapped.

> Elevator companies are eager to be the first to arrive because emergency services can do a great deal of damage to stalled elevators when they fight their way in to rescue panicked people.

II-D. UNFORTUNATE SUBSTITUTES FOR REAL ELEVATORS

Many libraries have used unfortunate substitutes for elevators, either to save money (elevators are expensive) or to save space. We know many libraries that are unhappy with their choices. And many users that are as well.

In most cases, frustrations are the result of a penny-wise and pound-foolish approach. If you are going to get a lift, get the best one. A good lift has a large platform and a large lifting capacity. It's easy for users to operate, and it has no places where they can be hurt by moving doors. In particular, the gap between the outside doors and the inside doors is small enough so that no children can be trapped.

There are a huge number of products available in this area. Our coverage is extremely brief because we think that while they may be suitable for home use, substitutes for real elevators are never suitable for libraries.

A standard substitute used by Carnegie-era libraries is a platform lift, either one sitting on the floor of a room at grade level or one enclosed in a shaft. Some lifts are placed outside buildings, next to entry stoops, and can move people from ground level to the main floor.

There are some reasons to use a lift instead of an elevator:

- Lifts can sometimes be fitted into smaller spaces than can elevators.
- Lifts are cheaper than elevators.

Lifts also have a number of problems.

- Lifts sometimes serve only the main floor of a library and not the basement, making the building only partially accessible.
- Lifts can require serious effort to open and close doors manually. Library staff may need to run down to the entry foyer, open the lift door for the user in a wheelchair, then run back upstairs to open the upper door.
- Lifts can be so small inside that no one can accompany the person using a wheelchair.
- Fitting a lift into a building may still require the construction of an exterior enclosure

for the lift. Some lifts are accessed directly from outside libraries rather than from a foyer, and people waiting to use a lift may end up standing outside in the rain.

We know of some libraries that have installed chair lifts on staircases. These can be platforms that provide a flat space large enough for a wheelchair. The lift maintains a fixed distance from the stairs and simply rides up following the stairs.

Remember that some users use lifts not because they are in wheelchairs, but because they cannot bend their legs or have bad balance and are afraid of falling on staircases. Because they will be standing up, they may find lifts of this type frightening.

A similar device is a lift that provides a seat running on rails. A person who uses a wheelchair can sit on the platform and ride up, while someone else carries the wheelchair upstairs. Or the library may have a loaner wheelchair waiting at the top of the stairs. Things are made more complicated if the person using the chair lift may have to be lifted on and then helped off again. Chair lifts are intended for home use and have no place in libraries.

One unfortunate result of cheap lifts is libraries with two entrances—an elegant front door and an ugly accessible entrance around the back.

II-E. DUMBWAITERS

Many older library buildings without elevators still have dumbwaiters for moving books from floor to floor. Some of the historic ones are not mechanized but are operated by hanging loops of rope. Because the hoist mechanisms provide mechanical advantage, one can end up pulling a lot of rope to move a couple of carts of books up a floor.

The advantage of dumbwaiters is that you can ship things from floor to floor without having a staff member accompany them. For example, Fred's library installed a dumbwaiter to make it possible for departmental staff members in two different departments to send books to a lending desk on a different floor instead of leaving their departments unstaffed. It was an unusual situation, but the staff in both departments still use the dumbwaiter daily.

III. Staircases

Libraries on more than one level all have staircases.

While some staircases are extremely attractive, the code requirements for staircases are extensive. Unfortunately, many older buildings have staircases that no longer meet building codes. Many staircases are falling hazards or terrify people with fear of heights, and old wooden staircases can make buildings fire traps.

Even staircases that meet today's building codes can be artistically interesting while otherwise pretty much disasters. Because of these problems, this section is full of admonitions of the "never do this again" variety.

III-A. VOCABULARY

Staircases have a number of technical terms. Some commonly encountered ones include:

- *Baluster*. An upright support found in staircases and railings. Building codes often require that the spacing of balusters be too close to allow children to fall through.

- *Guardrail*. An additional railing preventing users from falling off staircases. The handrails are inside the guardrails and lower. Guardrails are often installed on the edges of staircase openings.

- *Handrail*. A device to hold onto while using a staircase or looking over an architectural abyss. There are an impressive number of codes concerning handrails, and an even greater number of handrails that should have been banned but are still around.

- *Landing*. A resting area between groups of steps.

- *Newel post*. A post at the head or foot of a flight of stairs, supporting the end of the handrail.

- *Nosing*. The lead edge of a tread.

- *Riser*. The vertical portion of each step.

- *Step*. The combination of a tread and a riser. The final step is onto the arrival floor. Many building codes control the number of steps that can be built until there is a landing. We think codes can require too few landings.

- *Tread*. The horizontal portion of each step.

See also chapter 3, "The Basic Configuration of Successful Library Spaces"; chapter 11, "Accessibility"; and chapter 16, "Remodeling and Expanding Library Buildings."

III-B. BASIC STAIRCASE DESIGN

The basics of staircase design are straightforward, and there shouldn't be so many problems. But some owners and designers are hard to restrain when they hear the word "staircase."

- The most important thing is that users of staircases should be safe. And *feel* safe.

- Staircases should have steps of constant dimensions. The depths of the treads and the heights of the risers should be consistent.

- There should be no funny-shaped treads. Lots of old Carnegie-era libraries have pie-shaped treads on the staircases to their basements, and this is very definitely Not a Good Thing.

  Lots of libraries have curved staircases. This is also a bad idea, because none of the treads are rectangular, and the most comfortable portions of treads may be in their centers, where there may be no handrail. Given the amazing (and amazingly ill-advised) popularity of curved staircases in libraries, you may have to lay down the law to your designers. Sometimes repeatedly.

- Handrails should be in locations and diameters specified by codes. Some historic libraries have staircases with handrails set lower than current codes require, and walking down can be unnerving. Our personal opinion is that new or supplementary handrails should be installed, but the tensions between function and historic preservation may be hard to sort out.

  Some staircases have handrails that are too large to grasp. For example, some from the era of brutalist architecture have huge wooden beams for handrails. The ADA and most current codes provide required diameters, and there's no sane reason to do something else. Or to keep the old ones that can't be grabbed.

  Most codes restrict the distance between handrails on the opposite sides of a staircase to eight feet. If your staircase is wider, a central handrail is required

  Codes require handrails that begin before the first nosing of a staircase and run past the last nosing. Users shouldn't have to let go of the railing until they are off the staircase and standing on the floor.

Codes also require guardrails that are higher than the handrails. Typically these are 42 inches high.

- Staircases should be staircases and never combined with seating or shelving. Some amazingly gimmicky (and awful) combinations exist.

- Sidewalls of staircases should never be transparent. Nor should the sidewalls along the edges of drop-offs.

- Even if your codes allow it, you don't want railings that can be climbed like ladders. These should have been banned by building codes many years ago, but they're still being built. And children are still climbing them and still falling off.

- Staircases should not panic users who have a fear of heights. Especially if the alternative elevators have glass walls.

- People should not be able to walk under staircases and crack their heads on the underside of the steps. Staircases like this are banned by many building codes, but they're still around.

- Some insane older staircases have banister posts that hang down beneath the stairs, allowing people to walk under the stairs and tear their scalps open on the bottoms of the posts.

- The joints between the treads and the risers should make it instantly clear where the edges of the steps are. This is especially important for people walking downstairs.

- Extremely long flights of stairs can panic people starting down. They envision tripping and rolling endlessly downstairs, head over teakettle. Codes specify how many steps a staircase may have before there's a landing. Sometimes it's a lot more friendly to have the stairs make a 180-degree turn (with a rectangular landing and no pie-shaped steps) halfway up, but sometimes users are less disoriented if the stair runs in a straight line.

One library staircase featured on the cover of a book on library architecture written by the architect of the library in question has a flight of stairs so long that the staff of the library installed a kiddie gate at the top. For some reason, the kiddie gate doesn't show in the cover photo.

All libraries with staircases need enclosed staircases that serve as emergency exits. Codes are complex and change, so rely on your architects and engineers. In many cases you will be required to have "places of refuge" immediately inside the entrances to exit staircases. Places of refuge provide spaces for people who cannot negotiate exit staircases to wait to be rescued. They include sufficient flat space for wheelchairs and methods of informing emergency personnel that people are waiting for assistance.

Places of refuge are essential because elevators automatically shut off in case of emergency. It's a great deal easier and safer for emergency workers to carry people downstairs than to try to rescue them when they are trapped between floors in stalled elevators.

Safe public staircases are essential, but frequently there are compromises driven by the desire for dramatic appearance. However, if someone falls downstairs in your library, you'll probably be speaking with people specializing in insurance and lawsuits. If the design of your staircase blew off considerations of comfort and safety, the conversation will be unpleasant.

Unfortunately, all too many libraries have staircases where users get a terrified vise grip on the railings before walking downstairs.

Tripping and falling downstairs is a great deal worse than tripping and falling upstairs, so when in doubt, make things safer for people headed downward.

III-C. STRANGELY CONFIGURED STAIRCASES

Public buildings are full of staircases that don't just run in a straight, safe line. Some of these are ancient, but others are modern. We keep building them until building codes settle down and ban them, and then we invent new oddities.

Buildings abound in curved staircases. They're ornamental but otherwise seriously nasty. Each tread on a curved staircase is a trapezoid, deeper on one side of the staircase than the other. People climbing curved staircases may find the treads uncomfortably shallow on one side and uncomfortably deep on the other. But in the middle, where the treads are a comfortable depth, there may be no handrails to grab.

Some buildings have diagonal staircases, where the run of the handrail is not perpendicular to the run of the steps. Walking down a staircase designed this way is a pain, since you have to constantly work your way either to left or right. In some of the worst cases, people using diagonal staircases have to essentially cross their legs at each step.

III-D. ODDLY SHAPED TREADS

One of the main considerations in staircase design should be avoiding anything that might lead users to trip and fall.

People climbing staircases expect all treads to be completely rectangular and exactly the same. Cute shapes are an anathema. Varied tread widths are an anathema. Pie-shaped treads are an anathema.

Dangerously shaped treads are nothing new. Carnegie-era libraries specialized in basement staircases with pie-shaped treads as they turned corners. Even staff members took tumbles and broke limbs.

All staircases are potentially dangerous and therefore bad places for artistic experimentation. In this library, the handrails run diagonally to the run of the staircases, forcing users to either climb without using the rails or to walk crablike up the steps.

Curved staircases, like this one in a historic building on a university campus, cause a variety of problems. In this case, the treads on the outside of the curve are too deep to use comfortably, while those on the inside of the curve are too shallow for feet. As a result, everyone climbs the center of the staircase, where the treads are of a rational size and there is an extra handrail.

People climbing staircases expect the ends of the treads to butt up against flat surfaces. Unfortunately, some designers are bored with this expectation and create treads that stop short of the side wall. Even if users can't slip through the opening between the tread and the side wall, it's still unnerving to look down and imagine having your foot slip off the tread and get caught. And the opening serves no practical purpose whatsoever.

Some libraries have staircases with treads that blend into the sidewalls with a radius between the tread and the wall. Again, this is a cute design concept rather than a functional one, and users may find it unnerving. If they walk too close to the side wall, they can trip on the up-curved end of a tread. (We are not making this up. Fred tripped on such a tread in the main building of the Seattle Public Library.)

People using staircases should find it easy to spot the edges of the treads. If you will be installing a ceramic tile or carpeted staircase, you can help by putting contrastingly colored nosings on the edges of the treads. You can also help by making the treads and risers lighter or darker, although that doesn't help people walking downstairs, who need more protection.

The main point is that anything that interferes with depth perception or differentiation of treads and risers is dangerous, whether or not it appeals to the aesthetics of your designers.

Include in your building program a prohibition on all non-rectangular stairway treads.

III-E. FLOATING STAIRCASES

Floating staircases are one of the most prevalent and long-lasting bad design ideas in library architecture.

Some floating staircases have no visible means of support. They're connected to the floor above and the floor below, but they have no supporting columns, not even under landings. They may represent tours de force in structural engineering, but this almost certainly excites the designers more than it does the library users.

One of the major problems with floating staircases is the space beneath. If the space is open, people of any height can walk beneath the right

> Fred inherited a library with a concrete floating staircase between two floors. From the designers' point of view, it was the showplace of the building, but library users and staff disliked it intensely. Or just thought it was seriously stupid. When the building was expanded, it took a team of workers weeks to demolish the staircase, using jackhammers to dismember the concrete and using saws to cut the rebar.

part of the staircase and crease their foreheads on the lower edges of the staircase, although codes prohibit much of this now. And the space beneath the staircase tends to be filled either (good) with stuff to keep people from hitting their heads or (bad) stuff stuck there because the library has too little storage space anyway.

Other ways to keep people from bashing their heads on the undersides of floating staircases is to put raised platforms under the staircase or to install sets of railings to keep people from wandering under the staircases.

One way to prevent innocent passersby from bashing their heads on the undersides of floating staircases is to install protective railings.

A tidier way may be to just construct a closet under that portion of the staircase that comes within seven or eight feet of the floor.

The combination of atrium and floating staircase can be an evil one, but it has strong designer appeal. Never let it happen in your library, although you may be in for a battle to prevent it.

III-F. OPEN RISERS

One of the most popular design abominations is staircases with open risers.

Back before building codes started forcing sanity, designers created insane staircases. There were staircases consisting of treads extending like planks from walls, with handrails on the wall sides only, providing amazing opportunities to fall off the edge or even (for smaller users) to slip between the treads. Other staircases had handrails on the side of the staircase away from the wall, but with support posts only every few feet, allowing similar slipping through.

Eventually, codes required railings on both sides. Codes required that the openings between balusters (the vertical posts on railing systems) and between treads be limited to four inches, to make it impossible for infants to slip between or through, but climbers with fear of heights still get to look nervously between their feet.

The amazing thing is that there is absolutely no need or benefit to staircases with open risers. For the agony of users with fear of heights, there is no compensating exhilaration for those who enjoy looking down from above, for the open risers don't provide much of a view—just enough to upset the climbers with acrophobia.

As with other seriously bad ideas described in this chapter, the first thing to do is to put "There will be no open or transparent risers in staircases anywhere in the building" in your building program. Then follow up by checking the construction drawings and shop drawings, just to be sure that people paid attention to you, because they may say "Yeah, sure" and then just go ahead.

III-G. STAIRCASES IN ATRIA

Atria are multistory openings between floors.

Atria have some advantages:

- Users can look up or down and sometimes see where things on other floors are located.

- People (especially owners and designers and visiting tourists) can admire the dramatic open space.

- And that's about it.

Atria also cause many problems. Some are described in chapter 3 on "The Basic Configuration of Successful Library Spaces."

- Atria tempt designers to include floating staircases, with all of the attendant evils thereof. (That's the reason we mention atria in this chapter, although you'll find them assaulted in other chapters as well, since they are among the most avoidable stupidities in library design.)

- Atria transmit noise. If the upper levels are not glazed (glassed in), all the noises from the lower level are transmitted to the upper levels. And vice versa. The combination of terrazzo floor and lending operations on the ground level, open walls on the upper floors, and a major skylight can turn the space into something resembling a boiler factory.

- Atria waste energy. Heating and cooling a massive volume of unoccupied space is a remarkably silly idea. Atria may also complicate temperature control.

- Atria get in the way. Unless atria are over entry lobbies, they get in the way on upper floors, and users have to go out of their way to circumnavigate atria.

- For people with a fear of heights, having to walk near an open atrium can be terrifying. If the configuration of the building forces users to walk extremely close to the atrium railing, right at the edge of the drop-off, the designers should be spoken with severely.

- Even worse is being forced to walk on a bridge over an atrium.

- Maintaining light fixtures in atria can be a major challenge.

- People commit suicide in atria. Including library atria.

Showoff atria with showoff staircases are a major problem in library architecture. Sometimes they form the glamourous centers of library buildings. If you want a dramatic staircase, find a way to cope with the problems that may result. If you want to totally prevent one in your library, be sure you have a staff member or consulting librarian or campus architect who can say "no" to dysfunctional ideas. And stop them.

Staircases in atria often encourage hidden elevators:

- Traditionally, staircases and elevators are located side-by-side. People who don't want to climb find the elevator handy, and those who don't want to wait can scamper up the stairs.

- But buildings with monumental staircases in atria often have elevators hidden away, sometimes down unmarked side halls. The visitors who have no desire to use the staircases look around in bafflement, while the staircases tempt them to unwise action by whispering (much like Theda Bara), "Climb me, my fools."

What can you do?

- As usual, the first thing is to say "No atria, with or without staircases" in your building program. But you may have to fight your owners and designers anyway.

If you get overruled and stuck with an atrium:

- Don't let anyone put a floating staircase there.
- Insist that all levels of the atrium above the main floor be glazed.
- Put all light fixtures on electrically powered lifts, so that they can be lowered to the floor for servicing.
- Put the atrium on one side of the building, so users and staff don't have to circumnavigate it on upper floors.
- Make sure that the alternate elevator is close and clearly visible to people uneasily contemplating the staircase.

Whenever you have a huge opening with a straight drop of many stories, someone will look downward at the people far below and be tempted to explore the forces of gravity.

III-H. STAIRCASES WITH CENTRAL OPENINGS

Some traditional staircases are built in multi-story shafts with the stairs winding endlessly around the shafts and users able to look downward the entire length of the staircases. We've seen staircases in old hotels or business buildings where one could look down 20 stories or fall 20 stories or at least contemplate the possibility of falling 20 stories.

All of this seems unnecessarily unnerving and completely avoidable. As the familiar exhortation goes, "Just say no!"

III-I. GLASS WALLS AT THE HEADS AND FEET OF STAIRCASES

If staircases are enclosed by glass walls, you need some way to prevent people from arriving at the end of a flight of stairs and slamming directly into a wall.

This may sound like an unusual situation, but problems happen all the time. (Fred has seen collisions of this type a half-dozen times while visiting new library buildings.)

One thing designers do is to put some kind of decals on glass walls that keep people from running into them. If that's insufficient, you may need something more obvious, such as a railing in front of the glass wall.

III-J. STAIRCASES INCORPORATING FURNISHINGS

Some library spaces constructed in recent decades are a combination of staircases and a series of reader seating or book shelving areas. The steps are on one side of an open space, and the levels with shelving or seating on the other.

In a somewhat similar fashion, some staircases have standard-height steps on one side and double-height steps on the other, so people can sit and read on the double-height side. If that's their idea of a good time.

All of these combinations are amazingly (and spectacularly) wretched ideas. If there are steps, the reading or shelving areas are all inaccessible. Because there's no way to install continuous railings between the stairs and the tables or shelving, the stairs are less safe to climb.

Some libraries with features like this have even made the national news in uncomplimentary articles.

The solution is straightforward. Always state in your program or your instructions to your architects that "staircases will be staircases, and they will never be combined with any other library function."

If you have enough space, you could use ramps instead of staircases for designs with seating or shelving on a series of levels, but outside of being accessible in a nasty sort of way, they're just as bad.

III-K. STORY HOUR STRUCTURES WITH RISERS

Staircase-like structures frequently turn up in libraries. One common place is multilevel structures for story hour spaces in public libraries. There have also been story hour pits, with steps down from the main floor level.

Pits are easily dealt with. Ask any librarian who has accidentally fallen into one. Luckily, one can always fill in pits and be done with them, although it costs money to fill them in.

Story hour structures are very popular, but they require a few cautions:

- Don't make them out of concrete, for if you do you will immediately find you (a) don't like them and (b) can't afford to bring in jackhammers to remove them.

- If you make story hour structures out of wood with plywood tops, they will echo hollowly when people walk on them. The solution used by some stage set designers is to glue Homasote (a high-density pressed paper product) to the *undersides* of the plywood platforms, between the supporting timbers. (Sound control really matters in set design. When the Ghost of Hamlet's Father walks the battlements of Elsinore, it cuts into the dramatic impact if the battlements echo hollowly.)

- It is nearly impossible to carpet story hour structures that have curved edges. Keep the edges straight or be prepared to have a very unhappy relationship with your carpet firm.

- You will probably want some kind of padding under the carpet, but you'll need institutional-level padding that can be glued in place, not home carpet padding.

- Remember that structures like this are inaccessible to some users with disabilities. Even children need wheelchairs. Know what you will do to treat these users fairly.

- Kids like to jump. Be prepared for leaping from the highest to the lowest level in a single bound. Parents will be happy with the situation until someone gets hurt, whereupon they will blame the library.

At one time, firms that specialized in library furniture sold children's reading structures with upper levels. Between lack of accessibility and dangers of falling, there don't appear to be any defendable reasons for these today, and we've seen libraries remove them.

III-L. UNNECESSARY STAIRCASES

Even in modern libraries, some designers suggest staircases or ramps merely for architectural interest or to permit some interesting furniture arrangement.

This is another opportunity to stop seriously bad ideas quickly.

III-M. STAIRCASES AND FIRES

Building codes are particularly stringent when it comes to staircases, which are required to be far more fire-resistant than the rest of structures. Watch, for example, when new five- or six-story buildings are going up, where the staircase and elevator enclosures are constructed first as vertical chunks of masonry, and then the rest of the building filled in around them.

Codes require fire-resistant staircases. If your building has a dramatic floating staircase, it may not count as a safe fire exit. Or even as a staircase.

Special problems occur in ancient buildings like Carnegie-era public libraries, where upper floors may be served by only one staircase, the staircase is not in a fire-resistant shaft, and it's made of wood. If there are fires in buildings of that vintage, and no new fire-resistant stairs have been added, people on upper floors will probably burn to death unnecessarily. This will be a hard event to explain to your community.

IV. Railings

There's not a lot to say about railings, but it's important.

Here are a few major problems with railings.

IV-A. RAILINGS THAT CAN BE CLIMBED

These days, many designers come up with railings that have horizontal bars that can be climbed like ladders. These should be totally banned by building codes, but they're still around.

The problem is that children can easily climb the railings and fall off. And they do.

Some designers will argue that this is not an issue because a specific library is not for children, but unless you plan to card people at the door, children can get in. And fall.

Even if you can successfully eliminate children from your library, adults may also be tempted to climb railings.

The ridiculous thing about all of this is that climbable railings serve absolutely no purpose. It's a matter of somebody's idea of cute design trumping functionality and safety.

Your building program should state something like, "There will be no railings that can be climbed like ladders." Then check your construction drawings and shop drawings to be sure that no one is slipping one past you. As far as we can tell, climbable railings are always an enthusiasm of designers and owners, but never of library users or librarians.

IV-B. GLASS RAILINGS

Some designers want railings that are sheets of glass. They are probably safe, but they give people with any touch of acrophobia the willies.

We've heard designers say things to the effect of "Walking through our library will be like floating on air." This is a time to be Very Afraid. And to tell your designers something to the effect of, "Not a chance!"

Emphasizing their disregard for the safety of small children, the designers of this campus building used railings with horizontal balusters in the greatest possible quantities. Many visitors compare the structure to a movie set for *Riot in Cell Block Thirteen*. (The designers specified painted railings rather than brushed stainless steel, which means the railings have to be repainted frequently and still look ratty most of the time.)

This (non-library) building has balconies with railings that small children (and pretty much anyone else) can climb like ladders. And fall off. Regardless of the purpose of the building, unless you plan to card children at the door, they can get in and be injured. (The only reason for horizontal beams in railings is aesthetic, and that's not a good enough reason. Until building codes catch up and ban them, say "No" in your building program.)

As with other bad ideas listed in this chapter, the sad thing is that railings of this type are totally unnecessary. There are all kinds of substitutes that are less terrifying.

In many cases, you'll have to stop your designers even after you've shouted, "No!" Check the construction drawings and (particularly) shop drawings for signs of unwanted glass, just as you check for horizontal beams on railings.

> The central Minneapolis Public Library has a narrow walkway with glass railings crossing high above the floor of an atrium. Library users who need to reach the other side and who are usually able to conceal their slight tinges of acrophobia are sorely tried when they cross over. When in doubt, avoid walkways bridging huge atria, and if you are stuck with them, never let them have glass sides.

IV-C. PAINTED HANDRAILS

Lots of buildings have painted handrails. The problem is that the paint swiftly wears off.

If your library has major staircases with painted handrails, you'll have a choice of frequent repainting or constant shabbiness. (We know one library with lemon-yellow painted handrails. In addition to wearing off, lemon-yellow paint turns a nasty greenish color when it's dirty, and heavily used handrails soon get dirty.)

Many metallic surfaces cause equal problems. For instance, brass has to be lacquered if you don't want to polish it daily. Unfortunately, the lacquer soon wears off here and there, leaving the unpleasantly piebald look of mixed lacquered brass (shiny) and brass with lacquer worn off (dingy).

You can run into the same type of problem with colored door handles. Within a few years the color starts wearing off, and the door looks ugly. Unfortunately, colored door handles are in all the hardware catalogs, and they look great on opening day. Ratty-looking colored hand grabs are a constant in contemporary American buildings.

About the only thing that stands up to the constant rubbing that handrails and door handles receive is brushed stainless steel.

The same thing is true of doorknobs and newel posts.

If you *must* have painted handrails, seldom seen or used emergency exit staircases are a good place to put them.

IV-D. RAILINGS ON NARROW WALKWAYS

One thing that can accompany atria is narrow walkways around the edges.

In some cases, like hotels with large atria, the walkways usually are wide and the railings are comfortably chest high. People with a fear of heights can walk around the atria without being forced to look straight down.

Door handles are available in a wide range of colors to match building décor. Unfortunately, all colored handles seem to have the finish wear off. Luckily, there is no color to wear off brushed stainless steel. All door handles and handrails need to be made entirely of brushed stainless steel. (Brass is okay if you like daily polishing.)

But in other places the walkways are narrow and the railings less comforting. The New York University library, for example, has the reputation of people walking around the atrium while rubbing their shoulders against the outside wall due to the yawning abyss. (As a matter of fact, NYU spent a very great deal of money putting up an ornamental screen to provide psychic comfort and prevent the unwanted leaping that had led to suicides in the past.)

So, if you MUST have a big atrium surrounded by walkways, keep the walkways wide and the railings high. (Even better, of course, is to incorporate the phrase "no atria" into a number of places in your building program, and then be prepared to fight. Some designers have an uncanny desire for atria.)

IV-E. RAILINGS THAT CANNOT BE COMFORTABLY GRABBED

Too many railings are massive slabs that have to be gripped vise-like between the thumb and fingers. These fail to meet modern building codes, but there are a lot of older examples running around.

Talk with your designers about legal shapes and widths of handrails. With modern building codes, you're unlikely to get into trouble, but you may still have to cope with yesterday's dumb ideas.

IV-F. RAILINGS THAT PEOPLE CAN FALL THROUGH

Building codes bar them fiercely now, but many railings in days gone by had openings large enough for children (and adults) to fall through. Now the maximum opening is four inches.

If your library has railings—staircase railings or balcony railings—that fail to meet this code, you'll need to do something about it quickly.

IV-G. EXTRA HANDRAILS FOR CHILDREN

It's easy to add a second and lower handrail for children. This seems particularly suitable for public libraries and for grade schools.

Unlike the other railings described here, this is A Good Thing.

V. Ramps

Many libraries have ramps. Older libraries with main floors set above grades may have ramps from the sidewalk up to the main floor or down to a ground floor.

Some libraries have ornamental shifts in floor height in the middle of readings rooms,

You can make staircases safer and more comfortable for small children by installing a second (and lower) handrail.

sometimes with one or two steps stretching the length of the room. These require supplementary ramps.

Some libraries have stages at one end of their meeting rooms. Codes require that stages have ramps or lifts for access.

At the time this was written, the maximum legal slope for all but extremely short ramps was 1:12, or 12 feet of run for every single foot of rise, with a flat area for resting after every 25 feet. Ramps are all required to have handrails.

A legal sidewalk has a slope no steeper than 1:20 and does not require handrails.

Some large auditoriums have sloped floors. If your library will have one, check with your architects about the slope of the floor and make serious decisions if it's greater than 1:12. And provide places where users in wheelchairs can view performances.

Trying to move people between floors by means of ramps is a seriously (or an impressively amazingly) bad idea. If the top of one floor is 14 feet higher than the top of the floor below, the ramp will be 168 feet long, plus 30 additional feet for resting areas. Anyone who thinks this is a good idea should be fitted into a loaner wheelchair and asked to wheel it up a 198-foot ramp. (Fourteen feet from floor to floor is probably an absolute minimum difference in height. It assumes 10-foot ceilings and four feet for floor structure and MEP equipment.)

The only civilized way to move people between floors is with elevators.

In general, architects have quit designing buildings that require ramps to deal with purely aesthetic features, but there are vast numbers of older buildings that have had to provide ramps. The major use of ramps we see in well-designed modern libraries is for access to meeting room stages and similar platforms.

The main point is that ramps are makeshift adaptations, not desirable design features. Far too many promotional photos of buildings with endless ramps show users in wheelchairs whizzing happily downhill. But never struggling uphill.

Probably the worst ramps are exterior ramps. They can be icy or snowy. They can expose users to rain. And if they're less than about six feet wide, people going in opposite directions may have to reverse directions on the ramps to let each other pass.

An exterior ramp leading to a basement combines some of the worst possible library design errors, including the known tendency of water to flow downhill and flood basements.

The building codes involving ramps are more complex than outlined here. You need the assistance of your architects and engineers.

VI. Snappy Rules on Elevators, Staircases, Railings, and Ramps

1. The rights of people with disabilities overrule the rights of buildings to be cute.

2. The fear of heights is not covered by the Americans with Disabilities Act. But it should be. In the meantime, block insanely vertiginous design concepts, of which there are a lot running around.

3. Ramps can be unpleasantly long. For example, if it's eight feet up to the front door, a ramp will be a minimum of over 110 feet long. This is an amazingly uncivilized device, even if you can find a place to put it. And consider how much people will enjoy it in the winter or during a rainstorm. Or if it's too narrow for people to pass in opposite directions.

4. An open exterior ramp leading to the basement will sooner or later fill with rainwater and flood the basement. Most likely sooner.

5. If people suggest a library where you can look straight down at users a half-dozen floors below, ask them what they think the terminal velocity of a dropped dictionary might be.

6. If you intentionally design a library that is unnecessarily difficult for people with disabilities to use, shame on you. In addition, if you get sued, you'll lose.

7. As with other building codes, the requirements in the Americans with Disabilities Act are legal minimums, not ideals. Don't feel seriously smug about things if your building just barely squeaks through.

8. If you have a Carnegie-era library building with a main floor a number of steps above

grade, you'll either have to move to a different building or install an elevator. Historic buildings can be wonderful things, but there's a cost. Exterior ramps are unpleasant at best and an abomination in areas chillier than central Florida or wetter than Arizona.

9. No sane people climbing staircases want to look between their feet and see the floor below.

10. Atria can provide five minutes of "Wow!" followed by 50 years of major problems. That's a high price to pay for a little bit of "Wow!" (It's a little bit akin to the moment-on-the-lips-lifetime-on-the-hips situation, but much harder to correct.)

11. The undersides of floating staircases are wonderful places to bump one's head. And gash one's scalp.

12. Steps that serve no necessary purpose whatsoever serve no purpose whatsoever.

13. Long exterior ramps are an assault on library users and staff in nice weather, and impressively nasty in times of rain or ice.

14. If you have a high atrium surrounded by railings on every level, sooner or later someone may jump off. Universities are particularly prone to this. (While you're sitting at the lending desk at the bottom of the atrium, "splat" is not a comforting sound.)

15. Staircases should not terrify library users, who are nice people and deserve better treatment.

16. Make the edges of the treads on your staircases stand out. Especially to people walking downstairs.

17. If people using your staircases are gripping the railings in a white-knuckled sort of way, find out why.

18. Whether you say "atriums" or "atria," you don't want either one in your library.

19. Tell your owners and designers that atria with monumental staircases are one of the "most derivative and overworked clichés in architectural design." (We suspect that being accused of imitation bothers some owners and designers more than being accused of dysfunctional designs. So give it a shot.)

20. When it comes to vertiginous drop-offs and glass railings, the thoroughly watched designer gets away with a lot less.

21. Beware of designers pitching soaring spaces and terrifying staircases to groups like governing boards that will never have to actually ascend above the first floor. (The relationship between designers and governing boards can be a little like that between Svengali and Trilby.)

22. If you need an elevator, get an elevator. A real elevator.

23. A designer envisions a balcony overlooking a library atrium as an inspirational vantage point. A library manager wonders how long it will be before someone falls off.

24. If you have a 15,000-square-foot, two-story library, you don't need an elevator. You need a flatter library on a larger site. (Of course, if your library is an architectural monument, that complicates things.)

25. Libraries that have a choice in the matter keep the doors to their exterior balconies locked at all times.

26. There's no excuse for staircases with funny-shaped treads. (Pie-shaped or curved treads from 1905 are just as dangerous as weirdly artistic treads from 2020.)

27. For some reason, the entire area of atria, balconies, and artistically lethal staircases is dangerously alluring to owners and reviewers and designers of libraries. It's the duty of librarians to make them stop.

28. Staircases and elevators need to be close enough so that people who don't want to use one can look around and see the other. Side-by-side is particularly polite.

29. For people with a serious fear of heights, a glass-walled elevator is not a kindly alternative to a vertiginous staircase.

30. Ramps are excusable only when you have absolutely no other choice. Never build one because it's cute. And never build one out of doors if the vertical distance is more than a few inches.

31. Railings that can be climbed like ladders are an abomination and should have been banned by codes long ago.

32. Dramatic staircases inspire many owners and designers and tourists. Stopping them may be painful for everyone concerned, but it sometimes has to be done.

33. Some historic libraries have tiny two- or three-story stack units with narrow staircases for access. By the time we make them legal by removing inaccessible floors and widening the overly narrow aisles, the book storage capacity has been reduced by about 75 percent. In many expanded libraries, they just end up as modestly sized rooms with high ceilings.

34. What will you do when the historic staircase in your historic library has railings too low to be of any help?

35. A staircase is a staircase. It should never be a series of small rooms, each connected to the next by a few steps.

36. When evaluating proposed staircase designs, the only valuable opinions are those people who spend time in library buildings—library users and librarians—and the engineers who make sure that everything is legal. The opinions of owners, designers, and tourists are all good things to ignore.

37. Unfortunately, some of the worst design ideas in libraries involve connections between floors. And just when you think you've headed a foolish idea off at the pass, along comes another.

38. This chapter is full of detailed examples because there are so many genuinely awful elevators, staircases, railings, and ramps in libraries.

PART IV
Technical Issues

CHAPTER 31

Lighting

I. Introduction

I-A. ABOUT LIBRARY LIGHTING

Good lighting is essential in libraries, but far too many are badly lit.

Library lighting needs to be bright enough for users to read comfortably, including not only books open on tabletops but also books held vertically. It needs to illuminate the spines of books on shelves, even the top and bottom shelves in book stacks. It must never shine unpleasantly in people's eyes, even when they are looking straight up. It should never feature uneven illumination either because of bad choices of lighting design or because creating patterns of light and dark is more exciting to some owners and designers than is providing even illumination. It must allow furniture to be rearranged without requiring altered lighting. It must allow colors to be viewed accurately. It should include attractive lighting fixtures, but never if they lead to poorer lighting.

From the point of view of efficiency, lighting should conserve energy, have inexpensive components, and be easy to maintain.

Daylight is important in libraries. Making effective use of daylight can save energy, but daylight can be both a major benefit and a source of major problems. Windows that can admit direct sunlight require blinds, but far too many libraries have windows that force users and staff to move. Some staff members at service desks find that they are blinded by window light—and can't move.

When night falls, artificial lighting needs to seamlessly replace the missing daylight. Skylights illuminated by actual daylight, for example, cause too much glare by day and too much gloom by night. Some people like skylights in libraries, but they probably are visitors rather than library users.

Architectural design can have a major impact on the quality of lighting. Wide variations in paint colors can lead to uneven or strangely colored lighting. Ornamental soffits around the edges of rooms or over service desks always result in bad lighting. Ceilings work best when they're white, and libraries stuck with historic dark ceilings need careful lighting design. Very dark and very light working surfaces on counters cause problems with reflections and with contrast in brightness.

Light fixtures that produce high-quality library light hang down from ceilings and shine the light upward. Some people feel these fixtures spoil the otherwise clean lines of interior spaces, but the combination of clean lines and rotten lighting is always a rotten choice.

In recent years, library lighting has been complicated by the ever-increasing emphasis on energy conservation. The development of efficient light sources has been a benefit, and some libraries have also been able to save energy by cutting lighting levels in overly bright areas. But there have been a variety of bad ideas as well. Saving energy by making libraries too dim misses the whole point of libraries. The use of motion detectors to activate lighting has for the most part been a seriously bad idea, with lights going off and on unpleasantly, and with people having to grope their way into dark rooms in order to turn on the lights. Devices to automatically cut artificial lighting when daylight is sufficiently bright haven't worked well. Some energy-saving codes have been serious mistakes, and they come and go almost predictably.

Because of the importance of lighting in the day-to-day use and operation of libraries, and the impact that frequent or pervasive lighting problems can cause, it's important for librarians to understand how lighting systems work—and don't work.

I-B. A FEW COMMON LIGHTING TERMS

As in many other areas of library building design, familiarity with some of the basic vocabulary in the field is essential. Here are some of the terms and concepts we think you encounter most frequently in talking with lighting designers and contractors.

- *Artificial skylight.* A ceiling treatment that looks like a skylight but is really just artificial light in disguise. (It may be an old skylight that is roofed over and lighted artificially.)

- *Ballast.* A ballast is a transformer that provides current for fluorescent and HID lamps by increasing voltage to the point that power can jump the length of the lamp. The most efficient ballasts are electronic. Ballasts vary widely in quality, and manufacturers matter. Be careful about claimed "equivalents." See also "Driver" (below).

- *Color rendering index* (**CRI**). A measure of the accuracy with which a light source reproduces colors. CRI is supposed to vary from 0 to 100, with 100 the best, but some researchers feel that even light sources with CRIs of 100 reproduce reds poorly. It is now being replaced by the IES (Illuminating Engineering Society) TM (Technical Manual) 30 Method for Evaluating Light Source Color Rendition.

- *Color temperature.* Color temperature describes the warmth or coolness of lighting colors. It is measured in degrees Kelvin. The higher the number, the bluer the light. Many libraries choose lighting with a color temperature of 3500K.

- *Contrast.* Range in relative levels of light and dark. Libraries with lighting problems frequently have dark and light areas too close to each other. (That's why extremely light or dark tabletops and countertops cause eyestrain. They contrast too much with the books and papers on them.) Ill-considered dramatic lighting often has too much contrast.

- **Driver.** Drivers power LEDs the way that ballasts power fluorescent lamps, and they protect the LEDs from current fluctuations. Household LEDs have built-in drivers while most commercial LED light fixtures have external drivers.

- **Efficacy.** A measure of efficiency with which lamps convert electrical energy to visible light. The standard measure of lamp efficacy is lumens per watt. There is a wide range in lamp efficacy, with LEDs the best.

- **Fluorescent light.** The first major replacement for incandescent light, developed in the 1930s. Fluorescent light is far more efficient than incandescent light, and due to the relatively large sizes of the tubes it can lend itself to low-glare lighting.

- **Foot-candle.** The brightness of light falling on a surface is measured in foot-candles, sometimes abbreviated f-c. Eyestrain is far less when visible surfaces have fairly similar levels of foot-candles. See also *Lux*.

- **Glare.** Blindingly bright light that interferes with comfortable vision. Some designers specialize in glare.

- **HID.** Short for high-intensity discharge. An energy-efficient and compact light source, now obsolete in part because of its weirdly variable colors and unacceptable restrike time.

- **Incandescent lamps.** The "hot wire in a bottle." Edison's original lightbulb. The historical source of artificial light in libraries, with wonderful color rendering and easy dimming. But replaced almost entirely due to its inefficiency.

- **Lamp.** In the lighting trade, lightbulbs are called "lamps." To avoid confusion, never refer to light fixtures as lamps. Use a more specific term, such as "table lamp," to make clear what you are talking about.

- **Lamp nomenclature.** Many lamps have code numbers that describe the shape of the lamp and its diameter in eighths of an inch. For example, when a fluorescent lamp is labeled T-8, we know that it's a tubular lamp with a one-inch diameter. A G-40 is a globular lamp five inches in diameter.

- **LED.** Short for light-emitting diode. A highly efficient and fairly low-maintenance source of light that is currently the standard of the interior lighting industry. LEDs have been around for decades, mostly as colored indicator lights, but the development of white LEDs with high color quality has been very recent.

- **Light fixture.** A device to hold a light source and control or direct its output. See also luminaire.

- **Lumen.** The output of electric lamps is listed in "lumens." For example, a 100-watt incandescent lamp (ordinary lightbulb) emits about 1,500 lumens, while a 100-watt high-pressure sodium lamp (the pinky-orange lamps used to light some streets) emits about 15,000 lumens.

- **Luminaire.** A combination of a light fixture and the appropriate lamp.

- **Lux.** A measurement of brightness. The metric equivalent of the foot-candle is the lux, with 10 lux equal to about one foot-candle.

- **Metal halide.** Another obsolete lighting technology you don't want in your library.

- **Parabolic reflectors.** A parabola is a curve based on a specific mathematical formula.

Some lamps and light fixtures employ parabolas as reflectors. If a concentrated source of light is placed at the mathematical focal point of a parabolic reflector, all light emitted from the reflector emerges as a highly directional beam. Parabolic reflectors were in vogue years ago, but they shouldn't have been.

- *PAR lamps*. PAR stands for parabolic aluminized reflector. Some lamps that emit highly concentrated beams of light are identified as PAR lamps, which frequently behave like automobile headlights. There are no doubt great uses for them (such as lighting diamonds in jewelry store windows), but no uses in libraries.

- *Parabolic fixtures*. Some ceiling-mounted fluorescent fixtures use partial parabolic lenses that look like a group of open boxes suspended beneath the fluorescent tubes. These are not the vicious devices that PAR lamps are, but the light they put out is very significantly inferior to reflected uplighting. Say no.

- *Recessed downlight*. These fixtures appear as neat, round holes in ceilings. They combine tidy appearance with terrible light. Always say no before design work begins. And watch for them sneaking into drawings.

- *Sunlight*. Pleasant if properly controlled, but amazingly badly controlled in far too many libraries. No user or staff member should ever be forced to face direct sunlight. Far too many service desks face painfully blinding light at various times of day or year and give staff no place to move.

- *Visible light*. Visible light is the narrow portion of the electromagnetic spectrum that we can actually see. The electromagnetic spectrum runs from radio waves to gamma rays. Violet light has the shortest wavelength we can see, and red the longest. Infrared light has waves too long for us to see, and ultraviolet too short.

II. An Impressively Short History of Library Lighting in the Last Century

Into the twentieth century, libraries were designed with the necessity of relying on natural light. Windows served not to provide a pleasant view of the outside world or to bring in daylight for psychological reasons, but rather to light reading rooms.

The result of the dependence on natural light is seen everywhere in the reading rooms of libraries built before the Second World War. Both the great reading rooms in academic and research libraries and domestic-sized reading rooms in Carnegie-era public libraries depended on high windows to bring in light. Many of these windows had sills eight of more feet above the floor, to leave space for wall-mounted shelving below and to allow daylight to penetrate further into the interior space and reduce the need for candles or gas lighting, resulting in rooms with daylight but with no view of the world beyond. Some spaces managed both high windows for light and lower windows for view.

Before the coming of modern electric lighting, many libraries were forced to close after dark, sometimes leading to accusations that they were institutions for the elite. And during the day, libraries had to cope with situations where there was too much or too little light, and where direct sunlight made reading nearly impossible.

Since World War II, and particularly in the last few decades, libraries have relied heavily on artificial light. Artificial light has many advantages.

We can control direction and brightness, providing the amount of light we want where we want it and when we want it.

Artificial light also has downsides. It requires energy both to operate the lights and to eliminate heat generated by the lights. Although modern lighting saves both operating energy and cooling energy, it's generally not as cheap as daylight.

This chapter provides a practical review of artificial and natural lighting options in libraries, with recommendations on proven solutions and comments on several lighting concepts that frequently lead to trouble.

III. A Quick Formula for Good Library Lighting

This chapter on lighting is long and complex, but here's an easy formula for good library lighting: Provide bright, even, low-glare light everywhere. Bounce light off white ceilings. Be sure all vertical surfaces like the fronts of books are lighted. And never shine light directly into anyone's eyes.

Adamantly refuse to compromise on any of the points in this section, particularly when it comes to bouncing light off ceilings and preventing direct sunlight. Some people will insist on compromises, but stand firm in the sureness that you are right, that they are wrong, and that the libraries that have installed lighting to meet the following requirements are particularly happy.

- For artificial lighting, select an LED light source with a color rendering index of at least 85 and a color temperature of between 3000K and 3500K. (If you have an existing fluorescent light source that meets all the requirements in this section, the main reason to change is to save energy.)

- Require rooms with white ceilings between 10 and 20 feet high, with 11 to 15 preferable for most room sizes. Larger rooms require higher ceilings. All walls of all rooms should be in fairly light colors.

- Bounce 100 percent of all the light off the ceilings. Fixtures should be at least eight feet off the floor and at least two feet below the ceiling. Individual LEDs should be invisible to people standing on the floor.

- Use fixtures set end-to-end in parallel rows, with the rows parallel to the walls. All book aisles should be parallel to each other, and they should be perpendicular to the rows of light fixtures. Rows of fixtures should end no more than two feet from a wall.

- Spacing between the rows of light fixtures should be constant, but the space between the last row of fixtures and the adjacent wall should be half the width of the spaces between the rows of fixtures in the rest of the room.

- Have no soffits anywhere, particularly around the edges of rooms or over service desks.

- Arrange lighting to provide 60 foot-candles of brightness on tabletops and a minimum of 20 foot-candles on the spines of the lowest shelves of books.

- Natural light is always important, but all exterior glass that can admit direct sunlight must always have adjustable blinds. Window tinting or dark films are not "adjustable blinds" and are often a bad idea.

- Never have real skylights of any kind, which often lead to areas that are unpleasantly bright by day and unpleasantly dark by night. If you inherit beautiful historic skylights, Fred thinks you should roof them over and light them artificially. If you want skylights in your new library, light them artificially or see Joe.

- Devices that attempt to save energy by switching lights on and off automatically must always work properly. An amazing number do not, forcing people to walk into dark rooms, turning lights off when spaces are occupied, and failing in their attempts to deal with changes in sunlight. Test everything during construction and include all problems in your punch list.

Unfortunately, vast numbers of library buildings are not constructed to meet these requirements, making this chapter worth reading.

IV. General Lighting Concepts

A few general concepts are of concern everywhere in lighting, and you will need to be comfortable with them in order to talk about lighting with lighting designers, engineers, architects, and consulting librarians.

We want to be sure to repeat our essential premise that buildings work as assemblies of systems and that these systems are perceived through a complex set of physical and psychological components that make up our vision. For our purposes, the key is to recognize that our perception is based on sensing and processing light reflected by objects (people, walls, books) in the environment. Throughout this section, we focus a lot of attention on the light source and only obliquely refer to objects reflecting the light. Any assessment of a light source's performance is as much due to the nature of the materials that reflect the light to our eyes as it is about the nature of the source. As you read this chapter, you will come across points that make this clear: our preference for indirect light depends on a reflective surface to bounce the light back into the areas we inhabit. Be sure to see the chapter on walls, ceilings, and floors for more. Half of bad lighting is really a misalignment of finish selections and lighting design. The other half is overly direct lighting. (The halves are approximate.)

IV-A. ILLUMINATION LEVELS

The brightness of lighting falling on surfaces is measured in foot-candles. The derivation of the term can be found in many technical manuals, but what's important to librarians is the level of brightness needed in well-lighted libraries.

Foot-candle levels can be as high as 10,000 foot-candles in direct sunlight at noon. By contrast, the light of the full moon provides about 0.025 foot-candles. Parking lots are often lighted at 1 or 2 foot-candles. And most people can read regular print very comfortably under high-quality light of about 60 foot-candles.

Readers' ability to see is dependent not only on absolute foot-candle levels but also on relative levels. When people enter a building at high noon, their eyes take a few moments to adjust to the difference in light. And when they step back outside, they are momentarily blinded.

The main point here is that readers see best and least painfully when lighting levels are fairly even. Trying to read at a table that is lit by artificial light but has a band of direct sunlight falling across one end is an unpleasant experience. Trying to see books along a wall when the spines are lit at 20 foot-candles but windows every few feet provide hundreds of foot-candles is difficult. Trying to read book spines on high shelves can be totally impossible if you're looking into a skylight at the same time.

Problems with wide variations in brightness are one of the many reasons to reject with great vigor any suggestion that your library have skylights.

Readers' difficulties in dealing with contrast are the source of the problems that people have with reading tables and service counters with white or extremely dark tops. White tops reflect too much light and blind readers. Dark tops contrast too much with white paper, and the result is eyestrain. The reason that so many designers select finishes like natural birch and pale gray laminates for tabletops is not just aesthetics.

IV-B. CALCULATIONS

One problem libraries encounter in specifying illumination levels is that most commercial specification is in terms of light falling on tabletops, and many light fixtures are designed to direct light entirely downward. In libraries, however, many surfaces readers need to view are not horizontal. Readers hold books vertically and expect to have workable light falling on the pages. Light on bookshelves needs to illuminate spines rather than the top edges of the books. Flip bins for CDs and DVDs or children's picture books—particularly when overcrowded—allow only a narrow gap for light to fall on the front of the recording or book.

For this reason, librarians can't simply specify 60 foot-candles and get workable lighting. Although one can, for example, specify the number of foot-candles falling on vertical surfaces, our experience has been that it's equally important to tell designers exactly how we want our libraries lit.

Always insist that your designers provide you with calculations of foot-candles at tabletop level for all areas of your library, including the vertical surfaces of bottom shelves. These are generated by computer programs and should be part of basic design services. "Calcs" (to use the trendy term) provide illumination levels on a grid basis, so the calculations for a room may include a large matrix of numbers. In a well-lighted room, the numbers should be relatively even from edge to edge in all directions. (The placement of shelving can make a huge difference in illumination levels, so be sure your designers' calculation models include the effects of stacks of your intended height, orientation, and spacing.)

Although you can use various formulas and simple lighting calculators to estimate how much light your chosen light sources will deliver, this is something you really need to leave to professionals. The electrical engineers working on your building are the people you want to provide these calculations.

When you are reviewing calcs, watch in particular for light levels that fall off around the perimeters of rooms. This is a very common problem with some widely used styles of lighting, and you don't want it in your library. One major source of problems is soffits around the perimeters of rooms.

If the calculations show uneven lighting (or dim lighting on perimeters), your designers may say that the figures do not include all fixtures. At this point, you need to stop everything and have them rerun the calculations. Whether they want to or not, make them rerun the calcs. (This is a common problem. When Fred used to request calcs on proposed reading rooms, what was submitted almost never met this specification.)

IV-C. STANDARDS

The IES—the Illuminating Engineering Society (formerly the IESNA—the Illuminating Engineering Society of North America) publishes illumination standards.

IV-D. MODELING

Calculations don't tell the whole story. Libraries need soft, even light that falls on vertical surfaces as well as horizontal ones. Calcs tell us that the light is bright and uniform, but we need to specify proper fixtures before requesting that calcs be developed. Advances in design software such as building information modeling (BIM) now allow daylighting and electrical illumination to be modeled. Both should be required.

IV-E. GLARE

Glare is unwanted light that blinds us.

Because people live with glare every day, they tend to associate it with adequate lighting, and it's easy to assume that a lack of glare means dim light. But it's just the result of poorly chosen lighting options.

Glare comes in two varieties—direct glare and reflected glare.

IV-E-1. Direct Glare

Direct glare is just what it sounds like—a source of light shining directly in someone's eyes. Light may be simply too bright for reading. Glare frequently comes from direct sunlight, but with artificial light glare is more likely to be the result of overly directional lighting.

Direct lighting is a particular problem in libraries because people spend so much time looking upward at books on high shelves. Looking upward at a top shelf, only to find oneself staring into a brilliant light shining downward, is a truly unpleasant experience.

In addition to windows, typical sources of glare in libraries are ceiling-mounted lights that shine straight downward. The smaller and more concentrated the source, the worse the glare. You know your building has trouble with glare if you realize that an eye shade would make your life more comfortable.

Other nasty sources of direct glare are skylights and exterior windows with no blinds, unless the windows face straight north.

> Fred did consulting work for a library where the stacks were full of small skylights. Trying to read spines on tall shelving when a skylight is blazing right behind them is impossible, no matter what people claim to the contrary.

The best way to avoid direct glare from artificial lights is to have white ceilings and illuminate them as evenly as possible using suspended fixtures that shine 100 percent of the light straight up and are designed so no areas are brighter than they need to be to provide adequate light, and none are darker.

In addition to being unpleasant, direct glare is usually accompanied by unwanted shadows. Some lighting is so direct that readers cast shadows on their books when they lean over to read, or their hands cast dark shadows on their notes while they write.

Unfortunately, some of the kinds of artificial lighting most popular with designers create a great deal of direct glare. Of these, the greatest evil (and yet amazingly popular with owners and architects) is the so-called "recessed downlight" or "can light." Can lights are everywhere; look for round six-inch holes in the ceiling. If you don't believe can lights are nasty, just experiment by looking up into them.

To avoid direct glare in your library, start by informing your designers bluntly that you will accept no recessed downlights or skylights anywhere, for any purpose whatsoever. And hold them to it, since some designers will agree pleasantly and then use can lights anyway.

IV-E-2. Indirect Glare

Indirect glare consists of unpleasant reflections of concentrated light sources on shiny surfaces. This is frequently called "veiling reflectance," because the images of the lights reflected on the shiny surfaces "veil" the images people are trying to see. Anyone who has tried to read *National Geographic* under recessed downlights and has had to tilt the magazine endlessly to see the pictures knows all about veiling reflectance.

We can fight indirect glare in libraries first by avoiding shiny surfaces. Glass-covered tables, ancient curved cathode ray tube monitors, and other highly polished surfaces all reflect images too readily.

When computer monitors were first introduced into libraries, some libraries purchased tables with glass tops over rectangular openings, with monitors set beneath the openings, angling up toward the users. Unfortunately, veiling reflections on the glass tops made it almost impossible to see the monitors under the glass, and black plastic hoods were added to keep room light from falling on the glass. The result was users peering under hoods to see the monitors below. (Computer workstations of this type were also miserable for users with bifocals, who found themselves bending forward to see the monitors beneath the tabletops, then rearing backward to focus on their notes. The effect was a little like the bobbing toy birds that hook onto the rim of a glass of water, but less entertaining to watch if you are a nice person.)

A second way to fight indirect glare is to avoid concentrated light sources.

IV-F. COLOR RENDERING

A major concern in selecting light sources is the degree to which they portray colors accurately. Daylight and incandescent light both do a great job, but many other kinds of light cause problems. For example, cheap fluorescent lamps can put out such poor-quality light that customers in clothing stores have to carry clothes out into the sunshine just to see what the colors actually are.

The problem is due to the fact that many modern light sources are missing some of the wavelengths that make up white light. If a light source, for example, emits little or no light in the red end of the spectrum, red objects will appear black beneath it. Cheap fluorescent lamps tend to concentrate their light output in the yellow-green area of the spectrum, and red colors correspondingly are inaccurately portrayed.

The ability of light to portray colors accurately has until recently been described by color rendering index, usually abbreviated CRI. CRI ratings usually vary from 0 to 100, but low-pressure sodium light has a CRI of well below 0. High-quality fluorescent light has a CRI of at least 85, and we recommend that you accept nothing lower. With some LED lamps, it is possible to achieve ratings close to 100 CRI.

All respectable lamps should have boxes indicating CRI, but for some you need to check the web. If you can't find information on the CRI of a lamp, never buy it.

The push a few years ago for CFLs (compact fluorescent lamps) was ill-advised because CFLs have notoriously bad CRIs. The boxes of CFLs seldom mention color rendering indexes, and the manufacturers' websites steer clear of the subject. People who experiment with CFLs in their homes, particularly when they (for example) put an incandescent lamp in a fixture at one end of a sofa and a CFL in an identical fixture at the other end, note that the CFLs put out the nasty yellow-green light associated with cheap fluorescent tubes decades ago.

LEDs have taken over. They are tremendously efficient when it comes to energy use. In the past, they had a number of serious problems, including bad color rendering, bad color temperatures, and harsh directionality. But improvements have occurred rapidly.

A note on the limitations of CRI. There is a widespread feeling that CRI is becoming less effective at achieving desired results in the real world, especially for reds. While many lighting professionals and manufacturers will continue to work with CRI, IES (Illuminating Engineering Society) TM-30 provides an alternative, more comprehensive color index. CRI measures color fidelity with just eight color samples, while TM-30 uses 99. TM-30 also measures both color fidelity and color saturation. If you are concerned about reds being accurately illuminated, use TM-30.

However, at least for the time being, many engineers and manufacturers, as well as the world at large, still cite CRI, choosing the simple and familiar rather than the better and more comprehensive. And this book does too.

IV-G. COLOR TEMPERATURE

The color temperature of lighting is important to the mood and warmth of libraries.

Color temperature is measured in Kelvin. The higher the number, the bluer the light. For example, daylight has a color temperature of about 6,000K, while candlelight is about 1,800K. Incandescent light varies but averages about 3,000K.

If lighting has a high CRI, people can see colors accurately in a variety of color temperatures. In fact, only when light with two different color temperatures is visible at the same time are people aware of the difference. For example, when people walking in the twilight see lighted interiors, they realize how orange incandescent light is by comparison to daylight. Once they enter buildings and see only incandescent light, it generally ceases to seem warm.

Opinions differ, but the majority of people feel most comfortable when the color of the internal lighting is similar to that provided by incandescent lamps. Many fluorescent lamps are available with color temperatures of 3000K and 3500K. This is warm enough so that buildings look welcoming when people drive by at twilight and people's complexions look good, but cool enough for reading and for a sense of accurate color. LEDs are available in a wide range of color temperatures, including even adjustable CRI.

V. Types of Light Sources

To understand artificial lighting and its uses, it's important to review how artificial lighting works. There are four basic sources of artificial light found in most libraries:

- Incandescent (including quartz halogen)
- Fluorescent (including cold cathode fluorescent)
- HID (high-intensity discharge)
- LEDs (light-emitting diodes)

V-A. INCANDESCENT

Incandescent lamps are the kind we all grew up with, basically hot wires in bottles. They've been around for over a century, and they come in a wide variety of shapes, wattages, and colors. But limit your nostalgia. The Department of Energy (DOE) has announced it will eliminate them via regulation by 2025.

V-B. FLUORESCENT

Fluorescent lighting has been in use since the late 1930s. High-voltage (and very low amperage) electric current jumps the length of a tube, creating ultraviolet light, which is converted to visible light by phosphors that line the tube. Until the coming of LED technology, fluorescent lighting was almost a standard in non-residential buildings.

The advantages of fluorescent lighting are everyday technology (although becoming less common), efficiency (but poorer than LEDs), less blinding than incandescent or LEDs due to larger radiative surfaces, availability in a variety of color temperatures, reasonable bulb lifespans, and low replacement costs.

Disadvantages include very limited dimming capabilities, a wide variety of color rendering ratings, cheap ballasts that resulted in noise and flickering, and time delays between turning switches and lights coming on. All fluorescent lamps contain mercury, but some modern lamps have so little that they can simply be tossed in the trash. Look for green endcaps on lamps.

Small quartz halogen bulbs were popular with designers but have problems in libraries. They are extremely hot and unpleasant to look at directly. But they have the advantage of usually being burned out. (Quartz halogen bulbs are great for illuminating diamonds, but libraries are generally short of diamonds.)

Cold cathode fluorescent lamps are available in decorative curved shapes, but the cost of maintenance can be extraordinary. This library fixture is now disconnected because the cost of totally replacing burnt-out curved fluorescent lamps would probably exceed $25,000.

Libraries with regular fluorescent fixtures have had great luck replacing the tubes with LEDs that fit into the same fixtures, eliminating the need to purchase all new fixtures.

With improvements in LED lighting, all HID lighting is unsuited to libraries. Never let anyone install it, and if you have it look for replacements.

V-C. HIGH-INTENSITY DISCHARGE (HID)

High-intensity discharge lamps are part of a family of lighting that includes mercury vapor, sodium vapor, and metal halide. HID lighting is very widely used, particularly for outdoor illumination.

Of the three, mercury and sodium vapor lighting have unpleasant colors, and only metal halide is used in non-industrial indoor locations.

Metal halide lighting has the advantage of being efficient (although less efficient than LEDs), and its concentration can make it good for lighting very large spaces. It also has a lot of problems: It very often has funny and unpredictable colors, noisy ballasts, terrible delays in turning on once it's been turned off (restrike time), and mercury.

Our favorite problem is what the industry euphemistically calls "catastrophic end of service," which means that HID bulbs occasionally explode.

V-D. LIGHT-EMITTING DIODES (LEDS)

While the first edition of this book was being written, LEDs were emerging as a major source of lighting. Since then, much of their early promise has been realized and problem areas (including bad color rendering, bad color temperatures, and harsh directionality) have been addressed. LED lighting uses less energy, has a longer life, and requires less maintenance than other forms of lighting. And it now offers a high CRI and even lamps with adjustable color temperatures, ranging from 4000K during the day to 2700K by night.

The major points include:

- Light-emitting diodes are found everywhere. They are durable, and they are efficient to the point where they remain cool in use. LEDs have been used in indicator lamps and digital clocks for years, and now they are standard lighting technology.

- White LEDs are now widely available. One thing that has historically limited the use of LEDs for general lighting has been the absence of pleasant white colors. Most LEDs are intensely bright colors, particularly red and green. White LEDs were slow to be developed, and most of the early ones had an extremely unpleasant blue-white color that limited their use. This is no longer the case.

- Optics (lenses) are now used to recreate a consistent, omnidirectional light. This had been another limit to the use of LEDs. The right lens on a multiple LED lamp diffuses the light and evenly distributes it, offsetting individual LEDs directionality and producing a gentle, ambient light.

- In addition to great efficacy, LEDs tend to have a very long life, which makes them an attractive choice for light fixtures that are hard to reach.

- When you are selecting any item with white LEDs, always ask to see CRI (color rendering index) and color temperature information. You should require a CRI of at least 85. Color temperature should be similar to that of incandescent and warm fluorescent lighting, roughly 3000K to 3500K.

Fixtures that direct all or most of the light from LEDs straight downward are likely to provide extremely unpleasant illumination, but fixtures with a large indirect light component are available. Unfortunately, we've see some LED fixtures with vicious downlight in libraries.

When you are considering LED lighting, ask serious questions about maintenance.

- When individual LEDs and drivers start to burn out (and they will), how will you maintain the fixtures?

- Are the fixtures designed for individual LED replacement? Or will you have to completely replace the entire fixture? If you have to replace it, will matching fixtures still be available? If the fixtures have circuit boards, will they be available in the future?

- Where is the driver located and how do you get to it? In commercial fixtures, the LEDs and drivers are separate components, and the components with the shortest lifespans are the drivers. Frequently, the driver is replaced rather than the lamp or the fixture.

- There are three types of external drivers, and their input/output requirements must match the LED lamp: constant current, constant voltage, and AC LED drivers for use with lamps that already contain internal drivers. The drivers also control dimming capabilities. An LED driver should be paired with an LED lamp that uses 80 percent of its maximum rated wattage or it will overload the circuit. UL Class II drivers are rated for no risk of fire or electric shock. Class I drivers require safety protection when handling them, but they can handle more lamps.

- The key to LED drivers is to appropriately match the driver to the lamps and luminaires.

- Always use a reliable manufacturer. There is a better chance that matching fixtures and circuit boards will be available in the future.

One of the great things about fluorescent lighting is standardization. LED standards have evolved, and the best way to evaluate an LED product is an LM-79 report. This provides standardized measurements of efficacy and color quality of the entire luminaire. It is also used as the basis for the EPA Energy Star Qualified LED Lamp Program and Lighting Facts label. The DOE Light Facts program lists participating manufacturers. UL (Underwriters Laboratories) have done standardized testing of LEDs since 2009.

In all fairness, there are issues with LEDs as there are with any technology.

- Light output decreases gradually over the lifetime of the system. This can be offset by specifying lamps with initial lumen output greater than required.
- CRIs over 95 is available in white light LED but expensive. Typical LED CRIs are around 80, so achieving 85 is currently more expensive than using standard LEDs. Typical commercial lamps are 82. Test the lamp before you purchase a significant quantity. This is still an evolving technology.
- LED lamps will work only with LED-specific dimmer switches.
- Flicker can occur with poor drivers.
- LEDs need to be disposed of like other electronics (such as computers).

V-E. SELECTING LIGHT SOURCES

Here are our conclusions about sources of artificial light.

- In our opinion, by far the best current source of indoor lighting for libraries is the LED. It combines efficiency, standardizing (if not fully standardized) technology, reasonably priced lamps, available lamps with high CRIs, a variety of color temperatures, cool surfaces, availability of silent ballasts, and consistent color maintenance.
- Never select lamps with a CRI of less than 80. And higher is better.

Reflected uplighting can be installed in historic library rooms without creating aesthetically jarring effects. Designers are sometimes tempted to install clusters of chandeliers, but the effect can be overdone. (And lots of chandeliers with translucent bowls do a great job of displaying dead bugs.)

- We personally prefer lamps with a 3500K color temperature, but you may want to view a few installations before you decide.
- Don't buy cheap LEDs, no matter how many sleazy bulb salesmen darken your library door. Buy LEDs from recognized manufacturers and buy matching replacements.
- Never let people buy any old fluorescent lamps for your library. One of the worst lighting effects in any building is the piebald look that comes from the use of fluorescent lamps in a variety of colors. (Better yet, of course, convert to LEDs.)

VI. Lighting Strategies

VI-A. INTRODUCTION

We are going to focus here on the strategy part of a lighting concept. Keep in mind that this is only one part of a building- or space-specific concept. To be effective, a lighting concept is based on a wide variety of non-lighting, non-electrical building components, space uses, and an even wider range of users group (human) behaviors

CHAPTER 31: LIGHTING | 597

This photo of a waffle-slab ceiling shows two excellent lighting decisions. First, light is bounced off the ceiling rather than supplied by downlight fixtures set in the waffle openings.

And second, there is no special lighting for the service desk (located below the sign), making it possible to rearrange or relocate the desk without having to alter the lighting.

One of the best ways to light stack aisles in small or medium-sized libraries is with strip fixtures installed end-to-end and perpendicularly to the aisles. If the fixtures provide 100 percent uplight, like the ones in this library, users never have to look directly into a bright light source when they are looking at high shelves. (The end panels in this library have slat wall inserts for displaying a handful of books cover out.)

Uplighting fixtures work extremely well in strips. By lighting the ceiling fairly evenly, they allow almost unlimited reorganization of furnishings (particularly in children's departments like this one, where lower furnishings allow for even greater spread of light).

and abilities. Be sure to consider floor, wall, and ceiling color and texture, ceiling height (a big, big factor) and shape, locations of natural light sources, and other openings in both interior and exterior walls as you review fixture size, type, spacing, location, and direction. Think about what you want to happen in the space, how often you might change that use, how much flexibility you need in the area for traditional or non-traditional library services (pop-up or temporary/traveling exhibits and performances outside of the usual multi-purpose room as an example). All of this defines the work that the lighting system needs to accomplish and will be a factor in determining which strategy is most appropriate for a particular space. In reality, a good lighting concept will layer lighting strategies into a cohesive, functional whole that supports building occupants.

VI-B. UPLIGHTING

Uplighting consists of bouncing light off white ceilings. It's a simple strategy, and suspended uplight fixtures are widely available. Because the entire ceiling becomes a source of light, there are few problems with spotty illumination or glare. Well-designed uplighting allows the rearrangement of shelving, reader seating, computer workstations, and staff service desks without altering the lighting.

Some people complain that even uplighting is unexciting, or they dislike the hanging fixtures it requires. But they're out of luck.

Well-designed uplighting requires paying attention to the distance between the fixture and the ceiling, the distance from the ceiling to the top of the book stacks, the distance from the ceiling to horizontal work surfaces and the vertical faces of the lowest shelves, the distance from the ceiling to the floor, the spacing of the

Designers sometimes forget that light needs to fall on the spines of books (where the titles and call numbers are located) rather than the tops (where the cut edges of the pages seldom benefit from bright light.)

fixtures, the output of the fixtures, and the light distribution of the optics of the fixtures. These are all intertwined. An eight-foot-high ceiling with 84-inch-high book stacks arranged with code-minimum three-foot aisles is not the same as a room with 14-foot ceilings and with 60-inch high-sloped front book stacks with four-foot aisles.

Many fixtures provide a mix of uplighting and downlighting. Depending on the fixture, 75 to 90 percent of the light is directed upward and the remaining light directed downward through slots, translucent lenses, or perforations in the fixture. The locations of the perforations or lenses need to be considered to make sure that the fixtures do not become highly visible displays of dead bugs.

Although there are some fixtures that produce an attractive mixture of uplighting and downlighting, library users and staff are almost always very happy with 100 percent uplighting.

Some designers will suggest that so-called direct/indirect fixtures are equivalent to reflected uplighting. They're not, but they are often used when ceilings are too low for uplighting from suspended fixtures. See the description in the next section.

VI-C. DOWNLIGHTING

Downlight fixtures shine light directly from the ceiling (or other location) straight down on the area to be lighted.

Most of the common types of lighting fixtures are designed to produce downlight. Among these are all of the so-called "troffer" fixtures, light fixtures that are mounted directly in suspended ceiling grids. Troffers are usually two-by-four-foot fluorescent fixtures set flush with the ceiling, although two-by-two troffers are also popular. Troffers tend to have either parabolic grids, through which the fluorescent tubes are visible, or prism lenses. Troffers are relatively inexpensive and easy to install, but they direct most of their light straight downward. This means that the ceiling of the library is primarily in relative shadow, with the exception of the bright rectangles of light.

Light from fixtures of this type can be extremely spotty. If a stack aisle is located where there happens to be no fixture above, the result is books almost too dark to see. Libraries with ceiling-mounted fixtures over their stacks are constantly moving fixtures or adding extras, and even then they have problems with the ceiling grid not aligning correctly with the stack aisles. Because ceiling grids are laid out in multiples of two or four feet, and stacks almost never are, the result of troffers over stack aisles is always trouble, with some fixtures centered over aisles and others over the tops of shelves.

One way to avoid this problem is to run strip lights or troffers end-to-end and perpendicular to the aisles in the stacks. No matter how the shelving is moved to alter aisle width, light will still be over each aisle. In a similar way, a few libraries have been built with diagonal strip lights, allowing not only aisle width to be changed but also shelving to be rotated 90 degrees. To light the final aisles, the ends of strip lighting have to come within a foot or two of each side wall.

This library was originally equipped with only two rows of recessed downlights on the sides of the ceiling, leaving the center of the room so dark that a strip of fluorescent lights had to be retrofitted. (The original situation was made worse by the fact that the can lights were metal halide, which led them to overheat and shut down now and then. Because of the restrike time for metal halide lighting, the lights took about 15 minutes to come back on again, leaving impressively dark areas in a building that was already amazingly badly lighted.)

Fixtures can also be ceiling mounted with wrap-around lenses. These are better sources of library light than troffers, because the sides of the lenses provide at least a little illumination on the ceiling. But their brightness creates glare, and they tend to look extremely utilitarian.

Another type of ceiling-mounted fixture is the so-called "direct/indirect" fixture. In fixtures of this type, the lamps are hidden behind metal shields and shine upward inside the fixture, where light is reflected from white-painted surfaces. These provide somewhat less glare than other troffer fixtures, but the ceiling is still a dark area punctuated by bright rectangles.

Some direct/indirect fixtures have sections that hang down to project light sideways, where some of it reflects off adjacent ceilings. Other direct/indirect fixtures have perforated baffles where the light from fluorescent tubes is emitted directly but glare is reduced by the solid areas around the perforations.

By far the worst excrescence in the world of library lighting is the recessed downlight, also known as a "can light" because it is basically a lightbulb in a short, concealed tube. Downlights combine the worst of glare, spotty illumination, and harsh shadow, but they are oddly beloved of designers, librarians, and owners everywhere, whose standard approach is to lard ceilings with hundreds of can lights. *We recommend that at the beginning of the design process, you inform your architects and interior designers that you will accept absolutely no can lights for any purpose whatsoever.*

People who specify can lights tend to think that the only thing library lighting needs to accomplish is to brightly light tabletops. When laying out grids of can lights, they check the cones of illumination to be sure they overlap properly

Can lights (also known as "recessed downlights") are among the worst light fixtures possible in libraries. The lighting system visible in the ceiling of this room is spectacularly awful—a mixture of spotty illumination and horrible glare. Put "absolutely no recessed downlights" in your written building program.

Fred is entitled to say evil things about this lighting system because this picture was taken in a building he inherited and coped with for many years. In a subsequent remodeling, 100 percent of the can lights—not some weak proportion like 98 percent—went into dumpsters.

(Actually, the original lighting was even worse than in this picture, for the cans originally had black linings, wasting large amounts of energy and increasing the harsh verticality of the light emitted.)

The recessed downlights in this library work on library shelving only because the ceilings are high, the aisles unusually wide, and the shelving unusually low. But even then, if you are short and looking up at the top shelves, the lights may be blinding.

at 29 inches off the floor. But further from the floor, the light from the same can lights is incredibly spotty. The combination of can lights and book stacks is particularly nasty. And the glare is nasty too.

Luckily, for libraries with ceilings less than 10 feet high, there are lighting systems that are vastly better than can lights.

VI-D. TASK LIGHTING

Task lighting consists of supplying light only where it is needed.

Like anything else, task lighting can be done well or it can be done poorly. The basic concept of task lighting is an initially appealing one, and it comes down to purpose and execution to determine if that appeal is superficial or an integral component of a well-thought-out lighting concept. If we want superficial, we start by thinking, "Put light just where we need it for each task; we won't waste energy, and we'll have plenty of light for reading or other work." If we want integrated and effective, we'll start by thinking, "Let general room illumination handle most tasks (basic navigation, browsing the collection, most reading) and put a bit of extra light when needed for the few tasks and to support a number of building occupants that require higher light levels based on their abilities. We'll improve user productivity and satisfaction while reducing energy use."

If you think of task lighting as a way to reduce general illumination, you will be disappointed. The spottiness of task lighting in libraries can mean that users have to hunt for places with enough light to read. People can live with that in their homes, where we can navigate with our eyes closed, but in libraries we need to see everywhere, and spotty illumination is frustrating. The general illumination is the first layer and must do its job.

The other functional problem is that a great deal of task lighting is attached to our buildings. This means that we cannot relocate furniture or shelving or service without also relocating lighting. Ceiling or wall-mounted task lighting is a terrible idea, and libraries are full of surviving task lights that at one time illuminated a long-gone desk or table.

Think instead about task lighting as an element that supplements general illumination when needed, such as reading fine print. A small amount of task lighting may be useful for those with poorer-than-average eyesight, particularly with an aging population. This is better than over-illuminating the whole building and causing fatigue and eyestrain for those who do not need the added light.

One example of task lighting is supplementary lamps on study tables. Because they are individually controlled, users can turn them off or on as needed.

One persistent and extraordinarily bad idea in library lighting is the installation of soffits with downlights over service desks. If the shape of the soffit matches that of the desk below, the desk can never be reconfigured or relocated without ripping out both the soffit and the lights, plus often having to rip out and replace the sprinkler pipes inside the soffit. The whole idea of matching soffits and desks may seem attractive to you when your designer first suggests it, but you will eventually wish your building had greater flexibility in use. Like can lights in general, soffits over service desks are a good thing to ban before design work begins.

To prevent the obsolescence of permanent task lighting, some furniture or equipment comes with its own task lighting attached. This is common, for example, in the office system components used to create cubes, and it's possible to attach lighting units to book shelving.

These photographs demonstrate the foolishness of using architecturally mounted task lighting. The first lights were installed when a service desk was at the back of the skylight, at the rear of the photograph. When the service desk was rotated 90 degrees and moved to the left, the first set of lights no longer served any purpose, and a second set of lights was installed over the new location. The second (vertical) photo shows what happened when the desk was moved again, leaving the second set of lights also in the wrong place. The whole mess was solved (as it should have been from the beginning) by adding bright, indirect lighting to the room, taking advantage of the existing cove.

Lighting units attached to shelving can be centered over aisles on arms extending from shelving units, or they can be strip lights attached directly to the canopy tops of the shelving. The first approach leads to good light on the spines of books, but the second lights primarily the top edges of the books.

The trouble with shelf-mounted lighting is that it has to be connected to electric outlets in the floor, making it extremely hard to relocate shelving, since we cannot afford to locate floor outlets everywhere we might possibly need them. (Some shelving has lighting connected to ceiling electrical outlets by flexible electrical conduit, but this provides a serious industrial look.)

Task lights mounted on shelving are sometimes the only solution in historic rooms with very high, dark ceilings. In rooms like this, chandeliers may provide sufficient allover lighting for users to navigate safely, while table lamps and shelf lights provide the brighter light needed for finding books and for reading.

VI-E. LIGHTING IN NEW BUILDINGS

For most new buildings the lighting concept can be fairly straightforward: use indirect lighting wherever you can. This concept works because you have control over all the other factors, including ceiling height, window size, location, orientation, configuration, reflectance of adjacent surfaces, and so on. Work toward the higher end of the IES-recommended illumination levels. Integrate this with a realistic assessment of natural light.

Have windows, but always control direct sunlight. Review suggestions for task lighting, many of which are based on inadequate general lighting. Imagine standing at work counters, sitting at desks, and checking titles on the bottom shelf in the back of the collection.

By attaching stack lighting on arms extending from shelving, this library made it possible to relocate shelving and maintain the same lighting. Notice the curved brackets attached to the columns. Every other row of shelving needs to support brackets. (Of course, when the shelving is relocated, there will have to be some place in the floor to plug it in. And changing the width of the stack aisles may require different brackets.)

VI-F. LIGHTING IN OLD BUILDINGS WITH LOW CEILINGS (AND NO WAY TO RAISE THEM)

For many old buildings, the challenge to matching a "new building" lighting concept is the floor to ceiling height. Occasionally, you can raise the ceiling a bit, but more often than not the space above the ceiling is chock full of ducts, sprinkler piping, structure, and all sorts of other systems (the "guts" of the building). Even if you can afford to relocate all of this, the available space in many older buildings is minimal even after you've relocated all of the guts.

With no space within to suspend the preferred indirect lights, downlights become the only effective strategy for general illumination. You will still want to consider the other building factors that influence the effectiveness of the lights: window size, location, orientation, configuration, reflectance of adjacent surfaces, and so on. Work toward the higher end of the IES-recommended illumination levels. Integrate this with a realistic assessment of the natural light.

Be careful to address all of the potential pitfalls of downlight. Get some light on the ceiling using baffles, lenses, and reflectors. Consider supplemental fixtures whose task is to light the ceiling specifically to reduce contrast and glare. Imagine standing at work counters, sitting at desks, checking titles on the bottom shelf in the back of the collection. Ask whether you would ever end up working in your own shadow?

VII. Energy-Saving Ideas

With increasing concern about buildings that burn too much energy, lighting designers have sought ways to save energy while producing effective lighting. Some of these work well, but others cause trouble. Unfortunately, some really bad ideas are incorporated in building codes by people who understand energy saving but have no idea whatsoever of how libraries work. Review all proposed ideas with your entire team.

VII-A. EFFICIENT LIGHTING TECHNOLOGY

Improvements in lighting technology have made it possible to provide high-quality lighting with less power.

One of the easiest ways to improve efficiency is to get rid of all incandescent lighting. Decades ago, libraries were lighted with incandescent lamps, but they can no longer afford them. (This is another reason we object to quartz halogen lamps. In addition to creating unwanted glare, being dangerously hot, and burning out

> Years ago, Fred inherited a library with hundreds of 300-watt incandescent lamps in can lights with black linings. By changing lamp types—still incandescent—and painting the insides of the cans white, the library was able to provide good lighting with 75-watt lamps. The reduction of 225 watts per fixture saved another 75 watts in air conditioning load, for a total savings of 300 watts per light fixture. In essence, free lighting—although one could argue that replacing an incredibly stupid lighting system with a less stupid system hardly qualifies as "free." The white linings in the cans also made the light less unpleasantly directional. Library users commented on the "new lighting," and everyone was happy except the original designer.

This modern library in a converted gymnasium illustrates extremely traditional concepts of lighting that go with high, dark ceilings. Ceiling-mounted fixtures provide general lighting, while reading-level lighting is provided by special fixtures illuminating shelving and tables.
SOURCE: ENGBERG ANDERSON WITH ALICE RIEMENSCHNEIDER ASSOCIATES

too quickly, they are an extremely inefficient source of light.)

A major way to conserve electricity is to convert your library to LED lighting.

A second spinoff from efficient lighting is reduced air conditioning costs. For every three watts we save in lighting, we save about an additional watt in air conditioning load.

However, the savings are not huge, since lighting may be a quarter or less of a building's energy load.

VII-B. MOTION SENSOR SWITCHES

Many libraries and offices have motion sensor switches. When we enter rooms, the lights automatically turn on, and a few minutes after we leave they switch off again.

Some codes require motion sensor switches in public restrooms. Other codes, such as the 2018 IECC require that spaces have either vacancy sensors (auto off after 20 minutes) or central timeclocks that shut off the lights at a set time daily.

The major problem with motion sensors is that the lights won't go on until we grope our way into dark rooms and won't stay on when we sit still. One possible improvement is dual-function sensors (motion and infrared) that provide a greater level of accuracy. You can also check the aim of the sensors in your new building. And you can tell your designers and contractors in advance that lights will go on the moment doors are opened or be added to the punch list.

You can also make sure that no room with motion sensors is ever plunged into total darkness.

Be sure that a dim light remains on when the motion sensor lights go out.

> Motion sensor switches have been required in library restrooms for a number of years, but they often work badly. Fred encountered a library where the restroom motion sensors did not detect motion in some of the stalls. If anyone was in one of these stalls when the lights went out, no amount of frantic arm waving turned the lights back on. Sitting in a stall in a pitch-dark restroom helplessly waving one's arms in the air may lead to some kind of epiphany, but it is not a really good epiphany.

With motion sensor lighting in restrooms, it's also important that the lights come on when the door opens. No users—particularly in public buildings—want to grope their way into a dark room in the uncertain expectation that lighting may eventually come on. Accomplishing this requires motion sensors mounted on the ceilings, not the cheap motion sensors embedded in light switches.

In states that have adopted the IECC, libraries may find that even a large reading room is supposed to have energy management via either vacancy sensors, with lights in various areas of the room turning off when no one is there, or a time clock that shuts all the lights off at a set time each day. When vacancy sensors are used instead of time clocks for large, open public spaces, the result is lights flickering off and on in a single room—a singularly dreadful idea. The important part of the requirement is the provision that allows time clocks, especially because they can be set for closing times on different days and provide for the needs of cleaning crews.

VII-C. DAYLIGHT "HARVESTING" AND DAYLIGHT SENSORS

Some libraries are designed with sensors that turn lights off and on as daylight varies. Areas located near windows, for example, may not need much artificial light during the day. Utilizing (harvesting) controlled daylight to illuminate rooms when possible not only improves performance, reduces absenteeism, improves employee retention, and increases user satisfaction, but it also saves energy.

By the same token, areas located under skylights do not always need artificial light by day. (Skylights cause so much other trouble, however, that this is interesting rather than useful information.)

While light sensors work when night falls, some librarians tell us that sensors don't respond fast enough to work well during days when clouds come and go. Others report that the response times are too fast and that each wisp of a cloud results in switching the lights on or off. Much of this is the result of the difficulty and expense of dimming fluorescent lamps, and LED fixtures can work much better.

For years, librarians have simply turned lights off and on as outside conditions varied, and that continues to be a workable idea, even if it violates some codes.

It's better to install LED lighting and a light-control system. The LED lamps dim smoothly across the entire range of output, allowing the control system to ramp illumination up or down in infinitesimal amounts and blend the artificial and natural illumination seamlessly, eliminating the jarring jumps and noticeable lag times associated with stepped switching.

Here are some things you can do:

- When sensor-based systems are recommended, always visit another library with the kind of system being recommended for yours. If no such library exists, remember the first-kid-on-the-block effect many libraries experienced when purchasing early automation systems. Some designers talk endlessly about exciting buildings in the planning stages but stop talking about the buildings after they're built. So when in doubt, always insist on seeing a working example.

- Get specific information on warranties on sensors, and ask for full parts and labor that lasts for more than a year.

- Expect to have trouble getting daylight sensors to work properly. They tend to be fooled by reflections.

Even without daylight sensors, you can set up light switches so the lamps closest to the windows can be turned off and on separately using traditional light switches. You will have to tie these switches to a time clock to be code compliant. If you have both east and west windows, you'll want to switch the area next to each side separately.

VIII. Common Lighting Problems and How to Avoid Them

Although there are many ways of dealing with lighting problems, by far the best way is to stop bad ideas before they are implemented. Be sure people review your building plans carefully before your project is bid and constructed. Be sure to include your custodians and your consulting librarian.

Even with great planning and excellent drawings, things can go wrong in construction. Insist on a commissioning process during which the lighting is tested by the occupants of the building with designers, installers, and manufacturers making adjustments to programming as needed.

VIII-A. LACK OF FLEXIBILITY

If all of us have learned anything about libraries over the years, it's that they are constantly changing. Every few years, new demands alter the way librarians use spaces in their buildings, and within a few years after a library is constructed, staff start rearranging shelving, service desks, study tables, soft seating, computers, and other equipment.

Because libraries are always rearranging things, lighting needs to be all-purpose and flexible.

Unfortunately, designers are extremely fond of installing special-purpose lighting that assumes nothing will ever move. (Some argue that, although we moved things around constantly in the past, we now have arrived at the perfect solution and don't need to worry about times yet to come.)

The worst source of inflexibility is architecturally mounted task lighting, denounced in the previous section. Another major error is ceiling-mounted lights parallel to stack aisles, so stack aisles can't be relocated.

VIII-B. GLARE

High-glare lighting is always popular with designers because it brings drama and chiaroscuro. Uneven lighting is exciting. Picking out special features for brilliant illumination while leaving other areas dim is a characteristic of upscale merchandising. Unfortunately, libraries are a lot better off with big-box-store lighting than exciting lighting.

High-glare lighting is also popular because fixtures can be unobtrusive. Recessed downlights (always nasty in libraries) fit smoothly into ceilings, but they have nothing else to recommend them. Rectangular downlight fixtures at ceiling level can be a painful source of glare.

One of the best ways to avoid glare is to *avoid all direct lighting*. If you specify fixtures that provide 70 to 100 percent reflected uplight for your library, ban all fixtures that produce only downlight, and control direct daylight, glare should be minimal.

However, avoiding glare this way is difficult. We recommend you say "NO DIRECT LIGHT WHATSOEVER" in your building program and then watch your designers like hawks.

Another source of glare is lighting designed to produce "sparkle." This is not good library lighting.

And all windows that can admit direct sunlight need adjustable shades.

VIII-C. GLOOM

A number of architectural decisions result in libraries that are almost impossible to light effectively or attractively.

Probably the worst of these is dark surfaces. A dark ceiling makes it impossible to reflect light off the ceiling, forcing the library to use some kind of harsh, direct lighting. A bright light fixture in a dark ceiling is a lot nastier than a bright light fixture in a white ceiling. Shelving painted dark colors absorbs too much light (in addition to showing accumulated dust to great effect and freezing your color scheme for many decades to come). Tabletops in dark colors add to the gloom (and cause eyestrain). Although the occasional dark wall may be fun, dark walls suck up light rather than reflecting it.

Soffits that hang down to less than 10 feet from the floor are difficult or impossible to light with reflected uplight. The usual approach designers take is to fill soffits with recessed downlights, creating spotty illumination and glare in the process. Soffits that are painted any color except white on their undersides combine the worst features of dark ceilings and low ceilings.

Some older libraries have historic dark ceilings that need to remain their original colors. In this case, the original scheme of dim allover lighting and task lights on tables and shelves may be the only alternative. But it's insane to design new libraries that way.

VIII-D. DARK PERIMETERS

A surprising number of library rooms are too dark around the edges. This problem comes from a number of easily avoidable designs.

Perimeter soffits around the edges of rooms are a popular design detail, but they are almost always too dark underneath. Sometimes the situation is made worse by painting the undersides of the soffits a dark color. Because the soffits are close to the floor, designers tend to install rows of can lights in the soffits. The result is extremely spotty lighting near the bottom of the soffit, odd patterns of light and dark on the walls, and truly nasty direct glare for anyone who makes the mistake of looking upward.

The combination of perimeter soffits with downlights and perimeter shelving is found in many libraries, and it's always an unfortunate idea. Light on the books on the top shelves is irregular, the can lights cast harsh shadows (making it easy for users to block their own

The designers of this library failed to provide ceiling fixtures close enough to the side wall to light the last aisle of books, forcing the library to retrofit a strip light fixture.

The best way of lighting shelving of this type is illustrated in previous photos—strip fixtures running from wall to wall and perpendicular to the aisles. If the aisles are made wider or narrower, the lighting is still over the aisles, although there may be problems with the location of structural support columns. (Two-by-four-foot troffer fixtures, visible over the stacks, cause endless problems in libraries.)

light), and looking up at a top shelf often involves staring straight into the glare of a can light, making it nearly impossible to read the spines of the nearby books.

If architectural detail around the perimeter of a room is desired, crown moldings are far more attractive than soffits and don't cause illumination problems.

Another cause of dark perimeters is badly spaced light fixtures. If rows of fixtures are spaced six feet apart (for example) in a large room, the space between the last row of fixtures and the wall should be only three feet. This way, no place in the room is more than three feet from a fixture. Frequently, however, designers leave six feet between the last row of fixtures and the wall. Now everywhere in the room except the edges is within three feet of a fixture, but the walls can be up to six feet from the nearest fixture. In some libraries, the situation is even more extreme, with the last rows of fixtures even further from the walls.

We have even seen libraries where no lights were installed over the aisles closest to the walls, and new fixtures had to be awkwardly retrofitted.

VIII-E. ARCHITECTURAL FEATURES THAT COMPLICATE LIGHTING

A variety of architectural designs lead to lighting problems in libraries. Here are a few to watch out for. All of them are pains. All lead to bad lighting. Always so "no" to all of them up front.

- **Low ceilings.** It's hard to light any library space with a ceiling less than 10 feet high, because suspended (pendant) uplight fixtures need to be at least eight feet off the floor and a couple of feet below the ceiling.

  Low ceilings are particularly characteristic of libraries with balconies, where the ceilings over the balcony spaces and the spaces underneath the balconies are all too low to light.

- **Soffits.** We've mentioned problems with soffits endlessly. Soffits help to interrupt huge, boring expanses of ceiling, but they must not prevent the uniform use of reflected uplighting. Some new libraries feature unruly masses of soffits and promise nothing good for the future. It's a good thing to

In rooms with high or dark ceilings, one traditional way of lighting book shelving is with fixtures that extend from the shelving units. Doing this well may require some experimentation with your architects to select fixtures and the best way to install them.

Historic spaces with dark ceilings usually call for low-level ambient light with task lighting for shelving, reading areas, and staff desks. In the photograph with the dark ceiling (above), notice the task lighting on the shelving unit on the right.

The modern wing in the same library (right) has a white ceiling that allows reflected uplighting. (Libraries have used low-level general lighting with supplementary shelf and table lights for generations.)

tell your designers "No soffits" at the start of your project.

- **Dark ceilings.** The moment designers introduce dark ceilings they are forced to use direct lighting, with all the resulting problems with uneven illumination and glare. Librarians sometimes inherit historic dark ceilings, but there's no need to create new ones. If you have a (non-historic) dark ceiling in your library and paint it white, you will be amazed at how the character of the space changes. And how much energy you save.

- **Atria.** It's hard to light atria. Ceiling lights are too far from the floor to maintain unless they can be lowered to the floor. Many atria have downlights with the subtle look of railroad headlights. (Since atria also waste space and energy and cause problems with acoustics and user safety, you don't have to fall back on lighting problems alone as a reason to ban them from your building.)

- **Monumental staircases.** Always find out how the lamps in light fixtures over staircases will be changed. If the fixtures are not over landings, even tall ladders may not work, and renting lifts is expensive. LED lamps have long lives, but they eventually wear out. Have a plan! Consider using remote drivers in places that are easier to access than in the fixtures.

- *Windows that don't face straight north* and aren't equipped with movable blinds. Adding dark film to windows doesn't work well and makes people wonder why they wasted money on the windows in the first place.

- *Skylights*. Skylights are sources of manifest evil in libraries. When it comes to lighting, spaces under skylights are too dark by night and too bright by day. Looking up into skylights (and people have to look up at high shelves) is unpleasant, and the glare may make it impossible to see the shelves. Lighting areas under skylights at night is tricky, because reflected uplight doesn't work.

If you must have a skylight, Fred would suggest using "artificial skylights" with electric illumination.

Skylights should be banned from all libraries.

VIII-F. LIGHTING THAT IS HARD TO MAINTAIN

Some forms of lighting are notoriously difficult to maintain.

Among the questions that you (and your custodians) should ask when reviewing designs, one of the most important is how lamps will be changed.

In many libraries and other buildings, some lamps are almost impossible to reach.

Fred has been collecting photographs of unreachable light fixtures. Some require the construction of multistory scaffolds each time the lamp needs to be changed (and as a result, the lamps are never replaced once they burn out).

Here are some things you can do.

- Always check with your custodians before approving light fixtures and their placement. (Maintenance people at universities complain that they point out problems in lighting plans, only to find the buildings constructed unchanged and the maintenance staff stuck with trying to change the lamps. But it's still worth fighting for rationality.)

> A few years ago, a British library discovered that it had to relocate large quantities of shelving just to change the lamps.

When can lights are located high in the air over staircases, it's hard to figure out where to put a ladder or lift when lamps are changed. This campus building is notorious among the university's maintenance staff.

Always insist on very specific answers when you ask your designers how far-away devices will be serviced. ("Use a lift" is never a specific answer.)

The lonely light fixture high above the entrance to this area could not be reached from above, and the design of the doors at the bottom prevented a lift from being brought in. The university upon which this light fixture was inflicted replaced the bulb once by building a several-story scaffold, but after reviewing the cost they never replaced the bulb again.

- Begin with the requirement that all lamps can be changed by someone using an eight-foot stepladder. You may have to compromise but be extremely insistent that you have exact maintenance information.

- If your architect nonchalantly tells you that your custodian can "use a lift," insist that the lift and its storage space be included in the project budget. Require that someone verify that the lift can actually fit through the spaces it needs to, and that the furniture, such as shelving, will not have to be moved to make room for the lift.

> Fred knows a building at the University of Illinois where maintenance staff had to construct a three-story scaffold to change a lightbulb because a lift would not fit through the door. They changed it only once.

- If you have high chandeliers that can't be reached with a reasonable stepladder, insist that they be on electric drops so they can be serviced at floor level.

- Avoid fixtures that have to be disassembled in tricky ways before lamps can be changed. This requires close study of cut sheets for proposed fixtures. Fred's library had a fixture in an atrium that required two men standing on lifts to disassemble it in midair before lamps could be changed.

- Be particularly careful when your designers are proposing to locate light fixtures over staircases. Find out exactly where the person changing the lamp will stand. Even if your ceilings are reasonably low, the ceiling over a staircase may be impressively high, and there may be no way to reach the light fixtures once the construction scaffolding is removed.

- Stand guard over the brands of electronic ballasts supplied with your light fixtures. Even if you specify (for example) three fixtures with high-quality ballasts available

The attractive arch of lightbulbs over this service desk has to be kept turned off because there is no way to reach the bulbs when they burn out without building a scaffolding on top of the desk. (The library tried to place a large sheet of plywood on top of the service desk, but it didn't work.)

When neatly spaced bulbs are used as ornaments, any burnt-out bulb becomes an instant eyesore, spoiling an attractive design.

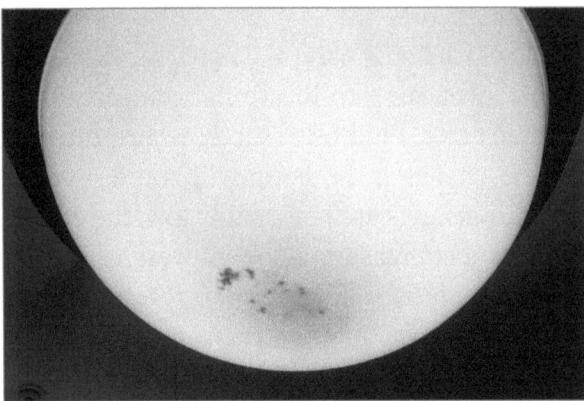

Luckily, fixtures are available with opaque central ornaments to hide the dead bugs. Unluckily, many designers don't select them. (Campus maintenance staffs describe removing endless bushels of dead bugs from light fixtures.)

locally, your contractor may ask to substitute something different as an "equivalent." Be sure your architect knows that you will not accept any fixture with a ballast not stocked in your best local area electric supply firm.

- Avoid multiple lamp types. There's no excuse for having more than a half-dozen or so different lamp types in a library. The cost and space required to warehouse 50 different lamp types can be depressing.

- Avoid extremely expensive lamps. For all unusual or specialized lighting, ask your designers to provide information on the replacement cost of lamps. Finding out that your clever light fixtures have lamps that cost $1,200 each and come from far overseas gives you a choice of stocking many thousands of dollars worth of lamps you may never use or waiting forever to get new ones when the old ones burn out.

- Avoid lamps that are expensive to dispose of. Inquire about mercury content and your specific ability to simply toss old lamps into the trash.

- Avoid fixtures that display dead bugs. Chandeliers with translucent bowls at the bottom can be handsome, but the effect is tempered by the handful of dead bugs in the center. (This is why some fixtures of this type have round finials in the center. The bugs are still gathered together there, but they can't be seen from the floor.)

Bugs are less attracted to certain wavelengths and color temperatures. Higher CRIs attract more bugs. Color temperatures over 5000K attract more bugs. CFLs and incandescent bulbs attract more bugs due to their light wavelengths being in the same range as the bugs' preferences.

- As much as possible, locate light switches in staff areas. This prevents users from playing with the lights. (Larger buildings will have lighting control systems and fewer individual switches. Access to the lighting control software needs to be limited.)

> One of Fred's earliest memories of public libraries is his stretching up to reach a long brass switch plate by the public entrance to the main reading room of the Detroit Lakes, Minnesota, Public Library and turning off all the lights one by one. His father reached him just as the last light went out.

- If you have fixtures with perforations, be sure that they are on the side of the fixture, where dead bugs won't show. Perforations are often used in strip fluorescent fixtures to provide an element of downlight. We find this unnecessary, but designers generally dislike 100 percent uplight.

- Require that installers save the instruction sheets for all light fixtures and give them to the library administration to be filed with other building data. Electricians, who deal with this equipment on a daily basis, will not find it puzzling when it needs attention in years to come, but the rest of us may need the instruction sheets.

VIII-G. BUYING LIGHTING

We have found a few helpful ideas when it comes to purchasing lighting.

- Negotiated government discounts. If you run a government-owned library, it's very much worth finding out whether your state has an agency that arranges centralized purchasing of items like electric lamps. In Illinois, government agencies were able to buy fluorescent lamps by a major manufacturer at about an 85 percent discount from list price. Depending on the agency, there may be simple requirements for participation, such as a formal motion by your governing agency.

- Lamps from major manufacturers. When you are specifying lighting for a building, stick with products from major manufacturers in the hope you will be able to buy matching lamps when yours burn out.

- Door-to-door lamp salesmen. There are some dubious high-pressure door-to-door salesmen who sell high-priced off-brand lamps, contending that these products are of a quality far superior to everyday lamps. Our experience suggests very much otherwise. Despite the persuasive sales literature, we find this kind of product expensive and of no better quality than standard lighting. We think you are far better off dealing with lamps manufactured by major manufacturers and stocked by large electrical firms. After a few experiences, Fred refused even to speak with lamp salesmen.

VIII-H. LIGHTING GIMMICKS

Every age has its own lighting gimmick.

One gimmick of a few years past was pendant lights, cute colored glass shapes hanging from the ceiling. The fixtures glowed attractively, but the lamp inside often projected a small circle of blazingly bright light straight downward. Unfortunately, no reader benefits from a spot of brilliant light in the middle of an otherwise dimly lit table.

Pendant lights with clear glass shades can be blinding to look at from any direction.

If your designer proposes pendant globe lights, check out an installation before you say "yes." Many can be found in recently decorated restaurants and bars.

One library Fred dealt with ripped out all of its pendant globe lights in terminal annoyance before he even had a chance to see them.

Ban them (or their current gimmicky replacements) before design work begins.

VIII-I. TROUBLESOME SECURITY LIGHTING

Most modern libraries are designed so that public areas are never completely dark. After all the lights have been shut off for the night, occasional fixtures have a lamp that stays illuminated at all times. This allows staff members to negotiate the darkened library on their way out the door at night without tripping over furniture or abandoned skateboards.

Night lights of this type work well, but they can cause trouble in meeting room or classroom spaces, where you may want to turn off all the lights. Always specify that there be some way to turn off security lights in these rooms.

Among the high-maintenance items in many libraries is the small battery-powered LED emergency lighting units that come on whenever the power fails. Even a medium-sized library can have dozens of them. The units are ingenious. While the power is on, they charge continuously, and the connection to the library's power supply provides constant information on whether the power is on or off.

Battery-powered units of this type are also prone to failure. Every time the fire marshals arrive to check your library, they'll find units that no longer work.

Another (albeit more expensive) option is to use a powerful central battery to power all the night lights in the building. Units of this type use an inverter, a device that changes the DC of the battery to the AC necessary to operate fluorescent light fixtures. When the time comes to construct your new library, you might inquire about this type of emergency lighting.

A third option is to connect the night lights to an emergency generator. This may make sense if there are other systems (such as drainage pumps) that need to work even if normal power is off.

VIII-J. HISTORIC LIGHTING FIXTURES

Although simple fluorescent strip uplight fixtures can be used effectively in historic buildings, there are situations where something more elaborate is required.

One of the easy solutions is to equip historic fixtures with relatively dim lamps and provide the actual uplighting from another source. LED lamps are now available in many historic sizes, including LEDs with filaments, in clear, amber, or frosted glass. Color temperatures can vary from 1800K to 3000K.

The Indianapolis Public Library had an extremely effective arrangement of this kind in its central hall. Great wagon-wheel fixtures hanging from the ceiling had visible lamps dim enough to avoid glare, while the real light came from invisible lamps on top of the fixtures, projecting light upward onto the ceiling.

To library users, the feeling was historic, and they didn't have to know that the visible lamps were there just to create a pleasant atmosphere.

Modern uplighting fixtures can also be incorporated in historic rooms with little feeling of inappropriateness, and they may be less obtrusive than the rows of hanging-bowl chandeliers that are sometimes used.

IX. Working with Natural Light

Natural light is undependable. It varies from too bright to too dark. And everyone wants it.

When we prepare building programs for new library structures, we always ask the staff what's most important in their workspaces. And they always tell us "windows."

Nothing is sadder than to do a post-occupancy study of a new library building where many of the staff are stuck in windowless basement rooms, along with storage and HVAC.

The importance of natural light is a major argument for avoiding basements in libraries. (Another and even better argument involves surprise adventures with water.)

Basements in houses provide inexpensive space, but basements in libraries are almost as expensive as floors above ground. It's hard to excuse them.

One way to provide natural light is through clearstory windows—windows set vertically in a roof. If the windows face directly north, as these do, the result can be wonderful lighting. If they face other directions, they let in direct sunlight, which tends to be blindingly awful.

IX-A. COMPASS POINTS MATTER

In the continental US at least, the direction of light matters a great deal.

- North light is by far the best light for reading and work. The sun almost never shines directly through north windows.

- West light is the worst. When the sun sets on summer evenings, light through western windows comes blasting in and takes out retinas. Libraries that have west windows without effective blinds find that computers can't be used at busy times in the afternoon and evening. If a library entrance faces west, staff members at a service desk facing the entrance may find that it's almost impossible to work late in the day with the direct sun in their faces.

- East light on summer mornings can be equally harsh, but libraries are seldom open at dawn. By the time libraries are ready for business, the sun is high enough in the sky for building overhangs or summer awnings to control unwanted light.

- South light is a mixed blessing. In the summer, the sun can be almost directly overhead, and building overhangs can keep the direct sun out of south windows. In the winter, when the sun is lower in the southern sky, some users enjoy sitting in sunny windows to read. But south light that falls directly on service desks or computers is always seriously nasty. Shades are essential.

These different qualities of daylight are another reason to have the long dimension of library buildings east-west. If the long walls face north and south, libraries maximize desirable north and south light and minimize problems with east and west light.

Since north entrances are always cold, one approach is to have a sheltered south entrance and concentrate reader seating on the north side of the building.

One can make a very good argument for avoiding west light entirely. If one end of the building must house HVAC gear and garages, why not make it the west end?

IX-B. CONTROLLING DAYLIGHT

Building designs are extremely subject to vogues and passing enthusiasms. In the 1960s we had an excess of glass boxes, and we seem to be there again.

Because glass walls are never as well insulated as the best masonry walls, we wonder why glass buildings continue to be constructed given the current emphasis on green architecture.

Some designers assure their clients that with modern glass, west light is no longer a problem. We think that with modern glass, west light can be *less* of a problem, but that you still will hate it if you don't have working blinds.

Libraries with glass walls can save a lot more energy by preventing daylight from falling on the outside of the glass than by blocking the daylight with blinds, particularly dark blinds. By the time daylight enters the building, much of the accompanying heat (solar gain) stays in the building. This is why awnings save more cooling energy than Venetian blinds.

> Unfortunately, some daylight is extremely difficult to control. For example, Fred consulted with a library that has a huge reading room with a cathedral ceiling. At one end of the room, the ridgepole was a few feet lower, and a chevron of glass connected the higher and lower cathedral ceilings. Unfortunately, the chevron faced west, and because of its configuration didn't lend itself to any kind of blinds. During the afternoon, light through the chevron passed slowly over the reading tables and computers, constantly forcing users to relocate until the library covered the glass chevron with a dark film.
>
> Another library Fred worked with had a cathedral ceiling with small dormers set high in the ceiling, also facing west. Because the dormers were set in the middle of slopes, they defied the installation of blinds and were a daily source of unpleasant glare.

[Above] This library copes with direct sunlight on its east windows by installing awnings that can be removed in the winter, when sunlight comes mostly from the south. (The awnings work because the sun is fairly high in the sky by the time the library opens in the morning. If the awnings were on the west side of the building, the setting sun would blast between the bottom edges of the awnings and the window sills, taking out the retinas of the people inside.) Awnings this large need to be lashed to frames in order to withstand the wind.

BENJAMIN HALPERN

[Right] This attractive library entrance faces south, which means that the daylight coming through the glass is brutal in the winter. When southern sunlight shines on the service desk inside the door, workers are blinded.

Given the extremely complex shapes of the windows, adding blinds would be difficult—if not impossible. The library could do as others have done and add dark gray film to the glass to block the sunlight, but that would spoil the appearance of things and make one wonder (as many other libraries have done in similar situations) why the designer provided the glass in the first place.

The easy way to control daylight is to control how and where windows are planned.

If you're already stuck with windows facing in bad directions, some possibilities include:

- Exterior awnings. These can look very attractive, as the photograph of awnings over the east terrace of Fred's former library indicate. By the time the library opens on summer mornings, the sun is high enough in the sky so that no light falls through the east windows. Awnings of this size need to be lashed to frameworks to prevent them from blowing away in strong winds. When the sun shifts to the south in the winter, the awnings and their frameworks can be dismantled to let light from the eastern sky enter the library.

- Vertical Venetian blinds. Vertical blinds offer an opportunity to angle the slats so that daylight is visible but sun doesn't enter. (Obviously this works only when light is striking the windows at an angle.) One problem with vertical blinds, however, is that they are fragile and frequently damaged by library users or by furniture bumping against them.

- Perforated vinyl blinds. Blinds of this type have been used very satisfactorily in a number of libraries. While blocking most of the sunshine, they still allow users to see what's outside the building. We recommend that you always use white blinds, which save cooling energy by bouncing some light back out the window and save lighting energy by bouncing interior light rather than absorbing it. By reflecting interior light, white blinds also improve illumination and make rooms look less dark when the blinds are pulled.

- Traditional Venetian blinds. Blinds with horizontal slats do a very effective job of blocking direct sunlight, although enough light leaks around the edges of the slats to prevent the near total blockage of light needed (for example) by some image projection systems. Remember that dark blinds absorb more heat than light blinds do and are somewhat less energy efficient during cooling seasons. And consider the fun of dusting Venetian blinds.

This library was equipped with high windows facing west. The resulting afternoon light was blinding. Fitting horizontal blinds into windows with sloped tops is nearly impossible, but the library found a good solution with vertical Venetian blinds.

CHAPTER 31: LIGHTING | **621**

[Right] One of the problems with historic skylights is figuring out how to provide light at night. This library has added a hanging electric fixture in the middle of the skylight. Other libraries have relied on task lighting, with lighting fixtures mounted on service desks and reading tables. Others have roofed over the skylights and lighted them electrically.

[Left] Avoid skylights. In this library, as the sun crosses the sky during the day, direct sunlight falls on these service desk computers, making them impossible to use.

[Left] Artificial skylights with constant illumination levels work a lot better than skylights that rely on the uncertainty of sunlight. But maintenance can be complex. To change the lights in this skylight or clean the translucent panes, workers span the area between the railings with long planks, place plywood sheets on the planks, and then stand on the assembly to change the lights and clean the glass. (The railings have the kind of horizontal balusters that encourage young visitors to climb up and fall over.)

Other libraries have rectangular west windows with blinds, topped by arched or triangular windows without blinds. Unfortunately, the western sun can be just as nasty when it comes through an arched window.

Another problem is so-called "monitor" structures, raised portions of the roof with vertical glass walls on some or all sides. Usually these cause nothing but trouble because there is no way to put blinds on the glass sides of the monitors.

When you visit libraries with vertical glass sections set high above the floor, look for signs of nasty glare. Also look for the retrospective installation of dark gray transparent material on the glass of windows that don't face north.

The moral of all this is never locate a west, south, or east window where you can't install a blind.

IX-C. SKYLIGHTS

Skylights offer a particularly effective example of unwanted light because it is difficult to block light that falls through skylights. Everyday shades and blinds don't work.

In a number of places in this book, we dwell on the fact that skylights and libraries are an extraordinarily bad combination. When it comes to lighting, areas under skylights are too bright by day and too dark by night. (Skylights also reflect noise and leak, but that's for other chapters.)

Libraries are full of examples of the negative effects of skylights on practical library lighting. For example, we know one library that has a cathedral ceiling in its children's department, with a skylight running along the peak. Since the ridge pole runs from north to south, a band of hot daylight crosses the department each day, as the sun moves from east to west over the building. When the band of light falls on the reference desk, all computer work must cease.

Another library has skylights over staff desks. Direct sun through the skylights made it impossible for staff members to work, so they installed horizontal rods on the ceiling and draped fabric panels under each skylight.

Another library with a huge skylight has large movable fabric panels running on wire tracks.

Once skylights have been installed in buildings, getting rid of them is expensive. The right time to say "no" (loudly) is when they are first proposed. Write "no skylights" in your building program. For Fred, writing "ABSOLUTELY no skylights" is even better.

Joe has seen enough poorly designed, constructed, positioned, and maintained skylights that he understands Fred's preference for blanket bans, but there are some truly spectacular spaces made humane and welcoming by skylights, and they can be favorite spaces for people in those buildings. Skylights are complex, and if you are not going to invest the design time, construction cost, and maintenance efforts in doing them well, don't do them at all. This is not the time for a "how hard can it be" attitude by anyone on the team, including the architect.

One favorite cliché in library design is to connect new and old buildings with large skylights. We know a number of libraries that were initially enthusiastic about this feature but came to hate it. Areas under huge skylights are hard to use. They're noisy, the sun fades the books, and light levels are seldom pleasant for reading. We think it's easy for spaces of this type to end up as noisy concourses, expensive structures to pass through rather than occupy.

The extremely negative effects of skylights can be tempered slightly by using translucent, insulated materials, but even then we find large skylights a major problem.

IX-D. EFFECTS OF UNWANTED DAYLIGHT

Daylight is vastly brighter than any artificial light used for general library illumination.

The contrast between direct sunlight and good artificial light is so great that it can be almost impossible to read under a mixture of the two.

Libraries with shelving subject to daily direct sunlight point to book spines and labels faded to uniform pale gray. Be sure to think through glass performance when you are replacing windows or designing a new building. There is a lot that can be done to reduce the UV radiation that degrades finishes, furnishings, and collections.

IX-E. VIEWS OF THE OUTSIDE WORLD

In historic libraries, windows served primarily to illuminate reading areas. In both great university libraries and in small Carnegie-era libraries, windows were set high in the walls, often above wall-mounted shelving.

Many readers today, however, want to be able to see the world go by while they are reading. What, one might ask rhetorically, could be more fun than reading new books while drinking coffee and keeping an eye on the passing throng?

With new buildings, setting windowsills about 24 or 30 inches from the floor is easy. But with expanded historic buildings, it's also easy to have lower windowsills. If the rest of the new windows match the older windows in all other ways, the difference in height of windowsills is not particularly noticeable.

X. A Final Word on Lighting (Because This Horse Might Not Be Dead Yet!)

Bad lighting is one of the most frequently encountered problems in both old and new library buildings. Much of this is the result of lazy integration of lighting into a building. New and evolving technologies, a wider array of functional users within libraries, increasing expectations for human comfort and support of visual perception, and demands for energy conservation mean that a simplistic approach to lighting is doomed.

This is not a license to experiment. It is unfortunate that functional library lighting is not exciting to some owners and designers, who want to bring in clouds of glorious but uncontrolled daylight, create exciting patterns of darkness and light, and use whatever is the current vogue in novelty lighting fixtures.

Creating excitement with light in a library is like creating excitement with steps in a nursing home.

XI. Snappy Rules on Lighting

1. There are a lot of snappy rules on lighting because library lighting is critically important and frequently done badly.

2. The best way to light a library is to bounce light off a white ceiling.

3. Never compromise on color rendering index (CRI). There's no need to accept anything less than 85.

4. Color temperature is of major importance. People like artificial lighting to be warm colored—about 3000K to 3500K.

5. Beware of overly expensive lamps (lightbulbs). Always inquire about unusual lamps before you approve fixtures. If your lamps cost over $1,000 each to replace (and some curved tube lamps do), they had better be more wonderful than one would believe possible.

6. Unless you suffer from a surfeit of storerooms and maintenance funds, severely limit the number of lamp types and fixtures.

7. Know how you will change your lamps. If your designer says "Use a lift," that is about as helpful as being told to "Use a screwdriver" when you ask how to rebuild the carburetor on your XKE.

8. For situations where lamps will be turned off and on frequently—meeting rooms, some restrooms, and rooms with detectors for natural light—avoid HID lighting, which has a lot of trouble starting and stopping.

9. Avoid direct lighting. The result is always glare and spotty illumination.

10. Any window that can admit direct sunlight needs a shading device. "Modern glass" is not a substitute.

11. If your designers insist that you're wrong about modern glass, demand that they show you an installation that works. And test it out in direct sunlight.

12. Avoid incandescent lamps. The worst are quartz halogen lamps, which are unfortunately beloved of some designers. (Luckily, most quartz halogen lamps in most libraries have the lifespan of gnats and are usually burned out.)

13. Avoid skylights with a passion. Areas under skylights are too dark by night, too bright by day, and noisy. And skylights leak. (Some owners and architects are seriously enamored of skylights, and you will have to be very firm.)

14. Be sure your lighting is bright enough. Anything less than 50 foot-candles of soft, even light is unacceptable, and 60 foot-candles is a lot better.

15. Entryways need to be bright and welcoming, even though all most people do is move on through them.

16. Architecturally mounted task lighting is evil. Or at the very least really, really dumb.

17. Perimeter soffits with recessed downlights are beloved of many designers, but they provide rotten light. So do soffits with recessed downlights over service desks.

18. Parabolic lenses in fluorescent light fixtures are designed to direct light straight downward, creating glare and bad light distribution.

19. Can lights (recessed downlights) are inevitably a terrible idea. Tell your designers from the start that you will have none of that.

20. Motion detectors may be called for in codes. Fight them passionately in reading rooms. When you are stuck with them in smaller rooms, insist that they be activated by the motion of doors, not by people entering a room.

21. Motion detectors can be paired with detectors that measure the presence of people in other ways, to reduce the chance of users and staff being plunged into darkness. Talk with your electrical engineers.

22. Avoid tricksy switching of lights in meeting rooms that will be used by people who have not received special training. Most intelligent and well-educated people have not received special training.

23. People who want to read with their books held vertically should be accommodated.

24. Be particularly wary of bits of windows too high above the floor to allow blinds. If they face any direction except due north, you'll end up retrofitting dark gray plastic films and wondering why you wasted money on the windows in the first place.

25. Be very afraid when people start talking about "glorious" light.

26. A favorite (and unsatisfactory) location for motion detectors in smaller spaces is in the box where the light switch would be located at the entrance to a room. Unfortunately, these are not activated by the motion of doors and force people to grope their way into dark rooms. Groping your way into a dark room (particularly a restroom) may seem adventurous, but in reality it's no fun at all.

27. Skylights are always evil in libraries. Tiny little skylights are lesser evils than huge skylights, but only because they're smaller. Always tell your designers "No skylights," and then watch them like hawks.

28. The combination of atrium, lending desk, ceramic tile floor, skylight, floating staircase, and open-sided balconies with railings that can be climbed like ladders is not just evil but evil in an almost Biblical sense. Unfortunately, the whole idea appeals passionately to some owners and designers, who will need to be sat upon firmly. (Reminding your designers that the whole arrangement is an extremely well-worn cliché may help more than pointing out it's spectacularly dysfunctional.)

29. With the exception of study rooms, program rooms, and faculty studies, put light switches where library users can't play around with them.

30. Instead of motion detectors for stack aisles, consider pressure switches, which won't let the lights go off just because a user is standing too quietly, or time clocks.

31. In days gone by, high windows in reading rooms served to provide light. These days lots of readers enjoy windows with sills low enough to allow them to see passing traffic while they read. You can have both.

32. Round lamps on tabletops are cute, but many of them don't provide useful lighting. If you want light for reading, the easiest approach is straight fixtures that run the length of the tabletops.

33. The light at the end of the tunnel is burned out again.

34. A "monitor" is a structure that rises above a roof and has glass on most or all of its sides. Since monitors do not have adjustable blinds, any glass that doesn't face straight north is too much glass. Stop monitors the first time you hear them mentioned, and say "NO MONITORS" in your building program. (If you have a paralyzing fear of reptiles, keep the phrase "monitor lizard" in mind.)

35. North-facing clearstory windows are a great idea. (On the other hand, clearstories

facing any direction except north are seriously nasty.)

36. If you have to install dark gray film on a window to block the glare, you should be asking yourself why you allowed anyone to install the window in the first place.

37. All windows that don't face directly north need a way to control direct sunlight. "Modern glass" can be amazing, but it is not magical. (You can often expect a fight from your owners or architects, who will be wrong but unusually determined.)

38. Recessed downlights (can lights) lead to elegant, unobstructed ceilings. But they also lead to impressively crappy lighting, a triumph of glamor over function, of glare and shadows over visibility. Ban them from day one (but expect to hear them suggested anyway).

PART IV
Technical Issues

CHAPTER 32

Electrical Systems

I. Introduction

I-A. ELECTRICAL SYSTEMS IN LIBRARIES

Libraries can be major users of electricity because of the importance of HVAC and lighting, and they can require an unusually extensive provision of electrical outlets (receptacles) because of the vast numbers of smaller electrical devices in use.

This chapter covers some basic points about electrical systems as they apply to libraries, concentrating in particular on areas that have caused problems in libraries. The chapter is less thorough than some other parts of the book because electrical systems are complicated. This is a time to rely on your electrical engineers, who are heroic.

Many electrical requirements are included in the National Electrical Code and local codes. They are not repeated here, since we assume you will have a legal building. And they are sufficiently complex to fill this book. Always remember, however, that codes are legal minimums, not necessarily ideals, and that saying "Our building meets all applicable codes" does not really give you bragging rights. And in case things seem simple, aspects of the codes seem to be updated on an annual basis.

Almost all libraries, including brand new ones, have fewer outlets than they need. Many libraries also have too few electrical circuits, particularly in areas where food is prepared and served.

For safety, all electrical circuits have automatic cutoff switches. In days gone by, circuits were equipped with fuses, but the modern thing is circuit breakers, which are resettable switches. You don't want fuses in your library. If you have them, this would be a really good time to upgrade.

Electrical systems of particular importance to libraries are also covered in some separate chapters, and the information there is by and large not covered in this chapter. See in particular chapter 28, "Staff Facilities"; chapter 31, "Lighting"; chapter 24, "Program, Activity, and Study Rooms"; and chapter 35, "Security."

627

I-B. NOMENCLATURE

Electrical service is pretty standard, although the details are impressively complex. When your building is being planned and constructed, it's a good thing to know what people are talking about. Here are some basic terms.

- *Breaker box.* See circuit breaker.

- *Circuit breaker.* A device that interrupts the flow of current when the amount of current is too high for the safety of the circuit. Modern circuit breakers are resettable switches. When in doubt, require "switch rated" breakers, which don't wear out in daily use. Breakers are clustered in electrical panels (also called load centers or breaker boxes).

- *Electrical room.* A room dedicated to electrical equipment. This could be the electrical service room (where power enters the building, flows through a master switch, and is routed to various electrical panels), an electrical distribution room (with clusters of electrical panels for receptacles, equipment, or lighting), or where the remote electrical panels are located.

- *Fuse.* A form of circuit breaker. A fuse has a strip of metal that melts when the amperage in the circuit reaches a specific level. A common problem is the use of fuses that allow unsafe levels of currents in wiring; for example, 30-amp fuses in circuits designed for 20 amps. (In days gone by, people would insert pennies behind fuses in fuse boxes, resulting in a complete loss of protection and occasional exciting fires.) If your library has fuse boxes, today would be a really good time to upgrade.

- *Ground.* Grounded outlets are required by modern building codes. Look for three openings in electrical outlets—two slots and a round opening.

- *Load.* The amount of power drawn from a circuit.

- *National Electrical Code* (**NEC**). The basic national code. Published by the National Fire Protection Association (NFPA).

- *Panel room.* See electrical room.

- *Receptacle.* A standard term for an electrical outlet where things can be plugged in.

- *Underwriters Laboratories.* Providers of UL certifications. These are not always required by law, but insurance companies can require certifications.

II. Electrical Circuits

An electrical circuit is composed of wiring, loads (electrical outlets, lighting, or other energy-consuming equipment), and a safety cutoff for situations where the circuit is overloaded, where something is wrong with the grounding, and so on.

A circuit is the path followed by current from the power source through whatever device is using power and then back to the power source. The electrical outlets, light fixtures, or other power users on a single path form a circuit. In modern buildings in the US, circuits for everyday use—lighting, outlets, and so on—are typically 20 amps each. Areas with many pieces of high-amperage equipment—such as kitchenettes—require a number of separate circuits.

Most wiring is 110 volts, but higher voltage wiring is required for some heavy-duty appliances, such as electric stoves, and a wide variety of equipment that most staff do not work with.

Far too many libraries—even brand new ones—have insufficient electrical wiring. Multiple separate circuits are particularly important in areas where food is prepared or served. Far too many meeting rooms and staff rooms have so few separate circuits that dinners or parties are impossible. Kitchenettes of all sorts are notorious for inadequate numbers of circuits. Some libraries end up running extension cords from other areas of the library where additional circuits are available. This is an extraordinarily bad idea.

To answer a question, extra electrical wiring costs more to install, but electrical wiring itself doesn't consume any power until you use it.

II-A. WIRING

II-A-1. Modern Wiring

Modern 110-volt wiring has three wires, including hot and cold plus ground. Grounded wiring is a lot safer. To check whether your library has grounded wiring, look for the third opening in electrical outlets—two vertical slots and a round hole.

Circuit breakers are designed to prevent situations where too much power flows through a circuit. By automatically disconnecting the circuit, a circuit breaker prevents damage resulting from overheated circuits.

Ground fault circuit interrupters (GFCI) are devices to prevent situations where faulty pieces of equipment short out through the bodies of people holding the equipment. GFCIs are required by codes in areas where people can touch extremely well-grounded items while they are holding faculty equipment. The common use of GFCIs is in rooms with plumbing—kitchens and restrooms.

In many areas of libraries, we keep adding more and more pieces of electrical equipment. Be sure you have enough circuits to cope with future needs. The most common problems seem to occur in food-service areas, but other possibilities are any areas with high-wattage equipment.

II-A-2. Legacy Wiring

Knob and tube wiring is a system used from the late nineteenth century through the late 1930s.

Instead of the modern three wires in a conduit (hot, cold, and ground), knob and tube systems strung individual wires through the walls. Wires were held away from nearby wood by ceramic "knobs," which supported wires above surfaces, and by ceramic "tubes," which allowed wires to pass through beams without touching the beams. Knob and tube wiring has no grounding wire.

In addition to general safety issues, because the positive and negative wires in knob and tube wiring are separated, they can have a negative effect on data transmission.

Obsolete wiring can depend on fuses rather than circuit breakers to protect circuits. If your library is old enough to have a fuse box, it's time to modernize your electrical system. With fuse boxes, it's too easy for someone to create a dangerous situation by putting in fuses with amperages too high for the wiring or by putting pennies behind the fuses. (If you have a fuse box, feel the wires coming out of it. If they're warm, turn things off and get help today. If they're cool, don't postpone past next week.)

Legacy wiring is obsolete and dangerous and basically asking for trouble.

II-B. CONDUIT

Conduit is piping for wiring. It protects wiring from people, and it protects people from wiring.

All wiring in all libraries should be in conduit, even though home wiring typically is not. Flexible metal conduit is available for situations where simple piping would be difficult to install.

For retrofitting spaces where new conduit cannot be inserted into a wall, surface-mounted systems are available. Surface-mounted conduit is often called "wire mold." It's not as nice looking as hidden wiring, but it's common in the backroom areas of libraries. The walls and trim in some Carnegie-era library buildings are covered with galvanized piping for wires because it was hard to hide added wiring.

Dual conductor wire mold is available for installations where both power and data cabling are needed. One conductor handles 110-volt wiring and the other data wiring. The separate passageways in the wire mold keep the 110-volt wiring from messing up data transmission in the other wiring.

II-C. ELECTRICAL PANELS

An electrical panel is a metal panel with a door in front and rows of circuit breakers inside. In "panel rooms," where the library's main power panels are located, major panels may just have massive switch levers for turning power to groups of panels (or even power to the entire library) off and on. (Some homes have plastic electrical panels, but we think libraries need metal.)

You want panels with circuit breakers, not fuses. See the section II-A-2 "Legacy Wiring."

Adding panels to older buildings can be a challenge, especially if the original electrical service is too small to power all of the building's equipment. All power should be routed through a single central switch to avoid the dangers of staff or repair teams being unaware of needing to turn off multiple power feeds in the building. Avoiding this problem by replacing an undersized electrical service with a larger one can be expensive because older electrical panels need to be reconnected to the new, larger supply. However, as expensive as this is, it's less costly—and less dangerous—than having to come back later and combine a multitude of separate power supplies.

II-D. ELECTRICAL OUTLETS

One of the most common errors in library design is the provision of too few electrical outlets. While meaning well, your designers are likely to try to save you money by limiting the number of outlets in your building.

The problem is that with the coming of universal laptops and other computers, library staff members and library users are constantly looking for places to plug things in. Batteries don't hold their charges long enough, and they may never do so.

So the basic rule is, provide an extraordinary number of electrical outlets.

Among other things, you will need:

- Electrical outlets on all reading tables. If a table has four chairs, it needs four outlets. (Think of students piling into the college library at exam time, with every chair taken and with every student carrying a laptop.)

- Outlets on reading tables should be on top of the tables rather than hidden beneath.

Why make library users crawl under tables looking for place to plug in their laptops? If it's an issue of aesthetics, attractive table lamps are available with outlets in their bases.

- Electrical outlets by all soft seating.
- Electrical outlets at all places computers are scheduled to be located.
- Electrical outlets at all places where self-check equipment will be located.
- Electrical outlets at all places where security gates will be located.
- Electrical outlets all over the place in spaces to be used for group study, especially if furniture is designed to be movable.
- Electrical outlets in places where electronic gadgets may replace shelving.
- Electrical outlets at all places where any of the equipment listed above may be located at any time in the future.
- What this means is that, except for permanent stack structures, libraries need outlets everywhere.
- Outlets spaced sufficiently closely together so that extension cords are never needed. Extension cords are a serious fire hazard. And people trip over them. Make your fire marshal and users happy with lots of outlets. (You can try to ignore unhappy users, but it's harder to ignore unhappy fire marshals.)

> One academic library Fred worked with had so few electrical outlets that the lending desk checked out extension cords to students for use with their laptop computers.

- Outlets on all sections of wall large enough to possibly have something plugged in. This means that a three-foot section of wall between two doors needs an electrical outlet.
- Heavy three-wire extension cords with built-in circuit breakers for situations where you are forced to use extension cords. These are not dime-store items.
- Outlets above tabletop level in staff work areas, to make it unnecessary for staff members to crawl under furniture—or pull furniture away from the wall—in order to plug things in.
- Tamper-resistant (childproof) outlets in ALL PUBLIC AREAS of all public libraries. They are more important in adult areas than in children's areas, because it's in adult areas that busy parents hand their car keys to their children to play with while the parents are using the library. (When children poke car keys into unprotected outlets, the result is excitement for everyone.) A blue dot on the face of the outlet indicates that it is tamper-resistant. Many people, architects included, tend to assume that childproof outlets are needed only in children's departments, but they are WRONG. In addition to saving uproar, childproof outlets add very little cost to construction. (Check your construction drawings to be sure that you're actually getting childproof outlets in ALL public areas. And then check installations, since drawings can be ignored or altered at the last second, or electricians can decide on their own that childproof outlets must be for children's departments only. Remember that the extra cost of a childproof outlet is impressively tiny.)
- Flush outlets in the middle of floors, so that furniture can be located on the boxes until the boxes are needed. A common brand is

Walker boxes, which have lids that open to provide access to both 110-volt outlets and data conduit. If you retrofit floor outlets they'll stick up. And if there's no floor below, you'll pay an astounding price. Considering that you'll need two or three trades to do the work, you may not even be able to find an interested contractor.)

- Computer tables with outlets that don't force library users with computers to sit facing walls. A great many users are spooked by this arrangement and don't sit there.

- Outlets not inserted by core drilling through concrete floors, because the outlets are kept in place by flanges resting on the floors, which means they always stick up a quarter of an inch or more.

- No so-called pedestal electrical outlets that stick up like tombstones above the floor. One still sees them, but they are killers, mercilessly tripping up the unwary. Libraries with pedestal outlets end up having to position furniture over them, regardless of whether the furniture blocks the movement of people through the building.

- Grounded electrical outlets. If your outlets don't have three openings (two vertical slots and one round opening), talk to electrical people.

- Checking correct wiring of electrical outlets is easy to do with a gadget called a "multimeter." It's a standard instrument used for measuring AC voltage and current, DC voltage and current, resistance, continuity, and other values. It plugs into outlets, with indicator lights that let you know whether everything is hooked up right. In older buildings, it's a great way to see whether the ground connection in outlets is actually hooked up. Checking outlets for correct wiring can be part of punch listing.

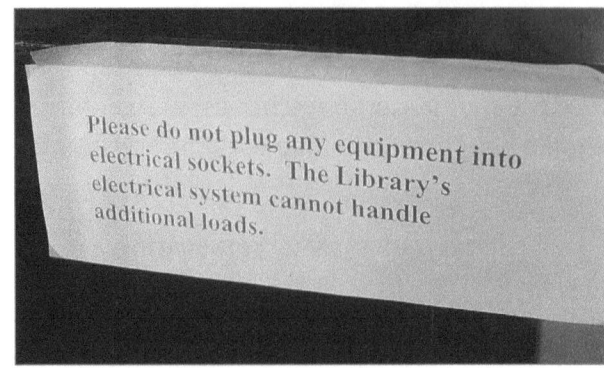

Far too many libraries—even brand-new ones—have insufficient electrical wiring. Kitchenettes are notorious for inadequate numbers of circuits, but historic buildings can be short of amperage almost anywhere. Economizing during remodeling or new construction can be a major mistake.

- A few libraries that have problems with grounding have separately grounded outlets for use with computers. They're colored orange.

- In staff workrooms, consider wall outlets installed above tabletop height. Staff will appreciate not having to crawl under furniture to plug stuff in. The director may need a workroom with outlets concealed for aesthetic reasons, but most other staff members will prefer easy access over hidden outlets.

- Outdoor electrical outlets. You will need a minimum of one on each side of your building and more if the sides of the building exceed 50 feet. Be sure the outlets are on a separate circuit (or separate circuits), so they can all be turned off when outdoor work is not taking place. Never tie outlets into adjacent indoor circuits. Weather-proof outlet covers are available, but being able to shut everything off is a lot better.

If you plan any sort of outdoor events, you may need vastly more outdoor wiring. Work with your architects and engineers.

[Right] Where electrical outlets are insufficient, the result can be flimsy and unattractive power poles, as seen in the center of this picture. (The lighting system visible in the ceiling of this room is spectacularly awful. See chapter 31, "Lighting.".)

[Below] Electrical outlets in the middle of floors need to be sufficiently flush with the floor to allow furniture to be placed on the outlet covers when outlets are not in use, and to prevent people from tripping over the outlets.

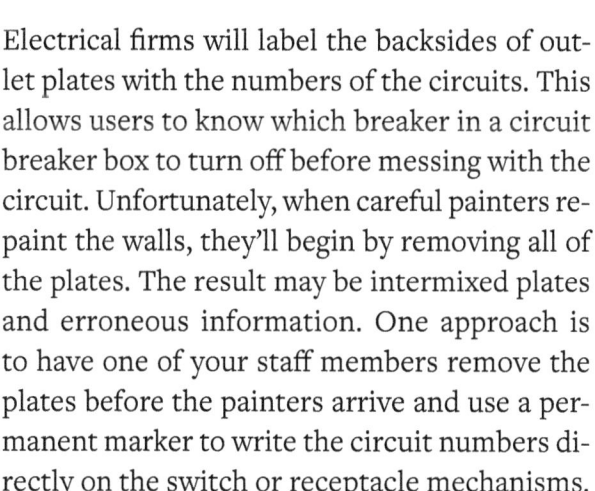

Electrical firms will label the backsides of outlet plates with the numbers of the circuits. This allows users to know which breaker in a circuit breaker box to turn off before messing with the circuit. Unfortunately, when careful painters repaint the walls, they'll begin by removing all of the plates. The result may be intermixed plates and erroneous information. One approach is to have one of your staff members remove the plates before the painters arrive and use a permanent marker to write the circuit numbers directly on the switch or receptacle mechanisms.

II-E. ELECTRICAL SWITCHES

Rooms that house the electrical switching gear for libraries are often called "panel rooms," which take their name from the electrical panels that house groups of circuit breakers. In very small libraries, electrical panels may be located in back rooms that house other functions, such as HVAC equipment or storage.

As with other MEP areas, the points included here deal mainly with errors that libraries encounter.

- One of the first rules of switch placement is to never put switches where users can mess about with them. (Unless you want users to mess about with the switches, such as the switches in program and meeting rooms and in study rooms and in faculty studies.)

- The easy place to put light switches for reading rooms is in a nearby office or staff corridor. Switches also work well behind service desks, but there's always a chance you'll relocate the desk someday and leave the switches alone and vulnerable.

- Key switches are available for use in situations where switches cannot be placed in areas limited to staff and you don't want users playing with switches. The "key" is usually just a flat strip of steel with a forked end that fits around a block in the switch.

- If you plan to use any of your circuit breakers as switches, be sure they're "switch rated." Or they'll break.

> Using circuit breakers in power panels as light switches is a seriously bad idea anyway. Some cities may require a union electrician to operate switches that are located in power panels, and you can't afford that. (Fred worked in a library set up this way, and he suspects that the electricians who shambled out of the basement at closing time were paid more than the department heads.)

- Motion-detector switches need to be in places where they can detect motion. The places where the light switches for rooms might be located are often not very workable. You will want to specify that the switches be operated by the motion of the entry door and NOT force people to grope their way into dark rooms.

- Unfortunately, in many situations in modern buildings, users have to grope their way into dark rooms. Remarks like "The triumph of energy codes over common sense and decency" occur to one.

II-F. EMERGENCIES

Things can occasionally go crazy electrically. One of the two feeds on two-phase wiring (not covered in this book) may be lost. Or seriously weird things may start happening.

The best thing to do may be to shut everything off, evacuate the building, and call for help.

> Calling for help can take time. Fred's library once had the power feed to the main electrical panels short out in an area accessible only to the power company. The fire chief arrived in about 30 seconds. The trucks were there in two minutes. The library staff evacuated the library building in two minutes (thanks to lots of previous rehearsals with the Urbana fire department). And the power company (necessary to disconnect the power supplies) took 45 minutes to turn up, while everyone stood outside and listened to the crashing and banging of short circuits.

III. Snappy Rules on Electrical Systems

1. The most important place for childproof (tamper-resistant) electrical outlets is in public library adult departments, because that's where parents hand their keys to their children to play with while the parents are occupied.

2. There's no such thing as too many electrical circuits in kitchenettes.

3. Fire marshals fear extension cords with good reason. If you have lots of extension cords, you will in turn learn to fear fire marshals. Have enough electrical outlets, and if you must buy extension cords, always buy heavy-duty three-conductor extension cords with circuit breakers.

4. Any section of wall located between two doors that is large enough for anything

that anyone might ever want to plug in can be placed there needs an electrical outlet.

5. When your architects ask you where you will be placing computers, always answer, "Anywhere we want." (But don't be surprised at the cost.)

6. Outlets around the walls and on the columns are never enough. Every library needs floor outlets.

7. Floor outlets that stick up are a pain. People trip over them, and they prevent you from putting furniture just where you want it.

8. Wall-mounted computer counters with outlets at the back force users to sit with their backs to the room. Lots of users don't like this much.

9. The easy way to add extra wiring to historic buildings is with wire mold or surface-mounted conduit. It's also the excessively ugly way, and one owners, librarians, and architects should be ashamed of.

10. The trickier your electrical gadgetry, the sooner it will fail in use and the more you will need to budget for repairs. Ordinary switches can last for many decades, but automatic ones probably won't.

11. Adding an extra outlet to a slab-on-grade floor is an adventure in spending money. You may even have trouble finding anyone willing to do the work. Specify enough outlets when you are planning your building, and check the construction drawings to be sure the outlets are actually there.

12. The "UL" labels on electrical gadgets mean that they have been tested and approved by the Underwriters' Laboratories, which are operated by the insurance industry. UL labels are not required by law, but many private concerns demand them.

13. The only fiscally responsible way to build a library is to include all the required circuits and conduits and outlets and switches on opening day. "We can add them later" is not a sign of fiscally clear thinking.

PART IV
Technical Issues

CHAPTER 33

HVAC

I. Introduction

HVAC is short for "heating, ventilating, and air conditioning." But no one involved in the industry ever says "heating, ventilating, and air conditioning." Saying "heating, ventilating, and air conditioning" takes too long, and when you deal with people in the field they'll get bored long before you finish. They just say "HVAC," pronounced "h-vac." So this chapter does too.

As librarians, we expect a lot from our HVAC systems: safe, comfortable, and habitable buildings. To meet this expectation, the system must:

- **Control temperature.** This frequently includes situations where some areas of a building (or even separate areas of single, large rooms) need to be heated while other areas need to be cooled at the same time, or where some areas need immediate and rapid cooling when hordes of users crowd abruptly into small meeting rooms.

- **Control relative humidity.** "Relative humidity" is the amount of moisture air contains compared to the maximum amount it can contain at that temperature. Warmer air can contain more moisture than colder air, so with a given amount of moisture in the air, raising the temperature lowers the relative humidity. Humidity control is essential for personal comfort, and it's extremely important for preserving books in research collections. All libraries need to avoid extremes. Public and school libraries may be satisfied with limiting relative humidity to something between 30 and 50 percent, but research libraries may need to limit humidity to extremely tight ranges.

- **Control the amount of carbon dioxide (CO_2) in the air.** Minor changes in CO_2 levels can make everyone feel uncomfortable or drowsy or short of fresh air. Crowded rooms with bad ventilation are often awash in excess CO_2.

- **Clean the air.** This includes removing unwanted particles (such as dust and pollen) and pathogens (such as molds, viruses, and bacteria). In the age of COVID, this is a renewed concern.

- **Eliminate odors.** Think fish TV dinners in staff lunchrooms, inadequate ventilation

637

in poorly designed restrooms, spray glue in staff graphic artist workrooms, and seriously unbathed users pretty much anywhere.

How we deal with all of these challenges depends on the nature of the building, its contents, and the construction and operating budget.

Librarians are frequently unhappy with climate control in their buildings:

- One room in a library can always be too hot, while the room next door is always too cold.
- Lots of study rooms are so badly ventilated that they have to be aired out between users.
- Air conditioning equipment is horrendously expensive and can wear out after about 20 years.
- Refrigerants are frequently banned, with resulting expenses for anyone whose cooling system uses the banned refrigerants.
- Meeting rooms can be so slow to cool down that the sweaty crowd that attends a meeting leaves before the room is comfortable, and the buildup of CO_2 during the meeting can make everyone uncomfortable.
- When an HVAC system goes awry, the rare book room in a university library can have its humidity abruptly soar to such heights that the books begin developing mold.
- Under-slab air ducts tend to fill with water or dust, or even worse, wet dust, leaving libraries worrying about all sorts of pathogens that flourish in dark, wet environments and having to arrange to have ducts vacuumed or pumped out often.
- Systems can require nearly constant maintenance that is beyond the skills of the library's regular maintenance staff.
- Underfloor air plenums can bounce underfoot, creeping out library users and staff.
- The floor grills of underfloor air plenums and underfloor air ducts frequently make it impossible to rearrange furniture.
- New and exciting concepts can be abandoned by the HVAC profession almost before the ribbon is cut.

All of this can (and does) happen because heating, ventilating, and air conditioning (HVAC) systems are extremely complex and expensive. HVAC systems can represent perhaps 25 percent of the total construction cost of a new library building. Cutting costs can result in serious cuts in quality, so the decisions made about HVAC systems are of extreme importance and not suitable for postponement.

If we tried to be really thorough in covering HVAC systems, this section would be huge, and it would be completely out of date by the time the book appeared. The systems are constantly changing in response to rising expectations for energy efficiency, comfort, control, and ease of maintenance. Given all of this, we are going to stick to a few of the basics:

- ***HVAC systems are extremely expensive*** and require extensive input from engineers. Even if you have a very small library, the planning of HVAC systems will be (or should be) in the hands of professional engineers, to whom your architects will subcontract the work. Many engineering firms are serious heroes. Make sure that you meet your engineers and talk through the systems planned for your building.
- ***HVAC systems use a large amount of energy***. People sometimes worry about the cost of library lighting. It's significant, but it's minor compared with HVAC.

- *Controlling humidity is extremely important*, and HVAC systems that are weak in that area are completely unsuited for library use.

- *All HVAC systems operate in concert with the rest of the building*. This includes roof, walls, and windows that enclose the space being conditioned. The electrical systems and the HVAC systems are entirely intertwined.

- *HVAC system design is a balancing act*. Systems must balance comfort, control, reliability, cost to operate, ease of maintenance, and installation cost. Be involved in the decisions that go into determining this balance. It should be no surprise that the lower the installation cost, the lower the ability to control temperature, humidity, air quality, energy costs, or maintenance costs. Don't skimp here.

- *Energy conservation requirements are not going away*. Your engineers will have to deal with increasingly complex energy-saving code requirements that are incorporated into building codes. Some libraries pursue more stringent conservation and sustainability standards than others do. LEED certification or participation in some other sustainable building program may place additional requirements on the HVAC system.

- *Most aspects of the HVAC system are governed by building codes and standards*. Based on building use, number of occupants, and other factors, minimum (and in some cases maximum) limits are established to govern occupant health and comfort as well as energy consumption and preservation of various collections. You do not need to know the specifics, but don't hesitate to ask what codes and standards are being followed. Ask about the library-specific requirements. Inquire as to any flexibility or limitations in determining design temperature and humidity levels.

II. Basic HVAC Vocabulary

HVAC is probably the most complex technology described in this book, with a large technical vocabulary. Here are a few of the terms you are most likely to encounter. (If people use terms you don't understand, ALWAYS stop the conversation to ask them what they're talking about.)

- *Air handler*. An air handler, or air-handling unit (abbreviated AHU), is a device used to regulate and circulate air as part of an HVAC system. An air handler is usually a large metal box containing a fan (often called a "blower"), heating or cooling elements, filters, and dampers. Air handlers usually are part of ductwork ventilation systems that distribute conditioned air throughout the building and return it to the AHU.

- *Carbon dioxide*. Excess carbon dioxide in the air can make people extremely uncomfortable. This can easily happen in crowded meeting rooms that have inadequate HVAC.

- *Chiller*. A device that removes heat from a liquid.

- *Coal gas*. Carbon monoxide gas produced through partial burning of coal. Also called "stove gas." It's extremely poisonous and has been replaced by natural gas and other less dangerous gases.

- *Condenser*. A component in the basic refrigeration cycle that ejects or removes heat from the system. The condenser is on the hot side of an air conditioner or heat pump. Condensers are heat exchangers and can transfer heat to air or to an intermediate fluid (such as water or an aqueous solution of ethylene glycol) to carry heat to a distant sink, such as ground (earth sink), a body of water, or air (as with cooling towers).

- *Constant air volume* (**CAV**). A system designed to provide constant airflow. This term is applied to HVAC systems that have variable supply-air temperature but constant airflow rates. Most residential forced-air systems are small CAV systems with on/off control.

- *Cooling tunnel.* A tunnel carrying cold water to one of a group of buildings that share a central cooling source. The cold water acts as a refrigerant in each building.

- *Dehumidification.* Lowering the moisture content of air to maintain desired humidity levels. See also Humidification.

- *Filtration.* The use of filters to remove particles from the air.

- *Geothermal systems.* Heating systems that take advantage of the heat differences between the air temperature at the surface of the ground and the earth temperature below ground.

- *Heat pump.* A device that transfers heat from a colder area to a hotter area by using mechanical energy. In cooler months, a heat pump pulls heat from the cold outdoor air and transfers it indoors, and in warmer months it pulls heat out of indoor air to cool your home. It is essentially a furnace and air conditioner all in one.

- *Heating tunnel.* A tunnel with hot water piping that connects a group of buildings sharing a central heating system.

- *Humidification.* Raising the moisture content of air to maintain desired humidity levels. See also Dehumidification.

- *Plenum.* An enclosed space inside a building or other structure, used for airflow. "Plenum" often refers to the space between a dropped ceiling and the structural ceiling or between a raised floor and the hard floor. Wiring and piping within plenums must be specially rated. Many underfloor plenums bounce underfoot, and users and librarians dislike that intensely.

- *Refrigerant.* An HVAC system chemical that transmits temperatures by changing back and forth from a liquid to a gas. Leaked refrigerants can cause all sorts of atmospheric problems and are consequently heavily regulated. Specific refrigerants are frequently banned, with serious financial implications for those who own HVAC systems that use those refrigerants.

- *Relative humidity.* The amount of water in air compared with the amount air can hold at that temperature. Changing the temperature of air can therefore change the relative humidity level. Saving energy by letting air temperatures rise or fall when buildings are closed will affect relative humidity.

- *Respiratory diseases.* COVID-19, MERS, SARS, tuberculosis, asthma, allergies, influenza, and varieties of pneumonia caused by Legionella bacteria, which frequently grow in enclosed, wet, dark spaces, such as some flooded under-slab air ducts.

- *Split system.* The combination of an outdoor unit and an indoor unit. This is the most common type of HVAC system.

- *Ultra Violet Germicidal Irradiation* (**UVGI**). The use of ultraviolet light for disinfection of water or air. UV systems work better with water than air because airborne particles can shield microorganisms within them. Direct exposure to UV radiation can be extremely dangerous to people, and the systems need to be very carefully shielded.

- *Under Floor Air Distribution* (**UFAD**). Air distribution in ducts under slabs or in underfloor air plenums. Libraries frequently report troubles with UFAD systems due to water collecting in air ducts and to floor grills that limit furniture locations.
- *Variable air volume* (**VAV**). An HVAC system that has a stable supply-air temperature and varies the airflow rate to meet temperature requirements.

III. HVAC Basics

There are a number of ways of controlling temperature, humidity, and air quality in libraries. A typical HVAC system addresses four key needs: heating, cooling, ventilating, and control. Common to all of them is their role in consuming or managing the consumption of energy. Most energy sources are becoming more expensive and more regulated as part of regional and national environmental policy and local interest.

Because heating, cooling, ventilating, and energy consumption are so intertwined, the energy consumption aspects of HVAC design are discussed in section IV, "Energy Conservation."

III-A. HEATING

Heating is most often generated by burning a fuel to heat air (in a furnace) or a liquid (in a boiler). In most libraries, the heating occurs on site, but there are some academic libraries, special libraries, school libraries, and municipal libraries that are part of campus, city-wide, or even multifunction building networks with centralized heating and cooling plants.

If you visit a university heating plant, watch for the heating tunnels that extend underground across campus and house steam, hot water, and chilled water pipes. Fraternity members are notorious for earning demerits while exploring the alluring mysteries of utility tunnels.

III-B. COOLING

Cooling is almost always done via direct expansion of a refrigerant.

One common way of providing properly conditioned air includes first cooling the air to the point where water condenses out (about 55 degrees) and lowers relative humidity, then reheating to achieve the desired comfort level. (Getting rid of air conditioner condensate is important, since in even a modest-sized building, the condensate can run like a hose in midsummer.)

As with heating, cooling is most often done on-site, but medical, academic, and some municipal libraries may have access to centralized chilled water plants. This chilled water is piped to the library equipment and replaces the need for a chemical refrigerant in the cooling coil.

III-C. VENTILATING

Ventilation involves moving fresh air into spaces and removing contaminated air. This circulation of fresh air is scaled to the number of occupants in the space, what they are doing (how active they are), and the amount of heating or cooling the conveyed air needs to accomplish. The fresh air is typically supplied via ducts and returned through air ducts or plenums. Air ducts can take up a lot of space, which can be a problem when libraries try to air condition older buildings.

III-C-1. Ducted Systems

Air ducts handle airflow through buildings. Larger ducts are rigid and usually made from galvanized sheet steel or aluminum. Flexible ducts (flex) are typically made of flexible plastic over a metal wire coil shaped like a tube.

Because air ducts take a lot of space, owners, architects, and engineers can be tempted to make a variety of mistakes.

- Undersized ducts. There are efficient dimensions for air ducts. If you try to save space by using undersized ducts, you're likely to have the happy sound of rushing air permeating your library.

- Oddly proportioned ducts. One of the major challenges in modernizing old library buildings is finding places in which to install air ducts. Preserving the form of the building can lead to oddly shaped ducts that constrain airflow, make noise, and interfere with light fixture and sprinkler head layout.

Retrofitting modern HVAC systems to historic libraries can be tricky because there may not be any space for air ducts. Before you make final decisions about acquiring or remodeling old buildings, talk extensively with your architects and engineers. See section VII of this chapter.

- Low ceiling heights and soffits. One bad side effect of overly low ceilings is air ducts enclosed in soffits dangling too close to the floor. Libraries need space above suspended ceilings for properly concealed air ducts.

- Underfloor ducts. As mentioned above, beware of underfloor air ducts, which can flood or lead to floor gratings that prevent furniture rearrangement.

III-C-2. Plenum Systems

Instead of using air ducts, some HVAC systems use plenums, which are open spaces above a ceiling or below a floor through which heated or cooled air flows everywhere rather than being limited by ductwork. The air moves between the plenum and the occupied spaces of the building through grills.

Plenums are a very common means of returning air from occupied spaces to an air-handling unit.

Wiring that runs loose through plenums needs to be "plenum rated." This used to be a lot more expansive than regular wire, but things aren't as bad as they used to be. There will be a lot of it (phones, data, and other low-voltage systems) and all of it must have insulation that has low-smoke and low-flame characteristics. In small buildings, plenums extend throughout the building, and any smoke developed in the plenum can go everywhere. In large buildings, codes require plenums to be partitioned into smaller sections to limit the risk of fire or smoke spread into other spaces.

Be very wary of underfloor plenums.

III-C-3. Natural Ventilation

Libraries are sometimes tempted to save energy by simply opening up buildings when the air is cool outside, saving money and enjoying the pleasant evening air.

Having a few windows that can be opened will help if your HVAC system fails and you have an emergency need for fresh air. However, open windows cause all sorts of problems with dust and humidity. They can also throw HVAC systems off balance. And a favorite way of stealing books from libraries with security systems is to drop the books out of windows into the shrubbery below. You never want windows that users can open, and you may have to give your staff stern warnings against "just opening a window." Locks on the inside are useful.

Your building program may have to stress the reasons for locking windows from both inside and outside the building, because some readers won't understand the need for inside locks.

If you've never spent time in a library without air conditioning and with low reading room ceilings in midsummer with the windows wide open and fans blowing everywhere, you have no idea how thick the air can feel and how much airborne dirt and crud can accumulate on the seats of chairs and the tops of books.

Some people call this "free air conditioning," but that seems to stretch the meaning of "free."

III-D. FILTRATION

This brings us to filtration. First, let's talk about what is in that airborne crud.

III-D-1. Contaminants and Pathogens

As this book is updated, there is renewed concern over the multiple variations of the SARS-Corona Virus-19 virus and how best to protect against transmission. We need to acknowledge that we are not experts regarding diseases, nor are we medical professionals or experts in public health or hygiene. We rely on the recommendations, guidelines, and regulations of a range of local, state, national, and international public health officials. The guidance changes as more is known about COVID, and this is true of any well-established or emerging pathogen.

The general rule appears to be that good airflow and good air filtration can help, but that they cannot completely solve problems.

III-D-2. Filters

Most systems rely on centralized filtration. The filters installed can vary in their effectiveness. The most common measure of effectiveness is the MERV rating. MERV stands for "Minimum Efficiency Reporting Value." Filters with higher ratings remove a larger percentage and broader range of crud from the air.

The higher the MERV rating the greater the airflow resistance. Buildings have to be designed to cope with this. A good library system is likely to have either MERV 9-12 or MERV 13-16 filters. Higher-level filters are usually found in healthcare areas or laboratories.

Regardless of size or rating, there are two things to keep in mind about all filters. First, keep filters clean. Change them at least four times per year, more often if you are in areas with poor air quality (think wildfires or smog). And second, no filter is of use if the edges are not tightly sealed. A lower-rated filter with a tight seal and good airflow rate may be more effective than a higher-rated filter with perimeter gaps and low airflow.

III-D-3. Protection against Diseases

Some people have discussed using ultraviolet light (UV-C) for disinfecting air. This is an area with possibilities and serious challenges. We started to include a section of this chapter on this topic, but we found so many cautions and details, including advanced air-handling equipment and the health risks of badly controlled radiation, that we finally decided to recommend you discuss the issues with your architects and engineers.

III-E. CONTROLS

Getting all of this to work together can be daunting. Even small buildings quickly outgrow a residential style approach to controls.

III-E-1. Zoning

Zoning involves providing separate temperature control for different areas of a library, allowing equipment to provide heat for one area of a building while simultaneously providing cooling for another. It may involve heating the side of a building that faces away from the sun while simultaneously cooling another side that faces the sun. Or it may involve providing a great deal of extra cooling and fresh air when a large number of people abruptly crowd into a meeting room.

The best number of rooms controlled by a thermostat is one. If you use one thermostat for two separate rooms, one of the rooms will probably be miserable to occupy.

If library users and staff can play with thermostats, they will. To prevent this, you can have locking thermostats or set thermostats remotely from your desktop. Or you can install locking transparent plastic boxes that enclose thermostats. The boxes have vent holes that allow the thermostats to sense the temperature in the room but prevent passersby from changing settings. In tricky situations where you can't control thermostats centrally, use key-operated thermostats.

Some systems forgo local control in favor of a centralized control. Target conditions for each room or zone are set electronically in a central

> In Fred's library, two staff members who shared a workroom had no temperature they both liked. The moment one left the room, the other changed the thermostat setting. Eventually they wore out the pneumatic thermostat. In desperation, Fred had a key-operated thermostat installed and kept the key in his desk. He offered to change the setting whenever they asked, but his staff were embarrassed to call him every 20 minutes, and all was well.

computer. Getting things set up right takes skill and time. It is the focus of the commissioning process described in chapter 15, "Construction," and in the section "Operations and Maintenance," located later in this chapter.

Much like thermostats in the decentralized approach to controls, you don't want everyone having access to the control system. Passwords should be guarded and given out to a limited number of trained, trusted individuals. Some (again, at least two) of those individuals should be on staff. Libraries that have centralized control systems and can't control their own thermostats directly tell us that they're seriously unhappy with this situation.

III-E-2. Humidity Control

Humidity control is particularly important to libraries because books are hygroscopic (absorb water) and are subject to mildew and mold. For archival collections and for academic libraries—particularly rare book rooms—tight control of humidity is essential.

Because the amount of water air can hold depends on air temperature, a library that has a desirable relative humidity of 50 percent can approach mildew levels if the temperature is dropped too low.

- Humidification is much more complicated than dehumidification. If done incorrectly, it can lead to unwanted condensation on interior surfaces. New buildings can be constructed to be compatible with humidification, but if you are considering converting an older building that will require humidification, be sure to check with engineers before buying the building or mentioning your plans in public.

- With either new or existing buildings, check the quality of the water in the area. Hard water is rough on humidifiers. You may need filters or softeners to condition the water that goes through your humidifier. We know too many libraries that spent too much money on humidification systems, only to have them ruined by bad water after a few years of operation or turned off because of the costs of keeping them up and running.

- Talking "paybacks." Planners talk in terms of "paybacks" for upgrades to more energy-efficient systems. The idea is that the increased efficiency of a new system will pay for its greater upfront installation cost.

  The great danger is that the new system can be nearly worn out before you start coming out ahead. Talk with your engineers. Designers tell us that paybacks of over about four years are dangerous from a purely economic point of view.

  If you replace an HVAC system that is in good operating condition with a new and expensive energy-efficient system, the potential for bad investment is even worse.

- Public policy and the cost of energy. If your HVAC design presumes specific policies like lower electric rates at night, what will you do if rates flatten out?

- Paying to get energy-efficient systems. Grants may be available to cover the extra cost of using a more energy-efficient system.

IV. Energy Conservation

The entire field of energy conservation in HVAC systems is amazingly complex and constantly changing. Our main concern is the transitory nature of approaches to energy conservation. Equipment can age more rapidly than one might hope.

- Be honest in comparison. All sorts of energy-saving systems are available. When you are comparing various conventional and energy-efficient HVAC systems, be sure to compare the very best conventional systems with the energy-saving systems. Some comparisons load the dice by using obsolete conventional systems for comparison.

IV-A. STRATEGIES TO REDUCE ENERGY USE

IV-A-1. Building Enclosure Strategies

- Increased insulation. While there is a limit, most buildings will benefit from additional insulation. There is greater benefit to adding insulation of a roof than to a wall because it is typically the largest surface and it faces the night sky, radiating heat into space.

- Well-maintained sealants. It's not glamorous, but it's effective. Think of cracked or missing sealants as an open zipper in your insulated jacket.

- Reflective roofs. Some libraries have installed white roof membranes rather than the usual black membranes or built-up roofs. The idea is that white membranes will reflect sunlight and help keep the building cooler. The warmer your climate (think south) the more this is true. The cooler your climate (think north) this may be counterproductive, because you miss out on the warming provided by sunlight on a black roof.

IV-A-2. Passive Ventilation and Cooling Strategies

Passive ventilation and cooling are often interrelated. They are the process of supplying air to and removing air from an indoor space without using mechanical systems, ideally in a way that improves thermal comfort. Natural ventilation in buildings is of two types.

- Cross ventilation. The strategy of cross ventilation relies on wind to pass through the building for the purpose of cooling the occupants.

- Stack ventilation. This strategy relies on the buoyancy of warm air to rise and exit through openings located at ceiling height. Cooler outside air replaces the rising warm air through carefully designed inlets placed near the floor. This buoyancy-driven ventilation/cooling is more reliable than wind-driven ventilation.

- Earth coupling. Direct earth coupling or earth sheltering occurs when a building uses earth as an insulating buffer for the walls, and occasionally the roof. The earth buffers the building from temperature extremes. The earth effectively provides insulation and limits infiltration.

IV-B. ALTERNATIVE ENERGY SOURCES

The majority of public libraries have stand-alone HVAC systems operated by a local utility or take advantage of some on-site alternative energy source such as wind, solar, or geothermal energy.

For all libraries, initial planning includes making sure that possible building sites have easy access to electric power, natural gas, and other necessary utilities.

IV-B-1. Ground Source Heat Pumps (GSHP)

Often and widely referred to as "geothermal heat pumps," this is a heating and cooling system that uses a heat pump to transfer heat to or from the earth. They can be much more energy efficient for HVAC and water heating than are electric or gas-fired devices, but they are more expensive to install. In addition, if the GSHP system can't keep up with the hottest and coldest days, you may need a source of supplemental heat or cooling. Libraries need to locate the "wells" where they are accessible in case repairs are needed.

IV-B-2. Photovoltaic Systems

Photovoltaic systems are popularly known as solar panels. The efficiency of these systems varies with temperature, altitude, latitude, orientation to the sun, tilt of the panels, cloud cover, and soiling, as well as the efficiency of the photocells and the area covered by the solar modules. Some systems are standalone, while others depend on supplementary electrical power.

Most standalone installations use battery technology to store electricity for demand during off-peak production.

The workability of solar power systems depends on the age of the panels. At the time this was written, cells lasted up to 30 years.

Our best advice is to plan for options. Consider whether making provisions to support solar panels on roofs and configuring electrical switch gear to shift between on-site and utility-provided energy makes sense. Monitor advances in technology related to output and lifespan. Consider tax incentives, rebates, or other inducements offered by utilities and government agencies to offset construction, operation, and replacement costs.

IV-C. GREEN BUILDING CERTIFICATION

There are a number of organizations that encourage and support sustainability throughout the construction and operation of buildings and neighborhoods. Their approaches and scopes differ. Some are focused on energy conservation alone, while others look at broader ranges of issues, often including water resource management and indoor air quality.

One is the LEED rating system (Leadership in Energy and Environmental Design) from the United States Green Buildings Council (USGBC). Although nongovernmental, the LEED program is referenced or incorporated into the building requirements of many jurisdictions. The LEED system awards points for various building attributes, with levels of compliance resulting in various levels of recognition.

The LEED system differs greatly from some building codes and aligns well with others. While codes describe standard solutions, the LEED system gives points for following current year ideas. As a result, following LEED can mean very little when it comes to long-term energy saving solutions. If you design a building for this year's points but don't build it for a few years, the points may no longer exist.

Rather than seek certification, many libraries use the system as a guide to issues that should be considered during the design, construction, and operation of facilities. And avoid the silly frustration of "chasing points."

V. Considerations of Function

V-A. "TYPICAL" LIBRARIES

In most libraries, and certainly in new or newly renovated buildings, the HVAC system will be by far the most complex and expensive system in the library, 25 percent or more of the overall cost of construction. There are a few basic points that apply to almost all libraries:

- ***HVAC equipment wears out.*** In fact, it can have a relatively short life. While ductwork and radiators can last for many years, the expected lifespan of HVAC machinery—furnaces, chillers, and so on—can be about 20 years. (Maybe 30 years if you buy high-end equipment and luck out.) This is one reason why remodeling an existing library or converting an old building to a library may cost a lot more than you expect.

- ***Systems need to be commissioned.*** When your new building is complete, hire an independent HVAC specialist (often called a "commissioning agent") to "commission" your equipment. It's far too complicated for anyone to evaluate by simply walking through the building or just noting that it "feels okay" today.

  The commissioning process is more than an inventory of parts. The system is run through startup, shutdown, emergency shutdown, and other procedures. This testing should occur in both the heating and cooling seasons if you are fortunate to live in such a delightful climate. Remember that the commissioning agent should (OR MUST?) be independent; not the installer, not the general contractor or one of their subcontractors, and not the design engineer. All three will balk and claim they can do this objectively (and some can) but unless you know, why risk it?

If you are not convinced of the merits of commissioning, you may have to do at anyway, since many building and energy conservation codes require some form of basic conditioning.

- **Get trained on how to operate your system.** As part of transferring control of your HVAC system to your library at the end of construction, the engineers and installers are supposed to provide full operating information and training.

Get everything in print, including copies of all equipment manuals, as-built drawings, and (most importantly) equipment warranties.

Anything explained or demonstrated in person needs to be saved as a video.

If you have in-house facilities people, have them attend these sessions.

The requirement for this training should not be a fixed number of hours but rather successful demonstration that the people being trained understand the systems and their operation. Yes: this means a test! Seriously, a passing score of 80 percent on a proficiency exam by your staff is a clear indicator of the quality of training they are getting.

- **Engage a professional service provider.** Try to have a year of service built into the construction contract or have your service provider present during this training. Having a service provider and the installer both present with the commissioning agent will undoubtedly be uncomfortable—but who cares?

V-B. RARE BOOKS AND ARCHIVES

There is much that can be written about the HVAC requirements of archives and rare book rooms—much more than we can include here. Suffice it to say that both have more stringent requirements that emphasize preservation of materials over the usual balance of preservation and human comfort.

The preservation of materials piece of that equation depends on the stability of temperature and humidity, with humidity being the key for most materials. Specific temperature limits are more often established to arrive at and maintain the necessary humidity level.

Ideal book storage temperatures are cooler than ideal user temperatures, and book storage areas may be kept as much as 20° F cooler than reading rooms.

Requirements vary by the type of material. Metals, cellulose acetate films, fabrics, leather and vellum bindings, and paper have differing requirements. If you hold various types of materials, you may need separate storage environments.

Most library archives attempt some balance between preservation and access. This typically involves a transitional space between the general areas of the building and the rigorously controlled archival and rare book storage spaces. These transitional spaces maintain the physical security and integrity of materials with controlled access and environmental isolation. Although these are most often room-sized spaces that serve as workspaces for staff and for researchers, they function as "airlocks," buffering the highly controlled environments inside the rare book and archives areas from the rest of the building and providing a balance of protection for the collection and comfort for occupants.

Even in these instances, libraries worry about the effects on books of moving them quickly to warmer areas, since moisture can condense on cold books as it does on cold beverage glasses. When the temperature differential between book storage areas and reading areas is very large, books may have to be allowed to warm up safely to prevent condensation.

V-C. CAMPUS BUILDINGS

Most public libraries probably have standalone HVAC systems, while many academic libraries and some medical or municipal libraries are part of campus-wide networks, including centralized heating plants. Central heating and/or chilling plants provide efficient use of energy for multiple buildings that comprise campuses. The specific library-related components of building HVAC systems must be compatible with the central plants, be accessible (ideally via tunnel networks for easy maintenance), and fit within the capacity of the central services. Control systems are also standardized across campuses to support servicing of the campus buildings. All of this usually comes with the planning, operational, and maintenance support of campus planning/facilities teams.

All of this is great, but libraries are more complex than typical campus buildings and need to be thought of in those terms. Because of the heavy use, specialized collection preservation, security requirements, and pervasive technology demands, there are added burdens on HVAC, electrical, security, and technology systems. Along with athletic facilities and laboratories, libraries need special planning attention. If your campus thinks of the library as just another space in just another building, beware!

VI. Common HVAC Systems

So with all this, what might you come across in the process of constructing or renovating a building? We've outlined a few of the more common systems, why you might be interested in them, and what concerns should be discussed in your evaluations with your engineers.

VI-A. UNITARY SYSTEMS

Rooftop units (RTUs) are very popular all-in-one heating and air conditioning systems. They are simple and compact, often referred to as "package units" because the complete HVAC unit is found all in one self-contained system. RTUs are regularly used on the rooftops of retail and small commercial and institutional buildings. They provide conditioned air to designated areas via building air ducts.

RTUs are typically low cost, with simple construction and maintenance. They don't take up any internal floor space, and they can be repaired or replaced from outside the building.

The disadvantages of RTUs include potentially shorter lifespans, delayed maintenance and upkeep because RTUs are out of sight, exposure to storm damage resulting from lightning or other weather damage, and difficulty servicing the units during inclement weather. You need to be rigorous in protecting roof surfaces from wear and from accidental damage by maintenance operations. Many roof warranties require rigorous documentation of access to the roof and frequent inspections to prevent damage from tools, supplies, and foot traffic.

VI-B. SPLIT SYSTEMS

As the name suggests, these systems consist of components in multiple locations. Typically, some sort of heat-rejecting piece of equipment (a chiller or condenser) is located outside the building while the heating and ventilating equipment is mounted inside the building. Pumps move refrigerants through insulated pipes connecting the exterior equipment to that located inside the building.

Constant air volume (CAV) systems use variable air temperature and constant airflow, while Variable Air Volume (VAV) systems keep constant temperature and variable airflow. CAV systems are better suited for single-zone applications where the load experiences little change, while VAV systems are the best option for multi-zone applications with constantly changing loads.

Split systems include Variable Refrigerant Flow (VFR) systems, which offer easier heating and cooling of individual rooms, particularly when there are historic low ceilings. But they can cost more to install and maintain. And they may not provide adequate humidity control.

VII. Old Libraries

In the days before air conditioning, libraries were usually heated by radiators, using either hot water or steam. Steam heat can be noisy. Steam-heated radiators have a single combined feed pipe and condensate return pipe. If you do not bleed air from the system, the radiators can clank a lot. By contrast, hot water radiators have two pipes and are a lot more acoustically subtle.

In some libraries, the means of heating shifted to a furnace supplying warm air to the occupied spaces. These early systems still did not have air conditioning. The small scale and simplicity of these units did a poor job of removing moisture from the air. Given the requirements for ventilated restrooms and meeting rooms, the amount of fresh air brought into the building could quickly drive humidity levels to uncomfortable and damaging levels.

As a result, many older libraries equipped with radiators or residential-style furnaces tried to introduce cooling by installing window air conditioners, which are inefficient users of power, noisy, and drip water as it condenses out of the air. On the plus side, they don't require air ducts.

Adding "real" air conditioning can be difficult, in part because there is typically no space to add ductwork. Care is required to preserve the look and character of an old building while providing comfort for occupants and a stable environment for collections.

Integrating modern cooling or humidification into old buildings has other challenges.

- Air conditioning makes the indoor air less humid as it makes it cooler. The water vapor in warm, outside air will try to move through the wall. At some point, usually the worst point, the vapor condenses and becomes liquid water within the wall.

- Adding humidification makes the building comfortable in winter, but humidification drives water vapor into the exterior walls from the inside, where it finds a place to condense into liquid water.

Because older buildings were not designed to get rid of this water, as a result the water can become a real problem, either by supporting growth of molds, mildew, and other "biologics" or by freezing, first cracking and then pushing the building components apart,

Newer buildings have materials and air gaps designed to slow the movement of water vapor into walls and to let the water that does condense in the wall find a way out rather than sitting within the wall assembly.

Adding modern HVAC systems to historic buildings is very complex. In the most extreme situations, architects may need to construct separate modern buildings inside historic buildings.

VIII. Operations and Maintenance

Operating HVAC systems is a complex undertaking. Here are just a few suggestions.

- Always know how to shut off your HVAC system. Sometimes you will be in a serious hurry. For instance, at times when dangerous gases are being drawn into your air intakes. Even if you have a facilities person or team, they are not always in the building.

> In Fred's library, a crew digging up a nearby street severed a gas pipe. The escaping gas rose happily into the air and was sucked into the library's air intakes. The staff had to immediately shut down the entire HVAC system, evacuate the building, and call the fire department. The moral is that staff need to know how to shut things down.

- Be diligent about maintenance. Annual and seasonal checks, tune-ups, and cleaning can extend the life of your system, protect occupant health, and keep costs down.

- Malfunctioning components put extra stress on the heating or cooling system. This is compounded by normal wear and tear and drastically reduces the life of your commercial HVAC unit by 8 to 15 years, depending on the type and quality of your equipment.

- Poor indoor air quality is especially bad for public buildings. People expect them to be healthy spaces.

- Preventative commercial grade HVAC maintenance can lower energy costs. The savings can range from 5 to 40 percent. Poor maintenance not only shortens the lifespans of equipment but leads to it working harder to accomplish its purpose.

- Don't wait until you have a problem to do maintenance.

- Have a maintenance schedule and follow it. Some things can be done by library staff, but others require outside expertise. A typical list should include:

  » Monitor for noises or smells.

  » Check thermostat settings and operations piping for corrosion leaks, and check seals for leaks.

  » Inspect wires and other electronic equipment, air ducts, and insulation.

  » Clean all components inside and out, with special attention to sumps, pans, and drains, as well as cabinets, gauges, switches, sensors, registers, and intakes.

  » Replace air filters.

- » Compare heating and cooling bills from previous years. Check quantities used, not prices.
- » Schedule professional maintenance.

IX. Snappy Rules on HVAC Systems

1. All occupied study rooms and staff workrooms need individual sensors. If two rooms share one sensor, the people in the room without the thermostat will almost certainly be very unhappy.

2. Modern HVAC equipment offers all sorts of tamper-resistant thermostats. You will like these.

3. If you buy a building with propane heating to convert to a library, it helps if you live in the Very Deep South or have a bizarrely large endowment. Natural gas is inexpensive, but propane is very much otherwise. People use propane because there's no natural gas available, not because propane has any special virtues of its own. If you have to choose between a site with natural gas and one that requires propane, the propane site needs to have a lot of compensating strengths.

4. If you install an energy-efficient system that takes advantage of lower nighttime costs rates for electric power, what will happen if lower nighttime rates are discontinued?

5. The amazingly complicated demands of modern HVAC systems are one of the many reasons to NEVER make any promises regarding modernizing an existing building without previous input from your architects and engineers.

6. Among the vast number of problems modernizing historic library buildings is finding space for HVAC ductwork, air handlers, and heating and refrigeration equipment, all of which are amazingly larger than old-time radiators and window air conditioners.

7. Unless you have the right kind of plenum system above grade level and with space to crawl inside it, all of the best ducts are overhead. Underground ducts and plenums can fill with water, facilitating Legionnaires' disease and needing to be pumped out. Immoveable grills in the floor can make necessary furniture placement or rearrangement nearly impossible. Unless there's space for overhead ducts on every floor of your building or two or three feet of surplus ceiling height to allow a plenum people can crawl through, pick a different building.

8. Existing air ducts under concrete floors can turn out to be lined with asbestos board. Know what you're getting into before you make any commitments to a building with under-slab air ducts. Tearing up an entire poured concrete floor to replace the ductwork may not cost as much as constructing an entirely new building, but it may come impressively close.

9. Opening the doors and windows in libraries can totally screw up HVAC systems, especially in library buildings larger than tract houses. Limit the opportunity to people in charge.

10. People trying to unload white elephant buildings may angrily deny what replacement HVAC systems can actually cost.

11. Some HVAC system installations result in all sorts of unsightly and surprisingly large equipment blossoming on the roofs

of beloved historic library buildings. But putting as much equipment as possible indoors can take a lot of space that could otherwise be used for library purposes. Move with caution.

12. One of the useful strengths provided by a reasonable command of HVAC terminology is that when you raise a question and the people involved in your building project say, "Don't you bother your little head about it," you can demonstrate your strength of vocabulary right before you deck them.

PART IV
Technical Issues

CHAPTER 34

Plumbing Systems

I. Introduction

I-A. ABOUT LIBRARY PLUMBING

By and large, libraries are not huge water users. We use water for restrooms, kitchenettes, technical services, handwashing, and fire sprinkler systems. The biggest demand for water can come from fire sprinkler systems, but even when they are activated they seldom operate at full capacity because sprinkler heads go off only where there's fire.

Libraries also cope with excess incoming water, particularly runoff from rain. And sometimes flooding.

If we make mistakes, they tend to lie in the direction of too few sources of water and bad preparation for flooding, both from rain and from plumbing run amok.

The majority of public libraries probably have standalone plumbing systems, while many academic libraries are part of campus-wide networks. For public libraries, planning includes making sure that possible sites have easy access to water supplies, sanitary sewers and storm sewers, or some other form of stormwater management, such as detention and retention ponds.

Along with quick reviews of basic points about plumbing, the chapter includes a number of issues that have caused libraries grief in the past.

Plumbing is a complex subject. When it comes to programming and designing your library, you'll mainly want to know how to discuss with your team the features you want and the features you definitely don't want. And you will rely on your campus architects, city authorities, and your own architects and engineers to make sure things are done correctly. The engineering team will include a civil engineer, a plumbing engineer, and a fire protection engineer.

On a daily basis, you mainly need to know what to do until the plumber arrives. This includes knowing how to turn off the entire water supply, how to turn off individual devices (such as faucets and toilets), how to cut the water to your sprinkler system when a sprinkler head fails and water is cascading all over everything, and how to cope with other wet emergencies.

> Most individual devices like sinks and toilets have small valves below their water inputs. To turn off a flush valve toilet that won't stop running, turn the attractive pipe cap facing you counterclockwise to remove it (don't scratch it), then use a large, flat-bladed screwdriver to tighten the valve (clockwise) under the cap. (Usually a plumber can rescue you quickly, but sometimes running water means chaos, and you can save the day.)

This chapter covers some aspects of plumbing systems that are not covered in other chapters. In addition to this chapter, see in particular chapter 9, "Site Selection"; chapter 24, "Program, Activity, and Study Rooms"; chapter 26, "Restrooms"; chapter 28, "Staff Facilities"; and chapter 35, "Security" (for fire-suppression systems).

I-B. VOCABULARY

- ***Domestic water.*** The "everyday" water used in a library—drinking water, handwashing, flushing toilets, cleaning, and so on. Any water not used for fire protection or irrigation is usually considered domestic water.

- ***Ejector pit.*** A reservoir that collects water (stormwater or wastewater) from areas that are below the levels of a building's outgoing sewer lines. The pits have pumps that pump the contents of the pits up to the outgoing piping and by this means "eject" them from the building. Ejector pits are common and need a couple of protections, including a redundant pump (in case one fails) and an alarm (if the level of water in the pit exceeds the level at which the pumps should run).

- ***Internal roof drain.*** A drain for removing rainwater and cleaning water from a roof. The alternative is having it run over the edges of the roof, hopefully into a gutter, and thence into a downspout. But in some instances, down the sides of the building. Good internal drains are paired with an overflow roof drain that drains water if the primary drain becomes clogged or blocked by debris.

- ***Irrigation.*** A system of applying water in a controlled manner to support the health of ground covers, shrubs, trees, and various other plantings.

- ***Insulation valve.*** A valve that stops the flow of fluids to a location without interrupting the flow to other locations on the same piping loop. (You have them under the kitchen sink and at the washing machine hook-ups.)

- ***Water room.*** A room in the library with valves for control of all of the library's incoming and outgoing water, including sprinkler systems.

- ***WC.*** A term used in many codes and plans to denote a toilet.

II. Water Supplies

II-A. WATER SERVICE

Incoming water service needs to be large enough to meet all of the building's needs. After entering the building, water is immediately split into specific uses—domestic, fire protection, irrigation—using valves. Each of these, as well as the incoming service, has some sort of backwater preventer to keep anything from working its way backward out of the building and contaminating the local water supply. There are distinct limits on how all of this can be arranged to avoid stagnant water that can breed contaminants and corrode piping. The space needs for all of this are surprisingly large, particularly because human beings need to be able to get at all of the valves quickly to operate them.

In small libraries, the valves can be in places like multifunction utility rooms, but larger libraries may have "water rooms" where all the valves are located.

II-B. DOMESTIC WATER

- Hot water heating. Hot water can be generated in centralized locations, much as in residential hot water heaters. This makes the system simple to service, easy to locate near a floor drain in case the water heater goes bad and spills its contents, and away from the public and most staff, who might choose ill-advised messing about with the system.

  The challenge is the distance between the hot water heater and the locations where you want to use the water. Workrooms, restrooms, lunchrooms, and program rooms can be far away from a central hot water heater. Insulating the hot water pipes and running a pump to keep the hot water circulating can reduce the time people have to wait for hot water where they need it.

  An alternative is remote water heaters located where people need hot water. So-called "electric resistance heaters" can quickly heat cold water where it's needed. These units need to be in spaces with floor drains, just in case…

- Water treatment. Many areas have water that can quickly damage piping or stain fixtures. Chemical treatment of the water can extend life expectancies and improve the "taste" of water. Have your water tested and talk with your engineers about the cost of installing, operating, and maintaining these treatment systems.

- Isolation valves. Anything attached to a pipe will need to be repaired or replaced one day. This is a lot easier and much less disruptive if the sink or urinal or toilet can be "isolated" from the rest of the system. This simply means that there are shutoff valves on either side of each fixture that when closed allow water to bypass that fixture and continue to supply other fixtures in the building. There is no need to drain the entire system to work on a particular fixture. When repair work is complete, the isolation valves are reopened and the fixture is restored to operational status. It is all too common to take these valves out to save a few dollars during construction.

II-C. FIRE PROTECTION

Fire-protection systems are required by building codes.

Medium and large buildings will want multiple zones in their systems, with each zone controlled by a valve so that work can be done on various floors or in different zones while the rest of the system remains operational.

Libraries with sprinkler systems need to train a large number of staff members on how to turn off the systems. If a sprinkler head fails and douses the library with water when there is no fire, the sooner the valves feeding the system are turned off, the less damage is done.

Libraries are at their most vulnerable when they are brand new and not enough people have yet been trained on shutting off the system. And buildings under construction are particularly vulnerable when workers are using torches and the sprinkler systems haven't yet been installed.

A variety of fire-protection methods are available, and specification and installation are specialized areas.

See chapter 35, "Security."

II-D. IRRIGATION AND MAINTENANCE WATER

II-D-1. Hose Bibs

Almost all libraries need external faucets (sometimes called hose bibs or sillcocks) for external access to water.

Hose bibs need to be freeze proof. A common way to do this is to have the valve for the hose bib inside the library where building heat will keep it from freezing. The external handles for hose bibs have long stems that reach inside the building to engage the actual valve.

Hose bibs also need to be vandal-proof. You don't want people messing with your water system. In some cases, the exterior control handles can simply be removed. Other handles lock.

To help prevent unauthorized use, all of the exterior hose bibs should be controlled by a valve inside the library. The valve (or valves, for a large building) should not affect any water access points inside the building, so that turning off the outside water does not limit any use of water inside the building.

Libraries need to work with their planners and grounds maintenance staff to determine the number of hose bibs needed. A minimum of one on each side of the building is necessary. After that, spacing is a matter of hose length. Hoses longer than about 50 feet are a pain to drag around, which means that hose bibs need to be less than about 75 feet apart, or even closer if water will be needed a long way from the building.

Rooftop water supplies are necessary to service rooftop mounted equipment and clean dirt from metal finishes. The mixture of dirt and rainwater in urban areas can create a mild acid that will eat away at metal finishes and stone copings. Keeping these surfaces clean will extend their lifespan.

Rooftop water supplies are also important for the maintenance of vegetated (green) roofs, which need watering during the first year. It's vastly easier if water is available nearby.

II-D-2. Irrigation Systems

Many communities regulate water use for landscaping purposes. Libraries typically look to limit water use for environmental and economic purposes because water is surprisingly expensive in some parts of the country. And many people are concerned that clean water is a limited resource. The selection of ground covers and other plantings will determine how much water is needed to maintain a healthy and attractive site. The selection of low or no-mow ground covers includes plants that need less watering, less mowing, and less fertilizing. Drought-tolerant and indigenous plantings will reduce the need for irrigation. If irrigation is needed to sustain the landscape, a system that controls time, duration, frequency, and volume of water distributed based on actual moisture content of the soil is essential. Various zones should be established so that plantings that need similar amounts of water are grouped together. Water should be supplied to the plants by emitters (drip lines or sprinkler heads) that focus water distribution where the plant can best take up the water.

III. Wastewater

Sanitary sewers carry away all sorts of indoor water from toilets, sinks, showers, bathtubs, dishwashers, clothes washers, and so on. Dealing with this "wastewater" is more often a more complex design issue than water supply. Using gravity as much as possible to move waste to the sanitary sewer or an ejector pit takes careful planning. Pipes need to slope at a sufficient rate to keep water flowing while still carrying solids. This requirement often leads to the waste line being the piece of hidden infrastructure that all other building systems need to work around. The exact route taken needs to be coordinated both during the planning of the building and by the contracting team as they nest the plumbing, HVAC, electrical, and other systems above the ceiling.

Existing sewers in brownfield sites can have a major influence on subsequent building designs.

Tapping into existing waste lines needs some investigation. Existing waste piping may not have the needed diameter to take the added load. It may not have sufficient slope to meet standards for positive drainage, and it may have corroded to the point where capacity and flow are reduced. In combination, low slope and internal corrosion can result in a need to add a new waste line or even replace the existing line.

For many rooms on the lowest floor of the building (ideally the first floor and not a basement) the waste lines are buried in the ground beneath the concrete floor slab. These lines need to slope, whether directly to the sanitary connection to local utilities or to an on-site storage and filtration system such as a septic field or septic tank. If all the piping is low enough, the waste may need to be collected in a waste pit and ejected by pumps up and then out to sewer or septic structures.

Whether you are expanding an existing library, converting another type of building, or acquiring a site with a previous use, it always seems that one or more of the utilities is in the wrong place for your needs. It's best to find this out early and budget accordingly. This is never more true than with sanitary lines, which are the most complicated to engineer and the most expensive to install or relocate. Good evaluation of existing conditions can head off a last-minute discovery of truly major costs.

A lot of things can go wrong. Primarily clogs and leaks. And leaks caused by clogs. Getting into waste piping is done through essential devices called "cleanouts," access points in the floor or wall where caps can be removed and various tools used to locate and remove blockages. Having lots of cleanouts is a good thing.

The sounds of water and other things running through waste piping are not pleasant. Locating these pipes behind insulated walls and acoustic ceilings helps maintain a welcoming ambience in a building. This is even a bigger deal in mixed-use buildings.

And remember one of the great favorite evils of library building design: staff toilets located directly next to staff lunchrooms. Watch your plans carefully, for the toilets turn up when you are least expecting them.

See chapter 18, "Shared Buildings"; chapter 24, "Program, Activity, and Study Rooms"; chapter 26, "Restrooms"; and chapter 28, "Staff Facilities," for details on waste line issues.

IV. Stormwater

Stormwater is one of the most regulated aspects of any project. Increases in storm events and concerns about the ability of antiquated infrastructures to handle large influxes of rain or meltwater, combined with concerns over the quality of water being returned to rivers and aquifers, mean that significant effort goes into managing the flow of surface water. As with water supply and wastewater, some of this is the domain of the civil engineer (where it is usually referred to as stormwater management) and includes anything outside the exterior walls of the building, and the plumbing engineer where it includes things like gutters and downspouts or interior roof drains.

The site portions of the overall system need extensive coordination with local utilities for connection to storm sewers or the development of on-site water management structures such as detention or retention basins. See also chapter 9, "Site Selection" (section II-D, "Surface Water Runoff Detention and Retention").

IV-A. STORM DRAINS

"Storm sewers" carry away surface runoff (including from roofs) and soil moisture. By contrast, "sanitary sewers" carry away all sorts of indoor water from toilets, sinks, showers and bathtubs, dish and clothes washers, and so on.

Not all towns have storm sewer systems. Small drainage ditches between streets and sidewalks are one of the warning signs of the absence of storm drains.

In a town with storm drains, sump pits embedded in basement floors collect water from under the floor slab of the basement and from the bottoms of window wells. As the sump fills with water, a float on the sump pump turns on the pump, which pumps water to the storm sewer outside. To prevent backflow, the highest point in the pipe between the sump pump and the storm sewer needs to be higher than the exterior storm drains. Codes may also require backwater valves in situations like this. If a gully washer leads to more water than the storm sewers can handle, the water backs up to exterior drains rather than to the library basement.

If a library has an open exterior staircase leading down to a basement door, the staircase needs a drain at the bottom. If the drain opening becomes clogged, rainwater coursing down the open staircase simply runs into the basement. The best way to avoid this problem is to have no basement. If you're stuck with a basement, enclosing the steps down to the basement door will help keep water from accumulating right outside the door.

Even worse, if the drain at the foot of the stairs is lower than the storm drain gratings on the street outside, stormwater will attempt to gush happily from the drain at the foot of the stairs. And flood the basement.

Many communities have found that careless construction led to numerous incorrect sewer connections, with sanitary drains leading to storm sewers and storm drains leading to sanitary sewers. Both of these errors lead to serious problems. Correcting them can be expensive and lead to angry confrontations between landowners and governments.

With crossed connections, during heavy rains, the rainwater from the storm drain system fills the sanitary sewer system, increasing the likelihood of toilets backing up. If some sanitary drains dump into the storm system, when the system backs up through your storm drains, the floodwater flowing into your basement will be even less fun.

Some communities have a combined sewer system with sanitary and stormwater mingled. Many are working at separating them. It's expensive and takes a long time, and it usually results in a system that is still combined but less prone to backups. With recent climate events on the rise, all we can say is "Good luck!"

In general, any space below grade is waiting eagerly to be flooded. Although your library may come pre-equipped with subterranean spaces, you'll be happier without them. In planning libraries, never forget that (a) basements aren't much cheaper per square foot than extra floors and (b) a heavy rain will not flood an alternative upper floor. Although it's not a water issue, upper floors also have natural light, which is a lot more fun than gloom and damp.

If you construct an open terrace below grade level, you will regret it deeply. Yet Joe is surprised at how often owners suggest this. The terrace will need storm drains. If the storm drain openings on the terrace are lower than the storm drain openings on the street outside, any water the storm sewers can't handle will back up onto your terrace and flow into your library. If you have backwater valves on your terrace drains to prevent this from happening, sooner or later a valve will clog and water will back up into your library. If none of your drains clog, and the backwater valves all continue to work, the water pressure can literally blow a valve out into the air, and water can fill your library anyway. Standing helplessly while you watch stormwater backing up relentlessly into your library is no fun at all (although watching sanitary sewer water backing up is even less fun).

IV-B. DETENTION AND RETENTION BASINS

"Detention basins" are areas designed to control the speed of water runoff by detaining the water during rainstorms to help prevent flooding. The general principle is that a detention basin fills quickly with water during a rainstorm. After the rain ends, the water drains away slowly until the basin is empty.

"Retention basins" by contrast retain part of the water at all times, serving as permanent ponds or lakes.

Detention and retention basins are frequently legally required when a development (such as a new library building or parking lot) decreases the amount of land that can absorb water and thereby increases the rate of runoff.

Since existing structures and paving may be grandfathered in, detention basins may be required only to deal with the reduction in permeable land area that results from a project.

If a library has a tight site with no space for a basin, it may find that it can receive compensating credit for its increased building or parking footprint by using pervious pavers in a parking lot or by adding a green roof.

One of the major downsides of required retention basins is neighborhoods dotted with lakes that harbor Canada geese. While geese are attractive and appealing creatures, they supposedly deposit more poop per pound of goose than cows do per pound of cow. Keeping lawns and parking lots sanitary around retention basins can be a difficult proposition. For this reason, detention basins rather than retention ponds seem more library friendly.

Retention ponds also provide one more place into which children can fall.

Detention ponds are not maintenance free. If you have a detention basin, you will need to make sure that the device that controls the speed of water exit does not plug up. You will also need to mow the basin when it is dry, and you may need to control plant species.

This is a once-over-extremely-lightly review of detention basins. Depending on where your library is located, it may be subject to a wide variety of rules. Just as your architects and engineers work with local authorities about zoning and building code requirements, they will need to work with them about water runoff control requirements.

You may also need to review with your architects and engineers what will happen when a rain "event" overstresses the capacity of your detention basin. "Hundred-year floods" seem to occur every half-dozen years now, and even the elderly among us will live to see more of them.

Our personal opinion is that limiting water runoff speed is a good thing, but "detained" water is a lot less of a problem than "retained" water. In addition to concerns about child safety and goose poop and mosquito breeding, retained water is water constantly lying around on your property.

V. Special Room Considerations

V-A. FOOD PREPARATION AND SERVICE AREAS

Chapter 24, "Program, Activity, and Study Rooms," and chapter 28, "Staff Facilities," include basic material on areas used for food preparation.

- Areas that are used for food preparation are subject to special requirements. Before planning any area of this type, you and your architects need to sit down with local public health service people to learn requirements.
- Depending on codes, an area used for preparing and serving food may need a three-drain sink, a grease trap, a separate hand-washing sink directly behind a service counter, and other plumbing.

> One library Fred worked with had no mop sink (although mop sinks are required on any floor that has a toilet). The custodian dealt with the situation by using one of the three drains in the sink in a food preparation area as a mop sink. This eventually led to serious consternation when word got around.

V-B. STAFF WORKROOM PLUMBING

Most library workrooms need running water. Unfortunately, it is often omitted, forcing library staff to carry water from other parts of their buildings. And retroactive plumbing is vastly more expensive than plumbing provided at the outset.

V-B-1. Washbasins

Public service departments need washbasins because librarians frequently deal with users who are obviously infected. This is particularly true in public library children's departments, where legions of sneezing kids can send librarians rushing back endlessly to wash their hands one more time, but it happens in all departments.

Any library department that deals with preparing materials for use, repairing them, preparing displays and artwork, and many other functions also needs access to running water.

Retrofitting running water and drains is a lot more difficult than installing them during construction, so postponing makes no economic sense unless you are absolutely sure you won't ever want them. And won't ever convert the room to another purpose that will benefit from running water.

Washbasins have to be large enough for serious use. Like basins in areas where food is prepared, sinks in workrooms need to be deep. They also need high gooseneck faucets to allow coffee urns and other large containers to be filled. Whether a sink will need one or two drains or three drains depends on its long-term use.

The best way to plan is probably to specify that sinks will be provided in all staff workrooms and then to decide which ones aren't really necessary.

V-B-2. Washers and Dryers

Some libraries have washing machines and dryers. Public library children's departments that have hand puppets or dress-up costumes or similar items used by children may want to be able to wash the items in the library instead of having staff take them home to wash in their home washing equipment.

If you think you may need a washer and dryer, you'll find it extremely hard to retrofit, because you will need hot and cold water supplies, a drain, a dryer vent, and probably a 220-volt power supply for the dryer. Even if you aren't quite sure, the time to install all of these connections (rough them in) is when you are constructing the building. You can always purchase the washer and dryer later (although the cost of providing the necessary connections will probably be far higher than the cost of the washer and dryer).

If space is very tight, apartment-type over-and-under washer/dryer combinations are available, but you may find standard equipment less maintenance trouble over the years. And the extra amount of space extremely minor.

V-C. CUSTODIAL WORKROOMS

Building codes may require that your library have a mop sink on any floor that has a restroom, but you're a lot better off having one on every floor.

A variety of mop sinks is available—primarily wall-mounted and floor-level sinks—and you and your custodians will need to consult with your architects. The custodians we've worked with like floor-mounted basins because it's easier to empty things into them, and because they can rinse out mops without holding them in midair.

A good way to organize storage space for cleaning equipment—supplies on shelves and floor space for cleaning carts, vacuum cleaners, and rug shampooers—is to store them all in rooms that hold mop sinks.

V-D. SEMPER PARATUS IS SEMPER FINE

When you have any doubts, adding plumbing when the building is being constructed is endlessly cheaper and neater and better integrated with your plumbing system and more practical in general than retrofitting it later. And often the difference between having or never having the fixture you need.

VI. Water "Features"

VI-A. INDOOR WATER FEATURES

Water features have been favorite design elements with many owners, architects, and interior designers over many years. They include such items as fountains, water walls, reflecting pools, and so on. The main concern of most librarians is the practical effects of interior water features.

Indoor water features have a few appealing aspects:

- Water features can be fun to look at.
- The sound of running water is pleasant.
- Water features provide unexpected fun. Just as with the Spanish Inquisition, no one expects a sudden water feature.

But indoor water features cause many problems:

- Users pitch coins into fountains, blocking the drains and leading to overflows.
- People drop things into fountains. Hopefully their own things, but sometimes the library's things.
- People fall in. Having a user or a mayor take a header into a fountain can spoil a library administrator's day.

> When John Moorman, coauthor of the first edition, was working at a university library, students put fish and frogs into the water features. In a way, it's a friendly gesture, and one that shows an attractive interest in biological studies, but there are probably downsides as well.

- Many librarians with indoor fountains worry about children drowning.
- Fountains can provide pleasant humidity when the air is dry, but they can also add unwanted extra humidity when the air is damp.
- The sound of running water is so persuasive that it sends nearby staff members rushing off to the restroom all day long. (We are not making this up. We know one library that had to turn off its fountain for this reason.)
- Most importantly, indoor water features can harbor Legionnaires' disease, which is a deal killer.

There are all sorts of architectural design concepts you do not want in your library. Few of them are more of a pain than indoor water features. No matter how exciting the picture painted by your designers may be, stop the conversation instantly. Rise up firmly and shout, *"We don't want any @#$% indoor water features."*

If you're stuck with an indoor water feature, just turn it off and convert it to a planter.

VI-B. OUTDOOR WATER FEATURES

Many libraries have fountains outside their buildings.

In most cases, these are the ideas of people who are not librarians.

Fountains can be high-maintenance items. They have to be cleaned. In climates with actual winters, fountains have to be drained and covered for winter. While a running fountain can be fun in the summer, a fountain with a tarp over it may not be all that cute in the winter.

Librarians whose buildings have fountains in front tell us they always worry about children falling in.

If you inherit a fountain, you can always cap the pipe, fill the fountain with dirt, and create a handsome flowerbed. We know librarians who have done this, and they are pleased with the improvement.

VII. Snappy Rules on Plumbing Systems

1. In addition to spreading Legionnaires' disease, indoor "water features" have many other nasty functions. There's no excuse for letting your owners or architects talk you into indoor water features. Shout "NO!" and "NOT A CHANCE!" and "NEVER BRING THIS UP AGAIN!" the moment the idea is first mentioned. (If it's brought up a second time, shout "@#$%&!")

2. Anyone who has dealt with children in a library knows that "infectious" does not apply just to laughter. All staff workrooms need washbasins in addition to the customary plentiful hand sanitizers.

3. Libraries are too often equipped with toy washbasins. You don't want any. Washbasins need to be seriously deep and have faucets high enough to allow coffee urns to be filled. (Bar sinks are toy washbasins.)

4. Expanding or retrofitting plumbing is expensive. Don't let people talk you into marginally adequate systems. It makes good sense to rough in plumbing when there is a reasonable chance you may want to add a sink or washer and dryer or other feature later.

5. If you have an open exterior staircase leading down to a basement door, sooner or later the drain at the bottom of the steps will plug up and rainwater will flow into your library. Enclose the staircase when you construct the building rather than retrofitting some sort of makeshift cover after a few floods.

6. Some washbasins may require garbage disposals, particularly in staff lunchrooms. (Imagine a performing group called the "Staff Room Cloggers.")

7. Undesired water is just one of the many exciting reasons that basements are such a bad idea in libraries.

8. If you construct an open terrace next to your library below grade level, you will regret it deeply. The terrace will need storm drains. If the storm drains openings on the terrace are lower than the storm drains openings on the street outside, any water the storm sewers can't handle will back up onto your terrace and flood your library. If you have backwater valves on your terrace drains to prevent this from happening, sooner or later a valve will clog or get a twig lodged in it, and water will back up and flood your library. If all the valves work correctly, pressure from the local storm drain system may literally blow one

out of one of the valves. And flood your library. You will not enjoy flooding in your library.

9. If your building site is small and your town requires water detention, explore credits (such as green roofs and permeable pavers) available to offset the new land you plan to occupy.

10. A happy library is a basement-less library.

11. All library employees should know how to turn off water. When the time comes to turn it off, you don't have time to look things up in a leisurely fashion or to wait for outside assistance. Extensive training of staff and labeling of valves helps.

12. A friend of Fred's in the insurance business says, "Basements are places you put things you really don't want."

PART IV
Technical Issues

CHAPTER 35

Security

I. Introduction

All libraries must be concerned with protecting users, staff, collections, and buildings.

Building codes play a major role in the determination of minimum security equipment, but it's important to remember that codes contain minimum requirements, not ideal requirements. There are a great many options for better structures and equipment that libraries should at least consider.

Of the many approaches to security, a surprising number are structural and involve no high-tech gear of any kind. These include site selection, construction materials, and physical arrangement of spaces. Starting with inherently secure buildings is a lot more sensible than beginning with mechanical security systems, and it should always come first.

Other approaches involve mechanical or electronic equipment. A wide variety of equipment is available to prevent unauthorized entry or exit, control access to secure areas, limit theft of library materials, oversee spaces, suppress fires, protect collections from water, and protect libraries and their staff members from lawsuits. While some equipment is easy to retrofit into most existing library buildings, other equipment involves a certain amount of advance planning.

We think that the time for a thorough review of all planned security is during the design phases of libraries—and the earlier this takes place, the easier it will be to keep your building secure.

Include your library building consultant in your security discussions, since consultants should have a significant amount of firsthand experience with library security problems.

Make sure that your architects and engineers are aware of your security plans from the beginning, and check with them about improvements and changes since this book was written.

The US insurance industry has been a dominant player in the creation of safer buildings, including the creation of many building codes and the development of the Underwriters Laboratories, which evaluates the safety of equipment of many types. Knowing what types of construction will lower your insurance rates is a great guide to some of the steps you can take to create a safer building. See chapter 36, "Insurance."

Some serious library security problems can result from badly designed shared buildings. See chapter 18, "Shared Buildings."

II. Security through Building Design

While many security systems consist of mechanical or electrical equipment, a large number of opportunities exist for designing library buildings that provide safety for people, collections, and equipment.

Here are a few everyday examples of what one might call "passive" security systems—designing buildings so that they are inherently secure.

The great advantage of passive systems is that the security technology does not wear out and need to be replaced. Buildings constructed without basements don't develop basements due to the passage of time.

II-A. FIRE-RESISTANT CONSTRUCTION

> "Fire *resistive*" is a category of construction type defined by the Insurance Services Office, and not what we are talking about here.

One of the easy ways to construct a safer library is to use fire-resistant materials.

In many cases, local building codes will limit the size of a library that can be built with wood-frame construction or other flammable materials. Some libraries even find that when the time comes to expand, the materials used in the original construction are not legal for a larger building, or even for the current building due to code changes.

You will want to review fire resistance with your architect at one of your first planning meetings. Be sure to discuss the implications of long-term future expansion and of insurance rates. One good approach is to require that your new library meet all applicable codes for a larger building.

It is essential that some areas of libraries be designed to be unusually fire resistant. The classic example is book returns that lead directly inside library buildings. Unfortunately, one of the standard causes of library fires is incendiaries in book returns. For instance, major fires at the Danbury, Connecticut, public library in 1996 and at the Auburn, Indiana, public library in 2017 were both started in book returns. While returns that lead directly into buildings are convenient for staff and help protect books, the receiving areas for returns of this type need to be capable of containing fires. Any fire in a book return is likely to result in the destruction of all the books in the return, but it's a nice thing if that's as far as the damage goes.

Just because construction materials are available and currently legal, this doesn't mean you want just any of them used in your library building.

Always review flammability of materials and specific needs of various kinds of installations. If you plan to use a material in a fashion different from how it is typically used, take care. For example, if you are considering gluing carpet to walls for decorative or acoustic purposes, be sure that the carpet you select meets fire standards for application on vertical surfaces. Carpet attached to walls must meet a higher standard because fires can burn their way vertically up walls, and carpet that is safe for the floor of your library may be a serious fire hazard on walls.

In many new libraries, any structural wood must be fire resistant. For example, blocking installed in steel stud walls for later mounting of plaques or other heavy objects should be treated to be fire resistant. And any work after your construction project is complete should also meet those standards.

II-B. FIRE-RESISTANT CONTENTS

Because of their book collections, libraries are inherently flammable.

To help alleviate future problems, library furnishings need to be fire resistant. Some of the most important requirements involve upholstered furniture. A great deal of soft seating sold in the US is filled with polyurethane foam that is almost explosively flammable and exudes cyanide gas when it burns. (Remember the Sofa Super Store fire in Charleston, South Carolina, in 2007, in which nine firefighters were killed.)

For many years, the standard for public buildings with polyurethane foam furniture was CAL 133, which specified chemicals required to make polyurethane foam less of a fire hazard. The CAL 133 specification has been altered, however, since the fire-prevention chemicals were also dangerous themselves. While CAL 133 required testing of entire items of furniture, new standards simply require testing of individual components. It's a lot less expensive for manufacturers, but it fails to test what happens when various materials are combined.

Unfortunately, despite its lethal qualities, polyurethane foam is still everywhere. Its continuing use is apparently a matter of 10 points for industry interests and 0 points for safety interests.

Due to the uncertain safety standards, our best advice is to simply avoid furniture with unnecessary padding, such as overstuffed armchairs.

II-C. FLOOD-RESISTANT CONSTRUCTION

Although major library floods are relatively rare, they occur in the US almost every year.

Floods are not fun. Wet books are frequently ruined by the time the heavily polluted flood waters finally recede. Freeze drying is frequently touted in the library literature as a treatment for saturated books, but it's expensive, books are never as good as new afterwards, and it doesn't work on coated paper.

One obvious way to protect libraries from floods is to build them on high ground and avoid basements, but for a variety of political, historical, and design reasons, these easy protections are sometimes ignored. It's hard to agree with any of the reasons.

II-C-1. Never Build on Floodplains

One of the easiest ways to protect your library from water is to always build on high ground.

Insurance maps showing the locations of floodplains are available for communities throughout the US. You may even find state regulations that forbid library construction on floodplains.

Even when they avoid floodplains, however, many libraries end up wet when flooding spreads beyond the limits of official floodplains. In recent years, the phrase "100-year flood" has become almost a joke, with 100-year floods seeming to occur in some communities every decade.

Many riverside towns have dike systems to protect low-lying areas, but (as the Mississippi River demonstrated in Louisiana in 2007 and the Cedar River in Iowa in 2008) dikes fail. We think that blissfully counting on the eternal efficacy of dikes is on par with believing everything one reads on the Internet.

Resist political pressure to build libraries in historic areas that can flood. If your town has a historic riverside section and a modern bluff-top section, you may find yourself under tremendous pressure from local historical organizations to locate your library where floods will sooner or later find it, rather than to locate it safely on high ground.

II-C-2. If You MUST Build on a Floodplain . . .

If (despite your best judgment) you have to build on a floodplain, you will encounter many restrictions established by the National Flood Insurance Program. Depend on your architects and engineers to be sure these requirements are met, and to explain to local governments during the site selection process what extra expenditures will be required and what troubles can ensue.

If a library is built on a floodplain, the lowest floor needs to be above the base flood elevation level, but elevators can continue down to grade level to provide essential accessibility.

Foundations must be stable under flooding conditions, and special construction materials are required, such as stainless steel connectors near saltwater.

Joe has constructed a very successful library on a site that was slightly below the flood level. But considering that floods seem to be higher and more frequent every year, keeping far away makes extremely good sense. Being only a foot or two above the maximum flood level this year may result in being below the flood level next year.

See chapter 9, "Site Selection," and the ASCE (American Society of Civil Engineers) standard 24, "Flood Resistant Design and Construction," for vastly more detail.

II-C-3. Never Put Books in Basements

We think that the evil allure of basements in libraries is driven primarily by ill-informed stinginess, but it can result in all manner of unpleasant outcomes.

When people construct houses with crawl spaces, the extra cost of basements is relatively modest because (almost) all they have to do is extend the walls, pour a floor, provide drainage tiles around the house foundation and under the floor slab, and supply a sump pump. Basements in houses are appealing because they hold all sorts of stuff, and they provide tornado shelters for houses that are almost always too flimsy to withstand storms.

But a basement in a library is not much cheaper than an extra floor above ground, and the floor above ground offers the advantages of the presence of natural light and the absence of unwanted water. By constructing a basement rather than an extra floor, you may save only 5 or 10 percent of the cost up front. And since a basement is more expensive to maintain after construction, in the long run there may be no difference in cost at all.

Basements are bad enough in traditional Carnegie-era buildings where the main floors are half a flight above grade and the basements half a flight below. But in modern buildings with grade-level main floors, basements are completely subterranean. If basement ceilings are high enough to allow good lighting and space is provided above the ceilings for mechanical systems, basement floors in these buildings may be 15 or more feet below grade, rather than five or six feet below grade in Carnegie-era buildings. And any flooding will be correspondingly worse.

Basements in modern libraries are also windowless, unless you can sneak in a skylight or two along the perimeter of the building. If your library opts for a basement rather than an extra floor, anyone who works in the basement (and there will be more and more of them as the number of staff members grows and the public areas above grade fill with new books and equipment) will be banished forever to windowless gloom.

When we talk with library staff members about what they want in workrooms, the word we hear most often is *daylight*.

There are plenty of examples of modern libraries with basements that flood. Relying on modern construction methods to keep your feet dry is not demonstrably an effective idea. Although maintaining water seals on all library floors is important, it's more difficult to do when basements are involved.

Sub-basements are of course even more dangerous. The deeper libraries burrow into the earth, the farther they are beneath the water table, and the greater the hydrostatic pressure becomes. One library has constructed a multi-deck underground structure near a lake, and to many observers the major question seems to be not "Will it leak?" but "When will it leak?"

Basements also tend to be more humid than spaces above grade level, and they require extra attention to monitoring humidity and to dehumidification equipment. High humidity is hard on books and unhealthy for people.

All basements are potentially subject to flooding. Mechanical systems like sump pumps exist for basements, and most of them appear to work most of the time. But they need backup sump pumps with supplementary power supplies, plus high water alarms to warn library staff when the flood waters are arriving more rapidly than the sump pumps can cope with them. Even if you have really satisfactory devices, why rely on mechanical gadgets when by building above ground you can have a library with passive systems to keep it dry?

Libraries have had huge numbers of people racing to move books out of the way of rising floodwaters. People rescuing books deserve great praise, but how much better is it to store books out of the way in the first place?

The main point is that basements in libraries cost nearly as much as additional upper floors. The main extra cost of building above ground is the extra cost of replacing concrete basement walls with more attractive walls and windows. And the extra doesn't amount to much.

From our point of view, there is absolutely no good reason for constructing basements in modern libraries. Libraries should build high, stay dry, and enjoy the view.

Plastic sheeting in this book stack unit protected shelving from water leaking through the terrace above by channeling the water into a variety of large containers that needed to be emptied during rainstorms. Unfortunately, the expensive circus tents retrofitted to the terrace didn't help with leakage. Over the years, as the rebar in the terrace began to rust, the water leaking into the shelving below turned the color of tea. (The last we knew, the leaking terrace and circus tents and plastic sheeting and receiving containers and tea-colored water were all still there, but the shelving had been removed.)

II-D. WINDSTORM-RESISTANT CONSTRUCTION

Windstorms are impressively present in the United States. Hurricanes are a particular threat in the Southeast, but at least we see them coming. Even if librarians don't know the strength of the hurricane or exactly where it will hit land, they know it's on its way. And architects can plan for predictably nasty hurricane weather. For example, glass damage can be a major factor, and there are systems for protecting windows.

Tornados are found almost anywhere, but especially in the Midwestern plains. They are far more difficult to predict than hurricanes and they can be far more devastating when they occur. Unlike even the strongest hurricanes, they can wreak virtually total destruction.

You should be able to rely on your architects and engineers for incorporating windstorm protection into your library building.

Even sturdy, modern libraries are vulnerable to tornadoes and hurricanes. Tornadoes in particular can rip off roofs and send shards of glass streaking like jet-propelled knives.

Because of the danger to roofs and windows, all library buildings need places of refuge where users and staff can find shelter from tornados and hurricanes.

- In large libraries with more than one floor, staff members need to designate places that have strong floors above them and are protected from possible flying glass. Although the roof may be yanked off the library, a concrete floor sturdy enough to hold library books will probably withstand a storm. Hallways beneath such a slab are great places of refuge. The current architectural enthusiasm for glass buildings makes us wonder about tornado safety in showplace libraries. For example, where will users of some new libraries where every vertical surface appears to be glass find shelter during a tornado?

- Single-story or wood-frame library buildings need to create internal rooms that can withstand the direct hit of a major tornado or hurricane. Commonly these are restrooms, which in most cases have no windows. One library with which Fred worked was a replacement for one destroyed by a tornado. In the new library, which houses the village hall, library, and an ESDA (Emergency Services and Disaster Agency) office, the restrooms have concrete walls and ceilings. One advantage of using restrooms for windstorm shelters is that they may be the only rooms in a library that will reliably have open floor space when the storm arrives, since library staff members cannot requisition restrooms for storage, filling them with program supplies, puppet storage racks, excess furniture, and neatly boxed miscellany, thereby making it impossible for panicked people to crowd in. It's hard to imagine a non-restroom storm shelter in a library that will not be filled—sooner or later—with stacked cartons of book sale books.

The trouble with windstorm damage is that everyone is painfully aware of the possibilities for a few years after a nearby storm, but they eventually forget, and as the years pass they sometimes don't want to spend the money to make their buildings more weather resistant.

II-E. EARTHQUAKE-RESISTANT CONSTRUCTION

Libraries need to rely on their architects, engineers, and shelving manufacturers for guidance on preparing for earthquakes. In addition to general building codes, there may be specific earthquake codes (as in California) or other construction requirements. And as with many other codes, requirements may be made more demanding after every major earthquake.

One of the major concerns is the stability of book shelving. Cantilever steel shelving units can topple like dominos, and libraries in earthquake-prone areas may be required to limit the height of units, to anchor the feet of the units to the floor, or to connect the tops of support posts with steel U channels that are anchored to walls. (Pictures of toppled shelving units are available and dramatic.)

Individual shelving units may also require the addition of gussets to strengthen the connections between the columns and the bases.

Some people suggest that carpeting or other soft materials under shelving will increase the likelihood of tipping by making it easier for shelving units to rock.

Some codes may also require solid walls to resist the tendency of buildings to tip during earthquakes. A main functional question may be whether solid walls interfere with design functions that rely on modular (post and beam) construction.

As with resistance to windstorms, libraries in earthquake-prone areas need the careful attention of architects and engineers.

II-F. LIMITED PUBLIC ENTRANCES

One of the core principles of good library design is limiting the number of entrances. Every entrance needs to be supervised by a staff member. Book theft detection systems require oversight by nearby staff who can see the security gates and the people using them. If a library is open 60 to 70 hours a week, that means a minimum of two full-time people to watch a single door. If a second entrance is at the end of an otherwise unstaffed hallway, the library staff member at the entrance may be so unprotected that two staff members need to be assigned there. And once staff members are supervising lesser-used multiple entries, what will they do between library users?

However, multiple entrances are among the first features many libraries and library users want, especially with large buildings that must be circumnavigated if they have single entrances. City leaders want public libraries with entrances facing both the sidewalks in front of libraries and the parking lots behind them. Some planners of community college libraries think it would be great to place the library in the middle of a sprawling building and have entrances from all directions. Campus officials feel that university libraries are such large buildings that they should have doors on more than one side, and the main floors of some academic libraries double as walkways through campuses.

Many of the people with whom you will have to work will insist that multiple entrances are essential. In all multiple entrance situations, it's tremendously important for university and city governments to make informed decisions and not feign surprise when the extra staffing bill arrives. When people pressure you to add extra entrances, always quote the cost of doing so in terms of extra staff, and ask whether they are proposing to pay the additional cost for eternity (or for the life of the library, whichever is less). (Fred has done this several times with town officials, who begin in grumpy disbelief at prospective staffing costs but then frequently back down on multiple entrances.)

> All of these may sound imaginary, but we've run into each of these situations. For instance, one major university library in Illinois closed all but one of its original entrances because of the high costs of staffing doors. And an Illinois community college was actually constructed with multiple entrances the way it's described above. The first year it was open, a substantial portion of the collection vanished, and the school had to go through complex restructuring in a partially successful attempt to correct the mess.

The only time multiple entrances don't lead to substantial extra expenditures are situations where:

- The library is so large it has interior distributor halls with a separate (supervised) entrance to each departmental library.
- The multiple entrances lead to a concourse that has a single entrance to the actual library.

At any rate, when issues of multiple entrances arise, review the costs and benefits carefully, including realistic (rather than optimistic) staffing costs.

II-G. GOOD SIGHT LINES

One of the easiest ways to provide safer libraries at no extra cost is to take great care with sight lines. Sight lines are direct open visual paths that allow library staff members to see what's going on around the building.

When you review the plans for your library, with furniture locations indicated, always ask yourself how your staff will keep an eye on the

Glass partitions are a great way to separate noisy areas from quiet areas while maintaining security.

In this case, the noise of the children's department in the background is prevented from disturbing people borrowing books and looking at new materials.

The same principle works with study rooms, which need to be glass boxes. (On the other hand, the children's department in this library is far more brightly lighted than the adjacent area, perhaps making the lobby seem gloomy by comparison.)

library and its users. And also ask whether people will be able to see what they'd rather not see.

II-G-1. Beneficial Sight Lines

- *Stack orientation.* For example, if staff members can see down stack aisles when seated at the reference desk, they can keep a much better eye on things than if the aisles are perpendicular to the desk. Although they won't be able to see all the aisles from the desk, staff can do so by taking a few steps backward and forward rather than having to walk the length of the library, peering into each aisle.

- *Internal windows.* Another way to maintain good sight lines is through the use of internal windows. Study rooms need glass walls on at least three sides. (A glass wall is a real glass wall, not a tiny window in a solid wall.) If staff workrooms have windows to the adjacent public areas of the library, staff members working at their desks are more aware of what's going on in the building. If children's departments are walled off for acoustic purposes, the use of glass walls permits better oversight.

- *Zigzag style entries to restrooms.* Zigzag entries (the kind airports use) can totally prevent unwelcome sight lines while eliminating both the problems with doors with dirty handles and the problems with total privacy that restrooms with doors provide.

II-G-2. Evil Sight Lines

The pursuit of better sight lines has also led to some really unfortunate ideas, and some accidental sight lines are real howlers.

- *Hidden corners.* If your library design requires staff to walk the length of a long room just to see what's going on in a back corner or in a small study room, you will spend a great deal of money in frustrated oversight. Study the architect's drawings for problem areas in time for changes to be made. You can always install video surveillance systems to cover hidden corners, but video systems are primarily useful in forensics—finding out what happened after the fact. Few libraries can station someone to stare at monitors by the hour waiting for the very occasional malfeasance. (Very obvious cameras, of course, may intimidate some people by merely being visible.)

- **Radiating book stacks.** Radiating stacks are an eternally appealing but extraordinarily bad concept. The general idea is to arrange shelving units so they radiate out from a central service point like the spokes of a wheel, enabling staff members seated there to look down all the aisles by simply twirling around. The first thing this accomplishes is the waste of expensive space. If aisles are wide enough near the service desk, they can be extraordinarily wide 50 feet away. Some libraries have tried to insert short sections of shelving at the far ends of the radiating aisles, but that leads to confused users—and it still wastes a great deal of space. For more examples of the evil of radiating shelves, see chapter 22, "Collection Storage and Display."

- **Full-view restrooms.** It always amazes us how many restrooms place users on full display whenever the doors are opened. For example, in many library restrooms (and those in other buildings, to be fair about things), gentlemen standing at the urinals are in plain view whenever the doors are opened. Even when there is no direct view of restroom action, it's often possible to see everything going on reflected in mirrors over the sinks. All of this can violate building codes. And we're not sure that users like to be watched while they're standing at sinks anyway. Single-user restrooms are often laid out so that the toilet is on proud display whenever the door is open. This strikes us as an unsatisfactory idea, particularly because the doors of unoccupied restrooms can stand open.

It's a good idea to check the proposed floor plans of your library to be sure that the only things visible when restroom doors are open are blank walls. See also chapter 26, "Restrooms," and chapter 28, "Staff Facilities."

II-H. NO PLACES WHERE PEOPLE CAN BE TRAPPED

One of the easiest ways to protect library users and staff is to avoid situations where people can be cornered.

II-H-1. Dead-End Book Aisles

An obvious example is avoiding dead-end book stack aisles. When faced with overcrowding, libraries are often tempted to eliminate cross aisles and use the space instead for additional shelving. The problem with dead-end aisles is that people can be cornered there.

Dead-end book aisles are banned by building and accessibility codes, but they may still exist from the days before codes dealt with them. And they're easy for library staff to create informally by just tucking extra shelving units at the end of aisles.

II-H-2. Service Desks with Only One Staff Exit

The staff areas of all service desks need more than one way out. This is extremely easy to arrange, but not all service desks are designed this way.

Some libraries have added swinging door panels labeled "staff only" to remind library users not to walk behind service desks. Door panels need to be single panels, so that a staff member can hold a door panel open with one hand and push a book truck through with the other. And door panels need latches so the doors can be locked open once library users get the idea.

II-I. PROVIDING SECURITY BY AVOIDING SHARED BUILDINGS

One source of serious security problems occurs in situations where multiple agencies share buildings.

Libraries are particularly subject to problems in this area because libraries have open spaces rather than individually locked public service spaces like classroom buildings. Once people are inside the library, they may have access to almost all the collections, computers, and other equipment. This is the main reason that shared elevators between libraries and classroom buildings are an unbelievably awful idea.

If non-library staff have keys to the building, everyone may have keys to the building.

A handy rule of thumb is that no one who does not report to the library director should have keys to the building.

See chapter 18, "Shared Buildings."

II-J. WINDOWS

One serious source of theft is windows that can be opened by library users. It's easy to open a window, drop a book into the bushes, and retrieve it later.

Having windows that open may be a good thing in case of HVAC failure, but you want to be sure that only staff members are able to open windows.

Academic libraries have had major thefts by people who lowered bags or baskets of books out of book stack windows.

II-K. READING AND ACTIVITY TERRACES

Exterior terraces always are an attractive concept, but you need to be sure that people cannot use terraces without first checking materials out. As with windows, it's easy to drop books off the edges of terraces for later retrieval.

Owners and designers are frequently enamored by the concept of reading terraces and try to argue that users won't actually drop books off the edges. They use the phrase "secure" reading terrace, but there's no such thing.

II-L. DANGEROUS ARCHITECTURAL FEATURES

A number of ill-considered but popular architectural features have led to injuries to users and staff. It's easy to say "No!" to all of them.

User and staff safety trumps cute design concepts.

II-L-1. Atria

Atria attract suicides. One major New York City library has had at least three.

We've argued against atria in many places in this book. Suicides are just one of many good reasons to oppose atria—although we think it's a sufficient reason.

II-L-2. Story Pits

Some libraries have constructed story pits in their children's departments. Sooner or later, someone falls in. Risers for children to sit on work just as well. But both are inaccessible.

The central point is, avoid uneven floors.

II-L-3. Oddly Configured Staircases

Staircases are sufficiently dangerous without making the treads odd shapes, without making the treads end before they touch the wall, without moving people diagonally, without having steps that go on forever, without terrifying people with acrophobia, and without lots of other seriously bad ideas.

As we get older, we are more conscious of the possibilities of falling downstairs.

II- L-4. Railings That Can Be Climbed Like Ladders

One of the most popular design features in modern architecture is railings with horizontal bars that can be climbed like ladders. People can (and do) fall off. Any sane building code would ban them, but we still see them everywhere.

II-L-5. Water Features

Owners and designers are so fond of water inside buildings that the whole concept has a name of its own—"water feature."

We don't know of any deaths in library water features, but librarians are constantly worried because people fall into water features with dismal (or exciting, if you enjoy the news) regularity, and water features harbor Legionnaires' disease.

Water features can also be a source of unwelcome noises. The sounds of loud water features can be extremely distracting, while the softer sounds of more gentle water features can be so suggestive that they send people rushing to the restrooms all day long.

II-L-6. Rooms with Artistically Sloped Floors

One vogue in architectural design of libraries has been sloped floors with reading or book collection areas every few feet vertically.

We think these are always an extremely bad idea.

III. Theft-Control Systems

For many libraries, one of the primary security problems is preventing users from stealing the collection.

Many of the attempted solutions to problems of book theft have implications for building design.

Much of theft control reflects the general assumption that theft of library materials is more a matter of opportunity than sophisticated criminal enterprise. For every thief practicing professional sleight-of-hand as he removes maps from atlases in rare book rooms, there are thousands of university students stealing research materials from book stacks and hundreds of thousands of middle-schoolers filching copies of skateboarding and teeny-bopper/rock-star magazines.

Librarians have to protect their collections not only against theft, but also against mutilation and hiding. Users cut pictures out of books. They hide items for later use or to keep other users from finding them.

In general, preventing book theft is the easiest problem to solve—or at least combat. However, the most determined thieves will get their materials no matter what security systems are in place. The theft of audio and video recordings is more difficult to prevent. Mutilation of materials can be almost impossible to prevent if it involves no attempt to remove anything larger than a sheet of paper from the library. And preventing theft of video games is nearly impossible.

III-A. TYPICAL HIGH-RISK MATERIALS

Most public librarians can predict the types of materials most likely to be stolen, although the types of materials stolen vary as the years go by. Books on sex, the occult, auto repair, and do-it-yourself anarchy disappear with predictable regularity. Non-print materials such as recordings of popular music and popular films would vanish almost instantly in many libraries if the materials were ever left lying around loose. And video games vanish almost instantly.

In particular, CDs and DVDs lend themselves to theft because they are in high demand and can easily be concealed in pockets. The side pockets on a man's sport coat, for example, can easily hold several hundred dollars worth of discs without bulging.

Interestingly, perhaps, the most frequently stolen or mutilated materials in public libraries are old high school yearbooks. People cut out pictures of friends or famous graduates. In most libraries, yearbooks have to be kept behind desks, and people consulting them have to be forced to sit directly in front of librarians.

In large academic and research libraries, the regular book stacks are full of materials that would be kept under lock and key in lesser libraries. The managers of rare book rooms in libraries like this are aware of the situation, but the rare book room stacks may be far too small to allow every valuable item to be sequestered.

The trend toward more open stacks saves library staff costs but can lead to greater stack thefts.

> One of the engaging variants on theft occurs in competitive academic environments, where students working on assignments hide key volumes from each other. Law school librarians, for instance, have told us about this practice, which in turn may tell us something about lawyers in training.

The carefully controlled clientele of special libraries makes theft a less pressing issue, particularly because physicians and lawyers may have 24/7 access to their libraries.

III-B. ECONOMIC MODELS

Every library contemplating theft-control systems sooner or later faces cost-benefit analysis, weighing the value of items stolen against the cost of security systems. Often analysis of this type underlies planning discussions, even when it is unvoiced.

The problem with this approach is attempting to set a cost on theft. In addition to the cash value of the stolen item, there are substantial costs for:

- Staff time keeping an eye on materials. This can be especially significant in archival and rare book collections.
- Staff time spent inventorying for theft. (Inventorying requires preliminary shelf

reading, and some large libraries can't even afford that.) In some large research libraries, the only staff time spent on missing materials is in response to snags—reports that requested items cannot be located. The fewer problems libraries have with theft, the less time they need to spend verifying what's actually there.

- Staff time wasted hunting for an item and finally coming to the conclusion that it is genuinely gone.
- Staff time spent deciding whether missing items should be replaced.
- Difficulty in locating replacements. Most books in most libraries are out of print.
- Dealing with irreplaceable items. Document collections and archives, for example, are full of unique materials. Unless collections have been digitized or duplicated, any small item that makes its way into a convenient briefcase or purse is probably gone forever.
- Staff time ordering and processing replacements. Particularly in the case of out-of-print materials purchased from small vendors, the combined costs for searching, ordering, cataloging, and check issuing can vastly exceed the cost of the item purchased.
- User alienation. If high-demand materials are frequently missing, or if requests for high-demand materials take forever to fill because the items need to be reordered, users may have a lower opinion of the library.

Some libraries have perennial problems locating materials in stacks. Whether this is due to theft, lack of shelf reading, or other problems, the result is a body of users who are unimpressed with the quality of their libraries.

For all of these reasons, we think that library theft and mutilation problems do not easily lend themselves to a simple economic analysis.

III-C. IMPROVED OVERSIGHT

One way of limiting theft and mutilation of materials lies in designing library buildings that lend themselves to improved collection oversight.

Here are some basic approaches:

- Concentration on excellent sight lines. The more users are aware of being watched, the less likely they are to remove items from collections.
- Strategic use of glass partitions. If there's no special need for privacy, avoid it.
- Careful positioning of staff points. A reference desk in the middle of a large room provides better staff oversight than one tucked into a corner. Two staff desks placed closely together waste potential oversight opportunities.

> A library school student Fred knew had been a high school football player. Years later he helped supervise the Chicago Public Library patent collection. In spite of being a fairly large person, he did not have to rely on size to discourage inappropriate behavior. Fred overheard him:
>
> Student supervisor: "Is this your razor blade?"
>
> Library user: "No, no! I have no idea where it came from."
>
> Student supervisor: "Then let's just take it away before someone gets hurt."

- Easily watched tables for people consulting theft-prone materials. Proposed floor plans need to be checked to make sure that tables are visible from service desks. (An associated management problem involves training staff members to insist that users consulting theft-prone materials use designated tables. Users who announce preferences for hidden tables in back corners may be telegraphing felonious intent.)

- Staffed exits. No library exit can be left unwatched unless it is an emergency exit with a very loud alarm and a security camera. Book theft security gates are a tremendous help, but they can easily be defeated when no one is watching. And they don't prevent mutilation, such as the theft of materials from archives or cutting of plates from rare books.

- Guard stations at exits. Guard stations where briefcases and purses carried by people leaving the building were inspected were common in large libraries before the advent of electronic theft-detection systems, and they may still be in use in some libraries.

- Coin-return lockers for briefcases and purses. Major archives or other collections of rare materials may permit users to bring in absolutely nothing, but in turn provide free yellow pads, pencils, and photocopies. (The problem with people using coin-return lockers as personal storerooms can be solved by emptying lockers nightly.)

- Theft-control gates that don't result in false alarms. If gates go off when nothing is being illicitly removed, library staff soon begin to just wave everyone through. And potential thieves note it.

Something similar can happen with oversensitive gates that constantly set off alarms when nothing is being stolen. Soon library staff simply wave users through when the gate alarms go off.

- Restrooms outside of theft-control gates. Restrooms provide a favorite place for removal of theft-control devices, particularly plastic anti-theft boxes on CDs and DVDs. They're also a great place for destructive reading of library materials. By arranging buildings so that nothing can be taken into a restroom before being checked out, libraries can prevent a number of problems.

- Windows that cannot be opened by users. One of the traditional ways of removing items from collections is to pitch them out the windows for later retrieval. Book stacks with windows that open for ventilation offer wonderful opportunities for theft. Users even bring ropes and baskets to lower stolen books into shrubbery below. All libraries planning new construction or remodeling need to specify ways to keep users from opening windows. A standard

> Years ago, Fred specified windows that couldn't be opened from inside, to prevent users tossing books out of windows, only to find that in the completed library the architect had provided windows with manual latches. When asked, the architect happily assured everyone that he had ignored the program requirement because custodians could check the library at closing time to be sure that all the windows were locked, thereby preventing would-be intruders from slithering into the library in the dark of the night. But he never thought to ask why the library wanted locking windows in the first place.

way is to avoid windows that can be opened, but some libraries like to be able to open windows in case of HVAC failure. Preventing users from opening windows can sometimes be as simple as removing cranks from casement windows. Other windows need key locks. Some libraries that start out with windows that can be opened end up having to bolt their windows shut. If you specify user-proof windows in your building program, be sure that your architect doesn't simply blow off the requirement in the mistaken assumption that the locks serve only to keep intruders out of the library at night.

The main reason to provide a few windows that can be opened is to provide emergency airflow during times of HVAC failure. In any other circumstances, they're just a nuisance. (Opening windows can also screw up the balance of properly functioning ventilation systems.)

Actually, a few libraries may be located in areas where mild and relatively dry climates allow occasional "free air conditioning" by simply opening windows. Libraries that plan to do this (and we think it's a seriously bad idea) need to figure out how to prevent people from chucking items out the windows. And how to keep dust and dirt from blowing into the building.

All of these security concepts have structural implications. If you want to employ them (or even keep your options open) you will want to be sure that they appear in your building program. You will also need to check proposed floor plans carefully to be sure the requirements have actually been followed.

Few non-librarians have had to cope with the everyday security problems that librarians know all too well. If owners and designers don't understand why librarians need specific features, they may decide to simply omit the features rather than ask.

III-D. SEQUESTERING THEFT-PRONE MATERIALS

Placing materials that are valuable or prone to mutilation and theft in closed areas is a traditional way of protecting collections. It's a major function of separate rare book rooms. In smaller libraries (particularly those without electronic theft control systems) shelving units behind lending desks are frequently provided for materials needing extra protection.

- Sequestering portions of collections requires advance planning in building programs. Even small libraries that need to protect AV collections or videogames must calculate the amount of space needed for storing materials.

- For efficient functioning, circulating materials stored behind desks need to be in the containers in which they will be lent. Some libraries try to store CDs and DVDs loose behind lending desks, retrieving them and inserting them in their boxes when users bring the empty boxes to the lending desks. This is a desperate solution for libraries that have too little space behind desks, but it wastes a great deal of staff time and provides extra wear and tear on the recordings. Given the painful fragility of DVDs, rough storage and extra handling are both bad ideas.

- High-demand materials stored behind lending desks need to be close at hand. Fred worked with one public library where lack of space behind the service desk and the inflexible design of the adjacent staff workroom forced the staff to store the DVD collection at the far end of the staff workroom. Every time someone wanted a DVD—and this happened every few minutes—a staff member had to walk a total of nearly 100 feet to retrieve it. Both the inadequate space behind the service desk and the inflexible room behind it were examples of poor original planning.

III-E. KEEPING UNAUTHORIZED PEOPLE OUT OF THE LIBRARY

For many great university libraries—particularly libraries in private universities—a central approach to security simply involves keeping unauthorized people entirely out of libraries.

The same approach can be taken by special libraries, which can limit access to corporate employees, and by school libraries, which can limit access by non-students.

The increased school security necessary after assaults on school children may result in fewer thefts by non-students, but student thefts may be unaffected.

Libraries that limit use by unauthorized people will need space for guard stations controlling access to the building.

They may also want to allow space for access gates using swipe cards or proximity cards carried by students and faculty.

III-F. ELECTRONIC THEFT-DETECTION SYSTEMS

Many medium-sized and large libraries use electronic theft-protection systems.

These systems include targets inserted into each book. When books that have not been properly checked out are carried through exit gates, alarms sound.

Systems that include checkout and theft detection in a single step lend themselves to self-check equipment. Other systems that involve two separate steps must be performed by library staff.

Some libraries use bypass systems. In these libraries, the targets inserted in books are never disabled. Users hand books to staff members, staff members check the books out, users walk through the exit gates, and staff members hand them the books. The systems are very much like those used in some mostly bygone video stores. One problem with bypass systems is that books or videos checked out at one institution can set off alarms in others.

As with library automation systems, the possibility of technical obsolescence is always around. For this reason, architectural spaces compatible with a variety of theft-detection systems are always desirable.

A major danger with electronic theft-detection systems is false alarms. After enough false alarms, library staff members start waving users through the gates whenever the alarms are activated. For this reason, it seems far better to adjust alarms so that they are slightly insensitive and miss a few items than to have alarms that are activated when they should not be.

III-F-1. Space Planning for Electronic Theft-Detection Systems

If your library is planning to install a theft-prevention system—either when it opens or at a later time—you will need to incorporate space for the associated equipment in your building plans.

All systems use some form of security gates. Be sure that your architect checks with the manufacturer of your equipment concerning space and electrical requirements, including distances between gates and other parts of your building. Some gates must be separate from metal structural components, and floor plans need to include space for separating gates from adjacent walls.

Bypass systems require constructing service counters attached to security gates, so that users can hand books to attendants, walk through the gates, and then collect their books on the far side before leaving the library. The design concept is very much like airport security gates. A bypass system will require extra staff and extra space for the service counter and accommodations for people entering and leaving the library, all plugged into an entryway.

Modern video surveillance systems include alarm inputs that can integrate with theft-detection systems and can be programmed to alert the security staff. These systems also tag the recorded video for easier future access and retrieval. Libraries need to make sure that there is physical space for high-resolution video cameras to photograph users when the gate alarms go off. For this reason, security gates directly next to exterior exit doors don't work well.

If you have older video surveillance equipment, you will want lights on top of your exit gates that flash whenever the audio alarm is activated. If the surveillance cameras can pick up the flashing light, you will be able to link specific faces with the alarms. (The beeping sound of the gates is not enough, since most surveillance systems do not include sound, and there will be no way to link a specific person with the alarm.)

In order for security gates to function, they have to be located with 15 or 20 feet of constantly staffed workstations and easily visible to staff working there.

III-F-2. Designing Buildings to Cope with Problems Due to Theft-Detection Systems

Some problems with theft-detection systems have architectural implications.

- Systems that include return slots that check items in are often somewhat slow because items need to be fed one at a time. Three or four parents with stacks of picture books can create a major bottleneck. Additional problems can occur if that bottleneck in turn affects the ability of other users to enter or leave the library. The moral is to be sure that there is enough elbow room around return points, as well as enough space for adding extra return points if they become necessary. And be sure you know what extra return points will cost.

- Any system failure affecting return slots will lead to massive numbers of books being returned manually, and libraries need space to receive them.

- Book transport systems can literally weave through library structures. There need to be ways to deal with items that jam the conveyor system. If the belt moves from floor to floor through a narrow tunnel, the library may need extraordinarily slender employees with no sense of claustrophobia to creep into the tunnel and retrieve books that have fallen off the belt.

- In costing out systems, be sure to have accurate information on the cost of maintenance and upkeep once warranties have expired.

- Double-check your proposed system's operating capacity. If your system has a single automatic sorting line, is it possible that use may increase to the point where the line cannot handle the load? Adding extra lines can be amazingly expensive if architectural spaces need to be created for them.

How will your book returns handle materials (such as books from other libraries) that do not use RFID tags?

- While magnetic theft-detection strips can be hidden in the spines of books, many brands of tags are usually extremely visible. Libraries have found that it's extremely easy for thieves to simply remove the tags from the books, and they find handfuls of RFID tags littering the stacks and restrooms. There's only so much that can be done, but placing public restrooms outside of security gates helps.

- Plastic security boxes with theft-detection targets require space plans. Some libraries use removable plastic boxes that encase DVDs and CDs. Theft-detection targets are built into the boxes. When a recording is checked out, a staff member uses a special key to remove the box. If you are planning to use plastic security boxes of this type, there are a number of space implications:

  - Recordings in security boxes take up more space than recordings without security boxes, and storage capacities of shelving and bins are reduced accordingly.

  - Removing and replacing security boxes takes time and may affect the number of workstations needed at a lending desk. (Be sure to try out sample boxes extensively before settling on a model. Some are extremely difficult to remove.)

  - You will need space under the lending desk to store security boxes as they are removed from recordings.

  - If your restrooms are inside your security gates, users may take recordings to the privacy of toilet stalls and try to break off the security boxes.

  - Some AV selection systems require special space planning. For example, if your library has DVD selection cards and keeps its video collection behind the lending desk, you need to plan additional space for the selection card equipment.

III-F-3. Self-check Equipment

We don't have numerical data, but we are convinced that self-check equipment plays an increasing role in many libraries. The tradeoffs typically involve efficiency in the use of staff time vs. equipment cost and potential user alienation.

Much self-check equipment interlocks with library security systems, with workstations that desensitize books as users check them out. But stand-alone self-check systems can easily be installed in libraries that do not have theft-detection equipment.

Allocating sufficient space for current and future self-check workstations is important. Vendors can provide advice, but we think that 75 square feet per workstation is about minimal. Spaces for future self-check workstations need both electrical outlets and data connections.

Many libraries with self-check equipment also opt for public shelving for holds and interlibrary loans, with the books wrapped in paper with the borrowers' names written on the spines, or with coded slips that make it extremely difficult to guess borrowers' names. If you plan to use this approach, be sure to leave space for the self-pickup shelving.

IV. Theft of Personal Possessions

All libraries are subject to miscellaneous theft. Billfolds vanish from users' ignored purses with dependable regularity. People break in and abscond with computers. Coats vanish. Staff purses are rifled. Students leave their laptops when they use restrooms, and they return to find their laptops gone.

What are some things that may help?

- Coin-return lockers for patrons. Perhaps because libraries are such comforting places, users tend to invite theft by putting down their purses and wandering off. If billfolds are removed and the purses left in place, it may be hours before the owners realize things are missing. One possible help for theft of purses and briefcases and other relatively small personal objects is coin-return lockers—if libraries can talk patrons into using them. The downside of coin-return lockers is patrons who use them for permanent personal storage. Plan to empty them every night.

- Some libraries have so many problems with purse theft that every reading table has a sign warning users not to leave their purses unattended.

- Lockers for staff. Many staff members without private workrooms simply sling their purses (or backpacks with billfolds) down in convenient corners of staff work areas. Inevitably, people sneak in and help themselves. Purse lockers are one option to help prevent theft. They come in stacks of four or five, and each stack occupies the same space as a school hallway locker. Unfortunately, many younger employees carry backpacks in which they keep their billfolds. Since the backpacks are too large for purse lockers, employees simply dump the backpacks and assume all will be well. To prevent theft from backpacks, consider purchasing half-height lockers in stacks of two, with enough space to hold backpacks. Lockers work better with hasps for padlocks than with built-in key locks. Staff frequently lose keys. Libraries can issue padlocks, keeping a record of the combination for each padlock. And bolt-cutters (always friendly pieces of equipment) can remove padlocks for which no one knows the combinations. For a single stack of lockers in a staff area, five square feet should be enough space.

- Coat storage for patrons. What we hear from libraries is that provisions for coat storage receive very little use and are generally a waste of space and money.

- Computer equipment tethers. Some laptop users who need to be away from their workstations for a few minutes don't want to shut down their computers. To help with this situation, a number of companies make tethers that allow computer components to be connected to tabletops.

V. Entrance and Exit Control Equipment

Providing proper control over entrances and exits is extremely important. You need to make it easy for your users and staff to go where they need, while at the same time keeping unauthorized people out. You need to make it easy for people to escape from your library during emergencies, but hard for them to leave through unauthorized exits when all is well.

V-A. BUILDING CODES

Due to a number of horrendous fires, building codes throughout the US are particularly detailed when it comes to fire safety. Unfortunately, some of the worst tragedies occur in spite of codes.

- For example, 602 people died in the Iroquois Theater fire in Chicago in 1903, due among other things to badly designed exits. The required asbestos safety curtain apparently burned, which makes one wonder about the type of "asbestos" used. In addition, City inspectors had been paid off to allow the theater to open before it was complete. Probably because the theater was in Chicago, no one went to jail.

- The situation in the 1942 Cocoanut Grove nightclub fire in Boston was similar, and 492 people died. In this case, some side doors to the club had been welded shut to keep people from sneaking in and out, fire doors opened inward, and the front door was a revolving door, which could handle very few people. Some decorations were flammable, and due to wartime restrictions the coolant in the air conditioning system was also flammable. The owner went to jail for violating even the loose building codes of the day. (In response to questions, it was "Cocoanut," not "Coconut.")

When your building is being designed, your architects will verify that it is in compliance with all applicable safety codes. Fire safety codes are complex, and you don't want to cut corners. Rely on your architects and engineers to make sure that exit doors, fire pull stations, fire alarm buzzers, fire extinguishers, sprinkler systems, and other devices meet or exceed codes in terms type, quantity, and placement.

As an example, one common violation of everyday exit safety codes is the use of double-cylinder locks in library entrances. A double-cylinder lock is opened by key from both sides, with no crash bar (panic bar) to open the door when people need to leave quickly. Fred has run into a number of small-town libraries with these locks. They are appealing because no one can break a pane of glass in the door and reach inside the library to unlock the door. But all one has to do is to imagine someone accidently locked into the library on the night that a fire breaks out.

> Fred worked with one library where the staff at the service desk inside the building had to hunt for almost five minutes to find the key to unlock the front door and let him in. The library was a 100-year-old building on three levels with wooden floors connected by only a wooden interior staircase. The fire exit from the second-story meeting room involved crawling through a window to a semi-flat roof, then scrambling down a vertical steel ladder. Even without worrying about the locked front door, if the elderly members of the Garden Club had been trapped on the second floor with the wooden staircase on fire, how many of them would have managed to crawl through the window and down the ladder?

Many code violations continue unabated in small towns because they have no fire marshals to make safety checks on public and commercial buildings. If you own one of these libraries, it's worthwhile hiring someone to perform a safety check.

It helps to remember that codes are only absolutely minimum requirements. Bragging that a library "meets all applicable codes" is a little like bragging "I didn't fail any courses this semester."

In general, evaluating exit code compliance is a job for experts, including architects, engineers, and fire marshals.

V-B. MODERN PANIC HARDWARE

Codes require that all doors used for emergency egress have panic hardware, otherwise known as crash bars. When panicked people flee a library, doors need to open quickly and easily. Any exit doors that require keys to open by people exiting the building are a major threat to life safety.

The problem with exit doors is that users can leave not only in case of fire but also in case of deep personal need to remove portions of the collection without benefit of checkout formalities.

To combat this, many libraries equip exit door hardware with alarms. If someone uses a panic bar to open a locked door, a loud alarm summons library staff. This is also useful in children's departments, where children can wander out of the library through fire exits.

The problem, of course, is that by the time a staff member arrives, the person who set off the alarm can be long gone.

One solution is to use "delayed egress" panic hardware with built-in time delays. When someone attempts to open a door using panic hardware, the alarm begins immediately, but the door does not open for perhaps 15 seconds, time for a staff member to find out what's going on. If the building's fire alarms have been activated, or power has failed, the time-delay function is disabled and the door opens immediately. (Codes require that all time-delay panic hardware needs to be labeled, so that people don't panic in emergencies and dash off to find other doors.)

Alarmed exits are frequently set off by accident, particularly in children's departments, where library staff may have to dash to the exits to keep small children from toddling out into traffic. All staff members need to be able to locate keys quickly to turn off exit alarms.

V-C. KEY SYSTEMS

The traditional way to provide access to buildings and rooms within them is through hierarchical keys. Each individual door usually has its own key.

In addition, master keys can be provided for various groups of doors, as needed by the owners of the building. It's possible to have a hierarchy of master keys, but the more levels that exist, the greater the chance that a random key made with the same blank will open an inappropriate door. The loss of master keys can be extraordinarily expensive. If a key opens every door in the library, replacing it will involve modifying every lock in the library and reissuing keys.

Another drawback with keys of all sorts is that there is never a record of who used a door and at what time.

For this reason, access-control systems (proximity cards, swipe cards, fobs, and keypads) make good sense for all doors that will be opened by a number of people.

For security, you may wish to have some doors that cannot be opened by any master key.

Typically, these might include the library's server rooms and rooms where sensitive records (such as personnel records) are stored.

Arranging keys takes planning. Problems occur when a crisis arises in a room and no one with a key is in the building.

V-D. PROXIMITY CARDS, SWIPE CARDS, FOBS, AND KEYPADS

A variety of modern access-control systems eliminate the expensive problem of lost keys.

In all of these systems, each person authorized to open any doors in the library—even a very limited number of doors on very limited occasions—is issued a swipe card or proximity key. Each card or key has a machine-readable code. Information on the key is transmitted to a central computer that checks whether the individual key is authorized to open that particular door at that particular time. If everything is in order, the door opens.

There are a very large number of advantages to systems of this type.

- Instead of representing a major cost for new locks and keys for an entire building, a lost swipe card or proximity key may cost only a couple of dollars. If staff members aren't sure whether they have their proximity cards, it's cheap and easy for the library to reprogram the system to deny access to the lost card and then issue the staff member a new card.

- Because swipe cards and proximity cards are vastly cheaper than actual keys, staff members may be less hesitant to admit they've mislaid them.

- The authorization for each card can be as complex as you wish. For example, a bookshelver's card may normally open only the door to the book-sorting room, but the computer can easily be reprogrammed to allow the same bookshelver (for example) to enter the library early on Wednesday mornings to empty the book drops, without being able to get in early any other mornings.

- The small computer that operates the system keeps track of exactly which cards were used on what doors at what times, providing a great deal of additional security information. For example, if a card is lost and disabled, the library can tell if anyone ever tried to use it afterwards. Use of individual doors can be tracked by time and person. Use of all doors can be tracked for a single person.

- Proximity and swipe card systems can also be programmed to automatically unlock doors, and more importantly lock them, in case staff forget to lock a door when the library is closing.

Good candidates for doors with swipe card or proximity card systems are those that need to be kept locked but are used by a number of people. Most of the time these will be doors between public and staff areas of the library.

> When Fred's library installed a proximity card system, it was under the supervision of the administrative office manager, who got a huge kick (initially, at least) out of watching the computer screen to see who was going through what doors. She said she could follow the progress of people through the building, not unlike the users of the Marauder's Map in the Harry Potter books.

Doors used by only one or two people—such as doors to private staff workrooms—are generally practical to operate with keys.

If you are considering some kind of swipe card or proximity card system, be sure to investigate it before you construct your building. Some good systems require special door hardware that may be more difficult or expensive to retrofit. You also need specific information on connections between access-control and alarm systems, and on how your library will function when the system inevitably needs to be repaired. Simply leaving all the doors unlocked doesn't work.

VI. Intrusion Alarms

Intrusion alarms are common and inexpensive. Every security company knows how to install them. The systems are easy to retrofit to libraries. And they work.

Intrusion alarms typically guard libraries in two ways.

- Detecting violations of the perimeter. If someone opens a door or window that should not be opened, the alarm system is activated.

- Motion detection. Wireless motion detectors in particular are easy to install. Just stick them up in appropriate places. Once the library is closed, detectors scattered throughout the building detect inappropriate motions and set off the alarm.

If people have hidden in the building until closing time, when they begin to move around the motion detectors pick up their presence.

Almost all intrusion alarms are linked to emergency services. Sometimes this is a direct link to the police, but often it is a link to the security company, which then in turn telephones the police dispatch center.

When staff are working after regular library hours, only the perimeter of the building (doors and windows) needs to be armed. Any attempt to enter will alert the staff.

When the building is completely empty of staff, both the perimeter and internal motion-detector sensors can be armed to detect anyone either entering the building or moving around inside.

If you are purchasing an intrusion alarm system, you may want an annunciator that tells which of the many detection units in your building was activated. This will help emergency services go directly to the area where the alarm was activated, and it will help you isolate individual detectors with a bad habit of sending out false alarms.

The downside of intrusion alarms is false alarms. For example, if a breeze from the HVAC system blows a piece of paper off a desktop, the motion may be picked up by a detector. To minimize these false alarms, detectors are available that combine PIR (passive infrared) detection of heat patterns with microwave detection of actual physical movement.

In almost every case, emergency personnel responding to an intrusion alarm when the library is closed will want a member of the library staff to join them while they search the building. Libraries need staff members who (a) live near the library and (b) are not spooked by wandering through the quiet library with the police.

As with all other technical equipment, alarm systems are improved regularly, and selecting places to install detectors requires experience. For these reasons, always consult with at least a couple of good firms before putting out an RFP for an intrusion alarm system. One of the most common complaints is that the systems come with a service contract that is automatically renewed with each service call. Any issues with the response time on a service call or reliability of the system can be hard to overcome if you are locked into this type of contract.

VII. Fire-Protection Systems

Fires in libraries are always a threatening possibility. Although it's relatively hard to set shelves packed with books on fire, once they are burning the amount of fuel they supply is impressive.

A wide variety of equipment is available to suppress fires. Although fire-suppression systems will protect collections from damage, they are designed first and foremost to preserve human life, and in the process of extinguishing flames they may soak parts of the collection.

Fire-protection systems are extensively specified by building codes, and many of the features included in new libraries are not a matter of choice.

Actual fires are different from movie fires. Instead of the drama of roaring flames, they often feature intense, black smoke that obscures everything. Even if exits are extraordinarily well marked, finding one's way through the murk can be extremely difficult.

VII-A. FIRE ALARM SYSTEMS

Basic components of fire alarm systems include the following. All are very much worthwhile, and almost all are specified by codes.

- Detectors. All libraries need heat and (particularly) smoke detectors with automatic links to emergency services. Your architect will specify detectors in places called for in local building codes. Detectors are particularly important in storage closets and attics, where fires have a particularly good chance of developing unnoticed.

- Warning horns and flashing lights. All buildings require audible and visual fire alarms to alert occupants. Alarm units combine electric buzzers with flashing strobe lights. Strobe lights are required by accessibility codes for hearing-impaired people who cannot hear alarms. As an alternative to buzzers, recorded spoken announcements are also possible, including instructions about how to exit the building. These are particularly useful because libraries—unlike school classrooms—do not have consistent occupancy, and fire drills for users cannot be held.

- Spoken announcement warnings. These are required in libraries with calculated occupancies of more than 1,000 people.

- Emergency exit signs. Illuminated "exit" signs are required at all exits. All exits have signs above their doors, but some jurisdictions require second signs at floor level. Exit signs above the doors are great for reminding people about how to get out, but during fires, dark smoke can rise to the ceiling, blocking the view of the upper exit signs. This can leave the lower signs visible to people who are trying to stay below the level of smoke while fleeing the fire. (We

- think both signs should be required by code.)

- Annunciators. All but the very smallest libraries should have annunciators located in their main entries. Annunciators are panels that tell arriving firefighters which detectors have been activated. In a complex building with dozens or even hundreds of spaces, firefighters could spend far too long trying to find out which detector set off the alarm. In the meantime, the fire can quickly spread.

- Pull stations. Fire codes will require pull stations that can be used manually by staff or users. Typically these are located by exits, so people can set off the alarms while leaving the building, rather than possibly heading off into the fire. The problem with pull stations is that many people are afraid to use them, particularly when doing so requires breaking a thin pane of glass or snapping a glass rod. Staff fire drills need to include the breaking of glass.

- Automatic linkages to fire services. Depending on local requirements, this linkage may be by way of an alarm company, which will receive your alarm notification and telephone your local emergency services, or it may ring directly in your local fire department.

- Knox Boxes. Many communities now require that major buildings have small safes built into exterior walls by their main entrances. The safes contain keys to the building, and emergency service personnel in turn carry keys that unlock the safes. Knox Boxes eliminate the need for emergency personnel to carry keys to many buildings. Hunting for the right key takes time, and safely keeping track of a large number of keys to secure areas can be a challenge. The whole Knox Box approach is very much like that used by real estate agents who store keys to houses in small safes attached to front door knobs. All participating agents carry a standard key that fits all boxes.

VII-B. SPRINKLER SYSTEMS

Sprinkler systems provide automatic fire suppression with water or various chemicals.

Librarians have a love/hate relationship with sprinkler systems. They save buildings and lives, but they can make a soggy mess out of collections.

Sprinkler systems are widely specified by building codes. Whether or not your building is required to have a sprinkler system depends on a number of variables, including square footage of the building, type of construction, and the degree to which the building facades are accessible to the fire department using their equipment.

Sprinkler systems can be required in libraries as small as 7,500 square feet, and all libraries of 12,000 square feet or more require sprinklers.

There are extremely good arguments for equipping all buildings with sprinkler systems.

VII-B-1. Fear of Sprinkler Systems

Librarians by and large fear sprinkler systems, associating them with massive water spillage and the ruin of book collections.

Part of librarians' fear of sprinkler systems is due to misrepresentation in the movies. When sprinkler systems are activated in movies, water immediately begins spraying from every sprinkler head in sight. But actual sprinkler heads are designed to provide water only where fires exist.

The great thing about sprinklers is that they genuinely do save lives.

The major frustrations with sprinkler systems occur when a sprinkler head discharges accidentally, dumping serious amounts of unwanted water upon the place beneath. Fred knows two libraries in central Illinois that were soaked by faulty sprinkler heads. One was a library where Fred was the consultant, which made him particularly self-conscious about the event.

We have seen several libraries that were carefully planned to be just small enough to slip under code requirement for sprinkler systems. Although this may seem like a clever idea at the time, it handicaps those who follow behind and may find that expansion is difficult or almost impossible. A classic example of this is libraries built at just under building area limit to avoid the necessity of sprinkler systems. Unfortunately, sooner or later they need to expand, and sprinkler systems have to be installed retroactively in spaces that may never have been designed for them.

Because the provision of sprinkler systems lowers insurance rates, the savings from avoiding sprinkler systems may be far less than the owners expected.

VII-B-2. Wet Pipe Systems

Everyday sprinkler systems have pipes permanently filled with water. Sprinkler heads are mounted on the pipes. Each sprinkler head includes a fusible link that melts when heat reaches a specific level. The melted link allows a valve to open. Water rushing from the pipe hits a diffuser that spreads it out into a spray pattern.

Wet pipe sprinkler systems are very widely used.

They have a few weaknesses:

- Even though water emerges only from the activated sprinkler head, it can still make a considerable mess.

- Sprinkler heads can be vandalized or accidentally damaged. Both of these problems can be limited by using sprinkler heads concealed by white metal discs that are even with the ceiling. When a fire occurs, the disc first falls off and the sprinkler head drops into place. When the fire becomes slightly hotter, the sprinkler head is activated.

- After being inside sprinkler pipes for a few years, water contains a combination of mold and corrosion, and it resembles India ink.

- After many years, sprinkler systems can develop leaks. Typically these are only pinholes, but they are still unwelcome. (Luckily, acoustic ceiling tile develops brown spots when it hears the word "leak.")

The important point is that when sprinkler systems are activated, only the heads over the fire open. The dramatic scenes in movies where all the heads open at once are exciting but total fantasies.

VII-B-3. Dry Pipe Systems

Dry pipe systems are used where there is danger of the water in wet pipe systems freezing.

In dry pipe systems, there is no water in the pipes until one or more sprinkler heads open. A small air pump creates enough air pressure within the sprinkler pipes to keep water out. When one or more sprinkler heads open, the compressed air in the pipes quickly rushes out through the sprinkler heads, followed by water.

Dry pipe systems have alarms to indicate that air pressure in pipes is dropping and that water could be creeping into freezing territory.

A common use of dry-pipe systems is when sprinkler pipes must be installed above the ceilings of older buildings, but even some modern buildings are freezing cold above their ceilings. Watch for ceiling tiles that have been removed to let heat into the spaces above.

VII-B-4. Pre-action Systems

Pre-action systems provide a fail-safe mechanism to prevent the accidental discharge of water due to failure of faulty or damaged sprinkler heads.

The sprinkler pipes in a pre-action system are dry at all times until the library's smoke detectors sense smoke in the building. At that time, the sprinkler pipes fill with water, ready for use if sprinkler heads open.

A small air compressor keeps the air in the sprinkler pipes slightly compressed at all times. If one or more sprinkler heads open when there is no water in the pipes, an alarm indicates that there may be faulty or damaged sprinkler heads.

Occasionally, the smoke detectors for pre-action systems are fooled by something other than the smoke of a fire, and the systems fill with water. For these situations, all pre-action systems have drain valves that allow technicians to drain the system after the detectors have been reset.

By requiring that both smoke detectors and sprinkler heads be activated before water is discharged, pre-action systems help to prevent water damage from faulty sprinkler heads.

> A library Fred worked with liked to hold cooking demonstrations in its community room, and the smoke and fumes kept activating the pre-action sprinkler system, filling the pipes with water. Everything worked in accordance with design, but the library had to call the sprinkler company occasionally to have the system drained.

Pre-action systems are more expensive than the standard wet-pipe and dry-pipe systems, but they are particularly important with collections that cannot be replaced. In our opinion, they are worth having in all libraries.

VII-B-5. Types of Sprinkler Heads

Sprinkler heads come in a variety of configurations, depending on whether water is ejected upward, downward, or to the side.

For rooms with acoustic ceilings, the most attractive sprinkler heads are concealed by white metal discs that fit relatively flush to the ceiling. When fires occur, the low-melting-point solder that holds the disc to the sprinkler unit melts, and the disc falls off, exposing the sprinkler head. The diffuser that directs the sprinkler water in a spray pattern then drops into place. When the temperature becomes slightly higher, the fusable link in the sprinkler opens and water escapes.

We like concealed sprinkler heads not only because they look less mechanical but also because they do not provide an attractive target for vandals. And custodians carrying stepladders are far less likely to bump into them.

VII-B-6. Inert Gas Systems

Some highly secure installations, such as military computers, are protected by systems that fill rooms with oxygen-free gas, stifling fires without the possibility of water damage.

These aren't for libraries, except for protective storage vaults for rare items.

Although these systems sound appealing, they can be used under only highly controlled situations, since people who are in rooms where the system deploy may have only a couple of minutes to leave the room before suffocating. Only spaces with access strictly limited to a few very highly trained personnel can afford to take a chance on quick suffocation.

VII-B-7. Powder Systems

A dry-chemical fire-suppression system makes use of a large tank that is filled with the dry-chemical powder and then pressurized. When the system is activated, either electrically or manually, the valve on the pressurized tank opens and the dry powder is released into a piping system and out the nozzles of the fire-suppression system. The use of dry chemicals reduces damage to valuable books and papers.

When dry-chemical systems are activated they have to be recharged.

VII-B-8. Shutting Off Sprinkler Systems

Libraries with sprinkler systems need to train a large number of staff members on how to turn off the systems. If a sprinkler head fails and douses the library with water when there is no fire, the sooner the valves feeding the system are turned off, the less damage is done.

Libraries are at their most vulnerable when they are brand new and not enough people have yet been trained on shutting off the system.

VII-C. ESCAPE ROUTES

All libraries need to plan escape routes. The less complex and more familiar these are, the less chance of loss of life in the case of fire.

As with other areas of fire safety, escape routes are much controlled by building codes and may need to be posted. Your architects and engineers should help you. Talk with them.

In general, users try to exit buildings using the doors by which they entered. Making it quick and easy for users to retrace their steps helps.

As we noted above, all fire codes require illuminated exit signs that remain illuminated when power fails. Older signs use tubular incandescent lamps, which burn out frequently and are therefore an incredible nuisance. Modern signs all depend upon LEDs. If your library still has incandescent signs, this week is a great time to replace them.

Keeping escape routes clear is made difficult by the fact that most fires are accompanied by thick, opaque smoke.

Because the areas clearest of smoke are by the floor, some codes now require additional illuminated exit signs at floor level. We think all codes should require them.

In buildings with more than one floor, codes may require "areas of refuge" in the entry areas of all emergency staircases where the areas do not align with ground level. The idea is that people who are fleeing a fire but cannot deal with stairs can wait in safety to be rescued. Because fire-exit staircases are built to withstand fires better than other spaces in a building, people waiting there are relatively safer. Areas of refuge need equipment that allows people waiting there to alert emergency personnel.

Codes require signs indicating areas of refuge.

One sign of the higher construction standards for staircases is that in some construction projects the staircases are the first things built. Until the rest of the building is constructed, the staircases stand alone like mysterious towers.

VII-D. PORTABLE FIRE EXTINGUISHERS

Fire codes require that portable fire extinguishers be located at specified locations in libraries. Depending on code requirements, these extinguishers can be in cabinets or directly hung on wall brackets.

Not all fire extinguishers are suitable for all fires. The standard types of extinguishers include:

- Class A—Burning wood, paper, cloth, plastics, etc.
- Class B—Burning liquids
- Class C—Electrical fires
- Type D—Burning metals

Most libraries will want multi-type extinguishers so that staff members do not have to be trained to identify fires and determine whether or not they can use a particular extinguisher. In addition, in a public building, a member of the public may decide to step in. Type ABC extinguishers are common in libraries.

Codes typically require fire extinguishers by exit doors.

All fire extinguishers require periodic inspection and maintenance, and they need to be completely serviced if they are used even very briefly.

As a practical note, staff training always has to emphasize first calling emergency services and only then attempting to use portable fire extinguishers to put out the fire. Untrained people using fire extinguishers may aim at the visible flames rather than at the burning material.

VIII. Humidity Control

Of all the dangers associated with poor-quality or malfunctioning HVAC systems, one of the greatest threats to libraries and their contents is high humidity.

Relative humidity describes the amount of water in the air compared with the maximum amount of water air can hold at that temperature. For any given amount of water in the air, when we lower the temperature, the relative humidity increases. In libraries, somewhere between 30 and 50 percent appears to be ideal, although rare book collections will require far tighter controls on humidity, such as +/- 0.5 percent.

When relative humidity exceeds about 70 percent, mildew and mold can form on books. Mold in particular can be extremely destructive, but mildew is not a lot of fun either.

The possibility of mold may seem remote, but it can strike even in hallowed halls. In 2008, for example, mold appeared on books in the stacks of a major university's rare book room.

If you have a collection of rare materials, you may want to invest in a recording hygrometer, which keeps a record of changes in relative humidity over time. Or you may want a humidity alarm.

For more information on humidity control, see chapter 33, "HVAC."

IX. Video Surveillance Systems

Libraries increasingly incorporate surveillance cameras in their security systems. Even if people don't notice them, surveillance cameras are everywhere.

Although a library might in theory station a staff member in front of a bank of monitors to watch for problems picked up by surveillance cameras, there would be little benefit. Instead, data recorded by cameras is typically checked after an event takes place. Because surveillance systems link images to times, it is possible to see what happened at a particular place at a particular time.

All modern video surveillance equipment uses solid-state memory. Because images make intensive use of memory, a library with a dozen video cameras may need a terabyte of storage.

Modern surveillance technology uses high-definition cameras that take even more storage space but balance that with great image clarity, which makes it easier to identify people and activities.

Data needs to be retained for about three weeks to give the library and law-enforcement employees time to download and preserve relevant images.

Modern surveillance systems use built-in video analytics to identify movement without the image. This allows the recording system to reduce its resolution or recording rates when no movement is detected but increase both when something happens within the view of the camera. The system also flags events for easier review and retrieval, reducing the amount of time spent in reviewing data.

Surveillance cameras should have motion sensors to allow the system to retain data whenever motion takes place. The system should retain data starting a few seconds before motion is detected by the camera and continuing a few seconds after motion ceases. Some cameras in busy locations may end up retaining data for virtually the entire time the library is open, while others in locations like fire escapes may retain only occasional data.

For reasons of personal privacy, video surveillance systems typically do not include sound recordings. However, the use of audio recording has increased in areas where interactions between staff and users can be uncomfortable or even threatening. To avoid violation of eavesdropping laws, you will need clearly posted notices that audio monitoring is taking place, warning people that they can be subject to accountability for what they say. Check with your security firm about requirements concerning privacy and sound recordings in your state.

IX-A. EQUIPMENT SPECIFICATIONS

Video cameras are typically tidy in appearance. Most are under plastic ceiling-mounted domes about six inches in diameter, and they are relatively unobtrusive. However, libraries with video surveillance systems may want to post notices to that effect on entry doors, both to warn people and to provide an extra incentive to good behavior.

Setting a high technical standard is important. Newspapers frequently feature blurred images of people holding up convenience stores, and these can be of little value. The specifications outlined below are typical of those found in high-quality systems. In particular, you never want to compromise on number of pixels per image, number of images per second, resolution, and light sensitivity.

The quality of surveillance equipment varies widely. If you are purchasing a system for your library, you will want to specify at a minimum:

- Cameras
    » Color images. It's much easier to recognize people with color images than with black and white images.
    » Sixteen images per second. For comparison, theatrical motion pictures use 24 images per second. Experts tell us that it is hard for people in law enforcement to make good use of data from cameras that record fewer than 16 images per second.
    » Motion activation.
    » Hot-spot motion detection, with the ability to exclude irrelevant motion within specified areas of a camera's view.
    » Minimum image capture rate of one image per second in the absence of detected motion.
    » Auto-iris.
    » Manual zoom lenses.
    » Resolution at a minimum of 1,080 horizontal lines for standard definition systems.
    » Light sensitivity rating of 0.5 lux. This is very dim light, the equivalent of about 0.05 footcandles or bright moonlight.
    » Cameras are also available with built-in infrared illumination to produce usable images in total darkness. Because the image depends on light emitted by the camera, the usability of the image depends on the distance between the subject and the camera.
    » Tamper-resistant protective domes.
    » Exterior cameras in vandal-resistant domes and outdoor environmental enclosures. Vandal-resistant domes might—for example—resist the impact of a 10-pound hammer.
- Central units.
    » Sufficient storage to retain at least three weeks of data.
    » Rate of recording adjustable on a camera-by-camera basis.
    » Image pixel count of no less than 720 by 486 for all images.
    » During alarm state, cameras will record a minimum of 16 images per second. "Alarm state" refers to times where cameras are detecting motion.
    » Pre-alarm buffer of two seconds at 16 images per second. Because surveillance systems are constantly recording and then eventually discarding non-alarm data, it's always possible to save data from shortly before motion is first detected.
    » Post-alarm recording of three seconds at 16 images per second.
    » All images to be matched to clock times. It's extremely important to be able to tie images to specific times.
- Installation.
    » Turn-key installation. All work required to install the system and set it in

operation should be preformed by the vendor, including any necessary architectural modification of the library.

» No surface-mounted wire conduit or exposed wire. As with all systems added to library buildings, no one wants new visible conduit or wire. Exposed wire trailing around is ugly, and conduit is unpleasantly industrial.

» All cable plenum rated. A plenum is an open space—such as the space under a floor or above a ceiling—that conducts air for an HVAC system. Plenum-rated cable is rated for installation inside plenums.

» Central unit(s) in a rack in the library's main server room (or other specified location). Note our suggestions on server room security.

Due to the large amount of data being transferred, your video surveillance cameras may require hard wiring for data transmission.

IX-B. COMMON CAMERA LOCATIONS

Libraries need to position surveillance cameras in locations where they have had previous problems or where they can anticipate serious problems arising.

For example, libraries may need to record the faces of people threatening staff members at service desks and causing trouble with computer workstations.

Cameras can be placed to record:

- Bike racks. One of the most important user of cameras is overseeing bicycle racks. In Fred's library, in the first week of operation the cameras recorded guys with bolt cutters going after the bike locks.

- Faces of people at computer workstations. Due to considerations of patron privacy, libraries will probably not want to be able to see screen images.

- Faces of people speaking to library staff at service desks. If users threaten staff members, libraries need images of the users, not of the staff.

- People exiting restrooms. (No matter how much vandalism takes place inside restrooms, libraries that place cameras inside restrooms are in violation of serious privacy laws that prohibit video surveillance in places where users can expect privacy, such as restrooms, dressing rooms, etc.)

- Elevator cabs. Adding a camera to an elevator will require coordination between a library's elevator company and its security company (who may not want to play nicely together), but if there are problems with vandalism in elevators, it will be worth the extra effort.

- License plates of cars passing through drive-up service lanes. Because of problems with inappropriate things placed in exterior book returns, some libraries will almost certainly want to record all use of returns.

- People using walk-up exterior book returns. Recorded for the same reason.

- All possible exits from children's departments. A children's department may need to record images of everyone leaving the department, including use of emergency exits, due to occasional abduction of children by non-custodial parents.

- Faces of people passing through security gates on the way out of the library. Because of the problems involved with sound recording, it's a good idea to have gates with lights that flash in addition to beeping when theft is detected, so that the record can match the face with the event.

- Situations where cash or credit cards are used.

X. Miscellaneous Issues in Patron and Staff Security

X-A. PANIC BUTTONS

Many libraries provide panic buttons at staff workstations.

Typical panic buttons are concealed beneath desktops or countertops. To prevent accidental activation, most consist of small boxes with recessed buttons.

Panic buttons can be linked to the library's emergency service dispatcher, but they also need annunciators at a heavily staffed service point (typically the library's central lending desk) so that staff members and emergency service responders will know not only that someone has pushed a button but also exactly where that button is located. It may also be possible to provide an annunciator for panic buttons at the main entrance to the library.

Police tell us they much prefer phone calls, because they then know what to expect when they arrive at the library.

Even if panic buttons are seldom or never used, they provide a better sense of security for staff members who are occasionally worried.

> In Fred's library, the only time a panic button was pressed was when a little girl crawled under the children's department reference desk and pushed the button. Afterwards, everyone agreed it had been a good test of the system, although there was universal puzzlement when the police arrived, since no one knew which of the many panic buttons in the building had been pressed and there appeared to be no trouble anywhere in the building.

X-B. PORTABLE ALARM DEVICES

Staff members can carry alarm devices. Some can have wireless connections to the library's panic button system, while others just make an incredible racket.

In our experience, the primary staff members who want equipment of this type are pages shelving books, who often end up sharing obscure corners of book stacks with people they would not like to meet in the proverbial dark alley.

Book stacks tend to absorb a lot of the noise from alarm devices that are not connected electronically to a central station, but portable alarm devices are amazingly loud up close and may serve their purpose for that reason alone.

> In Fred's library, the shriek of a lavalier alarm was so earsplitting up close that the creep involved raced from the library like a terrified rabbit. The staff a floor away couldn't hear the alarm, but it still worked well.

X-C. PUBLIC LIBRARY CHILDREN'S DEPARTMENTS

Children's departments in public libraries require special attention to security. Librarians worry about abduction by non-custodial parents, people with a history of child molestation hanging around, and unwatched toddlers wandering out of the building into traffic. Constructing children's libraries that prevent these kind of problems is always worthwhile.

Here are some basic principles:

- Children's departments should always be at the end of the line, never a passageway to other parts of the library. If the department is not a passageway, any adult unaccompanied by a child will be particularly evident.

> In the library Fred inherited when he became a library director, the only entrance for users with disabilities was a ramp that led people through the center of the children's department. A number of people who did not need the department's services would linger too long on their way through, to the frequent discomfort of the staff. When the library was expanded, the new children's department was at the end of a hall and through glass doors, and the unwanted lingering essentially ceased—all achieved by better design rather than by security systems.

- Children's departments benefit from glass walls separating them from the rest of the library. Glass walls provide separation without blocking staff oversight or making visitors feel uncomfortable or insecure about entering an unseen department. And they can do a great job of blocking sound if the adult department is right next door.

- No item of equipment required by adults, with the exception of parents, should be located within a children's department.

- If children toddle out of the children's department, they should have to pass directly—and conspicuously—by service desks before exiting the building.

- The hardest place to see is the back of the children's department.

- If your library has a video security system, the most important place for cameras may be the children's department.

> Fred consulted with one library where young children who toddled out of the children's department immediately found themselves next to an exterior automatic door that opened helpfully, encouraging them to wander into the street immediately outside.

XI. Public Relations Implications

Each time libraries install new security systems, they worry about negative patron responses. They worry that users will be offended by the implications of distrust. Some libraries decide not to install security systems because they are concerned about user reactions to being mistrusted. Others avoid searching bags or briefcases because of the intrusion involved.

Our experience, however, suggests that complainers are a smaller minority than library owners or directors expect. Almost all users say, "It's about time!" For example, as a graduate student Fred worked in a major metropolitan public library. When the library finally introduced guards who inspected briefcases, users who expressed themselves seemed uniformly pleased. Civil liberties was not an issue.

The main issues appear to be social rather than structural. If staff members are trained to always allow readers to save face, many problems can be averted. It's easy, for example, to apologize when users set off exit alarms, even when the dishonesty of the situation is fairly obvious.

If you decide to avoid having a security system because it may offend users, you can always provide the space necessary to install one later.

XII. Staff Training on Security

Staff training is a major part of maintaining library security. While some staff automatically take action when crises occur, others simply freeze and do nothing without prior training.

Among the things a library can do are:

- Assign each service desk an area of the library for which it is responsible. Desk responsibilities work far better than individual responsibilities, since the people on duty at any given place or time can vary greatly.

- Hold staff drills for crisis situations, working with your local fire and police departments. With the exception of school libraries, the people present in a library at any given time vary tremendously, and drills like school fire drills are not feasible.

- Train all of the staff, including those who are exclusively backroom staff.

- Remind staff to watch for occurrences that may not be crises but appear odd. And tell someone.

- Train everyone on the staff to call emergency numbers whenever a crisis occurs. Making 50 calls to 911 for the same emergency is infinitely better than making no calls at all, with each staff member assuming someone else would call.

- Drills need to involve repeats. The first time through, things always go wrong. At the end of the simulation, gather everyone together, review what went wrong, and then repeat the drill immediately.

Fred's library had annual fire drills, with the fire department providing a smoke generator and having a real fire truck pull up. The equipment made the drills memorable. When a fire actually occurred, the staff searched and evacuated the entire building in two minutes.

You can also hold fire extinguisher drills. Without training, many people aim the extinguisher at the flames rather than the burning material and completely miss the fire. However, the main point to make during staff training is to always call the fire department *before* trying to put out a fire.

Dealing with dangerous individuals involves much of the same procedure. Insist that all the staff call for help rather than just standing and watching.

XIII. Snappy Rules on Security

1. The correct number of entrances to a library is anything up to one. Or more if you have Enough Money.

2. If RFID tags are visible when they're installed in books, users with theft in mind may simply remove the tags.

3. The true cost of replacing a stolen book is vastly more than the value of the book.

4. When you are planning a library building, always ask what additional building codes will come into play when you expand it.

5. Basements cost almost as much as extra floors and can carry a terrible functional price in gloom and moisture and difficult maintenance. But they have an evil allure for people who don't know much about commercial-grade construction.

6. All entrances need to be staffed, whether or not they have security gates.

7. Never let your library be a passageway to someone else's turf.

8. Anyone who works in a library building must report to the director of the library. With the exceptions of service windows in library lobbies, shared facilities are seriously evil.

9. Provide tornado and hurricane shelters. If your library is destroyed by a tornado or hurricane, it's hard to explain why you skipped shelters to save a little money.

10. The best tornado and hurricane shelters are restrooms because no one will store book-sale books or puppet stages in them.

11. If it's obvious to library users how your book theft-detection system works, the serious thieves will circumvent it.

12. The lowest-cost and most effective theft-prevention system is keeping something theft-worthy behind a service desk. Or just locking it in a well-built room.

13. Automated book sorting is fun, but there's apparently no serious study of whether it saves money. Sorter bin envy is not a healthy emotion.

14. Meeting rooms and the restrooms that go with them need to be accessible from entryways.

15. When you need serious liability insurance coverage, you need serious liability insurance coverage.

16. The way to save money on insurance is to raise the deductible amount rather than cutting the total coverage.

17. Avoid places where staff and users can be trapped. Dead-end book aisles and service desks with only one way out are good examples of bad design. So are exit passages with a series of one-way doors. All of which exist despite codes.

18. Public library children's departments must not be passageways to other public areas of a library.

19. Always study your plans for ways to improve staff sight lines. Your architects will not always like this.

20. Group study rooms need to be glass boxes, with major sheets of glass on all interior sides. Audio privacy always, but video privacy never.

21. Codes provide a lot of detail on required security arrangements, but always show your plans to your most paranoid staff members. And to your building consultants if they have extensive backgrounds in library management.

22. If your library has an unenclosed ramp or staircase leading down to a basement entrance, sooner or later you'll have a

flooded basement. And most libraries don't have flood insurance.

23. Never store book sale books in your library's attic without first consulting your engineers or architects on whether your attic will handle the weight. Finding out experimentally that it doesn't work is not much fun.

24. If you decide to build a wood-framed library without a tornado shelter, have your rationale ready for your press interview the day after the tornado.

PART IV
Technical Issues

CHAPTER 36

Insurance

I. Introduction

I-A. INSURANCE COVERAGE IN LIBRARIES

Insurance coverage is essential for libraries.

Many libraries are covered by the insurance policies or other risk coverage systems of parent institutions. The directors of academic libraries, school libraries, and special libraries are not likely to be solely responsible for insurance arrangements, but public libraries frequently need to plan and negotiate their own coverage.

No matter which body is responsible for your library's coverage, you still want to review values with people in charge. For example, a university employee may seriously underestimate the value of a library collection.

Insurance developed from groups of ship owners who agreed to jointly cover lost ships belonging to members of the group. If the loss of a ship was a rare experience but devastating to the owner, sharing the risk made tremendous sense.

The same concept applies today. Insurance is for unaffordable losses, not for nuisance losses.

There may be no legal requirement to purchase building insurance. But depending on the nature of financing, libraries may be required to have insurance.

The US insurance industry has been a dominant player in the creation of safer buildings, including the creation of many building codes and the development of the Underwriters Laboratories, which evaluate the safety of equipment of many types. Knowing what types of construction will lower your insurance rates is a great guide to some of the steps you can take to create a safer building.

And if some aspect of your proposed new structure will greatly increase your insurance rates, you will probably want to review your design plans.

Although some insurance policies can be extremely complex, there are a few basic terms everyone should know. Some states improved the situation greatly by passing laws insisting that insurance policies be understandable by average high school graduates. Until then, many insurance policies gave the impression of attempting to make it impossible for clients to be sure what losses were actually covered.

In any case, risk management is a complicated area of operations for a library. It requires sound advice from a professional and periodic assessment to be sure that coverages fit the particulars of your situation.

I-B. BASIC INSURANCE VOCABULARY

- *Actual cash value*. What the property is worth right before the loss. Unlike replacement cost, ACV may take depreciation into account.
- *Agreed amount*. A value determined in advance by joint agreement of the parties.
- *Brokers or agents*. The people from whom you purchase your insurance coverage. (The terms have somewhat different legal meanings.)
- *Endorsements*. Increased or reduced coverage is provided to basic policies through the use of endorsements. Typically these appear as additional sheets of paper stapled to your basic policy and cited in the cover page of the policy.
- *Exclusions*. Losses not covered by specific policies.
- *Floater policy*. An all-risk policy covering specifically scheduled items. Items that lend themselves to theft are commonly insured this way. Works of art or valuable books that are at risk because they are on public display might be protected by floater policies.
- *Insured*. People in the insurance business refer to a customer as "the insured."
- *ISO*. The Insurance Services Office, which provides statistical, actuarial, underwriting, and other information to the insurance industry.
- *Loss adjustment*. The process of determining how much your insurance company will pay for your loss is called "adjusting," and the people who do this work are called "adjusters." Some companies use only their own employees as adjusters, while other companies use the services of independent insurance adjusting firms.
- *Mysterious disappearance*. Sometimes, things just vanish. We can't point to any specific theft incident. All we know is that something is missing. So-called floater policies can cover this kind of loss. They're too expensive for book collections, but you may want to cover objects that appeal to thieves and are continually at risk, such as laptops or artworks.
- *Perils*. Insurance industry talk for the sources of damages.
- *Premium*. The cost of the policy.
- *Replacement cost*. Cost to replace an item at today's prices rather than at the original cost, without any deduction for depreciation. In other words, the cost to rebuild the same type of building at the same location with similar materials.
- *Risk*. The type or amount of loss against which policies are issued. Also the propensity of an insured to have a loss. For example, young drivers pay higher rates than mature drivers because they have more accidents.

- **Scheduled.** Individual items specified for higher risk coverage. See "floater policy," above.

- **Settlement.** Most insurance companies are prepared to make partial payments almost immediately, to allow repair work to begin, with final details to be worked out at a later time. Beware of any company that pressures you to accept a final settlement soon after the loss. Sometimes adjusting can lead to major conflicts. After Hurricane Katrina, for example, insureds and underwriters sometimes disagreed on whether specific losses were due to windstorm (which the companies covered) or flood (which was excluded). A settlement is an agreement between the insured and the insurance company based on the type of policy and the demonstrated loss. If an agreement cannot be reached, most policies have an arbitration clause.

- **Underwriter.** The insurance company.

See also chapter 13, "Building Codes," And chapter 35, "Security."

II. Types of Insurance Coverage

Of these, the two key terms are *perils*, the sources of damage, and *risks*, the possible damages that may occur.

The major risks libraries insure against are injury to patrons, injury to employees, damage to structures and furnishings, theft of equipment, and damage to collections.

Liability insurance covers injuries to people and to property that does not belong to the library. Property insurance covers damage to the library and its contents from fire, windstorm, lightning, theft, flood, earthquake, and other perils. (Flood and earthquake coverage will usually involve an endorsement or a separate policy.)

Loss of business income is a major issue for some businesses, but it may not be important to libraries, which may elect not to have this coverage.

In general, insurance companies are far more worried about injuries to people than damages to buildings. Adjusters say that it's easy and straightforward to estimate losses if no one is hurt, but when people are hurt losses can be unpredictable and sometimes extremely high.

Additional forms of insurance are mentioned very briefly in "Other Insurance Not Relevant to Buildings," later in this chapter.

II-A. STRESS ON COVERING MAJOR LOSSES

As with all forms of insurance, the purpose of library insurance is to protect the institution from losses it cannot afford. Although the cost of replacing a stolen laptop or redecorating a small workroom may be frustrating in a year of tight budgets, purchasing insurance to cover small losses is usually a waste of money.

While some libraries purchase insurance directly, non-public libraries are usually part of larger organizations that manage risk. In some of these cases, the organization may "self-insure" itself, purchasing insurance coverage only for truly immense losses.

II-B. SETTING VALUES

When you meet with an insurance broker to develop coverage for your library, you will need to be prepared to set values on structure and contents. Here are some common ways of doing this.

- Buildings. When it comes to buildings, original construction costs are no guide to replacement costs, for the cost of construction can escalate from 3 to 8 percent a year.
    » Try to find out what buildings of similar quality are costing to construct per square foot at the time you arrange the policy. If it's been a few years, call your architect.
    » Some companies use computer programs to estimate the costs of buildings per square foot. But be careful, because libraries are generally expensive to construct, and computer programs may underestimate costs.
- Furnishings. Furnishings can usually be estimated by using formulas that architects use. If it's been a few years, call your architect. Again.
- Collections. In addition to furnishings, you will need to insure your collection. For ordinary collections that are not filled with valuable objects, a simple formula will probably be sufficient. Remember that the cost of replacing books is not only the purchase price but also the cost of ordering and processing, so be sure that your insurance company recognizes that it is insuring staff time as well as the cost of books and recordings.

Inflation is always a concern. You can review your policy frequently, or you can purchase an endorsement that increases your coverage based on the general rate of inflation or on actual building costs for your area.

A lot of older buildings tend to be underinsured if their owners or managers fail to pay attention to inflation.

II-C. DEDUCTIBLES

Property insurance always has a deductible amount. This amount is paid by the insured before the insurance company steps in to pay the balance. Deductible amounts keep insurance companies from being badgered by endless small claims (which would in turn lead to an increase in premiums). Most agencies that purchase insurance regard this approach as separating affordable and unaffordable losses. For example, if your library carries a $10,000 deductible, the insurance company will pay any insured loss, less the first $10,000.

Deductibles apply to each separate loss rather than to cumulative individual claims.

One of the easiest ways to cut the cost of insurance is to purchase policies with fairly high deductible amounts and thereby limit claims to very serious losses.

By contrast, liability insurance typically has no deductible amounts. If someone falls down the front steps of your library, your insurance company steps in and handles everything (up to the limits on your policy).

II-D. ENDORSEMENTS

Basic insurance policies can be extensively modified through the addition (or elimination) of coverage options. These are called "endorsements" and often consist of extra sheets attached to the basic printed policy.

The critical thing is knowing what losses are covered or not covered by your basic policy. For example, what will your policy do about mold in your library, and do you want to have better coverage?

II-E. UMBRELLA LIABILITY COVERAGE

Many libraries purchase what are called "umbrella" liability policies to cover extremely substantial losses in excess of coverage provided in basic policies.

Umbrella policies are typically sold in multiples of $1,000,000. The cost is relatively low because the chance of a loss in excess of the basic policy amount is also low.

The problem lies in predicting the size of losses. Insurance underwriters may be able to make coverage suggestions based on the experiences of other libraries.

> Carrying a multimillion-dollar policy may seem like overkill, but losses of this size do occur. For example, a few years ago a public library had an $8 million liability settlement but had only a $4 million umbrella policy. The city had to levy an additional $4 million in local taxes to make up the difference.

Unfortunately, there is no real way to know how large an umbrella policy should be, and most libraries appear to just decide informally what feels comfortable.

II-F. COINSURANCE CLAUSES

Many people are tempted to underinsure on the premise that their homes or libraries are unlikely to suffer a 100 percent loss. If the building and contents are worth (for example) $10 million, the library may assume that the loss from any event is unlikely to top $5 million, and try to insure for that lower amount.

This is not a smart thing to do. Historically, insurance companies dealt with this kind of planned underinsurance through the concept of "coinsurance," which held that a policy for half the value of the property would lead to a 50 percent payout in case of a loss. In this case, the owners of the property were assumed to be coinsurers, covering half of the loss themselves. To prevent intentional underinsurance, companies may have required, for example, that insurance be for at least 80 percent of replacement cost.

Having inadequate insurance can lead to abrupt and serious awakening when a library has losses and finds them only partially covered.

Today, companies and insureds typically take care of this situation through "agreed value" insurance, where both parties agree in advance on what things are worth, jointly signing off on a statement of values (SOV) based on 100 percent replacement cost.

II-G. SUBROGATION

When your library purchases insurance, you authorize your insurance company to act legally on your behalf.

For example, a number of years ago, Fred's library had a serious electrical fire. The library's insurance company paid the entire loss cheerfully, but it turned around and (successfully) sued the local power company *in the name of the library*.

When troubles occur, you should expect to see news articles listing your library as the active party in a lawsuit when it's really the insurance company suing or acting on your behalf. For example, if a child is seriously injured in your library, the news may report that the library is arguing against the liability settlement the child's family wants. You may feel uncomfortable about this, but that's the way policies are written and the law works. The policy will actually have a clause explaining that the insured must cooperate in this process.

II-H. PURCHASING INSURANCE POLICIES

As noted in the introduction to this chapter, many libraries are parts of larger institutions and do not purchase their own insurance. In addition, some independent libraries are members of cooperative groups that purchase insurance jointly for all members of the group.

Libraries that purchase their own insurance need to be sure that they understand how the system works, but libraries that are covered by larger agencies' insurance will want to know whether their own library coverage is adequate.

Insurance policies can be extremely detailed concerning risks covered and values assigned to building and contents. Library staff (or staff of parent organizations) need to be sure that the amount of coverage provided is appropriate.

Insurance can be purchased either by low bid or by using an independent broker to obtain bids from a number of underwriters. Both approaches have advantages, but as with all bidding situations, you will need a very carefully written bid document. This is not a job for a neophyte.

When prices for insurance get high, we recommend that you first explore increasing deductible amounts. The difference between the premiums on $1,000 deductible and $5,000 deductible policies can be significant.

One of the best ways to control insurance costs is to build a library that is an attractive risk to the insurance company. If insurance companies are eager to insure your library, that's one indication you have built well.

A number of elements will affect insurance cost. They include:

- *The age of the building*.

- *The quality of local fire-protection services* (**Fire Protection Class**). PC classes run from PC 1 (the best) to PC 10 (significantly other than the best). PC ratings are based on the technical competence and equipment of fire departments, access to water, and quality of dispatch services. A city is pleased when its fire department's PC rating improves because insurance rates for property within the city drop accordingly. PC ratings are provided by the Insurance Services Office (ISO).

- *Sprinkler systems*. Libraries with sprinklered buildings may be charged substantially lower rates, due both to the vastly reduced risk of fire loss and to the vastly reduced likelihood of injuries to occupants.

- *Other security systems*. Fire and intrusion alarms linked automatically to central dispatch services lower the likelihood of losses.

- *Type of construction*. Buildings that are harder to burn are cheaper to insure. The ISO (Insurance Systems Office, not

International Standards Organization) describes six levels of construction, listed here from poorest to best. Definitions of the terms are available from the industry or on the net.

- » Frame.
- » Joisted masonry.
- » Masonry non-combustible.
- » Non-combustible.
- » Modified fire resistive.
- » Fire resistive.

If your building meets all current building codes for a building twice that size, with a non-flammable exterior and no wooden components in the walls, floors, and roofs, everyone will be happier.

When you are figuring the actual cost of better construction or new safety equipment, always factor in any potential insurance savings. (Sometimes, of course, there are no savings, so always check with your insurers first.)

III. Possible Property Coverages

III-A. PROPERTY INSURANCE

Property insurance covers losses due to a variety of "perils." The difficulty with property insurance is that the possible sources of losses are so very many. In the insurance industry, "Basic" policies cover a wide range of losses, and "Broad" policies cover even more. But it's still hard to read the lists and be sure every peril you want covered is covered.

By contrast, "special form" coverage covers all losses not specifically exempted in the policy, helping eliminate horrible surprises. Some people call it "all risk," although there are still exclusions. Libraries that want to cover the additional risks work with their insurance carriers to arrange additional coverages. Most library insurance coverage is special form.

Common risks excluded from special form coverage may include fungus, war and terrorism, sewer backup, earthquakes and sinkholes, floods, and intentional tenant damage. In particular, earthquakes and floods can lead to major library losses.

III-B. FLOOD

Providing flood insurance is a problem for insurance companies because most property owners know whether or not they are in danger.

Insurance works by a large number of people sharing risks. For insurance to be successful as a business, many people have to buy insurance while only a very small number receive payments. When one person has a loss, the premiums paid by the others are pooled to pay the loss. However, if individual property owners can be fairly certain who will have a loss and who won't, those who are not threatened are not interested in purchasing insurance, and there is no business niche for the insurance company.

Property without flood insurance may not be covered for floods caused by other disasters, such as landslides, windstorms, earthquakes, and so on. Windstorm insurance, for example, may cover structural damage due to the windstorm itself but not damage due to flooding caused by (or associated with) the windstorm.

Because private insurance companies often do not foresee any profitable business in flood insurance for structures on floodplains, the US federal government created the National Flood Insurance Program (NFIP) in 1968. NFIP was motivated in part by the tremendous damage caused by the category 4 Hurricane Betsy in 1965. At that time, Betsy was the most expensive hurricane in US history.

This federal flood insurance is available in communities that have entered into agreements with the federal government to establish and enforce laws to manage floodplains by reducing flood risk to new construction. It may also be obtainable through your insurance broker.

NFIP is the primary program for flood insurance. Unfortunately, it loses billions of dollars every year due to political pressures to charge unrealistically low underwriting rates.

Critics feel that NFIP encourages additional construction in areas in danger of flooding, and that property owners may even hope to collect on both flood insurance and disaster relief. Critics also accuse this flood insurance of being a direct federal subsidy.

Although some flood insurance may be available for your library, we think the best possible advice is to *never build libraries in flood-prone areas.*

We think that sooner or later, people nationwide are going to get thoroughly tired of having to constantly bail out entities that insist on constructing and reconstructing buildings in areas prone to flooding, all at government expense. When that time comes, there may be even less assistance available to flooded libraries than there is now, and having built your library far above the raging waters will make even more sense.

III-C. OTHER PROPERTY RISKS

Other risks for which you might seek insurance on your library and its contents include:

- *Earthquakes*. Earthquake insurance is available as a separate endorsement, and it's an important issue. (Californians do not have a monopoly on earthquakes. They just have them more frequently.)

- *Sewer backup*. In Fred's library, for some obscure reason a child flushed his shirt down a toilet. The shirt made its way through the sewer pipes to the main sanitary sewer connection. Where it stopped, thereby blocking the library's entire sanitary sewer system and flooding the lowest area of the library—the auditorium—which had (until that moment) an attractive new carpet. And just as sanitary sewers can back up, so can storm sewers. (Reason #27 for avoiding basements.) Sewer backup will probably require a special endorsement on your policy.

- *Valuable objects*. (Personal property floater policies.) If you have expensive objects you want to protect from all risks (including dropping them on the floor or realizing that they used to be in your workroom but no longer are), you will need to schedule individual items for all-risk coverage. To do this, you will need exact descriptions, including serial numbers on equipment. The costs for this type of coverage are much higher than the costs of general insurance, but it may be worthwhile for items like laptops that are dragged everywhere and can be lost or lifted. Similar policies are available for expensive works of art that require special protection.

- *Exhibits*. In addition to its own valuable objects, a library may need to insure items that belong to other people and are currently on display at the library. One possibility is a general exhibit floater policy that covers unspecified exhibits up to a specified amount.

- *Loss of business income.* Many private businesses purchase this coverage to cover the loss of income when the business is closed due to an insurable loss. Because libraries do not generate much income from sales or fees, typically they do not purchase this kind of coverage. But the loss of income from fines and fees and copying can add up. Your policy can also pay salaries of employees if the library is closed because of a covered loss.

- *Theft of library property.* Property insurance also covers theft, but typically not the kind of theft from which libraries suffer. If someone breaks into your library at night and takes five computers, that is insurable theft. The police will be called in, paperwork will be filed, and everyone will agree on what happened and when. Most library theft, however, consists of things turning up missing. Sometime in the last six weeks (for example), someone lifted all of a library's James Bond DVDs. But the library doesn't know when or how it actually happened. From the point of view of the insurance industry, this is "mysterious disappearance" and not covered unless items are individually scheduled.

Coverage for any nonstandard risks is provided through endorsements, as described above.

III-D. BUILDER'S RISK INSURANCE

Builder's risk insurance covers the value of buildings while they are under construction and particularly vulnerable.

- The absence of locking doors and working security systems means that outsiders can wander into partially completed libraries, where they can commit vandalism or fall into unanticipated apertures.

- Partially completed buildings may be far more susceptible to damage because they are not yet fully enclosed, because sprinkler systems may not yet be functional, or because (for example) rows of roof trusses are not yet held firmly in place by sheathing. In addition, workers using torches are a fairly common source of fires in buildings under construction or repair. The combination of torches and the ancient timber of historic buildings being remodeled or expanded is particularly dangerous. As at Notre Dame.

As work on a new library building continues, the owner makes regular payment to the contractor for work completed and as a result owns increasingly large portions of the building.

Libraries can purchase their own builder's risk insurance, or they can require in their contracts with construction firms that the firms carry this insurance on the full project.

Builder's risk insurance typically ceases when the building is completed and the owners replace the builder's risk insurance with standard insurance.

III-E. WAR AND INSURRECTION

Coverage for losses due to war and insurrection is not provided by insurance policies.

Obviously, in case of the widespread destruction of war, no insurance company could provide coverage. Losses would be so widespread that companies would immediately go bankrupt.

But when it comes to riot and civil commotion, you will want to clarify coverages with your insurance company.

Given the potential for civil disobedience (consider, for example, angry citizens reacting to extremist groups you were legally unable to bar from your meeting room), you may want to make sure that your policies do not exclude damage resulting from events of this kind.

IV. Non-property Insurance

IV-A. AUTOMOTIVE

Many libraries own bookmobiles, vans, or other vehicles, and you will need comprehensive coverage (collision damage, storm damage, theft, liability, and so on).

Even if your library does not own a vehicle, you will want to be sure that your liability insurance covers any accidents that occur when library staff are operating vehicles while on library business. The term for this coverage is *non-owned auto liability*, and it may be added to your policy through an endorsement.

If, for example, your employees injure people while running errands for the library (even if not requested to do so by library management and driving their own cars), the library could be at the very least subject to a liability suit.

Automotive coverage of this type should be a standard component of liability policies, but it's important to check.

IV-B. LIABILITY

Even before the day of massive personal injury settlements, liability insurance for libraries was important. Now it is absolutely essential.

Liability insurance covers bodily injuries and property damages that are the fault of the library or its employees—or that just take place on library premises.

Although a handful of what appear to be insane settlements occur in liability cases and make the evening news, in most situations settlements are reasonable.

Obviously you can limit liability claims by keeping your building safe. Look for structural situations that can lead to personal injuries. And when your library is being designed, imagine what can go wrong with the more adventurous features of your new building.

The main secret in dealing with liability situations is to offer any help you can. Call emergency services, but *leave all talking to your insurance company*. The minute you start saying that you're sorry and that you've always known those steps were dangerous, you run the risk of getting your library into a tangle.

In order to avoid lawsuits and save insurance companies money, many liability policies include medical payment coverage that pays basic medical bills without assigning liability for the injuries. The coverage can be very broad, but limited to a few thousand dollars.

IV-C. OTHER INSURANCE NOT RELEVANT TO BUILDINGS

Most libraries carry a variety of insurance that has nothing to do with buildings. Some—such as workers' compensation insurance—may be required by law, but others are at the option of the library. The main reason for mentioning them here is because this coverage may be handled by the same firm that provides your other insurance.

- Workers' compensation insurance provides coverage for staff members injured on the job or traveling to and from the job. Rates vary with the risk to the worker. Because librarians live in a low-risk environment, the only members of the staff of the average library likely to be expensive to insure are the custodians. Insurance rates ("mod rates") are modified each year on the basis of the company's experience with each employer.
- Staff health and life insurance are typically regarded as benefits.
- Directors' and officers' liability ("D and O liability") covers malfeasance and torts by administrators. Boards and librarians most commonly are concerned about accusations of improper hiring and firing, so be sure that your insurance covers alleged civil rights violations. D and O liability coverage is usually an endorsement.

V. Action in Case of Loss

If you have a loss that you think may involve an insurance claim, your insurance policy will require you to contact your insurance company immediately. You will also want to contact your insurance broker.

If the loss involves theft or other criminal activity, you will need to inform law enforcement and file a police report. And have evidence that you did so.

The insurance company's adjuster will inspect (or hire an independent adjuster to inspect) the damage and write an estimate of repair costs. If you want to double-check, you can hire a "public adjuster" to write an estimate, but the costs of hiring your own adjuster are your responsibility.

In the case of serious structural damage, many insurance firms will hire engineering firms to assess structural damages. Depending on circumstances, a library may decide to arrange for its own inspection by a qualified engineering firm that represents the library rather than the insurance company, but that's at the library's cost.

VI. Snappy Rules on Insurance

1. Be careful to set adequate insurance values. The true cost of a book to a library can be vastly more than the purchase price of the book.
2. Constructing secure and fire-resistant buildings is a great way to cut insurance costs. Because it's a great way to cut covered losses.
3. Provide tornado and hurricane shelters. If your library is destroyed by a tornado or hurricane, and people are killed or badly injured, it's hard to explain why you skipped shelters in order to save a little money.
4. When you need serious liability insurance coverage, you need serious liability

insurance coverage. Settlements for injuries can be very large and extremely unpredictable.

5. The way to save money on insurance is to raise the deductible amount rather than cutting the total coverage. Losses covered should be truly painful, not merely annoying.

6. Always show your insurance plans to your most paranoid staff members. And to your building consultants if they have extensive backgrounds in library management.

7. If your insurance or alternative coverage is provided by a parent institution, talk with them carefully about the actual costs of library damage.

8. Store books where they can't be ruined by flood waters. Looking down from your high book stack window on the inundation that ends pleasantly below your bottom floor is infinitely more fun than looking down from the main floor of your library into your water-filled basement shelving.

9. Flood coverage is currently politics, not business, and sooner or later it may become far more expensive. Consider your long-term future and build comfortably out of the range of floods.

10. Be sure your insurance does not require you to purchase exact replacements of books or chairs or posters.

11. If your library has multiple locations, working with a single insurer may cut your total premiums.

About the Authors

FRED SCHLIPF has been hanging out in library buildings since the early 1940s (at about the age of four, he turned out all the lights in the Detroit Lakes [Minnesota] Public Library one evening—a happy moment that is still both bright and dark in his memory) and has been working for libraries and teaching about libraries and consulting on libraries since he was 17. He was a library school faculty member at the University of Illinois Urbana-Champaign for over 50 years, specializing in library buildings and library administration, and he spent nearly 33 years as director of The Urbana Free Library, the public library of Urbana, Illinois. He's done formal building consulting for about 200 libraries. He has a PhD from the Graduate Library School of the University of Chicago. He has served on dozens of committees and task forces of the American Library Association, the Illinois State Library, the Illinois Library Association, local library groups in Illinois, and the Illumination Engineering Society of North America. He has given presentations at many conferences. He was Illinois Librarian of the Year in 2000.

JOE HUBERTY grew up in a small branch of the Milwaukee Public Library and was doomed to be an architect after reading *Harold and the Purple Crayon*. Too many years later, he is a partner with Engberg Anderson Architects. He has spent the last 30+ years planning and designing award-winning and much-loved libraries across the nation, mostly so he can hang out with librarians. Joe sees architecture as a practical art that provides future-friendly, pragmatic, and functional space that is comfortable, aspirational, and inspirational. Libraries are the ultimate embodiment of the relationship between people, services, and space. His work for public and academic libraries has been the subject of multiple presentations at state and national conferences. Joe is a licensed architect in Alabama, Arizona,

Connecticut, Florida, Georgia, Illinois, Indiana, Iowa, Michigan, Missouri, New Jersey, New York, North Carolina, Oklahoma, Oregon, Utah, Virginia, and Wisconsin.

While not a part of the active updating of this second edition, **JOHN A. MOORMAN** was an essential voice in framing the first edition. He is owed much in the way of inspiration and guidance as well as practical content. All of that rose from his work as director of five public libraries and a multi-type library system, most recently the Decatur (Illinois) Public Library and the Williamsburg (Virginia) Regional Library. He has a PhD from the University of Illinois library school. He has been active in state and national library associations. When not working with buildings, he developed a specialty in legislative matters, served as a registered lobbyist, and chaired legislative-related committees for the Illinois and Virginia Library Associations. He is a past president of the Virginia Library Association and a lifelong elected honorary member of that association. Within the American Library Association (ALA) he served on the Public Library Association's Board of Directors, the ALA Council, and the ALA Executive Board, as well as served on and chaired many committees and task forces.

Index

A

academic agencies, 333-334
academic libraries
    adjacent land for expansion space, 298-299
    auditoriums in, 464
    building costs, 343
    conference rooms in, 469
    construction plaques for, 284
    entrances, multiple, 674
    expandability of, 19
    HVAC for, 649
    library buildings that include other academic agencies, 333-334
    meeting room capacities, 444
    shared buildings, combined public/academic libraries, 331
    shared buildings, problems of, 327-329
    shared buildings, rules on, 340-342
    shared meeting spaces, 332-333
    site needs of, 156
    site selection rules, 159-160
    sites, problematic, 126
    size of building footprint, 139
access hours
    of combined school and public library, 330
    of community center with public library, 332
    meeting rooms and, 446-447, 464
access-control systems
    for doors, 688
    proximity cards, swipe cards, fobs, keypads, 689-690
accessibility
    Americans with Disabilities Act, 191-193
    of auditoriums, 465
    building codes for, 189
    of collection storage equipment, 343
    conversion of house into library and, 322-323
    conversion of non-library buildings and, 311
    evaluation of, 57
    of historic entrances, 300
    improving, 204-206
    of large entry rooms, 40
    of libraries, xiv-xv
    library design for, 17, 19
    library tables and, 51
    of meeting rooms, 463
    of multi-deck shelving units, 408
    multi-floor openings and, 38
    for people with acrophobia, 199-203
    for people with claustrophobia, 204
    for people with limited eyesight, 195-198
    for people with limited hearing, 198-199
    for people with limited mobility, 193-195
    for people with limited senses of direction, 204
    for people with vertigo, 203
    problems of library buildings, 189-190
    problems with remodeling/expanding library buildings, 299-300
    of program/activity/study rooms, 463
    ramps, problems with, 579-580
    ramps as dysfunctional design, 63
    of restroom stall enclosures, 495-496
    restrooms, codes for, 491-492
    rules on, 206-208
    rules on elevators, staircases, railings, and ramps, 580-582
    of service desks, 418
    site topography and, 136
    of sound system for meeting room, 456
    stack aisle widths and, 407
    of staff lunchroom, 537-538
    of staff workrooms, 512
    of tables, 372-373, 374
accessibility codes
    amplification units, 456
    for basements, 32
    dead-end book aisles banned by, 676
    function of, 240
    for people with limited hearing, 198
    rule on, 207
    strobe lights for fire alarms, 691
    for tables, 51
accessories, 398-400
accreditation
    of architects, 105-106
    grant applications requirements, 75
    library building consultants and, 90
acoustic ceilings
    access for people with limited hearing, 198-199
    for program/activity/study rooms, 452
acoustic engineers
    hiring, 451
    involving in library design, 20
acoustic tile
    advantages of, 231
    for ceilings, 54, 231-232, 235
    importance of, 60
    issues with, 232
    on punch list, 273
acoustical engineering, 171
acoustical engineers, 38, 44, 60
acoustics
    access for people with limited hearing, 198-199
    artistic ceiling shapes and, 41-42
    of children's craft and story rooms, 476
    curved walls/round rooms and, 37
    dysfunctional designs for, 60
    evaluation of, 50
    library design for, 20
    noise in school libraries, 157
    of program/activity/study rooms, 449-452, 480
    rules about library spaces, 42
    service desks and, 440
ACP (aluminum composite panels), 217
acreage
    estimating site acreage, 144

acreage (cont'd)
    size of site, 138–144
acrophobia
    access for people with, 199–203
    evaluation of library buildings, 54–55
    library accessibility problems, 190
    multi-floor openings and, 38, 39
    rules on, 580
    staircase design and, 567
    staircases in atria and, 573
    stairs with open risers and, 572–573
acrylic polymers, 437
activity rooms
    See program, activity, and study rooms
actual cash value, 706
ADA
    See Americans with Disabilities Act
add alternates
    add/deduct alternates in cost estimates, 346
    bid openings and, 258–259
    definition of, 244
    overview of, 256–257
addendum, 244
adhesives, 212
adjacencies
    building program on, 83
    evaluating potential sites, 138
    remodeling/expansion of library and, 298–299
    site selection and, 157
    of staff workroom, 512
    of storage spaces, 553
adjacent transportation, 155–156
adjuster, 715
administrators
    design, involvement in, 163
    design process diary, 167
    interviews with, for building program input, 76–77
    library design decisions, involvement in, 18
    workrooms for, 516
adult department, 54
adverse possession, 240
advertising
    for bids, 254
    for construction management firm, 248
agency, 81
agents, 706
agreed amount, 706
agreed value insurance, 709
AIA
    See American Institute of Architects
air conditioning
    cooling process, 641

efficient lighting and, 606
HVAC, evaluation of, 51
HVAC problems, 638
obsolete or nonexistent, 310
for old libraries, 650–651
See also HVAC (heating, ventilating, and air conditioning)
air ducts
    remodeling/expanding library buildings, 304
    rules on, 652
    separately ducted, 220
    ventilation with, 641–642
air handler, 639
air handling, 472
air supplies/returns, 450
aisles
    ADA accessibility requirement for, 191
    aisle width in building program, 87
    cross aisles, 407–408
    shelving aisles, dysfunctional designs for, 63
    shelving aisles, evaluation of, 52
    width, end panels and, 400
    width for accessibility, 192
    See also stack aisles
alarms
    of electronic theft-detection systems, 683, 684
    for exit doors, 688
    fire alarm systems, 691–692
    intrusion alarms, 690–691
    portable alarm devices, 700
alcove, 471
Allerton (IL) District Library, design sample of
    floor plan, 178
    general features, 179
    main library room, 179–180
    program room, 179
    restrooms, 180
ALS (Assistive Listening System), 456
alternate bids, 256–257
alternates, 346
    See also add alternates
alternative energy sources, 646–647
aluminum, 217
aluminum composite panels (ACP), 217
American Best Bond Companies, 257–258
American Institute of Architects (AIA)
    accreditation of architects, 105
    awards, ignoring, 110
    basic services phases, 172
    contract forms by, 118–119
American Society for Testing and Materials (ASTM), 213

Americans with Disabilities Act (ADA)
    access for people with acrophobia, 202
    access for people with limited mobility, 193, 194
    accessibility for library users, 19
    building codes for accessibility, 189
    conversion of non-library buildings and, 311, 324
    handrail codes, 568–569
    lending desk height requirements, 424
    library accessibility requirements, 191–193
    ramps, allowance of, 206
    requirements as legal minimums, 580
    requirements of, 10
    restroom requirements, 493–494
    stack aisle width requirements, 407
    table requirements, 374
amplification equipment, 456
annunciators
    of fire alarm systems, 692
    for intrusion alarm, 690
    for panic buttons, 700
anti-tax groups, 355, 356
apaceDesign, 178
appearance, of library building, 46–47
application for payment
    See draws
aprons
    definition of, 373
    no aprons for library reading tables, 378
    tables without, recommendation for, 374
archaeological compliance survey, 147
archaeology, 147
architects
    accreditation of, 105–106
    awarding construction contracts, 260
    bidders, prequalification of, 254
    bonding and, 257–258
    building codes and, 239
    building costs and, 343
    building program design team, 73
    building program, ignoring, 93–94
    building program on architecture requirement, 84
    building program, review of, 92, 171–172
    building programs and, 72
    building programs by, 88–89
    building programs, purposes of, 73, 74, 75
    building programs, writing, 84
    change orders and, 276–277

INDEX | 721

for community center with public library, 332
construction, role in, 264–265
construction coordination meetings, 267–268
construction plaques and, 284
construction rules on, 287, 288
contract close-out, 278–279
contract documents, 184–187
conversion, cost of, 315–316
for conversion of non-library buildings, 324–325
for conversion project, 307, 308
cost estimating and, 345–346
design, rules on, 187–188
design development, 183–184
in design planning group, 163–164
design process, 162–163
design process, bad behavior during, 164–167
design process, owners behaving badly in, 169
design process steps, 169–174
design process work, 161–162, 169–170
design-build projects and, 250
display cases designed by, 489
draws/lien waivers/retainage, 275–276
errors, resolving, 271
FF&E estimates, 349
functional evaluation of current facilities and, 82
fundraising, assistance with, 181–183
furniture designed by, 392
government sites for public libraries and, 153
hiring
  architectural firms, locating, 98–99
  contracting with architects, 118–123
  design competitions, 123
  final selection, 117–118
  interviews, 111–117
  overview of, 97–98
  prior work of architectural firms, 99–101
  proposals, evaluation of, 109–110
  proposals from architectural firms, 108
  request for qualifications (RFQ), 101–108
  snappy rules on, 123–124
  teams, special problems with, 108–109
historic exteriors, matching, 296–298

interviewing
  information you are looking for, 112–114
  questions for, 114–117
  recommendations for, 110–112
library design decisions, involvement in, 18
pre-bid meetings/tours, 254–255
professional fees of, 350
proposals, evaluating, 109–110
remodeling/expansion, cost of, 290, 291
rules about, 3, 7, 8, 9, 10, 12, 13
rules for good/evil in library architecture, 3–16
rules on building programs, 95–96
schematic design, 174–183
school libraries, design of, 157
security plans and, 667
site acreage, estimates of, 144
for site selection, 158–159
site selection rules, 159, 160
sites, evaluation of potential, 126–129
storage spaces in building program, 553, 554–555
Substantial Completion/punch lists, 272–275
teamwork for library design/construction, 67–70
toxic chemicals in materials and, 212
understanding, 122
user seating and, 372
verification that construction matches drawings/specifications, 268–271
working with, 162–163
architectural drawings
  change orders and, 276–277
  in construction documents, 184–185
architectural features
  dangerous, 677–678
  that complicate lighting, 610–612
architectural firms
  donor insistence on particular firm, 361
  final selection of, 117–118
  interviews of architects, 110–117
  locating, 98–99
  multi-firm teams, problems with, 108–109
  prior work of, investigating, 99–101
  proposals, evaluating, 109–110
  proposals from, 108
architectural models, 182–183
architectural terracotta, 217
architecture
  as always about people, 162

architectural features of good libraries, 100
building program requirement about, 84
errors in library architecture, 100–101
good library design ideas, 17–23
matching historic exteriors, 296–298
archives
  HVAC requirements for, 648–649
  security of, 681
  theft from, 680
armchairs
  bad decisions on, 371
  evaluation of, 51
  flammability of, 669
  guidance on, 381–382
  problems with, 383–384
  for program/activity/study rooms, 447
  rule about, 391
  for staff lunchroom, 538
artificial lighting
  access for people with limited eyesight, 196
  color rendering, 591–592
  downlighting, 599–601
  evaluation of, 49–50
  fluorescent, 593–594
  glare and, 590–591
  good library lighting, formula for, 587
  guidance on, 583–584
  HID, 594
  in history of library lighting, 586–587
  incandescent, 593
  LED, 594–596
  for program/activity/study rooms, 449
  selection of, 596
  for staff workrooms, 513–514
  types of, 592–593
artificial skylight
  definition of, 584
  photo of, 621
  recommendation of, 20, 612
artistic design, 103–104
artworks
  on display in library, 483
  display/exhibit areas rules on, 489
  permanent works of art in libraries, 487
  wall spaces for hanging, 486
asbestos
  conversion of non-library buildings and, 313
  remodeling/expansion of library and, 292
  testing library building for, 212
  vinyl asbestos tile, 227–228

INDEX

assignable space, 85
assigned storage spaces, 548–549
Assistive Listening System (ALS), 456
ASTM (American Society for Testing and Materials), 213
atlas cases, 411
atria
    access for people with acrophobia, 200–201
    accessibility, improving, 205
    acoustics and, 50, 60
    architect insistence on, 103
    as dangerous feature, 677
    with floating staircase, 572
    high light fixtures, 49
    lighting problems, 611
    problems with, 3, 22, 37–38
    railings on narrow walkways, 578
    rules on, 3, 13, 206, 208, 581, 582
    shared facilities in single buildings, 335
    staircases in, 573–574
    walkways across, 201
attic
    storing books sale books in, 704
    weight of storage in, 15
attic stock
    of acoustic tile, 232
    assigned storage spaces for, 549
    of ceramic tile, 230
    definition of, 210
    of floor coverings, 224
    of flooring, 234
    storage space for, 555–556
attorneys
    See lawyers
audience, 445
audio amplification, 456
audiovisual equipment
    for program/activity/study rooms, 455–457
    storage closets for, 445, 458
auditoriums
    accessibility of, 463
    acoustics of, 452
    description of, 464–465
    planning issues involving, 465–466
    for program/activity/study rooms, 464–466
    slope of floors, 579
automated book-handling systems
    connection to service desks, 418
    rule on, 703
    space for, 426–427
automatic fixtures, 273, 508
automatic flush toilets, 494–495
automatic light switches, 588
automobile sales rooms, 323
automotive insurance, 714
awards
    AIA awards, ignoring, 110
    architectural glamor contests, 47
    library design awards for appearance, 104
    rule about, 124
awnings, exterior, 619, 620

B

backpacks, 424, 542, 686
Bacon, Francis
    on library building programs, 96
    on truth emerging, 15, 72
bake sales, 360, 367
balconies
    access for people with acrophobia, 200–201, 202
    avoidance of, 22
    dysfunctional designs for, 62, 63
    problems with, 38, 39
    rules on, 5, 10–11, 581, 582
ballast
    definition of, 584
    of metal halide lighting, 594
    quality of, 613–614
baluster
    bad staircases/handrails, 62
    definition of, 567
    horizontal, safety and, 577, 621
    openings between, 572
    sharp-edged, 191
    vertical, 56
bamboo floor, 229
bankruptcy, 257–259
banks, 317
barrel vault ceilings, 41
barricades, 438–439, 528
baseboards, 222–223, 233
basements
    avoidance of, 22, 32–34
    books in, flooding and, 670–671
    conversion of non-library buildings and, 312–313
    cost of, 703
    drawbacks of, 9
    in expanded historic buildings, 301
    exterior ramp leading to, 300, 580
    flooding from ramp/staircase, 15
    flooding of, 131, 703–704
    HVAC systems and, 293
    natural light and, 48, 617
    plumbing rules on, 665, 666
    rules on, 43, 44
    security and, 64
    shared buildings, library in basement, 342
    site selection rules, 159
    special libraries located in, 158
    staff workroom lighting and, 513
    storm drains and, 660–661
    subsurface water and, 133
"Basic" policies, 711
basic services phases, of design process, 172
battery
    LED emergency lighting, 616
    for solar panel systems, 646
beams, signing, 282
bearing strength, of floor, 223–224
bearing walls
    conversion problems, 312
    problems with remodeling/expansion, 292–293
    rules on remodeling/expanding library buildings, 304
bedbugs
    chairs infested by, 384
    washing toys/puppets, 527
benches
    padded benches, 386
    window seats, 386–387
bequests, 357–359
betterments, 104
bid, 244
bid and construction documents
    conversion of design into, 170
    design process to create, 161–162
    substitutions listed in, 186
bid bonds, 257
bid evaluation, 259
bid form, 244
bid openings, 258–259
bidders
    prequalification of, 254
    responsible/responsive, 244–245
bidding
    advertising for bids, 254
    alternate bids, 256–257
    alternatives to, 259–260
    awarding contracts, 260
    basic services phases, 172
    bid evaluation, 259
    bid openings, 258–259
    bonding, 257–258
    cost estimating and, 180, 181
    delivery methods, 245–248
    overview of, 243–244
    pre-bid meetings/tours, 254–255
    preparation for, 251–253
    prequalification of bidders, 254
    receipt deadlines, 258
    rules on, 260
    substitutions/equivalencies claims, 255–256

vocabulary for, 244–245
bids
  architect help construction bids, 170
  cost estimates and, 346
  higher bids for phased expansion projects, 302
  hiring architects by low bid, 118
  for insurance policies, 710
big box stores
  conversion, good reasons for, 308–309
  conversion to library, 319–320
bike racks, 699
bike storage, 543
BIM (building information management) systems, 176–177
blinds
  for daylight control, 618–622
  for natural light protection, 48
  perforated vinyl white roller blinds, 23
  for protection from sunlight, 587
  for staff workrooms, 512–513, 514, 529
board of trustees meeting
  location of conference room, 469
  rooms used for, 522
bond referendums, 356–357, 366
bonding
  bid bonds, 257
  bidding errors and, 259
  bidding rule about, 260
  payment bonds, 258
  performance bonds, 257–258
bonds
  definition of, 244
  referendums/bond issues, 356–357
  rules on, 366
book aisles
  See aisles; stack aisles
book displays, 430
book pickups, 429
book return slots
  automated book-handling system and, 427
  design problems of, 424–425
  storeroom precautions for, 556–557
  theft-detection systems and, 684–685
book returns
  automated book-handling systems, 426–427
  drive-up books returns with receiving rooms, 427–428
  external book return bins, 428–429
  fire resistant materials for, 668
  lending desk provisions for, 424–425
book sales
  assigned storage spaces for books, 549

book sale closets, 459
books, storage space for, 550
money raised by, 360, 367
storage closet for book sale books, 446
storing books in attic, 704
book transport systems
  automated book-handling systems, 426–427
  evaluation of, 421
book trucks, 519, 525–526
bookends, 398
books
  assigned storage spaces for, 548
  in basements, flooding and, 670–671
  bearing strength of floors and, 223–224
  collection space calculations, 86
  daylight, effects on, 623
  flooding, protection from, 716
  flooding and, 669
  humidity control for, 644–645, 696–697
  moving, costs of, 349
  site selection and weight of, 127
  theft of, 678–679
  upward expansion and, 142
booths, 386
breaker box, 628
bricks
  damaged brickwork, 274
  exterior wall rules, 233–234
  exterior walls made of, 213–214
  matching historic exteriors, 296
  proper installation of, 209
  for recognizing smaller donations, 362–363
"Broad" insurance policies, 711
broadloom carpet, 210, 225–227
brokers, 706
bronze sculptures, 487–488
brownfield sites
  dangers in dealing with, 136–137
  evaluating potential sites, 136–137
  existing sewers in, 659
  surface water runoff detention/ retention, 131
budget
  agreement on meaning of, 181
  architect interview question about, 116
  for commissioning, 270–271
buffet shelves, 537
bugs
  bedbugs, 384, 527
  lighting fixtures that display, 614
builder's risk insurance
  library purchase of, 276

overview of, 713
building codes
  for accessibility, 189
  additional codes, 240–241
  changing, 291
  code compliance problems, 313
  code inspections/occupancy permits, 271–272
  commissioning and, 270
  conversion of non-library buildings and, 326
  costs of remodeling/expanding and, 290
  disasters and, 238–239
  electrical codes, 627
  for electrical wiring, 294
  for elevators, 564
  enforcement of, 239
  for entrances/exits, 687–688
  for escape routes, 695–696
  existing structures, evaluation of, 173–174
  expansion, new code categories from, 291–292
  for fire-protection systems, 691
  historic buildings and, 146
  for HVAC systems, 639
  insurance and, 705
  municipal codes, 239
  overview of, 237–238
  public libraries in residential or commercial buildings, 335
  for railings, 579
  for ramps, 580
  remodeling/expanding library buildings, problems of, 291–292
  requirements as legal minimums, 580
  for restroom fixtures, 502
  for restrooms, 493–496
  rules on, 5, 241
  schools, conversion of, 316
  for security, 667
  site selection and, 128
  for sprinkler systems, 692, 693
  staff lunchroom stove and, 535
  for staircases, 567, 568–569, 576
  for strip malls, 318
building consultants
  See library building consultants
building costs
  capital costs, 344–346
  capital renewal/replacement costs, 352–353
  construction, 347
  estimating, 351
  furniture, fixtures, and equipment, 348–349
  moving, 349

building costs (cont'd)
- opening day collections for public libraries, 350
- operating costs, anticipating, 351–352
- overview of, 343–344
- professional fees, 350–351
- rules on, 353–354
- site acquisition, 346–347
- site development, 348
- temporary housing, 349
- utilities, 347–348
- vocabulary on, 344

building design, security through
- dangerous architectural features, 677–678
- earthquake-resistant construction, 673
- entrances, limited public, 673–674
- fire-resistant construction, 668–669
- fire-resistant contents, 669
- flood-resistant construction, 669–672
- importance of, 667
- reading/activity terraces, 677
- shared buildings, avoiding, 677
- sight lines, 674–676
- trapped, places where people can be, 676–677
- windows, 677
- windstorm-resistant construction, 672–673

building enclosure strategies, 645–646
building information management (BIM) systems, 176–177
building information modeling, 590
building inspectors, 271
building plans, 74
building programs
- architect interview question about, 115
- architects paying attention to, 98
- architectural firm, review of, 113
- basic points about, 72–73
- building costs and, 353
- conclusion about, 94
- contents of, 81–84
- for conversion of non-library buildings, 324
- description of, 71
- final review of, 92
- functions of, 71–72
- furniture specifications in, 374
- giving copies to architects, 108
- for grant application, 364, 365
- ignoring of, prevention methods, 93–94
- input on
  - consultants, observations by, 76
  - data from non-library sources, 80
  - focus groups, 78–79
  - staff/management interviews, 76–77
  - strategic plans, 80
  - surveys, 79–80
- librarian involvement in, lack of, 72
- library building consultants, hiring, 89–91
- on lighting, 196
- program review by architects, 165
- programming methods, 91–92
- purposes of, 73–76
- for remodeling/expanding library buildings, 289, 290, 303
- review of in design process, 171–172
- rules about, 3, 4, 6, 12, 15
- rules on, 95–96
- on site characteristics, 126
- for site selection, 158, 159
- site selection and, 153–154
- size, cutting down, 91–92
- space estimates using formulas, 94
- space estimating methods, 84–88
- on space needs, for site selection, 127
- for special libraries, 158
- on storage closets, 549
- storage spaces described in, 552–554, 555
- successive program drafts, 91
- two-phase building programs, 92–93
- writing, 88–89

bulletin boards
- complaints about, 486
- for graphic arts workroom, 524
- for staff lunchroom, 539
- for staff workrooms, 522

buried remains, 147
business records, storage space for, 548
buzzers, 691
bypass systems, 683, 684

C

cabinets
- for children's craft and story rooms, 475
- for kitchenettes, 550–551
- for staff lunchroom, 536–537
- storage cabinets for staff workrooms, 519, 520

CADD (computer-aided drawing and design) systems, 176–177
CAL 133, 669
calculation, of illumination levels, 589
call numbers
- range content labels, 409
- unbroken call number ranges, 405–406

can lights
- *See* recessed downlights

Canada geese, 661
canopies
- for cantilever steel shelving, 400
- rule about, 415

cantilever shelving
- accessories for, 398–400
- advantages of, 52, 395
- bookends for, 398
- compact shelving, 400–401
- depths of, 397–398
- earthquakes and, 673
- heights of, 396–397
- manufacturers of, 395
- overview of, 394
- paint finishes, 395–396
- rules about, 5, 414–415
- selection of, 393
- for staff workrooms, 519–520
- width of, 398

capital campaigns, 360–361
capital costs
- anticipating, 352–353
- definition of, 344
- estimating, 345–346
- projecting building costs prior to design, 344–345

car, 562
carbon dioxide (CO_2)
- buildup of, 638
- definition of, 639
- HVAC for control of, 637

card catalog, 61
card tubs, 439–440
Carnegie, Andrew, 483
Carnegie Corporation, 366
Carnegie Institute, Pittsburgh, 332
Carnegie Museums of Pittsburgh, 488
carpet squares, 462
carpet tile, 227
carpet yarns, 227
carpeting
- broadloom carpet for floor, 225–227
- cantilever shelving and, 395
- carpet patterns, 190
- evaluation of, 55
- flammability of, 668–669
- offgassing, 212
- for people with vertigo, 203
- for program/activity/study rooms, 452
- on punch list, 273
- rules on surfaces/materials for floors, 234
- under shelving, 673
- of story hour structures, 575

carrels, 376, 390

cash on hand, 356
cash settlement, 30
casters
   for chairs, 384-385
   for movable seating, 389
   shelving on, 409
cataloging, 77
cathedral ceilings
   acoustics with, 41-42
   daylight control and, 618
   with skylight, 622
   wooden, 232
CAV (constant air volume), 640, 650
CDs
   plastic boxes to encase, 685
   sequestering theft-prone materials, 682
   theft of, 679
ceilings
   access for people with limited eyesight, 196
   access for people with limited hearing, 198-199
   ceiling shapes, artistic, 41-42
   of churches, 322
   conversion of non-library buildings and, 325
   damaged ceiling tiles, 273
   dark, as dysfunctional design, 60
   dark, lighting of, 10, 608-609, 610
   dark, lighting problems from, 611
   downlighting and, 599-601
   energy problems and, 293-294
   evaluation of, 54
   height for meeting rooms, 463
   height for storage spaces, 553
   of huge reading rooms, 41
   light, bouncing off, 587, 623
   lighting old buildings with low ceilings, 604
   low, air ducts and, 642
   low, conversion and, 315
   low, lighting problems for, 610
   materials for
      acoustic tile, 231-232
      drywall, 232
      linear slot/perforated acoustic ceilings, 233
      plaster, 232
      wood, 232-233
   of multifunction meeting rooms, 468
   rules on surfaces/materials for, 234-235
   sound-absorbing ceiling tiles, 224
   surfaces/materials, 231-233
   uplighting, 598-599
   windows set into, 40
cement board, 219
central openings, staircases with, 574
ceramic tile
   for floor surface, 230
   for interior wall covering, 221
   for restroom floor covering, 509
   rules on, 234
ceremonies
   See public ceremonies
Certificate of Substantial Completion
   holdback money and, 275
   issued by architect, 272
   punch list and, 274
   warranties and, 278
CFLs (compact fluorescent lamps), 592
chair legs, 392
chair lifts, 195, 567
chair rails, 221-222, 233
chairs
   bad decisions about, 371
   booths, 386
   for children, 387
   for classrooms, 466
   for conference room, 446, 469
   evaluation of, 51
   flammability of, 669
   flammability standards for, 387
   furniture storage closets for, 458
   meeting room furniture storage space, 550
   padded benches, 386
   placement of, 387-389
   for program/activity/study rooms, 447
   quantity of/types of, 374-375
   rules on user seating, 390-392
   for seating at tables, 384-386
   selection of, 372
   soft seating, 381-384
   for staff conference rooms, 522-523
   for staff lunchroom, 538
   for staff workrooms, 518-519
   window seats, 386-387
   See also user seating
chandeliers
   dead bugs displayed in, 614
   maintenance of, 613
change orders
   architect help with, 170
   definition of, 262
   excessive number of, 105
   overview of, 276-277
   in remodeling projects, 305
   sloppy construction drawings and, 251
   from sloppy work, 166
changing tables
   accessibility and, 193
   for restrooms, 501
Charleston Sofa Store fire, 238
charrette, 175
check out/check in of library materials
   as lending desk function, 422
   lending workrooms for, 423-424
Checklist of Library Building Design Considerations (Sannwald), 77
Cheek, Lawrence, 59
chemicals, in construction materials, 211-212
Chicago Public Library, 204
Chicago Public Library Cultural Center, 295
childproof outlets
   in all public areas, 631
   importance of, 50-51
   placement of, 634
children
   climbable railings and, 576, 577
   display cases and, 489
   at ground breakings, 281
   handrails for, 579
   kiddie toilets, 494
   multilevel children's story structures, 476-477
   public library sites near schools, 155
   restroom accommodations for, 501-502
   seating for, 387
   tables for very young children, 377-378
   tables/chairs for, 381
   toilets, plugging of, 495
   water features and, 664
children's craft and story rooms
   acoustics of, 476
   children's supply closets, 458
   decoration of, 474
   floor coverings for, 474-475
   lighting for, 475-476
   location of, 474
   multilevel children's story structures, 476-477
   overview of, 473-474
   for program/activity/study rooms, 473-474
   public use of, 476
   restrooms next to, 476, 502
   room acoustics, 452
   sinks/cabinets for, 475
   sizes of, 474
   storage for, 475
   windows in, 475
children's departments
   assigned storage spaces for, 548
   chairs for, 383
   flip bins for, 410
   functional arrangement of rooms, 54

children's departments *(cont'd)*
   lighting for, 196
   novelty displays for children's books, 413
   security for, 701
   shelving height for, 396
   storage closets for program/activity/study rooms, 457
   storage spaces for, 556
   story hour structures with risers, 575
   video camera locations, 699
   workrooms of, 526–528
chiller, 639
chipboard
   avoidance of, 372
   no chipboard tabletops, 378
   staff lunchroom cabinets and, 537
   wooden shelving made from, 403
churches, conversion to library, 322
circuit breakers
   definition of, 628
   in electrical panels, 630
   as electrical switches, 627, 634
   function of, 629
circuits
   See electrical circuits
circulation space, 85
civil disobedience, insurance for, 713–714
civil engineer
   geotechnical engineers identified as, 102
   hiring architect and, 114
   for library plumbing system, 655
   site selection, input on, 127
   for stormwater system, 660
civil engineering, 170–171
classrooms
   design issues, 466–467
   furnishings for, 447–448
   for program/activity/study rooms, 466–467
   technology in, 466
claustrophobia, 204
cleanouts, 659
clearances
   between furnishings, 387–388
   for storage spaces, 553
clearstory windows
   access for people with limited eyesight, 196
   as dysfunctional design, 60
   north light from, 617
   north-facing, 625–626
   problems with natural light, 20
clients
   responsiveness of architects to client requests, 103

   satisfaction of, 102
closets
   audiovisual storage closets, 458
   book sale closets, 459
   in building program, 552–554
   for classrooms, 466
   coat storage for meeting rooms, 453–454
   computer storage closets, 459
   for cooperating groups, 459
   design guidance for storage closets, 549
   furniture storage closets, 448, 458
   for maker space equipment, 460
   for meeting room, 445–446, 550, 551
   for program/activity/study rooms, 457
   program/craft supplies closets, 458
clothes washers/dryers
   for children's workrooms, 526–527
   plumbing for, 663
   in staff workrooms, 515
CM
   See construction management firm
CM Agency (CM/A), 246–247
CM/A (construction management as advisor), 246–247
CMAR (construction management at risk), 247
CMU
   See concrete masonry unit
coal gas, 639
coat bars
   for meeting rooms, 453–454
   for staff coat storage, 541
coat closets, 541
coat hooks
   for meeting rooms, 453
   for staff conference rooms, 523
   for staff facilities, 540–541
   in staff restrooms, 540
coat racks, movable, 454
coat storage
   for meeting rooms, 445, 453–454
   for patrons, 686
   for program/activity/study rooms, 453–454
   for staff facilities, 540–541
   for staff lunchroom, 535
   for staff workrooms, 520–521
Cocoanut Grove nightclub fire, New York, 238, 687
code enforcement officials, 271
codes
   additional codes, 240–241
   for earthquake-resistant construction, 673
   site acquisition costs and, 347
   See also building codes

Coefficients of Friction, 225
coffee shop, in library, 423
coffeemakers, 535
coinsurance clauses, 709
collection storage/display
   atlas cases, 411
   compact shelving, 400–401
   dictionary stands, 412
   display shelves, 413
   flip bins, 410
   map cases, 411–412
   microfilm/microfiche cabinets, 412–413
   non-library shelving, 403
   overview of, 393–394
   rules on, 414–415
   shelving placement
      call-number ranges, unbroken, 405–406
      contents of shelving ranges, marking, 409
      cross aisles, 407–408
      curved shelving, 409–410
      electrical outlets and, 405
      floor strength for books, 403
      multi-deck shelving supported by columns, 408
      perimeter shelving, 403–404
      ranges of shelves in parallel rows, 404
      seismic issues, 408
      shelving on casters, 409
      stack aisle widths, 407
      stack aisles, dead-end, 404–405
      stack aisles, lighting, 406–407
      stack aisles, orientation for staff oversight, 405
   shelving with end-supported shelves, 402
   space required for, estimating, 414
   spinners, 410–411
   steel cantilever shelving
      advantages of, 395
      overview of, 394
      specifying, 395–400
   super high-density storage, 413
   wood shelving, 402–403
collections
   in cost estimates, 346
   insurance values, setting, 708
   opening day collections, 287
   opening day collections, cost estimate of, 350
   planning space for, 86–87
   shared buildings and, 339
color
   of desktop surfaces, 418

INDEX | **727**

of lighting for graphic arts workroom, 524
color rendering, 591–592
color rendering index (CRI)
　color rendering ratings, 591–592
　definition of, 584
　good library lighting, formula for, 587
　of LED lighting, 594–595, 596
　lighting for accessibility, 197
　limitations of, 592
　not compromising on, 624
　selection of light sources and, 596
color temperature
　definition of, 584
　good library lighting, formula for, 587
　importance of, 624
　of LED lighting, 594–595
　overview of, 592
colors
　dark surfaces, lighting and, 608–609
　of display cases, 485, 486
　of door handles, 578
　of grout, 507
　lighting for accessibility and, 197
　of roof coverings, 235
　of roofing, 218
　seating colors, bad choices on, 372
　of service desktops, 437
　of shelving, 52, 396
columns
　of buildings designed for extra floor, 314
　in cantilever shelving, 415
　floor strength and, 311
　in middle of shelving aisles, 52
　multi-deck shelving supported by, 408
　ornamental, 44
　service desk access and, 421
　stack aisle widths and, 407
　upward expansion and, 142
COM (customer's own materials), 373, 391
combined libraries/museums, 488
commercial buildings, 335–337
commercial businesses, 151–152
commissioning
　definition of, 262
　HVAC systems, 274
　overview of, 270–271
　of systems, process of, 647–648
commissioning agents
　commissioning process, 647–648
　fees for, 351
　proof of operation provided by, 270
community
　building program for presentations to, 74

building programs, data from non-library sources, 80
　focus groups and, 78, 79
　ground breakings and, 280–281
　library building consultant and, 91
　public ceremonies, purposes of, 279–280
　ribbon cuttings and, 286–287
　topping out ceremony and, 282–283
community agencies, 329
community centers
　with public libraries, 332
　shared buildings, rules on, 341
community rooms
　provisions for performers, 468
　seating capacity, 467–468
compact fluorescent lamps (CFLs), 592
compact shelving
　floor bearing strength and, 224
　overview of, 400–401
　rule about, 415
compass orientation
　See orientation
complete bid, 245
computer assistance, 431
computer classroom, 459
computer storage closets, 459
computer tables
　configuration of, 377
　electrical outlets for, 632, 635
　rule about, 392
computer workstations
　for graphic arts workroom, 523
　for staff lunchroom, 538–539
computers
　computer equipment tethers, 686
　computer storage closets, 459
　family computer rooms, 473
　indirect glare and, 591
　placement of, 4, 389
　reference desk placement near, 432
　wall-mounted computer counter, 12
concrete
　broadloom carpet for floor, 226
　for exterior walls, 216
　floor coverings for, 462
　flooring on top of, 224
　for interior walls, 219
　precast stone, 215–216
　stained concrete for floor surface, 228–229
concrete masonry unit (CMU)
　definition of, 210
　inner wall for brick walls, 213
　for interior walls, 219
condenser, 639–640
conduit, 271, 630
conference room chairs, 447

conference rooms
　ceiling height of, 463
　functions served by, 468–469
　furnishings for, 447–448
　furniture storage closets for, 458
　kitchenette for, 460–462
　location of, 469
　ownership of, 470
　room capacities, 445
　rules about, 480
　shared, 519
　space needed for, 446
　staff conference rooms, 522–523
　staff oversight, 470
　staff workroom rules, 529
conference tables
　in director's workroom, 530
　drawbacks of, 448
　in staff workrooms, 519
　storage space for, 551
confidence intervals, 80
connecting hallways, 21
constant air volume (CAV), 640, 650
construction
　architect's role in, 264–265
　architect's work during, 170
　builder's risk insurance for, 713
　building costs, components of, 347
　cheap, conversion of non-library building, 313, 320
　contract close-out, 278–279
　contractor's role in, 263–264
　contracts, awarding, 260
　coordination/quality control
　　code inspections/occupancy permits, 271–272
　　construction coordination meetings, 267–268
　　errors, resolving, 271
　　Substantial Completion/punch lists, 272–275
　　verification that construction matches drawings/specifications, 268–271
　earthquake-resistant, 673
　fire-resistant, 668–669
　flood-resistant, 669–672
　insurance, building construction and, 710–711
　librarian's role in, 265–267
　money for, 275–277
　phased expansion projects, 301–303
　post-occupancy inspection, 279
　process of, 261–262
　public ceremonies
　　beams, signing, 282
　　construction plaques, 284
　　cornerstones, laying, 281–282

construction (cont'd)
   public ceremonies (cont'd)
      donor receptions, 285
      donor recognition plaques, 284–285
      ground breakings, 280–281
      phase I completion events, 283
      planning for, 280
      purposes of, 279–280
      ribbon cuttings, 286–287
      rules on, 287–288
      topping out, 282–283
      tours of work in progress, 283–284
   recurring tasks, 277–278
   rules on, 287–288
   vocabulary for, 262–263
   windstorm-resistant, 672–673
construction administration, 170, 172, 264
construction control meeting, 262
construction coordination meetings, 267–268, 288
construction costs
   building costs, rules on, 353
   as component of building cost, 347
   in cost estimates, 345
   definition of, 344
   project costs, distinction between, 343–344
construction documents
   architect's responsibility for, 264
   basic services phases, 172
   cost of labor, 251–252
   design process to create, 161–162
   drawings in, 184–185
   overview of, 184–187, 251
   phased construction/interim facilities, 252–253
   specifications in project manual, 185
   on substitutions, 186
   value engineering, 252
construction drawings
   architect's responsibility for, 264
   change orders due to, 104
   definition of, 262
   overview of, 251
   verification that construction matches drawings/specifications, 268–271
construction industry, 117
construction management
   construction management as advisor, 246–247
   construction management at risk, 247
   definition of, 244
   description of, 243

   guaranteed maximum price, 247–248
   hiring construction management firms, 248–250
   professional fees of, 350
   selection of delivery method, 250
construction management as advisor (CM/A), 246–247
construction management at risk (CMAR), 247
construction management firm (CM)
   bidding process, 253
   bidding rule about, 260
   construction management as advisor, 246–247
   construction management at risk, 247
   cost estimating by, 347
   guaranteed maximum price, 247–248
   hiring, 248–250
   shop drawings, verification of, 268–269
   value engineering by, 252
construction manager
   construction rules on, 287
   guaranteed maximum price and, 248
   hiring, 248–250
   role of, 245
construction materials
   building code categories from expansion, 291
   building costs, rules on, 353
   cheap or fragile, in historic libraries, 295–296
   fire-resistant construction, 668–669
   fragile, evaluation of, 53
   matching historic, 303
   testing, 269–270
   See also surfaces/materials
construction meetings, 266
construction oversight, 105
construction plaques, 284
construction site
   advertising on, 288
   librarian visits to, 265–266
   maintenance, 277–278
   tours of work in progress, 283–284
construction workers
   signing beams, 282
   topping out ceremony for, 282–283
consultants, 350
   See also library building consultants
contact information, for authors, xvi
contaminants, 643
contingencies
   in construction budget, 277
   in cost estimates, 346
   definition of, 344

contractors
   bid evaluation, 259
   bid openings, 258–259
   bidders, prequalification of, 254
   bidding rules, 260
   bonding, 257–258
   builder's risk insurance, 713
   change orders and, 276–277
   construction, role in, 263–264
   construction contracts, awarding, 260
   construction coordination meetings, 267–268
   construction management and, 246–248
   construction rules on, 30, 287
   construction site maintenance, 277–278
   contract close-out, 278–279
   definition of, 244
   design-build projects and, 250
   errors, resolving, 271
   librarian's role in construction, 265–266
   local contractors, bid evaluation, 259
   phased expansion projects and, 302–303
   pre-bid meetings/tours, 254–255
   rules about, 7
   Substantial Completion/punch lists, 272–275
   substitutions/equivalencies claims, 255–256
contracts
   with architects, 118–123, 124
   construction contract close-out, 278–279
   construction contracts, awarding, 260
   construction documents, 184–187
   contractor's role in construction, 263, 264
   design rule about, 187, 188
   percentage of contract amount attributable to each step, 119
contrast
   definition of, 584–585
   illumination levels and, 588, 589
control, of library design, xv
controls, for HVAC, 644–645
conversion, of non-library buildings to public libraries
   bad reasons for, 309–310
   good reasons for, 308–309
   overview of, 307–308
   problems with
      accessibility, 311
      air conditioning, 310

asbestos, lead paint, hazardous materials, 313
basements, 312–313
bearing walls, 312
buildings designed for extra floor, 314
ceilings, low, 315
cheap construction, 313
code compliance, 313
electrical wiring/outlets, 314–315
expansion space, lack of, 311
floor strength, 310–311
high cost of conversions, 315–316
historic structures, 314
lighting, poor, 310
lighting, unworkable, 315
locations, 310
parking, 312
partitions/floors, unwanted, 310
utilities, lack of, 311

rules on, 325–326
summary of, 324–325
technical advice for, 347
types of buildings
- automobile sales rooms, 323
- banks, 317
- big box stores, 319–320
- churches, 322
- department stores, 317–318
- government buildings, abandoned, 323–324
- historic stores on courthouse squares, 320–322
- houses, 322–323
- schools, 316–317
- strip malls, 318

conveyance, 562
Coogan, Julie, 179
cookie-cutter building programs, 73
cooling
- by HVAC system, 641
- in older libraries, 650–651
- passive ventilating/cooling strategies, 646
- *See also* HVAC (heating, ventilating, and air conditioning)

cooling tunnel, 640
cooperating groups, 459
coordination/quality control
- code inspections/occupancy permits, 271–272
- construction coordination meetings, 267–268
- errors, resolving, 271
- Substantial Completion/punch lists, 272–275
- verification that construction matches drawings/specifications, 268–271

copier paper, 520
cork tile, 228
corner bracket, 373
corner protectors, 223, 233
cornerstones, 281–282
corporate grants, 365–366
cost estimates
- add alternates and, 256
- architect interview question about, 115
- of building costs, 351
- building costs, rules on, 353
- building costs, underestimating, 343
- of capital costs, 345–346
- for conversion of non-library buildings, 324–325, 326
- in design process, 177
- by fundraising consultant, 359
- for grant application, 364
- overview of, 181
- projecting building costs prior to design, 344–345
- for remodeling/expansion project, 290–291
- as schematic design deliverable, 180
- of site acreage, 144

cost estimators, 102, 115, 345
cost-benefit analysis, 679–680
costs
- of architect error in contract, 119
- of basements, 703
- of brownfield site cleanup, 136, 137
- of change orders, 276
- CM/A construction management and, 247
- construction management at risk, 247
- conversion, bad reasons for, 309
- of conversion of non-library buildings, 325, 326
- of conversions, 315–316
- guaranteed maximum price, 247–248
- of HVAC, 638
- of insurance, 710–711
- of labor in construction documents, 251–252
- multi-firm teams, problems with, 109
- of multiple entrances, 674
- owners who refuse to be realistic about, 168
- of phased expansion projects, 302, 303
- of remediation, 212
- of remodeling/expanding library buildings, 289, 290–291
- rules about, 11
- shared buildings for cost savings, 327–328, 329, 338
- site selection and, 129

value engineering, 252
See also building costs; construction costs

counters, 536
courthouse squares, historic stores on, 320–322
courtyards
- avoidance of, 22
- design guidance, 35–36
- dysfunctional designs for, 64

covenants
- description of, 240
- evaluating potential sites, 150–151
- rules on building codes, 241
- site selection and, 150–151

cover sheet, 184
COVID-19, 640, 643
craft rooms
See children's craft and story rooms
craft supplies, 527
craft supplies closet, 458
crash bars, 687, 688
credenza, 518
crenellations, 438–439, 441
CRI
See color rendering index
cross aisles
- rule about, 415
- shelving placement and, 407–408

cross sections, 180
cross ventilation, 646
curb cuts, 193
curved risers, 479
curved shelving
- problems with, 409–410
- rule on, 415

curved staircases
- access for people with limited eyesight, 197
- photo of, 571
- problems with, 568, 570

curved walls
- access for people with limited hearing, 199
- as bad idea, 133
- design challenges of, 37
- expense of, 26
- problems with, 8, 26, 28, 42, 88
- rule on, 9, 42
- for staff workrooms, 530

custodial supplies, 549
custodial workrooms, 663
customer's own materials (COM), 373, 391
cut pile carpet, 225
cut sheets, 186, 256, 262
cyanide gas, 669

D

Davis-Beacon Act, 251
daylight
    controlling, 618–622
    daylight harvesting/daylight sensors, 606
    effects of unwanted, 623
    in history of library lighting, 586–587
    working with, 583
    See also sunlight
daylight sensors, 606
DD (design development), 183–184
dead load, 223
dead-end stack aisles
    avoiding for security, 676
    as places where people can be trapped, 703
    problem with, 404–405
deadline, for bids, 258
deaf people, access for, 198–199
decision-making
    all parties involved in, 17–18
    architects, final selection of, 117–118
    teamwork for, 67–70
decoration
    for children's craft and story rooms, 476
    of staff lunchrooms, 539
deduct alternates, 346
deductibles
    for insurance, 708
    insurance policies, purchasing, 710
    for property insurance, 708
    raising, 715
deflection
    from compact shelving, 401
    floor strength and, 224
dehumidification, 640
delivery, 244
delivery methods
    construction management, 246–250
    design-bid-build projects, 245–246
    design-build projects, 250
    selection of, 243, 250–251
demolition drawings, 185
dents, 273
department stores
    conversion to library, 317–318
    rule on conversion of, 325
depth, of cantilever steel shelving, 397–398
design
    architect interview questions about, 115, 116
    artistic design *vs.* function, 103–104
    definition of, 161
    service desk design needs, 417–419
    of staircases, 568–570
    See also building design, security through; dysfunctional designs; library design
design award
    AIA awards, ignoring, 110
    as architectural glamour contests, 47
    library design awards for appearance, 104
design competitions
    architects and, 123
    problems with, 123
    rule on, 10, 124
design development, 172, 183–184
design process
    architects, working with, 162–163
    architects behaving badly, 164–167
    contract documents, 184–187
    design development, 183–184
    overview of, 161–162
    owners behaving badly, 167–169
    planning groups, 163–164
    rules on, 187–188
    schematic design
        cost estimating, 177, 181
        fundraising assistance, 181–183
        overview of, 174–175
        process, 175–180
    steps in
        basic services phases, 172
        engineering services, 170–171
        preliminary services, 172–174
        program review or verification, 171–172
    work of architects, 169–170
design team, 73
design-bid-build projects
    advertising for bids, 254
    bidding process, 253
    definition of, 244
    description of, 243
    overview of, 245–246
design-build projects
    bidding process, 254
    bidding rule about, 260
    definition of, 244
    overview of, 250
desks
    flexibility to move, 53
    reference and reader guidance desks, 430–432, 438
    for staff workrooms, 517–518
    See also lending desks; service desks
desktop surfaces
    color of, 418
    fragile, 437–438
    rules about, 441, 442
detectors, 691
detention basins
    function of, 131–132
    overview of, 661–662
    rule on, 666
    as site development cost, 348
diagonal staircases, 570
diary, 267, 274, 277
dictionary stands, 412
die-cutting equipment, 527
dike systems, 670
direct glare
    evaluation of, 49
    overview of, 590–591
direct lighting, 590, 608
"direct/indirect" fixture, 598–599, 600
direction
    See orientation
direction, sense of, 204
directors' and officers' liability insurance, 715
director's workrooms
    conference table in, 519, 530
    features of, 516
    furnishings for, 517
    storage for, 531
disabilities
    access for people with acrophobia, 199–203
    access for people with claustrophobia, 204
    access for people with limited eyesight, 195–198
    access for people with limited hearing, 198–199
    access for people with limited mobility, 193–195
    access for people with limited senses of direction, 204
    access for people with vertigo, 203
    accessibility, improving, 204–206
    accessibility problems of library buildings, 189–190
    accessibility rule on, 206–208
    Americans with Disabilities Act, 191–193
    building codes for accessibility, 189
    requirements, rules on, 10, 14
    rules on elevators, staircases, railings, and ramps, 580–582
disasters, 238–239
disclaimer, xv
diseases
    dishwashers for transmission prevention, 536
    filtration for protection against, 643–644
    Legionnaires' disease, 652
    respiratory diseases, 640

dishwasher, 536
display
 cases, 484–486, 489
 shelves, 413
 spaces for, 430
 See also collection storage/display
display and exhibit areas
 combined libraries/museums, 488
 display cases, 484–486
 exterior displays, 487–488
 open exhibit areas, 484
 overview of, 483
 permanent works of art, 487
 pinnable surfaces, 486–487
 policies on, 488–489
 rules on, 489
 security issues, 487
 suspicious attitude toward, 484
 wall spaces for hanging artworks, 486
disposable soap dispensers, 497–498
dissolution, of contract, 121
divider shelves, 400
domestic water, 656, 657
donations
 named categories for, 288
 recognizing smaller donations, 362–363
 record keeping of, 361–362
 spirit of community and, 4
donor receptions, 285
donor recognition plaques, 284–285, 287
donors
 art displays and, 489
 bequests, 357–359
 capital campaigns and, 360
 construction plaques for, 284
 conversions and, 309–310
 cost estimates and, 181
 donor recognition plaques, 284–285
 funding problems, 355
 lead gifts, 360–361
 library building on land owned by, 149–150
 library design process and, 18
 making the ask, 361
 naming opportunities for quiet reading rooms, 470, 471
 public ceremonies, purposes of, 279–280
 receptions for, 285
 recognition of, 362
 record keeping of fundraising, 361–362
 ribbon cuttings and, 286–287
 rules about, 11
 rules on funding, 366–367
 smaller donations, recognizing, 362–363

teamwork for library design/construction, 68, 69
 thanking, 6, 367
door handles
 brushed stainless steel, 22
 colored, 53, 578
 levers for, 191
 of restroom doors, 499, 508
door panels, 676–677
doorless restrooms, 505
doors
 access-control systems for, 689–690
 accessibility rule on, 208
 ADA accessibility requirements for, 191–192
 key systems for, 688–689
 locking doors for study room, 473
 panic hardware for, 688
 paper towels by door, 499
 restroom stall doors, 495–496
 to restrooms, 493
 security of, 56
 sound transmission and, 450
 to storerooms, 557
door-to-door lamp salesmen, 615
double-cylinder locks, 687
downlighting
 access for people with limited eyesight, 197
 "direct/indirect" fixture, 600
 as dysfunctional design, 59–60
 glare from, 590–591, 608
 light fixtures with mix of uplighting and, 598
 lighting in old buildings with low ceilings, 604
 for meeting rooms, 451
 recessed downlights, 586, 599, 600–601, 624, 626
 troffers, 599–600
drafting tables, 524
drafts, of building program, 91
drawers
 for kitchenettes, 550–551
 for staff lunchroom, 536–537
drawings
 change orders and, 276
 construction documents, 184–185
 as not precious in design process, 163
 renderings, 181
 in schematic design process, 175–176
 verification that construction matches drawings/specifications, 268–271
 See also construction drawings; shop drawings
draws
 architect responsibility for, 264–265

definition of, 262
 overview of, 275
drills, staff, 702
driver
 definition of, 585
 LED lighting maintenance, 595
drive-through services, 140
drive-up book returns, 427–428
drive-up lending service windows, 429
driveways
 drive-up book returns and, 427
 as site development cost, 348
 space required for, 139–140
 video camera locations, 699
dry pipe systems, 693–694
dryers
 clothes washers/dryers, 515, 526–527, 663
 for hand drying, 498–499
drywall
 for ceilings, 232
 health problems from, 211
 for interior walls, 219
 painted drywall, 220–221
 preventing damage to walls, 221–222
dual conductor wire mold, 630
ductwork, 293–294
 See also air ducts
dumbwaiter, 562, 567
durability
 of service desks, 417–418
 of storage spaces, 554
DVDs
 plastic boxes to encase, 685
 sequestering theft-prone materials, 682
 theft of, 679
dysfunctional designs
 acoustics, 60
 balconies/walkways, 63
 courtyards, 64
 donors and, 361
 elevators, cheap substitutes for, 63
 entrances, multiple public, 64
 funny-shaped interior spaces, 64
 inflexibility, 60–61
 introduction to, 59
 lighting, 59–60
 ramps, 63
 security, 64
 shelving, 63
 sight lines, 63
 soffits, 62
 staircases/handrails, 62–63
 storage space, insufficient, 64
 unexpandability, 62
 ventilation, 60
 water features, indoor, 64

732 | INDEX

dysfunctional designs *(cont'd)*
   wiring, 64

E

earth coupling, 646
earthquakes
   earthquake insurance, 712
   earthquake-resistant construction, 673
   shelving placement and, 408
easements, 148
east light, 618
echo, 50
economic models, of theft-control systems, 679–680
edge banding, 378
edges, for end panels, 399
efficacy, 585
EIFS (External Insulation Finishing Systems)
   cheap construction of commercial buildings, 313
   definition of, 210
   evaluation of construction materials, 53
   for exterior walls, 216
ejector pit, 656
electric eye
   on elevators, 565
   faucets, 497, 540
   soap dispensers, 498
electric traction elevators, 562, 564
electrical circuits
   automatic cutoff switches of, 627
   conduit, 630
   electrical outlets, 630–633
   electrical panels, 630
   electrical switches, 633–634
   electrical wiring, 629
   for kitchenettes, 461, 464, 480
   for meeting rooms, 454–455
   overview of, 628–629
   rule on, 634
   for staff lunchroom, 537, 544
electrical codes
   description of, 240
   National Electrical Code, 627, 628
electrical conduit, 294–295
electrical outlets
   conversion of non-library buildings and, 314–315
   for flexibility of space, 53
   insufficient number of, 60–61
   lack of in libraries, 627
   for meeting rooms, 454–455
   movable seating and, 389
   need for, 50

   overview of, 630–633
   rules on, 4, 5, 6, 12, 634–635
   rules on remodeling/expanding library buildings, 304
   shelving placement and, 405
   for staff conference rooms, 523
   for staff workrooms, 514, 530
   for study rooms, 472
   for tables, 373, 374, 378, 390, 391
   for technical services workrooms, 526
electrical panels, 630, 633–634
electrical room, 628
electrical switches, 273
electrical systems
   electrical circuits
      conduit, 630
      electrical outlets, 630–633
      electrical panels, 630
      electrical switches, 633–634
      electrical wiring, 629
      overview of, 628–629
   emergencies and, 634
   overview of, 627
   rules on, 634–635
   vocabulary for, 628
electrical wiring
   conversion of non-library buildings and, 314–315
   correct wiring of outlets, 632
   dysfunctional designs for, 64
   for electrical circuits, 628–629
   errors, resolving, 271
   evaluation of, 50–51
   modern/legacy wiring, 629
   in plenums, 642
   for program/activity/study rooms, 454–455
   remodeling/expanding, problems with, 294–295
   rules on, 304, 634–635
   for service desks, 418
   for staff workrooms, 514
electronic equipment
   See equipment
electronic theft-detection systems
   description of, 683
   problems with, 684–685
   self-check equipment, 685–686
   space planning for, 683–684
elements, protection from, 55
elevations, 180
elevators
   access for people with acrophobia, 199, 201, 202
   access for people with limited mobility, 193–195
   for accessibility, 19

   accessibility, improving, 205
   accessibility problems of libraries, 190
   accessibility rule on, 206, 207
   ADA accessibility requirements for, 191, 192
   basements in expanded historic buildings, 301
   cheap substitutes for, 63
   dumbwaiters, 567
   enclosed exit staircases and, 569
   as essential, 562
   hidden, staircases in atria and, 573–574
   for historic library, 300
   historic stores, conversion of, 321
   located near stairs, 7
   options for, 564–566
   problems with, 561–562
   real elevators, need for, 563–564
   rules on, 10, 11, 12, 14, 580–581, 582
   rules on remodeling/expanding library buildings, 304
   shared buildings and, 329
   shared elevators in shared buildings, 340–341
   shared facilities in single buildings, 334–335
   staircase, proximity to, 21
   substitutes for real elevators, 566–567
   terminology for, 562–563
   upward expansion and, 142
   video cameras in, 699
emergencies
   building codes for entrances/exits, 687–688
   electrical systems and, 634
   elevator response to, 564–565
   panic hardware for, 688
emergency exits
   enclosed exit staircases, 569
   from program rooms, 464
   signs for escape routes, 695–696
   signs of fire alarm systems, 691–692
emergency lighting units, 616
emergency services
   fire alarm system and, 692
   intrusion alarms linked to, 690
   liability situations and, 714
   panic buttons linked to, 700
   training staff to call, 702
eminent domain, 150
end panels
   for cantilever steel shelving, 399–400
   marking contents of shelving ranges, 409
   mechanical-assist shelving and, 401

INDEX

rule about, 415
shelving with end-supported shelves, 402
signs for shelving aisles, 414
end runs, 165
endorsements
for addition of coverage options, 708–709
definition of, 706
end-supported shelves, 402
energy codes, 240
energy conservation
daylight control for, 618–620
daylight "harvesting"/daylight sensors, 607
HVAC system requirements for, 639
in HVAC systems, 645–647
LED lighting for, 594
lighting, problems with, 584
lighting technology, efficient, 604–606
motion sensor switches for lighting, 606
energy consumption
atria as energy wasters, 573
historic library buildings as energy hogs, 293-294
by HVAC systems, 638, 641
enforcement, of building codes, 239
engineering studies, 82
engineers
architect interview question about, 114
in architectural firm RFQ, 102
building codes and, 239
for community center with public library, 332
for conversion of non-library buildings, 324, 325
conversion project, input on, 307
engineering services in design process, 170–171
HVAC system, input on, 638
library planning meetings and, 69
for library plumbing systems, 655
professional fees of, 350
questioning, 68
remodeling/expansion, cost of, 290, 291
security plans and, 667
for site selection, 158
sites, evaluation of potential, 126–129
structural evaluation of current facilities, 82
entrance and exit control
building codes, 687–688
importance of, 686
key systems, 688–689

modern panic hardware, 688
proximity cards, swipe cards, fobs, keypads, 689–690
service desks for, 432–432
entrances
combined school and public libraries, 330
desks for entrance/exit control, 432–433
elements, protection from, 55
entrance and exit control equipment, 686–690
historic entrances, remodeling/expansion issue, 300
for large entry rooms with radiating wings, 40
multiple public entrances, 64
number of, 7, 27
orientation of, 26–27, 147–148, 617
parking lot location and, 312
placement of, 27
problems with remodeling/expanding library buildings, 300
rules about, 42
rules on remodeling/expanding library buildings, 304
of school library, 157
security, evaluation of, 56
security rules about, 702, 703
security with limited public entrances, 673–674
site acquisition costs and, 347
south-facing entrances, 4
staffed entrances for security, 48
entry foyers
meeting rooms accessible from, 447
program rooms accessible from, 479–480
restroom location near, 502
restrooms as tornado shelters and, 505
entry ramps, exterior, 14
entry rooms, 40
entryways, 11
environmental contamination, 173
Environmental Protection Agency (EPA), 137, 173
equipment
assigned storage spaces for, 548
audiovisual equipment for meeting rooms, 455–457
audiovisual storage closets, 458
closets for maker space equipment, 460
cost of FF&E, 348–349
cut sheets of, 186
entrance and exit control equipment, 686–690

excluded from general bids, 253
for food preparation/serving in staff lunchroom, 535–538
for graphic arts workroom, 523–524
in maker spaces, 477
meeting room storage space for, 550
operating costs, 351–352
phased expansion projects, warranties on equipment, 302–303
for restrooms, 493, 494–501
for staff workrooms, 521–522
storage space for, 553
storage spaces for mechanical equipment, 551–552
storage spaces, rules on, 555, 556
video surveillance systems, 697–699
equivalencies, 255–256
errors
bidding, 259
change orders from, 276–277
contractor errors, resolving, 271
escalation, 346
escalator, 563
escape routes, 695–696
estimates
See cost estimates
evaluation
of architect proposals, 109–110
of bids, 259
of current facilities in building program, 82
of service desks, 421
evaluation of library buildings
accessibility, 57
acoustics, 50
acrophobia, 54–55
appearance of building, 46–47
artificial light, 49–50
ceilings, 54
electrical wiring, 50–51
expandability, 56–57
flexibility, 53
floor coverings, 55
fragile construction materials, 53
furnishings, 51–52
HVAC, 51
library staff and, 46
natural light, 48–49
ornamental spaces, 55
protection from elements, 55
reasons for evaluating on your own, 45–46
room arrangement, functional, 54
security, 55–56
staff service points, 47–48
storage, 53
water features, 57

evaluation of library buildings (cont'd)
   welcome, sense of, 47
evaluation of potential sites
   adjacent uses, 138
   archaeology, 147
   brownfield sites, 136–137
   covenants, 150–151
   easements, 148
   expansion land, acquisition of, 150
   floodplains, 133
   historic buildings/neighborhoods, 145–146
   land ownership, 149–150
   orientation to compass, 147–148
   professional assistance in, 126–129
   site configuration, 133
   site topography, 133–135
   size, 138–144
   soil conditions, 129–130
   subsurface water, 132
   surface water runoff detention/retention, 131–132
   utilities, 130–131
events
   See public ceremonies
exclusions, 706
executive summaries, 74
exhaust fans
   for graphic arts workroom, 524
   for restrooms, 500
   for staff lunchroom, 535, 537
   for staff restrooms, 540
exhibit areas
   See display and exhibit areas
exhibit floater policy, 487
exhibits, insurance for, 712
existing structures
   accessibility, improving, 205
   on brownfield sites, 136–137
   construction drawings for remodel, 185
   cost of removing, 129
   evaluation of, 172–173
   See also conversion, of non-library buildings to public libraries; historic libraries; remodeling/expanding library buildings
exit control
   desks for entrance/exit control, 432–433
   entrance and exit control equipment, 686–690
   as lending desk function, 422
   placement of service desks for, 420–421
   for theft control, 681
   See also entrance and exit control

exits
   emergency exit signs, 691–692
   emergency exits from program rooms, 464
   escape routes, 695–696
   exit staircases, 569
   panic hardware for doors, 688
   video camera locations, 699–700
expandability
   evaluation of, 56–57
   library design for, 19
expansion
   building codes and, 237–238
   evaluation of existing structure by architect, 169
   evaluation of existing structures, 172–173
   restrooms and, 504
   review of, 290
   site, review of, 150
   unexpandability, dysfunctional design and, 62
   See also remodeling/expanding library buildings
expansion space
   for academic libraries, 156
   adjacent land for, 298–299
   lack of, conversion and, 311
   of library building, 35
   library sites with no room for, 125
   site size and, 140–144
expenses, 120–121
   See also costs
experts, on historic library design, 146
extension cords
   electrical outlet spacing and, 631
   electrical outlets and, 50
   rule on, 634
   violation of fire codes, 239
exterior awnings, 619, 620
exterior book pickups, 429
exterior book return bins, 428–429
exterior displays, 487–488
exterior finishes, 296–298
exterior ramps, 580
exterior walls
   aluminum composite panels, 217
   architectural terracotta, 217
   brick, 213–214
   cheap construction of commercial buildings, 313
   concrete, 216
   EIFS, 216
   natural stone, 214–215
   phenolic resin panels, 217
   precast stone, 215–217
   rules on surfaces/materials for, 233–235

   siding, 216–217
external configuration of library buildings, 26–27
External Insulation Finishing Systems
   See EIFS (External Insulation Finishing Systems)
eyesight, people with limited
   accessibility rule on, 206
   library accessibility for, 195–198

F

fact sheet, 281
faculty studies, 478
FAIA (Fellow of the American Institute of Architects), 105
false alarms
   of electronic theft-detection systems, 683
   of intrusion alarms, 690
   of theft-control gates, 681
family computer rooms, 473
family restrooms, 502
faucets, automatic, 273
fax machines, 430
fear of heights
   See acrophobia
feasibility studies, 174
fees
   in architect contract, 120–121
   of fundraising consultant, 360
   professional fees, in cost estimates, 350–351
Fellow of the American Institute of Architects (FAIA), 105
feminine hygiene products, 500, 540
FF&E
   See furniture, fixtures, and equipment
fiber-cement, 217
file storage
   for staff workrooms, 520
   for technical services workrooms, 525
filters, 643
filtration
   of air by HVAC, 637
   definition of, 640
   by HVAC system, 643–644
finishes, 400
fir tree, 282–283
fire
   book return slots and, 427, 428
   building codes and, 238
   building codes for entrances/exits, 687
   buildings violating codes, 239
   drills, 702
   kitchenettes and, 460, 461

plenum systems and, 642
protection of library from, 22
staff lunchroom stove and, 535
staircases and, 576
fire alarm systems, 691–692
fire extinguishers, portable, 696, 702
fire prevention codes, 240
fire protection engineer, 655
fire safety codes
   for entrances/exits, 687–688
   for portable fire extinguishers, 696
fire-protection services (Fire Protection Class), 710
fire-protection systems
   escape routes, 695–696
   fire alarm systems, 691–692
   insurance cost and, 710
   portable fire extinguishers, 696
   sprinkler systems, 691–695
   sprinkler systems, training on, 657
fire-resistant construction, 668–669
fire-resistant contents, 669
fiscal responsibility, 104–105
501(c)(3) foundations
   bequest through, 360
   for fundraising, 361
   overview of, 363–364
   for private fundraising discussions, 360
   as source of funding, 363–364
fixtures
   for children's restrooms, 501
   cost of FF&E, 348–349
   excluded from general bids, 253
   on punch list, 273
   for restrooms, 493, 494–501
   for restrooms, building codes on, 493–494
   for restrooms, number of, 502
   for restrooms, rules on, 508, 509
   table lamps, 380, 391
   See also light fixtures
flammability
   of construction materials, 668–669
   of soft seating, 383
   standards for chairs, 387
   of upholstered furniture, 390, 669
flashing lights, of fire alarm systems, 691
flat fee method, 120
flexibility
   of architect team, 113
   costs cut by, 17
   evaluation of, 53
   inflexibility from dysfunctional designs, 60–61
   inflexibility of service desks, 434–437
   library design for, 18–19

of library supply company service desks, 440
of lighting, lack of, 608
modular furnishings for staff workrooms, 513
of service desks, 417
shelving on casters and, 409
of staff workroom furnishings, 517
of storage spaces, 554
flip bins
   for collection storage/display, 410
   description of, 399
floater policy, 706
floating staircases
   access for people with acrophobia, 202
   with atria, 573
   as dysfunctional design concept, 62
   fires and, 576
   problems with, 571–572
   protective railings under, 191
   rule on, 581
flood insurance, 711–712, 716
flooding
   of basement, 703
   detention/retention basins and, 661–662
   from exterior ramp, 300
   flood-resistant construction, 669–672
   insurance for, 711–712, 716
   library on floodplains and, 133
   library plumbing and, 655
   rules on plumbing, 665
   sewer backup insurance, 712
   site selection, buildable site, 128
   site selection rules, 159, 160
   storm drains and, 660–661
floodplains
   evaluating potential sites, 133
   never build on, 669–670
flood-resistant construction, 669–672
floor boxes, 265–266
floor coverings
   for children's craft and story rooms, 474–475
   evaluation of, 55
   for program/activity/study rooms, 462–463
   for restrooms, 507, 509
floor drains, 491, 507
floor plans
   building programs and, 93, 94
   building programs do not include, 84
   placement on north walls, 204
   as schematic design deliverable, 180
   traffic flows and, 40–41
floor space
   for children's craft and story rooms, 474

for performers, 468
for staff workrooms, 519
for technical services workrooms, 525–526
floor strength
   for books, 16, 60, 403
   of churches, 322
   for collection storage/display, 414
   for compact shelving, 401
   conversion of non-library buildings and, 325, 326
   department store conversion and, 317–318
   of historic stores, 321
   of houses, library conversion and, 323
   importance of, 4
   insufficient, conversion and, 310–311
   for shelving, 393, 403, 415
floors
   access for people with limited eyesight, 198
   bearing strength, 223–224
   of big box stores, 319
   buildings designed for extra floor, 314
   conversion problems, 310
   floor surfaces
      bamboo, 229
      broadloom carpet, 225–227
      carpet tile, 227
      carpet yarns, 227
      ceramic tile, 230
      cork tile, 228
      hardwood, 229–230
      linoleum, 229
      loose floor mats, 231
      overview of, 224–225
      poured epoxy, 228
      recycled tires, 228
      rubber tile, 228
      stained concrete, 228–229
      terrazzo, 229
      vinyl tile, 227–228
      walk-off mats, 230
   ornamental openings between, 37–39
   rules on surfaces/materials for, 234–235
   sloped, 678
   strength of, basements and, 312–313
   strength of, evaluation of, 173
   strong, for expansion, 143, 144
fluorescent lamps
   color rendering, poor, 591
   color temperature and, 592
   selection of light sources, 596
fluorescent light, 585
fluorescent lighting
   advantages/disadvantages of, 593–594
   downlight fixtures, 599–600

fluorescent lighting (cont'd)
    replacing with LEDs, 594
flush outlets, 631–632, 633
flush-tank toilets, 494–495
flush-valve toilets
    recommendation for, 494–495
    rule on always using, 508
    for staff restrooms, 540
    turning off, 656
foam insulation, 212
fobs, 689–690
focus groups, 78–79, 95
folding chairs, 447
folding tables, 447–448
food
    for ground breakings, 281
    for ribbon cuttings, 287
    for topping out ceremony, 283
food preparation/service areas
    plumbing system for, 662
    staff lunchroom
        accessibility, 537–538
        buffet shelves, 537
        cabinets/drawers, 536–537
        counters/sinks, 536
        dishwashers, 536
        exhaust fans, 537
        microwaves, coffeemakers, 535
        plumbing connections/electrical
            circuits, 537
        refrigerators, 536
        stoves, 535
    See also kitchenettes
foot-candles
    calculation of, 589
    definition of, 585
    illumination levels, 588–589
    rule on, 624
footings
    of buildings designed for extra floor,
        314
    remodeling/expansion and, 304
    upward expansion and, 142
footprint, building, 139
formaldehyde, 211
formulas, for space estimates, 94
fortress desks, 438–439
foundation board members, 361
fountains
    problems with, 664–665
    as site development cost, 348
    See also water features
foyers
    meeting rooms accessible from, 447
    program rooms accessible from,
        479–480
    restroom location near, 502
friends of the library, 361

"fritted" glass, 48
frosted glass, 48
fuel tanks, buried, 137
functional evaluation, of current
    facilities, 82
functional location, 296
functional needs, 34
functionality
    artistic design vs. function, 103–104
    of service desks, 417
funding
    for construction projects, rules
        about, 11
    problems with, 355–356
    rules on, 366–367
    sources of
        bequests, 357–359
        501(c)(3) foundations, 363–364
        fundraising, 359–363
        grants, 364–366
        money on hand, 356
        mortgages, 359
        referendums/bond issues, 356–357
        savings set aside from operating
            funds, 356
        special appropriations, 366
fundraising
    capital campaigns, 360
    donor recognition, 362–363
    501(c)(3) foundations for, 363–364
    fundraising consultants, 359–360
    lead gifts, 360–361
    making the ask, 361
    professional fees, 350
    record keeping, 361–362
    at ribbon cuttings, 287
    rules on funding, 366–367
    schematic design for assistance with,
        181–183
    as source of funding, 359–363
fundraising consultants
    legitimate, 8
    library design process and, 18
    services of, 359–360
    work for fees or salaries, 367
furnaces, 650
furnishings
    circulation space and, 85
    evaluation of, 51–52
    excluded from general bids, 253
    for faculty studies, 478
    fire-resistant, 669
    insurance values, setting, 708
    in library, evaluation of, 51–52
    for program/activity/study rooms,
        447–448
    for quiet reading rooms, 471
    ribbon cuttings and, 286

    for staff lunchroom, 538
    for staff workrooms, 513, 517–522,
        529, 530
    staircases incorporating, 574–575
    for storage spaces, 553–554
    for study rooms, 472
furniture
    accessibility of, 190
    assigned storage spaces for, 548
    chair rails and, 222
    for comfort of library users, xiv
    conference room space and, 446
    cost of FF&E, 348–349
    design rule on, 188
    fire-resistant furnishings, 669
    flexibility to move, 53
    furniture placement drawings, 185
    in library, evaluation of, 51–52
    meeting/program room storage
        spaces, 549–550
    moving library and, 349
    new, selecting, 375–376
    ordering of furniture, 375–376
    placement in schematic design, 119,
        177
    polyurethane foam, dangers of, 211
    for program/activity/study rooms,
        447–448
    rules about, 7, 8, 15, 16
    rules on user seating, 390–392
    space estimation for, 87–88
    for staff conference rooms, 522–523
    for staff lunchroom, 538
    for staff workrooms, 513, 529, 530
    "T"-shaped furniture layout, 5
    vocabulary for, 373
    See also user seating
furniture, fixtures, and equipment
    (FF&E)
    building costs, components of,
        348–349
    in cost estimates, 346
    definition of, 344
furniture storage closets
    guidance on, 458
    for meeting rooms, 445, 550
    for program/activity/study rooms,
        448
fuse, 628
fuse box, 629

G

game tables, 377
garage, 552
garbage disposal units, 536
gate, 563
gender-neutral restrooms, 504

general contractor
  CMAR and, 247
  construction coordination meetings, 267–268
  design-bid-build projects, 245–246
  draws/lien waivers/retainage, 275–276
  role of, 245
  See also contractors
geotechinical engineers
  architect interview question about, 114
  in architectural firm RFQ, 102
  consulting professionals in architectural team, 106
  engineering services in design process, 170
  soil conditions of site, input on, 127
geothermal heating systems, 130
geothermal systems, 640
GFCI (ground fault circuit interrupters), 629
gifts
  lead gifts, 360–361
  making the ask, 361
  smaller donations, recognizing, 362–363
gimmicks, lighting, 615–616
glare
  access for people with limited eyesight, 195, 196
  definition of, 585, 590
  direct glare, 49, 590–591
  high-glare lighting, 608
  indirect glare, 591
  lighting problems, 608
  modern glass and, 148
  from recessed downlights, 600, 601
  rules about, 9
  from skylights, 583
glass
  for desktop surfaces, 437
  excess, library orientation and, 148
  modern glass, 188, 624
  multi-deck shelving with glass floors, 408
  railings, 201
  railings, problems with, 576–577
glass walls
  for children's departments, 701
  daylight, controlling, 618–620
  elevators with, 202
  at heads/feet of staircases, 574
  for sight lines, 675
  for study rooms, 464, 471, 472, 480–481
  for theft control, 680
glides, for table legs, 379
gloom, 583, 608–609

GMP (guaranteed maximum price), 247–248
governing bodies, 163
government bonds, 356–357
government buildings
  conversion to library building, 323–324
  public libraries in shared government buildings, 334
government discounts, 615
government grants
  deadlines for, 366
  grant applications, 364, 365
  rule on, 367
government sites, for public libraries, 152–153
graffiti
  in restrooms, prevention of, 507
  surfaces resistant to, 496
grandfathering
  code enforcement involves, 239
  water retention zoning changes, 299
grants
  building programs and, 72, 75
  grant applications, 364–365
  rules on funding, 367
  shared buildings and, 339
  as source of funding, 364–366
graphic arts workroom, 523–524
graves, 147
green board, 219
green building certification, 647
green materials, 235
green roofs
  detention/retention basins and, 661, 666
  rooftop water supplies for, 658
  runoff control of, 132
  zoning and, 299
greenfield sites, 136
Grenfell Tower fire, London, 239
ground, 628
ground breakings
  in construction process, 267
  definition of, 262
  overview of, 280–281
  rules about, 8
ground fault circuit interrupters (GFCI), 629
ground loop system, 456
ground source heat pumps (GSHP), 646
grounded electrical outlets, 632
grounded wiring, 629
groundwater, 22
group workrooms
  rules on, 530, 531
  for staff, 513
grout, 230, 507

growth, plan for, xv
GSHP (ground source heat pumps), 646
guaranteed maximum price (GMP), 247–248
guard stations
  at exits for theft control, 681
  for keeping unauthorized people out of library, 683
guardrail, 568

H

hallways, 21
hand drying
  dryers on punch list, 277
  for restrooms, 498–499
  rule on, 508
handrails
  accessibility and, 205
  definition of, 568
  design of, 568–569
  dysfunctional designs for, 62–63
  painted, problems of, 577–578
  width/shape of, 578–579
  See also railings
hard copies, 108
hardwood, 229–230, 234
health problems, from surfaces/materials, 211–213
hearing, people with limited, 198–199
heat pump, 640
heating
  HVAC, evaluation of, 51
  by HVAC system, 641
  with natural gas, 12
  See also HVAC (heating, ventilating, and air conditioning)
heating tunnel, 640
height
  of cantilever shelving, 396–397
  of reference desks, 431
  seated *vs.* standing-height lending desks, 424
  for storage spaces, 59
hidden corners, 675–676
high school yearbooks, 679
high-density storage
  of academic libraries, 156
  close to library, 159
  super high-density storage, 413
high-glare lighting, 608
high-intensity discharge (HID) lighting
  avoiding, 624
  definition of, 585
  overview of, 594
highways, 155–156
hinged tilting shelves, 398–399

hiring
  architects
    architectural firms, locating, 98–99
    contracting with architects, 118–123
    design competitions, 123
    final selection, 117–118
    interviews, 110–117
    overview of, 97–98
    prior work of architectural firms, investigating, 99–101
    proposals, evaluation of, 109–110
    proposals from architectural firms, 108
    request for qualifications (RFQ), 101–108
    rules about, 123–124
    teams, special problems with, 108–109
  construction management firms, 248–250
  library building consultants, 89–90
historic buildings
  basements in, 301
  construction limitations in historic district, 129
  converting to library, 314
  elevators for, 192
  evaluating potential sites, 145–146
  historic exteriors, matching, 296–298
  remodeling, cost of, 290–291
  rules controlling, 240–241
historic entrances
  basements in expanded historic buildings, 301
  problems with, 300
  rules on remodeling/expanding library buildings, 304
historic libraries
  access for people with limited mobility, 194
  accessibility, improving, 204–205
  accessibility problems of, 189–190
  air ducts in, 642
  basements in expanded historic buildings, 301
  elevator issues for, 562, 563–564
  historic entrances, remodeling/expansion issue, 300
  in history of library lighting, 586–587
  HVAC and, 650–651
  HVAC rules about, 652–653
  large entry rooms with radiating wings, 40
  lighting fixtures, historic, 616–617
  lighting in old buildings with low ceilings, 604
  matching historic exteriors, 296–298
  perimeter shelving in, 403–404
  problems with remodeling/expanding library buildings, 291–301
  ramps for, 580–581
  "River City" sites, 153–154
  rules about, 12
  rules on remodeling/expanding library buildings, 303–305
  service desks, obsolete, 438
  staircases of, 582
historic light fixtures, 616
historic remains, 129
historic stores on courthouse squares, 320–322
historical preservation regulations, 129
history, of library lighting, 586–587
hoistway, 563
holds, 422
Homasote, 477, 575
homeless population, 154
homeless shelter, 154, 160
hooks, 496
  See also coat hooks
horizontal display cases, 486
hose bibs, 658
hot water heating, 657
houses, conversion to library, 322–323
Huberty, Joe
  contact information for, xvi
  information about, 717–718
  introduction to book, xiii–xvi
humidification
  complications of, 645
  definition of, 640
  of older libraries, 650–651
humidity
  in basements, 671
  control of, 696–697
  control with HVAC, 637, 639, 644–645
  HVAC for rare books/archives, 648–649
  in older libraries, 650–651
Hunters Point branch of Queens Borough (New York) Public Library, 193
hurricane shelters, 715
hurricanes
  flood insurance and, 712
  shelters, rule on providing, 703
  windstorm-resistant construction, 672–673
HVAC (heating, ventilating, and air conditioning)
  air conditioning, obsolete or nonexistent, 310
  bad ventilation, 60
  for campus buildings, 649
  commissioning, 270
  controls, 644–645
  conversion of non-library buildings and, 324
  cooling, 639
  drawings, 185
  energy conservation, 645–647
  evaluation of, 51
  filtration, 643–644
  heating, 641
  humidity control, 696–697
  for meeting rooms, 480
  moving out of library during construction, 253
  old libraries and, 650–651
  operating costs, 351–352
  operations/maintenance, 651–652
  overview of, 637–639
  phased expansion projects, warranties on equipment, 302–303
  problems with remodeling/expanding library buildings, 293–294
  for program/activity/study rooms, 443, 453
  on punch list, 274
  for rare books and archives, 648–649
  rules on, 652–653
  shared buildings and, 339
  split systems, 640, 650
  supplies, storage space for, 552
  for typical libraries, 647–648
  unitary systems, 649–650
  ventilating, 641–643
  vocabulary for, 639–641
Hyatt Regency Hotel, Kansas City, 201
hydraulic elevator
  advantages/disadvantages of, 564
  definition of, 563
  safety of, 565–566
hypodermic needles, 500, 540

I

IBC (International Building Code)
  adopted by many municipalities, 239
  enforcement of, 240
  sprinkler system for expanded building, 291–292
  used by local communities, 237
ice dispensers, 536
ID services
  benefit of combined services, 337
  shared space arrangement for, 341
  student service facilities, 333
ideas, 78–79
Illuminating Engineering Society (IES), 590, 592

illumination
  even, 583
  levels, 588–589
  modeling, 590
incandescent lamps
  avoiding, 624
  definition of, 585
  description of/examples of, 593
  getting rid of, 604–606
index tables, 377
indicators, for shelving, 86–87
indirect glare, 591
individual workrooms, 516–517
indoor water features
  problems of, 664
  rule on, 665
  See also water features
inert gas systems, 694–695
infants
  changing tables for, 501
  infant seats, 381, 502
inflation, 708
inflexibility
  dysfunctional designs that cause, 60–61
  of service desks, 434–435
information desks, 433
infrared system, 456
inherited walls, 34–35
input
  building program for user input, 76
  on building programs, 76–80
inscribed paving brick, 362–363
inspections
  code inspections/occupancy permits, 271–272
  of elevators, 566
  post-occupancy inspection, 279
insulation
  of older houses, 323
  for reducing energy use, 645
  of roof coverings, 218
insulation valve, 656
insurance
  automotive, 714
  bonding, 257–258
  builder's risk insurance, 713
  coinsurance clauses, 709
  deductibles, 708
  directors' and officers' liability, 715
  endorsements, 708–709
  flood, 711–712
  liability, 714
  liability and property insurance, 707
  library policy on displays/exhibits, 488
  loss, actions in case of, 715
  major losses, covering, 707

overview of, 705–706
for permanent works of art, 487
property, 711
property risks, 712–713
purchasing insurance policies, 710–711
rules on, 703, 715–716
security and, 667–668
staff health and life insurance, 715
subrogation, 709–710
umbrella liability coverage, 709
values, setting, 708
vocabulary for, 706–707
for war/insurrection, 713–714
workers' compensation, 715
Insurance Services Office (ISO), 706, 710
insured, 706
interim facilities, 252–253
interior designers
  architect interview question about, 115
  furniture ordering by, 375–376
  professional fees of, 350
  staff workroom furnishings and, 518
interior walls
  ceramic tile, 221
  materials for, 219–220
  painted drywall, 220–221
  plaster, 221
  preventing damage to, 221–223
  rules on surfaces/materials for, 233
  sound transmission/reflection and, 220
  wood paneling, 221
interlibrary loans
  as lending desk function, 422
  lending workrooms for, 423
  space for sorting, 430
internal layout/room shapes
  basements, avoiding, 32–34
  expansion space, 35
  functional needs and, 34
  inherited walls, 34–35
  labyrinths, 29
  sight lines, 29–30
  strangely shaped spaces, 28
  wayfinding, assisting, 30–31
Internal Revenue Service (IRS), 363–364
internal roof drain, 656
internal windows, 675
International Building Code
  See IBC (International Building Code)
interviews
  of architects
    guidance on, 110–114

    questions for, 114–117
    rule about, 124
  of architectural firms, 102
  for hiring construction management firm, 248, 249–250
  number of firms you plan to interview in RFQ, 107
  with staff/management for building program, 76–77
intrusion alarms, 690–691
inventory
  of existing furniture, 375
  for theft control, 679–680
Iroquois Theater fire, Chicago, 238, 687
irrigation
  definition of, 656
  hose bibs, 658
  systems, 658
IRS (Internal Revenue Service), 363–364
ISO (Insurance Services Office), 706, 710
isolation valves, 657

J

joints, 384, 392

K

Kelvin, 592
key systems, 688–689
keypads, 689–690
keys
  access-control systems and, 689
  Knox Boxes for, 692
  for restrooms, 505
  to shared buildings, 677
kick blocks, 399
kiddie toilets, 494
kitchenettes
  electrical circuits for, 454–455, 464, 480, 628–629
  for meeting rooms, 445–446
  plumbing system for, 662
  for program/activity/study rooms, 460–462
  for staff lunchroom, 535–538
  storage for, 550–551
  stove in staff lunchroom, 534
knob and tube wiring
  in old libraries, 294
  replacing, 315
  safety issues of, 629
Knox Boxes, 692

L

label holders, 542

labels
  for artworks on display, 489
  for permanent works of art, 487
  range content labels, 409
labor costs, 251–252
labyrinths, 29
lactation rooms, 539, 544
ladders
  for lamp changing, 612–613
  storage of, 551, 552, 555
laminates
  as fragile desktop surface, 437
  on service desks, 440
  for tables, 378
laminators, 524
lamp, 585
lamp nomenclature, 585
lamps
  lighting that is hard to maintain, 612–615
  rules on, 624
  See also light fixtures; table lamps
land, adjacent, 298–299
land ownership
  acquisition of expansion land, 150
  evaluating potential sites, 149–150
  site selection rule on, 160
landing, 568
landscaping
  irrigation/maintenance water, 658
  as site development cost, 348
  site size and, 140
laptops
  electrical outlets for meeting rooms, 454
  electrical outlets/data ports for, 50
  security, provisions for, 380, 390
  Wi-Fi for meeting rooms, 455
latex paint, 220–221
laws
  on bid and construction documents, 161–162
  on bonds, 357
  on employing architects, 124
  on 501(c)(3) foundations, 364
  on hiring architects, 98, 118
  owners wanting to do illegal things, 169
  prevailing wage laws, 251–252
lawsuits, 709–710
lawyers
  for awarding construction contracts, 260
  bequests to library and, 358

for bond issues, 357
  for bond referendums, 356–357
  for contract with architects, 121
  501(c)(3) foundation, setting up, 363–364
lead
  in construction materials, 211
  conversion of non-library buildings and, 313
  remodeling/expansion of library and, 292
lead gifts, 360–361
lecterns, 468
LED (light-emitting diode), 585
LED lighting
  access for people with limited eyesight, 197
  advantages of, 594–595
  for auditoriums, 468
  color rendering by, 591–592
  daylight sensors and, 607
  for display cases, 485
  emergency lighting units, 616
  for energy conservation, 606
  energy saving with, 19–20
  good library lighting, formula for, 587
  issues with, 595–596
  in library, evaluation of, 49
  lighting vocabulary, 585
  maintenance questions about, 595
  for meeting rooms, 449
  selection of light sources, 596
LEED (Leadership in Energy and Environmental Design)
  description of, 240
  green building certification, 647
  LEED-certified building, 106, 177
leg clearance, of tables, 378
legal standing, 148
Legionnaires' disease
  HVAC system rule and, 652
  from indoor water features, 5, 64, 202, 664, 665, 678
lending agency, 359
lending desks
  additional lending desk spaces, 429–430
  automated book-handling systems, 426–427
  book return, provisions for, 424–425
  desktop surfaces, fragile, 437–438
  drive-up books returns with receiving rooms, 427–428
  exterior book pickups, 429

external book return bins, 428–429
  functions of, 422
  lending service windows, 429
  lending workrooms, 423–424
  location of, 41
  obsolete features in, 439–440
  with off-desk workspaces, 425
  placement of, 422–423
  planning for, 421–422
  queuing space, 426
  seated *vs.* standing-height, 424
  service desk rules, 441
  sorting rooms, 426
  staff spaces, 423
  visual barricades on user sides of, 425–426
lending service windows, 429
lending workrooms, 423–424
letter of support, 365
leveling screws, 399
leveling zone, 563
levers, 191
liability insurance
  for displays/exhibits, 488
  guidance on, 714
  no deductibles for, 708
  non-owned auto liability insurance, 714
  risks covered by, 707
  rule on, 715–716
  umbrella liability coverage, 709
librarians
  accessibility input from, 190
  architect references and, 110
  architects, understanding of, 122–123
  architects, working with, 162–163
  architects behaving badly in design process, 164–167
  architectural firm references, 99–100
  architectural firms, locating, 98–99
  on building program planning team, 94
  building program, review of, 92
  building programs and, 71–73
  building programs, purposes of, 73–76
  construction, role in, 265–267
  construction plaques and, 284
  construction process and, 261–262
  in design planning group, 164
  design process, owners behaving badly in, 167–169
  evaluation of library buildings, 45–57

library design decisions, involvement in, 17
roving librarian concept, reference desk and, 431–432
rules on building programs, 96
service desk design needs, 417–419
shared buildings, problems of, 327–329
sprinkler systems and, 692–693
storage spaces and, 545–547
teamwork for library design/ construction, 67–70
workers' compensation insurance, 714–715

libraries
accessibility problems of, 189–190
building program, contents of, 81–84
combined libraries and museums, 488
history of library lighting, 586–587
shared buildings, problems of, 327–329
space estimating methods, 84–88
tours of, 100–101
user seating, bad decisions on, 371–372
See also historic libraries

library architecture, rules for good/evil in, 3–16

library building consultants
architect interview question about, 115
architects, working with, 166, 167
architects ability to work with, 113
architectural firms, locating, 98–99
architectural firms, references, 99–100
building program by, 88
building program design team, 73
building program, ignored by owners/ architects, 93–94
building program, methods for, 91–92
building program, review of, 92
for building programs, 71, 72
building programs, input by, 76
construction documents and, 186
conversion of non-library buildings and, 325
conversion project, input on, 307
at design meeting, 16
in design planning group, 164
in design process, importance of, 171–172
hiring, 89–90

hiring separately from architects, 124
at interviews of architects, 112
interviews with staff/management, 76–77
knowledge of libraries, 97
planning meetings, presence at, 74
public meetings, participation in, 183
remodeling/expansion design, review of, 290
reporting to architectural firm, 106
rules on building programs, 96
at schematic design meetings, 175
in security discussions, 667
for site selection, 158
sites, evaluation of potential, 126–128
teamwork for library design/ construction, 67–70

library buildings
accessibility problems of, 189–190
ADA accessibility requirements for, 191–193
evaluation of existing structures, 172–173
expansion space for, 140–144
external configuration of, 26
functionality of buildings designed by architectural firm, 102–103
insurance values, setting, 708
rules about, 15
See also evaluation of library buildings; remodeling/expanding library buildings; shared buildings

library design
accessibility, 19
acoustics, 20
basics of, xiv–xv
building program as framework for, 73–74
connecting hallways, 21
expandability, 19
flexibility, 18–19
introduction to, 17–18
lighting, effective, 19–20
low-maintenance designs, 22
popular designs that cause problems, 22–23
problems, strategies for avoiding, 67–70
room shapes, functional, 21
rules on, 23
safe environments, 22
staircases, 20–21
teamwork for, 67

library directors
architectural firm references, 99–100
individual workrooms and, 516
workroom furnishings, 517, 519
workroom storage, 531

library experience
architect interview questions about, 115–116
of architecture firm, 109–110

library name, 362

library policy, on displays/exhibits, 488–489

library site
See site selection

library spaces, configuration of
Allerton (IL) District Library, design sample of
floor plan, 178
general features, 179
main library room, 179–180
program room, 179
restrooms, 180

ceiling shapes, artistic, 41–42
external configuration
building shapes, 26
entrances, number of, 27
entrances, orientation of, 26–27
entrances, placement of, 27

features that require extreme care
courtyards, 35–36
curved walls/round rooms, 37
large entry rooms with radiating wings, 40
ornamental openings between floors, 37–39
reading rooms, huge, 39
windows set into ceilings, 40

internal layout/room shapes
basements, avoiding, 32–34
expansion space, 35
functional needs and, 34
inherited walls, 34–35
labyrinths, 29
sight lines, 29–30
strangely shaped spaces, 28
wayfinding, assisting, 30–31

rules on, 42–44
schematic designs for, 25–26
traffic flows, 40–41

library staff
See staff

library supply company service desks, 440

licensing
    architect interview question about, 117
    of architects to practice in state, 105
lien waivers, 258, 275–276
lifespan, of HVAC equipment, 647
lifts
    advantages of/problems of, 566–567
    definition of, 563
    inexpensive, problems with, 194–195
light fixtures
    definition of, 585
    downlight fixtures, 599–601
    evaluation of, 49, 50
    glare and, 590–591
    good library lighting, formula for, 587
    historic, problems with, 616–617
    LED fixtures, 595
    lighting that is hard to maintain, 612–615
    placement of, dark perimeters and, 609–610
    rules on lighting, 623–626
    for stack aisles, 406–407
    for staircases in atria, 573
    storage space for, 555
    substitutions for, 255, 256
    uplighting, 596, 597, 598–599
light switches
    guidance on, 633–634
    location in staff areas, 615
    location of, 50
    for restrooms, 506
    rules on, 7, 11, 625, 635
    for stack aisles, 406
light-emitting diode
    See LED lighting
lighting
    access for people with limited eyesight, 195–197, 198
    accessibility, improving, 205
    accessibility problems of libraries, 190
    accessibility rule on, 206
    artificial lighting
        evaluation of, 49–50
        fluorescent, 593–594
        high-intensity discharge (HID), 594
        incandescent, 593
        light-emitting diodes (LEDs), 594–596
        recommendations for, 19–20
        selection of, 596
        types of, 592–593
    of atria, 200
    for auditoriums, 466
    bad lighting, 623
    in book storage areas, 415
    bright/low-glare lighting for library, xiv
    calculations of, 589
    ceiling materials and, 231, 232–233, 235
    for children's craft and story rooms, 475–476
    color rendering, 591–592
    color temperature, 592
    for compact shelving, 401
    conversion of non-library building and, 315
    for display cases, 485
    downlighting, 599–601
    dysfunctional designs for, 59–60
    energy-saving ideas for, 604–607
    gimmicks, 615–616
    glare, 590–591
    good library lighting, formula for, 587–588
    for graphic arts workroom, 524
    history library lighting, 586–587
    illumination, modeling, 590
    illumination levels, 588–589
    meeting room ceiling height and, 463
    by mirrors in restrooms, 499–500
    motion detector lighting, on punch list, 273
    movable seating and, 389
    multi-floor openings and, 37–38
    natural light
        compass orientation and, 617–618
        daylight, controlling, 618–622
        daylight, effects of unwanted, 623
        evaluation of, 48–49
        recommendations for, 20
        skylights, 622–623
        working with, 617
    in new buildings, 603
    in old buildings with low ceilings, 604
    overview of, 583–584
    problems
        architectural features that complicate lighting, 610–612
        buying lighting, 615
        dark perimeters, 609–610
        flexibility, lack of, 608
        glare, 608
        gloom, 608–609
        historic lighting fixtures, 616–617
        lighting gimmicks, 615–616
        security lighting, 616
    for program/activity/study rooms, 449
    of reading rooms, 39
    for restrooms, 506
    of restrooms, problems with, 491–492
    rules on, 4, 6, 7, 11, 13, 14, 15, 623–626
    for service desks, 418, 435, 438–439, 440
    skylights and, 40
    of stack aisles, 406–407
    of staff workrooms, 513–514
    standards for, 590
    for storage closets, 457, 549
    for storage spaces, 554
    task lighting, 601–603
    for technical services workrooms, 526
    uplighting, 596, 597, 598–599
    vocabulary for, 584–586
limestone, 214–215, 296
Lincoln, Abraham, 487
linear slot acoustic ceilings, 233
linoleum, 210, 228
lips (backstops), 398
listening
    architects ignoring clients, 164, 165
    in design process, 163
    skills of architects, 103, 113
live load, 223
LM-79 report, 595
load, 628
local activist groups, 146
local contractors, 259
local government
    bequests and, 358
    funding problems, 355
    government sites for public libraries, 152–153
    occupancy permit issued by, 271–272
local matching funds, 365
local planning agencies, 146
location
    of children's craft and story rooms, 474
    combined school and public libraries, 330
    of conference room, 469
    conversion, bad location for, 310
    conversion, good reasons for, 308
    conversion of big box stores and, 320
    historic stores, conversion of, 320
    of individual workrooms, 516
    of program/activity/study rooms, 446–447
    of restrooms, 493, 494, 502–503
    schools, conversion of, 316
    of staff lunchroom, 534–535
    of staff mailboxes, 542
    of staff restrooms, 533
    of staff workrooms, 512
    of storage spaces, 545, 547
    of technical services workrooms, 526

See also site selection
lockers
    for lending workrooms, 424
    for prevention of theft of personal possessions, 686
    for purse storage, 541–542
    for theft control, 681
locking doors, 473
locks
    double-cylinder locks, 687
    for file storage cabinets, 520
    for restroom doors, 504–505
    for windows, 681–682
Longfellow, Henry Wadsworth, 487
long-range plans, 81
loop antennas, 199
loop pile carpet, 225
loose floor mats, 231
loss adjustment, 706
losses
    insurance actions in case of, 715
    loss of business income, 707, 713
    major losses, covering, 707
    types of insurance coverage, 707
    umbrella liability coverage for, 709
louvers, 450
loveseats, 382
low slope roofs, 218
low-maintenance designs, 22
lumen, 585
luminaire, 585
lunchrooms
    See staff lunchrooms
lux, 585

M

machine tables, 377
magazines, 471
mailboxes
    for staff, 533, 542–543
    staff mailboxes, size of, 544
maintenance
    of brick walls, 214
    capital renewal/replacement costs, 353
    construction site maintenance, 277–278
    custodial workrooms, plumbing for, 663
    of elevators, 566
    of floor coverings, 225
    of fountains, 665
    of HVAC systems, 638, 651–652
    of LED lighting, 595
    lighting that is hard to maintain, 612–615
    low-maintenance library designs, 22
    operating costs, anticipating, 351–352
    problems from bad designs, 64
    of restroom toilets, 494
    for restrooms, 507
    shared buildings and, 339–340
maintenance staff, 99
maintenance water, 658
maker spaces
    closets for equipment, 460
    description of, 477–478
manual light switches, 506
manufacturers
    buying furniture from, 375–376
    buying lighting from major manufacturers, 615
    warranties from, 279
map cases, 411–412
marble, 215
master keys, 688
materials
    See construction materials; surfaces/materials
mats, 230–231
mechanical equipment, storage spaces for, 551–552
mechanical-assist shelving, 401
media
    at ground breakings, 281
    responding to questions from, 183
    at ribbon cuttings, 286
meeting rooms
    access for people with limited hearing, 199
    accessibility of, 463
    acoustics of, 449–452
    audiovisual equipment for, 455–457
    building program, two-phase, 92–93
    ceiling height of, 463
    coat storage for, 453–454
    electrical wiring for, 454–455
    floor coverings for, 462–463
    footprint size and, 139
    functional arrangement of rooms, 54
    furnishings for, 447–448
    HVAC for, 453
    kitchenette for, 460–462
    lighting for, 449
    location of, 446–447
    multipurpose rooms/community rooms, 467–468
    noise, control of, 443
    private use of, 478–479
    public libraries in shared government buildings, 334
    rectangular room configuration for, 444
    required room spaces, 445–446
    room capacities, determining, 444–445
    rules on, 13, 479–481
    security for, 464
    shared buildings, 327
    shared meeting rooms rules, 341
    shared meeting spaces, 332–333, 338, 339
    storage space for, 64, 549–551, 556
    See also program, activity, and study rooms
meetings
    architect at public meetings, 183
    building program, final review of, 92
    building program meetings, 94
    construction coordination meetings, 267–268
    construction meetings, 266
    minutes of, 187
    pre-bid meetings, 254–255
    private meetings of 501(c)(3) foundations, 364
    on schematic design, 175
    teamwork for library design/construction, 67–70
MEP systems
    acoustic tile for access to, 231
    engineering services in design process, 170
    evaluation of condition of, 173
MERV (Minimum Efficiency Reporting Value) rating, 643
metal halide lighting
    advantages/disadvantages of, 594
    definition of, 585
    photo example of, 599
microfiche cabinets, 412–413
microfilm cabinets, 412–413
microwave, 460, 535
Minimum Efficiency Reporting Value (MERV) rating, 643
Minneapolis Public Library, 201, 577
minutes, 164–165, 176
mirrors, 499–500, 508
Misselhorn, Mark, 178
mobility, people with limited, 193–195
models, architectural, 182–183
modern glass, 148, 188
modesty panels, 518
modular desks
    for flexibility, 420, 436
    importance of, 441
modular furnishings
    modular office system workstations, 518
    modular tables, 448
    for staff workrooms, 513, 517
moisture, 224
    See also humidity

mold/mildew
  green board for interior walls, 219
  humidification and, 650–651
  humidity control and, 696–697
money
  change orders, 276–277
  combined public and academic libraries, 331
  for construction, 275–277
  draws/lien waivers/retainage, 275–276
  on hand, as funding source, 356
  as most important construction material, 355, 366
  punch list and, 274–275
  shared buildings to save money, 329
  See also building costs; costs; funding
monitor windows
  access for people with limited eyesight, 196
  blinds for, 5
  daylight control and, 622
  as dysfunctional design, 60
  problems with natural light, 20
  rule on, 625
monumental staircases
  lighting problems, 611
  rule on, 581
monumentality, 417, 434
Moorman, John
  daytime shelters, 154
  first edition of book, xiii
  information about, 718
  restroom design without ventilation and, 104
  storeroom of library and, 546
  water feature story of, 664
mop basins, 500–501, 556
mop sink, 662, 663
mortar, 213, 214
mortgages, 359, 366
motion detectors
  of intrusion alarms, 690
  on punch list, 273
  rules on, 624, 625
motion sensor lights
  problems with, 198, 584, 491–492
  for restrooms, 49–50, 506
  for stack aisles, 406
  for staff restrooms, 540
  switches, 606, 634
  towel dispenser, 499
  for video surveillance cameras, 697
movability
  of display cases, 485, 489
  movable desks, 436–437
  movable furniture, 390
  movable room dividers, 13, 14, 451–452

movable seating, 389
movable walls, 473
moving
  of cantilever shelving, 395
  in cost estimates, 346, 349
  of library during construction, 261–262
  phased expansion projects and, 301–303
multi-deck shelving supported by columns, 408
multi-firm teams
  architect interview question about, 116–117
  as mostly window dressing, 110
  problems with, 108–109
  rule about hiring, 122
multi-floor openings, 37–39
multifunction desks, 433
multifunction meeting rooms
  furnishings for, 447–448
  kitchenette for, 460–462
  provisions for performers, 468
  seating capacity, 467–468
multilevel children's story structures, 476–477, 575
multimeter, 632
multipurpose rooms/community rooms, 467–468
municipal authorities, 127
municipal codes, 239
museums, combined with libraries, 488
mysterious disappearance, 706

N

Naestved, Denmark, 152
naming opportunities
  planning, 366
  program rooms offer, 443–444
  for quiet reading rooms, 470, 471
  for recognition of donors, 362
  rule about, 4
National Electrical Code (NEC), 240, 627, 628
National Fire Protection Association (NFPA) code, 240
National Flood Insurance Program, 670, 711–712
National Register of Historic Places, 145, 146
Native American graves, 147
Native American Graves Preservation and Repatriation Act (NAGPRA) of 1990, 147
natural gas, 311
natural light
  compass orientation and, 617–618

conversion problem, 310
daylight, controlling, 618–622
daylight, effective use of, 583
daylight, effects of unwanted, 623
direct sunlight, prevention of, 587
evaluation of, 48–49
in history of library lighting, 586
library design recommendations, 20
for program/activity/study rooms, 449
skylights, 622–623
for staff workrooms, 513, 514
working with, 617
natural stone, 214–215
NEC (National Electrical Code), 240, 627, 628
needs
  architect interviews and, 113
  building costs and, 353
  building programs as statements of needs, 74–75
  library design compatible with, 17
  space estimation for, 84–88
  special site needs of libraries, 151–158
neighborhoods, 150–151
neighbors, 137
new buildings, lighting in, 603
New York University Library, 200, 578
newel post, 568
newspapers, 471
NFPA (National Fire Protection Association) code, 240
night lights, 616
noise
  access for people with limited hearing, 198–199
  accessibility problems of libraries, 190
  adjacent uses and, 138
  atria transmit, 200, 573
  ceiling materials and, 231–232
  community center with public library and, 332
  of drive-up book returns, 428
  interior walls for controlling, 220
  library as passageway and, 335
  multi-floor openings and, 37
  of program/activity/study rooms, 443
  public libraries in shared government buildings, 334
  public library site, adjacent transportation, 155
  in quiet reading rooms, 471
  in school libraries, 157
  shared buildings and, 340
  study rooms, sound control for, 471–472
  from waste piping, 657

See also sound
non-library buildings
    See conversion, of non-library buildings to public libraries
non-library shelving, 403
non-owned auto liability insurance, 714
NORC, 80
north light
    as best light for reading/work, 617
    clearstory windows for, 617
    orientation of library, 148
    for reading, 49
nosing, 568–569, 571
nylon, 210

O

occupancy permit, 262, 271–272
odors, 637–638
off-desk workspaces, 418, 425
office, 529
office supplies, 548
open exhibit areas, 484
open risers, 62, 572–573
open terrace
    below grade level, 12
    flooding from, 665–666, 672
    storm drains for, 661
opening day collections, 350
openings, between floor, 37–39
operating costs, 343, 351–352
operating funds, 356
operation, of HVAC systems, 648, 651–652
opinion, difference of, 75
ordinances
    existing structures and, 173
    historic buildings/neighborhoods, 145
orientation
    of entrances, 26–27
    evaluating potential sites, 147–148
    natural light and, 617–618
    site selection and, 147–148
ornamental openings between floors, 37–38
ornamental spaces, 55
O'Rourke, P. J., 3
Our Lady of the Angels school fire, Chicago, 238
outdoor displays, 485–486
outdoor electrical outlets, 632
outdoor equipment, 551, 555
outdoor program space, 14
outdoor water features, 664–665
outlet boxes, 50
outline specifications, 177, 180
out-of-town firm, 108–109, 110
outward expansion, 141

overly specific number technique, 87
oversight, 105
    See also security; staff oversight
overstuffed furniture
    avoidance of, 373
    polyurethane foam, dangers of, 211, 212
    problems with, 52
owners
    architects, final selection of, 117–118
    architects behaving badly in design process, 164–167
    bonding and, 257–258
    building program design team, 73
    building program, evaluation of current facilities in, 82
    building program, ignoring, 93–94
    on building program planning team, 72
    building program, review of, 92
    building programs by, 89
    change orders and, 104, 276–277
    CM/A construction management and, 246–247
    contract close-out, 278–279
    conversions, reasons for, 309
    in design planning group, 164
    design process, bad behavior during, 167–169
    punch list and, 274
    shared buildings and, 339–340
    storage spaces and, 554
    teamwork for library design/construction, 67–70
owners' rep, 262–263
ownership
    combined libraries and museums and, 488
    of conference rooms, 470
    display/exhibit areas rule on, 489
    of library buildings, 326
    public library in residential/commercial buildings, 337
    site selection, land ownership and, 149–150

P

padded benches, 386
padding, 575
paint
    on cantilever shelving, 395–396
    for interior walls, 219, 220
    lead paint, remodel/expansion of library and, 292
    painted drywall, 220–221
    painted handrails, 577–578
    punch list and, 273

panic buttons, 433, 700
panic hardware, 686
paper shredders, 521
paper towels, 498–499
paperbacks, 410–411
PAR lamps, 586
parabolic fixtures, 197, 586
parabolic lenses, 624
parabolic reflectors, 585–586
parallel rows, shelving in, 404, 414
parents
    changing tables for, 501
    family restrooms, 502
    infant seats for restrooms, 502
park, 154
parking
    big box stores, conversion of, 320
    for combined school and public libraries, 330
    during construction process, 261
    conversion, good reasons for, 308
    conversion of non-library buildings and, 324
    historic stores, conversion of, 321, 322
    oddly shaped sites and, 128
    phased expansion project and, 302
    problems of building conversion, 312
    schools, conversion of, 316
    secure location for library site, 154
    as site development cost, 348
    space required for, 139–140
    survey on users walking to library, 153
Parsons Design tables, 373
partitions
    conversion problems, 310
    glass partitions, 198
    good excuse for, 43
    in historic stores, 321
    sound transmission, limiting, 450
partner in charge
    in architect contract, 120
    architects, final selection of, 117–118
    bait and switch of, 124
    interview questions about, 114, 116
passageways
    individual workrooms as, 516
    libraries must never serve as, 335
    staff workrooms as, 512, 530
passive systems
    dangerous architectural features, 677–678
    earthquake-resistant construction, 673
    entrances, limited public, 673–674
    fire-resistant construction, 668–669
    fire-resistant contents, 669
    flood-resistant construction, 669–672

passive systems (cont'd)
  reading/activity terraces, 677
  security through building design, 668
  shared buildings, avoiding, 677
  sight lines, 674–676
  trapped, places where people can be, 676–677
  windows, 677
  windstorm-resistant construction, 672–673
pathogens, 643
pathways, 420
patrons
  See users
patterns
  access for people with vertigo, 203
  in broadloom carpet, 226
  of carpet tiles, 227
pavers, 362–363
paybacks, 645
payment
  bills handled by architect, 264–265
  draw, 262
  draws/lien waivers/retainage, 275–276
payment bonds, 258
PC ratings, 710
pedestal electrical outlets, 632
pendant lights, 615–616
people mover, 563
perforated acoustic ceilings, 233
perforated vinyl blinds, 620
performance bonds, 257–258
performers, 445, 468
perils, 706, 707, 711
perimeter shelving, 403–404
perimeter soffits, 624
perimeters
  dark, lighting design and, 609–610
  illumination levels, calculation, 589
  intrusion alarms and, 690
periodicals, 398–399
permanent exhibits, 488, 489
permanent works of art, 487, 489
permitting, 350
personal possessions, theft of, 686
phase I completion events, 283
phased construction, 252–253
phased expansion projects
  advantages of, 301
  problems with, 301–303
  reasons for, 303
phenolic resin panels, 217
phone application, 456
photocopiers, 430
photographs
  by architects, 112
  of existing library in grant application, 365

of ribbon cutting, 287
photovoltaic systems, 646–647
physical layout
  See library spaces, configuration of
pianos, 468
pinnable backs, 485, 486
pinnable surfaces, 486–487
pipes
  of sprinkler systems, 693
  for wastewater, 659
placement
  of lending desks, 422–423
  of reference desks, 432
  of service desks, 420–421
  of user seating in library, 387–389
  See also location
places of refuge
  enclosed exit staircases, 569
  fire-exit staircases, 695–696
  shelters from tornadoes/hurricanes, 672–673
planning
  building programs, purposes of, 73
  for conference rooms, 469–470
  for donor recognition, 362
  for lending desks, 421–422
  long-range plans in building program, 81
  meeting room capacity, 467–468
  meetings, 67–70
  planning team for building program, 72
  process, steps of, 6
  for public ceremonies, 280
  for restroom maintenance, 507
  for service desks, 417
  for staff workrooms, 511–512
planning groups
  design planning groups, 163–164
  in design process, 163–164
  teamwork for library design/construction, 67–70
planning studies, 360
plantings, 140
plaques
  construction plaques, 284
  donor recognition plaques, 284–285, 287
  for recognition of grant, 366
  for recognizing smaller donations, 362–363
plaster, 221, 232
platform lift, 566
plenum
  definition of, 640
  floors, 199, 200
  problems with HVAC, 638
  system, ventilating with, 642

video surveillance system and, 699
plumbing
  drawings, 185
  public libraries in residential or commercial buildings, 335, 337
  rules on remodeling/expanding library buildings, 304
  for staff lunchroom, 537
plumbing codes
  description of, 240
  on number of fixtures for restrooms, 502
  unisex restrooms and, 540
plumbing engineer, 655
plumbing systems
  for custodial workrooms, 663
  for food preparation/service areas, 662
  overview of, 655–656
  rules on, 665–666
  for staff workrooms, 662–663
  stormwater, 660–662
  vocabulary for, 656
  wastewater, 659
  for water features, 664–665
  water supplies, 656–658
plunger locks, 520
police
  intrusion alarms and, 690
  library located next to, 152
  panic buttons and, 700
  theft of library property and, 713, 715
policy
  on display and exhibit areas, 483, 488–489
  for storage spaces, 556
politicians
  assistance from, 146
  at ground breakings, 280–281
politics
  bond referendums and, 357
  conversion, good reasons for, 309
  of conversion of non-library buildings, 325
  special appropriations for fundraising, 366
pollution
  adjacent uses and, 138
  asbestos/other pollutants, remodel/expansion and, 292
  of brownfield sites, 137
  conversion of non-library buildings and, 313
  existing structures, evaluation of, 173
polyurethane foam
  definition of, 210
  flammability of, 383, 669
  toxicity of, 211

in upholstered furniture, 212, 390–391
portable alarm devices, 700
portable fire extinguishers, 696
post-occupancy inspection, 279
poured epoxy, 228
powder systems, 695
power driven shelving, 401
power poles, 627
pre-action systems, 694
pre-bid meetings, 254–255
precast, 210
precast stone, 215–216
preliminary services
   of design process, 172–174
   evaluation of existing structures, 172–173
   feasibility studies, 173
premium, 706, 710
prequalification, 244, 254
preservation, 648–649
press releases, 281
pressure sensors, 406
pressure switches, 198
prevailing wage, 244, 251–252
printers, 521, 524
privacy
   individual workrooms for, 516
   privacy panels for carrels, 380
   of staff lunchroom, 534
   of staff workrooms, 513
private use, of program rooms, 478–479
problems
   with architect teams, 108–109
   with atria, 3, 22, 37–38, 573–574
   conversion of non-library buildings
      accessibility, 311
      air conditioning, 310
      asbestos, lead paint, hazardous materials, 313
      basements, 312–313
      bearing walls, 312
      buildings designed for extra floor, 314
      ceilings, low, 315
      cheap construction, 313
      code compliance, 313
      electrical wiring/outlets, 314–315
      expansion space, lack of, 311
      floor strength, 310–311
      high cost of conversions, 315–316
      historic structures, 314
      lighting, poor, 310
      lighting, unworkable, 315
      locations, 310
      parking, 312
      partitions/floors, unwanted, 310
      utilities, lack of, 311
   errors in library architecture, 100–101

with funding, 355–356
with lighting, 607–617
with railings, 576–579
remodeling/expanding library buildings
   accessibility, 299–300
   adjacent land, 298–299
   asbestos/other pollutants, 292
   basements in expanded historic buildings, 301
   bearing walls, 292–293
   building codes, changing, 291
   building codes, new code categories from expansion, 291–292
   cheap or fragile construction materials, 295–296
   electrical wiring, 294–295
   functional location, poor, 296
   historic entrances, 300
   historic exteriors, matching, 296–298
   HVAC, 293–294
   room arrangements, 301
   windows, 295
with restrooms, 491–493
of service desks, 434–440
of shared buildings, 327–329
with soft seating, 383–384
with staircases, 567
teamwork for decision-making and, 67–70
products, in specification books, 251
professional assistance, 126–129
professional fees, 350–351
professional publications, 345
program, activity, and study rooms
   accessibility of, 463
   acoustics of, 449–452
   audiovisual equipment for, 455–457
   ceiling height of, 463
   coat storage for, 453–454
   electrical wiring for, 454–455
   floor coverings for, 462–463
   furnishings for, 447–448
   HVAC for, 453
   kitchenettes, 460–462
   lighting for, 449
   locating rooms in buildings, 446–447
   overview of, 443–444
   private use of, 478–479
   rectangular room configuration, 444
   required room spaces, 445–446
   room capacities, determining, 444–445
   rules on, 12, 479–481
   security of, 464
   storage closets, 457–460

   storage spaces for, 549–551, 556
   types of
      auditoriums, 464–466
      children's craft and story rooms, 473–476
      classrooms, 466–467
      conference/seminar rooms, 468–470
      faculty studies, 478
      maker spaces, 477–478
      multilevel children's story structures, 476–477
      multipurpose rooms/community rooms, 467–468
      quiet reading rooms, 470–471
      study rooms, 471–473
program equipment, 550
program/craft supplies closets, 458
programmers
   See library building consultants
programs
   See building programs
project cost
   building costs, rules on, 343
   construction costs *vs.*, 343–344
   in cost estimates, 345–346
   definition of, 344
   rule about, 3, 4
project equipment, 523
project lists, 101–102, 105
project narratives, 365
project-end celebrations, 284–287
projection systems
   ceiling height and, 463
   for meeting rooms, 455–456
   room dividers and, 451
proof of operation, 270
propane, 311, 652
property insurance
   deductibles, 708
   earthquake, 712
   exhibits, 712
   flood insurance, 711–712
   loss of business income, 713
   overview of, 711
   risks covered by, 707
   sewer backup, 712
   theft of library property, 713
   valuable objects, 712
property risks, 712–713
proposals
   from architectural firms, 108
   directions on where to send copies of, 106
   evaluating, 109–110
   specific information in RFQ, 106–108
protection
   from elements, 55

protection (cont'd)
　of storage spaces, 545, 554–555
proximity cards, 689–690
public areas, workspaces in, 528
public ceremonies
　beams, signing, 282
　construction plaques, 284
　in construction process, 267
　cornerstones, laying, 281–282
　donor receptions, 285
　donor recognition plaques, 284–285
　ground breakings, 280–281
　phase I completion events, 283
　planning for, 280
　purposes of, 279–280
　ribbon cuttings, 286–287
　rules on, 287–288
　topping out, 282–283
　tours of work in progress, 283–284
public handouts, 281
public libraries
　adjacent land for expansion space, 298, 299
　auditoriums in, 465
　building costs, 343
　combined community centers with public libraries, 332
　conference rooms in, 468–470
　construction plaques for, 284
　expandability of, 19
　expansion space and, 142, 143
　funding, sources of, 356–357
　land ownership, site selection and, 149–150
　library sites with no room for expansion, 125
　meeting rooms, capacities of, 444–445
　poor functional locations, 296
　program, activity, and study rooms, private use of, 478–479
　quiet reading rooms in, 470–471
　in residential or commercial buildings, 335–337
　security for children's departments, 701
　shared buildings, combined public and academic libraries, 331
　shared buildings, combined school and public libraries, 330–331
　shared buildings, problems of, 327–329
　shared buildings, rules on, 340–342
　in shared government buildings, 334
　shared meeting spaces, 332–333
　site choice, push for, 126
　site selection rules, 159–160
　size of building footprint, 139
　special site needs of, 151–156
　See also conversion, of non-library buildings to public libraries
Public Library Association, xiii
public meetings, 183
public relations, 701–702
public service desks
　See service desks
public sorting shelves, 426, 430
public use
　of children's craft and story rooms, 476
　of staff conference rooms, 522
publicity, 286
pull stations, 692
punch lists
　architect verification of, 265
　architects that blow off, 167
　definition of, 263
　final punch lists, 272–273
　floor drains for restrooms, 507
　librarian and, 265, 266
　list of items to include in, 273–274
　restroom equipment, checking, 508
　ribbon cuttings and, 286
　rules on, 287
　working with contractors/architects on, 274–275
purchasing
　of furniture, 375–376
　lighting, 615
purse storage
　coin-return lockers for patrons, 686
　purse lockers, 541–542
　for staff facilities, 533
　for staff lunchroom, 535
　for staff workrooms, 520–521
push buttons, 406
"push survey," 79

Q

QBS (qualifications based selection) laws, 118
quality, cost of, 354
+623quality control
　construction coordination meetings, 267–268
　construction in accordance with drawings/specifications, 268–271
　errors, resolving, 271
questions
　for architect interviews, 113–117
　for focus groups, 78
　for hiring construction management firm, 249–250
　for interviews of architects, 112
　for interviews with staff/management, 76–77
　for surveys, 79
queuing space, 426
quiet reading rooms, 470–471

R

radiating book stacks, 676
radiators, 650
radio frequency system, 456
rail, 373
railings
　accessibility, improving, 205
　ADA accessibility requirements for, 191
　climbable, 569, 576, 577
　codes require, 572
　dangers of, 678
　dysfunctional designs for, 62
　extra handrails for children, 579
　glass, 576–577
　glass railings next to drop-offs, 201
　hard to grab, 578–579
　on narrow walkways, 578
　painted handrails, 577–578
　rules on, 581, 582
　security of, 56
　that people can fall through, 579
　See also handrails
railroads, 155–156
rainwater, 131–132
ramps
　access for people with limited eyesight, 198
　access for people with limited mobility, 193–195
　accessibility rule on, 206, 207
　in auditoriums, 465
　dysfunctional designs for, 63
　elevator options and, 565
　for historic entrance, 300
　historic stores, conversion of, 321
　problems with, 192, 561–562, 579–580
　requirements for, 579
　rules on, 580–581, 582
Rana Plaza collapse, Dhaka, 238–239
range content labels, 409
rare book departments
　HVAC problems and, 638
　HVAC requirements for, 648–649
　theft from, 679
　workroom for, 528
reader guidance, 431
　See also reference and reader guidance desks
reading
　illumination levels and, 588–589

lighting for comfortable reading, 583
reading pits, 198
reading rooms
  evaluation of acoustics, 50
  in historic libraries, 293
  huge, 39
  lighting for, 197
  quiet reading rooms, design of, 470–471
  on top floors, 42–43
  total square footage for small reading room, 87
reading tables
  electrical outlets for, 6, 630–631
  facing shelving, 393
  height for, 15
  placement next to shelving, 388
  requirement for, 378–380
  rules about, 391, 392
reading terraces
  as dysfunctional design, 64
  problems of, 23
  rules about, 4, 44
  security issues, 56
  security through building design, 677
receipt deadlines, 258
receiving bins, 423, 424–425
receiving rooms, 427
receptacle, 628
recessed downlights
  definition of, 586
  direct glare from, 590–591
  glare from, 608
  photo examples of, 599, 600, 601
  problems with, 600–601
  rule on, 624, 626
recognition
  donor recognition rule, 367
  grant terms about, 366
record drawings
  architect failure to deliver, 121
  checking, 277
  definition of, 263
  review of in contract close-out, 278–279
record keeping, 361–362
rectangular rooms, 21, 444
rectangular tables, 376–377, 390
recurring tasks, construction, 277–278
recycled tires, 228
reference and reader guidance desks
  changes in reference service, 430–431
  desktop surfaces, 438
  functions of, 431
  heights of, 431
  number of service points at, 431
  placement of, 432
  roving librarian concept and, 431–432
  storage at, 432
references
  for architects, 102
  for architectural firms, 99–100
  for construction management firm, 249
  for proposal evaluation, 110
referendums, bond, 356–357
reflective roofs, 645–646
refrigerants
  banned, 638
  cooling via expansion of, 641
  definition of, 640
refrigerators, 521, 536
relative humidity
  control of, 696–697
  definition of, 640
  description of, 637
remediation
  of asbestos/other pollutants, 292
  costs of, 212
  definition of, 210
remodeling
  bequests and, 358
  building code rule on, 241
  building costs, rules on, 353
  change orders due to, 104
  construction drawings for, 185
  evaluation of existing structures, 172–173
  rules on, 11
remodeling/expanding library buildings
  comparative costs, 290–291
  introduction to, 289
  library relocation during construction, 261–262
  phased construction/interim facilities, 252–253
  phasing expansion projects, 301–303
  problems with
    accessibility, 299–300
    adjacent land, 298–299
    asbestos/other pollutants, 292
    basements in expanded historic buildings, 301
    bearing walls, 292–293
    building codes, changing, 291
    building codes, new code categories from expansion, 291–292
    cheap or fragile construction materials, 295–296
    electrical wiring, 294–295
    functional location, poor, 296
    historic entrances, 300
    historic exteriors, matching, 296–298
    HVAC, 293–294
  room arrangements, 301
  windows, 295
  rules on, 303–305
  See also conversion, of non-library buildings to public libraries
remote water heaters, 657
renderings, 181–182, 281
rented buildings
  interim facilities for library, 253
  for library during construction process, 265–266
  public libraries in, 149
  shared buildings, library in rented building, 341
  shared buildings, rules on, 341
repairs
  bequests and, 358
  capital renewal/replacement costs, 352–353
replacement cost, 706
replacements
  cost of, 702
  insurance requirements, 716
  staff time for dealing with, 680
request for qualifications (RFQ), 101–108
reserve reading functions, 422
residential buildings, public libraries in, 335–337
resilient flooring, 462
respiratory diseases, 640
responsibility, 246, 247
responsible, 244
responsible bidder, 245
responsive, 244–245
responsive bidder, 245
restrooms
  accessible stalls in, 192–193, 207
  ADA accessibility requirements for, 191
  for auditoriums, 465
  building codes for, 493–494
  building program, two-phase, 93
  ceramic tile for, 221
  children/infants, accommodations for, 501–502
  combined school and public libraries and, 333
  community center with public library, 332
  family restrooms, 502
  fixtures/equipment
    feminine hygiene products, 500
    hand drying, 498–499
    hypodermic needles, 500
    mirrors, 499–500
    mop basins, 500–501
    shelves, 500

fixtures/equipment (cont'd)
  soap dispensers, 497–498
  stall enclosures, 495–496
  toilets, 494–495
  urinals, 496–497
  ventilation, 500
  washbasins, 497
 full-view, 676
 lighting
  light distribution, 506
  manually switched, 506
  motion sensor lights, 49–50, 506, 606
 maintenance, planning for, 507
 meeting room location and, 447
 next to children's craft and story rooms, 476
 problems with, 491–493
 punch list and, 273
 rules on, 12, 508–509
 security for
  doors/sight lines, 56
  restrooms as tornado shelters, 505–506
  single-user restrooms, 505
  staff oversight, 504–505
  video surveillance, 505
 shared buildings rule for, 341
 shared meeting spaces and, 333
 size/location of
  expansion, implications for, 504
  fixtures, number of, 502
  gender-neutral restrooms, 504
  locations, 502–503
  staff restrooms, 503–504
 for staff, 539–540
 staff workrooms and, 515
 theft control and, 681
 with tornado-resistance construction, 6
 video camera locations, 699
 washbasins, 8
 for windstorm shelters, 673
 zigzag entries for, 675
retail sites, for public libraries, 151–152
retainage
 definition of, 263
 overview of, 276
 punch list and, 274–275
retention basins
 function of, 131
 as habitat for geese, 132
 overview of, 661–662
 as site development cost, 348
return slots
 See book return slots
review
 of building programs, 92, 93

program review by architects, 165
of submittals, 268–269
rezoning, of site for library, 128
RFID tags, 685, 703
RFQ (request for qualifications)
 artistic design/function balance, 103–104
 change orders, number of, 104–105
 client satisfaction, 102
 construction oversight, responsibility for, 105
 functionality of buildings designed by firm, 102–103
 for hiring construction management firm, 248
 information to include in, 106–108
 interview plan in, 111
 library work done by firm, 101–102
 listening skills, 103
 people proposed for project, 102, 105–106
 questions to ask in, 105–106
 responsiveness to client requests, 103
ribbon cutting
 definition of, 263
 guidance on, 286–287
 rule on, 8, 288
risers
 colored, for people with limited eyesight, 197
 definition of, 568
 open risers, banning, 202
 staircase design basics, 568, 569
 staircases with open risers, 572–573
 story hour risers, 476–477
 story hour structures with risers, 575
risks
 definition of, 706
 insurance policies, purchasing, 710–711
 property risks, insurance for, 712–713
 types of insurance coverage and, 707
"River City" sites, 153–154
rocking chair, 221, 383
Roman bricks, 214
roofs
 green roofs, 132
 HVAC equipment on, 652
 internal roof drain, 656
 reflective, for reducing energy use, 645–646
 roof coverings, 218, 235
 upward expansion and, 142
 windstorm-resistant construction, 672–673
rooftop units (RTUs), 649–650
rooftop water supplies, 658
room arrangements, 301

room capacity
 of children's craft and story rooms, 474
 determining, 444–445
room dividers, 451–452
 See also partitions
room reservations, 478–479
room shapes
 dysfunctional designs, 64
 evaluation of, 54
 functional shapes, 21
 round rooms, design challenges of, 37
 strangely shaped spaces, 28
rooms
 with diagonal walls, 40
 functional arrangement, evaluation of, 54
 large entry rooms with radiating wings, 40
 See also program, activity, and study rooms
round rooms, 21, 37
round service desks, 434–435
round tables, 377, 390
roving librarian concept, 431–432, 441
RTUs (rooftop units), 649–650
rubber tile, 228
rules
 on accessibility, 206–208
 on bidding, 243–244, 260
 on building codes, 241
 on building costs, 353–354
 on building programs, 96
 on collection storage/display, 414–415
 on construction, 287–288
 on conversion of non-library buildings to public libraries, 325–326
 on design process, 187–188
 on display and exhibit areas, 489
 on electrical systems, 634–635
 on elevators, staircases, railings, and ramps, 580–582
 entire list of, 3–16
 on funding, 366–367
 on hiring architects, 123–124
 on HVAC, 652–653
 on insurance, 715–716
 on library design, 23
 on library spaces, configuration of, 42–44
 on lighting, 623–626
 on plumbing systems, 665–666
 on program, activity, and study rooms, 479–481
 on public ceremonies, 287–288
 on remodeling/expanding library buildings, 303–305

on restrooms, 508-509
on security, 702-704
on service desks, 441-442
on shared buildings, 340-342
on site selection, 159-160
snappy rules, inclusion of, xiii
on staff facilities, 543-544
on staff workrooms, 529-531
on storage spaces, 555-557
on surfaces/materials, 233-235
on user seating, 390-392
runoff
detention/retention basins for, 661-662
storm drains for, 660-661
rusticated
definition of, 210
stone, 215

S

Sannwald, William, 77
safes, 692
safety
electrical wiring and, 629
indoor water features and, 664
placement of service desks for, 420-421
of railings, problems with, 576-579
safe spaces, library design for, 22
staircase design and, 568-570
staircases and fires, 576
tours of work in progress and, 283
See also security
safety codes, 62, 290
samples, of furniture, 376
sandstone, 215
sanitary sewer
sewer backup insurance, 712
storm drain connections to, 660-661
wastewater systems, 659
savings, funding from, 356
SBC (Standard Building Code), 237
scheduled, definition of, 707
scheduling
ground breakings, 280
of interviews with architectural firms, 107, 111
of payments in contract with architect, 121
ribbon cuttings, 286
shared meeting spaces and, 333
schematic designs
in architect contract, 119, 121
architects, working with, 167
basic services phases, 172
cost estimating, 180, 181
design rule on, 188

example of, 178-180
fundraising assistance, 175-180
for grant application, 365
overview of, 174-175
process, 175-180
for remodeling/expansion, 290
for staff workrooms, 528-529
Schlipf, Fred
contact information for, xvi
information about, 717
introduction to book, xiii-xvi
school libraries
building costs, 343
funding, sources of, 356-357
library sites, problematic, 125-126
shared buildings, combined school and public libraries, 330-331
shared buildings, problems of, 328
shared buildings, rules on, 340-342
shared facilities in single buildings, 334-335
shared meeting spaces, 332-333
special site needs of, 156-157
storage spaces for classroom equipment, 556
strong floors, need for, 144
school shootings, 328, 331
schools
conversion to library, 316-317
public library sites near, 155
SCOF (Static Coefficient of Friction), 225
screened porches
avoidance of, 23
as miserable idea, 44
rule about, 10
sealants, 645
sealing, 462
seating
capacity of multifunction meeting rooms, 467
for staff lunchroom, 538
for staff workrooms, 518-519
See also chairs; user seating
Seattle Public Library, 59, 204
secluded spaces, 539
secure storage, 521, 525
security
academic library buildings that include other academic agencies, 333-334
balconies and, 39
of book return slots, 427
building design for
dangerous architectural features, 677-678
earthquake-resistant construction, 673

entrances, limited public, 673-674
fire-resistant contents, 669
fires-resistant construction, 668-669
flood-resistant construction, 669-672
reading/activity terraces, 677
shared buildings, avoiding, 677
sight lines, 674-676
trapped, places where people can be, 676-677
windows, 677
windstorm-resistant construction, 672-673
for children's craft and story rooms, 474
children's departments in public libraries, 701
combined school and public libraries and, 331
desks for entrance/exit control, 432-433
of display and exhibit areas, 483, 487
for display cases, 486
dysfunctional designs for, 63-64
elevators and, 563
entrance and exit control
building codes, 687-688
importance of, 686-687
key systems, 688-689
modern panic hardware, 688
proximity cards, swipe cards, fobs, keypads, 689-690
entrances, number of, 48
evaluation of, 55-56
fire-protection systems
escape routes, 695-696
fire alarm systems, 691-692
portable fire extinguishers, 696
sprinkler systems, 692-695
historic entrances and, 300
humidity control, 696-697
intrusion alarms, 690-691
lending desk placement for, 422-423
library design for, xiv
for meeting rooms, 457
of office supplies, 548
overview of, 667-668
panic buttons, 700
personal possessions, theft of, 686
portable alarm devices, 700
of program/activity/study rooms, 443, 464
public relations implications, 701-702
purse storage and, 541-542
restroom location and, 503
for restrooms, 504-506, 508

security (cont'd)
- rules on, 12, 702–703
- secure locations for library site, 154–155
- secure storage for staff workrooms, 520
- security systems, insurance cost and, 710
- for service desks, 418–419
- service desks and, 433–434
- service desks, placement of, 420–421
- service desks, security for staff, 433–434
- shared buildings and, 340
- shared buildings, problems of, 328, 329
- shared elevators and, 334–335
- single-user restrooms and, 505
- site selection for public libraries and, 151
- staff training on, 702
- theft-control systems
  - economic models, 679–680
  - electronic theft-detection systems, 683–686
  - high-risk materials, 679
  - oversight, improved, 680–682
  - overview of, 678–679
  - theft-prone materials, sequestering, 682–683
  - unauthorized people, keeping out of library, 683
- traffic flows and, 41
- video surveillance systems
  - camera locations, 699–700
  - equipment specifications, 697–699
  - overview of, 697
security boxes, 685
security gates
- of electronic theft-detection systems, 683–684
- space for, 429
- video camera locations, 699–700
security lighting, 616
seismic issues, 408
self-check equipment
- space for, 429–430
- for theft control, 683, 685
self-service lending, 422
seminar rooms
- furnishings for, 447–448
- overview of, 468–470
service counters
- color of, 589
- services on, evaluation of, 51

service desks
- aisles, orientation for best staff oversight, 405
- design needs of, 417–419
- for entrance/exit control, 432–433
- evaluation of proposed, 421
- information desks, 433
- lending desks
  - additional lending desk spaces, 429–430
  - automated book-handling systems, 426–427
  - book return, provisions for, 424–425
  - drive-up books returns with receiving rooms, 427–428
  - exterior book pickups, 429
  - external book return bins, 428–429
  - functions of, 422
  - lending service windows, 429
  - lending workrooms, 423–424
  - with off-desk workspaces, 425
  - placement of, 422–423
  - planning for, 421–422
  - queuing space, 426
  - seated vs. standing-height, 424
  - sorting rooms, 426
  - staff spaces, 423
  - visual barricades on user sides of, 425–426
- library supply company service desks, 440
- multifunction desks, 433
- with only one staff exit, 676–677
- panic buttons for, 700
- placement of, 420–421
- problems in design of
  - acoustics, 440
  - desktop surfaces, fragile, 437–438
  - fortress desks, 438–439
  - inflexibility, 434–437
  - monumentality, 434
  - obsolete desks, persistence of, 438
  - obsolete features in lending desks, 439–440
  - soffits/bad lighting, 440
- reference and reader guidance desks, 430–432
- rules on, 13, 441–442
- security for staff and, 433–434
- soffits over, 602
- task lighting, architecturally mounted, 602
- typical functions of, 419–420
- work counters behind, 528

service points
- evaluation of, 47–48
- number of, 431
service standards/restrictions, 81–82
setbacks, 140, 238
settlement, 707
sewer backup insurance, 712
sewers
- cost of relocating, 130
- wastewater system, 659
shadows, 590
shape
- of meeting rooms, 444
- of site for library, 128
- strangely shaped spaces, 28
shared buildings
- academic library buildings that include other academic agencies, 333–334
- benefits of, 327, 337–338
- challenges of, 338–339
- combined community centers with public libraries, 332
- combining types of libraries, 330–331
- problems of, 327–329
- public libraries in residential or commercial buildings, 335–337
- public libraries in shared government buildings, 334
- reasons for, claimed, 338
- rules on, 340–342
- security by avoiding, 677
- shared facilities in single buildings, 334–335
- shared meeting spaces, 332–333
- things to clarify in advance, 339–340
shared meeting spaces, 332–333
"Sharps" containers, 500
sheetrock, 219
shelters
- public library sites near, 154, 160
- tornado/hurricane, 715
- windstorm shelters, 672–673, 703
shelves
- buffet shelves for staff lunchroom, 537
- of display cases, 485, 486
- for restrooms, 500
shelving
- ADA accessibility requirements for, 192
- call-number ranges, unbroken, 405–406
- on casters, 409
- chairs placed next to, 388
- for children's supply closets, 458
- compact shelving, 400–401

contents of shelving ranges, marking, 409
cross aisles, 407–408
curved shelving, 409–410
curved walls and, 37
dysfunctional designs for, 63
earthquakes and, 673
electrical outlets and, 405
with end-supported shelves, 402
evaluation of, 52
on exterior walls, 296
floor strength for books, 403
functional arrangement of rooms, 54
lending desk staff spaces, 423
for lending workrooms, 423–424
light fixtures extending from, 610
lighting units attached to, 602, 603
multi-deck shelving supported by columns, 408
non-library shelving, 403
perimeter shelving, 403–404
planning space for collections, 86–87
ranges of shelves in parallel rows, 404
rules on, 5, 6, 8, 9, 414–415
seismic issues, 408
selection of, 393
service desks and, 421
sight lines and, 675, 676
stack aisle widths, 407
stack aisles, dead-end, 404–405
stack aisles, lighting, 406–407
stack aisles, orientation for staff oversight, 405
for staff workrooms, 519–520
staircases incorporating, 574–575
steel cantilever shelving, 394–400
for technical services workrooms, 525
wood shelving, 402–403
shelving ranges, 409
shop drawings
architect's responsibility for, 264
definition of, 263
librarian review of, 266–267
verification that construction matches drawings/specifications, 268–269
showers, for staff, 543
"sick building syndrome," 211
side chairs, 384–386
sidewalks, 348
siding, for exterior walls, 216–217
sight lines
dysfunctional designs for, 63
funding problems and, 356
importance of, 10
maintaining, 29–30
to meeting rooms, 447
into restrooms, 503
rules on, 43
for safe environments, 22
for security, 674–676, 703
security through building design, 674–676
service desks, evaluation of proposed, 421
service desks, security for staff, 433
staff service points and, 47–48
for study rooms, 472
for theft control, 680
signs
for emergency exits, 695
lettering on, 198
marking contents of shelving ranges, 409
for people with limited sense of directions, 204
for shelving aisles, 414
for welcoming library, 47
simplicity, library design for, xv
single-user restrooms
paper towels flushed in, 499
security issues of, 505
sight lines into, 676
single-user tables, 376
sinks
for children's craft and story rooms, 475
for children's workrooms, 526
in kitchenette for meeting room, 460
for lending workrooms, 424
mop sinks, 663
plumbing for, 662
plumbing for staff workrooms, 663
plumbing rules on, 665
for staff conference rooms, 523
for staff facilities, 533
for staff lunchroom, 536
for staff workrooms, 514, 530
site
acquisition costs, 346–347
adjacent land, 298–299
configuration of, 135
development costs, 348
for library, rules about, 14
topography, 133–136
site plans
construction drawing of, 184–185
as schematic design deliverable, 180
site selection
architect assistance with, 169
building codes, rules on, 241
codes related to, 240, 241
evaluating potential sites
adjacent uses, 138
archaeology, 147
brownfield sites, 136–137
covenants, 150–151
easements, 148
expansion land, acquisition of, 150
floodplains, 133
historic buildings/neighborhoods, 145–146
land ownership, 149–150
orientation to compass, 147–148
professional assistance in, 126–129
site configuration, 133
site topography, 133–136
size, 138–144
soil conditions, 129–130
subsurface water, 132
surface water runoff detention/retention, 131–132
utilities, 130–131
flat sites for accessibility, 205, 207
as group process, 68
introduction to, 125–126
poor functional locations, 296
rules on, 159–160, 305
site acquisition costs, 346–347
special site needs of libraries
academic libraries, 156
public libraries, 151–156
school libraries, 156–157
special libraries, 158
summary of, 158–159
size
of elevators, 563–564
of staff workrooms, 511–512, 528–529
size of site
acreage needed, 138–139
building footprint, 139
estimating site acreage, 144
expansion space, 140–144
parking/driveways, 139–140
plantings/landscaping, 140
setbacks, 140
skylights
access for people with limited eyesight, 196
accessibility rule on, 207
artificial, 20, 584, 621
avoiding, 624
in children's craft and story rooms, 475
drawbacks of, 4, 23
as dysfunctional design, 59
energy lost with, 293
glare from, 590, 591
glare/gloom from, 583
in historic libraries, 295
light control with, 40

skylights (cont'd)
    lighting and, 587–588, 589
    lighting problems from, 612, 622–623
    problems with, 48
    in staff workrooms, 514
slat-wall inserts, 400
sled bases, 384
sliding wire book supports, 398
sloped roofs, 218
slope-top tables, 381
smoke detectors, 691, 694
snappy rules
    See rules
soap dispensers, 497–498
social events, for donors, 363
sofas
    bad decisions on, 371
    guidance on, 383
    lend themselves to misuse, 52
    rule about, 390
    for staff lunchroom, 538
soffits
    above service points, 48
    accessibility rule on, 207
    air ducts and, 642
    avoidance of, 23
    as bad idea, 7
    dark perimeters from perimeter
        soffits, 609–610
    dysfunctional designs for, 62
    gloom from bad lighting, 609
    lighting and, 587
    lighting problems from, 610–611
    in meeting rooms, 449
    over service desks, 602
    perimeter, 54, 624
    perimeter shelving and, 404
    service desks and, 417, 435, 440, 441
    warning against, 235
soft seating
    armchairs, 381–382
    loveseats, 382
    problems with, 383–384
    rocking chairs, 383
    rules about, 390
    sofas, 383
soil borings, 137
soil conditions
    checking soil of potential sites,
        129–130
    site selection and, 127
solar panels, 646–647
sorting rooms, 426
sound
    sound absorbing panels, 450
    sound absorption of acoustic tile, 231
    sound control for study rooms,
        471–472

sound insulation for restrooms, 491
sound transmission, 220, 449–451
sound-absorbing materials, 220
    See also acoustics; noise
sound system, 281, 456
south light, 615
south-facing entrances, 147–148
space
    in building program, 74
    building program space calculations,
        83–84
    building programs, space-cutting,
        91–92
    for children's workrooms, 527
    for collection storage/display,
        estimating, 414
    for electronic theft-detection
        systems, 683–684
    evaluation of potential sites and,
        126–127
    expandability of library, 19
    flexibility of, xiv
    interviews with staff/management
        about, 76–77
    lack of space in phased expansion
        project, 302, 303
    lending desk spaces, additional,
        429–430
    lending desks, queuing space for, 426
    for lending workrooms, 423–424
    long-range plans in building
        program, 81
    needs, conversion and, 309
    planning space for collections, 86–87
    poaching, building programs and, 75
    remodeling/expanding library
        buildings, 290
    required room spaces, 445–446
    room shapes, functional, 21
    shape of, 9
    shapes for library rooms, 13
    shared buildings and, 339
    site size, 138–144
    staff workroom sizes, 511–512,
        528–529
    between tables, 378
    user seating, clearances for, 387–388,
        391
    See also floor space; library spaces,
        configuration of
space estimation
    building program space calculations,
        83–84
    methods of, 84–88
    putting numbers together, 87–88
    space estimates using formulas, 94
spalling, 210, 215
speakers, 280, 286

special appropriations, 366
"special form" insurance coverage, 711
special libraries
    conference rooms in, 469
    funding projects with money on
        hand, 356
    problematic library sites, 126
    shared buildings, problems of, 329
    special site needs of, 158
    strong floors, need for, 144
    unauthorized people, keeping out of
        library, 683
specialized workrooms
    children's departments, 526–528
    graphic arts, 523–524
    rare book departments, 528
    technical services, 524–526
specification books, 251
specifications, 185–186
spinners, 410–411, 414
splat, 373
split system, 640, 650
spoken announcement warnings, 691
spray booths, 524
sprinkler heads, 694
sprinkler systems
    ceiling height and, 315
    in construction documents, 185
    cutting water to, 655–656
    dry pipe systems, 693–694
    fear of, 692–693
    function of, 692
    inert gas systems, 694–695
    insurance cost and, 710
    for library, evaluation of, 56
    powder systems, 695
    pre-action systems, 694
    required for larger libraries, 237–238
    requirement for building expansion,
        291–292
    shutting off, 695
    sprinkler heads, types of, 694
    staff training on turning off, 657
    wet pipe systems, 693
square footage
    planning space for collections, 86–87
    putting space estimate numbers
        together, 87–88
    small reading room, total square
        footage for, 87
    space calculations, 83–84
    table in building program, 93
square tables, 376
stack aisles
    ADA accessibility requirement for,
        191
    aisle width in building program, 87
    dead-end, avoiding, 676

    dead-end, problem with, 404–405, 703
    lighting, 49, 406–407, 597
    orientation for staff oversight, 405
    rules on, 8
    security, evaluation of, 55
    sight lines for, 675, 676
    width, selection of, 394, 407
    width for accessibility, 192
    width of, 8, 414
stack ventilation, 646
stacking chairs, 447
staff
    aisles, orientation for best staff oversight, 405
    at construction meetings, 266
    design process, time for, 188
    evaluation of library buildings, 46
    fortress desks and, 438–439
    information desks and, 433
    interviews with, for building program input, 76–77
    lending desk staff spaces, 423
    lending desks, 423
    lending desks, provisions for book returns, 424–425
    lending workrooms, 423–424
    lockers for, 686
    panic buttons for, 700
    phased expansion project and, 302
    reference and reader guidance desks and, 431–432
    security of staff areas, 56
    security training for, 702
    service desk design needs, 417–419
    service desks, evaluation of proposed, 421
    service desks, placement of, 420–421
    service desks, security for, 433–434
    staff costs, controlling, 351–352
    storage places, location of, 547
    tours of libraries and, 100
    training on building systems, 278
    trapped, places where people can be, 676–677
    workers' compensation insurance, 715
staff facilities
    bike storage, 543
    coat storage, 540–541
    features often omitted from, 533
    lunchrooms, 534–539
    mailboxes, 542–543
    purse storage, 541–542
    restrooms, 539–540
    rules on, 543–544
    showers, 543
    staff conference rooms, 522–523

    thermostats for, 5
staff health and life insurance, 715
staff lunchrooms
    bulletin boards, 539
    computer workstations in, 538–539
    decoration of, 539
    entertainment for, 539
    food preparation/serving, 535–538
    functions of, 534
    lactation rooms, 539
    location of, 534–535
    rules on, 543–544
    seating, 538
    secluded spaces, 539
    staff restrooms next to, 533, 543
    vending machines, 538
staff oversight
    of conference rooms, 470
    of entrances, 673–674
    as lending desk function, 422
    of quiet reading rooms, 470–471
    as reference desk function, 431
    of restrooms, 504–505
    security for study/meeting rooms, 464
    service desk design for, 418
    service desks rule about, 441
    service desks, security for staff, 433
    sight lines for, 674–676
    of study rooms, 472
    for theft control, 680–681
    theft-control systems, cost-benefit analysis of, 679–680
    windows from staff workrooms for, 512–513
staff restrooms
    guidance on, 539–540
    location of, 493, 503–504, 533, 534–535
    next to staff lunchrooms, 533, 534–535
    rules on, 508, 543, 544
    size/location of, 502–504
staff service points, 47–48
staff workrooms
    arrangement/adjacencies, 511
    building program, two-phase, 93
    clothes washers/dryers, 515
    electrical outlets for, 632
    electrical wiring for, 514
    example of bad design, 546
    furnishings
        equipment, 521–522
        equipment, spaces with shared, 522
        open floor space, 519
        seating, 518–519
        storage, 519–521
        work surfaces, 517–518
    individual workrooms, 516–517

    lighting, 513–514
    modular furnishings for, 513
    overview of, 511
    placement of, 44
    plumbing systems for, 662–663
    privacy of, 513
    restrooms and, 515
    rules on, 44, 529–531
    size of, 511–512
    size requirements for, 528–529
    specialized workrooms
        children's departments, 526–528
        graphic arts, 523–524
        rare book departments, 528
        technical services, 524–526
    staff conference rooms, 522–523
    storage for, 515
    temperature control for, 515
    ventilation for, 515
    washbasins in, 663, 665
    water for, 514
    windows to rest of library, 512–513
    workspaces in otherwise public areas, 528
stages, 468, 579
staggered stud walls, 220
stained concrete, 228–229, 462
stains, prevention of, 462
staircases
    access for people with acrophobia, 202
    accessibility, improving, 205
    accessibility rule on, 207
    acrophobia, evaluation of stairs, 54–55
    ADA accessibility requirements for, 192
    in atria, 573–574
    broadloom carpet on, 226
    with central openings, 574
    ceramic tile for, 230
    curved, problems with, 568, 570, 571
    dangerous features of, 678
    design, basics of, 568–570
    dysfunctional designs for, 62–63
    fire-exit staircases, 695–696
    fires and, 576
    floating, protective railings under, 191
    floating staircases, 571–572
    glass walls at heads/feet of, 574
    historic entrances and, 300
    historic stores, conversion of, 321
    incorporating furnishings, 574–575
    monumental, 38, 188
    monumental, space needs and, 85
    with open risers, 572–573
    problematic designs, 20–21, 22
    problems with, 561–562, 567

staircases (cont'd)
   rules on, 5, 7, 10, 11, 13, 14, 581, 582
   rules on good library design, 23
   shared facilities in single buildings, 334–335
   story hour structures with risers, 575
   treads, 570–571
   unnecessary, 576
   upward expansion and, 142
   vocabulary for, 567–568
stall enclosures, 495–496
stand end labels, 198
Standard Building Code (SBC), 237
Standard Oil Building, Chicago, 215
standards
   for HVAC systems, 639
   for LED lighting, 595
   for lighting, 590
   review of service standards in building program, 81–82
standing seam metal roofs, 218
standing-height desks, 424, 518
starter-added shelving, 394
state historic preservation agencies, 146
state library agencies, 99
state library conferences, 99
Static Coefficient of Friction (SCOF), 225
steel cantilever shelving
   See cantilever shelving
step, definition of, 568
steps
   access for people with acrophobia, 202
   access for people with limited eyesight, 197–198
   accessibility issues of remodel/expansion, 299
   rules on, 581
   See also staircases
stone
   for desktop surfaces, 437
   natural stone for library buildings, 214–215
   precast stone, 215–216
stonework
   damaged, 274
   matching historic exteriors, 296
stools, 387
storage
   bike storage for staff, 543
   for children's craft and story rooms, 475
   for children's workrooms, 527, 528
   coat storage for meeting rooms, 453–454
   coat storage for staff, 540–541
   evaluation of, 53
   furniture storage for meeting rooms, 448
   for graphic arts workroom, 524
   high-density storage units of academic libraries, 156
   library sites, problematic, 126
   for meeting rooms, 445–446
   purse storage for staff, 541–542
   at reference desks, 432
   for staff lunchroom, 536–537
   for staff workrooms, 515, 519–521, 530
   super high-density storage, 413
   for technical services workrooms, 525, 526
   in window seats, 385–389
   See also collection storage/display
storage cabinets, 519, 520
storage closets
   audiovisual storage closets, 458
   book sale closets, 459
   in building programs, 552–553
   computer storage closets, 459
   for cooperating groups, 459
   design guidance for, 549
   furniture storage closets, 458
   for maker space equipment, 460
   for meeting room, 445–446
   for meeting rooms, 464
   for program/activity/study rooms, 457–460, 479, 480, 481
   program/craft supplies closets, 458
   rules on, 556
storage spaces
   assigned, 548–549
   building program interviews about, 77
   building program, two-phase, 93
   in building programs, 552–554
   dysfunctional designs for, 64
   evaluation of, 53
   library need for, 9
   locations of, 547
   for mechanical equipment, 551–552
   meeting/program room storage spaces, 549–551
   need for, 43
   overview of, 545–547
   for program rooms, 13
   protecting from people who covet, 554–555
   rules on, 555–557
stores, historic, 320–322
storm drains
   best practices for, 660–661
   for open terrace, 665–666
stormwater
   detention/retention basins, 661–662
   plumbing systems, 660–662
   storm drains, 660–661
   system for managing, 660
story hour pits
   avoiding, 477
   as dangerous feature, 677–678
   filling in, 575
story hour structures
   multilevel children's story structures, 476–477
   with risers, design cautions about, 575
story rooms
   See children's craft and story rooms
storytelling collections, 527
stove
   in kitchenette for meeting room, 460, 461
   in staff lunchroom, 534, 535, 543, 544
strategic plans, 80, 81, 96
stretchers, 373
strip malls, 313, 317
structural bays, 337
structural drawings, 184
structural evaluation, of current facilities, 82
structural issues, 337
student service facilities, 333
students
   academic library buildings that include other academic agencies, 333–334
   combined public and academic libraries, 331
   combined school and public libraries, 330–331
   public library sites near schools, 155
   shared buildings and, 329
study rooms
   access for people with limited hearing, 198, 199
   accessibility of, 463
   evaluation of acoustics, 50
   furnishings for, 472
   locking doors for, 473
   movable walls for, 473
   for program/activity/study rooms, 471–473
   room capacities, determining, 444–445
   rule on, 13, 43, 480–481
   security for, 464
   security rule for, 703
   supervision of, 9, 472
   thermostats for, 5
   vital features of, 471–472
   See also program, activity, and study rooms
study tables, 6

style
   of architectural firm, 109
   furniture vocabulary, 373
   matching existing architecture, 122
sub-basements, 671
subcontractor, 245
submittal
   definition of, 263
   librarian review of, 266–267
   verification that construction matches drawings/specifications, 268–269
subrogation, 709–710
Substantial Completion
   process of, 272
   punch lists, 272–275
substitutions
   in bidding process, 255–256
   in construction documents, 186
subsurface water, 132
suicide
   atria and, 22, 38, 60, 200, 201, 578, 677
   multi-floor openings and, 38, 39
sump pumps, 660, 671
sunlight
   access for people with limited eyesight, 196
   control of, 586
   prevention of direct, 587
   skylights, problems of, 612, 622–623
   See also natural light; skylights
super high-density storage, 413
supervision
   See staff oversight
surface water, 131–132
surface-mounted conduit, 630
surfaces/materials
   accessibility problems of libraries, 190
   ceilings, 231–233
   dark, lighting and, 608–609
   desktop surfaces, 441
   desktop surfaces, fragile, 437–438
   exposed surfaces in/on library buildings, 209
   exterior walls, 213–214
   floor surfaces, 224–231
   floors, bearing strength of, 223–224
   health problems, 211–213
   interior walls, 219–223
   problems with remodeling/expanding library buildings, 295–296
   roof coverings, 218
   rules on, 233–235
   sound-absorbing surfaces, 199
   vocabulary for, 210–211
   See also construction materials

surveys
   for building programs, 79–80, 95
   professional fees, 350
   rules about, 15
swipe cards, 689–690
switches
   electrical switches, 273
   motion sensor switches, 606, 634
   pressure switches, 198
   See also light switches

T

table lamps, 380, 391
table legs, 374, 378–379
tables
   accessibility rule on, 208
   adaptations based on age of users, 381
   chairs for seating at, 384–386
   clearances for, 387–388
   for conference room, 446
   configurations of, 376–378
   essential requirements for, 378–380
   evaluation of, 51, 52
   furniture storage closets for, 458
   for graphic arts workroom, 524
   guidance on choice of, 372–373
   meeting room furniture storage space, 550
   options for, 380
   placement of, 387–389
   for program/activity/study rooms, 447–448
   quantity of/types of, 374–375
   rules about, 6
   rules on user seating, 390–392
   for staff conference rooms, 522–523
   for staff lunchroom, 538
   for study rooms, 472
   tables on wheels, 448
   theft control, oversight for, 681
tabletops, 378, 379
tarps, 462–463
task lighting
   architecturally mounted, 602, 608
   description of, 601
   dysfunctional designs, 60
   mounted on shelving, 601, 602–603
   photo examples of, 601, 602, 603
taxes
   bequests and, 358
   501(c)(3) foundations for fundraising, 363–364
   referendums/bond issues, 356–357
teams
   architect team, interviews of, 112–113

architect teams, local architect/out-of-town library architects, 98
architect teams, special problems with, 108–109
library experience of architect team, 109–110
teamwork
   design as team sport, 163–164
   design process as team effort, 162
   for library design/construction, 67
   problems, strategies for avoiding, 67–70
technical experts, 18
technical services
   assigned storage spaces for, 549
   location of, 41
   workroom for, 524–526
technology
   in classrooms, 466
   for interviews of architectural firms, 111–112
telephone switchboard, 422
telephones
   for staff conference rooms, 523
   for staff workrooms, 521, 530
television sets, 539
temperature
   control for staff workrooms, 515
   control with HVAC, 637
   controls, zoning, 644
   HVAC for rare books/archives, 648–649
   HVAC problems and, 638
temporary displays
   artworks, wall spaces for hanging, 486
   in libraries, 483
   political overtones in, 488
   rule on, 489
temporary housing, 346, 349
terraces
   See open terrace; reading terraces
terracotta, architectural, 217, 295–296
terrazzo
   definition of, 210
   for floor surface, 224, 229
   rule on, 234
testing
   commissioning, 270–271
   definition of, 263
   professional fees for, 351
   verification that construction matches drawings/specifications, 269–270
thanks
   to all of your donors, 6, 367
   public ceremonies for, 279
theatrical performances, 465

theft
    of personal possessions, 686
    theft-prone materials, 682–683
theft of library property insurance, 713
theft-control gates, 681
theft-control systems
    economic models, 679–680
    electronic theft-detection systems, 683–686
    high-risk materials, 679
    oversight, improved, 680–682
    overview of, 678–679
    rule on, 703
    theft-prone materials, sequestering, 682–683
    unauthorized people, keeping out of library, 683
thermostat
    for individual rooms, 5
    for meeting rooms, 480
    rules on, 652
    for staff workrooms, 515, 530
    zoning, 644
3-D printers, 477
time limits, on bequests, 359
time-and-materials-not-to-exceed (NTE) charge, 120
timing of testing, 270
title
    clear title for grant application, 365
    full title for conversions, 309–310
    library building on land that library does not have title to, 149–150
TM-30, 592
toaster ovens, 535
toilet paper dispensers, 496
toilets
    automatic, on punch list, 273
    building codes on, 493–494
    building program, two-phase, 93
    for children's restrooms, 501
    number of, 502
    for restrooms, 494–496
    rules on, 12, 14, 508, 509
    for staff restrooms, 540
    stall enclosures for, 495–496
    turning off, 656
top rail, 373
topography, site, 133–136
topping out, 282–283
"tornado" approach, 77, 290
tornado shelters
    basements as, 670
    in library, 15
    restrooms as, 505–506, 508–509
    rules on providing, 703, 715
tornadoes, windstorm-resistant construction, 672–673

tours
    of library at ribbon cutting, 287
    pre-bid tours of library, 255, 260
    prior work of architectural firms, investigating, 100–101
    of work in progress, 283–284
toxic materials
    danger of, 209–210
    health problems from, 211–213
traffic flows, 40–41
training
    on fire extinguishers, 696
    on HVAC system operation, 648
    security training for staff, 702
    on sprinkler systems, 657, 695
    of staff on building systems, 278
transportation, adjacent, 155–156
trash, 277–278
traveling exhibits, 484
travertine, 215
treads
    of curved staircases, 570
    definition of, 568
    oddly shaped, 568, 570–571, 678
    rules on, 581, 582
    staircase design basics, 569
    staircases with open risers, 572
Triangle Shirtwaist factory fire, Greenwich Village, 238
trim, 273
tripping hazards, 195
troffers, 197, 599
truncated domes, 193
tuckpointing, 211, 214
two-phase building programs
    guidance on, 92–93
    for library expansion, 141
    restrooms and, 504
    rule about, 96
    space for construction/expansion with, 127
two-phase construction, 252–253
two-position chairs, 384

U

Ultra Violet Germicidal Irradiation (UVGI), 640–641
ultraviolet light, 643–644
umbrella liability coverage, 709
unassignable space, 85
unauthorized people, keeping out of library, 683
Under Floor Air Distribution (UFAD), 641
underfloor ducts, 641
underwriter, 707, 709

Underwriters Laboratories (UL)
    evaluation of safety of equipment, 667–668, 705
    testing/approval of electrical gadgets, 635
    UL certifications from, 628
union labor
    bidding rule about, 260
    competency of, 287
    prevailing wages and, 251
unisex restrooms, 503, 504, 540
unitary systems, 649–650
United States Green Buildings Council (USGBC), 647
university libraries
    funding problems, 355–356
    shared buildings, problems of, 327–329
    shared buildings, rules on, 340–342
    unauthorized people, keeping out of library, 683
    See also academic libraries
University of Chicago, 156
University of Illinois, 143, 613
upholstered furniture
    flammability of, 383, 669
    rule about, 390–391, 392
upholstery
    avoidance of, 373
    evaluation of, 51
    rule about, 392
uplighting
    for high-quality library light, 584
    historic lighting fixtures and, 616–617
    overview of, 598–599
    photo examples of, 596, 597, 611
upward expansion, 141–143
urinals, 496–497
used book sale displays, 430
user input, 76, 95
user seating
    chairs, 381–387
    for classrooms, 466
    furniture vocabulary, 373
    ordering of furniture, 375–376
    overview of, 371–373
    placement of, 387–389
    quantities/types of, 374–375
    rules on, 390–392
    tables, 376–381
users
    access for people with acrophobia, 199–203
    access for people with claustrophobia, 204
    access for people with limited eyesight, 195–198
    access for people with limited

hearing, 198–199
access for people with limited mobility, 193–195
access for people with limited senses of direction, 204
ADA accessibility requirements for library, 191–193
combined public and academic libraries, 331
combined school and public libraries and, 330–331
dead-end stack aisles and, 404–405
fortress desks and, 438–439
lending desk functions, 422
library design decisions, involvement in, 17
parking at library, 312
phased expansion project and, 302
security systems, public relations implications, 701–702
stairs, elevators, ramps, problems with, 561–562
theft of personal possessions, 686
USGBC (United States Green Buildings Council), 647
utilities
    of big box stores, 320
    building costs, components of, 347–348
    connections, 348
    connections, conversion and, 308
    conversion of non-library buildings and, 311
    cost of, as component of building cost, 347–348
    definition of, 344
    evaluating potential sites, 130–131
    relocation of, 348
UVGI (Ultra Violet Germicidal Irradiation), 640–641

V

valuable objects, 712
value engineering, 245, 252
values
    for insurance, reviewing, 705
    for insurance, setting, 708, 715
    insurance policies, purchasing, 710–711
vandalism
    of children's restrooms, 501
    graffiti in restrooms, 507
    in restrooms, 504–505
variable air volume (VAV), 641, 650
Variable Refrigerant Flow (VFR) systems, 650
VAT (vinyl asbestos tile), 227–228, 292

vaults, 317
VCT (vinyl composition tile), 227
vehicles, 552, 714
veiling reflectance, 591
vending machines, 538
veneer, 399
Venetian blinds, 620
ventilation
    dysfunctional designs for, 60
    for graphic arts workroom, 524
    HVAC, evaluation of, 51
    HVAC problems and, 638
    by HVAC system, 641–643
    passive ventilating/cooling strategies, 646
    for restrooms, 492, 500, 508
    for staff workrooms, 515
    See also HVAC (heating, ventilating, and air conditioning)
vertical display cases, 486
vertigo, 190, 183
video cameras
    equipment specifications, 697–699
    locations for, 699–700
    of video surveillance systems, 697
video recording, 456
video surveillance
    in elevator, 564
    of hidden corners, 675–676
    of restrooms, 505
    space for, 684
video surveillance systems
    camera locations, 699–700
    for children's departments, 701
    equipment specifications, 697–699
    overview of, 697
vinyl
    definition of, 211
    for exterior wall siding, 217
    for floor covering, 225
    pollution from manufacture of, 212
vinyl asbestos tile (VAT), 227–228, 292
vinyl baseboards, 222
vinyl blinds, 620
vinyl composition tile (VCT), 227
vinyl siding, 233
vinyl tile
    for children's craft and story rooms, 474–475
    for floor surface, 227–228
    for meeting room floors, 462
    for restrooms, 507
vinyl wallpaper, 223
visibility, of study rooms, 471
visible light, 586
vision
    access for people with limited eyesight, 195–198

lighting concepts and, 588
visitor seating, 519
visual barricades, 425–426
vocabulary
    for bidding, 244–245
    for building costs, 344
    for construction, 262–263
    for electrical systems, 628
    for elevators, 562–563
    for furniture, 373
    for HVAC, 639–641
    for insurance, 706–707
    for lighting, 584–586
    for plumbing systems, 656
    for staircases, 567–568
    for surfaces/materials, 210–211

W

wages, 251–252, 328
walking bridges, 38–39
walk-off mats, 211, 230
walkways
    across atria, 201, 577
    dysfunctional designs for, 63
    railings on narrow walkways, 578
wall shelving, 525
wall spaces for hanging artworks, 486
wall surfaces, pinnable, 486–487
wall-mounted display case, 486
wall-mounted toilets, 494–495
wall-mounted washbasins, 497
wallpaper, vinyl, 223
walls
    bearing walls, conversion problems, 312
    bearing walls, remodel/expansion and, 292–293
    construction materials of, 209
    curved, banning, 205
    curved interior walls, acoustics and, 199
    curved walls/round rooms, 37
    curved/diagonal exterior walls, 8
    double-stud walls for limiting sound transmission, 450–451
    earthquake-resistant construction, 673
    exterior walls, materials for, 213–217
    glass walls, daylight control and, 618–620
    glass walls for study rooms, 471, 472, 480–481
    interior walls, materials for, 219–223
    movable walls for study room, 473
    rooms with diagonal walls, 40
    rules on, 42, 43

walls (cont'd)
  rules on remodeling/expanding library buildings, 304
  rules on surfaces/materials for, 233–235
  wall coverings for restrooms, 507
  See also curved walls; glass walls
war/insurrection insurance, 713–714
warranties
  phased expansion projects, warranties on equipment, 302–303
  post-occupancy inspection, 279
  on roofs, 218
  what to include in, 278
washbasins
  bat handles for, 191
  building codes on, 493–494
  lighting for, 506
  plumbing for, 663
  for restrooms, 497
  rules on, 8, 665
  soap dispensers and, 497–498
  for staff restrooms, 540
washers/dryers
  for children's workrooms, 526–527
  plumbing for, 663
  for staff workrooms, 515
waste line, 659
wastewater, 659
water
  infiltration problems of existing structures, 173
  sprinkler systems, 692–695
  for staff workrooms, 514
  surface water runoff detention/retention, 131–132
  for technical services workrooms, 525
  See also flooding; plumbing systems
water features
  access for people with acrophobia, 202–203
  avoidance of, 22
  as dangerous feature, 678
  as dysfunctional design, 64
  evaluation of, 57
  indoor, 664
  outdoor, 664–665
  plumbing systems for, 664–665
  rule on, 10, 665
  service desks and, 419
water retention
  as site development cost, 348
  zoning requirements for, 299
water room, 656, 657
water service, 656–657
water supplies
  domestic water, 657

fire protection, 657–658
irrigation/maintenance water, 658
plumbing systems, 656–659
water service, 656–657
water treatment, 657
water vapor, 650–651
waterless urinals, 496–497
wayfinding, 30–31
WC, 656
weight, 127–128
welcome, 46, 47
welded frame shelving
  description of, 394
  disassembly/reassembly of, 395
  replacement of components of, 396
west light
  daylight control for, 622
  glass walls and, 617
  library building direction, 49
  orientation of library, 148
  as worst light, 617
wet pipe systems, 693
wheelchairs
  access for people with limited mobility, 193–195
  accessibility issues of remodel/expansion, 299–300
  accessibility rules, 207, 208
  ADA accessibility requirements for, 192, 193
  elevator options and, 565
  lifts and, 566–567
  meeting rooms, accessibility of, 463
  ramps, struggle with, 579–580
Wheeler, Joseph, 151
WHO (World Health Organization), 211
width
  of cantilever steel shelving, 398
  of cross aisles, 408
Wi-Fi service, 51
window air conditioners, 650
window seats, 386–387
windows
  access for people with limited eyesight, 196
  in basements, lack of, 671
  big box store conversion and, 320
  blinds for, 5, 7
  blinds for natural light, 48
  for children's craft and story rooms, 473, 475
  for children's workrooms, 527
  of churches, 322
  conversion problems, 310
  daylight, control of, 618–622
  department store conversion and, 318
  direct glare from, 590
  dysfunctional designs for, 59

lighting problems from, 611–612
lighting rules and, 624, 625–626
matching historic exteriors, 296
in meeting rooms, 449
for natural light, 586, 616
north windows, 148
opening, rule on, 652
perimeter shelving and, 404
problems with natural light, 20
problems with remodeling/expanding library buildings, 295
remodel/expansion issues, 293–294
remodeling/expansion of historic buildings, 295
rules about, 6
rules on remodeling/expanding library buildings, 305
seating by, 388
security, evaluation of, 55–56
security through building design, 677
service desks and, 441
for staff workrooms, 512–513, 514, 529
theft control and, 681–682
ventilation, open windows for, 642–643
for views of outside world, 623
windows set into ceilings, 40
windstorm insurance, 711
windstorm shelters, 673, 703
windstorm-resistant construction, 672–673
wire management troughs, 380
wireless signals (Wi-Fi), 455
wiring
  See electrical wiring
women's restrooms
  feminine hygiene products in, 500
  number of fixtures for, 492, 493–494
wood
  for ceilings, 232–233
  fire-resistant, 669
  paneling for interior wall covering, 221
  shelving, 402–403, 413
  siding for exterior walls, 216–217
  wooden desktops, 437
  wooden story hour risers, 477
work counters, 528, 530
work surfaces
  for children's workrooms, 527
  for staff workrooms, 517–518
  for technical services workrooms, 525
work tables, 518
workers' compensation insurance, 715
workroom, 12
World Health Organization (WHO), 211
Wright, Frank Lloyd, 214
written agreements, 340

Y
Yeats, William Butler, 59

Z
zigzag entries, 675
zoning
    changes, 238
    description of, 240
    existing structures, conformance with local zoning, 173, 174
    library site size and changes in, 299
    rules on building codes, 241
    for separate temperature controls, 644
    site acquisition costs, 347
    site selection and, 128
    site size and, 139–140
Zoom, 107

You may also be interested in . . .

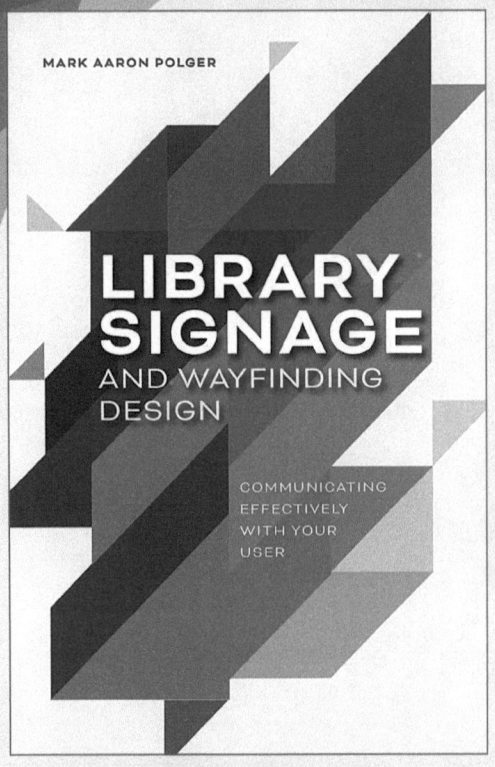

ISBN: 978-0-8389-3785-3

ISBN: 978-0-8389-4991-7

ISBN: 978-0-8389-1831-9

ISBN: 978-1-78330-383-0

For more titles, visit **alastore.ala.org**